438
433
436   } 282-283
485
493

510 } Compare + Contrast
514 }

The Norton Reader

Shorter Edition

FIFTH EDITION

W. W. NORTON & COMPANY, INC.
also publishes

THE NORTON ANTHOLOGY OF AMERICAN LITERATURE
edited by Ronald Gottesman et al.

THE NORTON ANTHOLOGY OF ENGLISH LITERATURE
edited by M.H. Abrams et al.

THE NORTON ANTHOLOGY OF MODERN POETRY
edited by Richard Ellmann and Robert O'Clair

THE NORTON ANTHOLOGY OF POETRY
edited by Arthur M. Eastman et al.

THE NORTON ANTHOLOGY OF SHORT FICTION
edited by R. V. Cassill

THE NORTON ANTHOLOGY OF WORLD MASTERPIECES
edited by Maynard Mack et al.

THE NORTON FACSIMILE OF
THE FIRST FOLIO OF SHAKESPEARE
prepared by Charlton Hinman

THE NORTON INTRODUCTION TO LITERATURE
edited by Carl E. Bain, Jerome Beaty, and J. Paul Hunter

and the

NORTON CRITICAL EDITIONS

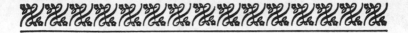

The Norton Reader

An Anthology of Expository Prose

FIFTH EDITION

Arthur M. Eastman, *General Editor*
VIRGINIA POLYTECHNIC INSTITUTE AND STATE UNIVERSITY

Caesar R. Blake
UNIVERSITY OF TORONTO

Hubert M. English, Jr.
UNIVERSITY OF MICHIGAN

Joan E. Hartman
COLLEGE OF STATEN ISLAND,
CITY UNIVERSITY OF NEW YORK

Alan B. Howes
UNIVERSITY OF MICHIGAN

Robert T. Lenaghan
UNIVERSITY OF MICHIGAN

Leo F. McNamara
UNIVERSITY OF MICHIGAN

James Rosier
UNIVERSITY OF PENNSYLVANIA

Shorter Edition

W · W · NORTON & COMPANY *New York* · *London*

Library of Congress Cataloging in Publication Data

Eastman, Arthur M   1918–   ed.
    The Norton Reader. Shorter

Includes bibliographical references and index.
    1. College readers.   I. Title.
PE1122.E3   1980   808.88′8   79–28421

ALL RIGHTS RESERVED
Published simultaneously in Canada
by George J. McLeod Limited, Toronto

W. Norton & Company, Inc., 500 Fifth Avenue, New York, N.Y. 10110

PRINTED IN THE UNITED STATES OF AMERICA

3 4 5 6 7 8 9 0

ISBN 0-393-95113-8

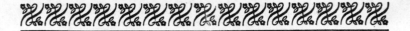

Contents

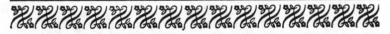

EDUCATION

LANGUAGE AND COMMUNICATION

LITERATURE AND THE ARTS

SIGNS OF THE TIMES

PEOPLE, PLACES

HUMAN NATURE

ETHICS

POLITICS AND GOVERNMENT

HISTORY

SCIENCE

PHILOSOPHY AND RELIGION

Exam

493
344
510–514
1

2/1/84
p179
438
433
p436

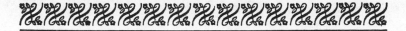

An Index of Essays Illustrative of Rhetorical Modes and Devices

Thesis[1]

1. The section headings of this index are treated more fully in the Notes on Composition, p. 669.

MEANS OF DEVELOPMENT

STYLE

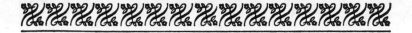

Preface

The Fifth Edition of *The Norton Reader,* Shorter Edition, maintains the size and quality of the Fourth Edition. Of its 128 selections, 60 are new. The new play an especially prominent part in Personal Report, which may strike our old friends as a shade more cheerful than its predecessors; in Education, which ranges from how children learn to the professional training of businessmen; in Signs of the Times—inevitably; and, to name but one other section, in Science, where all five selections are fresh.

Annotation has been slightly increased, acknowledging that students who read this book will have been born in the early 1960s and will regard as history what to their predecessors and teachers is common knowledge. The publication date has been added at the end of each selection at the right margin, with the date of composition (when significantly earlier) at the left. When a writing was originally addressed to a special audience, such as a convocation or a particular reader, this has been indicated too, unless stated within the work itself.

New in this edition is the section Human Nature, which brings together essays exploring individual and collective human behavior. The section formerly called People has expanded fruitfully, the editors think, to People, Places. The final section, hitherto called On Religion or, most recently, Last Things, is now more precisely labeled Philosophy and Religion. (As these examples show, section titles have abandoned the slightly archaic "On . . ." with which they were formerly introduced; for example, On Mind is now simply Mind.)

Additions, of course, come at the price of deletions which, although made on advice from teachers who have used the Fourth Edition, inevitably cause some regret. But 68 selections continue from the past as having stood the test of time, witness in Personal Report essays by Maya Angelou, Loren Eiseley, Wallace Stegner, Dylan Thomas, and E. B. White. Users of earlier editions, in other words, will find a wealth of tried and proved material here. And

xvii

our basic principles of selection remain largely unchanged. Contemporary essays are set beside earlier pieces, easy and entertaining essays beside those that challenge and stretch the mind; the Prose Forms rubrics continue to offer alternative angles of attack for the writing of full-scale essays; women writers discuss experiences and ideas which are distinctively female and those which are not. Continuing to present not only different kinds and styles of prose writing but different authorial perspectives, we now offer many selections by Canadians: Robertson Davies, Margaret Laurence, Fredelle Bruser Maynard, and Joyce Maynard, and many others.

The essays in the *Reader* are gathered into sections titled according to major fields of human concern, some of them familiar ground to students—Personal Report, Education, Mind, Language and Communication—and others inviting ventures into more specialized kinds of knowledge, such as History, Science, Philosophy and Religion. These and others of the rubrics correspond to the divisions of the liberal-arts curriculum. The ordering remains essentially unchanged—unobtrusive, we think, yet logical, reflective of the individual's enlarging experience. Essays within a topical division can be read together for contrasts in point of view; moreover, on gaining familiarity with the text, and perhaps with the aid of Craig B. Snow's *A Guide to the Norton Reader*, teachers will discover thematic links among the different sections. For example, Eiseley's "The Brown Wasps" in Personal Report ties in with Momaday's "The Way to Rainy Mountain" in People, Places, and both of these have in common the theme of intimations of mortality with two essays at the end of Human Nature: Sewall's "A Sense of the Ending" and Kübler-Ross' "On the Fear of Death." And not all selections about ethical issues are to be found within the limits of the section called Ethics. Instructors interested in exploring different manifestations of the same voice through differing subjects and tones will find a fair number of authors represented by two or more selections—Joan Didion, Ralph Waldo Emerson, Benjamin Franklin, E. B. White, and several others.

Besides subject matter for class discussion and writing assignments, the *Reader* offers many models for rhetorical and stylistic emulation, both in An Album of Styles and elsewhere. Teachers who prefer to organize their courses rhetorically will, we hope, find useful the Index of Essays Illustrative of Rhetorical Modes and Devices. Other pedagogical aids include study questions on content and rhetoric for many of the essays, and at the end of the book the Notes on Composition—a précis of basic rhetorical principles and an explanation of basic terminology, with examples from the *Reader*.

It is a pleasure to acknowledge the help we received in bringing the Fifth Edition to completion. Most especially the senior editors welcome as partner Joan E. Hartman, whose engagement with the *Reader* dates back to the Third Edition when, with Carol Ohmann, she nominated many pieces by women; we are glad she has joined us as a fully collaborating editor. John W. N. Francis of the Norton staff has contributed far more to this edition than we could have expected, and his colleagues at Norton—especially Jennifer E. Sutherland, who helped us particularly with the selection of Canadian essays, and Gordon E. Massman, who compiled many of the bio-bibliographical notices for the new essayists—also deserve our warm thanks.

Thanks are also extended to the many dedicated teachers who, by drawing on their classroom experiences with *The Norton Reader* and by giving generously of their time to answer our questionnaires, have offered a wealth of ideas and suggestions for its improvement. These include: Gilbert Allen, Furman University; Frank W. Bliss, Davidson College; Dorothy Boerner, University of Maryland; William Bracy, Beaver College; James Brazell, Trenton State College; M. Bryant, Drake University; Cheryl Calver, University of Lethbridge; Mark Coleman, Georgia College; Henry Davis, Jr., Spring Hill College; Helen Deese, University of California, Riverside; Joseph DeRocco, Bridgewater State College; Douglas M. Doty, Pace University; Marilyn Edelstein, State University of New York, Buffalo; Richard N. Erlich, Miami University of Ohio; Eileen B. Evans, South Dakota State University; F. L. Fennell, Loyola University; Peter A. Fischer, University of Houston, Clear Lake; Delmont F. Fleming, Mary Washington College; William Foltz, University of Hawaii; Jim French, University of Nebraska; Robert W. Gladish, Academy of the New Church; David Goslee, University of Tennessee; David Gottlieb, Capitol Institute of Technology; Robert Greene, Washburn University; Edward A. Hagan, Western Connecticut State College; George Haich, Georgia State University; Jon Hake, Florissant Valley Community College; S. Hallgarth, William Woods College; John Hanes, Duquesne University; Paul R. Harrison, Florissant Valley Community College; James Hawley, State University of New York, Agricultural and Technical College, Morrisville; Bruce Henricksen, Loyola University; John S. Hillman, Essex Community College; Marilyn Hilpert, California State College, Stanislaus; Mark Hochberg, Juniata College; David Hoddeson, Rutgers University, Newark; Virginia Hohman, University of Central Arkansas; Clark Holtzman III, St. Louis University; Betty Hughes, Beaufort County Technical Institute; Clarence Johnson, New Jersey Institute of Technology; R. A. Johnson, Mount Holyoke College; Peggy Knapp, Carnegie-Mellon University; Don Knefel, Loras College; Teo Locker, Fresno City College; Barbara Lootens, Purdue University, North Central Campus; William Lucas, Peninsula College; Madeleine Lynch, San Joaquin Delta College; Steven Malanca, University of Maryland; Patricia Miller, Albion College; David Noveshen, Catonsville Community College; M. G. O'Hara, Muscatine Community College; Charlotte F. Otten, Calvin College; J. Michael Pilz, Bucks County Community College; David J. Popowski, Mankato State University; David G. Pugh, Western Michigan University; Jane R. Pugh, Case Western Reserve University; Richard E. Ray, Indiana University of Pennsylvania; Russell Rutter, Illinois State University; Marilyn B. Saveson, Mansfield State College; Carmen Schmersahl, Mount St. Mary's College; Arthur Schneider, Palm Beach Junior College; Christopher Schneider, Wright City College; William T. Schroder, College of Santa Fe; Melvin Schroeder, Canisius College; F. A. Shirley, Wheaton College; Martha S. Smith, Elon College; Robert Smith, Highlands University; John J. Soldo, Eastern New Mexico University; S. H. Statham, Los Angeles Valley College; Gary R. Stephens, New York Institute of Technology; Massie C. Stinson, Jr., Longwood College; George C. Storey, Ursinus College; John Stratton, University of Arkansas, Little Rock; Margaret A. Strom, George Washington University; G. Sutton, Bethune-Cookman College; Charles Tidwell, Canadian Union College; R. Tranquilla, St. Vincent College; Roald Tweet, Augustana College; Larry Watson, University of Wisconsin, Stevens Point; Joyce Yochheim, Ashland College; Tryna Zeedyk, Waubonsee Community College; Karl Zender, University of California, Davis.

ARTHUR M. EASTMAN

The Norton Reader

Shorter Edition

FIFTH EDITION

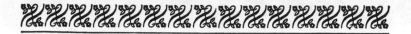

Personal Report

DYLAN THOMAS
Memories of Christmas

One Christmas was so much like another, in those years, around the sea-town corner now and out of all sound except the distant speaking of the voices I sometimes hear a moment before sleep, that I can never remember whether it snowed for six days and six nights when I was twelve or whether it snowed for twelve days and twelve nights when I was six; or whether the ice broke and the skating grocer vanished like a snowman through a white trap-door on that same Christmas Day that the mince-pies finished Uncle Arnold and we tobogganed down the seaward hill, all the afternoon, on the best tea-tray, and Mrs. Griffiths complained, and we threw a snowball at her niece, and my hands burned so, with the heat and the cold, when I held them in front of the fire, that I cried for twenty minutes and then had some jelly.

All the Christmases roll down the hill towards the Welsh-speaking sea, like a snowball growing whiter and bigger and rounder, like a cold and headlong moon bundling down the sky that was our street; and they stop at the rim of the ice-edged, fish-freezing waves, and I plunge my hands in the snow and bring out whatever I can find; holly or robins or pudding, squabbles and carols and oranges and tin whistles, and the fire in the front room, and bang go the crackers, and holy, holy, holy, ring the bells, and the glass bells shaking on the tree, and Mother Goose, and Struwelpeter[1] —oh! the baby-burning flames and the clacking scissorman!—Billy Bunter[2] and Black Beauty, Little Women and boys who have three helpings, Alice and Mrs. Potter's badgers,[3] penknives, teddy-bears

---

1. The title character of *Struwelpeter* (*Slovenly Peter*), *or Merry Tales and Funny Pictures*, a children's book originally in German, by Dr. Heinrich Hoffmann, containing gaily grim admonitory narratives in verse about little Pauline, for example, who played with matches and got burned up; or the little boy who sucked his thumbs until the tall scissorman cut them off.

2. The humorous fat boy in Frank Richards' tales of English school life.

3. Beatrix Potter, creator of *Peter Rabbit* and other animal tales for children, among them *The Tale of Mr. Tod*, a badger.

—named after a Mr. Theodore Bear, their inventor, or father, who died recently in the United States—mouth-organs, tin-soldiers, and blancmange, and Auntie Bessie playing "Pop Goes the Weasel" and "Nuts in May" and "Oranges and Lemons" on the untuned piano in the parlor all through the thimble-hiding musical-chairing blind-man's-buffing party at the end of the never-to-be-forgotten day at the end of the unremembered year.

In goes my hand into that wool-white bell-tongued ball of holidays resting at the margin of the carol-singing sea, and out come Mrs. Prothero and the firemen.

It was on the afternoon of the day of Christmas Eve, and I was in Mrs. Prothero's garden, waiting for cats, with her son Jim. It was snowing. It was always snowing at Christmas; December, in my memory, is white as Lapland, though there were no reindeers. But there were cats. Patient, cold, and callous, our hands wrapped in socks, we waited to snowball the cats. Sleek and long as jaguars and terrible-whiskered, spitting and snarling they would slink and sidle over the white back-garden walls, and the lynx-eyed hunters, Jim and I, fur-capped and moccasined trappers from Hudson's Bay off Eversley Road, would hurl our deadly snowballs at the green of their eyes. The wise cats never appeared. We were so still, Eskimo-footed arctic marksmen in the muffling silence of the eternal snows—eternal, ever since Wednesday—that we never heard Mrs. Prothero's first cry from her igloo at the bottom of the garden. Or, if we heard it at all, it was, to us, like the far-off challenge of our enemy and prey, the neighbor's Polar Cat. But soon the voice grew louder. "Fire!" cried Mrs. Prothero, and she beat the dinner-gong. And we ran down the garden, with the snow-balls in our arms, towards the house, and smoke, indeed, was pouring out of the dining-room, and the gong was bombilating, and Mrs. Prothero was announcing ruin like a town-crier in Pompeii. This was better than all the cats in Wales standing on the wall in a row. We bounded into the house, laden with snowballs, and stopped at the open door of the smoke-filled room. Something was burning all right; perhaps it was Mr. Prothero, who always slept there after midday dinner with a newspaper over his face; but he was standing in the middle of the room, saying "A fine Christmas!" and smacking at the smoke with a slipper.

"Call the fire-brigade," cried Mrs. Prothero as she beat the gong.

"They won't be there," said Mr. Prothero, "it's Christmas."

There was no fire to be seen, only clouds of smoke and Mr. Prothero standing in the middle of them, waving his slipper as though he were conducting.

"Do something," he said.

And we threw all our snowballs into the smoke—I think we

missed Mr. Prothero—and ran out of the house to the telephone-box.

"Let's call the police as well," Jim said.

"And the ambulance."

"And Ernie Jenkins, he likes fires."

But we only called the fire-brigade, and soon the fire-engine came and three tall men in helmets brought a hose into the house and Mr. Prothero got out just in time before they turned it on. Nobody could have had a noisier Christmas Eve. And when the firemen turned off the hose and were standing in the wet and smoky room, Jim's aunt, Miss Prothero, came downstairs and peered in at them. Jim and I waited, very quietly, to hear what she would say to them. She said the right thing, always. She looked at the three tall firemen in their shining helmets, standing among the smoke and cinders and dissolving snowballs, and she said: "Would you like something to read?"

Now out of that bright white snowball of Christmas gone comes the stocking, the stocking of stockings, that hung at the foot of the bed with the arm of a golliwog dangling over the top and small bells ringing in the toes. There was a company, gallant and scarlet but never nice to taste though I always tried when very young, of belted and busbied and musketed lead soldiers so soon to lose their heads and legs in the wars on the kitchen table after the tea-things, the mince-pies, and the cakes that I helped to make by stoning the raisins and eating them, had been cleared away; and a bag of moist and many-colored jelly-babies and a folded flag and a false nose and a tram-conductor's cap and a machine that punched tickets and rang a bell; never a catapult; once, by a mistake that no one could explain, a little hatchet; and a rubber-buffalo, or it may have been a horse, with a yellow head and haphazard legs; and a celluloid duck that made, when you pressed it, a most unducklike noise, a mewing moo that an ambitious cat might make who wishes to be a cow; and a painting-book in which I could make the grass, the trees, the sea, and the animals any color I pleased: and still the dazzling sky-blue sheep are grazing in the red field under a flight of rainbow-beaked and pea-green birds.

Christmas morning was always over before you could say Jack Frost. And look! suddenly the pudding was burning! Bang the gong and call the fire-brigade and the book-loving firemen! Someone found the silver three-penny-bit with a currant on it; and the someone was always Uncle Arnold. The motto in my cracker read:

> Let's all have fun this Christmas Day,
> Let's play and sing and shout hooray!

and the grown-ups turned their eyes towards the ceiling, and Auntie Bessie, who had already been frightened, twice, by a clockwork mouse, whimpered at the sideboard and had some elderberry wine. And someone put a glass bowl full of nuts on the littered table, and my uncle said, as he said once every year: "I've got a shoe-nut here. Fetch me a shoehorn to open it, boy."

And dinner was ended.

And I remember that on the afternoon of Christmas Day, when the others sat around the fire and told each other that this was nothing, no, nothing, to the great snowbound and turkey-proud yule-log-crackling holly-berry-bedizined and kissing-under-the-mistletoe Christmas when *they* were children, I would go out, school-capped and gloved and mufflered, with my bright new boots squeaking, into the white world on to the seaward hill, to call on Jim and Dan and Jack and to walk with them through the silent snowscape of our town.

We went padding through the streets, leaving huge deep footprints in the snow, on the hidden pavements.

"I bet people'll think there's been hippoes."

"What would you do if you saw a hippo coming down Terrace Road?"

"I'd go like this, bang! I'd throw him over the railings and roll him down the hill and then I'd tickle him under the ear and he'd wag his tail . . ."

"What would you do if you saw *two* hippoes . . . ?"

Iron-flanked and bellowing he-hippoes clanked and blundered and battered through the scudding snow towards us as we passed by Mr. Daniel's house.

"Let's post Mr. Daniel a snowball through his letter box."

"Let's write things in the snow."

"Let's write 'Mr. Daniel looks like a spaniel' all over his lawn."

"Look," Jack said, "I'm eating snow-pie."

"What's it taste like?"

"Like snow-pie," Jack said.

Or we walked on the white shore.

"Can the fishes see it's snowing?"

"They think it's the sky falling down."

The silent one-clouded heavens drifted on to the sea.

"All the old dogs have gone."

Dogs of a hundred mingled makes yapped in the summer at the sea-rim and yelped at the trespassing mountains of the waves.

"I bet St. Bernards would like it now."

And we were snowblind travelers lost on the north hills, and the great dewlapped dogs, with brandy-flasks round their necks, ambled and shambled up to us, baying "Excelsior."[4]

We returned home through the desolate poor sea-facing streets

4. "Higher"—recalling Henry Wadsworth Longfellow's poem "Excelsior," in which a traveler who has adopted that word as his motto perishes while climbing a dangerous, snowy mountain trail, and is found by monks of Saint Bernard and their "faithful hound."

where only a few children fumbled with bare red fingers in the thick wheel-rutted snow and catcalled after us, their voices fading away, as we trudged uphill, into the cries of the dock-birds and the hooters of ships out in the white and whirling bay.

Bring out the tall tales now that we told by the fire as we roasted chestnuts and the gaslight bubbled low. Ghosts with their heads under their arms trailed their chains and said "whooo" like owls in the long nights when I dared not look over my shoulder; wild beasts lurked in the cubby-hole under the stairs where the gas-meter ticked. "Once upon a time," Jim said, "there were three boys, just like us, who got lost in the dark in the snow, near Bethesda Chapel, and this is what happened to them . . ." It was the most dreadful happening I had ever heard.

And I remember that we went singing carols once, a night or two before Christmas Eve, when there wasn't the shaving of a moon to light the secret, white-flying streets. At the end of a long road was a drive that led to a large house, and we stumbled up the darkness of the drive that night, each one of us afraid, each one holding a stone in his hand in case, and all of us too brave to say a word. The wind made through the drive-trees noises as of old and unpleasant and maybe web-footed men wheezing in caves. We reached the black bulk of the house.

"What shall we give them?" Dan whispered.

" 'Hark the Herald'? 'Christmas comes but Once a Year' ?"

"No," Jack said: "We'll sing 'Good King Wenceslas.' I'll count three."

One, two, three, and we began to sing, our voices high and seemingly distant in the snow-felted darkness round the house that was occupied by nobody we knew. We stood close together, near the dark door.

> Good King Wenceslas looked out
> On the Feast of Stephen.

And then a small, dry voice, like the voice of someone who has not spoken for a long time, suddenly joined our singing: a small, dry voice from the other side of the door: a small, dry voice through the keyhole. And when we stopped running we were outside *our* house; the front room was lovely and bright; the gramophone was playing; we saw the red and white balloons hanging from the gas-bracket; uncles and aunts sat by the fire; I thought I smelt our supper being fried in the kitchen. Everything was good again, and Christmas shone through all the familiar town.

"Perhaps it was a ghost," Jim said.

"Perhaps it was trolls," Dan said, who was always reading.

"Let's go in and see if there's any jelly left," Jack said. And we did that.

1945

WALLACE STEGNER
The Town Dump

The town dump of Whitemud, Saskatchewan, could only have been a few years old when I knew it, for the village was born in 1913 and I left there in 1919. But I remember the dump better than I remember most things in that town, better than I remember most of the people. I spent more time with it, for one thing; it had more poetry and excitement in it than people did.

It lay in the southeast corner of town, in a section that was always full of adventure for me. Just there the Whitemud River left the hills, bent a little south, and started its long traverse across the prairie and international boundary to join the Milk. For all I knew, it might have been on its way to join the Alph[1]: simply, before my eyes, it disappeared into strangeness and wonder.

Also, where it passed below the dumpground, it ran through willowed bottoms that were a favorite campsite for passing teamsters, gypsies, sometimes Indians. The very straw scattered around those camps, the ashes of those strangers' campfires, the manure of their teams and saddle horses, were hot with adventurous possibilities.

It was as an extension, a living suburb, as it were, of the dumpground that we most valued those camps. We scoured them for artifacts of their migrant tenants as if they had been archaeological sites full of the secrets of ancient civilizations. I remember toting around for weeks the broken cheek strap of a bridle. Somehow or other its buckle looked as if it had been fashioned in a far place, a place where they were accustomed to flatten the tongues of buckles for reasons that could only be exciting, and where they made a habit of plating the metal with some valuable alloy, probably silver. In places where the silver was worn away the buckle underneath shone dull yellow: probably gold.

It seemed that excitement liked that end of town better than our end. Once old Mrs. Gustafson, deeply religious and a little raddled in the head, went over there with a buckboard full of trash, and as she was driving home along the river she looked and saw a spent catfish, washed in from Cypress Lake or some other part of the watershed, floating on the yellow water. He was two feet long, his whiskers hung down, his fins and tail were limp. He was a kind of fish that no one had seen in the Whitemud in the three or four years of the town's life, and a kind that none of us children had ever seen anywhere. Mrs. Gustafson had never seen one like him either; she perceived at once that he was the devil,

1. The imaginary, mysterious river of Samuel Taylor Coleridge's poem "Kubla Khan."

and she whipped up the team and reported him at Hoffman's elevator.

We could hear her screeching as we legged it for the river to see for ourselves. Sure enough, there he was. He looked very tired, and he made no great effort to get away as we pushed out a half-sunken rowboat from below the flume, submerged it under him, and brought him ashore. When he died three days later we experimentally fed him to two half-wild cats, but they seemed to suffer no ill effects.

At that same end of town the irrigation flume crossed the river. It always seemed to me giddily high when I hung my chin over its plank edge and looked down, but it probably walked no more than twenty feet above the water on its spidery legs. Ordinarily in summer it carried about six or eight inches of smooth water, and under the glassy hurrying of the little boxed stream the planks were coated with deep sun-warmed moss as slick as frogs' eggs. A boy could sit in the flume with the water walling up against his back, and grab a cross brace above him, and pull, shooting himself sledlike ahead until he could reach the next brace for another pull and another slide, and so on across the river in four scoots.

After ten minutes in the flume he would come out wearing a dozen or more limber black leeches, and could sit in the green shade where darning needles flashed blue, and dragonflies hummed and darted and stopped, and skaters dimpled slack and eddy with their delicate transitory footprints, and there stretch the leeches out one by one while their sucking ends clung and clung, until at last, stretched far out, they let go with a tiny wet *puk* and snapped together like rubber bands. The smell of the river and the flume and the clay cutbanks and the bars of that part of the river was the smell of wolf willow.

But nothing in that end of town was as good as the dumpground that scattered along a little runoff coulee dipping down toward the river from the south bench. Through a historical process that went back, probably, to the roots of community sanitation and distaste for eyesores, but that in law dated from the Unincorporated Towns Ordinance of the territorial government, passed in 1888, the dump was one of the very first community enterprises, almost our town's first institution.

More than that, it contained relics of every individual who had ever lived there, and of every phase of the town's history.

The bedsprings on which the town's first child was begotten might be there; the skeleton of a boy's pet colt; two or three volumes of Shakespeare bought in haste and error from a peddler, later loaned in carelessness, soaked with water and chemicals in a house fire, and finally thrown out to flap their stained eloquence in the prairie wind.

Broken dishes, rusty tinware, spoons that had been used to mix paint; once a box of percussion caps, sign and symbol of the carelessness that most of those people felt about all matters of personal or public safety. We put them on the railroad tracks and were anonymously denounced in the *Enterprise*. There were also old iron, old brass, for which we hunted assiduously, by night conning junkmen's catalogues and the pages of the *Enterprise* to find how much wartime value there might be in the geared insides of clocks or in a pound of tea lead[2] carefully wrapped in a ball whose weight astonished and delighted us. Sometimes the unimaginable outside world reached in and laid a finger on us. I recall that, aged no more than seven, I wrote a St. Louis junk house asking if they preferred their tea lead and tinfoil wrapped in balls, or whether they would rather have it pressed flat in sheets, and I got back a typewritten letter in a window envelope instructing me that they would be happy to have it in any way that was convenient for me. They added that they valued my business and were mine very truly. Dazed, I carried that windowed grandeur around in my pocket until I wore it out, and for months I saved the letter as a souvenir of the wondering time when something strange and distinguished had singled me out.

We hunted old bottles in the dump, bottles caked with dirt and filth, half buried, full of cobwebs, and we washed them out at the horse trough by the elevator, putting in a handful of shot along with the water to knock the dirt loose; and when we had shaken them until our arms were tired, we hauled them off in somebody's coaster wagon and turned them in at Bill Anderson's pool hall, where the smell of lemon pop was so sweet on the dark pool-hall air that I am sometimes awakened by it in the night, even yet.

Smashed wheels of wagons and buggies, tangles of rusty barbed wire, the collapsed perambulator that the French wife of one of the town's doctors had once pushed proudly up the planked sidewalks and along the ditchbank paths. A welter of foul-smelling feathers and coyote-scattered carrion which was all that remained of somebody's dream of a chicken ranch. The chickens had all got some mysterious pip at the same time, and died as one, and the dream lay out there with the rest of the town's history to rustle to the empty sky on the border of the hills.

There was melted glass in curious forms, and the half-melted office safe left from the burning of Bill Day's Hotel. On very lucky days we might find a piece of the lead casing that had enclosed the wires of the town's first telephone system. The casing was just the right size for rings, and so soft that it could be

---

2. An alloy used for lining the chests in which tea was stored and transported.

whittled with a jackknife. It was a material that might have made artists of us. If we had been Indians of fifty years before, that bright soft metal would have enlisted our maximum patience and craft and come out as ring and metal and amulet inscribed with the symbols of our observed world. Perhaps there were too many ready-made alternatives in the local drug, hardware, and general stores; perhaps our feeble artistic response was a measure of the insufficiency of the challenge we felt. In any case I do not remember that we did any more with the metal than to shape it into crude seal rings with our initials or pierced hearts carved in them; and these, though they served a purpose in juvenile courtship, stopped something short of art.

The dump held very little wood, for in that country anything burnable got burned. But it had plenty of old iron, furniture, papers, mattresses that were the delight of field mice, and jugs and demijohns that were sometimes their bane, for they crawled into the necks and drowned in the rain water or redeye that was inside.

If the history of our town was not exactly written, it was at least hinted, in the dump. I think I had a pretty sound notion even at eight or nine of how significant was that first institution of our forming Canadian civilization. For rummaging through its foul purlieus I had several times been surprised and shocked to find relics of my own life tossed out there to rot or blow away.

The volumes of Shakespeare belonged to a set that my father had bought before I was born. It had been carried through successive moves from town to town in the Dakotas, and from Dakota to Seattle, and from Seattle to Bellingham, and Bellingham to Redmond, and from Redmond back to Iowa, and from there to Saskatchewan. Then, stained in a stranger's house fire, these volumes had suffered from a house-cleaning impulse and been thrown away for me to stumble upon in the dump. One of the Cratchet girls had borrowed them, a hatchet-faced, thin, eager, transplanted Cockney girl with a frenzy, almost a hysteria, for reading. And yet somehow, through her hands, they found the dump, to become a symbol of how much was lost, how much thrown aside, how much carelessly or of necessity given up, in the making of a new country. We had so few books that I was familiar with them all, had handled them, looked at their pictures, perhaps even read them. They were the lares and penates, part of the skimpy impedimenta of household gods we had brought with us into Latium.[3] Finding those three thrown away was a little like finding my own name on a gravestone.

And yet not the blow that something else was, something that

3. The region of Italy settled by the Trojans after their defeat by the Greeks in the Trojan War. Later, in Roman families, the lares and penates were the ancestral household gods; they came to embody the continuity of the family.

impressed me even more with the dump's close reflection of the town's intimate life. The colt whose picked skeleton lay out there was mine. He had been incurably crippled when dogs chased our mare, Daisy, the morning after she foaled. I had labored for months to make him well; had fed him by hand, curried him, exercised him, adjusted the iron braces that I had talked my father into having made. And I had not known that he would have to be destroyed. One weekend I turned him over to the foreman of one of the ranches, presumably so that he could be cared for. A few days later I found his skinned body, with the braces still on his crippled front legs, lying on the dump.

Not even that, I think, cured me of going there, though our parents all forbade us on pain of cholera or worse to do so. The place fascinated us, as it should have. For this was the kitchen midden of all the civilization we knew; it gave us the most tantalizing glimpses into our lives as well as into those of the neighbors. It gave us an aesthetic distance from which to know ourselves.

The dump was our poetry and our history. We took it home with us by the wagonload, bringing back into town the things the town had used and thrown away. Some little part of what we gathered, mainly bottles, we managed to bring back to usefulness, but most of our gleanings we left lying around barn or attic or cellar until in some renewed fury of spring cleanup our families carted them off to the dump again, to be rescued and briefly treasured by some other boy with schemes for making them useful. Occasionally something we really valued with a passion was snatched from us in horror and returned at once. That happened to the mounted head of a white mountain goat, somebody's trophy from old times and the far Rocky Mountains, that I brought home one day in transports of delight. My mother took one look and discovered that his beard was full of moths.

I remember that goat; I regret him yet. Poetry is seldom useful, but always memorable. I think I learned more from the town dump than I learned from school: more about people, more about how life is lived, not elsewhere but here, not in other times but now. If I were a sociologist anxious to study in detail the life of any community, I would go very early to its refuse piles. For a community may be as well judged by what it throws away —what it has to throw away and what it chooses to—as by any other evidence. For whole civilizations we have sometimes no more of the poetry and little more of the history than this.

1959

QUESTIONS

1. Stegner begins his reminiscence of the town dump by saying that it had "poetry and excitement" in it. In what ways does he seek

to convey those qualities to the reader?

2. Is Stegner's description of the dump and its surroundings vivid? Where does his writing directly appeal to the senses, and which senses are called into play?

3. In his second paragraph Stegner speaks of the Alph, the "sacred river" of Coleridge's poem "Kubla Khan." Why? How does allusion to that poem help him convey the strangeness and wonder he then felt?

4. In paragraphs 5-8 Stegner departs, as he had departed to a lesser degree in the two preceding paragraphs, from his description of the dump. Explain how that departure is justified and whether the writing there is appropriate to the essay as a whole.

5. Why does Stegner say (p. 9) that finding the three volumes of Shakespeare in the dump was "a little like finding my own name on a gravestone"? What is the purpose and effect of his allusion to Virgil's Aeneid in the sentence just before that?

6. Through what particular details does Stegner portray the dump as a record of his childhood? How is it shown to be also a record of the brief history of the town? In what respects does it reflect and suggest more widely yet, European and American history and culture and, ultimately, the ancient past, the foundations of civilization? Explain how and to what effect Stegner's focus on the dump enables these considerations to widen in scope but remain associated.

MARGARET LAURENCE

Where the World Began

A strange place it was, that place where the world began. A place of incredible happenings, splendors and revelations, despairs like multitudinous pits of isolated hells. A place of shadow-spookiness, inhabited by the unknowable dead. A place of jubilation and of mourning, horrible and beautiful.

It was, in fact, a small prairie town.

Because that settlement and that land were my first and for many years my only real knowledge of this planet, in some profound way they remain my world, my way of viewing. My eyes were formed there. Towns like ours, set in a sea of land, have been described thousands of times as dull, bleak, flat, uninteresting. I have had it said to me that the railway trip across Canada is spectacular, except for the prairies, when it would be desirable to go to sleep for several days, until the ordeal is over. I am always unable to argue this point effectively. All I can say is—well, you really have to live there to know that country. The town of my childhood could be called bizarre, agonizingly repressive or cruel at times, and the land in which it grew could be called harsh in the violence of its seasonal changes. But never merely flat or uninteresting. Never dull.

In winter, we used to hitch rides on the back of the milk sleigh, our moccasins squeaking and slithering on the hard rutted snow of the roads, our hands in ice-bubbled mitts hanging onto the box edge of the sleigh for dear life, while Bert grinned at us through his great frosted mustache and shouted the horse into speed, daring us to stay put. Those mornings, rising, there would be the perpetual fascination of the frost feathers on windows, the ferns and flowers and eerie faces traced there during the night by unseen artists of the wind. Evenings, coming back from skating, the sky would be black but not dark, for you could see a cold glitter of stars from one side of the earth's rim to the other. And then the sometime astonishment when you saw the Northern Lights flaring across the sky, like the scrawled signature of God. After a blizzard, when the snowplow hadn't yet got through, school would be closed for the day, the assumption being that the town's young could not possibly flounder through five feet of snow in the pursuit of education. We would then gaily don snowshoes and flounder for miles out into the white dazzling deserts, in pursuit of a different kind of knowing. If you came back too close to night, through the woods at the foot of the town hill, the thin black branches of poplar and chokecherry now meringued with frost, sometimes you heard coyotes. Or maybe the banshee wolf-voices were really only inside your head.

Summers were scorching, and when no rain came and the wheat became bleached and dried before it headed, the faces of farmers and townsfolk would not smile much, and you took for granted, because it never seemed to have been any different, the frequent knocking at the back door and the young men standing there, mumbling or thrusting defiantly their requests for a drink of water and a sandwich if you could spare it. They were riding the freights, and you never knew where they had come from, or where they might end up, if anywhere. The Drought and Depression were like evil deities which had been there always. You understood and did not understand.

Yet the outside world had its continuing marvels. The poplar bluffs and the small river were filled and surrounded with a zillion different grasses, stones, and weed flowers. The meadowlarks sang undaunted from the twanging telephone wires along the gravel highway. Once we found an old flat-bottomed scow, and launched her, poling along the shallow brown waters, mending her with wodges of hastily chewed Spearmint, grounding her among the tangles of yellow marsh marigolds that grew succulently along the banks of the shrunken river, while the sun made our skins smell dusty-warm.

My best friend lived in an apartment above some stores on Main Street (its real name was Mountain Avenue, goodness knows why), an elegant apartment with royal-blue velvet curtains. The back roof, scarcely sloping at all, was corrugated tin, of a furnace-like warmth on a July afternoon, and we would sit there drinking lemonade and looking across the back lane at the Fire Hall. Sometimes our vigil would be rewarded. Oh joy! Somebody's house burning down! We had an almost-perfect callousness in some ways. Then the wooden tower's bronze bell would clonk and toll like a thousand speeded funerals in a time of plague, and in a few minutes the team of giant black horses would cannon forth, pulling the fire wagon like some scarlet chariot of the Goths, while the firemen clung with one hand, adjusting their helmets as they went.

The oddities of the place were endless. An elderly lady used to serve, as her afternoon tea offering to other ladies, soda biscuits spread with peanut butter and topped with a whole marshmallow. Some considered this slightly eccentric, when compared with chopped egg sandwiches, and admittedly talked about her behind her back, but no one ever refused these delicacies or indicated to her that they thought she had slipped a cog. Another lady dyed her hair a bright and cherry orange, by strangers often mistaken at twenty paces for a feather hat. My own beloved stepmother wore a silver fox neckpiece, a whole pelt, *with the embalmed (?) head still on*. My Ontario Irish grandfather said, "sparrow grass," a more interesting term than asparagus. The town dump was known as "the nuisance grounds," a phrase fraught with weird connotations, as though the effluvia of our lives was beneath contempt but at the same time was subtly threatening to the determined and sometimes hysterical propriety of our ways.

Some oddities were, as idiom had it, "funny ha ha"; others were "funny peculiar." Some were not so very funny at all. An old man lived, deranged, in a shack in the valley. Perhaps he wasn't even all that old, but to us he seemed a wild Methuselah figure, shambling among the underbrush and the tall couchgrass, muttering indecipherable curses or blessings, a prophet who had forgotten his prophecies. Everyone in town knew him, but no one knew him. He lived among us as though only occasionally and momentarily visible. The kids called him Andy Gump,[1] and feared him. Some sought to prove their bravery by tormenting him. They were the medieval bear baiters, and he the lumbering bewildered bear, half blind, only rarely turning to snarl. Everything is to be found in a town like mine. Belsen,[2] writ small but with the same ink.

All of us cast stones in one shape or another. In grade school,

---

1. Chinless character in a comic strip popular in the 1920s and 1930s.   2. The Nazi concentration camp Bergen-Belsen.

among the vulnerable and violet girls we were, the feared and despised were those few older girls from what was charmingly termed "the wrong side of the tracks." Tough in talk and tougher in muscle, they were said to be whores already. And may have been, that being about the only profession readily available to them.

The dead lived in that place, too. Not only the grandparents who had, in local parlance, "passed on" and who gloomed, bearded or bonneted, from the sepia photographs in old albums, but also the uncles, forever eighteen or nineteen, whose names were carved on the granite family stones in the cemetery, but whose bones lay in France.[3] My own young mother lay in that graveyard, beside other dead of our kin, and when I was ten, my father, too, only forty, left the living town for the dead dwelling on the hill.

When I was eighteen, I couldn't wait to get out of that town, away from the prairies. I did not know then that I would carry the land and town all my life within my skull, that they would form the mainspring and source of the writing I was to do, wherever and however far away I might live.

This was my territory in the time of my youth, and in a sense my life since then has been an attempt to look at it, to come to terms with it. Stultifying to the mind it certainly could be, and sometimes was, but not to the imagination. It was many things, but it was never dull.

The same, I now see, could be said for Canada in general. Why on earth did generations of Canadians pretend to believe this country dull? We knew perfectly well it wasn't. Yet for so long we did not proclaim what we knew. If our upsurge of so-called nationalism seems odd or irrelevant to outsiders, and even to some of our own people (*what's all the fuss about?*), they might try to understand that for many years we valued ourselves insufficiently, living as we did under the huge shadows of those two dominating figures, Uncle Sam and Britannia. We have only just begun to value ourselves, our land, our abilities. We have only just begun to recognize our legends and to give shape to our myths.

There are, God knows, enough aspects to deplore about this country. When I see the killing of our lakes and rivers with industrial wastes, I feel rage and despair. When I see our industries and natural resources increasingly taken over by America, I feel an overwhelming discouragement, especially as I cannot simply say "damn Yankees." It should never be forgotten that it is we ourselves who have sold such a large amount of our birthright for a mess of plastic Progress. When I saw the War Measures Act being

---

3. That is, who had been killed in World War I. The Canadian war dead were buried in Canadian cemeteries in northeastern France and Belgium.

invoked in 1970,[4] I lost forever the vestigial remains of the naïve wish-belief that repression could not happen here, or would not. And yet, of course, I had known all along in the deepest and often hidden caves of the heart that anything can happen anywhere, for the seeds of both man's freedom and his captivity are found everywhere, even in the microcosm of a prairie town. But in raging against our injustices, our stupidities, I do so *as family*, as I did, and still do in writing, about those aspects of my town which I hated and which are always in some ways aspects of myself.

The land still draws me more than other lands. I have lived in Africa and in England, but splendid as both can be, they do not have the power to move me in the same way as, for example, that part of southern Ontario where I spent four months last summer in a cedar cabin beside a river. "Scratch a Canadian, and you find a phony pioneer," I used to say to myself in warning. But all the same it is true, I think, that we are not yet totally alienated from physical earth, and let us only pray we do not become so. I once thought that my lifelong fear and mistrust of cities made me a kind of old-fashioned freak; now I see it differently.

The cabin has a long window across its front western wall, and sitting at the oak table there in the mornings, I used to look out at the river and at the tall trees beyond, green-gold in the early light. The river was bronze; the sun caught it strangely, reflecting upon its surface the near-shore sand ripples underneath. Suddenly, the crescenting of a fish, gone before the eye could clearly give image to it. The old man next door said these leaping fish were carp. Himself, he preferred muskie, for he was a real fisherman and the muskie gave him a fight. The wind most often blew from the south, and the river flowed toward the south, so when the water was wind-riffled, and the current was strong, the river seemed to be flowing both ways. I liked this, and interpreted it as an omen, a natural symbol.

A few years ago, when I was back in Winnipeg, I gave a talk at my old college. It was open to the public, and afterward a very old man came up to me and asked me if my maiden name had been Wemyss. I said yes, thinking he might have known my father or my grandfather. But no. "When I was a young lad," he said, "I once worked for your great-grandfather, Robert Wemyss, when he had the sheep ranch at Raeburn." I think that was a moment when I realized all over again something of great importance to me. My

---

4. By Prime Minister Pierre Elliott Trudeau, citing an "apprehended insurrection" in the wake of terrorist kidnapings by the separatist FLQ (Front de Libération du Québec). Under the provisions of this act, the armed forces took over many police functions, and certain civil liberties—notably habeas corpus— were suspended so that suspected terrorists could be held in jail without being charged.

long-ago families came from Scotland and Ireland, but in a sense that no longer mattered so much. My true roots were here.

I am not very patriotic, in the usual meaning of that word. I cannot say "My country right or wrong" in any political, social or literary context. But one thing is inalterable, for better or worse, for life.

This is where my world began. A world which includes the ancestors—both my own and other people's ancestors who become mine. A world which formed me, and continues to dô so, even while I found it in some of its aspects, and continue to do so. A world which gave me my own lifework to do, because it was here that I learned the sight of my own particular eyes.

1970

RUSSELL BAKER

Summer Beyond Wish

A long time ago I lived in a crossroads village of northern Virginia and during its summer enjoyed innocence and never knew boredom, although nothing of consequence happened there.

Seven houses of varying lack of distinction constituted the community. A dirt road meandered off toward the mountain where a bootleg still supplied whisky to the men of the countryside, and another dirt road ran down to the creek. My cousin Kenneth and I would sit on the bank and fish with earthworms. One day we killed a copperhead which was basking on a rock nearby. That was unusual.

The heat of summer was mellow and produced sweet scents which lay in the air so damp and rich you could almost taste them. Mornings smelled of purple wisteria, afternoons of the wild roses which tumbled over stone fences, and evenings of honeysuckle.

Even by standards of that time it was a primitive place. There was no electricity. Roads were unpaved. In our house there was no plumbing. The routine of summer days was shaped by these deficiencies. Lacking electric lights, one went early to bed and rose while the dew was still in the grass. Kerosene lamps were cleaned and polished in an early-morning hubbub of women, and children were sent to the spring for fresh water.

This afforded a chance to see whether the crayfish population had multiplied. Later, a trip to the outhouse would afford a chance to daydream in the Sears, Roebuck Catalogue, mostly about shotguns and bicycles.

With no electricity, radio was not available for pacifying the young. One or two people did have radios that operated on mail-order batteries about the size of a present-day car battery, but these were not for children, though occasionally you might be invited in to hear "Amos 'n' Andy."

All I remember about "Amos 'n' Andy" at that time is that it was strange hearing voices come out of furniture. Much later I was advised that listening to "Amos 'n' Andy" was racist and was grateful that I hadn't heard much.

In the summer no pleasures were to be had indoors. Everything of delight occurred in the world outside. In the flowers there were hummingbirds to be seen, tiny wings fluttering so fast that the birds seemed to have no wings at all.

In the heat of mid-afternoon the women would draw the blinds, spread blankets on the floor for coolness and nap, while in the fields the cattle herded together in the shade of spreading trees to escape the sun. Afternoons were absolutely still, yet filled with sounds.

Bees buzzed in the clover. Far away over the fields the chug of an ancient steam-powered threshing machine could be faintly heard. Birds rustled under the tin of the porch roof.

Rising dust along the road from the mountains signaled an approaching event. A car was coming. "Car's coming," someone would say. People emerged from houses. The approaching dust was studied. Guesses were hazarded about whom it might contain.

Then—a big moment in the day—the car would cruise past.

"Who was it?"

"I didn't get a good look."

"It looked like Packy Painter to me."

"Couldn't have been Packy. Wasn't his car."

The stillness resettled itself as gently as the dust, and you could wander past the henhouse and watch a hen settle herself to perform the mystery of laying an egg. For livelier adventure there was the field that contained the bull. There, one could test his courage by seeing how far he dared venture before running back through the fence.

The men drifted back with the falling sun, steaming with heat and fatigue, and washed in tin basins with water hauled in buckets from the spring. I knew a few of their secrets, such as who kept his whisky hidden in a mason jar behind the lime barrel, and what they were really doing when they excused themselves from the kitchen and stepped out into the orchard and stayed out there laughing too hard.

I also knew what the women felt about it, though not what they thought. Even then I could see that matters between women and men could become very difficult and, sometimes, so difficult that they spoiled the air of summer.

At sunset people sat on the porches. As dusk deepened, the light-ning bugs came out to be caught and bottled. As twilight edged into night, a bat swooped across the road. I was not afraid of bats then, although I feared ghosts, which made the approach of bed-time in a room where even the kerosene lamp would quickly be doused seem terrifying.

I was even more afraid of toads and specifically of the toad which lived under the porch steps and which, everyone assured me, would, if touched, give me warts. One night I was allowed to stay up until the stars were in full command of the sky. A woman of great age was dying in the village and it was considered fit to let the children stay abroad into the night. As four of us sat there we saw a shooting star and someone said, "Make a wish."

I did not know what that meant. I didn't know anything to wish for.

1978

QUESTIONS

1. Baker attempts to describe a boyhood summer of perfect content-ment and fulfillment. Do you think he succeeds? If so, can you indicate those features of his manner, his style, as well as his choice of what to talk about, that are designed to convey that sense of perfect contentment?

2. The essay is written by a man looking back upon his boyhood. Are there any places in the essay where we seem to hear the boy himself—that is, where the writing expresses things just as the boy (not the older man) would experience them? Why does Baker choose to treat these particular things this way?

3. Near the beginning Baker says that "nothing of consequence hap-pened there." Do you agree? Are any unusual happenings described? In what way might they be important—"of conse-quence"?

4. Do you find the conclusion of the essay effective? Why, or why not? What details substantiate the thought conveyed in the con-clusion?

MAYA ANGELOU

Graduation

The children in Stamps[1] trembled visibly with anticipation. Some adults were excited too, but to be certain the whole young population had come down with graduation epidemic. Large classes

1. A town in Arkansas.

were graduating from both the grammar school and the high school. Even those who were years removed from their own day of glorious release were anxious to help with preparations as a kind of dry run. The junior students who were moving into the vacating classes' chairs were tradition-bound to show their talents for leadership and management. They strutted through the school and around the campus exerting pressure on the lower grades. Their authority was so new that occasionally if they pressed a little too hard it had to be overlooked. After all, next term was coming, and it never hurt a sixth grader to have a play sister in the eighth grade, or a tenth-year student to be able to call a twelfth grader Bubba. So all was endured in a spirit of shared understanding. But the graduating classes themselves were the nobility. Like travelers · with exotic destinations on their minds, the graduates were remarkably forgetful. They came to school without their books, or tablets or even pencils. Volunteers fell over themselves to secure replacements for the missing equipment. When accepted, the willing workers might or might not be thanked, and it was of no importance to the pregraduation rites. Even teachers were respectful of the now quiet and aging seniors, and tended to speak to them, if not as equals, as beings only slightly lower than themselves. After tests were returned and grades given, the student body, which acted like an extended family, knew who did well, who excelled, and what piteous ones had failed.

Unlike the white high school, Lafayette County Training School distinguished itself by having neither lawn, nor hedges, nor tennis court, nor climbing ivy. Its two buildings (main classrooms, the grade school and home economics) were set on a dirt hill with no fence to limit either its boundaries or those of bordering farms. There was a large expanse to the left of the school which was used alternately as a baseball diamond or basketball court. Rusty hoops on swaying poles represented the permanent recreational equipment, although bats and balls could be borrowed from the P.E. teacher if the borrower was qualified and if the diamond wasn't occupied.

Over this rocky area relieved by a few shady tall persimmon trees the graduating class walked. The girls often held hands and no longer bothered to speak to the lower students. There was a sadness about them, as if this old world was not their home and they were bound for higher ground. The boys, on the other hand, had become more friendly, more outgoing. A decided change from the closed attitude they projected while studying for finals. Now they seemed not ready to give up the old school, the familiar paths and classrooms. Only a small percentage would be continuing on to college —one of the South's A & M (agricultural and mechanical) schools, which trained Negro youths to be carpenters, farmers, handymen, masons, maids, cooks and baby nurses. Their future rode heavily on their shoulders, and blinded them to the collective joy that had pervaded the lives of the boys and girls in the grammar school graduating class.

Parents who could afford it had ordered new shoes and ready-made clothes for themselves from Sears and Roebuck or Montgomery Ward. They also engaged the best seamstresses to make the floating graduating dresses and to cut down secondhand pants which would be pressed to a military slickness for the important event.

Oh, it was important, all right. Whitefolks would attend the ceremony, and two or three would speak of God and home, and the Southern way of life, and Mrs. Parsons, the principal's wife, would play the graduation march while the lower-grade graduates paraded down the aisles and took their seats below the platform. The high school seniors would wait in empty classrooms to make their dramatic entrance.

In the Store I was the person of the moment. The birthday girl. The center. Bailey[2] had graduated the year before, although to do so he had had to forfeit all pleasures to make up for his time lost in Baton Rouge.

My class was wearing butter-yellow piqué dresses, and Momma launched out on mine. She smocked the yoke into tiny crisscrossing puckers, then shirred the rest of the bodice. Her dark fingers ducked in and out of the lemony cloth as she embroidered raised daisies around the hem. Before she considered herself finished she had added a crocheted cuff on the puff sleeves, and a pointy crocheted collar.

I was going to be lovely. A walking model of all the various styles of fine hand sewing and it didn't worry me that I was only twelve years old and merely graduating from the eighth grade. Besides, many teachers in Arkansas Negro schools had only that diploma and were licensed to impart wisdom.

The days had become longer and more noticeable. The faded beige of former times had been replaced with strong and sure colors. I began to see my classmates' clothes, their skin tones, and the dust that waved off pussy willows. Clouds that lazed across the sky were objects of great concern to me. Their shiftier shapes might have held a message that in my new happiness and with a little bit of time I'd soon decipher. During that period I looked at the arch of heaven so religiously my neck kept a steady ache. I had taken to smiling more often, and my jaws hurt from the unaccustomed activ-

2. The author's brother.

ity. Between the two physical sore spots, I suppose I could have been uncomfortable, but that was not the case. As a member of the winning team (the graduating class of 1940) I had outdistanced unpleasant sensations by miles. I was headed for the freedom of open fields.

Youth and social approval allied themselves with me and we trammeled memories of slights and insults. The wind of our swift passage remodeled my features. Lost tears were pounded to mud and then to dust. Years of withdrawal were brushed aside and left behind, as hanging ropes of parasitic moss.

My work alone had awarded me a top place and I was going to be one of the first called in the graduating ceremonies. On the classroom blackboard, as well as on the bulletin board in the auditorium, there were blue stars and white stars and red stars. No absences, no tardinesses, and my academic work was among the best of the year. I could say the preamble to the Constitution even faster than Bailey. We timed ourselves often: "WethepeopleoftheUnited Statesinordertoformamoreperfectunion . . ." I had memorized the Presidents of the United States from Washington to Roosevelt in chronological as well as alphabetical order.

My hair pleased me too. Gradually the black mass had lengthened and thickened, so that it kept at last to its braided pattern, and I didn't have to yank my scalp off when I tried to comb it.

Louise and I had rehearsed the exercises until we tired out ourselves. Henry Reed was class valedictorian. He was a small, very black boy with hooded eyes, a long, broad nose and an oddly shaped head. I had admired him for years because each term he and I vied for the best grades in our class. Most often he bested me, but instead of being disappointed I was pleased that we shared top places between us. Like many Southern Black children, he lived with his grandmother, who was as strict as Momma and as kind as she knew how to be. He was courteous, respectful and soft-spoken to elders, but on the playground he chose to play the roughest games. I admired him. Anyone, I reckoned, sufficiently afraid or sufficiently dull could be polite. But to be able to operate at a top level with both adults and children was admirable.

His valedictory speech was entitled "To Be or Not to Be." The rigid tenth-grade teacher had helped him write it. He'd been working on the dramatic stresses for months.

The weeks until graduation were filled with heady activities. A group of small children were to be presented in a play about buttercups and daisies and bunny rabbits. They could be heard throughout the building practicing their hops and their little songs that sounded like silver bells. The older girls (nongraduates, of course) were assigned the task of making refreshments for the night's festivities. A tangy scent of ginger, cinnamon, nutmeg and chocolate wafted around the home economics building as the budding cooks made samples for themselves and their teachers.

In every corner of the workshop, axes and saws split fresh timber as the woodshop boys made sets and stage scenery. Only the graduates were left out of the general bustle. We were free to sit in the library at the back of the building or look in quite detachedly, naturally, on the measures being taken for our event.

Even the minister preached on graduation the Sunday before. His subject was, "Let your light so shine that men will see your good works and praise your Father, Who is in Heaven." Although the sermon was purported to be addressed to us, he used the occasion to speak to backsliders, gamblers and general ne'er-do-wells. But since he had called our names at the beginning of the service we were mollified.

Among Negroes the tradition was to give presents to children going only from one grade to another. How much more important this was when the person was graduating at the top of the class. Uncle Willie and Momma had sent away for a Mickey Mouse watch like Bailey's. Louise gave me four embroidered handkerchiefs. (I gave her crocheted doilies.) Mrs. Sneed, the minister's wife, made me an undershirt to wear for graduation, and nearly every customer gave me a nickel or maybe even a dime with the instruction "Keep on moving to higher ground," or some such encouragement.

Amazingly the great day finally dawned and I was out of bed before I knew it. I threw open the back door to see it more clearly, but Momma said, "Sister, come away from that door and put your robe on."

I hoped the memory of that morning would never leave me. Sunlight was itself young, and the day had none of the insistence maturity would bring it in a few hours. In my robe and barefoot in the backyard, under cover of going to see about my new beans, I gave myself up to the gentle warmth and thanked God that no matter what evil I had done in my life He had allowed me to live to see this day. Somewhere in my fatalism I had expected to die, accidentally, and never have the chance to walk up the stairs in the auditorium and gracefully receive my hard-earned diploma. Out of God's merciful bosom I had won reprieve.

Bailey came out in his robe and gave me a box wrapped in Christmas paper. He said he had saved his money for months to pay for it. It felt like a box of chocolates, but I knew Bailey wouldn't save money to buy candy when we had all we could want under our noses.

He was as proud of the gift as I. It was a soft-leather-bound copy of a collection of poems by Edgar Allan Poe, or, as Bailey and I called him, "Eap." I turned to "Annabel Lee" and we walked up and down the garden rows, the cool dirt between our toes, reciting the beautifully sad lines.

Momma made a Sunday breakfast although it was only Friday. After we finished the blessing, I opened my eyes to find the watch on my plate. It was a dream of a day. Everything went smoothly and to my credit. I didn't have to be reminded or scolded for anything. Near evening I was too jittery to attend to chores, so Bailey volunteered to do all before his bath.

Days before, we had made a sign for the Store, and as we turned out the lights Momma hung the cardboard over the doorknob. It read clearly: CLOSED. GRADUATION.

My dress fitted perfectly and everyone said that I looked like a sunbeam in it. On the hill, going toward the school, Bailey walked behind with Uncle Willie, who muttered, "Go on, Ju." He wanted him to walk ahead with us because it embarrassed him to have to walk so slowly. Bailey said he'd let the ladies walk together, and the men would bring up the rear. We all laughed, nicely.

Little children dashed by out of the dark like fireflies. Their crepe-paper dresses and butterfly wings were not made for running and we heard more than one rip, dryly, and the regretful "uh uh" that followed.

The school blazed without gaiety. The windows seemed cold and unfriendly from the lower hill. A sense of ill-fated timing crept over me, and if Momma hadn't reached for my hand I would have drifted back to Bailey and Uncle Willie, and possibly beyond. She made a few slow jokes about my feet getting cold, and tugged me along to the now-strange building.

Around the front steps, assurance came back. There were my fellow "greats," the graduating class. Hair brushed back, legs oiled, new dresses and pressed pleats, fresh pocket handkerchiefs and little handbags, all homesewn. Oh, we were up to snuff, all right. I joined my comrades and didn't even see my family go in to find seats in the crowded auditorium.

The school band struck up a march and all classes filed in as had been rehearsed. We stood in front of our seats, as assigned, and on a signal from the choir director, we sat. No sooner had this been accomplished than the band started to play the national anthem. We rose again and sang the song, after which we recited the pledge of allegiance. We remained standing for a brief minute before the choir director and the principal signaled to us, rather desperately I thought, to take our seats. The command was so unusual that our carefully rehearsed and smooth-running machine was thrown off. For a full minute we fumbled for our chairs and bumped into each other awkwardly. Habits change or solidify under pressure, so in our state of nervous tension we had been ready to follow our usual assembly pattern: the American national anthem, then the pledge of allegiance, then the song every Black person I knew called the Negro National Anthem. All done in the same key, with the same passion and most often standing on the same foot.

Finding my seat at last, I was overcome with a presentiment of worse things to come. Something unrehearsed, unplanned, was going to happen, and we were going to be made to look bad. I distinctly remember being explicit in the choice of pronoun. It was "we," the graduating class, the unit, that concerned me then.

The principal welcomed "parents and friends" and asked the Baptist minister to lead us in prayer. His invocation was brief and punchy, and for a second I thought we were getting on the high road to right action. When the principal came back to the dais, however, his voice had changed. Sounds always affected me profoundly and the principal's voice was one of my favorites. During assembly it melted and lowed weakly into the audience. It had not been in my plan to listen to him, but my curiosity was piqued and I straightened up to give him my attention.

He was talking about Booker T. Washington, our "late great leader," who said we can be as close as the fingers on the hand, etc. . . . Then he said a few vague things about friendship and the friendship of kindly people to those less fortunate than themselves. With that his voice nearly faded, thin, away. Like a river diminishing to a stream and then to a trickle. But he cleared his throat and said, "Our speaker tonight, who is also our friend, came from Texarkana to deliver the commencement address, but due to the irregularity of the train schedule, he's going to, as they say, 'speak and run.'" He said that we understood and wanted the man to know that we were most grateful for the time he was able to give us and then something about how we were willing always to adjust to another's program, and without more ado—"I give you Mr. Edward Donleavy."

Not one but two white men came through the door off-stage. The shorter one walked to the speaker's platform, and the tall one moved to the center seat and sat down. But that was our principal's seat, and already occupied. The dislodged gentleman bounced around for a long breath or two before the Baptist minister gave him his chair, then with more dignity than the situation deserved, the minister walked off the stage.

Donleavy looked at the audience once (on reflection, I'm sure that he wanted only to reassure himself that we were really there), adjusted his glasses and began to read from a sheaf of papers.

He was glad "to be here and to see the work going on just as it was in the other schools."

At the first "Amen" from the audience I willed the offender to immediate death by choking on the word. But Amens and Yes, sir's began to fall around the room like rain through a ragged umbrella.

He told us of the wonderful changes we children in Stamps had in store. The Central School (naturally, the white school was Central) had already been granted improvements that would be in use in the fall. A well-known artist was coming from Little Rock to teach art to them. They were going to have the newest microscopes and chemistry equipment for their laboratory. Mr. Donleavy didn't leave us long in the dark .over who made these improvements available to Central High. Nor were we to be ignored in the general betterment scheme he had in mind.

He said that he had pointed out to people at a very high level that one of the first-line football tacklers at Arkansas Agricultural and Mechanical College had graduated from good old Lafayette County Training School. Here fewer Amen's were heard. Those few that did break through lay dully in the air with the heaviness of habit.

He went on to praise us. He went on to say how he had bragged that "one of the best basketball players at Fisk sank his first ball right here at Lafayette County Training School."

The white kids were going to have a chance to become Galileos and Madame Curies and Edisons and Gauguins, and our boys (the girls weren't even in on it) would try to be Jesse Owenses and Joe Louises.

Owens and the Brown Bomber were great heroes in our world, but what school official in the white-goddom of Little Rock had the right to decide that those two men must be our only heroes? Who decided that for Henry Reed to become a scientist he had to work like George Washington Carver, as a bootblack, to buy a lousy microscope? Bailey was obviously always going to be too small to be an athlete, so which concrete angel glued to what country seat had decided that if my brother wanted to become a lawyer he had to first pay penance for his skin by picking cotton and hoeing corn and studying correspondence books at night for twenty years?

The man's dead words fell like bricks around the auditorium and too many settled in my belly. Constrained by hard-learned manners I couldn't look behind me, but to my left and right the proud graduating class of 1940 had dropped their heads. Every girl in my row had found something new to do with her handkerchief. Some folded the tiny squares into love knots, some into triangles, but most were wadding them, then pressing them flat on their yellow laps.

On the dais, the ancient tragedy was being replayed. Professor Parsons sat, a sculptor's reject, rigid. His large, heavy body seemed devoid of will or willingness, and his eyes said he was no longer with us. The other teachers examined the flag (which was draped stage right) or their notes, or the windows which opened on our now-famous playing diamond.

Graduation, the hush-hush magic time of frills and gifts and congratulations and diplomas, was finished for me before my name was called. The accomplishment was nothing. The meticulous maps, drawn in three colors of ink, learning and spelling decasyllabic words, memorizing the whole of *The Rape of Lucrece*[3]—it was for nothing. Donleavy had exposed us.

We were maids and farmers, handymen and washerwomen, and anything higher that we aspired to was farcical and presumptuous.

Then I wished that Gabriel Prosser and Nat Turner[4] had killed all whitefolks in their beds and that Abraham Lincoln had been assassinated before the signing of the Emancipation Proclamation, and that Harriet Tubman[5] had been killed by that blow on her head and Christopher Columbus had drowned in the *Santa Maria*.

It was awful to be a Negro and have no control over my life. It was brutal to be young and already trained to sit quietly and listen to charges brought against my color with no chance of defense. We should all be dead. I thought I should like to see us all dead, one on top of the other. A pyramid of flesh with the whitefolks on the bottom, as the broad base, then the Indians with their silly tomahawks and teepees and wigwams and treaties, the Negroes with their mops and recipes and cotton sacks and spirituals sticking out of their mouths. The Dutch children should all stumble in their wooden shoes and break their necks. The French should choke to death on the Louisiana Purchase (1803) while silkworms ate all the Chinese with their stupid pigtails. As a species, we were an abomination. All of us.

Donleavy was running for election, and assured our parents that if he won we could count on having the only colored paved playing field in that part of Arkansas. Also—he never looked up to acknowledge the grunts of acceptance—also, we were bound to get some new equipment for the home economics building and the workshop.

He finished, and since there was no need to give any more than the most perfunctory thank-you's, he nodded to the men on the stage, and the tall white man who was never introduced joined him at the door. They left with the attitude that now they were off to something really important. (The graduation ceremonies at Lafayette County Training School had been a mere preliminary.)

The ugliness they left was palpable. An uninvited guest who wouldn't leave. The choir was summoned and sang a modern

---

3. A narrative poem of 1,855 lines, by Shakespeare.
4. Leaders of Virginia slave rebellions in 1800 and 1831 respectively.

5. Nineteenth-century black abolitionist, a "conductor" on the Underground Railroad.

arrangement of "Onward, Christian Soldiers," with new words pertaining to graduates seeking their place in the world. But it didn't work. Elouise, the daughter of the Baptist minister, recited "Invictus,"[6] and I could have cried at the impertinence of "I am the master of my fate, I am the captain of my soul."

My name had lost its ring of familiarity and I had to be nudged to go and receive my diploma. All my preparations had fled. I neither marched up to the stage like a conquering Amazon, nor did I look in the audience for Bailey's nod of approval. Marguerite Johnson, I heard the name again, my honors were read, there were noises in the audience of appreciation, and I took my place on the stage as rehearsed.

I thought about colors I hated: ecru, puce, lavender, beige and black.

There was shuffling and rustling around me, then Henry Reed was giving his valedictory address, "To Be or Not to Be." Hadn't he heard the whitefolks? We couldn't *be*, so the question was a waste of time. Henry's voice came out clear and strong. I feared to look at him. Hadn't he got the message? There was no "nobler in the mind" for Negroes because the world didn't think we had minds, and they let us know it. "Outrageous fortune"? Now, that was a joke. When the ceremony was over I had to tell Henry Reed some things. That is, if I still cared. Not "rub," Henry, "erase." "Ah, there's the erase." Us.

Henry had been a good student in elocution. His voice rose on tides of promise and fell on waves of warnings. The English teacher had helped him to create a sermon winging through Hamlet's soliloquy. To be a man, a doer, a builder, a leader, or to be a tool, an unfunny joke, a crusher of funky toadstools. I marveled that Henry could go through with the speech as if we had a choice.

I had been listening and silently rebutting each sentence with my eyes closed; then there was a hush, which in an audience warns that something unplanned is happening. I looked up and saw Henry Reed, the conservative, the proper, the A student, turn his back to the audience and turn to us (the proud graduating class of 1940) and sing, nearly speaking,

> "Lift ev'ry voice and sing
> Till earth and heaven ring
> Ring with the harmonies of Liberty ..."

It was the poem written by James Weldon Johnson. It was the music composed by J. Rosamond Johnson. It was the Negro national anthem. Out of habit we were singing it.

---

6. An inspirational poem by the nineteenth-century poet William Ernest Henley, once very popular for occasions such as this one.

Our mothers and fathers stood in the dark hall and joined the hymn of encouragement. A kindergarten teacher led the small children onto the stage and the buttercups and daisies and bunny rabbits marked time and tried to follow:

> "Stony the road we trod
> Bitter the chastening rod
> Felt in the days when hope, unborn, had died.
> Yet with a steady beat
> Have not our weary feet
> Come to the place for which our fathers sighed?"

Each child I knew had learned that song with his ABC's and along with "Jesus Loves Me This I Know." But I personally had never heard it before. Never heard the words, despite the thousands of times I had sung them. Never thought they had anything to do with me.

On the other hand, the words of Patrick Henry had made such an impression on me that I had been able to stretch myself tall and trembling and say, "I know not what course others may take, but as for me, give me liberty or give me death."

And now I heard, really for the first time:

> "We have come over a way that with tears
> has been watered,
> We have come, treading our path through
> the blood of the slaughtered."

While echoes of the song shivered in the air, Henry Reed bowed his head, said "Thank you," and returned to his place in the line. The tears that slipped down many faces were not wiped away in shame.

We were on top again. As always, again. We survived. The depths had been icy and dark, but now a bright sun spoke to our souls. I was no longer simply a member of the proud graduating class of 1940; I was a proud member of the wonderful, beautiful Negro race.

Oh, Black known and unknown poets, how often have your auctioned pains sustained us? Who will compute the lonely nights made less lonely by your songs, or the empty pots made less tragic by your tales?

If we were a people much given to revealing secrets, we might raise monuments and sacrifice to the memories of our poets, but slavery cured us of that weakness. It may be enough, however, to have it said that we survive in exact relationship to the dedication of our poets (include preachers, musicians and blues singers).

1969

LAURENCE SHEEHAN

How to Play Second Base

Second base is the most important position in baseball. Nobody realizes. A lot of coaches don't even bother to tell their second basemen the first thing about the job. They don't think second base is worth the effort.

The unfortunate name of second base is partly to blame. It just sounds like a hand-me-down. I think the ill-fated manager Joe McCarthy of the Boston Red Sox also once said something like second base is neither first nor third. That was the situation when I was playing for Centerville School, and I doubt if it's improved much since then, not at Centerville or in the majors.

Why is second base so important? Because when an easy grounder or a high pop-up is hit to that position, and you kick it away, or misjudge it and let it bounce on your head, the whole team gets demoralized. The shortstop comes over and says, Too bad the school bus didn't clip you this morning. The first baseman slaps his leg and laughs. The pitcher gives you the finger in front of everybody. Of course there may not be that many people at the game, so the public humiliation won't count for much. Centerville hardly ever drew a crowd because it was always in last place in its division, thanks in part to slight miscalculations by the second baseman.

I got my little sister Evie to come a lot when games were played at Legion Field in our neighborhood. But she didn't understand baseball. She would see me strike out on three consecutive pitches, or get run through by a steaming grounder. But she wouldn't find such happenings interesting enough to report to our parents. I'd have to tell them myself at supper.

You might say that for Evie my baseball failings went in one eye and out the other. She was a lousy fan. I sometimes wondered why I had her come to the games at all, which I did starting when I made the team in sixth grade and got my uniform. I don't think she even knew what number I wore (9—The Thumper's[1] own!). Anyway, if it weren't for the bubble gum my black pal Herman kept giving her, she probably would have stopped coming long before she finally did. Herman played third. She would chew gum or eat an apple or orange from home, and watch out that no one stole our gloves when we were at bat, but basically Evie paid no attention to what was going on. She usually sat on the opposing

1. Boston Red Sox star Ted Williams.

team's bench, to my great embarrassment. It was closer to the water fountain.

Back to second base now. There are tips that can make anybody play this position better and I'd like to pass them along.

By the way, I didn't mean to imply I minded my teammates groaning and hooting at my errors. I mean I minded, but I understood. And basically we had a close-knit infield. It wasn't any dream infield, such as the Bosox built around the great Bobby Doerr and Johnny Pesky in the same years I was at Centerville, but we had a pretty good team feeling. Erwin, our regular pitcher, would put up with four or five errors in one inning before going to the finger. Lover Boy, the first baseman, would laugh at errors and kid a lot, but actually he didn't care where the ball went or even who won. His mind was always on his girlfriends who were waiting for him up in the nearly empty stands. Bert, our team captain at short, would come over after I'd let one go through my legs, and say, "All right, let's get back in this game now." And of course Herman, who never made an error himself over at third, would not get upset by anything I did. Or anybody did. He was the coolest cucumber on the squad.

Not even State Street's Butch Mendoza, the division's Home Run King and number-one razzer, could get through to Herman. We had no regular coaches on the bases. Older players on each team did the job. Mendoza liked to do it for State Street. He'd coach first base and rib Lover Boy about his shaggy hair and his white cleats, and Lover Boy would nod and smile, probably not even hearing Butch's taunts, too busy dreaming about those girls of his up in the stands and about his plans for them all after the game. When Butch coached third he liked to rib Herman about his color. "Hey, boy, where's your watermelon today?" he'd say, or "How come you're not picking cotton this week?" At that time blacks were few and far between in our town, no matter what grammar school you went to, and Butch probably thought of Herman as a foreigner. The important thing is, Herman paid no attention to Butch and never did make an error before his eyes.

I'll spare the outfielders on Centerville. Like most outfielders they were hotshots, and I suppose because they managed to get more hits and runs than anyone else, they had a right to parade around out there and editorialize on every move the infielders made.

Now, then, the hardest play to handle is the infield fly. I say anytime a ball goes higher than it goes farther, it is going to be a son of a gun to catch. In my playing days, half the time I wouldn't even know when one of those high pops was entering my territory. I'd need to hear Lover Boy call over, "Hey, little man, here comes trouble!"

Anyway, you've got to get set. A good thing is to get your feet in motion. And bend your neck back far enough so your eyes see more than the brim of the baseball cap. Everything about school uniforms is fine except the brims on the caps. They are made for adult heads, and if you stand 4 feet 3 and weigh 75 pounds, the hat will be like an awning on your forehead. The only thing you'll be able to see without any strain is your feet, which as I said should be in motion anyway—as you commence dancing into position to make a stab at the catch.

Of course, once you get your head tilted back far enough so you can see past the brim of your cap, you risk being temporarily blinded by the sun. Even on cloudy days it is possible for the sun to come out just at the crucial instant and make you lose sight of the damn ball, assuming you ever saw it in the first place.

Another bad thing about the high fly is that it gives you too much time to think. Like the drowning man, a ten-year-old tends to experience all the important moments in his life while waiting for a baseball to drop. Moments such as when you saw your name on the Centerville School baseball roster for the first time.

To tell the truth, the reason I got to play second base for Centerville for three years in a row is that my growth was stunted at the time, and provided I didn't swing at the ball when I was up to bat, opposing pitchers tended to walk me. My strike zone was about the size of a civics workbook. If I waited out the pitchers, I could count on getting on base almost every time.

Not that I wouldn't go for the hit once in a while. I would pretend to miss the signal telling me to wait for the walk that would invariably come from the third-base coach when I was up. The signal was always the same: doff cap, scratch left knee, blow nose in hanky, in that order. By the end of the season every team in the division knew all our coaching signals, but it was too confusing to try to change them.

Anyway, sometimes I would just ignore the signal and go for the hit. Each time I missed the ball, of course, the third-base coach would slam his cap on the ground or throw his hanky down, mad as can be. The opposing team's catcher would grin and hold the ball up in front of my eyes for my inspection before tossing it back to the mound. I would ignore all this and just dig in deeper with my cleats and take a couple of fierce practice swings. Digging in was itself a problem because the batter's box was furrowed over from other stances. Following the example of The Thumper and Vern Stephens and other Beantown sluggers, the boys in our division liked to get a really firm hold on the planet when at bat. They would dig and kick with their cleats like dogs tearing up the ground after peeing, and the result would be a set of gullies in the batter's box among which I was supposed to find a place to stand. I had the narrow stance that comes with a 4-foot, 3-inch frame, and sometimes I had one foot on a hillside and the other in a gully. No wonder my average was low.

That's really part of the story of how Herman and I got to be friends—we were built the same. We were the only two to make the team in sixth grade. Herman made it on his talent in spite of his size and I made it on my size in spite of my talent. In a way we came up together from the minors. Also we tended to sit right near each other in classrooms because our last names started with the same initial and in those days everything was done alphabetically, from choking on cod-liver-oil pills to taking cover in the lavatory during practice A-bomb attacks.

Now about the high fly. Your own thoughts are not the only distractions when you're looking for a ball somewhere up there in the blinding blue infinity of outer space. People are chattering all around you. Once I heard my sister call to me, "Hey, I'm going to play on the swings now, OK?" Another time, when we were playing State Street, Butch Mendoza hit a real rainmaker somewhere in my neighborhood. Running down the line to first, Butch had plenty of time on his hands, so he hollered, "Hey, kid, you're gonna miss it, you're gonna miss it!" Of course I was; nobody had to broadcast it.

State Street always won the division and usually went on to win the town title by beating the leader of the other division. They were tough boys at State Street. If they didn't beat you in the game, they'd beat you up afterwards. A lot of the State Street players had stayed back in grades a couple of times, which gave them the edge of experience over the boys at Centerville. I don't know how old Butch was. I did hear once that when he finally graduated from State Street he was eligible for the draft. That may have been an exaggeration, but no question, he was big. He would pole tremendous flies that our outfielders wouldn't even bother running for. There was no proper fence at Legion Field such as they have at Fenway Park, and after a certain point, say 250 feet out, the field slanted sharply into an old cemetery and it was the devil finding the ball if it got that far.

Butch and one other boy in our division were the only ones who could reach the cemetery, so it really wasn't a problem. The other boy played for Mount Carmel but I don't remember his name. He missed a lot of the games, anyway, because he often had to work on his family's farm after school. Mount Carmel was in the town's last rural section and boasted a number of hayseeds on its squad, boys with eyebrows that grew together and hard bones.

The only other good team in our division was Spring Glen. It always amazed me how the rich families who lived in the Spring Glen section of town could produce so many ballplayers. As far as I could tell, Ted Williams, Dom DiMaggio, Walt Dropo, Birdie Tebbetts, Billy Goodman, and the rest all came from humble backgrounds. On that basis I used to think there was some connection between rough childhoods and good batting averages, which is why I sometimes wished my own house would burn down, to give me an edge.

My final advice on high pops is to play them on the first bounce. Just let the ball drop and say you thought the infield fly rule was in effect. Of course the infield fly rule is in effect only when two or more players are on base, and then the batter is automatically out. Actually, though, high infield flies are never hit to the second baseman when the rule happens to apply. That is one of the unfair parts a second baseman learns to live with.

I could go into what kind of glove to buy and how to keep it oiled and such, but you probably know all that. Anyway the glove doesn't make the ballplayer. When I was named to the team in sixth grade, I talked my folks into buying me a nice new glove with a big web and all, in honor of the miracle. But the only thing I ever caught in it was a cold—that's what Lover Boy always said. In comparison, Herman's glove looked like it had come off the world's last buffalo. It had no padding and hardly any webbing and one of the fingers was always coming unstitched. But Herman nabbed everything that came anywhere near third base.

I guess Evie knew Herman's glove was magical even though she hardly watched the action, because she would hold it in her lap for him between innings. Mine she just kept handy. Herman would pay her off in bubble gum for the service.

Now for grounders. I used to practice fielding grounders all winter by flinging a ball against the concrete wall in our basement. It drove my parents batty and scarred the patio furniture in storage and worst of all it taught me how to catch only one kind of grounder—the grounder that comes directly at you and bounces into your glove at knee level. In three years of play in our division, this particular type of ground ball was never once hit to my position.

The key thought at second is not to catch the grounder, anyway, but to stop it. That keeps the right fielder off your back and if you manage to find the ball after it's bounced off your knee or chest, you still might be able to get it to first in time for the out. A danger here is to get so excited about actually getting the ball in your bare hand that you send it sailing over the first baseman's head and over by the swings. So concentrate on the throw to first during infield warm-up at the start of every inning. This is when the first baseman throws a few grounders to the other infielders to loosen them up.

Lover Boy was always careful to give me a grounder underhanded, so I would be more likely to catch it and not have to trot out into shallow center to get the ball back again.

Maybe even more important than handling pops and stopping ground balls with your chin if necessary is the second baseman's role in boosting team spirit. A lot of boosting comes in the form of infield chatter in support of the pitcher. "Come on you kid, come on you babe," is a proven morale-booster. So are "No hitter no hitter up there" and "Chuck it in there, baby."

I was practically the psychological cornerstone of the Centerville infield because Erwin, our regular pitcher, was lefthanded. In the course of winding up, especially when there were men on base—as there usually were—Erwin would always pause briefly and be forced to look in my direction, as a southpaw, before collecting his energies for the assault on the strike zone. Sometimes he had a faintly disgusted look which seemed to say, "Well, I suppose you're getting ready to make another error." But I knew the importance of giving him confidence and I would stare right back and say, "Come on you kid come on you babe no hitter no hitter."

Erwin sucked on Life Savers during a game, which I don't approve of for a second baseman. If the second baseman gets knocked down by a runner, or happens to trip of his own accord, with a Life Saver in his mouth, it is quite possible he will get the candy jammed in his throat. I chewed gum and recommend the same. Chewing gum keeps your mouth from getting dry as a resin bag on those hot, dusty days when baseball was meant to be played, and it relaxes your jaw muscles, which are the first to freeze up under tension.

Covering the bag properly is another important duty. I never had much practice taking throws from the catcher, to put out base stealers, because in such cases the Centerville catchers either threw the ball way into the outfield or hit poor Erwin with it as he tried to get out of the way. I did handle throws from the outfield a lot. Naturally our outfielders had to show off their powerful throwing arms so, on an attempted double, say, I would face two means of extinction: (1) breaking my hand on the hard throw from the field, or (2) getting run over from behind by the base runner.

Actually I never got spiked or knocked down by runners, but there were many close calls. By far the most dangerous man on base in the division was Butch Mendoza, as you might have guessed by what I've mentioned about him already. Once Butch knocked Herman on his ass coming into third. Right away we had to bring in a young kid at Herman's position who was about as bad as I was out there. I remember Lover Boy saying, "My, my, we are now fielding a hole at second and a sieve at third!"

Herman was nowhere near the base and Butch should have been called out for running outside his normal course. He deliberately picked Herman off because of Herman's color and maybe even more because of Herman's indifference to Butch's many taunts. He should have been called out, but even the umpires were afraid of Butch Mendoza in those days. He was three times Herman's height and twice his weight, I'd guess. So Herman got carted off by Bert and Erwin and me, wind knocked out of him, and as it turned out, one arm busted.

In the meantime, I remember, Evie got up from the State Street bench, where she was sitting, naturally, and hit Butch with what was left of the apple she'd been chomping on. Got him in the face with her apple core after he'd crossed home plate. She turned and ran toward home and Butch was too surprised and out of breath anyway to do much about it. He just looked confused. I felt like catching up with Evie and buying her a Popsicle for trying to avenge Herman as she had done. I guess I knew, even as I helped cart off Herman, who was chewing his bubble gum like crazy at the time, to keep from crying probably—I guess I knew Butch had done something he would be ashamed of in later years, provided he ever stopped to think about it. And little Evie had done something she'd never stop to think about, because she was at that age when you can deal with villains cleanly.

In any case I couldn't have walked out on Centerville even though we were losing by about 12 to 3 at the time. We got Herman settled down and took the field again and finished the last two or three innings. I think State Street got a couple more runs off us, to rub it in. We never got on base again, but that didn't make any difference—we stuck it out. That's really about the last thing I wanted to pass along about the job of playing second base, whether you're winning or losing, or making five errors per game, or seeing one of your teammates get a bad break, or losing your only fan. Stick it out. That's what second base is all about.

1974

QUESTIONS

1. Did Sheehan care very much about playing baseball when he was a boy? What details in the essay support your answer? What is his attitude now?
2. From its title the essay would seem to promise instruction in playing second base. Do you learn how to do it? Do you learn anything else?
3. Why does Sheehan begin to tell you how to play the infield pop-up and then digress only to return to the topic later, doing this several times? Does he have trouble sticking to the topic, or is the essay organized, ordered to any point?

4. How would you describe Sheehan's tone, and his approach to the reader? What are some of the details of word choice, use of language, upon which you base your description of his style?
5. What is the role in the essay of Evie? Does her presence and behavior help to characterize Sheehan's attitude toward his subject now? What, for example, is being told us in the next-to-last paragraph, when Evie throws the apple core at Butch? What is the effect of the statement "she was at that age when you can deal with villains cleanly"?
6. Sheehan suggests that second base has an unfortunate name, that it "sounds like a hand-me-down" (p. 29). Can you think of any activities at which you have been a loser, so that you can speak about them with similar authority? Try an essay on "How to Play Second Fiddle," "How to Play Second String," "How to Have Second Thoughts," "How to Get a Second Chance," or "Loving in the Second City."

HUGH MacLENNAN

On Living in a Cold Country

I was twenty-one before I met a live writer; before I met, one might say, my fate. It was on my first voyage to England, where I was going to study: I had never been away from home before.

It is difficult for me to remember now how naïve I was then. I had worked and played hard, and had been equipping myself for twentieth-century life by studying Latin and Greek. I had never been outside the little province of Nova Scotia since the cessation of the period known to the psychologists as childhood amnesia (in my infancy, I'm told, I was in England for several months), and the polyglot passengers aboard that ship fascinated me, for the ship had sailed from New York and her ultimate destination was Antwerp. At Halifax, where I lived, she had stopped for half a day to take on two thousand barrels of apples, two elderly ladies, and myself.

Prowling about the ship after we got to sea, I had observed a sloppily dressed man of indeterminate age lounging in the smoke-roof or brooding over the ocean with his elbows on the railing. I could not imagine what his profession was, but the cut of his suit was American—in those days even I could distinguish an American suit from an English one—and his face looked as though some things I had never heard of had sunk into it and stayed there. When he told me he was a writer, I was impressed. When he later informed me that he was engaged on a three-hundred-thousand-word novel about Lincoln, in three sections of equal length, and in three different styles, I was reverent.

"The first section will be in the style of Mark Twain," he explained. "Why? Because that is the only style that fits the mood of Lincoln's youth. The second section"—he paused and assessed me with giveaway, spaniel's eyes—"will be in the style of Henry James."

In those days I had heard of Henry James, but only barely.

"You see, Lincoln's middle period was one of doubts, hesitations, and parentheses. He was a Hamlet in Illinois. Shakespeare would have made a success of *Hamlet* if he had written it in novel form in the style of Henry James."

The third section was to be written in the style of a writer I had not even heard about barely; it was to be written in the style of the last chapter of James Joyce's *Ulysses*.

"The choice is obvious," the writer explained. "Lincoln's third period was the presidency, and presidents, by the very nature of their jobs, can't think. They haven't the time. The stuff just pours through them."

I had never heard of this ship-met writer before, and perhaps I have already said enough to explain why I have never heard of him since. Yet he abides with me. I learned more from him about the trade of writing than I learned from any other teacher except Experience herself.

One night over his sixth drink he said that writing would be easy if it weren't for what he called "all the other things that went along with it," and that the chief of these other things were three insoluble problems. "Money," he said, "Women, and Liquor," and he pronounced each word as though a capital letter stood before it.

Much of what he had been saying had sounded strange to me, but this rang a familiar note. I admitted that my father had told me much the same thing the day before I sailed, but had not limited the three problems to writers. According to him, Money, Women, and Liquor were the three problems of every man who ever lived, nor were they (according to him) insoluble. With the first I was to be thrifty; the other two I was entirely to avoid.

The writer observed me gloomily: "If you take that advice, your Oedipus will be screaming before you're thirty."

I told him I had an *Oedipus* in my stateroom, and added guiltily that I ought to be studying it at that particular moment.

"My God," he said, "do you still think Oedipus is a play? But to get back—money you must have for obvious reasons, but too much is worse than too little. A high standard of living invariably produces a low standard of prose. But women and liquor, these are even more essential than money. They're necessary food for your subconscious. You need them to awaken your guilts." After ordering another drink, he sighed: "But the trouble with liquor is it's apt to leave you with nothing else *but* your subconscious. And alcoholic remorse, I'm sorry to say, is an uncreative remorse."

The next morning on deck he was obviously suffering from alcoholic remorse, and as we leaned on the railing and stared down at the yard-wide band of white brine seething along the vessel's flank, he told me he was feeling sorry for me.

"Because you want to be a writer," he said, "and you haven't a chance."

I felt myself flushing, for in those days I never told my love. I pretended that all I wished to be was a scholar.

"What gives you the idea I want to write?" I asked.

"When I met a man I know will be no good for anything else, I always know he's going to get the bug sooner or later, and probably sooner."

"Well, supposing I do? Why do you say I haven't a chance?"

"You aren't decadent enough. In fact, you're not decadent at all, and as you're twenty-one already, I doubt if you'll become decadent in time for it to matter. Frankly, your country has ruined any chance you might ever have had of becoming a writer."

"What's my country to do with it?"

"It's a cold country. In the entire history of the human race, no important art has ever come out of a cold country."

"But Canada can also get very hot," I protested.

He shook his head. "No. Canada is a cold country because that's what the world believes it is. Wait till you begin talking to editors and you'll remember that I told you so."

Some twenty years later I was talking with an editor and I did remember that he had told me so. By that time I had been writing long enough to be acutely aware of the first of the Three Problems, and this editor belonged to a super-colossal magazine that paid super-colossal fees. I wanted one of those fees to finance six months' work on a novel. While we ate lunch, with a tableful of bilingual lawyers across the aisle discussing a case with Gallic gestures, the editor informed me that what he wanted was "a real, true-to-life piece on Canada." For a subject I could take my pick of Eskimos, trappers, Mounties, or husky dogs, and if I could manage to work all four of them into the same piece, it would be perfect, providing it met the literary standards of his magazine. While we talked, the temperature was ninety degrees, and the editor was feeling it, for he had come north clad in heavy worsteds. Mopping his forehead, he explained that this would be what he called a "duty-piece." His magazine sold several hundred thousand copies in Canada every month, and occasionally the management felt it a duty to print some Canadian material. I must have made a comment about there being no Eskimos, trappers, or husky dogs within fifteen hundred miles of where we were sitting, for he cut me short with a gesture.

"No, they're imperative. In an African duty-piece you stress the heat and the jungle. In an English duty-piece you stress how old everything is. A French duty-piece has got to be romantic, but at the same time we like an angle showing the French are also practical and getting themselves orientated to the up-to-date. But in a Canadian duty-piece you simply have to go heavy on the snow and the cold."

But to return to that morning at sea—for some reason my newly met American writer had taken an interest in me. After saying that he believed in Voltaire's[1] way of dealing with aspiring young authors ("If I had a son who wanted to write, I'd strangle him out of sheer good nature"), he asked me how I'd been living "up there," his notion of Canada being a red-painted roof on top of the North American house.

"Well actually," I told him, "and so much for your idea of my living in a cold country, for the past eleven years I've been living in a tent."

"In a *what?*"

"The first time in eleven years that I've slept between four walls was my first night aboard this ship. Well yes, I suppose it does sound a little odd."

"It sounds *very* odd." His eyes opened wide at me. "Indeed, it sounds so odd that it may indicate possibilities for you. Continue. Tell me about it."

So I told him.

In those days in Halifax the life was not much different from life in a village, even though we had the harbor, the university, the hospitals, the Government House,[2] the curfew gun on the Citadel, and the memory of the explosion which had smashed a third of the town a few years before. Behind every house was some sort of back yard—the word "yard" had probably reached us from New England Loyalists[3]—and most of these had a kitchen garden, a few fruit trees, and a one-horse stable which might or might not have been converted into a one-car garage. In the early 1920s there was still a faint smell of stable behind the houses and a reasonably strong smell of it in the streets. Each yard was separated from its neighbors by a rough board fence on the top of which prowling tomcats sat in the nights and howled at the female cats they knew were inside the houses.

In the summer of my eleventh year I went to a boys' camp where

---

1. Eighteenth-century French writer.
2. Official residence of the lieutenant governor of Nova Scotia.
3. Many of the New England colonists who remained loyal to the British crown during the American Revolution resettled in Nova Scotia and New Brunswick.

we slept under canvas, and when I returned to Halifax, the weather was so hot I could not sleep well indoors. Heat waves are rare in Nova Scotia, but when they come, the salt humidity sticks to your skin. My father reminded me of a little tent in the basement he had used years ago for fishing trips and he said it was probably moldy in spots. It was, but I got it out, pitched it in the back yard, installed a battered old hospital cot and a packing case to hold a saucer with a candle in it, and that night I slept beautifully. The next day I told my parents I intended to stay out in the tent until school began.

But when school began on the first of September it was still warm, so I decided to stay out until it got cold. Then in the first week of October the mornings were cool enough, but there was dew on the ripe apples and pears, and waking up in such air was a sensual experience as delicious as any I can remember. I told my parents I intended staying out until it got really cold. Three weeks later I woke to see the tent walls sagging and a foot of snow on the ground. Presumably this was really cold, but I told my parents I had slept so well I would stay out until it got impossibly cold.

It never did. The Canadian climate in the early 1920s had a mean average temperature three to four degrees lower than it has now, and this, meteorologists tell me, represents a substantial differential. Nowadays the temperature seldom drops below zero in Halifax, though the salt humidity of a Maritime climate makes zero feel as cold as twenty-five below on the prairies. But it often got below zero in Halifax when I was a boy, and one night in my first January in the tent the thermometer fell to seventeen below, and the trees cracked like guns in the frost. Once more I slept beautifully, and after that night I decided to remain outside indefinitely.

It seemed perfectly natural to do this. I used to wear in the winters two pairs of flannel pajamas, a pair of woolen socks, and a red beret. When I emerged from the back door in this regalia I carried a hot-water bottle (it was bad the night it broke) to warm the blankets before my own body-heat sustained a modest furnace inside of them. The only part of me that ever got cold in the tent was my nose. And here is an item for anyone who does not already know it: a cold nose is a better sedative than a quarter-grain Seconal.

Phenomena belonging to the science of physics became high poetry on the really cold nights. My breath made snow, real snow. As it issued warm from my nose and mouth, it mounted to the canvas under the ridge-pole and turned into a delicate cloud in the still, frigid air. When it congealed, it was converted into a filmy snowmist, which descended and settled on top of the bed. Once I woke with a bright orange sun flaring into the tent and found myself warm under a quarter-inch layer of the softest snow I ever saw, each crystal dancing in the eye of that Austerlitz sunrise.[4]

But congealed breath made another problem, an uncomfortable chin. In the vicinity of the mouth, when you sleep out in sub-zero weather, your breath does not turn into snow but into ice, and ice irritates the skin. Having been helpless all my adulthood in the presence of the most elementary technical problem, it gives me a certain satisfaction to relate how I dealt with this one when I was ten years old and resourceful. I asked my mother for an old sheet, cut it crosswise into strips a foot wide, and each night when I tucked myself in by candle light I laid this length of sheeting under my jaw. Whenever I woke with ice irritating me, I shifted the sheeting to a dry place. After a while this routine became so automatic that I was unconscious of it.

A more serious problem was the one of waking up in the morning.

In those days my family kept a maid from Newfoundland called Sadie, a fisherman's daughter from the little island of Ramea off the southern coast of the Ancient Colony.[5] Ramea is barren, but the water surrounding it is so abundant in codfish that in Cabot's time the density of the cod impeded the motion of his ships. Ramea's climate is a little milder than Labrador's, but some of Sadie's tales of *her* experience of living in a cold country made Halifax seem like a sultry port in a sugar island. Sometimes the salt sea froze out a distance of two miles from the shore of Ramea, and when this happened, if the fishermen wanted food, they had to haul their dories over the treacherous, spongy, salt-water ice to deep water, and then haul them back in the evening with the catch. More than one man Sadie knew was drowned doing things like this. So to her, warmth was a thing you hoarded. When her Newfoundland friends, seamen all, visited her kitchen, the fog was so thick you could barely see through it, for while the men smoked shag in cutty pipes, the stove glowed cherry-red as it brewed the gallons of tea they drank. Happy in a hundred-degree temperature, the Newfoundlanders conversed in a dialect I could hardly understand, for the speech of their outports is the speech that was used by common folk in western England in Shakespeare's time.

Newfoundlanders are polite people, and Sadie never said straight out that I was crazy. But she did say it was no part of her duty to wade through the snow of a zero morning in order to waken a small

---

4. That is, a dazzling sunrise, revealing all. The expression refers to the Battle of Austerlitz (1805), one of Napoleon's greatest victories: when the sun rose on the morning of the battle and dispersed the heavy mist, the enemy was revealed to have fallen into Napoleon's trap.

5. Newfoundland, the "Ancient Colony," was probably first claimed for England in 1497 by John Cabot, who discovered the famous Grand Banks fisheries. It became an English colony formally in 1853.

boy who had a perfectly comfortable room indoors. My mother agreed with her; indeed, I suspect her of hoping that this would settle the matter, for she knew I would never wake up in time for school if left to myself.

However, there was a chandler's shop along the Halifax water-front which boasted that it sold everything from a needle to an anchor, and displayed in its window an anchor and a sailmaker's needle to prove it. Thither I repaired one afternoon when school was out, and came home lugging a four-pound gong of the kind they used to place on the outside of school walls to ring in the children from recess. This gong I installed inside the tent, and ran a cord from its clapper through a row of pulleys to the kitchen window. After boring a hole through the window-frame, I thrust the cord inside for Sadie to pull. And at seven-thirty the next morning, pull she did—with the vigor of a fisher girl heaving on a halyard.

The noise was appalling, for this was a gong which was meant to be audible for a quarter of a mile. I was out of the tent and inside the house before I was even awake. My father feared the police would intervene if the gong was used again. My mother, ever hopeful, telephoned the neighbours to apologize and to ask if they had been disturbed. She was told by all of them that they were delighted with the gong. They all got up at seven-thirty, and if they could be assured the gong would always ring, they would not have to worry about setting their own alarm clocks.

Now all the problems about sleeping in the tent were solved and I settled in for the years and the seasons that lay ahead. The little bells on the horses pulling milkmen's sleighs, jingling past on the street beyond the fence at six o'clock in the morning, used to reach through the walls of sleep like the bells of elfland. In the foggy springtimes I fell asleep with my ears filled with the groans, snores, and musical clangs of the fog signals and bell-buoys of Halifax harbor. When summer came, I often read by candlelight before falling asleep, and with the passage of seasons and years moved the passage of education and even of history.

I was sleeping in the tent when I learned how to translate the invaluable information that on the second day before the Kalends of June, Caesar moved his camp and marched his legions a distance of ten miles to a place where he made another camp. I was sleeping in the tent when, years later, I made my first acquaintance with communism in the form of Plato's *Republic*. I was in the tent the night when Lindbergh, after having spent the previous day flying over Nova Scotia, was dodging the ice-making clouds over the Atlantic. To the tent I returned at two o'clock in the morning the night Tunney beat Dempsey in Philadelphia, which also happened to be the first night I ever wore a dinner jacket or went to a Government House Ball.

Such was the story I told my writer-friend, and when I had finished I said: "So you see—it wasn't such a cold country after all."

He was silent a while, possibly engrossed in thoughts of Lincoln, probably worrying about his liver, and I felt embarrassed to have spoken so much about myself. But he seemed to have heard, for finally he turned and spoke.

"You'll never go back to that again, of course."

"I don't see why not."

"You must have slept without movement to have gotten away with it. If you'd moved in your sleep, you'd have disturbed the blankets and let in the cold."

"I did sleep without movement."

The spaniel eyes were prophetic: "Well, you have given me clear proof that your days of sleeping without movement are numbered. This avoidance of the house where your parents were sleeping, this compulsive crawling away from their vicinity and *into* that little tent in the back yard—if that doesn't indicate an Oedipus complex of magnitude, I don't know what else it indicates. A little while— and remember I told you so—and it will burst out. A little while, and your guilts will make you thrash and writhe in your sleep, and the last thing you'll ever think of doing will be to sleep in the tent with your lost innocence."

He stared out over the sea: "No, I can't help you. You're going to be a writer, all right."

1978

QUESTIONS

1. At the close of the essay, the older man says, "You're going to be a writer, all right." How does he know? And why does he tell the young man that he cannot help him? Does this concluding remark reflect back upon the sentence that opens the essay? What is the relationship, exactly, between the two men?

2. Early in the essay MacLennan says he equipped himself for twentieth-century life by studying Latin and Greek. Does that seem a good preparation for life? Is there evidence elsewhere in the essay for MacLennan's having equipped himself by that kind of study? What is his attitude as revealed by that remark?

3. Why does the editor say, on p. 38, that "a real, true-to-life piece on Canada" has to include Eskimos, trappers, Mounties, or husky dogs, or better yet, all four? What subjects might you include in "a real, true-to-life piece" on the United States written along similar lines? What is MacLennan saying, through this account of "duty-pieces," about people's expectations concerning real life? What is he saying about writing?

4. The editor says that "in a Canadian duty-piece you simply have to go heavy on the snow and the cold" (p. 39). Does MacLennan "go heavy" on the snow and the cold in what he tells

about his eleven years of living in a tent? Is this selection a "duty-piece" or true to life? Does the title of the selection help you in answering that question?

JOAN DIDION
On Going Home

I am home for my daughter's first birthday. By "home" I do not mean the house in Los Angeles where my husband and I and the baby live, but the place where my family is, in the Central Valley of California. It is a vital although troublesome distinction. My husband likes my family but is uneasy in their house, because once there I fall into their ways, which are difficult, oblique, deliberately inarticulate, not my husband's ways. We live in dusty houses ("D-U-S-T," he once wrote with his finger on surfaces all over the house, but no one noticed it) filled with mementos quite without value to him (what could the Canton dessert plates mean to him? how could he have known about the assay scales, why should he care if he did know?), and we appear to talk exclusively about people we know who have been committed to mental hospitals, about people we know who have been booked on drunk-driving charges, and about property, particularly about property, land, price per acre and C-2 zoning and assessments and freeway access. My brother does not understand my husband's inability to perceive the advantage in the rather common real-estate transaction known as "sale-leaseback," and my husband in turn does not understand why so many of the people he hears about in my father's house have recently been committed to mental hospitals or booked on drunk-driving charges. Nor does he understand that when we talk about sale-leasebacks and right-of-way condemnations we are talking in code about the things we like best, the yellow fields and the cotton-woods and the rivers rising and falling and the mountain roads closing when the heavy snow comes in. We miss each other's points, have another drink and regard the fire. My brother refers to my husband, in his presence, as "Joan's husband." Marriage is the classic betrayal.

Or perhaps it is not any more. Sometimes I think that those of us who are now in our thirties were born into the last generation to carry the burden of "home," to find in family life the source of all tension and drama. I had by all objective accounts a "normal" and a "happy" family situation, and yet I was almost thirty years old before I could talk to my family on the telephone without crying after I had hung up. We did not fight. Nothing was wrong. And yet some nameless anxiety colored the emotional charges between me and the place that I came from. The question of whether or not you could go home again was a very real part of the sentimental and largely literary baggage with which we left home in the fifties; I suspect that it is irrelevant to the children born of the fragmentation after World War II. A few weeks ago in a San Francisco bar I saw a pretty young girl on crystal take off her clothes and dance for the cash prize in an "amateur-topless" contest. There was no particular sense of moment about this, none of the effect of romantic degradation, of "dark journey," for which my generation strived so assiduously. What sense could that girl possibly make of, say, *Long Day's Journey into Night?*[1] Who is beside the point?

That I am trapped in this particular irrelevancy is never more apparent to me than when I am home. Paralyzed by the neurotic lassitude engendered by meeting one's past at every turn, around every corner, inside every cupboard, I go aimlessly from room to room. I decide to meet it head-on and clean out a drawer, and I spread the contents on the bed. A bathing suit I wore the summer I was seventeen. A letter of rejection from *The Nation*, an aerial photograph of the site for a shopping center my father did not build in 1954. Three teacups hand-painted with cabbage roses and signed "E.M.," my grandmother's initials. There is no final solution for letters of rejection from *The Nation* and teacups hand-painted in 1900. Nor is there any answer to snapshots of one's grandfather as a young man on skis, surveying around Donner Pass in the year 1910. I smooth out the snapshot and look into his face, and do and do not see my own. I close the drawer, and have another cup of coffee with my mother. We get along very well, veterans of a guerrilla war we never understood.

Days pass. I see no one. I come to dread my husband's evening call, not only because he is full of news of what by now seems to me our remote life in Los Angeles, people he has seen, letters which require attention, but because he asks what I have been doing, suggests uneasily that I get out, drive to San Francisco or Berkeley. Instead I drive across the river to a family graveyard. It has been vandalized since my last visit and the monuments are broken, overturned in the dry grass. Because I once saw a rattlesnake in the grass I stay in the car and listen to a country-and-Western station. Later I drive with my father to a ranch he has in the foothills. The

1. A powerful domestic tragedy by the modern American playwright Eugene   O'Neill, based on his early life.

man who runs his cattle on it asks us to the roundup, a week from
Sunday, and although I know that I will be in Los Angeles I say, in
the oblique way my family talks, that I will come. Once home I
mention the broken monuments in the graveyard. My mother
shrugs.

I go to visit my great-aunts. A few of them think now that I am
my cousin, or their daughter who died young. We recall an anecdote about a relative last seen in 1948, and they ask if I still like
living in New York City. I have lived in Los Angeles for three years,
but I say that I do. The baby is offered a horehound drop, and I am
slipped a dollar bill "to buy a treat." Questions trail off, answers are
abandoned, the baby plays with the dust motes in a shaft of afternoon sun.

It is time for the baby's birthday party: a white cake, strawberry-
marshmallow ice cream, a bottle of champagne saved from another
party. In the evening, after she has gone to sleep, I kneel beside the
crib and touch her face, where it is pressed against the slats, with
mine. She is an open and trusting child, unprepared for and unaccustomed to the ambushes of family life, and perhaps it is just as
well that I can offer her little of that life. I would like to give her
more. I would like to promise her that she will grow up with a sense
of her cousins and of rivers and of her great-grandmother's teacups,
would like to pledge her a picnic on a river with fried chicken and
her hair uncombed, would like to give her *home* for her birthday,
but we live differently now and I can promise her nothing like that.
I give her a xylophone and a sundress from Madeira, and promise to
tell her a funny story.

1966

QUESTIONS

1. Does the author take a single attitude, or several, toward
   "home"? Try to specify the attitude, or attitudes.
2. The author speaks of herself at home as "paralyzed by the
   neurotic lassitude engendered by meeting one's past at every
   turn" (p. 45). What details in the essay help explain that
   feeling?
3. What does the author mean by "the ambushes of family life"
   (above)?
4. Explain whether the essay gives you any clues as to why so
   much of the talk at home is ". . . about people we know who
   have been committed to mental hospitals, about people we
   know who have been booked on drunk-driving charges, and
   about property . . . (p. 44)?
5. If you have read or seen the play, explain the appropriateness
   of the author's reference (p. 45) to Eugene O'Neill's Long
   Day's Journey into Night.

6. *In her concluding sentence the author tells us she gives as birth-day gifts to her daughter "a xylophone and a sundress from Madeira." Are these appropriate? Why, or why not? Explain why she would like to give other gifts.*

JOYCE MAYNARD

Four Generations

My mother called last week to tell me that my grandmother is dying. She has refused an operation that would postpone, but not prevent, her death from pancreatic cancer. She can't eat, she has been hemorrhaging, and she has severe jaundice. "I always prided myself on being different," she told my mother. "Now I *am* different. I'm yellow."

My mother, telling me this news, began to cry. So I became the mother for a moment, reminding her, reasonably, that my grandmother is eighty-seven, she's had a full life, she has all her faculties, and no one who knows her could wish that she live long enough to lose them. Lately my mother has been finding notes in my grandmother's drawers at the nursing home, reminding her, "Joyce's husband's name is Steve. Their daughter is Audrey." In the last few years she hadn't had the strength to cook or garden, and she's begun to say she's had enough of living.

My grandmother was born in Russia, in 1892—the oldest daughter in a large and prosperous Jewish family. But the prosperity didn't last. She tells stories of the pogroms and the cossacks who raped her when she was twelve. Soon after that, her family emigrated to Canada, where she met my grandfather.

Their children were the center of their life. The story I loved best, as a child, was of my grandfather opening every box of Cracker Jack in the general store he ran, in search of the particular tin toy my mother coveted. Though they never had much money, my grandmother saw to it that her daughter had elocution lessons and piano lessons, and assured her that she would go to college.

But while she was at college, my mother met my father, who was blue-eyed and blond-haired and not Jewish. When my father sent love letters to my mother, my grandmother would open and hide them, and when my mother told her parents she was going to marry this man, my grandmother said if that happened, it would kill her.

Not likely, of course. My grandmother is a woman who used to crack Brazil nuts open with her teeth, a woman who once lifted a car off the ground, when there was an accident and it had to be moved. She has been representing her death as imminent ever since I've known her—twenty-five years—and has discussed, at length, the distribution of her possessions and her lamb coat. Every time we said goodbye, after our annual visit to Winnipeg, she'd weep and say she'd never see us again. But in the meantime, while every other relative of her generation, and a good many of the younger ones, has died (nursed usually by her), she has kept making knishes, shopping for bargains, tending the healthiest plants I've ever seen.

After my grandfather died, my grandmother lived, more than ever, through her children. When she came to visit, I would hide my diary. She couldn't understand any desire for privacy. She couldn't bear it if my mother left the house without her.

This possessiveness is what made my mother furious (and then guilt-ridden that she felt that way, when of course she owed so much to her mother). So I harbored the resentment that my mother—the dutiful daughter—would not allow herself. I—who had always performed specially well for my grandmother, danced and sung for her, presented her with kisses and good report cards—stopped writing to her, ceased to visit.

But when I heard that she was dying, I realized I wanted to go to Winnipeg to see her one more time. Mostly to make my mother happy, I told myself (certain patterns being hard to break). But also, I was offering up one more particularly fine accomplishment: my own dark-eyed, dark-skinned, dark-haired daughter, whom my grandmother had never met.

I put on my daughter's best dress for our visit to Winnipeg, the way the best dresses were always put on me, and I filled my pockets with animal crackers, in case Audrey started to cry. I scrubbed her face mercilessly. On the elevator going up to her room, I realized how much I was sweating.

Grandma was lying flat with an IV tube in her arm and her eyes shut, but she opened them when I leaned over to kiss her. "It's Fredelle's daughter, Joyce," I yelled, because she doesn't hear well anymore, but I could see that no explanation was necessary. "You came," she said. "You brought the baby."

Audrey is just one, but she has seen enough of the world to know that people in beds are not meant to be so still and yellow, and she looked frightened. I had never wanted, more, for her to smile.

Then Grandma waved at her—the same kind of slow, finger-flexing wave a baby makes—and Audrey waved back. I spread her toys out on my grandmother's bed and sat her down. There she stayed, most of the afternoon, playing and humming and sipping on her bottle, taking a nap at one point, leaning against my grandmother's leg. When I cranked her Snoopy guitar, Audrey stood up on the bed and danced. Grandma wouldn't talk much anymore, though every once in a while she would say how sorry she was that she wasn't having a better day. "I'm not always like this," she said.

Mostly she just watched Audrey. Sometimes Audrey would get off the bed, inspect the get-well cards, totter down the hall. "Where is she?" Grandma kept asking. "Who's looking after her?" I had the feeling, even then, that if I'd said, "Audrey's lighting matches," Grandma would have shot up to rescue her.

We were flying home that night, and I had dreaded telling her, remembering all those other tearful partings. But in the end, I was the one who cried. She had said she was ready to die. But as I leaned over to stroke her forehead, what she said was, "I wish I had your hair" and "I wish I was well."

On the plane flying home, with Audrey in my arms, I thought about mothers and daughters, and the four generations of the family that I know most intimately. Every one of those mothers loves and needs her daughter more than her daughter will love or need her some day, and we are, each of us, the only person on earth who is quite so consumingly interested in our child.

Sometimes I kiss and hug Audrey so much she starts crying—which is, in effect, what my grandmother was doing to my mother, all her life. And what makes my mother grieve right now, I think, is not simply that her mother will die in a day or two, but that, once her mother dies, there will never again be someone to love her in quite such an unreserved, unquestioning way. No one else who believes that, fifty years ago, she could have put Shirley Temple out of a job, no one else who remembers the moment of her birth. She will only be a mother, then, not a daughter anymore.

Audrey and I have stopped over for a night in Toronto, where my mother lives. Tomorrow she will go to a safe-deposit box at the bank and take out the receipt for my grandmother's burial plot. Then she will fly back to Winnipeg, where, for the first time in anybody's memory, there was waist-high snow on April Fool's Day. But tonight she is feeding me, as she always does when I come, and I am eating more than I do anywhere else. I admire the wedding china (once my grandmother's) that my mother has set on the table. She says (the way Grandma used to say to her, of the lamb coat), "Some day it will be yours."

1979

LOREN EISELEY
The Brown Wasps

There is a corner in the waiting room of one of the great Eastern stations where women never sit. It is always in the shadow and over-hung by rows of lockers. It is, however, always frequented—not so much by genuine travelers as by the dying. It is here that a certain element of the abandoned poor seeks a refuge out of the weather, clinging for a few hours longer to the city that has fathered them. In a precisely similar manner I have seen, on a sunny day in midwin-ter, a few old brown wasps creep slowly over an abandoned wasp nest in a thicket. Numbed and forgetful and frost-blackened, the hum of the spring hive still resounded faintly in their sodden tissues. Then the temperature would fall and they would drop away into the white oblivion of the snow. Here in the station it is in no way dif-ferent save that the city is busy in its snows. But the old ones cling to their seats as though these were symbolic and could not be given up. Now and then they sleep, their gray old heads resting with pain-ful awkwardness on the backs of the benches.

Also they are not at rest. For an hour they may sleep in the gasp-ing exhaustion of the ill-nourished and aged who have to walk in the night. Then a policeman comes by on his round and nudges them upright.

"You can't sleep here," he growls.

A strange ritual then begins. An old man is difficult to waken. After a muttered conversation the policeman presses a coin into his hand and passes fiercely along the benches prodding and gesturing toward the door. In his wake, like birds rising and settling behind the passage of a farmer through a cornfield, the men totter up, move a few paces and subside once more upon the benches.

One man, after a slight, apologetic lurch, does not move at all. Tubercularly thin, he sleeps on steadily. The policeman does not look back. To him, too, this has become a ritual. He will not have to notice it again officially for another hour.

Once in a while one of the sleepers will not awake. Like the brown wasps, he will have had his wish to die in the great droning center of the hive rather than in some lonely room. It is not so bad here with the shuffle of footsteps and the knowledge that there are others who share the bad luck of the world. There are also the whis-tles and the sounds of everyone, everyone in the world, starting on journeys. Amidst so many journeys somebody is bound to come out all right. Somebody.

Maybe it was on a like thought that the brown wasps fell away from the old paper nest in the thicket. You hold till the last, even if

50

it is only to a public seat in a railroad station. You want your place in the hive more than you want a room or a place where the aged can be eased gently out of the way. It is the place that matters, the place at the heart of things. It is life that you want, that bruises your gray old head with the hard chairs; a man has a right to his place.

But sometimes the place is lost in the years behind us. Or sometimes it is a thing of air, a kind of vaporous distortion above a heap of rubble. We cling to a time and place because without them man is lost, not only man but life. This is why the voices, real or unreal, which speak from the floating trumpets at spiritualist seances are so unnerving. They are voices out of nowhere whose only reality lies in their ability to stir the memory of a living person with some fragment of the past. Before the medium's cabinet both the dead and the living revolve endlessly about an episode, a place, an event that has already been engulfed by time.

This feeling runs deep in life; it brings stray cats running over endless miles, and birds homing from the ends of the earth. It is as though all living creatures, and particularly the more intelligent, can survive only by fixing or transforming a bit of time into space or by securing a bit of space with its objects immortalized and made permanent in time. For example, I once saw, on a flower pot in my own living room, the efforts of a field mouse to build a remembered field. I have lived to see this episode repeated in a thousand guises, and since I have spent a large portion of my life in the shade of a nonexistent tree, I think I am entitled to speak for the field mouse.

One day as I cut across the field which at that time extended on one side of our suburban shopping center, I found a giant slug feeding from a runnel of pink ice cream in an abandoned Dixie cup. I could see his eyes telescope and protrude in a kind of dim, uncertain ecstasy as his dark body bunched and elongated in the curve of the cup. Then, as I stood there at the edge of the concrete, contemplating the slug, I began to realize it was like standing on a shore where a different type of life creeps up and fumbles tentatively among the rocks and sea wrack. It knows its place and will only creep so far until something changes. Little by little as I stood there I began to see more of this shore that surrounds the place of man. I looked with sudden care and attention at things I had been running over thoughtlessly for years. I even waded out a short way into the grass and the wild-rose thickets to see more. A huge black-belted bee went droning by and there were some indistinct scurryings in the underbrush.

Then I came to a sign which informed me that this field was to be the site of a new Wanamaker suburban store. Thousands of obscure lives were about to perish, the spores of puffballs would go smoking off to new fields, and the bodies of little white-footed mice would be crunched under the inexorable wheels of the bulldozers. Life disappears or modifies its appearances so fast that everything takes on an aspect of illusion—a momentary fizzing and boiling with smoke rings, like pouring dissident chemicals into a retort. Here man was advancing, but in a few years his plaster and bricks would be disappearing once more into the insatiable maw of the clover. Being of an archaeological cast of mind, I thought of this fact with an obscure sense of satisfaction and waded back through the rose thickets to the concrete parking lot. As I did so, a mouse scurried ahead of me, frightened of my steps if not of that ominous Wanamaker sign. I saw him vanish in the general direction of my apartment house, his little body quivering with fear in the great open sun on the blazing concrete. Blinded and confused, he was running straight away from his field. In another week scores would follow him.

I forgot the episode then and went home to the quiet of my living room. It was not until a week later, letting myself into the apartment, that I realized I had a visitor. I am fond of plants and had several ferns standing on the floor in pots to avoid the noon glare by the south window.

As I snapped on the light and glanced carelessly around the room, I saw a little heap of earth on the carpet and a scrabble of pebbles that had been kicked merrily over the edge of one of the flower pots. To my astonishment I discovered a full-fledged burrow delving downward among the fern roots. I waited silently. The creature who had made the burrow did not appear. I remembered the wild field then, and the flight of the mice. No house mouse, no *Mus domesticus*, had kicked up this little heap of earth or sought refuge under a fern root in a flower pot. I thought of the desperate little creature I had seen fleeing from the wild-rose thicket. Through intricacies of pipes and attics, he, or one of his fellows, had climbed to this high green solitary room. I could visualize what had occurred. He had an image in his head, a world of seed pods and quiet, of green sheltering leaves in the dim light among the weed stems. It was the only world he knew and it was gone.

Somehow in his flight he had found his way to this room with drawn shades where no one would come till nightfall. And here he had smelled green leaves and run quickly up the flower pot to dabble his paws in common earth. He had even struggled half the afternoon to carry his burrow deeper and had failed. I examined the hole, but no whiskered twitching face appeared. He was gone. I gathered up the earth and refilled the burrow. I did not expect to find traces of him again.

Yet for three nights thereafter I came home to the darkened room and my ferns to find the dirt kicked gaily about the rug and the burrow reopened, though I was never able to catch the field mouse within it. I dropped a little food about the mouth of the burrow, but it was never touched. I looked under beds or sat reading with one ear cocked for rustlings in the ferns. It was all in vain; I never saw him. Probably he ended in a trap in some other tenant's room.

But before he disappeared I had come to look hopefully for his evening burrow. About my ferns there had begun to linger the insubstantial vapor of an autumn field, the distilled essence, as it were, of a mouse brain in exile from its home. It was a small dream, like our dreams, carried a long and weary journey along pipes and through spider webs, past holes over which loomed the shadows of waiting cats, and finally, desperately, into this room where he had played in the shuttered daylight for an hour among the green ferns on the floor. Every day these invisible dreams pass us on the street, or rise from beneath our feet, or look out upon us from beneath a bush.

Some years ago the old elevated railway in Philadelphia was torn down and replaced by a subway system. This ancient El with its barnlike stations containing nut-vending machines and scattered food scraps had, for generations, been the favorite feeding ground of flocks of pigeons, generally one flock to a station along the route of the El. Hundreds of pigeons were dependent upon the system. They flapped in and out of its stanchions and steel work or gathered in watchful little audiences about the feet of anyone who rattled the peanut-vending machines. They even watched people who jingled change in their hands, and prospected for food under the feet of the crowds who gathered between trains. Probably very few among the waiting people who tossed a crumb to an eager pigeon realized that this El was like a food-bearing river, and that the life which haunted its banks was dependent upon the running of the trains with their human freight.

I saw the river stop.

The time came when the underground tubes were ready; the traffic was transferred to a realm unreachable by pigeons. It was like a great river subsiding suddenly into desert sands. For a day, for two days, pigeons continued to circle over the El or stand close to the red vending machines. They were patient birds, and surely this great river which had flowed through the lives of unnumbered generations was merely suffering from some momentary drought.

They listened for the familiar vibrations that had always heralded an approaching train; they flapped hopefully about the head of an occasional workman walking along the steel runways. They passed from one empty station to another, all the while growing hungrier. Finally they flew away.

I thought I had seen the last of them about the El, but there was a revival and it provided a curious instance of the memory of living things for a way of life or a locality that has long been cherished. Some weeks after the El was abandoned workmen began to tear it down. I went to work every morning by one particular station, and the time came when the demolition crews reached this spot. Acetylene torches showered passersby with sparks, pneumatic drills hammered at the base of the structure, and a blind man who, like the pigeons, had clung with his cup to a stairway leading to the change booth, was forced to give up his place.

It was then, strangely, momentarily, one morning that I witnessed the return of a little band of the familiar pigeons. I even recognized one or two members of the flock that had lived around this particular station before they were dispersed into the streets. They flew bravely in and out among the sparks and the hammers and the shouting workmen. They had returned—and they had returned because the hubbub of the wreckers had convinced them that the river was about to flow once more. For several hours they flapped in and out through the empty windows, nodding their heads and watching the fall of girders with attentive little eyes. By the following morning the station was reduced to some burned-off stanchions in the street. My bird friends had gone. It was plain, however, that they retained a memory for an insubstantial structure now compounded of air and time. Even the blind man clung to it. Someone had provided him with a chair, and he sat at the same corner staring sightlessly at an invisible stairway where, so far as he was concerned, the crowds were still ascending to the trains.

I have said my life has been passed in the shade of a nonexistent tree, so that such sights do not offend me. Prematurely I am one of the brown wasps and I often sit with them in the great droning hive of the station, dreaming sometimes of a certain tree. It was planted sixty years ago by a boy with a bucket and a toy spade in a little Nebraska town. That boy was myself. It was a cottonwood sapling and the boy remembered it because of some words spoken by his father and because everyone died or moved away who was supposed to wait and grow old under its shade. The boy was passed from hand to hand, but the tree for some intangible reason had taken root in his mind. It was under its branches that he sheltered; it was from this tree that his memories, which are my memories, led away into the world.

After sixty years the mood of the brown wasps grows heavier

upon one. During a long inward struggle I thought it would do me good to go and look upon that actual tree. I found a rational excuse in which to clothe this madness. I purchased a ticket and at the end of two thousand miles I walked another mile to an address that was still the same. The house had not been altered.

I came close to the white picket fence and reluctantly, with great effort, looked down the long vista of the yard. There was nothing there to see. For sixty years that cottonwood had been growing in my mind. Season by season its seeds had been floating farther on the hot prairie winds. We had planted it lovingly there, my father and I, because he had a great hunger for soil and live things growing, and because none of these things had long been ours to protect. We had planted the little sapling and watered it faithfully, and I remembered that I had run out with my small bucket to drench its roots the day we moved away. And all the years since it had been growing in my mind, a huge tree that somehow stood for my father and the love I bore him. I took a grasp on the picket fence and forced myself to look again.

A boy with the hard bird eye of youth pedaled a tricycle slowly up beside me.

"What'cha lookin' at?" he asked curiously.

"A tree," I said.

"What for?" he said.

"It isn't there," I said, to myself mostly, and began to walk away at a pace just slow enough not to seem to be running.

"What isn't there?" the boy asked. I didn't answer. It was obvious I was attached by a thread to a thing that had never been there, or certainly not for long. Something that had to be held in the air, or sustained in the mind, because it was part of my orientation in the universe and I could not survive without it. There was more than an animal's attachment to a place. There was something else, the attachment of the spirit to a grouping of events in time; it was part of our morality.

So I had come home at last, driven by a memory in the brain as surely as the field mouse who had delved long ago into my flower pot or the pigeons flying forever amidst the rattle of nut-vending machines. These, the burrow under the greenery in my living room and the red-bellied bowls of peanuts now hovering in midair in the minds of pigeons, were all part of an elusive world that existed nowhere and yet everywhere. I looked once at the real world about me while the persistent boy pedaled at my heels.

It was without meaning, though my feet took a remembered path. In sixty years the house and street had rotted out of my mind. But the tree, the tree that no longer was, that had perished in its first season, bloomed on in my individual mind, unblemished as my father's words. "We'll plant a tree here, son, and we're not going to move any more. And when you're an old, old man you can sit under it and think how we planted it here, you and me, together."

I began to outpace the boy on the tricycle.

"Do you live here, Mister?" he shouted after me suspiciously. I took a firm grasp on airy nothing—to be precise, on the bole of a great tree. "I do," I said. I spoke for myself, one field mouse, and several pigeons. We were all out of touch but somehow permanent. It was the world that had changed.

1971

QUESTIONS

1. Eiseley writes of old men in train stations, brown wasps, a field mouse, pigeons near the El, and his own return to his boyhood home in Nebraska. What do these matters have in common? Can you state the essay's theme?

2. Some psychologists study animal behavior in order to learn about human behavior, but many of them write about animals in a very different fashion. Do you think that Eiseley's way of relating the behavior of animals to human behavior makes sense? If you are studying psychology, it might be interesting to compare a selection from your textbook with this essay.

3. Would Eiseley agree with Henry David Thoreau's remarks in "Observation" (pp. 98–99)? If so, in what particular ways would he agree?

4. Eiseley's essay contains sentences like "We cling to a time and place because without them man is lost, not only man but life" (p. 51) and also sentences like "A boy with the hard bird eye of youth pedaled a tricycle slowly up beside me" (p. 55). What is the difference between these two kinds of sentences? Can you show how Eiseley manages to connect one kind with the other?

5. In "Once More to the Lake" (pp. 56–62) E. B. White describes his return to a lake he had known years earlier. What reflections arise in his mind on this occasion? Are they similar to, or different from, Eiseley's thoughts upon returning to his Nebraska home and the nonexistent tree?

E. B. WHITE

Once More to the Lake

One summer, along about 1904, my father rented a camp on a lake in Maine and took us all there for the month of August. We all got ringworm from some kittens and had to rub Pond's Extract on our arms and legs night and morning, and my father rolled over in a canoe with all his clothes on; but outside of that the vacation was a success and from then on none of us ever thought there was any place in the world like that lake in Maine. We returned summer after summer—always on August 1st for one month. I have since become a salt-water man, but sometimes in summer there are days when the restlessness of the tides and the fearful cold of the sea water and the incessant wind which blows across the afternoon and into the evening make me wish for the placidity of a lake in the woods. A few weeks ago this feeling got so strong I bought myself a couple of bass hooks and a spinner and returned to the lake where we used to go, for a week's fishing and to revisit old haunts.

I took along my son, who had never had any fresh water up his nose and who had seen lily pads only from train windows. On the journey over to the lake I began to wonder what it would be like. I wondered how time would have marred this unique, this holy spot— the coves and streams, the hills that the sun set behind, the camps and the paths behind the camps. I was sure the tarred road would have found it out and I wondered in what other ways it would be desolated. It is strange how much you can remember about places like that once you allow your mind to return into the grooves which lead back. You remember one thing, and that suddenly reminds you of another thing. I guess I remembered clearest of all the early mornings, when the lake was cool and motionless, remembered how the bedroom smelled of the lumber it was made of and of the wet woods whose scent entered through the screen. The partitions in the camp were thin and did not extend clear to the top of the rooms, and as I was always the first up I would dress softly so as not to wake the others, and sneak out into the sweet outdoors and start out in the canoe, keeping close along the shore in the long shadows of the pines. I remembered being very careful never to rub my paddle against the gunwale for fear of disturbing the stillness of the cathedral.

The lake had never been what you would call a wild lake. There were cottages sprinkled around the shores, and it was in farming country although the shores of the lake were quite heavily wooded. Some of the cottages were owned by nearby farmers, and you would live at the shore and eat your meals at the farmhouse. That's what our family did. But although it wasn't wild, it was a fairly large and undisturbed lake and there were places in it which, to a child at least, seemed infinitely remote and primeval.

I was right about the tar: it led to within half a mile of the shore. But when I got back there, with my boy, and we settled into a camp near a farmhouse and into the kind of summertime I had known, I could tell that it was going to be pretty much the same as it had been before—I knew it, lying in bed the first morning, smelling the bedroom, and hearing the boy sneak quietly out and go off along the shore in a boat. I began to sustain the illusion that he was I, and therefore, by simple transposition, that I was my father. This sensation persisted, kept cropping up all the time we were there. It was not an entirely new feeling, but in this setting it grew much stronger. I seemed to be living a dual existence. I would be in the middle of some simple act, I would be picking up a bait box or laying down a table fork, or I would be saying something, and suddenly it would be not I but my father who was saying the words or making the gesture. It gave me a creepy sensation.

We went fishing the first morning. I felt the same damp moss covering the worms in the bait can, and saw the dragonfly alight on the tip of my rod as it hovered a few inches from the surface of the water. It was the arrival of this fly that convinced me beyond any doubt that everything was as it always had been, that the years were a mirage and there had been no years. The small waves were the same, chucking the rowboat under the chin as we fished at anchor, and the boat was the same boat, the same color green and the ribs broken in the same places, and under the floor-boards the same fresh-water leavings and débris—the dead helgramite,[1] the wisps of moss, the rusty discarded fishhook, the dried blood from yesterday's catch. We stared silently at the tips of our rods, at the dragonflies that came and went. I lowered the tip of mine into the water, tentatively, pensively dislodging the fly, which darted two feet away, poised, darted two feet back, and came to rest again a little farther up the rod. There had been no years between the ducking of this dragonfly and the other one—the one that was part of memory. I looked at the boy, who was silently watching his fly, and it was my hands that held his rod, my eyes watching. I felt dizzy and didn't know which rod I was at the end of.

We caught two bass, hauling them in briskly as though they were mackerel, pulling them over the side of the boat in a businesslike manner without any landing net, and stunning them with a blow on the back of the head. When we got back for a swim before lunch, the lake was exactly where we had left it, the same number of inches from the dock, and there was only the merest suggestion of a breeze. This seemed an utterly enchanted sea, this lake you could leave to its own devices for a few hours and come back to, and find that it had not stirred, this constant and trustworthy body of water. In the shallows, the dark, water-soaked sticks and twigs, smooth and old, were undulating in clusters on the bottom against the clean ribbed sand, and the track of the mussel was plain. A school of minnows swam by, each minnow with its small individual shadow, doubling the attendance, so clear and sharp in the sunlight. Some of the other

1. The nymph of the May-fly, used as bait.

campers were in swimming, along the shore, one of them with a cake of soap, and the water felt thin and clear and unsubstantial. Over the years there had been this person with the cake of soap, this cultist, and here he was. There had been no years.

Up to the farmhouse to dinner through the teeming, dusty field, the road under our sneakers was only a two-track road. The middle track was missing, the one with the marks of the hooves and the splotches of dried, flaky manure. There had always been three tracks to choose from in choosing which track to walk in; now the choice was narrowed down to two. For a moment I missed terribly the middle alternative. But the way led past the tennis court, and something about the way it lay there in the sun reassured me; the tape had loosened along the backline, the alleys were green with plantains and other weeds, and the net (installed in June and removed in September) sagged in the dry noon, and the whole place steamed with midday heat and hunger and emptiness. There was a choice of pie for dessert, and one was blueberry and one was apple, and the waitresses were the same country girls, there having been no passage of time, only the illusion of it as in a dropped curtain—the waitresses were still fifteen; their hair had been washed, that was the only difference—they had been to the movies and seen the pretty girls with the clean hair.

Summertime, oh summertime, pattern of life indelible, the fade-proof lake, the woods unshatterable, the pasture with the sweetfern and the juniper forever and ever, summer without end; this was the background, and the life along the shore was the design, the cottagers with their innocent and tranquil design, their tiny docks with the flagpole and the American flag floating against the white clouds in the blue sky, the little paths over the roots of the trees leading from camp to camp and the paths leading back to the outhouses and the can of lime for sprinkling, and at the souvenir counters at the store the miniature birch-bark canoes and the post cards that showed things looking a little better than they looked. This was the American family at play, escaping the city heat, wondering whether the newcomers in the camp at the head of the cove were "common" or "nice," wondering whether it was true that the people who drove up for Sunday dinner at the farmhouse were turned away because there wasn't enough chicken.

It seemed to me, as I kept remembering all this, that those times and those summers had been infinitely precious and worth saving. There had been jollity and peace and goodness. The arriving (at the beginning of August) had been so big a business in itself, at the railway station the farm wagon drawn up, the first smell of the pine-laden air, the first glimpse of the smiling farmer, and the great importance of the trunks and your father's enormous authority in such matters, and the feel of the wagon under you for the long ten-mile haul, and at the top of the last long hill catching the first view of the lake after eleven months of not seeing this cherished body of water. The shouts and cries of the other campers when they saw you, and the trunks to be unpacked, to give up their rich burden. (Arriving was less exciting nowadays, when you sneaked up in your car and parked it under a tree near the camp and took out the bags and in five minutes it was all over, no fuss, no loud wonderful fuss about trunks.)

Peace and goodness and jollity. The only thing that was wrong now, really, was the sound of the place, an unfamiliar nervous sound of the outboard motors. This was the note that jarred, the one thing that would sometimes break the illusion and set the years moving. In those other summertimes all motors were inboard; and when they were at a little distance, the noise they made was a sedative, an ingredient of summer sleep. They were one-cylinder and two-cylinder engines, and some were make-and-break and some were jump-spark,[2] but they all made a sleepy sound across the lake. The one-lungers throbbed and fluttered, and the twin-cylinder ones purred and purred, and that was a quiet sound too. But now the campers all had outboards. In the daytime, in the hot mornings, these motors made a petulant, irritable sound; at night, in the still evening when the afterglow lit the water, they whined about one's ears like mosquitoes. My boy loved our rented outboard, and his great desire was to achieve singlehanded mastery over it, and authority, and he soon learned the trick of choking it a little (but not too much), and the adjustment of the needle valve. Watching him I would remember the things you could do with the old one-cylinder engine with the heavy flywheel, how you could have it eating out of your hand if you got really close to it spiritually. Motor boats in those days didn't have clutches, and you would make a landing by shutting off the motor at the proper time and coasting in with a dead rudder. But there was a way of reversing them, if you learned the trick, by cutting the switch and putting it on again exactly on the final dying revolution of the flywheel, so that it would kick back against compression and begin reversing. Approaching a dock in a strong following breeze, it was difficult to slow up sufficiently by the ordinary coasting method, and if a boy felt he had complete mastery over his motor, he was tempted to keep it running beyond its time and then reverse it a few feet from the dock. It took a cool nerve, because if you threw the switch a twentieth of a second too soon you would catch the flywheel when it still had speed enough to go up past center, and the boat would leap ahead, charging bull-fashion at the dock.

We had a good week at the camp. The bass were biting well and the sun shone endlessly, day after day. We would be tired at night

2. Methods of ignition timing.

and lie down in the accumulated heat of the little bedrooms after the long hot day and the breeze would stir almost imperceptibly outside and the smell of the swamp drift in through the rusty screens. Sleep would come easily and in the morning the red squirrel would be on the roof, tapping out his gay routine. I kept remembering everything, lying in bed in the mornings—the small steamboat that had a long rounded stern like the lip of a Ubangi, and how quietly she ran on the moonlight sails, when the older boys played their mandolins and the girls sang and we ate doughnuts dipped in sugar, and how sweet the music was on the water in the shining night, and what it had felt like to think about girls then. After breakfast we would go up to the store and the things were in the same place—the minnows in a bottle, the plugs and spinners disarranged and pawed over by the youngsters from the boys' camp, the fig newtons and the Beeman's gum. Outside, the road was tarred and cars stood in front of the store. Inside, all was just as it had always been, except there was more Coca-Cola and not so much Moxie and root beer and birch beer and sarsaparilla. We would walk out with a bottle of pop apiece and sometimes the pop would backfire up our noses and hurt. We explored the streams, quietly, where the turtles slid off the sunny logs and dug their way into the soft bottom; and we lay on the town wharf and fed worms to the tame bass. Everywhere we went I had trouble making out which was I, the one walking at my side, the one walking in my pants.

One afternoon while we were there at that lake a thunderstorm came up. It was like the revival of an old melodrama that I had seen long ago with childish awe. The second-act climax of the drama of the electrical disturbance over a lake in America had not changed in any important respect. This was the big scene, still the big scene. The whole thing was so familiar, the first feeling of oppression and heat and a general air around camp of not wanting to go very far away. In midafternoon (it was all the same) a curious darkening of the sky, and a lull in everything that had made life tick; and then the way the boats suddenly swung the other way at their moorings with the coming of a breeze out of the new quarter, and the premonitory rumble. Then the kettle drum, then the snare, then the bass drum and cymbals, then crackling light against the dark, and the gods grinning and licking their chops in the hills. Afterward the calm, the rain steadily rustling in the calm lake, the return of light and hope and spirits, and the campers running out in joy and relief to go swimming in the rain, their bright cries perpetuating the deathless joke about how they were getting simply drenched, and the children screaming with delight at the new sensation of bathing in the rain, and the joke about getting drenched linking the generations in a strong indestructible chain. And the comedian who waded in carrying an umbrella.

When the others went swimming my son said he was going in

too. He pulled his dripping trunks from the line where they had hung all through the shower, and wrung them out. Languidly, and with no thought of going in, I watched him, his hard little body, skinny and bare, saw him wince slightly as he pulled up around his vitals the small, soggy, icy garment. As he buckled the swollen belt suddenly my groin felt the chill of death.

1941

QUESTIONS

1. White had not been back to the lake for many years. What bearing has this fact on the experience which the essay describes?
2. What has guided White in his selection of the details he gives about the trip? Why, for example, does he talk about the road, the dragonfly, the bather with the cake of soap?
3. How do the differences between boats of the past and boats of today relate to or support the point of the essay?
4. What is the meaning of White's last sentence? What relation has it to the sentence just preceding? How has White prepared us for this ending?
5. How would the narrative differ if it were told by the boy? What details of the scene might the boy emphasize? Why? Show what point the boy's selection of details might make.

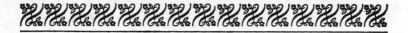

Prose Forms: Journals

Occasionally one catches oneself having said something aloud, obviously with no concern to be heard, even by oneself. And all of us have overheard, perhaps while walking, a solitary person muttering or laughing softly or exclaiming abruptly. Something floats up from the world within, forces itself to be expressed, takes no real account of the time or the place, and certainly intends no conscious communication.

With more self-consciousness, and yet without a specific audience, one sometimes speaks out at something that has momentarily filled his attention from the world without. A sharp play at the ball game, the twist of a political speech, an old photograph—something from the outer world impresses the mind, stimulates it, focuses certain of its memories and values, interests and needs. Thus stimulated, one may wish to share an experience with another, to inform or amuse that person, to rouse him or her to action or persuade someone to a certain belief. Often, though, the person experiencing may want most to talk to himself, to give a public shape in words to thoughts and feelings but for the sake of a kind of private dialogue. Communication to another may be an ultimate desire, but the immediate motive is to articulate the experience for oneself.

To articulate, to shape the experience in language for one's own sake, one may keep a journal. Literally a day-book, the journal enables one to write down something about the experiences of a day which for a great variety of reasons may have been especially memorable or impressive. The journal entry may be merely a few words to call to mind a thing done, a person seen, a menu enjoyed at a dinner party. It may be concerned at length with a political crisis in the community, or a personal crisis in the home. It may even be as noble as it was with some pious people in the past who used the journal to keep a record of their consciences, a periodic reckoning of their moral and spiritual accounts. In its most public aspect, the idea of a journal calls to mind the newspaper or the record of proceedings like the Congressional Record. In its most closely private form, the journal becomes the diary.

For the person keeping a journal, whatever he experiences and wants to hold he can write down. But to get it down on paper begins another adventure. For he has to focus on what he has experienced, and to be able to say what, in fact, the experience is. What of it is new? What of it is remarkable because of associations in the memory it stirs up? Is this like anything I—or others— have experienced before? Is it a good or a bad thing to have happened? And why, specifically? The questions multiply themselves quickly, and as the journalist seeks to answer the appropriate ones, he begins to know what it is he contemplates. As one tries to find the words that best represent this discovery, the experience becomes even more clear in its shape and meaning. We can imagine Emerson going to the ballet, being absorbed in the spectacle, thinking casually of this or that association the dancer and the movements suggest. When he writes about the experience in his journal, a good many questions, judgments, and speculations get tied up with the spectacle, and it is this complex of event and his total relation to it that becomes the experience he records. The simple facts of time, place, people, and actions drop down into one's consciousness and set in motion ideas and feelings which give those facts their real meaning to oneself.

Once this consciousness of events is formulated in words, the journal-keeper has it, not only in the sense of understanding what has been seen or felt or thought, but also in the sense of having it there before him to contemplate long after the event itself. When we read a carefully kept journal covering a long period and varied experiences, we have the pleasure of a small world re-created for us in the consciousness of one who experienced it. Even more, we feel the continuity, the wholeness, of the writer. Something of the same feeling is there for the person who kept the journal: a whole world of events preserved in the form of their experienced reality, and with it the persistent self in the midst of that world. That world and that self are always accessible on the page, and ultimately, therefore, usably real.

Beyond the value of the journal as record, there is the instructive value of the habit of mind and hand journal keeping can assure. One begins to attend more carefully to what happens to and around oneself. One learns the resources of language as a means of representing what one sees, and gains skill and certainty in doing justice to experience and to one's own consciousness. And the journal represents a discipline. It brings together an individual and a complex environment in a relation that teaches the individual something of himself or herself, something of the world, and something of the meaning of their relation. There is scarcely a moment in a person's life when he is not poised for the lesson. When it comes with the promise of special force, there is the almost irresistible temptation to catch the impulse, give it form, make it permanent, assert its meaning. And so one commits oneself to language. To have given up one's experience to words is to have begun marking out the limits and potential of its meaning. In the journal that meaning is developed and clarified to oneself primarily. When the whole intention of the development and the clarification is the consideration of another reader, the method of the journal redirects itself to become that of the essay.

JOAN DIDION: On Keeping a Notebook

" 'That woman Estelle,'." the note reads, " 'is partly the reason why George Sharp and I are separated today.' *Dirty crepe-deChine wrapper, hotel bar, Wilmington RR, 9:45 a.m. August Monday morning.*"

Since the note is in my notebook, it presumably has some meaning to me. I study it for a long while. At first I have only the most general notion of what I was doing on an August Monday morning in the bar of the hotel across from the Pennsylvania Railroad station in Wilmington, Delaware (waiting for a train? missing one? 1960? 1961? why Wilmington?), but I do remember being there. The woman in the dirty crepe-de-Chine wrapper had come down from her room for a beer, and the bartender had heard before the reason why George Sharp and she were separated today. "Sure," he said, and went on mopping the floor. "You told me." At the other end of the bar is a girl. She is talking, pointedly, not to the man beside her but to a cat lying in the triangle of sunlight cast through the open door. She is wearing a plaid silk dress from Peck & Peck, and the hem is coming down.

Here is what it is: the girl has been on the Eastern Shore, and now she is going back to the city, leaving the man beside her, and all she can see ahead are the viscous summer sidewalks and the 3 a.m. long-distance calls that will make her lie awake and then sleep drugged through all the steaming mornings left in August (1960? 1961?). Because she must go directly from the train to lunch in New York, she wishes that she had a safety pin for the hem of the plaid silk dress, and she also wishes that she could forget about the hem and the lunch and stay in the cool bar that smells of disinfectant and malt and make friends with the women in the crepe-de-Chine wrapper. She is afflicted by a little self-pity, and she wants to compare Estelles. That is what that was all about.

Why did I write it down? In order to remember, of course, but exactly what was it I wanted to remember? How much of it actually happened? Did any of it? Why do I keep a notebook at all? It is easy to deceive oneself on all those scores. The impulse to write things down is a peculiarly compulsive one, inexplicable to those who do not share it, useful only accidentally, only secondarily, in the way that any compulsion tries to justify itself. I suppose that it begins or does not begin in the cradle. Although I have felt compelled to write things down since I was five years old, I doubt that my daughter ever will, for she is a singularly blessed and accepting child, delighted with life exactly as life presents itself to her, unafraid to go to sleep and unafraid to wake up. Keepers of private notebooks are a different breed altogether, lonely and resistant re-arrangers of things, anxious malcontents, children afflicted apparently at birth with some presentiment of loss.

My first notebook was a Big Five tablet, given to me by my mother with the sensible suggestion that I stop whining and learn to amuse myself by writing down my thoughts. She returned the tablet to me a few years ago; the first entry is an account of a woman who believed herself to be freezing to death in the Arctic night, only to find, when day broke, that she had stumbled onto the Sahara Desert, where she would die of the heat before lunch. I have no idea what turn of a five-year-old's mind could have prompted so insistently "ironic" and exotic a story, but it does reveal a certain predilection for the extreme which has dogged me into adult life; perhaps if I were analytically inclined I would find it a truer story than any I might have told about Donald Johnson's birthday party or the day my cousin Brenda put Kitty Litter in the aquarium.

So the point of my keeping a notebook has never been, nor is it now, to have an accurate factual record of what I have been doing or thinking. That would be a different impulse entirely, an instinct for reality which I sometimes envy but do not possess. At no point have I ever been able successfully to keep a diary; my approach to daily life ranges from the grossly negligent to the merely absent, and on those few occasions when I have tried dutifully to record a day's events, boredom has so overcome me that the results are mysterious at best. What is this business about "shopping, typing piece, dinner with E, depressed"? Shopping for what? Typing what piece? Who is E? Was this "E" depressed, or was I depressed? Who cares?

In fact I have abandoned altogether that kind of pointless entry; instead I tell what some would call lies. "That's simply not true," the members of my family frequently tell me when they come up against my memory of a shared event. "The party was *not* for you, the spider was *not* a black widow, *it wasn't that way at all*." Very likely they are right, for not only have I always had trouble distinguishing between what happened and what merely might have happened, but I remain unconvinced that the distinction, for my purposes, matters. The cracked crab that I recall having for lunch the day my father came home from Detroit in 1945 must certainly be embroidery, worked into the day's pattern to lend verisimilitude; I was ten years old and would not now remember the cracked crab. The day's events did not turn on cracked crab. And yet it is precisely that fictitious crab that makes me see the afternoon all over again, a home movie run all too often, the father bearing gifts, the child weeping, an exercise in family love and guilt. Or that is what it was to me. Similarly, perhaps it never did snow that August in Vermont; perhaps there never were flurries in the night wind, and maybe no one else felt the ground hardening and summer already dead even as we pretended to bask in it, but that was how it felt to me, and it might as well have snowed, could have snowed, did snow.

How it felt to me: that is getting closer to the truth about a notebook. I sometimes delude myself about why I keep a notebook, imagine that some thrifty virtue derives from preserving everything observed. See enough and write it down, I tell myself, and then some morning when the world seems drained of wonder, some day when I am only going through the motions of doing what I am supposed to do, which is write—on that bankrupt morning I will simply open my notebook and there it will all be, a forgotten account with accumulated interest, paid passage back to the world out there: dialogue overheard in hotels and elevators and at the hatcheck counter in Pavillon (one middle-aged man shows his hat check to another and says, "That's my old football number"); impressions of Bettina Aptheker and Benjamin Sonnenberg and Teddy ("Mr. Acapulco") Stauffer; careful *aperçus* about tennis bums and failed fashion models and Greek shipping heiresses, one of whom taught me a significant lesson (a lesson I could have learned from F. Scott Fitzgerald, but perhaps we all must meet the very rich for ourselves) by asking, when I arrived to interview her in her orchid-filled sitting room on the second day of a paralyzing New York blizzard, whether it was snowing outside.

I imagine, in other words, that the notebook is about other people. But of course it is not. I have no real business with what one stranger said to another at the hat-check counter in Pavillon; in fact I suspect that the line "That's my old football number" touched not my own imagination at all, but merely some memory of something once read, probably "The Eighty-Yard Run." Nor is my concern with a woman in a dirty crepe-de-Chine wrapper in a Wilmington bar. My stake is always, of course, in the unmentioned girl in the plaid silk dress. *Remember what it was to be me:* that is always the point.

It is a difficult point to admit. We are brought up in the ethic that others, any others, all others, are by definition more interesting than ourselves; taught to be diffident, just this side of self-effacing. ("You're the least important person in the room and don't forget it," Jessica Mitford's governess would hiss in her ear on the advent of any social occasion; I copied that into my notebook because it is only recently that I have been able to enter a room without hearing some such phrase in my inner ear.) Only the very young and the very old may recount their dreams at breakfast, dwell upon self, interrupt with memories of beach picnics and favorite Liberty lawn dresses and the rainbow trout in a creek near Colorado Springs. The rest of us are expected, rightly, to affect absorption in other people's favorite dresses, other people's trout.

And so we do. But our notebooks give us away, for however dutifully we record what we see around us, the common denominator of all we see is always, transparently, shamelessly, the implacable "I." We are not talking here about the kind of notebook that is patently for public consumption, a structural conceit for binding together a series of graceful *pensées*;[1] we are talking about something private, about bits of the mind's string too short to use, an indiscriminate and erratic assemblage with meaning only for its maker.

And sometimes even the maker has difficulty with the meaning. There does not seem to be, for example, any point in my knowing for the rest of my life that, during 1964, 720 tons of soot fell on every square mile of New York City, yet there it is in my notebook, labeled "FACT." Nor do I really need to remember that Ambrose Bierce liked to spell Leland Stanford's[2] name "£eland $tanford" or that "smart women almost always wear black in Cuba," a fashion hint without much potential for practical application. And does not the relevance of these notes seem marginal at best?:

In the basement museum of the Inyo County Courthouse in Independence, California, sign pinned to a mandarin coat: "This MANDARIN COAT was often worn by Mrs. Minnie S. Brooks when giving lectures on her TEAPOT COLLECTION."
Redhead getting out of car in front of Beverly Wilshire Hotel, chinchilla stole, Vuitton bags with tags reading:

> MRS LOU FOX
> HOTEL SAHARA
> VEGAS

Well, perhaps not entirely marginal. As a matter of fact, Mrs. Minnie S. Brooks and her MANDARIN COAT pull me back into my own childhood, for although I never knew Mrs. Brooks and did not visit Inyo County until I was thirty, I grew up in just such a world, in houses cluttered with Indian relics and bits of gold ore and ambergris and the souvenirs my Aunt Mercy Farnsworth brought back from the Orient. It is a long way from that world to Mrs. Lou Fox's world, where we all live now, and is it not just as well to

---

1. Thoughts, reflections.
2. A nineteenth-century American millionaire.

remember that? Might not Mrs. Minnie S. Brooks help me to remember what I am? Might not Mrs. Lou Fox help me to remember what I am not?

But sometimes the point is harder to discern. What exactly did I have in mind when I noted down that it cost the father of someone I know $650 a month to light the place on the Hudson in which he lived before the Crash?[3] What use was I planning to make of this line by Jimmy Hoffa: "I may have my faults, but being wrong ain't one of them"? And although I think it interesting to know where the girls who travel with the Syndicate have their hair done when they find themselves on the West Coast, will I ever make suitable use of it? Might I not be better off just passing it on to John O'Hara? What is a recipe for sauerkraut doing in my notebook? What kind of magpie keeps this notebook? *"He was born the night the Titanic went down."* That seems a nice enough line, and I even recall who said it, but is it not really a better line in life than it could ever be in fiction?

But of course that is exactly it: not that I should ever use the line, but that I should remember the woman who said it and the afternoon I heard it. We were on her terrace by the sea, and we were finishing the wine left from lunch, trying to get what sun there was, a California winter sun. The woman whose husband was born the night the *Titanic* went down wanted to rent her house, wanted to go back to her children in Paris. I remember wishing that I could afford the house, which cost $1,000 a month. "Someday you will," she said lazily. "Someday it all comes." There in the sun on her terrace it seemed easy to believe in someday, but later I had a low-grade afternoon hangover and ran over a black snake on the way to the supermarket and was flooded with inexplicable fear when I heard the checkout clerk explaining to the man ahead of me why she was finally divorcing her husband. "He left me no choice," she said over and over as she punched the register. "He has a little seven-month-old baby by her, he left me no choice." I would like to believe that my dread then was for the human condition, but of course it was for me, because I wanted a baby and did not then have one and because I wanted to own the house that cost $1,000 a month to rent and because I had a hangover.

It all comes back. Perhaps it is difficult to see the value in having one's self back in that kind of mood, but I do see it; I think we are well advised to keep on nodding terms with the people we used to be whether we find them attractive company or not. Otherwise they turn up unannounced and surprise us, come hammering on the

<hr>

3. The stock market crash of 1929.

mind's door at 4 a.m. of a bad night and demand to know who
deserted them, who betrayed them, who is going to make amends.
We forget all too soon the things we thought we could never forget.
We forget the loves and the betrayals alike, forget what we whispered and what we screamed, forget who we were. I have already
lost touch with a couple of people I used to be; one of them, a seventeen-year-old, presents little threat, although it would be of some
interest to me to know again what it feels like to sit on a river levee
drinking vodka-and-orange-juice and listening to Les Paul and Mary
Ford and their echoes sing "How High the Moon" on the car radio.
(You see I still have the scenes, but I no longer perceive myself
among those present, no longer could even improvise the dialogue.)
The other one, a twenty-three-year-old, bothers me more. She was
always a good deal of trouble, and I suspect she will reappear when
I least want to see her, skirts too long, shy to the point of aggrava-
tion, always the injured party, full of recriminations and little hurts
and stories I do not want to hear again, at once saddening me and
angering me with her vulnerability and ignorance, an apparition all
the more insistent for being so long banished.

It is a good idea, then, to keep in touch, and I suppose that keeping in touch is what notebooks are all about. And we are all on our
own when it comes to keeping those lines open to ourselves: your
notebook will never help me, nor mine you. *"So what's new in the
whiskey business?"* What could that possibly mean to you? To me it
means a blonde in a Pucci bathing suit sitting with a couple of fat
men by the pool at the Beverly Hills Hotel. Another man
approaches, and they all regard one another in silence for a while.
"So what's new in the whiskey business?" one of the fat men finally
says by way of welcome, and the blonde stands up, arches one foot
and dips it in the pool, looking all the while at the cabaña where
Baby Pignatari is talking on the telephone. That is all there is to
that, except that several years later I saw the blonde coming out of
Saks Fifth Avenue in New York with her California complexion
and a voluminous mink coat. In the harsh wind that day she looked
old and irrevocably tired to me, and even the skins in the mink coat
were not worked the way they were doing them that year, not the
way she would have wanted them done, and there is the point of
the story. For a while after that I did not like to look in the mirror,
and my eyes would skim the newspapers and pick out only the
deaths, the cancer victims, the premature coronaries, the suicides,
and I stopped riding the Lexington Avenue IRT[4] because I noticed
for the first time that all the strangers I had seen for years—the

4. A New York City subway line; one of its stops is the Grand Central railway terminal.

man with the seeing-eye dog, the spinster who read the classified pages every day, the fat girl who always got off with me at Grand Central—looked older than they once had.

It all comes back. Even that recipe for sauerkraut: even that brings it back. I was on Fire Island when I first made that sauerkraut, and it was raining, and we drank a lot of bourbon and ate the sauerkraut and went to bed at ten, and I listened to the rain and the Atlantic and felt safe. I made the sauerkraut again last night and it did not make me feel any safer, but that is, as they say, another story.

1968

RALPH WALDO EMERSON: *from* Journal

I like to have a man's knowledge comprehend more than one class of topics, one row of shelves. I like a man who likes to see a fine barn as well as a good tragedy.   [1828]

The Religion that is afraid of science dishonors God and commits suicide.   [1831]

The things taught in colleges and schools are not an education, but the means of education.   [1831]

Don't tell me to get ready to die. I know not what shall be. The only preparation I can make is by fulfilling my present duties. This is the everlasting life.   [1832]

My aunt [Mary Moody Emerson] had an eye that went through and through you like a needle. "She was endowed," she said, "with the fatal gift of penetration." She disgusted everybody because she knew them too well.   [1832]

I am sure of this, that by going much alone a man will get more of a noble courage in thought and word than from all the wisdom that is in books.   [1833]

I fretted the other night at the hotel at the stranger who broke into my chamber after midnight, claiming to share it. But after his lamp had smoked the chamber full and I had turned round to the wall in despair, the man blew out his lamp, knelt down at his bedside, and made in low whisper a long earnest prayer. Then was the relation entirely changed between us. I fretted no more, but respected and liked him.   [1835]

I believe I shall some time cease to be an individual, that the eternal tendency of the soul is to become Universal, to animate the last extremities of organization. [1837]

It is very hard to be simple enough to be good. [1837]

A man must have aunts and cousins, must buy carrots and turnips, must have barn and woodshed, must go to market and to the black-smith's shop, must saunter and sleep and be inferior and silly. [1838]

How sad a spectacle, so frequent nowadays, to see a young man after ten years of college education come out, ready for his voyage of life—and to see that the entire ship is made of rotten timber, of rotten, honeycombed, traditional timber without so much as an inch of new plank in the hull. [1839]

A sleeping child gives me the impression of a traveler in a very far country. [1840]

In reading these letters of M.M.E. I acknowledge (with surprise that I could ever forget it) the debt of myself and my brothers to that old religion which, in those years, still dwelt like a Sabbath peace in the country population of New England, which taught privation, self-denial, and sorrow. A man was born, not for prosperity, but to suffer for the benefit of others, like the noble rock-maple tree which all around the villages bleeds for the service of man.[1] Not praise, not men's acceptance of our doing, but the Spirit's holy errand through us, absorbed the thought. How dignified is this! how all that is called talents and worth in Paris and in Washington dwindles before it! [1841]

All writing is by the grace of God. People do not deserve to have good writing, they are so pleased with bad. In these sentences that you show me, I can find no beauty, for I see death in every clause and every word. There is a fossil or a mummy character which pervades this book. The best sepulchers, the vastest catacombs, Thebes and Cairo, Pyramids, are sepulchers to me. I like gardens and nurseries. Give me initiative, spermatic, prophesying, man-making words. [1841]

When summer opens, I see how fast it matures, and fear it will be short; but after the heats of July and August, I am reconciled, like one who has had his swing, to the cool of autumn. So will it be with the coming of death. [1846]

---

1. The sap of the rock or sugar maple is collected and made into maple syrup.

In England every man you meet is some man's son; in America, he may be some man's father. [1848]

Every poem must be made up of lines that are poems. [1848]

Love is necessary to the righting the estate of woman in this world. Otherwise nature itself seems to be in conspiracy against her dignity and welfare; for the cultivated, high-thoughted, beauty-loving, saintly woman finds herself unconsciously desired for her sex, and even enhancing the appetite of ·her savage pursuers by these fine ornaments she has piously laid on herself. She finds with indignation that she is herself a snare, and was made such. I do not wonder at her occasional protest, violent protest against nature, in fleeing to nunneries, and taking black veils. Love rights all this deep wrong. [1848]

Natural Aristocracy. It is a vulgar error to suppose that a gentleman must be ready to fight. The utmost that can be demanded of the gentleman is that he be incapable of a lie. There is a man who has good sense, is well informed, well-read, obliging, cultivated, capable, and has an absolute devotion to truth. He always means what he says, and says what he means, however courteously. You may spit upon him—nothing could induce him to spit upon you—no praises, and no possessions, no compulsion of public opinion. You may kick him—he will think it the kick of a brute—but he is not a brute, and will not kick you in return. But neither your knife and pistol, nor your gifts and courting will ever make the smallest impression on his vote or word; for he is the truth's man, and will speak and act the truth until he dies. [1849]

Love is temporary and ends with marriage. Marriage is the perfection which love aimed at, ignorant of what it sought. Marriage is a good known only to the parties—a relation of perfect understanding, aid, contentment, possession of themselves and of the world—which dwarfs love to green fruit. [1850]

I found when I had finished my new lecture that it was a very good house, only the architect had unfortunately omitted the stairs. [1851]

This filthy enactment [The Fugitive Slave Law[2]] was made in the nineteenth century, by people who could read and write. I will not obey it, by God. [1851]

Henry [Thoreau] is military. He seemed stubborn and implacable; always manly and wise, but rarely sweet. One would say that, as

2. A law enacted in 1850 to compel the   to their owners.
arrest of runaway slaves and their return

Webster could never speak without an antagonist, so Henry does not feel himself except in opposition. He wants a fallacy to expose, a blunder to pillory, requires a little sense of victory, a roll of the drums, to call his powers into full exercise. [1853]

Shall we judge the country by the majority or by the minority? Certainly, by the minority. The mass are animal, in state of pupilage, and nearer the chimpanzee. [1854]

All the thoughts of a turtle are turtle. [1854]

Resources or feats. I like people who can do things. When Edward and I struggled in vain to drag our big calf into the barn, the Irish girl put her finger into the calf's mouth, and led her in directly. [1862]

George Francis Train said in a public speech in New York, "Slavery is a divine institution." "So is hell," exclaimed an old man in the crowd. [1862]

You complain that the Negroes are a base class. Who makes and keeps the Jew or the Negro base, who but you, who exclude them from the rights which others enjoy? [1867]

HENRY DAVID THOREAU: *from* Journal

As the least drop of wine tinges the whole goblet, so the least particle of truth colors our whole life. It is never isolated, or simply added as treasure to our stock. When any real progress is made, we unlearn and learn anew what we thought we knew before. [1837]

Not by constraint or severity shall you have access to true wisdom, but by abandonment, and childlike mirthfulness. If you would know aught, be gay before it. [1840]

It is the man determines what is said, not the words. If a mean person uses a wise maxim, I bethink me how it can be interpreted so as to commend itself to his meanness; but if a wise man makes a commonplace remark, I consider what wider construction it will admit. [1840]

Nothing goes by luck in composition. It allows of no tricks. The best you can write will be the best you are. Every sentence is the result of a long probation. The author's character is read from title-page to end. Of this he never corrects the proofs. We read it as the essential character of a handwriting without regard to the flourishes. And so of the rest of our actions; it runs as straight as a ruled line through them all, no matter how many curvets about it. Our whole life is taxed for the least thing well done: it is its net result. How we eat, drink, sleep, and use our desultory hours, now in these indifferent days, with no eye to observe and no occasion [to] excite us, determines our authority and capacity for the time to come. [1841]

What does education often do? It makes a straight-cut ditch of a free, meandering brook. [1850]

All perception of truth is the detection of an analogy; we reason from our hands to our head. [1851]

To set down such choice experiences that my own writings may inspire me and at last I may make wholes of parts. Certainly it is a distinct profession to rescue from oblivion and to fix the sentiments and thoughts which visit all men more or less generally, that the contemplation of the unfinished picture may suggest its harmonious completion. Associate reverently and as much as you can with your loftiest thoughts. Each thought that is welcomed and recorded is a nest egg, by the side of which more will be laid. Thoughts accidentally thrown together become a frame in which more may be developed and exhibited. Perhaps this is the main value of a habit of writing, of keeping a journal—that so we remember our best hours and stimulate ourselves. My thoughts are my company. They have a certain individuality and separate existence, aye, personality. Having by chance recorded a few disconnected thoughts and then brought them into juxtaposition, they suggest a whole new field in which it was possible to labor and to think. Thought begat thought. [1852]

It is pardonable when we spurn the proprieties, even the sanctities, making them stepping-stones to something higher. [1858]

There is always some accident in the best things, whether thoughts or expressions or deeds. The memorable thought, the happy expression, the admirable deed are only partly ours. The thought came to us because we were in a fit mood; also we were unconscious and did not know that we had said or done a good thing. We must walk consciously only part way toward our goal, and then leap in the dark to our success. What we do best or most perfectly is what we have most thoroughly learned by the longest practice, and at length it falls from us without our notice, as a leaf from a tree. It is the *last* time we shall do it—our unconscious leavings. [1859]

The expression "a *liberal* education" originally meant one worthy of freemen. Such is education simply in a true and broad sense.

But education ordinarily so called—the learning of trades and professions which is designed to enable men to earn their living, or to fit them for a particular station in life—is *servile*. [1859]

WOODY ALLEN: Selections from the Allen Notebooks

Following are excerpts from the hitherto secret private journal of Woody Allen, which will be published posthumously or after his death, whichever comes first.

Getting through the night is becoming harder and harder. Last evening, I had the uneasy feeling that some men were trying to break into my room to shampoo me. But why? I kept imagining I saw shadowy forms, and at 3 A.M. the underwear I had draped over a chair resembled the Kaiser on roller skates. When I finally did fall asleep, I had that same hideous nightmare in which a woodchuck is trying to claim my prize at a raffle. Despair.

I believe my consumption has grown worse. Also my asthma. The wheezing comes and goes, and I get dizzy more and more frequently. I have taken to violent choking and fainting. My room is damp and I have perpetual chills and palpitations of the heart. I noticed, too, that I am out of napkins. Will it never stop?

Idea for a story: A man awakens to find his parrot has been made Secretary of Agriculture. He is consumed with jealousy and shoots himself, but unfortunately the gun is the type with a little flag that pops out, with the word "Bang" on it. The flag pokes his eye out, and he lives—a chastened human being who, for the first time, enjoys the simple pleasures of life, like farming or sitting on an air hose.

Thought: Why does man kill? He kills for food. And not only food: frequently there must be a beverage.

Should I marry W.? Not if she won't tell me the other letters in her name. And what about her career? How can I ask a woman of her beauty to give up the Roller Derby? Decisions . . .

Once again I tried committing suicide—this time by wetting my nose and inserting it into the light socket. Unfortunately, there was a short in the wiring, and I merely caromed off the icebox. Still obsessed by thoughts of death, I brood constantly. I keep wondering if there is an afterlife, and if there is will they be able to break a twenty?

I ran into my brother today at a funeral. We had not seen one another for fifteen years, but as usual he produced a pig bladder from his pocket and began hitting me on the head with it. Time has helped me understand him better. I finally realize his remark that I am "some loathsome vermin fit only for extermination" was said more out of compassion than anger. Let's face it: he was always much brighter than me—wittier, more cultured, better educated. Why he is still working at McDonald's is a mystery.

Idea for story: Some beavers take over Carnegie Hall and perform *Wozzeck*.[1] (Strong theme. What will be the structure?)

Good Lord, why am I so guilty? Is it because I hated my father? Probably it was the veal-parmigian' incident. Well, what *was* it doing in his wallet? If I had listened to him, I would be blocking hats for a living. I can hear him now: "To block hats—that is everything." I remember his reaction when I told him I wanted to write. "The only writing you'll do is in collaboration with an owl." I still have no idea what he meant. What a sad man! When my first play, *A Cyst for Gus*, was produced at the Lyceum, he attended opening night in tails and a gas mask.

Today I saw a red-and-yellow sunset and thought, How insignificant I am! Of course, I thought that yesterday, too, and it rained. I was overcome with self-loathing and contemplated suicide again— this time by inhaling next to an insurance salesman.

Short story: A man awakens in the morning and finds himself transformed into his own arch supports (This idea can work on many levels. Psychologically, it is the quintessence of Kruger, Freud's disciple who discovered sexuality in bacon.)

How wrong Emily Dickinson was! Hope is not "the thing with feathers." The thing with feathers has turned out to be my nephew. I must take him to a specialist in Zurich.

I have decided to break off my engagement with W. She doesn't understand my writing, and said last night that my *Critique of Metaphysical Reality* reminded her of *Airport*. We quarreled, and she brought up the subject of children again, but I convinced her they would be too young.

---

1. A lurid and dissonant opera by the modern composer Alban Berg. Carnegie Hall is a famous concert hall in New York City.

Do I believe in God? I did until Mother's accident. She fell on some meat loaf, and it penetrated her spleen. She lay in a coma for months, unable to do anything but sing "Granada" to an imaginary herring. Why was this woman in the prime of life so afflicted—because in her youth she dared to defy convention and got married with a brown paper bag on her head? And how can I believe in God when just last week I got my tongue caught in the roller of an electric typewriter? I am plagued by doubts. What if everything is an illusion and nothing exists? In that case, I definitely overpaid for my carpet. If only God would give me some clear sign! Like making a large deposit in my name at a Swiss bank.

Had coffee with Melnick today. He talked to me about his idea of having all government officials dress like hens.

Play idea: A character based on my father, but without quite so prominent a big toe. He is sent to the Sorbonne[2] to study the harmonica. In the end, he dies, never realizing his one dream—to sit up to his waist in gravy. (I see a brilliant second-act curtain, where two midgets come upon a severed head in a shipment of volleyballs.)

While taking my noon walk today, I had more morbid thoughts. What *is* it about death that bothers me so much? Probably the hours. Melnick says the soul is immortal and lives on after the body drops away, but if my soul exists without my body I am convinced all my clothes will be too loose-fitting. Oh, well . . .

Did not have to break off with W. after all, for as luck would have it, she ran off to Finland with a professional circus geek. All for the best, I suppose, although I had another of those attacks where I start coughing out of my ears.

Last night, I burned all my plays and poetry. Ironically as I was burning my masterpiece, *Dark Penguin*, the room caught fire, and I am now the object of a lawsuit by some men named Pinchunk and Schlosser. Kierkegaard was right.

1972

---

2. The University of Paris.

Mind

ROBERTSON DAVIES

A Few Kind Words for Superstition

In grave discussions of "the renaissance of the irrational" in our time, superstititon does not figure largely as a serious challenge to reason or science. Parapsychology, UFO's, miracle cures, transcendental meditation and all the paths to instant enlightenment are condemned, but superstition is merely deplored. Is it because it has an unacknowledged hold on so many of us?

Few people will admit to being superstitious; it implies naïveté or ignorance. But I live in the middle of a large university, and I see superstition in its four manifestations, alive and flourishing among people who are indisputably rational and learned.

You did not know that superstition takes four forms? Theologians assure us that it does. First is what they call Vain Observances, such as not walking under a ladder, and that kind of thing. Yet I saw a deeply learned professor of anthropology, who had spilled some salt, throwing a pinch of it over his left shoulder; when I asked him why, he replied, with a wink, that it was "to hit the Devil in the eye." I did not question him further about his belief in the Devil: but I noticed that he did not smile until I asked him what he was doing.

The second form is Divination, or consulting oracles. Another learned professor I know, who would scorn to settle a problem by tossing a coin (which is a humble appeal to Fate to declare itself), told me quite seriously that he had resolved a matter related to university affairs by consulting the *I Ching*.[1] And why not? There are thousands of people on this continent who appeal to the *I Ching*, and their general level of education seems to absolve them of super-

---

1. A Chinese work of divination.

stition. Almost, but not quite. The *I Ching*, to the embarrassment of rationalists, often gives excellent advice.

The third form is Idolatry, and universities can show plenty of that. If you have .ever supervised a large examination room, you know how many jujus, lucky coins and other bringers of luck are placed on the desks of the candidates. Modest idolatry, but what else can you call it?

The fourth form is Improper Worship of the True God. A while ago, I learned that every day, for several days, a $2 bill (in Canada we have $2 bills, regarded by some people as unlucky) had been tucked under a candlestick on the altar of a college chapel. Investigation revealed that an engineering student, worried about a girl, thought that bribery of the Diety might help. When I talked with him, he did not think he was pricing God cheap, because he could afford no more. A reasonable argument, but perhaps God was proud that week, for the scientific oracle went against him.

Superstition seems to run, a submerged river of crude religion, below the surface of human consciousness. It has done so for as long as we have any chronicle of human behavior, and although I cannot prove it, I doubt if it is more prevalent today than it has always been. Superstition, the theologians tell us, comes from the Latin *supersisto*, meaning to stand in terror of the Deity. Most people keep their terror within bounds, but they cannot root it out, nor do they seem to want to do so.

The more the teaching of formal religion declines, or takes a sociological form, the less God appears to great numbers of people as a God of Love, resuming his older form of a watchful, minatory power, to be placated and cajoled. Superstition makes its appearance, apparently unbidden, very early in life, when children fear that stepping on cracks in the sidewalk will bring ill fortune. It may persist even among the greatly learned and devout, as in the case of Dr. Samuel Johnson, who felt it necessary to touch posts that he passed in the street. The psychoanalysts have their explanation, but calling a superstition a compulsion neurosis does not banish it.

Many superstitions are so widespread and so old that they must have risen from a depth of the human mind that is indifferent to race or creed. Orthodox Jews place a charm on their doorposts; so do (or did) the Chinese. Some peoples of Middle Europe believe that when a man sneezes, his soul, for that moment, is absent from his body, and they hasten to bless him, lest the soul be seized by the Devil. How did the Melanesians come by the same idea? Superstition seems to have a link with some body of belief that far antedates the religions we know—religions which have no place for such comforting little ceremonies and charities.

People who like disagreeable historical comparisons recall that when Rome was in decline, superstition proliferated wildly, and that something of the same sort is happening in our Western world today. They point to the popularity of astrology, and it is true that sober newspapers that would scorn to deal in love philters carry astrology columns and the fashion magazines count them among their most popular features. But when has astrology not been popular? No use saying science discredits it. When has the heart of man given a damn for science?

Superstition in general is linked to man's yearning to know his fate, and to have some hand in deciding it. When my mother was a child, she innocently joined her Roman Catholic friends in killing spiders on July 11, until she learned that this was done to ensure heavy rain the day following, the anniversary of the Battle of Boyne, when the Orangemen[2] would hold their parade. I knew an Italian, a good scientist, who watched every morning before leaving his house, so that the first person he met would not be a priest or a nun, as this would certainly bring bad luck.

I am not one to stand aloof from the rest of humanity in this matter, for when I was a university student, a gypsy woman with a child in her arms used to appear every year at examination time, and ask a shilling[3] of anyone who touched the Lucky Baby; that swarthy infant cost me four shillings altogether, and I never failed an examination. Of course, I did it merely for the joke—or so I thought then. Now, I am humbler.

1978

2. Protestant Irish. The Battle of the Boyne (1690), the final and decisive defeat of the forces of British Catholicism, made Protestantism secure as the official religion of Great Britain.
3. Then about twenty-five cents.

QUESTIONS

1. What is Davies' definition of superstition?
2. There is a certain quaintness about the names for the four forms of superstition. Why do you think Davies chose such names? Does his division of superstition into these four forms serve to clarify the nature or function of superstitions you know about?
3. Can superstition exist without religion? In what ways can it substitute for religion?
4. Write an essay describing the nature and function of a superstition you know about. In his conclusion Davies suggests two perspectives on the subject—a joking one and the later, "humbler," one. Which comes more naturally to you as the point of view in your essay? Or do you have a different perspective of your own?

BENJAMIN FRANKLIN

The Convenience of Being "Reasonable"

I believe I have omitted mentioning that, in my first voyage from Boston, being becalmed off Block Island, our people set about catching cod, and hauled up a great many. Hitherto I had stuck to my resolution of not eating animal food, and on this occasion I considered, with my master Tryon,[1] the taking every fish as a kind of unprovoked murder, since none of them had, or ever could do us any injury that might justify the slaughter. All this seemed very reasonable. But I had formerly been a great lover of fish, and, when this came hot out of the frying-pan, it smelled admirably well. I balanced some time between principle and inclination, till I recollected that, when the fish were opened, I saw smaller fish taken out of their stomachs; then thought I, "if you eat one another, I don't see why we mayn't eat you." So I dined upon cod very heartily, and continued to eat with other people, returning only now and then occasionally to a vegetable diet. So convenient a thing it is to be a *reasonable creature*, since it enables one to find or make a reason for everything one has a mind to do.

1791

1. "When about 16 years of age, I happened to meet with a book written by one [Thomas] Tryon [*The Way to Health, Wealth, and Happiness*, 1682] recommending a vegetable diet. I determined to go into it. * * * My refusing to eat flesh occasioned an inconveniency, and I was frequently chid for my singularity" [Franklin, *Autobiography*].

WILLIAM GOLDING

Thinking as a Hobby

While I was still a boy, I came to the conclusion that there were three grades of thinking; and since I was later to claim thinking as my hobby, I came to an even stranger conclusion—namely, that I myself could not think at all.

I must have been an unsatisfactory child for grownups to deal with. I remember how incomprehensible they appeared to me at first, but not, of course, how I appeared to them. It was the headmaster of my grammar school who first brought the subject of thinking before me—though neither in the way, nor with the result he intended. He had some statuettes in his study. They stood on a high cupboard behind his desk. One was a lady wearing nothing but a bath towel. She seemed frozen in an eternal panic lest the bath towel slip down any farther; and since she had no arms, she was in an unfortunate position to pull the towel up again. Next to her, crouched the statuette of a leopard, ready to spring down at the top drawer of a filing cabinet labeled A-AH. My innocence interpreted this as the victim's last, despairing cry. Beyond the leopard was a naked, muscular gentleman, who sat, looking down, with his chin on his fist and his elbow on his knee. He seemed utterly miserable.

Some time later, I learned about these statuettes. The headmaster had placed them where they would face delinquent children, because they symbolized to him the whole of life. The naked lady was the Venus of Milo. She was Love. She was not worried about the towel. She was just busy being beautiful. The leopard was Nature, and he was being natural. The naked, muscular gentleman was not miserable. He was Rodin's Thinker, an image of pure thought. It is easy to buy small plaster models of what you think life is like.

I had better explain that I was a frequent visitor to the headmaster's study, because of the latest thing I had done or left undone. As we now say, I was not integrated. I was, if anything, disintegrated; and I was puzzled. Grownups never made sense. Whenever I found myself in a penal position before the headmaster's desk, with the statuettes glimmering whitely above him, I would sink my head, clasp my hands behind my back and writhe one shoe over the other.

The headmaster would look opaquely at me through flashing spectacles.

"What are we going to do with you?"

Well, what *were* they going to do with me? I would writhe my shoe some more and stare down at the worn rug.

"Look up, boy! Can't you look up?"

Then I would look up at the cupboard, where the naked lady was frozen in her panic and the muscular gentleman contemplated the hindquarters of the leopard in endless gloom. I had nothing to say to the headmaster. His spectacles caught the light so that you could see nothing human behind them. There was no possibility of communication.

"Don't you ever think at all?"

No, I didn't think, wasn't thinking, couldn't think—I was simply waiting in anguish for the interview to stop.

"Then you'd better learn—hadn't you?"

On one occasion the headmaster leaped to his feet, reached up and plonked Rodin's masterpiece on the desk before me.

"That's what a man looks like when he's really thinking."

I surveyed the gentleman without interest or comprehension.

"Go back to your class."

Clearly there was something missing in me. Nature had endowed the rest of the human race with a sixth sense and left me out. This must be so, I mused, on my way back to the class, since whether I had broken a window, or failed to remember Boyle's Law, or been late for school, my teachers produced me one, adult answer: "Why can't you think?"

As I saw the case, I had broken the window because I had tried to hit Jack Arney with a cricket ball and missed him; I could not remember Boyle's Law because I had never bothered to learn it; and I was late for school because I preferred looking over the bridge into the river. In fact, I was wicked. Were my teachers, perhaps, so good that they could not understand the depths of my depravity? Were they clear, untormented people who could direct their every action by this mysterious business of thinking? The whole thing was incomprehensible. In my earlier years, I found even the statuette of the Thinker confusing. I did not believe any of my teachers were naked, ever. Like someone born deaf, but bitterly determined to find out about sound, I watched my teachers to find out about thought.

There was Mr. Houghton. He was always telling me to think. With a modest satisfaction, he would tell me that he had thought a bit himself. Then why did he spend so much time drinking? Or was there more sense in drinking than there appeared to be? But if not, and if drinking were in fact ruinous to health—and Mr. Houghton was ruined, there was no doubt about that—why was he always talking about the clean life and the virtues of fresh air? He would spread his arms wide with the action of a man who habitually spent his time striding along mountain ridges.

"Open air does me good, boys—I know it!"

Sometimes, exalted by his own oratory, he would leap from his desk and hustle us outside into a hideous wind.

"Now, boys! Deep breaths! Feel it right down inside you—huge draughts of God's good air!"

He would stand before us, rejoicing in his perfect health, an open-air man. He would put his hands on his waist and take a tremendous breath. You could hear the wind, trapped in the cavern of his chest and struggling with all the unnatural impediments. His body would reel with shock and his ruined face go white at the unaccustomed visitation. He would stagger back to his desk and collapse there, useless for the rest of the morning.

Mr. Houghton was given to high-minded monologues about the good life, sexless and full of duty. Yet in the middle of one of these monologues, if a girl passed the window, tapping along on her neat little feet, he would interrupt his discourse, his neck would turn of itself and he would watch her out of sight. In this instance, he seemed to me ruled not by thought but by an invisible and irresistible spring in his nape.

His neck was an object of great interest to me. Normally it bulged a bit over his collar. But Mr. Houghton had fought in the First World War alongside both Americans and French, and had come—by who knows what illogic?—to a settled detestation of both countries. If either country happened to be prominent in current affairs, no argument could make Mr. Houghton think well of it. He would bang the desk, his neck would bulge still further and go red. "You can say what you like," he would cry, "but I've thought about this—and I know what I think!"

Mr. Houghton thought with his neck.

There was Miss Parsons. She assured us that her dearest wish was our welfare, but I knew even then, with the mysterious clairvoyance of childhood, that what she wanted most was the husband she never got. There was Mr. Hands—and so on.

I have dealt at length with my teachers because this was my introduction to the nature of what is commonly called thought. Through them I discovered that thought is often full of unconscious prejudice, ignorance and hypocrisy. It will lecture on disinterested purity while its neck is being remorselessly twisted toward a skirt. Technically, it is about as proficient as most businessmen's golf, as honest as most politicians' intentions, or—to come near my own preoccupation—as coherent as most books that get written. It is what I came to call grade-three thinking, though more properly, it is feeling, rather than thought.

True, often there is a kind of innocence in prejudices, but in those days I viewed grade-three thinking with an intolerant contempt and an incautious mockery. I delighted to confront a pious lady who hated the Germans with the proposition that we should love our enemies. She taught me a great truth in dealing with grade-three thinkers; because of her, I no longer dismiss lightly a mental process which for nine-tenths of the population is the nearest they will ever get to thought. They have immense solidarity. We had better respect them, for we are outnumbered and surrounded. A crowd of grade-three thinkers, all shouting the same thing, all warming their hands at the fire of their own prejudices, will not thank you for pointing out the contradictions in their beliefs. Man is a gregarious animal, and enjoys agreement as cows will graze all the same way on the side of a hill.

Grade-two thinking is the detection of contradictions. I reached grade two when I trapped the poor, pious lady. Grade-two thinkers do not stampede easily, though often they fall into the other fault and lap behind. Grade-two thinking is a withdrawal, with eyes and ears open. It became my hobby and brought satisfaction and loneliness in either hand. For grade-two thinking destroys without having the power to create. It set me watching the crowds cheering His Majesty and King and asking myself what all the fuss was about, without giving me anything positive to put in the place of that heady patriotism. But there were compensations. To hear people justify their habit of hunting foxes and tearing them to pieces by claiming that the foxes liked it. To hear our Prime Minister talk about the great benefit we conferred on India by jailing people like Pandit Nehru and Gandhi. To hear American politicians talk about peace in one sentence and refuse to join the League of Nations in the next. Yes, there were moments of delight.

But I was growing toward adolescence and had to admit that Mr. Houghton was not the only one with an irresistible spring in his neck. I, too, felt the compulsive hand of nature and began to find that pointing out contradiction could be costly as well as fun. There was Ruth, for example, a serious and attractive girl. I was an atheist at the time. Grade-two thinking is a menace to religion and knocks down sects like skittles. I put myself in a position to be converted by her with an hypocrisy worthy of grade three. She was a Methodist—or at least, her parents were, and Ruth had to follow suit. But, alas, instead of relying on the Holy Spirit to convert me, Ruth was foolish enough to open her pretty mouth in argument. She claimed that the Bible (King James Version) was literally inspired. I countered by saying that the Catholics believed in the literal inspiration of Saint Jerome's *Vulgate*,[1] and the two books were different. Argument flagged.

At last she remarked that there were an awful lot of Methodists, and they couldn't be wrong, could they—not all those millions? That was too easy, said I restively (for the nearer you were to Ruth, the nicer she was to be near to) since there were more Roman Catholics than Methodists anyway; and they couldn't be wrong, could they—not all those hundreds of millions? An awful flicker of doubt appeared in her eyes. I slid my arm around her waist and murmured breathlessly that if we were counting heads, the Buddhists were the boys for my money. But Ruth had *really* wanted to do me good, because I was so nice. She fled. The combination of my arm and those countless Buddhists was too much for her.

That night her father visited my father and left, red-cheeked and

---

1. The Latin Bible as revised in the fourth century A.D. by Jerome and used thereafter as the authoritative text for Roman Catholic ritual.

indignant. I was given the third degree to find out what had happened. It was lucky we were both of us only fourteen. I lost Ruth and gained an undeserved reputation as a potential libertine.

So grade-two thinking could be dangerous. It was in this knowledge, at the age of fifteen, that I remember making a comment from the heights of grade two, on the limitations of grade three. One evening I found myself alone in the school hall, preparing it for a party. The door of the headmaster's study was open. I went in. The headmaster had ceased to thump Rodin's Thinker down on the desk as an example to the young. Perhaps he had not found any more candidates, but the statuettes were still there, glimmering and gathering dust on top of the cupboard. I stood on a chair and rearranged them. I stood Venus in her bath towel on the filing cabinet, so that now the top drawer caught its breath in a gasp of sexy excitement. "A-ah!" The portentous Thinker I placed on the edge of the cupboard so that he looked down at the bath towel and waited for it to slip.

Grade-two thinking, though it filled life with fun and excitement, did not make for content. To find out the deficiencies of our elders bolsters the young ego but does not make for personal security. I found that grade two was not only the power to point out contradictions. It took the swimmer some distance from the shore and left him there, out of his depth. I decided that Pontius Pilate was a typical grade-two thinker. "What is truth?" he said, a very common grade-two thought, but one that is used always as the end of an argument instead of the beginning. There is still a higher grade of thought which says, "What is truth?" and sets out to find it.

But these grade-one thinkers were few and far between. They did not visit my grammar school in the flesh though they were there in books. I aspired to them, partly because I was ambitious and partly because I now saw my hobby as an unsatisfactory thing if it went no further. If you set out to climb a mountain, however high you climb, you have failed if you cannot reach the top.

I _did_ meet an undeniably grade-one thinker in my first year at Oxford. I was looking over a small bridge in Magdalen Deer Park, and a tiny mustached and hatted figure came and stood by my side. He was a German who had just fled from the Nazis to Oxford as a temporary refuge. His name was Einstein.

But Professor Einstein knew no English at that time and I knew only two words of German. I beamed at him, trying wordlessly to convey by my bearing all the affection and respect that the English felt for him. It is possible—and I have to make the admission—that I felt here were two grade-one thinkers standing side by side; yet I doubt if my face conveyed more than a formless awe. I would have given my Greek and Latin and French and a good slice of my English for enough German to communicate. But we were divided; he was as inscrutable as my headmaster. For perhaps five minutes we stood together on the bridge, undeniable grade-one thinker and breathless aspirant. With true greatness, Professor Einstein realized that my contact was better than none. He pointed to a trout wavering in midstream.

He spoke: *"Fisch."*

My brain reeled. Here I was, mingling with the great, and yet helpless as the veriest grade-three thinker. Desperately I sought for some sign by which I might convey that I, too, revered pure reason. I nodded vehemently. In a brilliant flash I used up half of my German vocabulary.

"Fisch. Ja Ja."

For perhaps another five minutes we stood side by side. Then Professor Einstein, his whole figure still conveying good will and amiability, drifted away out of sight.

I, too, would be a grade-one thinker. I was irreverent at the best of times. Political and religious systems, social customs, loyalties and traditions, they all came tumbling down like so many rotten apples off a tree. This was a fine hobby and a sensible substitute for cricket, since you could play it all the year round. I came up in the end with what must always remain the justification for grade-one thinking, its sign, seal and charter. I devised a coherent system for living. It was a moral system, which was wholly logical. Of course, as I readily admitted, conversion of the world to my way of thinking might be difficult, since my system did away with a number of trifles, such as big business, centralized government, armies, marriage. . . .

It was Ruth all over again. I had some very good friends who stood by me, and still do. But my acquaintances vanished, taking the girls with them. Young women seemed oddly contented with the world as it was. They valued the meaningless ceremony with a ring. Young men, while willing to concede the chaining sordidness of marriage, were hesitant about abandoning the organizations which they hoped would give them a career. A young man on the first rung of the Royal Navy, while perfectly agreeable to doing away with big business and marriage, got as rednecked as Mr. Houghton when I proposed a world without any battleships in it.

Had the game gone too far? Was it a game any longer? In those prewar days, I stood to lose a great deal, for the sake of a hobby.

Now you are expecting me to describe how I saw the folly of my ways and came back to the warm nest, where prejudices are so often called loyalties, where pointless actions are hallowed into custom by repetition, where we are content to say we think when all we do is feel.

But you would be wrong. I dropped my hobby and turned professional.

If I were to go back to the headmaster's study and find the dusty statuettes still there, I would arrange them differently. I would dust Venus and put her aside, for I have come to love her and know her for the fair thing she is. But I would put the Thinker, sunk in his desperate thought, where there were shadows before him—and at his back, I would put the leopard, crouched and ready to spring.

1961

QUESTIONS

1. Why does Golding at the end of his essay return to the three statuettes? Have the statuettes anything to do with the three kinds of thinking described in the essay? Why would Golding rearrange the statuettes as he does in the final paragraph?
2. It has been said: "Third-rate thinkers think like everybody else because everybody else thinks the same way. Second-rate thinkers think differently from everybody else because everybody else thinks the same way. First-rate thinkers think." Does this saying correspond to Golding's message? Would you modify it in any way in light of what he writes?
3. Does Golding's anecdote about Einstein have any bearing upon his account of the three categories of thinking?
4. What are the special attractions and what are the penalties of grade-three thinking? Grade-two? Grade-one?
5. Are Golding's three categories all-encompassing? If so, how? If not, what additional ones would you add?
6. Are Golding's categories useful for assessing the value of a person's statements? Choose several selections in this book and examine them by Golding's implied criteria.
7. William Golding is the author of the novel Lord of the Flies. If you have read that work, do you see in his depiction of characters and events any manifestations of the three categories of thinking?

CARL SAGAN

The Abstractions of Beasts

"Beasts abstract not," announced John Locke, expressing mankind's prevailing opinion throughout recorded history: Bishop Berkeley[1] had, however, a sardonic rejoinder: "If the fact that brutes abstract not be made the distinguishing property of that sort

1. John Locke, English philosopher, author of *An Essay Concerning Human Understanding* (1690); Bishop George Berkeley, Irish philosopher, author of *A Treatise Concerning the Principles of Human Knowledge* (1710).

of animal, I fear a great many of those that pass for men must be reckoned into their numbers." Abstract thought, at least in its more subtle varieties, is not an invariable accompaniment of everyday life for the average man. Could abstract thought be a matter not of kind but of degree? Could other animals be capable of abstract thought but more rarely or less deeply than humans?

We have the impression that other animals are not very intelligent. But have we examined the possibility of animal intelligence carefully enough, or, as in François Truffaut's poignant film *The Wild Child*, do we simply equate the absence of our style of expression of intelligence with the absence of intelligence? In discussing communication with the animals, the French philosopher Montaigne remarked, "The defect that hinders communication betwixt them and us, why may it not be on our part as well as theirs?"

There is, of course, a considerable body of anecdotal information suggesting chimpanzee intelligence. The first serious study of the behavior of simians—including their behavior in the wild—was made in Indonesia by Alfred Russel Wallace, the co-discoverer of evolution by natural selection. Wallace concluded that a baby orangutan he studied behaved "exactly like a human child in similar circumstances." In fact, "orangutan" is a Malay phrase meaning not ape but "man of the woods." Teuber recounted many stories told by his parents, pioneer German ethologists who founded and operated the first research station devoted to chimpanzee behavior on Tenerife in the Canary Islands early in the second decade of this century. It was here that Wolfgang Kohler performed his famous studies of Sultan, a chimpanzee "genius" who was able to connect two rods in order to reach an otherwise inaccessible banana. On Tenerife, also, two chimpanzees were observed maltreating a chicken: One would extend some food to the fowl, encouraging it to approach; whereupon the other would thrust at it with a piece of wire it had concealed behind its back. The chicken would retreat but soon allow itself to approach once again—and be beaten once again. Here is a fine combination of behavior sometimes thought to be uniquely human: cooperation, planning a future course of action, deception and cruelty. It also reveals that chickens have a very low capacity for avoidance learning.

Until a few years ago, the most extensive attempt to communicate with chimpanzees went something like this: A newborn chimp was taken into a household with a newborn baby, and both would be raised together—twin cribs, twin bassinets, twin high chairs, twin potties, twin diaper pails, twin babypowder cans. At the end of three years, the young chimp had, of course, far outstripped the young human in manual dexterity, running, leaping, climbing and other motor skills. But while the child was happily babbling away, the chimp could say only, and with enormous difficulty, "Mama,"

"Papa," and "cup." From this it was widely concluded that in language, reasoning and other higher mental functions, chimpanzees were only minimally competent: "Beasts abstract not."

But in thinking over these experiments, two psychologists, Beatrice and Robert Gardner, at the University of Nevada, realized that the pharynx and larynx of the chimp are not suited for human speech. Human beings exhibit a curious multiple use of the mouth for eating, breathing and communicating. In insects such as crickets, which call to one another by rubbing their legs, these three functions are performed by completely separate organ systems. Human spoken language seems to be adventitious. The exploitation of organ systems with other functions for communication in humans is also indicative of the comparatively recent evolution of our linguistic abilities. It might be, the Gardners reasoned, that chimpanzees have substantial language abilities which could not be expressed because of the limitations of their anatomy. Was there any symbolic language, they asked, that could employ the strengths rather than the weaknesses of chimpanzee anatomy?

The Gardners hit upon a brilliant idea: Teach a chimpanzee American sign language, known by its acronym Ameslan, and sometimes as "American deaf and dumb language" (the "dumb" refers, of course, to the inability to speak and not to any failure of intelligence). It is ideally suited to the immense manual dexterity of the chimpanzee. It also may have all the crucial design features of verbal languages.

There is by now a vast library of described and filmed conversations, employing Ameslan and other gestural languages, with Washoe, Lucy, Lana and other chimpanzees studied by the Gardners and others. Not only are there chimpanzees with working vocabularies of 100 to 200 words; they are also able to distinguish among nontrivially different grammatical patterns and syntaxes. What is more, they have been remarkably inventive in the construction of new words and phrases.

On seeing for the first time a duck land quacking in a pond, Washoe gestured "waterbird," which is the same phrase used in English and other languages, but which Washoe invented for the occasion. Having never seen a spherical fruit other than an apple, but knowing the signs for the principal colors, Lana, upon spying a technician eating an orange, signed "orange apple." After tasting a watermelon, Lucy described it as "candy drink" or "drink fruit," which is essentially the same word form as the English "water melon." But after she had burned her mouth on her first radish, Lucy forever after described them as "cry hurt food." A small doll placed unexpectedly in Washoe's cup elicited the response "Baby in my drink." When Washoe soiled, particularly clothing or furniture, she was taught the sign "dirty," which she then extrapolated as a general term of abuse. A rhesus monkey that evoked her displeasure was repeatedly signed at: "Dirty monkey, dirty monkey, dirty monkey." Occasionally Washoe would say things like "Dirty Jack, gimme drink." Lana, in a moment of creative annoyance, called her trainer "You green shit." Chimpanzees have invented swear words. Washoe also seems to have a sort of sense of humor; once, when riding on her trainer's shoulders and, perhaps inadvertently, wetting him, she signed: "Funny, funny."

Lucy was eventually able to distinguish clearly the meanings of the phrases "Roger tickle Lucy" and "Lucy tickle Roger," both of which activities she enjoyed with gusto. Likewise, Lana extrapolated from "Tim groom Lana" to "Lana groom Tim." Washoe was observed "reading" a magazine—i.e., slowly turning the pages, peering intently at the pictures and making, to no one in particular, an appropriate sign, such as "cat" when viewing a photograph of a tiger, and "drink" when examining a Vermouth advertisement. Having learned the sign "open" with a door, Washoe extended the concept to a briefcase. She also attempted to converse in Ameslan with the laboratory cat, who turned out to be the only illiterate in the facility. Having acquired this marvelous method of communication, Washoe may have been surprised that the cat was not also competent in Ameslan. And when one day Jane, Lucy's foster mother, left the laboratory, Lucy gazed after her and signed: "Cry me. Me cry."

Boyce Rensberger is a sensitive and gifted reporter for the *New York Times* whose parents could neither speak nor hear, although he is in both respects normal. His first language, however, was Ameslan. He had been abroad on a European assignment for the *Times* for some years. On his return to the United States, one of his first domestic duties was to look into the Gardners' experiments with Washoe. After some little time with the chimpanzee, Rensberger reported, "Suddenly I realized I was conversing with a member of another species in my native tongue." The use of the word tongue is, of course, figurative: it is built deeply into the structure of the language (a word that also means "tongue"). In fact, Rensberger was conversing with a member of another species in his native "hand." And it is just this transition from tongue to hand that has permitted humans to regain the ability—lost, according to Josephus,[2] since Eden—to communicate with the animals.

In addition to Ameslan, chimpanzees and other nonhuman primates are being taught a variety of other gestural languages. At the Yerkes Regional Primate Research Center in Atlanta, Georgia, they

---

2. First-century Jewish general and historian.

are learning a specific computer language called (by the humans, not the chimps) "Yerkish." The computer records all of its subjects' conversations, even during the night when no humans are in attendance; and from its ministrations we have learned that chimpanzees prefer jazz to rock and movies about chimpanzees to movies about human beings. Lana had, by January 1976, viewed *The Developmental Anatomy of the Chimpanzee* 245 times. She would undoubtedly appreciate a larger film library.

* * * The machine provides for many of Lana's needs, but not all. Sometimes, in the middle of the night, she forlornly types out: "Please, machine, tickle Lana." More elaborate requests and commentaries, each requiring a creative use of a set grammatical form, have been developed subsequently.

Lana monitors her sentences on a computer display, and erases those with grammatical errors. Once, in the midst of Lana's construction of an elaborate sentence, her trainer mischievously and repeatedly interposed, from his separate computer console, a word that made nonsense of Lana's sentence. She gazed at her computer display, spied her trainer at his console, and composed a new sentence: "Please, Tim, leave room." Just as Washoe and Lucy can be said to speak, Lana can be said to write.

At an early stage in the development of Washoe's verbal abilities, Jacob Bronowski and a colleague wrote a scientific paper denying the significance of Washoe's use of gestural language because, in the limited data available to Bronowski, Washoe neither inquired nor negated. But later observations showed that Washoe and other chimpanzees were perfectly able both to ask questions and to deny assertions put to them. And it is difficult to see any significant difference in quality between chimpanzee use of gestural language and the use of ordinary speech by children in a manner that we unhesitatingly attribute to intelligence. In reading Bronowski's paper I cannot help but feel that a little pinch of human chauvinism has crept in, an echo of Locke's "Beasts abstract not." In 1949, the American anthropologist Leslie White stated unequivocally: "Human behavior is symbolic behavior; symbolic behavior is human behavior." What would White have made of Washoe, Lucy and Lana?

These findings on chimpanzee language and intelligence have an intriguing bearing on "Rubicon" arguments[3]—the contention that the total brain mass, or at least the ratio of brain to body mass, is a useful index of intelligence. Against this point of view it was once

3. Those assuming a definitive boundary between different kinds of intelligence. The allusion is to the river Rubicon, in ancient times the boundary between Rome and its "barbaric" Germanic provinces.

argued that the lower range of the brain masses of microcephalic humans overlaps the upper range of brain masses of adult chimpanzees and gorillas; and yet, it was said, microcephalics have some, although severely impaired, use of language—while the apes have none. But in only relatively few cases are microcephalics capable of human speech. One of the best behavioral descriptions of microcephalics was written by a Russian physician, S. Korsakov, who in 1893 observed a female microcephalic named "Masha." She could understand a very few questions and commands and could occasionally reminisce on her childhood. She sometimes chattered away, but there was little coherence to what she uttered. Korsakov characterized her speech as having "an extreme poverty of logical associations." As an example of her poorly adapted and automaton-like intelligence, Korsakov described her eating habits. When food was present on the table, Masha would eat. But if the food was abruptly removed in the midst of a meal, she would behave as if the meal had ended, thanking those in charge and piously blessing herself. If the food were returned, she would eat again. The pattern apparently was subject to indefinite repetition. My own impression is that Lucy or Washoe would be a far more interesting dinner companion than Masha, and that the comparison of microcephalic humans with normal apes is not inconsistent with some sort of "Rubicon" of intelligence. Of course, both the quality and the quantity of neural connections are probably vital for the sorts of intelligence that we can easily recognize.

Recent experiments performed by James Dewson of the Stanford University School of Medicine and his colleagues give some physiological support to the idea of language centers in the simian neocortex—in particular, like humans, in the left hemisphere. Monkeys were trained to press a green light when they heard a hiss and a red light when they heard a tone. Some seconds after a sound was heard, the red or the green light would appear at some unpredictable position—different each time—on the control panel. The monkey pressed the appropriate light and, in the case of a correct guess, was rewarded with a pellet of food. Then the time interval between hearing the sound and seeing the light was increased up to twenty seconds. In order to be rewarded, the monkeys now had to remember for twenty seconds which noise they had heard. Dewson's team then surgically excised part of the so-called auditory association cortex from the left hemisphere of the neocortex in the temporal lobe. When retested, the monkeys had very poor recall of which sound they were then hearing. After less than a second they could not recall whether it was a hiss or a tone. The removal of a comparable part of the temporal lobe from the right hemisphere produced no effect whatever on this task. "It looks," Dewson was reported to say, "as if we removed the structure in the monkeys' brains that may be analogous to human language centers." Similar studies on rhesus monkeys, but using visual rather than auditory stimuli, seem to show no evidence of a difference between the hemispheres of the neocortex.

Because adult chimpanzees are generally thought (at least by zoo-keepers) to be too dangerous to retain in a home or home environment, Washoe and other verbally accomplished chimpanzees have been involuntarily "retired" soon after reaching puberty. Thus we do not yet have experience with the adult language abilities of monkeys and apes. One of the most intriguing questions is whether a verbally accomplished chimpanzee mother will be able to communicate language to her offspring. It seems very likely that this should be possible and that a community of chimps initially competent in gestural language could pass down the language to subsequent generations.

Where such communication is essential for survival, there is already some evidence that apes transmit extragenetic or cultural information. Jane Goodall observed baby chimps in the wild emulating the behavior of their mothers and learning the reasonably complex task of finding an appropriate twig and using it to prod into a termite's nest so as to acquire some of these tasty delicacies.

Differences in group behavior—something that it is very tempting to call cultural differences—have been reported among chimpanzees, baboons, macaques and many other primates. For example, one group of monkeys may know how to eat bird's eggs, while an adjacent band of precisely the same species may not. Such primates have a few dozen sounds or cries, which are used for intra-group communication, with such meanings as "Flee; here is a predator." But the sound of the cries differs somewhat from group to group: there are regional accents.

An even more striking experiment was performed accidentally by Japanese primatologists attempting to relieve an overpopulation and hunger problem in a community of macaques on an island in south Japan. The anthropologists threw grains of wheat on a sandy beach. Now it is very difficult to separate wheat grains one by one from sand grains; such an effort might even expend more energy than eating the collected wheat would provide. But one brilliant macaque, Imo, perhaps by accident or out of pique, threw handfuls of the mixture into the water. Wheat floats; sand sinks, a fact that Imo clearly noted. Through the sifting process she was able to eat well (on a diet of soggy wheat, to be sure). While older macaques, set in their ways, ignored her, the younger monkeys appeared to grasp the importance of her discovery, and imitate it. In the next generation, the practice was more widespread; today all macaques on the island are competent at water sifting, an example of a cultural tradition among the monkeys.

Earlier studies on Takasakiyama, a mountain in northeast Kyushu inhabited by macaques, show a similar pattern in cultural evolution. Visitors to Takasakiyama threw caramels wrapped in paper to the monkeys—a common practice in Japanese zoos, but one the Takasakiyama macaques had never before encountered. In the course of play, some young monkeys discovered how to unwrap the caramels and eat them. The habit was passed on successively to their playmates, their mothers, the dominant males (who among the macaques act as babysitters for the very young) and finally to the subadult males, who were at the furthest social remove from the monkey children. The process of acculturation took more than three years. In natural primate communities, the existing nonverbal communications are so rich that there is little pressure for the development of a more elaborate gestural language. But if gestural language were necessary for chimpanzee survival, there can be little doubt that it would be transmitted culturally down through the generations.

I would expect a significant development and elaboration of language in only a few generations if all the chimps unable to communicate were to die or fail to reproduce. Basic English corresponds to about 1,000 words. Chimpanzees are already accomplished in vocabularies exceeding 10 percent of that number. Although a few years ago it would have seemed the most implausible science fiction, it does not appear to me out of the question that, after a few generations in such a verbal chimpanzee community, there might emerge the memoirs of the natural history and mental life of a chimpanzee, published in English or Japanese (with perhaps an "as told to" after the by-line).

If chimpanzees have consciousness, if they are capable of abstractions, do they not have what until now has been described as "human rights"? How smart does a chimpanzee have to be before killing him constitutes murder? What further properties must he show before religious missionaries must consider him worthy of attempts at conversion?

I recently was escorted through a large primate research laboratory by its director. We approached a long corridor lined, to the vanishing point as in a perspective drawing, with caged chimpanzees. They were one, two or three to a cage, and I am sure the accommodations were exemplary as far as such institutions (or for that matter traditional zoos) go. As we approached the nearest cage, its two inmates bared their teeth and with incredible accuracy let fly great sweeping arcs of spittle, fairly drenching the lightweight suit of the facility's director. They then uttered a staccato of short shrieks, which echoed down the corridor to be repeated and amplified by other caged chimps, who had certainly not seen us, until the corridor fairly shook with the screeching and banging and rattling of bars. The director informed me that not only spit is apt to fly in such a situation; and at his urging we retreated.

I was powerfully reminded of those American motion pictures of the 1930s and '40s, set in some vast and dehumanized state or federal penitentiary, in which the prisoners banged their eating utensils against the bars at the appearance of the tyrannical warden. These chimps are healthy and well-fed. If they are "only" animals, if they are beasts which abstract not, then my comparison is a piece of sentimental foolishness. But chimpanzees *can* abstract. Like other mammals, they are capable of strong emotions. They have certainly committed no crimes. I do not claim to have the answer, but I think it is certainly worthwhile to raise the question: Why, exactly, all over the civilized world, in virtually every major city, are apes in prison?

For all we know, occasional viable crosses between humans and chimpanzees are possible. The natural experiment must have been tried very infrequently, at least recently. If such off-spring are ever produced, what will their legal status be? The cognitive abilities of chimpanzees force us, I think, to raise searching questions about the boundaries of the community of beings to which special ethical considerations are due, and can, I hope, help to extend our ethical perspectives downward through the taxa on Earth and upwards to extraterrestial organisms, if they exist.

* * *

1977

HENRY DAVID THOREAU
Observation

There is no such thing as pure *objective* observation. Your observation, to be interesting, *i.e.* to be significant, must be *subjective*. The sum of what the writer of whatever class has to report is simply some human experience, whether he be poet or philosopher or man of science. The man of most science is the man most alive, whose life is the greatest event. Senses that take cognizance of outward things merely are of no avail. It matters not where or how far you travel—the farther commonly the worse—but how much alive you are. If it is possible to conceive of an event outside to humanity, it is not of the slightest significance, though it were the explosion of a planet. Every important worker will report what life there is in him. It makes no odds into what seeming deserts the poet is born. Though all his neighbors pronounce it a Sahara, it will be a paradise to him; for the desert which we see is the result of the barrenness of our experience. No mere willful activity whatever, whether in writing verses or collecting statistics, will produce true poetry or science. If you are really a sick man, it is indeed to be regretted, for you cannot accomplish so much as if you were well. All that a man has to say or do that can possibly concern mankind, is in some shape or other to tell the story of his love—to sing, and, if he is fortunate and keeps alive, he will be forever in love. This alone is to be alive to the extremities. It is a pity that this divine creature should ever suffer from cold feet; a still greater pity that the coldness so often reaches to his heart. I look over the report of the doings of a scientific association and am surprised that there is so little life to be reported; I am put off with a parcel of dry technical terms. Anything living is easily and naturally expressed in popular language. I cannot help suspecting that the life of these learned professors has been almost as inhuman and wooden as a rain-gauge or self-registering magnetic machine. They communicate no fact which rises to the temperature of blood-heat. It doesn't all amount to one rhyme.

JACOB BRONOWSKI

The Reach of Imagination

For three thousand years, poets have been enchanted and moved and perplexed by the power of their own imagination. In a short and summary essay I can hope at most to lift one small corner of that mystery; and yet it is a critical corner. I shall ask, What goes on in the mind when we imagine? You will hear from me that one answer to this question is fairly specific: which is to say, that we can describe the working of the imagination. And when we describe it as I shall do, it becomes plain that imagination is a specifically *human* gift. To imagine is the characteristic act, not of the poet's mind, or the painter's, or the scientist's, but of the mind of man.

My stress here on the word *human* implies that there is a clear difference in this between the actions of men and those of other animals. Let me then start with a classical experiment with animals and children which Walter Hunter thought out in Chicago about 1910. That was the time when scientists were agog with the success of Ivan Pavlov in forming and changing the reflex actions of dogs, which Pavlov had first announced in 1903. Pavlov had been given a Nobel prize the next year, in 1904; although in fairness I should say that the award did not cite his work on the conditioned reflex, but on the digestive gland.

Hunter duly trained some dogs and other animals on Pavlov's lines. They were taught that when a light came on over one of three tunnels out of their cage, that tunnel would be open; they could escape down it, and were rewarded with food if they did. But once he had fixed that conditioned reflex, Hunter added to it a deeper idea: he gave the mechanical experiment a new dimension, literally—the dimension of time. Now he no longer let the dog go to the lighted tunnel at once; instead, he put out the light, and then kept the dog waiting a little while before he let him go. In this way Hunter timed how long an animal can remember where he has last seen the signal light to his escape route.

The results were and are staggering. A dog or a rat forgets which one of three tunnels has been lit up within a matter of seconds—in Hunter's experiment, ten seconds at most. If you want such an animal to do much better than this, you must make the task much simpler: you must face him with only two tunnels to choose from. Even so, the best that Hunter could do was to have a dog remember for five minutes which one of two tunnels had been lit up.

I am not quoting these times as if they were exact and universal: they surely are not. Hunter's experiment, more than fifty years old now, had many faults of detail. For example, there were too few animals, they were oddly picked, and they did not all behave consistently. It may be unfair to test a dog for what he *saw*, when he commonly follows his nose rather than his eyes. It may be unfair to test any animal in the unnatural setting of a laboratory cage. And there are higher animals, such as chimpanzees and other primates, which certainly have longer memories than the animals that Hunter tried.

Yet when all these provisos have been made (and met, by more modern experiments) the facts are still startling and characteristic. An animal cannot recall a signal from the past for even a short fraction of the time that a man can—for even a short fraction of the time that a child can. Hunter made comparable tests with six-year-old children, and found, of course, that they were incomparably better than the best of his animals. There is a striking and basic difference between a man's ability to imagine something that he saw or experienced, and an animal's failure.

Animals make up for this by other and extraordinary gifts. The salmon and the carrier pigeon can find their way home as we cannot: they have, as it were, a practical memory that man cannot match. But their actions always depend on some form of habit: on instinct or on learning, which reproduce by rote a train of known responses. They do not depend, as human memory does, on calling to mind the recollection of absent things.

Where is it that the animal falls short? We get a clue to the answer, I think, when Hunter tells us how the animals in his experiment tried to fix their recollection. They most often pointed themselves at the light before it went out, as some gun dogs point rigidly at the game they scent—and get the name *pointer* from the posture. The animal makes ready to act by building the signal into its action. There is a primitive imagery in its stance, it seems to me; it is as if the animal were trying to fix the light on its mind by fixing it in its body. And indeed, how else can a dog mark and (as it were) name one of three tunnels, when he has no such words as *left* and *right*, and no such numbers as *one, two, three?* The directed gesture of attention and readiness is perhaps the only symbolic device that the dog commands to hold on to the past, and thereby to guide himself into the future.

I used the verb *to imagine* a moment ago, and now I have some ground for giving it a meaning. *To imagine* means to make images and to move them about inside one's head in new arrangements. When you and I recall the past, we imagine it in this direct and homely sense. The tool that puts the human mind ahead of the animal is imagery. For us, memory does not demand the preoccupation that it demands in animals, and it lasts immensely longer, because we fix it in images or other substitute symbols. With the same symbolic vocabulary we spell out the future—not one but many futures, which we weigh one against another.

I am using the word *image* in a wide meaning, which does not restrict it to the mind's eye as a visual organ. An image in my usage is what Charles Peirce called a *sign*, without regard for its sensory quality. Peirce distinguished between different forms of signs, but there is no reason to make his distinction here, for the imagination works equally with them all, and that is why I call them all images.

Indeed, the most important images for human beings are simply words, which are abstract symbols. Animals do not have words, in our sense: there is no specific center for language in the brain of any animal, as there is in the human being. In this respect at least we know that the human imagination depends on a configuration in the brain that has only evolved in the last one or two million years. In the same period, evolution has greatly enlarged the front lobes in the human brain, which govern the sense of the past and the future; and it is a fair guess that they are probably the seat of our other images. (Part of the evidence for this guess is that damage to the front lobes in primates reduces them to the state of Hunter's animals.) If the guess turns out to be right, we shall know why man has come to look like a highbrow or an egghead: because otherwise there would not be room in his head for his imagination.

The images play out for us events which are not present to our senses, and thereby guard the past and create the future—a future that does not yet exist, and may never come to exist in that form. By contrast, the lack of symbolic ideas, or their rudimentary poverty, cuts off an animal from the past and the future alike, and imprisons him in the present. Of all the distinctions between man and animal, the characteristic gift which makes us human is the power to work with symbolic images: the gift of imagination.

This is really a remarkable finding. When Philip Sidney in 1580 defended poets (and all unconventional thinkers) from the Puritan charge that they were liars, he said that a maker must imagine things that are not. Halfway between Sidney and us, William Blake said, "What is now proved was once only imagined." About the same time, in 1796, Samuel Taylor Coleridge for the first time distinguished between the passive fancy and the active imagination, "the living Power and prime Agent of all human Perception." Now we see that they were right, and precisely right: the human gift is the gift of imagination—and that is not just a literary phrase.

Nor is it just a literary gift; it is, I repeat, characteristically human. Almost everything that we do that is worth doing is done in the first place in the mind's eye. The richness of human life is that we have many lives; we live the events that do not happen (and some that cannot) as vividly as those that do; and if thereby we die a thousand deaths, that is the price we pay for living a thousand lives. (A cat, of course, has only nine.) Literature is alive to us because we live its images, but so is any play of the mind—so is chess: the lines of play that we foresee and try in our heads and dismiss are as much a part of the game as the moves that we make. John Keats said that the unheard melodies are sweeter, and all chess players sadly recall that the combinations that they planned and which never came to be played were the best.

I make this point to remind you, insistently, that imagination is the manipulation of images in one's head; and that the rational manipulation belongs to that, as well as the literary and artistic manipulation. When a child begins to play games with things that stand for other things, with chairs or chessmen, he enters the gateway to reason and imagination together. For the human reason discovers new relations between things not by deduction, but by that unpredictable blend of speculation and insight that scientists call induction, which—like other forms of imagination—cannot be formalized. We see it at work when Walter Hunter inquires into a child's memory, as much as when Blake and Coleridge do. Only a restless and original mind would have asked Hunter's questions and could have conceived his experiments, in a science that was dominated by Pavlov's reflex arcs and was heading toward the behaviorism of John Watson.[1]

Let me find a spectacular example for you from history. What is the most famous experiment that you had described to you as a child? I will hazard that it is the experiment that Galileo is said to have made in Sidney's age, in Pisa about 1590, by dropping two unequal balls from the Leaning Tower. There, we say, is a man in the modern mold, a man after our own hearts: he insisted on questioning the authority of Aristotle and St. Thomas Aquinas, and seeing with his own eyes whether (as they said) the heavy ball would reach the ground before the light one. Seeing is believing.

Yet seeing is also imagining. Galileo did challenge the authority of Aristotle, and he did look at his mechanics. But the eye that Galileo used was the mind's eye. He did not drop balls from the Leaning Tower of Pisa—and if he had, he would have got a very doubtful answer. Instead, Galileo made an imaginary experiment in his head, which I will describe as he did years later in the book he wrote after the Holy Office silenced him: the *Discorsi . . . intorno a due nuove scienze*,[2] which was smuggled out to be printed in the Netherlands in 1638.

Suppose, said Galileo, that you drop two unequal balls from the tower at the same time. And suppose that Aristotle is right—suppose that the heavy ball falls faster, so that it steadily gains on the light ball, and hits the ground first. Very well. Now imagine the same experiment done again, with only one difference: this time the two unequal balls are joined by a string between them. The heavy ball will again move ahead, but now the light ball holds it back and acts as a drag or brake. So the light ball will be speeded up and the heavy ball will be slowed down; they must reach the ground together because they are tied together, but they cannot reach the ground as quickly as the heavy ball alone. Yet the string between them has turned the two balls into a single mass which is heavier than either ball—and surely (according to Aristotle) this mass should therefore move faster than either ball? Galileo's imaginary experiment has uncovered a contradiction; he says trenchantly, "You see how, from your assumption that a heavier body falls more rapidly than a lighter one, I infer that a (still) heavier body falls more slowly." There is only one way out of the contradiction: the heavy ball and the light ball must fall at the same rate, so that they go on falling at the same rate when they are tied together.

1. Watson, a forerunner of B. F. Skinner (p. 377), argued that all human behavior consists of conditioned reflexes in response to environmental stimuli.

2. *Treatise . . . on Two New Sciences.*

In 1630, after publishing his heretical theory that the earth moves around the sun, Galileo was forced by the Inquisition to recant it under threat of torture.

This argument is not conclusive, for nature might be more subtle (when the two balls are joined) than Galileo has allowed. And yet it is something more important: it is suggestive, it is stimulating, it opens a new view—in a word, it is imaginative. It cannot be settled without an actual experiment, because nothing that we imagine can become knowledge until we have translated it into, and backed it by, real experience. The test of imagination is experience. But then, that is as true of literature and the arts as it is of science. In science, the imaginary experiment is tested by confronting it with physical experience; and in literature, the imaginative conception is tested by confronting it with human experience. The superficial speculation in science is dismissed because it is found to falsify nature; and the shallow work of art is discarded because it is found to be untrue to our own nature. So when Ella Wheeler Wilcox died in 1919, more people were reading her verses than Shakespeare's; yet in a few years her work was dead. It had been buried by its poverty of emotion and its trivialness of thought: which is to say that it had been proved to be as false to the nature of man as, say, Jean Baptiste Lamarck and Trofim Lysenko[3] were false to the nature of inheritance. The strength of the imagination, its enriching power and excitement, lies in its interplay with reality—physical and emotional.

I doubt if there is much to choose here between science and the arts: the imagination is not much more free, and not much less free, in one than in the other. All great scientists have used their imagination freely, and let it ride them to outrageous conclusions without crying "Halt!" Albert Einstein fiddled with imaginary experiments from boyhood, and was wonderfully ignorant of the facts that they were supposed to bear on. When he wrote the first of his beautiful papers on the random movement of atoms, he did not know that the Brownian motion which it predicted could be seen in any laboratory. He was sixteen when he invented the paradox that he resolved ten years later, in 1905, in the theory of relativity, and it bulked much larger in his mind than the experiment of Albert Michelson and Edward Morley[4] which had upset every other physicist since 1881. All his life Einstein loved to make up

---

3. Lamarck was a French biologist (1744–1829) who held that characteristics acquired by experience were biologically transmittable. Lysenko is a Russian biologist (1898–   ) who has held that hereditary properties of organisms could be changed by manipulating the environment.

4. Physicists had believed space to be filled with an ether which made possible the propagation of light and magnetism; the Michelson-Morley experiment proved this untrue. Einstein, an outsider, always claimed not to have heard of the experiment until after he published his special theory of relativity, which not only accounted for the Michelson-Morley findings but resolved such paradoxes as the impossibility of distinguishing qualitatively between gravity and the pull caused by the acceleration of an elevator, or lift.

teasing puzzles like Galileo's, about falling lifts and the detection of gravity; and they carry the nub of the problems of general relativity on which he was working.

Indeed, it could not be otherwise. The power that man has over nature and himself, and that a dog lacks, lies in his command of imaginary experience. He alone has the symbols which fix the past and play with the future, possible and impossible. In the Renaissance, the symbolism of memory was thought to be mystical, and devices that were invented as mnemonics (by Giordano Bruno, for example, and by Robert Fludd) were interpreted as magic signs. The symbol is the tool which gives man his power, and it is the same tool whether the symbols are images or words, mathematical signs or mesons. And the symbols have a reach and a roundness that goes beyond their literal and practical meaning. They are the rich concepts under which the mind gathers many particulars into one name, and many instances into one general induction. When a man says *left* and *right*, he is outdistancing the dog not only in looking for a light; he is setting in train all the shifts of meaning, the overtones and the ambiguities, between *gauche* and *adroit* and *dexterous*, between *sinister* and the sense of right. When a man counts *one*, *two*, *three*, he is not only doing mathematics; he is on the path to the mysticism of numbers in Pythagoras and Vitruvius and Kepler, to the Trinity and the signs of the Zodiac.

I have described imagination as the ability to make images and to move them about inside one's head in new arrangements. This is the faculty that is specifically human, and it is the common root from which science and literature both spring and grow and flourish together. For they do flourish (and languish) together; the great ages of science are the great ages of all the arts, because in them powerful minds have taken fire from one another, breathless and higgledy-piggledy, without asking too nicely whether they ought to tie their imagination to falling balls or a haunted island. Galileo and Shakespeare, who were born in the same year, grew into greatness in the same age; when Galileo was looking through his telescope at the moon, Shakespeare was writing *The Tempest* and all Europe was in ferment, from Johannes Kepler to Peter Paul Rubens, and from the first table of logarithms by John Napier to the Authorized Version of the Bible.

Let me end with a last and spirited example of the common inspiration of literature and science, because it is as much alive today as it was three hundred years ago. What I have in mind is man's ageless fantasy, to fly to the moon. I do not display this to you as a high scientific enterprise; on the contrary, I think we have more important discoveries to make here on earth than wait for us, beckoning, at the horned surface of the moon. Yet I cannot belittle the fascination which that ice-blue journey has had for the imagination of men, long before it drew us to our television screens to watch the tumbling astronauts. Plutarch and Lucian, Ariosto and Ben Jonson wrote about it, before the days of Jules Verne and H. G. Wells and science fiction. The seventeenth century was heady with new dreams and fables about voyages to the moon. Kepler wrote one full of deep scientific ideas, which (alas) simply got his mother accused of witchcraft. In England, Francis Godwin wrote a wild and splendid work, *The Man in the Moone*, and the astronomer John Wilkins wrote a wild and learned one, *The Discovery of a New World*. They did not draw a line between science and fancy; for example, they all tried to guess just where in the journey the earth's gravity would stop. Only Kepler understood that gravity has no boundary, and put a law to it—which happened to be the wrong law.

All this was a few years before Isaac Newton was born, and it was all in his head that day in 1666 when he sat in his mother's garden, a young man of twenty-three, and thought about the reach of gravity. This was how he came to conceive his brilliant image, that the moon is like a ball which has been thrown so hard that it falls exactly as fast as the horizon, all the way round the earth. The image will do for any satellite, and Newton modestly calculated how long therefore an astronaut would take to fall round the earth once. He made it ninety minutes, and we have all seen now that he was right; but Newton had no way to check that. Instead he went on to calculate how long in that case the distant moon would take to round the earth, if indeed it behaves like a thrown ball that falls in the earth's gravity, and if gravity obeyed a law of inverse squares. He found that the answer would be twenty-eight days.

In that telling figure, the imagination that day chimed with nature, and made a harmony. We shall hear an echo of that harmony on the day when we land on the moon, because it will be not a technical but an imaginative triumph, that reaches back to the beginning of modern science and literature both. All great acts of imagination are like this, in the arts and in science, and convince us because they fill out reality with a deeper sense of rightness. We start with the simplest vocabulary of images, with *left* and *right* and *one*, *two*, *three*, and before we know how it happened the words and the numbers have conspired to make a match with nature: we catch in them the pattern of mind and matter as one.

1967

QUESTIONS

1. How does the Hunter experiment provide Bronowski with the ground for defining the imagination?

2. Bronowski discusses the work of Galileo and Newton in the middle and at the end of his essay; what use does he make of their work? Does it justify placing them in the central and final positions?

3. On page 101 Bronowski attributes the imagination to a "configuration" in the brain. Configuration seems vague here; what else shows uncertainty about exactly what happens in the brain? Does this uncertainty compromise the argument of this essay?

4. What function is given to the mind by the title metaphor of reaching (later extended to symbols on page 105)? What words does Bronowski use to indicate the objects reached for? What is the significance of his selecting these words?

ISAAC ASIMOV

The Eureka Phenomenon

In the old days, when I was writing a great deal of fiction, there would come, once in a while, moments when I was stymied. Suddenly, I would find I had written myself into a hole and could see no way out. To take care of that, I developed a technique which invariably worked.

It was simply this—I went to the movies. Not just any movie. I had to pick a movie which was loaded with action but which made no demands on the intellect. As I watched, I did my best to avoid any conscious thinking concerning my problem, and when I came out of the movie I knew exactly what I would have to do to put the story back on the track.

It never failed.

In fact, when I was working on my doctoral dissertation, too many years ago, I suddenly came across a flaw in my logic that I had not noticed before and that knocked out everything I had done. In utter panic, I made my way to a Bob Hope movie—and came out with the necessary change in point of view.

It is my belief, you see, that thinking is a double phenomenon like breathing.

You can control breathing by deliberate voluntary action: you can breathe deeply and quickly, or you can hold your breath altogether, regardless of the body's needs at the time. This, however, doesn't work well for very long. Your chest muscles grow tired, your body clamors for more oxygen, or less, and you relax. The automatic involuntary control of breathing takes over, adjusts it to the body's needs and unless you have some respiratory disorder, you can forget about the whole thing.

Well, you can think by deliberate voluntary action, too, and I don't think it is much more efficient on the whole than voluntary breath control is. You can deliberately force your mind through channels of deductions and associations in search of a solution to some problem and before long you have dug mental furrows for yourself and find yourself circling round and round the same limited pathways. If those pathways yield no solution, no amount of further conscious thought will help.

On the other hand, if you let go, then the thinking process comes under automatic involuntary control and is more apt to take new pathways and make erratic associations you would not think of consciously. The solution will then come while you *think* you are *not* thinking.

The trouble is, though, that conscious thought involves no muscular action and so there is no sensation of physical weariness that would force you to quit. What's more, the panic of necessity tends to force you to go on uselessly, with each added bit of useless effort adding to the panic in a vicious cycle.

It is my feeling that it helps to relax, deliberately, by subjecting your mind to material complicated enough to occupy the voluntary faculty of thought, but superficial enough not to engage the deeper involuntary one. In my case, it is an action movie; in your case, it might be something else.

I suspect it is the involuntary faculty of thought that gives rise to what we call "a flash of intuition," something that I imagine must be merely the result of unnoticed thinking.

Perhaps the most famous flash of intuition in the history of science took place in the city of Syracuse in third-century B.C. Sicily. Bear with me and I will tell you the story—

About 250 B.C., the city of Syracuse was experiencing a kind of Golden Age. It was under the protection of the rising power of Rome, but it retained a king of its own and considerable self-government; it was prosperous; and it had a flourishing intellectual life.

The king was Hieron II, and he had commissioned a new golden crown from a goldsmith, to whom he had given an ingot of gold as raw material. Hieron, being a practical man, had carefully weighed the ingot and then weighed the crown he received back. The two weights were precisely equal. Good deal!

But then he sat and thought for a while. Suppose the goldsmith had subtracted a little bit of the gold, not too much, and had substituted an equal weight of the considerably less valuable copper. The resulting alloy would still have the appearance of pure gold, but the goldsmith would be plus a quantity of gold over and above his fee. He would be buying gold with copper, so to speak, and Hieron would be neatly cheated.

Hieron didn't like the thought of being cheated any more than you or I would, but he didn't know how to find out for sure if he had been. He could scarcely punish the goldsmith on mere suspicion. What to do?

Fortunately, Hieron had an advantage few rulers in the history of the world could boast. He had a relative of considerable talent. The relative was named Archimedes and he probably had the greatest intellect the world was to see prior to the birth of Newton.

Archimedes was called in and was posed the problem. He had to determine whether the crown Hieron showed him was pure gold, or was gold to which a small but significant quantity of copper had been added.

If we were to reconstruct Archimedes' reasoning, it might go as follows. Gold was the densest known substance (at that time). Its density in modern terms is 19.3 grams per cubic centimeter. This means that a given weight of gold takes up less volume than the same weight of anything else! In fact, a given weight of pure gold takes up less volume than the same weight of *any* kind of impure gold.

The density of copper is 8.92 grams per cubic centimeter, just about half that of gold. If we consider 100 grams of pure gold, for instance, it is easy to calculate it to have a volume of 5.18 cubic centimeters. But suppose that 100 grams of what looked like pure gold was really only 90 grams of gold and 10 grams of copper. The 90 grams of gold would have a volume of 4.66 cubic centimeters, while the 10 grams of copper would have a volume of 1.12 cubic centimeters; for a total value of 5.78 cubic centimeters.

The difference between 5.18 cubic centimeters and 5.78 cubic centimeters is quite a noticeable one, and would instantly tell if the crown were of pure gold, or if it contained 10 per cent copper (with the missing 10 per cent of gold tucked neatly in the goldsmith's strongbox).

All one had to do, then, was measure the volume of the crown and compare it with the volume of the same weight of pure gold.

The mathematics of the time made it easy to measure the volume of many simple shapes: a cube, a sphere, a cone, a cylinder, any flattened object of simple regular shape and known thickness, and so on.

We can imagine Archimedes saying, "All that is necessary, sire, is to pound that crown flat, shape it into a square of uniform thickness, and then I can have the answer for you in a moment."

Whereupon Hieron must certainly have snatched the crown away and said, "No such thing. I can do that much without you; I've studied the principles of mathematics, too. This crown is a highly satisfactory work of art and I won't have it damaged. Just calculate its volume without in any way altering it."

But Greek mathematics had no way of determining the volume of anything with a shape as irregular as the crown, since integral calculus had not yet been invented (and wouldn't be for two thousand years, almost). Archimedes would have had to say, "There is no known way, sire, to carry through a non-destructive determination of volume."

"Then think of one," said Hieron testily.

And Archimedes must have set about thinking of one, and gotten nowhere. Nobody knows how long he thought, or how hard, or what hypotheses he considered and discarded, or any of the details.

What we do know is that, worn out with thinking, Archimedes decided to visit the public baths and relax. I think we are quite safe in saying that Archimedes had no intention of taking his problem to the baths with him. It would be ridiculous to imagine he would, for the public baths of a Greek metropolis weren't intended for that sort of thing.

The Greek baths were a place for relaxation. Half the social aristocracy of the town would be there and there was a great deal more to do than wash. One steamed one's self, got a massage, exercised, and engaged in general socializing. We can be sure that Archimedes intended to forget the stupid crown for a while.

One can envisage him engaging in light talk, discussing the latest news from Alexandria and Carthage, the latest scandals in town, the latest funny jokes at the expense of the country-squire Romans— and then he lowered himself into a nice hot bath which some bumbling attendant had filled too full.

The water in the bath slopped over as Archimedes got in. Did Archimedes notice that at once, or did he sigh, sink back, and paddle his feet awhile before noting the water-slop. I guess the latter. But, whether soon or late, he noticed, and that one fact, added to all the chains of reasoning his brain had been working on during the period of relaxation when it was unhampered by the comparative stupidities (even in Archimedes) of voluntary thought, gave Archimedes his answer in one blinding flash of insight.

Jumping out of the bath, he proceeded to run home at top speed through the streets of Syracuse. He did *not* bother to put on his clothes. The thought of Archimedes running naked through Syracuse has titillated dozens of generations of youngsters who have heard this story, but I must explain that the ancient Greeks were quite lighthearted in their attitude toward nudity. They thought no more of seeing a naked man on the streets of Syracuse, than we would on the Broadway stage.

And as he ran, Archimedes shouted over and over, "I've got it! I've got it!" Of course, knowing no English, he was compelled to shout it in Greek, so it came out, *"Eureka! Eureka!"*

Archimedes' solution was so simple that anyone could understand it—once Archimedes explained it.

If an object that is not affected by water in any way, is immersed in water, it is bound to displace an amount of water equal to its own volume, since two objects cannot occupy the same space at the same time.

Suppose, then, you had a vessel large enough to hold the crown and suppose it had a small overflow spout set into the middle of its side. And suppose further that the vessel was filled with water exactly to the spout, so that if the water level were raised a bit higher, however slightly, some would overflow.

Next, suppose that you carefully lower the crown into the water. The water level would rise by an amount equal to the volume of the crown, and that volume of water would pour out the overflow and be caught in a small vessel. Next, a lump of gold, known to be pure and exactly equal in weight to the crown, is also immersed in the water and again the level rises and the overflow is caught in a second vessel.

If the crown were pure gold, the overflow would be exactly the same in each case, and the volume of water caught in the two small vessels would be equal. If, however, the crown were of alloy, it would produce a larger overflow than the pure gold would and this would be easily noticeable.

What's more, the crown would in no way be harmed, defaced, or even as much as scratched. More important, Archimedes had discovered the "principle of buoyancy."

And was the crown pure gold? I've heard that it turned out to be alloy and that the goldsmith was executed, but I wouldn't swear to it.

How often does this "Eureka phenomenon" happen? How often is there this flash of deep insight during a moment of relaxation, this triumphant cry of "I've got it! I've got it!" which must surely be a moment of the purest ecstasy this sorry world can afford?

I wish there were some way we could tell. I suspect that in the history of science it happens *often*; I suspect that very few significant discoveries are made by the pure technique of voluntary thought; I suspect that voluntary thought may possibly prepare the ground (if even that), but that the final touch, the real inspiration, comes when thinking is under involuntary control.

But the world is in a conspiracy to hide the fact. Scientists are wedded to reason, to the meticulous working out of consequences from assumptions to the careful organization of experiments designed to check those consequences. If a certain line of experiments ends nowhere, it is omitted from the final report. If an inspired guess turns out to be correct, it is *not* reported as an inspired guess. Instead, a solid line of voluntary thought is invented after the fact to lead up to the thought, and that is what is inserted in the final report.

The result is that anyone reading scientific papers would swear that *nothing* took place but voluntary thought maintaining a steady clumping stride from origin to destination, and that just can't be true.

It's such a shame. Not only does it deprive science of much of its glamour (how much of the dramatic story in Watson's *Double Helix* do you suppose got into the final reports announcing the great discovery of the structure of DNA?[1]), but it hands over the important process of "insight," "inspiration," "revelation" to the mystic.

The scientist actually becomes ashamed of having what we might call a revelation, as though to have one is to betray reason—when actually what we call revelation in a man who has devoted his life to reasoned thought, is after all merely reasoned thought that is not under voluntary control.

Only once in a while in modern times do we ever get a glimpse into the workings of involuntary reasoning, and when we do, it is always fascinating. Consider, for instance, the case of Friedrich August Kekule von Stradonitz.

In Kekule's time, a century and a quarter ago, a subject of great interest to chemists was the structure of organic molecules (those associated with living tissue). Inorganic molecules were generally simple in the sense that they were made up of few atoms. Water molecules, for instance, are made up of two atoms of hydrogen and one of oxygen (H_2O). Molecules of ordinary salt are made up of one atom of sodium and one of chlorine ($NaCl$), and so on.

Organic molecules, on the other hand, often contained a large number of atoms. Ethyl alcohol molecules have two carbon atoms, six hydrogen atoms, and an oxygen atom (C_2H_6O); the molecule of ordinary cane sugar is $C_{12}H_{22}O_{11}$, and other molecules are even more complex.

Then, too, it is sufficient, in the case of inorganic molecules generally, merely to know the kinds and numbers of atoms in the molecule; in organic molecules, more is necessary. Thus, dimethyl ether has the formula C_2H_6O, just as ethyl alcohol does, and yet the two are quite different in properties. Apparently, the atoms are arranged

---

1. I'll tell you, in case you're curious. None! [Asimov's note]. How Francis Crick and James Watson discovered the molecular structure of this vital substance is told in Watson's autobiographical book, *The Double Helix*.

differently within the molecules—but how to determine the arrangements?

In 1852, an English chemist, Edward Frankland, had noticed that the atoms of a particular element tended to combine with a fixed number of other atoms. This combining number was called "valence." Kekule in 1858 reduced this notion to a system. The carbon atom, he decided (on the basis of plenty of chemical evidence) had a valence of four; the hydrogen atom, a valence of one; and the oxygen atom, a valence of two (and so on).

Why not represent the atoms as their symbols plus a number of attached dashes, that number being equal to the valence. Such atoms could then be put together as though they were so many Tinker Toy units and "structural formulas" could be built up.

It was possible to reason out that the structural formula

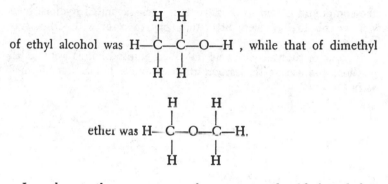

of ethyl alcohol was $H—C—C—O—H$, while that of dimethyl

ether was $H—C—O—C—H$.

In each case, there were two carbon atoms, each with four dashes attached; six hydrogen atoms, each with one dash attached; and an oxygen atom with two dashes attached. The molecules were built up of the same components, but in different arrangements.

Kekule's theory worked beautifully. It has been immensely deepened and elaborated since his day, but you can still find structures very much like Kekule's Tinker Toy formulas in any modern chemical textbook. They represent oversimplifications of the true situation, but they remain extremely useful in practice even so.

The Kekule structures were applied to many organic molecules in the years after 1858 and the similarities and contrasts in the structures neatly matched similarities and contrasts in properties. The key to the rationalization of organic chemistry had, it seemed, been found.

Yet there was one disturbing fact. The well-known chemical benzene wouldn't fit. It was known to have a molecule made up of equal numbers of carbon and hydrogen atoms. Its molecular weight was known to be 78 and a single carbon-hydrogen combination had a weight of 13. Therefore, the benzene molecule had to contain six carbon-hydrogen combinations and its formula had to be C_6H_6.

But that meant trouble. By the Kekule formulas, the hydrocarbons (molecules made up of carbon and hydrogen atoms only) could easily be envisioned as chains of carbon atoms with hydrogen atoms attached. If all the valences of the carbon atoms were filled with hydrogen atoms, as in "hexane," whose molecule looks like this—

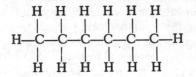

the compound is said to be saturated. Such saturated hydrocarbons were found to have very little tendency to react with other substances.

If some of the valences were not filled, unused bonds were added to those connecting the carbon atoms. Double bonds were formed as in "hexene"—

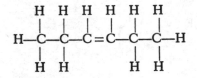

Hexene is unsaturated, for that double bond has a tendency to open up and add other atoms. Hexene is chemically active.

When six carbons are present in a molecule, it takes fourteen hydrogen atoms to occupy all the valence bonds and make it inert —as in hexane. In hexene, on the other hand, there are only twelve hydrogens. If there were still fewer hydrogen atoms, there would be more than one double bond; there might even be triple bonds, and the compound would be still more active than hexene.

Yet benzene, which is C_6H_6 and has eight fewer hydrogen atoms than hexane, is *less* active than hexene, which has only two fewer hydrogen atoms than hexane. In fact, benzene is even less active than hexane itself. The six hydrogen atoms in the benzene molecule seem to satisfy the six carbon atoms to a greater extent than do the fourteen hydrogen atoms in hexane.

For heaven's sake, why?

This might seem unimportant. The Kekule formulas were so beautifully suitable in the case of so many compounds that one might simply dismiss benzene as an exception to the general rule.

Science, however, is not English grammar. You can't just categorize something as an exception. If the exception doesn't fit into the general system, then the general system must be wrong.

Or, take the more positive approach. An exception can often be made to fit into a general system, provided the general system is broadened. Such broadening generally represents a great advance and for this reason, exceptions ought to be paid great attention.

For some seven years, Kekule faced the problem of benzene and tried to puzzle out how a chain of six carbon atoms could be completely satisfied with as few as six hydrogen atoms in benzene and yet be left unsatisfied with twelve hydrogen atoms in hexene.

Nothing came to him!

And then one day in 1865 (he tells the story himself) he was in Ghent, Belgium, and in order to get to some destination, he boarded a public bus. He was tired and, undoubtedly, the droning beat of the horses' hooves on the cobblestones, lulled him. He fell into a comatose half-sleep.

In that sleep, he seemed to see a vision of atoms attaching themselves to each other in chains that moved about. (Why not? It was the sort of thing that constantly occupied his waking thoughts.) But then one chain twisted in such a way that head and tail joined, forming a ring—and Kekule woke with a start.

To himself, he must surely have shouted "Eureka," for indeed he had it. The six carbon atoms of benzene formed a ring and not a chain, so that the structural formula looked like this:

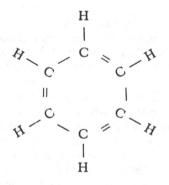

To be sure, there were still three double bonds, so you might think the molecule had to be very active—but now there was a difference. Atoms in a ring might be expected to have different properties from those in a chain and double bonds in one case might not have the properties of those in the other. At least, chemists could work on that assumption and see if it involved them in contradictions.

It didn't. The assumption worked excellently well. It turned out that organic molecules could be divided into two groups: aromatic and aliphatic. The former had the benzene ring (or certain other similar rings) as part of the structure and the latter did not. Allowing for different properties within each group, the Kekule structures worked very well.

For nearly seventy years, Kekule's vision held good in the hard field of actual chemical techniques, guiding the chemist through the jungle of reactions that led to the synthesis of more and more molecules. Then, in 1932, Linus Pauling applied quantum mechanics to chemical structure with sufficient subtlety to explain just why the benzene ring was so special and what had proven correct in practice proved correct in theory as well.

Other cases? Certainly.

In 1764, the Scottish engineer James Watt was working as an instrument maker for the University of Glasgow. The university gave him a model of a Newcomen steam engine, which didn't work well, and asked him to fix it. Watt fixed it without trouble, but even when it worked perfectly, it didn't work well. It was far too inefficient and consumed incredible quantities of fuel. Was there a way to improve that?

Thought didn't help; but a peaceful, relaxed walk on a Sunday afternoon did. Watt returned with the key notion in mind of using two separate chambers, one for steam only and one for cold water only, so that the same chamber did not have to be constantly cooled and reheated to the infinite waste of fuel.

The Irish mathematician William Rowan Hamilton worked up a theory of "quaternions" in 1843 but couldn't complete that theory until he grasped the fact that there were conditions under which $p \times q$ was *not* equal to $q \times p$. The necessary thought came to him in a flash one time when he was walking to town with his wife.

The German physiologist Otto Loewi was working on the mechanism of nerve action, in particular, on the chemicals produced by nerve endings. He awoke at 3 A.M. one night in 1921 with a perfectly clear notion of the type of experiment he would have to run to settle a key point that was puzzling him. He wrote it down and went back to sleep. When he woke in the morning, he found he couldn't remember what his inspiration had been. He remembered he had written it down, but he couldn't read his writing.

The next night, he woke again at 3 A.M. with the clear thought once more in mind. This time, he didn't fool around. He got up, dressed himself, went straight to the laboratory and began work. By

5 A.M. he had proved his point and the consequences of his findings became important enough in later years so that in 1936 he received a share in the Nobel prize in medicine and physiology.

How very often this sort of thing must happen, and what a shame that scientists are so devoted to their belief in conscious thought that they so consistently obscure the actual methods by which they obtain their results.

1971

QUESTIONS

1. Does Asimov argue that science ought to abandon reasoned thought in favor of intuition?
2. What does Asimov find wrong about scientific reports as they are customarily written? Do you agree? If scientific writing were not strictly reasonable wouldn't there be a danger of misrepresenting science?
3. Is cultivation of "the Eureka phenomenon" encouraged in any of the science courses you may have taken or are now taking? Why, or why not?
4. Have you ever experienced anything like "the Eureka phenomenon" Asimov describes? If so, write out an account of what happened. Tell what your feelings were when the phenomenon occurred. Did you ever report the discovery in just that way to any one else (to a teacher, for example)? If so, what was the other person's response?
5. In the preceding essay J. Bronowski discusses imagination and science. Are there points on which Asimov and Bronowski would seem to be in agreement concerning science?

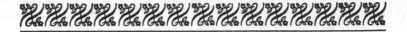

Education

MARGARET DONALDSON

The Desire to Learn

At a very early age, human babies show signs of a strong urge to master the environment. They are limited in what they can do by the slow development of their skill in controlling their own movements. Thus it is fair to call them "helpless" in the sense that they cannot manage the environment well enough to survive unaided. This makes it all the more interesting to discover that the urge to manage the environment is already there at this time of helplessness and that it does not appear to derive from anything else or to depend on any reward apart from the achieving of competence and control.

For some time past it has been widely accepted that babies—and other creatures—learn to do things because certain acts lead to "rewards"; and there is no reason to doubt that this is true. But it used also to be widely believed that effective rewards, at least in the early stages, had to be directly related to such basic physiological "drives" as thirst or hunger. In other words, a baby would learn if he got food or drink or some sort of physical comfort, not otherwise.

It is now clear that this is not so. Babies will learn to behave in ways that produce results in the world with no reward except the successful outcome. For an example of work which shows this clearly we may turn to some studies carried out by Hanus Papoušek.

Papoušek began by using milk in the normal way to "reward" the babies he studied and so teach them to carry out some simple movements, such as turning the head to one side or the other. Then he noticed that an infant who had had enough to drink would refuse the milk but would still go on making the learned response with clear signs of pleasure. So he began to study the children's responses in situations where no milk was provided. He quickly found that children as young as four months would learn to turn their heads to right or left if the movement "switched on" a display of lights—and indeed that they were capable of learning quite complex sequences of head turns to bring about this result. For instance, they could learn to make alternating turns to left and right; or to make double alternating turns (two left, two right); or to make as many as three consecutive turns to one side.

Papoušek's light display was placed directly in front of the infants and he made the interesting observation that sometimes they would not turn back to watch the lights closely although they would "smile and bubble" when the display came on. Papoušek concluded that it was not primarily the sight of the lights which pleased them, it was the success they were achieving in solving the problem, in mastering the skill. If he is right in this—and there is a considerable amount of other confirming evidence—then we may conclude that there exists a fundamental human urge to make sense of the world and bring it under deliberate control.

Papoušek argues further that what his babies are doing as they try to achieve this control is matching incoming information about the world against some sort of inner "standard." And this amounts to saying that they are already engaged in building some kind of "model" of bits of the world—some mental representation of what it is like. They then experience satisfaction when the fit between the model and the world is good, dissatisfaction when it is bad—that is, when the expected result fails to occur, when the lights do not go on. Papoušek reports "increased tension and finally upsetness and signs of displeasure" in the latter case.

Now on even the simplest notion of what is involved in adaptation, it can come as no surprise that dissatisfaction arises when prediction fails. As soon as a species abandons reliance on instinctual patterns of behavior and begins to rely instead on building inner representations and making predictions, then it becomes critical for survival to get the predictions right. Thus the realization of incongruity between our notion of the world and what it turns out to be like should naturally lead us to want to understand it better. And many different theories about the growth of intelligent thought stress that this kind of cognitive conflict is unacceptable to us, that it is something we try to get rid of. After the early stages, the conflict may be between different parts of our world model. If we come to face the fact that we hold two inconsistent beliefs we find this uncomfortable. And so we should. For it is axiomatic that the different parts of a model must fit together.

* * * It is not only when incongruities are forced on us by events that we try to resolve them. Sometimes we positively seek them out, as if we liked having to deal with things that we do not understand, things that challenge us intellectually. But * * * we may, on the

contrary, become afraid of meeting incongruity, afraid of realizing that we are wrong, and we may then take steps to defend ourselves against this recognition by avoiding situations that are likely to give rise to it. We may withdraw.

These are sharply contrasted responses and the difference between them is of crucial educational importance. Education should aim to encourage the readiness to come to grips with incongruity and even to seek it out in a positive fashion, enjoying challenge. Equally, it should aim to discourage defense and withdrawal. But often it seems in effect to do exactly the opposite. The reasons for this cannot become clear without consideration of another topic: the development of the self-image.

We are beings who ask questions; we are beings who make value judgments, holding some things good and important, others bad or worthless; and we are beings who build models of the world. In the course of time, these models come to include some representation of ourselves as part of the world. It is thus inevitable that we should arrive at the question: of what value am I? And it is also inevitable that the answer should matter to us a great deal.

When a child first asks this question, how is he to get the answer? One obvious way will be to try to discover what value other people place upon him. With increasing maturity, when he has perhaps managed to develop a more independent value system of his own, the judgments of others may come to matter less. But while he is still a young child they are bound to exert powerful influence on his self-esteem.

I have been arguing that there is a fundamental human urge to be effective, competent, and independent, to understand the world and to act with skill. I am reminded of a little girl of eighteen months, verbally somewhat precocious, who, when she was offered help with anything, was given to saying firmly: "Can man'ge." To this basic urge to "manage" there is added in our kind of culture very strong social approval of certain kinds of competence. It is arguable that in some ways we do *not* encourage competence—that we keep our children too dependent for too long, denying them the opportunity to exercise their very considerable capacity for initiative and responsible action. This is perhaps hard to avoid in a complex urban society with a highly developed technology. Yet within the educational system at least there is certainly strong social approval of competence in the more disembedded skills of the mind. So the child who succeeds in coping with these new challenges when he enters school will be highly valued by his teachers—and all too often the one who initially fails will not. In either case the child will quickly discover how he is judged to be doing. That he has often made up his mind about his cognitive competence even before he comes to school is emphasized by Marion Blank, who reports the occurrence of remarks like "I'm dumb," "I can't," "I'm stupid," and "I don't know how to do things" from certain kindergarten children faced by some cognitive demand.

There can be no doubt that if we decide we cannot cope with a particular kind of challenge we tend to give up and avoid it. Bruner[1] draws a sharp distinction between "coping" and "defending" which he likens to the distinction between "playing tennis on the one hand and fighting like fury to stay off the tennis court altogether on the other." People do of course differ in the extent to which they persevere in the teeth of persistent failure. Robert the Bruce[2] is said to have observed the tenacity of a spider and resolved to try again. But a spider has presumably no self-image to disturb it, and Robert the Bruce was a mature man who doubtless had a strong and resilient one.

Szasz[3] has this to say on the subject:

Definers (that is, persons who insist on defining others) are like pathogenic microorganisms: each invades, parasitizes, and often destroys his victim; and, in each case, those whose resistance is low are the most susceptible to attack. Hence, those whose immunological defenses are weak are most likely to contract infectious diseases; and those whose social defenses are weak—that is, the young and the old, the sick and the poor, and so forth—are most likely to contract invidious definitions of themselves.

If the child is defined as a failure he will almost certainly fail, at any rate in the things which the definers value; and perhaps later he will hit out very hard against those who so defined him.

So we know at least something to avoid. But we must contrive to avoid it not merely at the surface of our behavior. If we do not genuinely respect and value the children, I am afraid they will come to know.

Yet important as it is to avoid infecting the children with "invidious definitions," it is not enough. More than this is called for. When it comes to self-esteem, not even a young child depends entirely for his judgments on the views of others. For he can often see quite well for himself how he is doing. Paquita McMichael, in an interesting study of the relation between early reading skills and the self-image, concluded that there was a good deal of objective truth in the children's assessments of their competence. "When they agreed that they were not able to do things as well as some other children they were admitting to a reality."

1. Jerome S. Bruner, American psychologist and educator.
2. Robert I, fourteenth-century king of Scotland.
3. T. S. Szasz, contemporary psychologist.

Thus a very important part of the job of a teacher—or of a parent in a teaching role—is to guide the child toward tasks where he will be able objectively to do well, but not too easily, not without putting forth some effort, not without difficulties to be mastered, errors to be overcome, creative solutions to be found. This means assessing his skills with sensitivity and accuracy, understanding the levels of his confidence and energy, and responding to his errors in helpful ways.

Most teachers would accept this, I daresay, but it is not at all easy to achieve in practice and there is no general formula for success. However, a valuable discussion of teaching episodes where just this kind of thing is being attempted is given in Marion Blank's book *Teaching Learning in the Preschool*. She argues that it is essential to permit errors to occur but that the effectiveness of any teaching critically depends on how the wrong responses are then handled by the teacher. She makes many specific practical suggestions about this but she acknowledges that it is not possible at the moment to give rules for the exact application of her technique—it remains an art. Obviously much depends on the child's personality. Ways that work with a passive withdrawn child will not work with a hyperactive impulsive one. And if the child is functioning very poorly it is necessary to concentrate on helping him over his difficulties without too much delay.

It should be noted that Blank developed her techniques for use in a one-to-one teaching situation. She fully recognizes the difficulties of applying them with a group. It remains true that the kinds of teaching decision with which she is concerned are of pervasive importance and that there must surely be gain from any enhanced awareness of them.

The traditional way of encouraging children to want to learn the things that we want to teach is by giving rewards for success: prizes, privileges, gold stars. Two grave risks attend this practice. The first is obvious to common sense, the second much less so.

The obvious risk is to the children who do not get the stars, for this is just one way of defining them as failures. The other risk is to all of the children—"winners" and "losers" alike. There is now a substantial amount of evidence pointing to the conclusion that if an activity is rewarded by some extrinsic prize or token—something quite external to the activity itself—then that activity is less likely to be engaged in later in a free and voluntary manner when the rewards are absent, and it is less likely to be enjoyed.

This has now been demonstrated in numerous experiments with people of ages ranging from three or four years to adulthood.

One study, by M. R. Lepper and his colleagues, was carried out in a nursery school. Some of the children were given materials to draw with and were told that they would get a prize for drawing, which they duly did. Other children were given the same materials but with no prizes or talk of prizes. Some days afterward all of the children were given the opportunity to use these same materials again in a situation where lots of other toys were also available to them. The question was: would the groups differ in the amount of time which they spent in drawing? One might have expected that those who had been rewarded would return more eagerly to the situation which had been "reinforced." But the opposite happened. The children who had been rewarded spent a smaller proportion of their time drawing.

If one takes as criterion not the time freely spent on an activity but the person's own statement of how much it has been enjoyed, the same sort of thing is found: extrinsic material reward tends to decrease enjoyment. Children (and adults) who have been given prizes for doing something tend to say that they like it less well than children who have been given none. And there is even some evidence to suggest that the quality of what is produced may decline.

These findings obviously lead on at once to a further question: if you tell a child he is doing well, are you also rewarding him and hence perhaps running the same sort of risk as if you give him a prize? For, after all, verbal approval is a kind of prize. And certainly, like a material object, it is extrinsic to the activity itself—something added on at the end.

The available evidence suggests that the effects of telling someone he has done well are not the same as those of giving him a prize. For instance, R. Anderson, S. T. Manoogian and J. S. Reznick carried out a study very similar to the one by Lepper and his colleagues (see above) except that there were two extra conditions, in one of which the children were praised for their drawings. The results from Lepper's study were confirmed: the giving of material rewards was related to a decrease in time spent on the activity later. But the giving of verbal encouragement had the opposite effect. And this is just as well. If it were not so, teachers would have to face a disconcerting dilemma. For children must know how they are doing. As we have seen, they often have a shrewd idea of this themselves—and some tasks make it very evident. The young children who were given the task of balancing blocks on a narrow bar could see for themselves whether the blocks stayed in place or fell off. So they could develop theories, discover the inadequacies of these theories, and develop better theories, all without external reward of any kind. This is part of the justification for "discovering learning." But it is not equally possible in all kinds of learning to contrive situations where the child will see for himself the outcome of his efforts.

Frequently he must be told. He must be told: "Good, you've got that right!" or: "No, that's wrong.[4] Try again."

Such comments do more, of course, than merely give objective knowledge of results. They are unquestionably not neutral. But perhaps it is relevant to an understanding of the difference between words of praise and gold stars to draw a distinction between reward and recognition and to acknowledge how strong a need we have to communicate achievement to our fellow men and see it confirmed in their eyes. Thus Gerard Manley Hopkins,[5] who considered that his vocation as a Jesuit was incompatible with the publication of his poetry in his lifetime, reveals in his letters—especially his letters to Robert Bridges—how hard this was for him: "There is a point with me in matters of any size when I must absolutely have encouragement as much as crops rain . . ." He goes on bravely, " . . . afterwards I am independent." But many of us do not reach this kind of independence ever. And young children are certainly unlikely to have done so.

The final condition which Anderson and her colleagues included in their study (see page 123) is relevant here. In this condition the experimenter began by declaring an interest in "how boys and girls draw pictures"—and thereafter firmly refused to manifest this interest in any way. A child might show a picture, trying, as the report of the study puts it, "to elicit some recognition or validation." But he got none. The experimenter ignored all such overtures, turning his face away and saying: "I've got work to do." It is not surprising to learn that the children who received this treatment showed the greatest drop of all in the time which they later spent in drawing.

This still leaves us with the question of why extrinsic material rewards tend to produce effects of damaging kinds. The explanation which fits the known facts most nearly would seem to be that we enjoy best and engage most readily in activities which we *experience as freely chosen*. We do not like being controlled, we like controlling ourselves. Insofar as reward is seen as a means of controlling our behavior, it tends to diminish our interest and our pleasure. Of course we may work hard to get the reward at the time and for so long as we expect more reward to be forthcoming, but we will be less likely to go on with the activity when the reward is withdrawn.

This is strikingly illustrated by the following story (quoted by E. L. Deci in his book *Intrinsic Motivation*).

---

4. Notice that, if the child is told "That's good" whether he has really done well or not, the informational value of the comment is destroyed. It is a subtle art to give genuine information and to encourage at the same time [Donaldson's note].

5. Nineteenth-century English poet and priest, whose poems were first published in 1918, in an edition prepared by his friend and fellow poet Robert Bridges.

In a little Southern town where the Klan was riding again, a Jewish tailor had the temerity to open his little shop on the main street. To drive him out of the town the Kleagle of the Klan set a gang of little ragamuffins to annoy him. Day after day they stood at the entrance of his shop. "Jew! Jew!" they hooted at him. The situation looked serious for the tailor. He took the matter so much to heart that he began to brood and spent sleepless nights over it. Finally out of desperation he evolved a plan.

The following day, when the little hoodlums came to jeer at him, he came to the door and said to them, "From today on any boy who calls me 'Jew' will get a dime from me." Then he put his hand in his pocket and gave each boy a dime.

Delighted with their booty, the boys came back the following day and began to shrill. "Jew! Jew!" The tailor came out smiling. He put his hand in his pocket and gave each of the boys a nickel, saying, "A dime is too much—I can only afford a nickel today." The boys went away satisfied because, after all, a nickel was money, too.

However, when they returned the next day to hoot at him, the tailor gave them only a penny each.

"Why do we only get a penny today?" they yelled.

"That's all I can afford."

"But two days ago you gave us a dime, and yesterday we got a nickel. It's not fair, mister."

"Take it or leave it. That's all you're going to get!"

"Do you think we're going to call you 'Jew' for one lousy penny?"

"So don't!"

And they didn't.

All of this leads to a central dilemma for those who want to teach the young. There is a compelling case for control. The young child is not capable of deciding for himself what he should learn: he is quite simply too ignorant. And he needs our help to sustain him through the actual process of learning. Whitehead[6] puts it vividly: "After all the child is the heir to long ages of civilization and it is absurd to let him wander in the intellectual maze of men in the Glacial Epoch."

On the other hand, we should never forget the children who, having learned to shout "Jew" for a dime, would not then shout it when the payment came to an end. And there is clear evidence that if we try to exercise the control not by reward but by punishment the negative effects are even greater. If, when they leave us, our pupils turn away from what we have taught them, the teaching has surely been in vain.

Those who are most keenly aware of this latter danger tend to call themselves "progressive" and to advocate "freedom." Those who are most keenly aware of the former danger—the danger of leaving children to wander in the intellectual mazes of prehistory—

6. Alfred North Whitehead (1861–1947), American philosopher and educator.

are the advocates of "formal education" and of "discipline."

I can see only one way out of this dilemma: it is to exercise such control as is needful with a light touch and never to relish the need. It is possible after all for control to be more or less obtrusive, more or less paraded. Also a great deal will depend on what the teacher sees the aim of the control to be. If the ultimate aim of the control is to render itself unnecessary, if the teacher obviously wants the children to become competent, self-determining, responsible beings and believes them capable of it, then I am convinced that the risk of rejection of learning will be much diminished. We come back thus to the question of whether the teacher truly respects the children and lets them see it. If this condition is met, then the guidance of learning within a structured environment will not be seen as the action of a warder behind prison bars.

1978

JOHN HOLT
How Teachers Make Children Hate Reading

When I was teaching English at the Colorado Rocky Mountain School, I used to ask my students the kinds of questions that English teachers usually ask about reading assignments—questions designed to bring out the points that *I* had decided *they* should know. They, on their part, would try to get me to give them hints and clues as to what I wanted. It was a game of wits. I never gave my students an opportunity to say what they really thought about a book.

I gave vocabulary drills and quizzes too. I told my students that every time they came upon a word in their book they did not understand, they were to look it up in the dictionary. I even devised special kinds of vocabulary tests, allowing them to use their books to see how the words were used. But looking back, I realize that these tests, along with many of my methods, were foolish.

My sister was the first person who made me question my conventional ideas about teaching English. She had a son in the seventh grade in a fairly good public school. His teacher had asked the class to read Cooper's *The Deerslayer*. The choice was bad enough in itself; whether looking at man or nature, Cooper was superficial, inaccurate and sentimental, and his writing is ponderous and ornate. But to make matters worse, this teacher had decided to give the book the microscope and x-ray treatment. He made the students look up and memorize not only the definitions but the derivations of every big word that came along—and there were plenty. Every chapter was followed by close questioning and testing to make sure the students "understood" everything.

Being then, as I said, conventional, I began to defend the teacher, who was a good friend of mine, against my sister's criticisms. The argument soon grew hot. What was wrong with making sure that children understood everything they read? My sister answered that until this class her boy had always loved reading, and had read a lot on his own; now he had stopped. (He was not really to start again for many years.)

Still I persisted. If children didn't look up the words they didn't know, how would they ever learn them? My sister said, "Don't be silly! When you were little you had a huge vocabulary, and were always reading very grown-up books. When did you ever look up a word in a dictionary?"

She had me. I don't know that we had a dictionary at home; if we did, I didn't use it. I don't use one today. In my life I doubt that I have looked up as many as fifty words, perhaps not even half that.

Since then I have talked about this with a number of teachers. More than once I have said, "according to tests, educated and literate people like you have a vocabulary of about twenty-five thousand words. How many of these did you learn by looking them up in a dictionary?" They usually are startled. Few claim to have looked up even as many as a thousand. How did they learn the rest?

They learned them just as they learned to talk—by meeting words over and over again, in different contexts, until they saw how they fitted.

Unfortunately, we English teachers are easily hung up on this matter of understanding. Why should children understand everything they read? Why should anyone? Does anyone? I don't, and I never did. I was always reading books that teachers would have said were "too hard" for me, books full of words I didn't know. That's how I got to be a good reader. When about ten, I read all the D'Artagnan stories and loved them. It didn't trouble me in the least that I didn't know why France was at war with England or who was quarreling with whom in the French court or why the Musketeers should always be at odds with Cardinal Richelieu's men. I didn't even know who the Cardinal was, except that he was a dangerous and powerful man that my friends had to watch out for. This was all I needed to know.

Having said this, I will now say that I think a big, unabridged dictionary is a fine thing to have in any home or classroom. No book is more fun to browse around in—*if* you're not made to. Children, depending on their age, will find many pleasant and interesting things to do with a big dictionary. They can look up funny-sounding words, which they like, or words that nobody else in the class has ever heard of, which they like, or long words, which they like, or forbidden words, which they like best of all. At a certain age, and particularly with a little encouragement from parents or teachers, they may become very interested in where words came from and when they came into the language and how their meanings have changed over the years. But exploring for the fun of it is very different from looking up words out of your reading because you're going to get into trouble with your teacher if you don't.

While teaching fifth grade two years or so after the argument with my sister, I began to think again about reading. The children in my class were supposed to fill out a card—just the title and author and a one-sentence summary—for every book they read. I was not running a competition to see which child could read the most books, a competition that almost always leads to cheating. I just wanted to know what the children were reading. After a while it became clear that many of these very bright kids, from highly literate and even literary backgrounds, read very few books and deeply disliked reading. Why should this be?

At this time I was coming to realize, as I described in my book *How Children Fail*, that for most children school was a place of danger, and their main business in school was staying out of danger as much as possible. I now began to see also that books were among the most dangerous things in school.

From the very beginning of school we make books and reading a constant source of possible failure and public humiliation. When children are little we make them read aloud, before the teacher and other children, so that we can be sure they "know" all the words they are reading. This means that when they don't know a word, they are going to make a mistake, right in front of everyone. Instantly they are made to realize that they have done something wrong. Perhaps some of the other children will begin to wave their hands and say, "Ooooh! O-o-o-oh!" Perhaps they will just giggle, or nudge each other, or make a face. Perhaps the teacher will say, "Are you sure?" or ask someone else what he thinks. Or perhaps, if the teacher is kindly, she will just smile a sweet, sad smile—often one of the most painful punishments a child can suffer in school. In any case, the child who has made the mistake knows he has made it, and feels foolish, stupid, and ashamed, just as any of us would in his shoes.

Before long many children associate books and reading with mistakes, real or feared, and penalties and humiliation. This may not seem sensible, but it is natural. Mark Twain once said that a cat that sat on a hot stove lid would never sit on one again—but it would never sit on a cold one either. As true of children as of cats. If they, so to speak, sit on a hot book a few times, if books cause them humiliation and pain, they are likely to decide that the safest thing to do is to leave all books alone.

After having taught fifth-grade classes for four years I felt quite sure of this theory. In my next class were many children who had had great trouble with schoolwork, particularly reading. I decided to try at all costs to rid them of their fear and dislike of books, and to get them to read oftener and more adventurously.

One day soon after school had started, I said to them, "Now I'm going to say something about reading that you have probably never heard a teacher say before. I would like you to read a lot of books this year, but I want you to read them only for pleasure. I am not going to ask you questions to find out whether you understand the books or not. If you understand enough of a book to enjoy it and want to go on reading it, that's enough for me. Also I'm not going to ask you what words mean.

"Finally," I said, "I don't want you to feel that just because you start a book, you have to finish it. Give an author thirty or forty pages or so to get his story going. Then if you don't like the characters and don't care what happens to them, close the book, put it away, and get another. I don't care whether the books are easy or hard, short or long, as long as you enjoy them. Furthermore I'm putting all this in a letter to your parents, so they won't feel they have to quiz and heckle you about books at home."

The children sat stunned and silent. Was this a teacher talking? One girl, who had just come to us from a school where she had had a very hard time, and who proved to be one of the most interesting, lively, and intelligent children I have ever known, looked at me steadily for a long time after I had finished. Then, still looking at me, she said slowly and solemnly, "Mr. Holt, do you really mean that?" I said just as solemnly, "I mean every word of it."

Apparently she decided to believe me. The first book she read was Dr. Seuss's *How the Grinch Stole Christmas*, not a hard book even for most third graders. For a while she read a number of books on this level. Perhaps she was clearing up some confusion about reading that her teachers, in their hurry to get her up to "grade level," had never given her enough time to clear up. After she had been in the class six weeks or so and we had become good friends, I very tentatively suggested that, since she was a skillful rider and loved horses, she might like to read *National Velvet*. I made my sell as soft as possible, saying only that it was about a girl who loved and rode horses, and that if she didn't like it, she could put it back. She tried it, and though she must have found it quite a bit harder than what she had been reading, finished it and liked it very much.

During the spring she really astonished me, however. One day, in one of our many free periods, she was reading at her desk. From a glimpse of the illustrations I thought I knew what the book was. I said to myself, "It can't be," and went to take a closer look. Sure enough, she was reading *Moby Dick*, in the edition with woodcuts by Rockwell Kent. When I came close to her desk she looked up. I said, "Are you really reading that?" She said she was. I said, "Do you like it?" She said, "Oh, yes, it's neat!" I said, "Don't you find parts of it rather heavy going?" She answered "Oh, sure, but I just skip over those parts and go on to the next good part."

This is exactly what reading should be and in school so seldom is—an exciting, joyous adventure. Find something, dive into it, take the good parts, skip the bad parts, get what you can out of it, go on to something else. How different is our mean-spirited, picky insistence that every child get every last little scrap of "understanding" that can be dug out of a book.

For teachers who really enjoy doing it, and will do it with gusto, reading aloud is a very good idea. I have found that not just fifth graders but even ninth and eleventh graders enjoy it. Jack London's "To Build a Fire" is a good read-aloud story. So are ghost stories, and "August Heat," by W. F. Harvey, and "The Monkey's Paw," by W. W. Jacobs, are among the best. Shirley Jackson's "The Lottery" is sure-fire, and will raise all kinds of questions for discussion and argument. Because of a TV program they had seen and that excited them, I once started reading my fifth graders William Golding's *Lord of the Flies*, thinking to read only a few chapters, but they made me read it to the end.

In my early fifth-grade classes the children usually were of high IQ, came from literate backgrounds and were generally felt to be succeeding in school. Yet it was astonishingly hard for most of those children to express themselves in speech or in writing. I have known a number of five-year-olds who were considerably more articulate than most of the fifth graders I have known in school. Asked to speak, my fifth graders were covered with embarrassment; many refused altogether. Asked to write, they would sit for minutes on end, staring at the paper. It was hard for most of them to get down a half page of writing, even on what seemed to be interesting topics or topics they chose themselves.

In desperation I hit on a device that I named the Composition Derby. I divided the class into teams, and told them that when I said, "Go," they were to start writing something. It could be about anything they wanted, but it had to be about something—they couldn't just write "dog dog dog dog" on the paper. It could be true stories, descriptions of people or places or events, wishes, made-up stories, dreams—anything they liked. Spelling didn't count, so they didn't have to worry about it. When I said, "Stop," they were to stop and count up the words they had written. The team that wrote the most words would win the derby.

It was a success in many ways and for many reasons. The first surprise was that the two children who consistently wrote the most words were two of the least successful students in the class. They were bright, but they had always had a very hard time in school. Both were very bad spellers, and worrying about this had slowed down their writing without improving their spelling. When they were free of this worry and could let themselves go, they found hidden and unsuspected talents.

One of the two, a very driven and anxious little boy, used to write long adventures, or misadventures, in which I was the central character—"The Day Mr. Holt Went to Jail," "The Day Mr. Holt Fell Into the Hole," "The Day Mr. Holt Got Run Over," and so on. These were very funny, and the class enjoyed hearing me read them aloud. One day I asked the class to write a derby on a topic I would give them. They groaned; they liked picking their own. "Wait till you hear it," I said. "It's 'The Day the School Burned Down.' "

With a shout of approval and joy they went to work, and wrote furiously for 20 minutes or more, laughing and chuckling as they wrote. The papers were all much alike; in them the children danced around the burning building, throwing in books and driving me and the other teachers back in when we tried to escape.

In our first derby the class wrote an average of about ten words a minute; after a few months their average was over 20. Some of the slower writers tripled their output. Even the slowest, one of whom was the best student in the class, were writing 15 words a minute. More important, almost all the children enjoyed the derbies and wrote interesting things.

Some time later I learned that Professor S. I. Hayakawa, teaching freshman English, had invented a better technique. Every day in class he asked his students to write without stopping for about half an hour. They could write on whatever topic or topics they chose, but the important thing was not to stop. If they ran dry, they were to copy their last sentence over and over again until new ideas came. Usually they came before the sentence had been copied once. I use this idea in my own classes, and call this kind of paper a Non-Stop. Sometimes I ask students to write a Non-Stop on an assigned topic, more often on anything they choose. Once in a while I ask them to count up how many words they have written, though I rarely ask them to tell me; it is for their own information. Sometimes these papers are to be handed in; often they are what I call private papers, for the students' eyes alone.

The private paper has proved very useful. In the first place, in any English class—certainly any large English class—if the amount the students write is limited by what the teacher can find time to correct, or even to read, the students will not write nearly enough. The only remedy is to have them write a great deal that the teacher does not read. In the second place, students writing for themselves will write about many things that they would never write on a paper to be handed in, once they have learned (sometimes it takes a while) that the teacher means what he says about the papers' being private. This is important, not just because it enables them to get things off their chest, but also because they are most likely to write well, and to pay attention to how they write, when they are writing about something important to them.

Some English teachers, when they first hear about private papers, object that students do not benefit from writing papers unless the papers are corrected. I disagree for several reasons. First, most students, particularly poor students, do not read the corrections on their papers; it is boring, even painful. Second, even when they do read these corrections, they do not get much help from them, do not build the teacher's suggestions into their writing. This is true even when they really believe the teacher knows what he is talking about.

Third, and most important, we learn to write by writing, not by reading other people's ideas about writing. What most students need above all else is practice in writing, and particularly in writing about things that matter to them, so that they will begin to feel the satisfaction that comes from getting important thoughts down in words and will care about stating these thoughts forcefully and clearly.

Teachers of English—or, as some schools say (ugh!), Language Arts—spend a lot of time and effort on spelling. Most of it is wasted; it does little good, and often more harm than good. We should ask ourselves, "How do good spellers spell? What do they do when they are not sure which spelling of a word is right?" I have asked this of a number of good spellers. Their answer never varies. They do not rush for a dictionary or rack their brains trying to remember some rules. They write down the word both ways, or several ways, look at them and pick the one that looks best. Usually they are right.

Good spellers know what words look like and even, in their writing muscles, feel like. They have a good set of word images in their minds, and are willing to trust these images. The things we do to "teach" spelling to children do little to develop these skills or talents, and much to destroy them or prevent them from developing.

The first and worst thing we do is to make children anxious about spelling. We treat a misspelled word like a crime and penalize the misspeller severely; many teachers talk of making children develop a "spelling conscience," and fail otherwise excellent papers because of a few spelling mistakes. This is self-defeating. When we are anxious, we don't perceive clearly or remember what we once perceived. Everyone knows how hard it is to recall even simple things when under emotional pressure; the harder we rack our brains, the less easy it is to find what we are looking for. If we are anxious enough, we will not trust the messages that memory sends us. Many children spell badly because although their first hunches about how to spell a word may be correct, they are afraid to trust them. I have often seen on children's papers a word correctly spelled, then crossed out and misspelled.

There are some tricks that might help children get sharper word images. Some teachers may be using them. One is the trick of air writing; that is, of "writing" a word in the air with a finger and "seeing" the image so formed. I did this quite a bit with fifth graders, using either the air or the top of a desk, on which their fingers left no mark. Many of them were tremendously excited by this. I can still hear them saying, "There's nothing there, but I can see it!" It seemed like black magic. I remember that when I was little I loved to write in the air. It was effortless, voluptuous, satisfying, and it was fun to see the word appear in the air. I used to write "Money Money Money," not so much because I didn't have any as because I liked the way it felt, particularly that *y* at the end, with its swooping tail.

Another thing to help sharpen children's image-making machinery is taking very quick looks at words—or other things. The conventional machine for doing this is the tachistoscope. But these are expensive, so expensive that most children can have few chances to use them, if any at all. With some three-by-five and four-by-eight file cards you can get the same effect. On the little cards you put the words or the pictures that the child is going to look at. You hold the larger card over the card to be read, uncover it for a split second with a quick wrist motion, then cover it up again. Thus you have a tachistoscope that costs one cent and that any child can work by himself.

Once when substituting in a first-grade class, I thought that the children, who were just beginning to read and write, might enjoy some of the kind of free, nonstop writing that my fifth graders had. One day about 40 minutes before lunch, I asked them all to take pencil and paper and start writing about anything they wanted to. They seemed to like the idea, but right away one child said anxiously, "Suppose we can't spell a word."

"Don't worry about it," I said. "Just spell it the best way you can."

A heavy silence settled on the room. All I could see were still pencils and anxious faces. This was clearly not the right approach. So I said, "All right, I'll tell you what we'll do. Any time you want to know how to spell a word, tell me and I'll write it on the board."

They breathed a sigh of relief and went to work. Soon requests for words were coming fast; as soon as I wrote one, someone asked me another. By lunchtime, when most of the children were still busily writing, the board was full. What was interesting was that most of the words they had asked for were much longer and more complicated than anything in their reading books or workbooks. Freed from worry about spelling, they were willing to use the most difficult and interesting words that they knew.

The words were still on the board when we began school next day. Before I began to erase them, I said to the children, "Listen, everyone. I have to erase these words, but before I do, just out of curiosity, I'd like to see if you remember some of them."

The result was surprising. I had expected that the child who had asked for and used a word might remember it, but I did not think many others would. But many of the children still knew many of the words. How had they learned them? I suppose each time I wrote a word on the board a number of children had looked up, relaxed yet curious, just to see what the word looked like, and these images and the sound of my voice saying the word had stuck in their minds until the next day. This, it seems to me, is how children may best learn to write and spell.

What can a parent do if a school, or a teacher, is spoiling the language for a child by teaching it in some tired way? First, try to get them to change, or at least let them know that you are eager for change. Talk to other parents; push some of these ideas in the PTA; talk to the English department at the school; talk to the child's own teacher. Many teachers and schools want to know what the parents want.

If the school or teacher cannot be persuaded, then what? Perhaps all you can do is try not to let your child become too bored or discouraged or worried by what is happening in school. Help him meet the school's demands, foolish though they may seem, and try to provide more interesting alternatives at home—plenty of books and conversation, and a serious and respectful audience when a child wants to talk. Nothing that ever happened to me in English classes at school was as helpful to me as the long conversations I used to have every summer with my uncle, who made me feel that the difference in our ages was not important and that he was really interested in what I had to say.

At the end of her freshman year in college a girl I know wrote home to her mother, "Hooray! Hooray! Just think—I never have to take English any more!" But this girl had always been an excellent English student, had always loved books, writing, ideas. It seems unnecessary and foolish and wrong that English teachers should so often take what should be the most flexible, exciting, and creative of all school courses and make it into something that most children can hardly wait to see the last of. Let's hope that we can and soon will begin to do much better.

1967

QUESTIONS

1. What are the major indictments Holt makes and what alternatives does he propose?
2. Here are two accounts of a young boy's going to school, the second a summary or précis of the first. Determine what has been removed from the original in the summary. Then write a short comparison of original and summary from Holt's educational point of view, as it can be inferred from his essay.

His days were rich in formal experience. Wearing overalls and an old sweater (the accepted uniform of the private seminary), he sallied forth at morn accompanied by a nurse or a parent and walked (or was pulled) two blocks to a corner where the school bus made a flag stop. This flashy vehicle was as punctual as death: seeing us waiting at the cold curb, it would sweep to a halt, open its mouth, suck the boy in, and spring away with an angry growl. It was a good deal like a train picking up a bag of mail. At school the scholar was worked on for six or seven hours by half a dozen teachers and a nurse, and was revived on orange juice in midmorning. In a cinder court he played games supervised by an athletic instructor, and in a cafeteria he ate lunch worked out by a dietitian.

—E. B. White, "Education"

His days followed a set routine. He wore overalls and an old sweater, as everyone else did in his school. In the morning, a parent or nurse walked the two blocks with him to the corner where he met the school bus. The bus was always on time. During the six or seven hours of the school day, he had six teachers. The school also employed a nurse and a dietitian. Games were supervised. The children ate in the cafeteria. Orange juice was served during the morning session.

—End-of-Year Examinations in English for college bound students grades 9-12, Commission on English.

FREDELLE BRUSER MAYNARD

The Windless World

I remember the dog. He was a Spitz, I think, or a mongrel with a Spitzy tail, and he balanced on his hind legs on the cover of the Canadian Primer. There was an old woman, too—I learned afterward that she was Mother Goose—contained, like the dog, within a sharp black circle. The angle of the old lady's scarf, blown forward with stiffly outthrust fringe, suggested wind, but the world of the figures was windless. The blackish, olive-tinted sky seemed absolutely serene; the meadow flowers, each separate on its tuft of careful grass, were still and perfect as the matching flowers on Mother Goose's gown. What was she saying, her pointing finger outlined against the sculptured scarf? Surely nothing so insipid as "Bow-wow-wow, whose dog art thou?" Momentous as an Egyptian hieroglyph on the door of an unopened tomb, the picture haunted me through all the hours in prairie schoolrooms. It mingled with the smell of chalk dust and eraser crumbs, of crude ink splashed into inkwells by unsteady jug-bearers, of apples and pencil shavings and gum. Perhaps it was only when I left the Canadian Readers, in grade six, that I knew for sure the message frozen on those parted lips. The voice of the reader was the voice of the Union Jack: Be Brave (red); Be Pure (white); Be True Blue.

Every autumn, after Labor Day, we got a new book. What a moment that was, the crisp stacks of readers lined up at the head of each row as we sat in the approved position, eyes front, hands folded, waiting for the signal: "Take one and pass them back." The sour green binding looked unpromising enough. After Books I and II, with their cover pictures, the Nelson Publishing Company made no further concessions to frivolity. Books III, IV, and V presented a uniform front, a Canadian coat of arms with the lion, the unicorn, and the fought-for crown poised above a shaky maple leaf spray.[1] A *mari usque ad mare,* the banner read. From sea to sea, from September to September, the contents of those books were imprinted on the minds of young Canadians. In the small towns where I lived, there was little competition from other influences. We had no library, no magazine stands (or comic books); the radio was dominated by sopranos and the phonograph required cranking.

1. The Canadian coat of arms, like the British, has a shield with St. Edward's crown above and the English lion and the Scottish unicorn on either side—"fighting" for the crown, according to a nursery rhyme. The shield itself has five divisions, with the bottom one containing three maple leaves on a stem.

So I read the readers. All through the years, I have remembered the thrilling stories of Horatius and Robin Hood. Fragments of verses, memorized long ago for the school inspector's visit, have blown about the borders of adult consciousness. "Let me live in a house by the side of the road/And be a friend to man." "Those behind cried 'Forward!' and those before cried 'Back!' " Were the Canadian Readers so rich as in retrospect they seemed? I often wondered. And then, in the musty basement of a Winnipeg bookstore, I found them—a full glorious set. Books I to V. Magic casements opening on the foam by faery seas—or windows on a petrified forest? I could scarcely wait to know.

I have gone all through the Canadian Readers now, starting with "Tom Tinker had a dog" and ending with Kipling's *Recessional*. A strange journey. A journey in search of myself, perhaps, but even more in search of the attitudes which molded my generation, and of a long since vanished world. It is easy to criticize the readers. What an extraordinary list of authors, for example: there is no Milton, no Shakespeare except for a snippet from *Julius Caesar* and a scene from *As You Like It*. There is not one song from Blake or Burns or Water de la Mare. Longfellow, however, is most plentifully represented; so is James Whitcomb Riley. Much of the material is anonymous—for reasons which to the mature judgment seem clear. Imperialists abound. Kipling, Edward Shirley, Sir Henry Newbolt, Canon F. G. Scott blow their bugles mightily.

> Children of the Empire, you are brothers all;
> Children of the Empire, answer to the call;
> Let your voices mingle, lift your heads and sing;
> "God save dear old Britain, and God save Britain's king."

And behind them—a formidable array—march battalions of female poets with resonant triple names: Hannah Flagg Gould, Agnes Maule Machar, Julia Augusta Schwarz. Looking now at "The Crocus's Song" and "Christmas" ("Every mile is as warm as a smile,/And every hour is a song") I can understand why I thought, as a child, that poetry must be easy to write.

* * *

Illustrations for the Canadian Readers include a good deal of amateurish line drawing, dark blurred photographs, and acres of third-rate academy painting. Sometimes the pictures bear directly on the text, sometimes they are just vaguely related in feeling, as when "Dog of Flanders," about a boy and his dog, is introduced by the painting of a girl and her sheep. Landscape studies predominate, but it is a landscape startlingly irrelevant to the experience of the audience. Apart from some amusing "oriental" scenes, the world of the readers is English: indoors, nannies and beautifully groomed children at teatime; outdoors, a fairyland of stone walls and hawthorns where blackbirds sing from the blooming apple boughs. To the child who rode to school on horseback, past sloughs and wheatfields and elevators, the visions of Rosa Bonheur[2] must have been outlandish as Aladdin.

In addition to being remote, the world of the readers is limited. An adult today is struck by a peculiarly English class consciousness. For example, the account of a rogue named Greene, who led the mutiny against Henry Hudson, begins with a raised-monocle observation to the effect that "this Greene was of respectable connections." Not surprisingly, it's a man's world. The few women celebrated are those who prove themselves in war the equal of men— Boadicea, Laura Secord, Florence Nightingale, Edith Cavell.[3] (There is one essay called "A Pioneer Woman," but the achievements of its heroine are a sad anticlimax. "Mrs. Lajimodière was not, of course, expected to carry a load or to use a paddle, but the journey from Montreal to Pembina must have been one of great hardship to her. She had often to pass the whole day seated on the bottom of the canoe." We are not told whether she carried a parasol.) Even more serious is the indifference, through all five volumes, to people of other lands. There is the British Empire, and beyond that a wasteland inhabited by funny little people like Oogly the Eskimo and Ning Ting "away over in an eastern country called China." Japan is a place where "there isn't a sofa or chair," where one eats without a fork and rides in neat little rickshaws. You will find "in Japan that your horse is a man." Not surprising, I guess, to a child who, in the phonetic tables accompanying Book I, is given the series "nap, rap, gap, *Jap*." There are Indians in these stories, but not the Sioux or Cree of any Canadian's real experience. Gorgeously outfitted in buckskin, they sit under giant oaks whispering their secrets to squirrels. They have never seen a reservation, and they have no embarrassing Problems.

Perhaps it is unfair to protest, in material for the primary grades, the absence of any scholarly or scientific spirit. Still, it does seem that the borders between real and fanciful might have been more clearly defined. In grade three the student learns how umbrellas were invented (an elf, threatened with a soaking, uproots a toad-

2. Nineteenth-century French artist whose sympathetic paintings of animals were extremely popular in England and North America.

3. *Boadicea*: usual misspelling of the name of Boudicca, first-century Celtic queen who led a revolt against the Romans in Britain; *Laura Secord*: Canadian woman who during the War of 1812 walked nineteen miles through American-occupied territory to warn the Canadian militia of an impending attack; *Florence Nightingale*: the founder of modern nursing, famous for her care of wounded soldiers during the Crimean War; *Edith Cavell*: English nurse in Belgium, executed by the Germans for helping Allied prisoners to escape during World War I.

stool) and how James Watt discovered the principle of steam. He passes, without change in style or tone, from Robinson Crusoe, to Lord Nelson.[4] (I suspect that most little readers found Crusoe the more credible of the two.) Imaginary events are "proved" by the real existence of places named. Allan-a-Dale's marriage? "To this day you can still see the ruins of the great abbey in which it took place." The Pied Piper? "If you go to Hamelin, the people will show you the hill and the river." *Quod erat demonstrandum.*[5] Even historical material is presented with a curious indifference to fact. Florence Nightingale is described as having personally cared for 10,000 sick. We are told how Sir Philip Sidney looked when he offered a dying soldier his last cup of water—but not the name of the "great battle" just fought. Did the teachers of the 1920s fill in the blanks, supply the necessary correctives? Perhaps some did. But in the one-room schools of my acquaintance the teacher, often fresh out of Normal School, was glad if she had time to hear us recite. Anything else was extra and impossible.

* * *

In order that our chubby childhood might be secure from temptation, the readers lectured us continually. "Teach us to bear the yoke in youth" was the burden of the inappropriately named "Children's Song." "Teach us to rule ourselves alway,/Controlled and cleanly night and day." Goodness was a full-time job, *that* was clear. How we marveled at the story of David Livingstone,[6] a perfect lad even before Africa beckoned. "When he swept the room for his mother, there was no leaving of dust in dark corners where it might not be noticed, no dusting round in circles and not underneath." At ten, this paragon earned his own living at a cotton mill: up at five, then fourteen hours at the loom, a Latin grammar (bought with his first earnings) propped at eye level. "It might have been supposed," ran the text, "that after fourteen hours at the factory, David would have been glad to rest or play when he got home at night." But no. Home from work, he hurried off to night school; home from night school, he pored over his books until Mother blew out the candle. Of course, "whenever there was a Missionary Meeting held within walking distance he was always there." At the looms, too, joining threads, "he began to weave his plan of service for his Master." And from all the grueling routine he emerged fresh as a sprig of Scots heather. "Whenever a holiday came round he showed what a splendid out-of-door boy he was as well."

4. Horatio Nelson, the famous British admiral who routed Napoleon's fleet at the Battle of Trafalgar (1805).

5. Literally, "which was to be demonstrated"; used at the conclusion of a geometrical proof to state that it is complete.

6. Nineteenth-century Scottish missionary remembered for his explorations in central Africa.

Few of us could have hoped to emulate this noble life—for one thing, cotton mills were scarce on the Canadian prairies—but we were given plenty of help. Poems, stories, biographies—all uplifted. There were tongues in the trees, books in the running brooks, sermons in stones, and Good in everything. Literally. What does the crocus say, deep in the snow?

> I will peer up with my bright little head
> I will peer up with my bright little head.

giving us a lesson to borrow, that

> Patient today, through its gloomiest hour
> We come out the brighter tomorrow.

Willows demonstrate helpfulness; rabbits, the rewards of unselfishness. Sunbeams discover that "in seeking the pleasures/Of others [we've] filled to the full [our] own measure." Hens are punctual; bees, naturally, industrious; horses know how important it is to "Do your best wherever you are, and keep up your good name." * * * Over and over again, we are reminded that though intelligence and tender feeling are goods, there is one Good greater far. With the anonymous singer of Book IV, we cheerfully learn to say,

> Head, you may think; Heart, you may feel;
> But, Hand you shall work alway.

I can smile, now, at the naïve moralizing of the Canadian Readers. It did no harm; perhaps many children profited. But one aspect, one direction, of the material still seems to me pernicious, unforgivable: the exaltation of empire and the glorification of war. Through the whole five volumes, only two selections suggest in any way the virtues of peace. One is about a statue of Christ erected in the Andes, the other a rather pallid account of the League of Nations. Drowning out these faint whispers, the drums of war beat loud. This is a world where little boys dream of battle. "I will try to be very good," says Jackanapes, son of a father killed at Waterloo. "But I should like to be a soldier." His grandfather's old heart swells with pride. "You shall, my boy, you shall." A tale of powder-monkeys, for the third grade, describes the thrill of children on warships "going about [their] work amid the smoke and thunder of the guns, and seeing men struck down beside them by the fire of the enemy." A bit dangerous, of course, "but it was a fine training for the boys." Some of them even become admirals, and in this world making admiral is a big thing. Columbus was an admiral. So was Sir Cloudesley Shovell and Grenville and Raleigh and Drake.

> Admirals all, for England's sake . . .
> They left us a kingdom none can take,
> The realm of the circling sea.

If the kingdom must be won with human lives, that is a pity, certainly. But the true Briton sees these things *sub specie aeternitatis*.[7]

> Though our only reward be the thrust of a sword
> And a bullet in heart or brain,
> What matters one gone, if the flag float on,
> And Britain be Lord of the Main!

Four years after the close of the First World War, schoolchildren are invited to admire a battle for the Yser Canal, "an inferno of destruction and death." Shells burst, flames cloud the moon, and the great guns roar. "It was glorious," writes the author. "It was terrible. It was inspiring." Poet Laureate John Masefield describes the battle of Gallipoli[8] in terms which emphasize, ultimately, its dreadful brilliance. Within hours, he speculates of a departing troop ship, one tenth of the men "would have looked their last on the sun, and be a part of foreign earth or dumb things that the tides push." One third would be "mangled, blinded, or broken, lamed, made imbecile, or disfigured"; the rest would suffer agonies in the trenches. Still, the little readers are reminded "these things were but the end they asked, the reward they had come for, the unseen cross upon the breast. All that they felt was a gladness of exultation that their young courage was to be used. They went like kings in a pageant to the imminent death."

One can smile, now, at the Canadian Readers. Naïve, jingoistic, unscholarly, sentimental, moralistic—they were all these. And yet the fact remains that they were also memorable and moving. Few children of this generation will cherish their memories of Dick and Jane. But who could forget Jack Cornwall, the hero of the Battle of Jutland, or Madeleine, the heroine of Verchères?[9] What are Spot and Puff compared with Bruin, the Canadian bear who terrorized a lumber camp, and gentle Patrasche, who pulled a milk cart for love? The world of the readers was a world of heroes. And in the end it didn't much matter, I think, that these heroes were dedicated to purposes which a modern finds questionable—the invincibility of the British fleet, or the glories of empire. What mattered greatly, to all of us who succumbed to its spell, was the vision of men committed to a principle beyond self. I think of Grace Darling, rowing out to a shipwreck through furious seas; of plucky little Pierre, who stole through the German lines to bring news that would save his village; of Captains Scott's last journey,[1] and the dying Oates, who

7. That is, in proper perspective in the eternal scheme of things.

8. Futile and costly Allied attack on the Gallipoli Peninsula, in Turkey, in 1915.

9. Madeleine de Verchères in 1692, at the age of fourteen, led the defense of her family's seigneurial fort on the St. Lawrence River against an Iroquois raid, persevering until she was relieved eight days later.

1. Captain Robert Falcon Scott, Antarctic explorer; after reaching the South Pole in 1912, he and all the members of his expedition died during their return journey.

walked out into the blizzard to relieve others of responsibility for his care. In the end, the British Empire became a kind of metaphor —for honor, dignity, unselfishness, and courage. In today's schoolbooks, the captains and the kings depart—and what is left is the kid next door.

Along with the sense of the heroic the readers communicated something equally valuable, a sense of the importance of the individual. Every man *mattered*. Any man might become great. Little Antonio, who carved a lion out of butter for a rich man's table, becomes a famous sculptor; honest Michael, an ordinary Dutch sailor, risks death rather than betray his master and rises "step by step till he became an admiral." Whatever stone you cast into the waters carried reverberations to distant shores. John Cornwall, mortally wounded but still manning a gun, wins "a renown that can never fade so long as men reverence . . . Duty and Honor." The story of Grace Darling's brave deed "was told all over Europe and America. High and low, rich and poor, united to sing her praises and extol her bravery." It is not true, I see now, that Alan McLeod, V.C., "left behind an undying story and an immortal name." (Who *was* Alan McLeod?) But I am glad that I grew up believing in such a possibility.

The vision of the Canadian Readers was limited; it focused almost exclusively on a Protestant, Anglo-Saxon ideal. But it was always a moral vision. Open a modern school anthology and you will be struck with its efficient treatment of man as a social being: here is the real world of real children working, playing, or, as the psychologists would say, interacting. Open the Canadian Readers and you will find an often passionate concentration on what makes a man a *man*. This is true from the very beginning. Consider, for example, the First Reader story of "The Little Blue Egg." A boy, a decent chap really, takes just one peep at the nest, and then—they are *so* pretty—just one egg. The bird will surely not miss it. But at night, the egg safely hidden, he cannot sleep. However deep he huddles into the bedclothes he hears at the window a voice louder than any bird: BRING BACK MY LITTLE BLUE EGG. Compare this with an episode from a modern grade one reader.

> Sally found a big white egg.
> "I will take this," she said.
> "It looks like a ball."

Her brother sets her straight.

> "You funny girl," laughed Dick.
> "I cannot play ball with that egg.
> You must take it to Grandmother."
> Away Sally ran to the house.

Sally has learned, I suppose, a useful lesson. An egg is an egg is not a ball. But it's a far cry from the deep moral shudder communicated by that long-ago tale of the fatal blue egg.

Instead of the familiar—in vocabulary, situation, and scene—the Canadian Readers confronted us constantly with the unfamiliar, the strange. It was not a bad idea. "Sleep, baby, sleep!" runs a poem in the primer. "The large stars are the sheep;/The little stars are the lambs, I guess,/The bright moon is the shepherdess./Sleep, baby, sleep." Any first-grade teacher knows that "shepherdess" is a hard word for six-year-olds—but how nice that we heard it so young. As for the unfamiliar scenery presented in the Academy paintings; we had all seen enough tractors, and one mile of prairie is much like another. The images of orchards and castle walls were not baffling but liberating; they gave us room to grow.

A final observation about the Canadian Readers. Theirs was a world of extraordinary security and joy. The pages shine with birds and stars and flowers. * * * Above all, it was a solid, comfortable, ordered universe, where evil was always vanquished and right enthroned.

> Truth shall conquer at the last,
> For round and round we run,
> and ever the right comes uppermost,
> And ever is justice done.

And what was truth? It was not various and shifting, but a standard clear to rational man. "Teach us," we sang in "Land of Our Birth," "The Truth whereby the Nations live." *The Truth*, in capital letters—single, absolute, in all times and places infallible. Perhaps it is the sense which, in the end, makes the intellectual landscape of the readers remote as the Land of Oz. Chicken Little set out, in the primer, to tell the king the sky was falling, but we knew it was only a leaf. For this was indeed the windless world.

How could we have guessed the sky would ever fall?

1972

QUESTIONS

1. At the end of her essay, Maynard quotes from the poetry in her reader. What conclusions does she draw from this rather unpromising material? What specific words in her commentary show her attitude and conclusions?

2. Maynard's essay ends with a somewhat changed point of view. Where does the transition occur? What is the intellectual content of this change? Is she moving to larger considerations or simply different ones?

3. In describing her education, Maynard implies a good deal about herself. Characterize her as she presents herself in this essay. Is

she recognizably a product of the education she describes?

4. *Fredelle Bruser Maynard is the mother of Joyce Maynard, who writes about her grandmother in "Four Generations" (pp. 47–49). Compare and contrast, as far as the materials permit, the personalities and circumstances of the three women.*

WILLIAM ZINSSER

College Pressures

Dear Carlos: I desperately need a dean's excuse for my chem midterm which will begin in about 1 hour. All I can say is that I totally blew it this week. I've fallen incredibly, inconceivably behind.

Carlos: Help! I'm anxious to hear from you. I'll be in my room and won't leave it until I hear from you. Tomorrow is the last day for . . .

Carlos: I left town because I started bugging out again. I stayed up all night to finish a take-home make-up exam & am typing it to hand in on the 10th. It was due on the 5th. P.S. I'm going to the dentist. Pain is pretty bad.

Carlos: Probably by Friday I'll be able to get back to my studies. Right now I'm going to take a long walk. This whole thing has taken a lot out of me.

Carlos: I'm really up the proverbial creek. The problem is I really *bombed* the history final. Since I need that course for my major I . . .

Carlos: Here follows a tale of woe. I went home this weekend, had to help my Mom, & caught a fever so didn't have much time to study. My professor . . .

Carlos: Aargh! Trouble. Nothing original but everything's piling up at once. To be brief, my job interview . . .

Hey Carlos, good news! I've got mononucleosis.

Who are these wretched supplicants, scribbling notes so laden with anxiety, seeking such miracles of postponement and balm? They are men and women who belong to Branford College, one of the twelve residential colleges at Yale University, and the messages are just a few of the hundreds that they left for their dean, Carlos Hortas—often slipped under his door at 4 A.M.—last year.

But students like the ones who wrote those notes can also be found on campuses from coast to coast—especially in New England and at many other private colleges across the country that have high academic standards and highly motivated students. Nobody could doubt that the notes are real. In their urgency and their gallows humor they are authentic voices of a generation that is panicky to succeed.

My own connection with the message writers is that I am master of Branford College. I live in its Gothic quadrangle and know the students well. (We have 485 of them.) I am privy to their hopes and fears—and also to their stereo music and their piercing cries in the dead of night ("Does anybody *ca-a-are?*"). If they went to Carlos to ask how to get through tomorrow, they come to me to ask how to get through the rest of their lives.

Mainly I try to remind them that the road ahead is a long one and that it will have more unexpected turns than they think. There will be plenty of time to change jobs, change careers, change whole attitudes and approaches. They don't want to hear such liberating news. They want a map—right now—that they can follow unswervingly to career security, financial security, Social Security and, presumably, a prepaid grave.

What I wish for all students is some release from the clammy grip of the future. I wish them a chance to savor each segment of their education as an experience in itself and not as a grim preparation for the next step. I wish them the right to experiment, to trip and fall, to learn that defeat is as instructive as victory and is not the end of the world.

My wish, of course, is naïve. One of the few rights that America does not proclaim is the right to fail. Achievement is the national god, venerated in our media—the million-dollar athlete, the wealthy executive—and glorified in our praise of possessions. In the presence of such a potent state religion, the young are growing up old.

I see four kinds of pressure working on college students today: economic pressure, parental pressure, peer pressure, and self-induced pressure. It is easy to look around for villains—to blame the colleges for charging too much money, the professors for assigning too much work, the parents for pushing their children too far, the students for driving themselves too hard. But there are no villains; only victims.

"In the late 1960s," one dean told me, "the typical question that I got from students was 'Why is there so much suffering in the world?' or 'How can I make a contribution?' Today it's 'Do you think it would look better for getting into law school if I did a double major in history and political science, or just majored in one of them?'" Many other deans confirmed this pattern. One said: "They're trying to find an edge—the intangible something that will look better on paper if two students are about equal."

Note the emphasis on looking better. The transcript has become a sacred document, the passport to security. How one appears on paper is more important than how one appears in person. A is for Admirable and B is for Borderline, even though, in Yale's official system of grading, A means "excellent" and B means "very good." Today, looking very good is no longer good enough, especially for students who hope to go on to law school or medical school. They know that entrance into the better schools will be an entrance into the better law firms and better medical practices where they will make a lot of money. They also know that the odds are harsh, Yale Law School, for instance, matriculates 170 students from an applicant pool of 3,700; Harvard enrolls 550 from a pool of 7,000.

It's all very well for those of us who write letters of recommendation for our students to stress the qualities of humanity that will make them good lawyers or doctors. And it's nice to think that admission officers are really reading our letters and looking for the extra dimension of commitment or concern. Still, it would be hard for a student not to visualize these officers shuffling so many transcripts studded with As that they regard a B as positively shameful.

The pressure is almost as heavy on students who just want to graduate and get a job. Long gone are the days of the "gentleman's C," when students journeyed through college with a certain relaxation, sampling a wide variety of courses—music, art, philosophy, classics, anthropology, poetry, religion—that would send them out as liberally educated men ·and women. If I were an employer I would rather employ graduates who have this range and curiosity than those who narrowly pursued safe subjects and high grades. I know countless students whose inquiring minds exhilarate me. I like to hear the play of their ideas. I don't know if they are getting As or Cs, and I don't care. I also like them as people. The country needs them, and they will find satisfying jobs. I tell them to relax. They can't.

Nor can I blame them. They live in a brutal economy. Tuition, room, and board at most private colleges now comes to at least $7,000, not counting books and fees. This might seem to suggest that the colleges are getting rich. But they are equally battered by inflation. Tuition covers only 60 percent of what it costs to educate a student, and ordinarily the remainder comes from what colleges receive in endowments, grants, and gifts. Now the remainder keeps being swallowed by the cruel costs—higher every year—of just opening the doors. Heating oil is up. Insurance is up. Postage is up. Health-premium costs are up. Everything is up. Deficits are up. We are witnessing in America the creation of a brotherhood of paupers —colleges, parents, and students, joined by the common bond of debt.

Today it is not unusual for a student, even if he works part time at college and full time during the summer, to accrue $5,000 in loans after four years—loans that he must start to repay within one year after graduation. Exhorted at commencement to go forth into the world, he is already behind as he goes forth. How could he not feel under pressure throughout college to prepare for this day of reckoning? I have used "he," incidentally, only for brevity. Women at Yale are under no less pressure to justify their expensive education to themselves, their parents, and society. In fact, they are probably under more pressure. For although they leave college superbly equipped to bring fresh leadership to traditionally male jobs, society hasn't yet caught up with this fact.

Along with economic pressure goes parental pressure. Inevitably, the two are deeply intertwined.

I see many students taking pre-medical courses with joyless tenacity. They go off to their labs as if they were going to the dentist. It saddens me because I know them in other corners of their life as cheerful people.

"Do you want to go to medical school?" I ask them.

"I guess so," they say, without conviction, or "Not really."

"Then why are you going?"

"Well, my parents want me to be a doctor. They're paying all this money and . . ."

Poor students, poor parents. They are caught in one of the oldest webs of love and duty and guilt. The parents mean well; they are trying to steer their sons and daughters toward a secure future. But the sons and daughters want to major in history or classics or philosophy—subjects with no "practical" value. Where's the payoff on the humanities? It's not easy to persuade such loving parents that the humanities do indeed pay off. The intellectual faculties developed by studying subjects like history and classics—an ability to synthesize and relate, to weigh cause and effect, to see events in perspective—are just the faculties that make creative leaders in business or almost any general field. Still, many fathers would rather put their money on courses that point toward a specific profession—courses that are pre-law, pre-medical, pre-business, or, as I sometimes heard it put, "pre-rich."

But the pressure on students is severe. They are truly torn. One part of them feels obligated to fulfill their parents' expectations; after all, their parents are older and presumably wiser. Another part tells them that the expectations that are right for their parents are not right for them.

I know a student who wants to be an artist. She is very obviously an artist and will be a good one—she has already had several modest local exhibits. Meanwhile she is growing as a well-rounded person and taking humanistic subjects that will enrich the inner resources out of which her art will grow. But her father is strongly opposed. He thinks that an artist is a "dumb" thing to be. The student vacillates and tries to please everybody. She keeps up with her art somewhat furtively and takes some of the "dumb" courses her father wants her to take—at least they are dumb courses for her. She is a free spirit on a campus of tense students—no small achievement in itself—and she deserves to follow her muse.

Peer pressure and self-induced pressure are also intertwined, and they begin almost at the beginning of freshman year.

"I had a freshman student I'll call Linda," one dean told me, "who came in and said she was under terrible pressure because her roommate, Barbara, was much brighter and studied all the time. I couldn't tell her that Barbara had come in two hours earlier to say the same thing about Linda."

The story is almost funny—except that it's not. It's symptomatic of all the pressures put together. When every student thinks every other student is working harder and doing better, the only solution is to study harder still. I see students going off to the library every night after dinner and coming back when it closes at midnight. I wish they would sometimes forget about their peers and go to a movie. I hear the clacking of typewriters in the hours before dawn. I see the tension in their eyes when exams are approaching and papers are due: *"Will I get everything done?"*

Probably they won't. They will get sick. They will get "blocked." They will sleep. They will oversleep. They will bug out. *Hey Carlos, help!*

Part of the problem is that they do more than they are expected to do. A professor will assign five-page papers. Several students will start writing ten-page papers to impress him. Then more students will write ten-page papers, and a few will raise the ante to fifteen. Pity the poor student who is still just doing the assignment.

Once you have twenty or thirty percent of the student population deliberately overexerting," one dean points out, "it's bad for everybody. When a teacher gets more and more effort from his class, the student who is doing normal work can be perceived as not doing well. The tactic works, psychologically."

Why can't the professor just cut back and not accept longer papers? He can, and he probably will. But by then the term will be half over and the damage done. Grade fever is highly contagious and not easily reversed. Besides, the professor's main concern is with his course. He knows his students only in relation to the course and doesn't know that they are also overexerting in their other courses. Nor is it really his business. He didn't sign up for dealing with the student as a whole person and with all the emotional baggage the student brought along from home. That's what deans, masters, chaplains, and psychiatrists are for.

To some extent this is nothing new: a certain number of professors have always been self-contained islands of scholarship and shyness, more comfortable with books than with people. But the new pauperism has widened the gap still further, for professors who actually like to spend time with students don't have as much time to spend. They also are overexerting. If they are young, they are busy trying to publish in order not to perish, hanging by their finger nails onto a shrinking profession. If they are old and tenured, they are buried under the duties of administering departments—as departmental chairmen or members of committees—that have been thinned out by the budgetary axe.

Ultimately it will be the students' own business to break the circles in which they are trapped. They are too young to be prisoners of their parents' dreams and their classmates' fears. They must be jolted into believing in themselves as unique men and women who have the power to shape their own future.

"Violence is being done to the undergraduate experience," says Carlos Hortas. "College should be open-ended: at the end it should open many, many roads. Instead, students are choosing their goal in advance, and their choices narrow as they go along. It's almost as if they think that the country has been codified in the type of jobs that exist—that they've got to fit into certain slots. Therefore, fit into the best-paying slot.

"They ought to take chances. Not taking chances will lead to a life of colorless mediocrity. They'll be comfortable. But something in the spirit will be missing."

I have painted too drab a portrait of today's students, making them seem a solemn lot. That is only half of their story; if they were so dreary I wouldn't so thoroughly enjoy their company. The other half is that they are easy to like. They are quick to laugh and to offer friendship. They are not introverts. They are unusually kind and are more considerate of one another than any student generation I have known.

Nor are they so obsessed with their studies that they avoid sports and extracurricular activities. On the contrary, they juggle their crowded hours to play on a variety of teams, perform with musical and dramatic groups, and write for campus publications. But this in turn is one more cause of anxiety. There are too many choices. Academically, they have 1,300 courses to select from; outside class they have to decide how much spare time they can spare and how to spend it.

This means that they engage in fewer extracurricular pursuits than their predecessors did. If they want to row on the crew and play in the symphony they will eliminate one; in the '6os they would have done both. They also tend to choose activities that are self-limiting. Drama, for instance, is flourishing in all twelve of Yale's residential colleges as it never has before. Students hurl themselves into these productions—as actors, directors, carpenters, and technicians—with a dedication to create the best possible play, knowing that the day will come when the run will end and they can get back to their studies.

They also can't afford to be the willing slave of organizations like the *Yale Daily News*. Last spring at the one-hundredth anniversary banquet of that paper—whose past chairmen include such once and future kings as Potter Stewart, Kingman Brewster, and William F. Buckley, Jr.—much was made of the fact that the editorial staff used to be small and totally committed and that "newsies" routinely worked fifty hours a week. In effect they belonged to a club; Newsies is how they defined themselves at Yale. Today's student will write one or two articles a week, when he can, and he defines himself as a student. I've never heard the word Newsie except at the banquet.

If I have described the modern undergraduate primarily as a driven creature who is largely ignoring the blithe spirit inside who keeps trying to come out and play, it's because that's where the crunch is, not only at Yale but throughout American education. It's why I think we should all be worried about the values that are nurturing a generation so fearful of risk and so goal-obsessed at such an early age.

I tell students that there is no one "right" way to get ahead— that each of them is a different person, starting from a different point and bound for a different destination. I tell them that change is a tonic and that all the slots are not codified nor the frontiers closed. One of my ways of telling them is to invite men and women who have achieved success outside the academic world to come and talk informally with my students during the year. They are heads of companies or ad agencies, editors of magazines, politicians, public officials, television magnates, labor leaders, business executives, Broadway producers, artists, writers, economists, photographers, scientists, historians—a mixed bag of achievers.

I ask them to say a few words about how they got started. The students assume that they started in their present profession and knew all along that it was what they wanted to do. Luckily for me, most of them got into their field by a circuitous route, to their surprise, after many detours. The students are startled. They can hardly conceive of a career that was not pre-planned. They can hardly imagine allowing the hand of God or chance to nudge them down some unforeseen trail.

1979

QUESTIONS

1. By beginning with quotations from student notes to the counseling dean Zinsser seeks to establish the problem of college pressures as a concrete personal reality; then he seeks to generalize, using those personal statements to represent also the situation of other students at other colleges. Does this plan work? What makes the statements sound authentic, or inauthentic?

2. On p. 145 Zinsser names four kinds of pressure on college students. Are there others? Are they all equally strong? What counterpressures exist? What would be necessary for a state of equilibrium? Would those changes or that state be desirable?

3. In describing the four kinds of pressure, Zinsser has to make transitions. One of these ("Along with economic pressure . . ." [p. 147]) is loose. Could it be tightened? Should it be? What about the others? What are the logical relations among the four kinds of pressure?

4. On p. 150 Zinsser refers to "the blithe spirit" inside the "driven" college student. Willard Gaylin, in "What You See Is the Real You" (pp. 438–440), rejects such analyses. Which view do you find more persuasive? Why?

5. In the New York Times for May 14, 1970, Fred Hechinger reported an apparent increase in cheating by college students and pointed out that, historically, cheating occurs when grades are used to determine success in competition for economic and social rewards. He then concluded that some people are wondering if this process is not damaging the colleges, if "the economic and political system is improperly exploiting the educational system." By making "system" the subject of the clause, he avoided having to say who in particular is responsible for the problem. Write an essay in which you show who is responsible for the problem; or show that the problem doesn't exist, or isn't important; or redefine the problem to lead to different conclusions.

PETER COHEN

"What Would *You* Do?"
The Case Method of Business Education

September 19, [1968]: The case method is to the Harvard Business School what the crooked tower is to Pisa. The Harvard Business

School invented the method; the Harvard Business School succeeded with it; the Harvard Business School swears by it, and we
have to put up with it, every grinding minute of every grinding day.
There are no lectures, no labs, few textbooks even. Only cases,
cases, and more cases.

In its outward appearance, a case is a bundle of mimeographed
pages—some thirty to forty on the average—written in a heavy-
handed, lumbering prose that creaks from an overload of nouns. It
describes a real event (although the names may be disguised) that
happened in the course of some real business campaign, at times
giving a general's grand view, at times a corporal's blurred impressions; it reports on the conditions in the trenches and bunkers of
the business front; on the progress of armies of salesmen marching
against each other, of supply convoys streaming down channels of
distribution. It is a factual listing of men, money, and materials
risked; of brilliant victory, of losses beyond imagination.

It often begins with grandiose flourishes: "For J. Hamilton Peacock, chairman of the board of the First Haverhill National Bank,
planning was not a luxury . . ." Invariably it ends with a question
that is beginning to haunt us in our sleep: "What would *you* do?"

These aren't the "case histories" people get in law or medical
school. You know, and here is what the judge said. Or there is what
the doctor ordered. Our cases have no ending. They just kind of
dump the whole mess into your lap—tables, columns, exhibits, and
all—and you can't run away from it because tomorrow ninety-four
people—the entire Section—will be waiting for your decision. You
may not be the guy the professor calls on "to lay out the case," but
then again you may, which makes for a lot of motivation.

Three cases a day; sixty, maybe a hundred, maybe more than a
hundred pages a night. You almost read yourself to death, just to
find out what the *problem* is. And then, of course, you need *a
solution.*

Here you are, a strapping production manager, or financial vice-
president, or marketing executive, alone in a jungle of unfamiliar
terms of technology, with no lecture notes, no fundamentals, or formulas to go by; with, perhaps, a reading list and a textbook and an
equally confused, dry-mouthed roommate. And if you haven't done
so already, you do a lot of growing up in a hurry, because you've got
a problem. And no time. And little help. And something like your
life depending on your finding a solution.

* * *

January 24, [1969]: The answer to the Butcher Polish case was so
obvious, it had to be wrong. Green Stripe, a high-quality, liquid,
self-polishing wax is Butcher Polish's best seller. And although
Butcher is a small, family-owned company, Green Stripe is holding

its own against nationally advertised brands of much larger companies. Butcher's problem seems to be that Green Stripe isn't sold in enough places and that the places, where it is sold—hardware, grocery, and variety stores—don't have enough customers to build up the sales volume of which Green Stripe is capable.

The answer had to be: supermarkets! That they should go for the big-volume outlets.

"You must be aware," Professor Poole interrupted, "that supermarket shelves are crowded as they are?"

"Yes, sir, I am." Leroi was very sure. "That's why I recommend the heavy advertising. Make the product known! Create a lot of new customers."

"What about the money? The advertising money?" Poole, who had waited patiently for Leroi to get all the way out, was beginning to apply saw to limb.

"I believe," Leroi said with somewhat less conviction, "that they should cut their high retailer's margin. The dealers are making more money off Butcher's products than off anyone else's."

"Fine," Professor Poole said, "but you have thought, haven't you, what this will do to the retailers? Mr. Baxter, you want to address this point?"

"I would like to say this," Baxter said eagerly, "that so far what has sold Green Stripe wasn't advertising at all—page three of the case—they are doing almost no advertising. What they are doing is giving the advertising money to the retailers in the form of a high margin. That's what's selling the product. That's why the dealers are pushing it."

"And if you cut that margin . . ." Poole was encouraging Baxter to go on.

"If you cut that margin, you cut yourself off from all your present dealers. You no longer have any channels of distribution."

That's where the catch was! By changing your outlets, you weren't just changing your outlets, you were changing your whole marketing strategy. After you saw the case laid out as we did, you really had to admit, Butcher does have a strategy and a coherent one at that. Now it may not be the most dynamic, and, what's worse, there may be no way of changing it short of selling out to a big conglomerate, but it *is* a strategy: You let the corner grocer sell the product by paying him a high margin. By letting the corner grocer sell, you don't really need a lot of advertising. Which gives you the money to pay for the grocer's margin. You let the grocer *push* the goods out the door. As opposed to what Butcher's competitors are doing: going to the big-volume supermarkets where you don't have anybody pushing the goods. Where, consequently, you can save yourself the high grocer's margin. Which you then have to use for advertising, to sell by *pulling* the goods out the door.

Two major marketing strategies; one, the opposite of the other; each effective under very different circumstances: *push* or *pull*.

That's first-year marketing for you. "Marketing" which really means no more than what it actually says: getting the goods from the door of the factory to the people waiting for it in the market. Yet, a job which has come a long way since the days when you packed your widgets into a couple of wicker baskets, loaded them onto a cart, pushed the cart to the market in the town square; and advertised the widgets by shouting louder than your competitor.

* * *

January 28, [1969]: LaRue Textiles is a large mill, dominating the little town of Tugaloo, Alabama. Their problem, like the problems of the companies in the preceding PBE[1] cases, is how to survive the conflicting claims of black and white pressure groups; the second trying to block any and all exits from the status quo; the first yanking, at times violently, at the social and employment patterns built on a long and unfortunate tradition of segregation.

The Equal Employment Opportunity provisions of the Civil Rights Act of 1964: LaRue Textiles gingerly but determinedly goes along. And right away you have white backlash, intimidation by the Ku Klux Klan. A speech by a black congressman in Tugaloo is called off "for security reasons" by the town's mayor. CORE[2] is reacting. Demands, ultimatums almost, are presented to Tugaloo and LaRue textiles.

What would *you* do?

The consensus seems to be: Abide by the law but go slow. *Don't rock the boat!*

John Reddick, who hadn't said a word, held up his hand. "I'm disturbed," he said, and in the little pause following you could almost hear his insides burn. "I'm very disturbed.

"See, you've been telling the black man for years: Just wait and it will get better. Well, we've listened. And we've waited.

"We have waited too goddamn long.

"Look what happened to the Jews," Reddick said. "You in here, you may not be like that. But a lot of people in this country are. We aren't going to take any chances. We aren't going to let this happen again. You want to know how urgent it is? You *really* want to know? You want to know how much it takes to stop a lot of traffic in this country? A few bombs in a few places—that's all it takes."

After an instant of disbelief that Reddick had really said what he

---

1. Planning in the Business Environment.

2. The Congress of Racial Equality, a black activist political group.

said, a big argument started. Kaplan[3] accused Reddick of making the same sick generalizations that he, Reddick, had said white people were making. That Reddick is seeing whites not as people but as a category.

And the more people talked—and from here on Reddick kept quiet for the most part—the more the whole thing moved away, got hung up in abstractions. With the naïve belief in the power of argument, one guy after another tried to sum it all up cleanly and logically. But their big words melted like snowflakes on the seething surface of Reddick's barely controlled emotions.

* * *

[*March* 12, 1969:] The Blitz Company is having so many problems that one production class wasn't enough to sort them all out. The difficulty at first had seemed minor: Recent shipments have been an average of nine days late and Alfred Jodal, president, is worried about the loyalty of Blitz' customers.

Should he change the company's method of production scheduling? There really isn't any. That is, the president, the sales manager, and a newly hired supervisor are doing one kind of scheduling; the design engineer and the shop foreman are doing another.

The reason the shop foreman does his own scheduling is that he usually has to wait a couple of days before the raw material for an order arrives. And the raw material doesn't arrive because the treasurer who buys it doesn't keep enough of it in stock.

So before the president does anything about the *method* of scheduling, he should make someone clearly *responsible* for it. And, of course, he should talk to the treasurer about the firm's raw-material procurement. Which brings up the question of how large Blitz' stocks should be; because anything above what's needed not only ties up cash but even costs storage charges.

The way the Blitz Company works, no method can solve its scheduling problem. Its production bottlenecks shift around like so many clouds because Blitz almost never makes the same product two days in a row. Small orders, large orders; orders requiring few, and others requiring many operations; rush and regular orders, and nearly every order based on a different kind of basic design. The problem is as much what to offer as how to make it.

But the most formidable obstacle to a smoother operation is the layout of the plant itself, the design of the various work stations. The place was set up to minimize installation costs and to protect the various departments from one another's dust and odors. Little attention was paid to the flow of work. So people keep walking back and forth. Some of their tools, which may have been cheap to buy,

3. One of the older students, with a law degree.

are turning out to be very expensive in terms of added labor. What would it cost to change the layout? How much would the president have to figure for more efficient tools?

Here is one of those cases where, rather than being chairman or president, you're content to be a first-year nothing at the Harvard Business School.

1973

QUESTIONS

1. Cohen's journal format focuses his discussion on particular, limited experiences; it also tends to fragment that discussion. Can you write a thesis sentence for his essay? and, then, logical transitions from one entry to another? If you can't, would you say his discussion lacks unity?

2. In the first sentence Cohen speaks of the "crooked tower" of Pisa, where you might have expected the more conventional reference to the "leaning tower." Does this change seem to be meaningful, or is it just a variation to avoid the cliché?

3. This essay constitutes a personal report from one of the selective graduate schools that college students are competing to get into. Does Cohen sound like a winner? What seem to be the demands placed on him at the Harvard Business School? How good a preparation is college for meeting these demands?

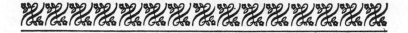

Language
and Communication

ROSE K. GOLDSEN

Literacy Without Books: Sesame Street

"Sesame Street" is a quality product turned out with care, fore-thought, and impressive investments of money, time, talent, and good will. Rejected by the commercial networks, the program is as different from materials they broadcast to children as a Mercedes-Benz is from a Volkswagen. In contrast to commercial television's aim to amass as many children as possible into the vastest markets conceivable, "Sesame Street" tries to gather as many preschool children as possible into the vastest nursery school conceivable. Still, while commercial producers may include in their program-specifications virtually any "message" that "works" to attract children to the set, "Sesame Street" may not. Specifications drawn up by the Children's Television Workshop, insist on only "prosocial" messages, even if it means losing viewers.[1]

"Sesame Street" is produced and distributed by Children's Television Workshop (CTW), which also franchises the sale of Sesame Street products. The first cycle of Sesame Street programs made its debut in November 1969 in this country and the series has been going strong ever since. Nineteen seventy-six marked the eighth cycle in the domestic series: which means that hundreds of these charming programs will have been broadcast and repeated, broadcast and repeated, coast to coast. At least fifteen million U.S. children have seen numerous episodes of "Sesame Street" during their preschool years. The few who may not have seen the shows know

---

1. "For example, even if televised aggression were found to be effective in holding children's attention, we would simply refuse to use it." Gerald S. Lesser, *Children and Television* (New York: Random House, 1974), p. 31 [Goldsen's note].

about them anyway, having picked up the information from their peers and their general surroundings. One result is that "Sesame Street" characters and the "Sesame Street" slant on learning and on childhood are now entrenched in this country's thought-environment. The program has penetrated the culture of childhood so that three-year-olds who may never have heard of Paul Bunyan, Johnny Appleseed, or Brer Rabbit are almost certain to know Big Bird, Kermit the Frog, and the Cookie Monster.

In these respects, of course, "Sesame Street" is no more and no less educational than any other kind of television program the children watch. The difference is that educators and governments define the series as curricular materials, while the rest of television has not yet been officially approved on so widespread a scale by the educational establishment.

The Content and Format

> Sunny day, keeping the clouds away
> On my way to where the air is sweet,
> Can you tell me how to get
> How to get to Sesame Street?

That's the signature song. When that tune comes over the speaker, preschool children within earshot run toward the television screen. They bounce with the bounciness of the tune, hum the melody, sing the words; they rock back and forth, jump or skip in time to the familiar beat. The song tells them the show is about to start.

Each program follows essentially the same format. About forty segments are spliced together to fill fifty-four minutes of broadcast time. About eight of the segments are live dramatic action that takes place on Sesame Street. The rest of the segments are animations, puppet sequences, and film clips that make up the CTW library, now available for worldwide sale and distribution.[2]

The show opens with a street scene. Number 123 Sesame Street is the house in which Gordon and Susan, a black couple, live. Bob, a white man, lives there, too. They are all great friends with each other and with all the people and creatures who live in the neighborhood or pass through it. That includes Maria—a beautiful chocolate-colored teenager said to be Puerto Rican (she speaks perfect unaccented English), Luis—a young Chicano, and muppets and puppets in assorted shapes and sizes. The cast of Sesame Street is integrated in every sense, not only by race, but by species, as it were, with regulars like Kermit the Frog, Ernie, Bert, Little Bird,

2. In 1975, overseas versions of "Sesame Street" in four different languages were accepted for broadcast in sixty-nine countries [Goldsen's note].

and Big Bird (who is as tall as Wilt Chamberlain but clumsy and slow-witted).

Oscar the Grouch ("the only grouch on Sesame Street") lives in a garbage can. He is another regularly appearing muppet—a word which collapses "monster" and "puppet" into a single portmanteau word.[3] The charming and fanciful creatures it refers to were created and copyrighted by Muppets, Inc., and belong to that company. The word *muppet*, however, has found its way into the English language and belongs to all English speakers forevermore.

Another regular on the show is Mr. Hooper, the elderly, white owner of a combination general store and candystore. He is kindly, understanding, warm, generous, hardworking, honest, friendly, and helpful to everyone. His store is a sort of central gathering place for the people and creatures of the neighborhood. He is the only character consistently addressed and referred to as "Mr."

Children are seen in some of the segments during each program. Their voices and laughter and shouts are frequently heard off-camera. They are not, however, cast as regulars on the show, and are rarely addressed by name. So far, on "Sesame Street" only the adults, muppets, and puppets have emerged from anonymity.

Each show tells a story about an event which is dramatized on the street. Gordon may star one day, Bob another; or it might be Mr. Hooper or Susan in the leading role. Sometimes there's a guest star like Jose Feliciano or Bill Cosby, Julie Andrews, Judy Collins. The drama of the day is divided into separate segments that are spotted throughout the fifty-four minutes the program lasts. Whatever the problem is that troubles Gordon or Bob or Susan or Mr. Hooper or Big Bird, the conflict is stated, faced, and ultimately resolved to everyone's satisfaction before the fifty-four-minute hour comes to a close. It's the same format the children get used to as they watch "Get Smart" or "Bonanza" or "Gilligan's Island" or "Bewitched"—or any other show on commercial television, for that matter.

* * *

It should surprise no one to learn that test results from this country and from almost every country in which evaluation studies have been made consistently show that the children who watch the program learn to recognize the letters and numbers and concepts "Sesame Street" tries to convey. After all, it is a common enough observation that even the dullest preschoolers recognize the characters' television features. Children throughout the country know the

3. From Lewis Carroll, *Through the Looking-Glass*: when two words are melded into one, their two meanings are "packed up in one word," like the two compartments which fold together to make the kind of suitcase called a portmanteau.

Jolly Green Giant and associate him with the Niblets he symbolizes for LeSueur industries. They incorporate commercials in their play ("How'd you like a nice Hawaiian punch?"). They recognize Mother Nature and Ronald McDonald and Fred Flintstone and Mr. Clean and Mr. Coffee and Rosie the waitress and Madge the manicurist and Cora the country storekeeper and Mr. Whipple and Mr. Goodwin, and easily associate them with the products they stand for: margarine, hamburgers and fast foods, vitamins, cleaning liquid, filters, paper towels, dish-washing detergent, coffee, toilet paper and toothpaste. In the same way, of course, they come to recognize the letter Y, just as they recognize the letter S that Superman wears emblazoned on his super-manly chest. They learn the concept *below*, associating it with the tree falling in the forest just as they learn that slow means fast when Steve Austin, the bionic man, races to someone's rescue at eight frames per minute,[4] but slow means slow in the Burger King commercial when the waitress for a rival hamburger chain fills a special order in the same slow motion.

It's just as easy to interest the children in the little dramas enacted by Susan and Mr. Hooper as it is to interest them in the dramas enacted on the same television screens by the Cartwrights of "Bonanza." or Gilligan and his friends, or Louis Erskine of "The FBI," or anyone else in the long array of glamorous and attractive stars that enter their lives so frequently.

While it remains to be seen whether "Sesame Street" actually provides preschool children with the fundamental skills they will need later to explore the world books and literature can open to them, it is clear that the series teaches them to read not books, but television. They learn, for example, to piece together the day's drama, unifying it into a continuous story in spite of all the interruptions. This skill will stand them in good stead, helping them to "read" the commercial television programs "Sesame Street" in all its versions imitates. The offstage laughter of the behind-the-scene audience teaches them to "read" the laugh track that now defines humor all over the world. They learn to "read" drum rolls and fanfares, voice-overs and pixillations.[5] They even learn to "read" what in other contexts would be puzzling statements directly contrary to lived experience, accepting them as television's acceptable constructions of false experience. Although there are frequent references to colors seen on the screen, the many children watching black-and-

---

4. After experimenting with various camera effects to convey the notion of Steve's extraordinary speed and power, the producers hit upon the slow-action technique as most effective [Goldsen's note].

5. "Pixillation" refers to speeded up, jerky movements reminiscent of the silent movies unreeled just a bit too fast [Goldsen's note].

white sets see no colors. After their first puzzlement wears off, these children learn to live quite comfortably with the contradiction, just as they learn to live with television's constant claims that good guys always thwart bad guys, the law is always on the side of justice, action is the same as drama, and using this or that brand of tooth-paste guarantees love.

This is a kind of hyperbole that audiences raised on television have learned to take for granted. It is quite different from fantasy's playful weaving back and forth between a world of imagination and a world of daily experience, thus extending the horizons of each. Television's hyperbole constructs irreality as reality. Behavior that would call down punishment and censure if anyone were to engage in it is demonstrated as perfectly normal and acceptable. Examples: walking into someone's house unannounced; commenting about the odors or dinginess of the wash; frying a loaf of bread in deep fat; discussing publicly discharges from the body's nether regions; exclaiming rhapsodically about the color of the water in the toilet bowl; wolfing down one's food and smacking the lips over it, and so on. Adults who already know the rules can take these nonplayful exaggerations with the necessary grain of salt, even smile at them. For children who have not yet internalized the rules, however, this "puffery" is just as much a part of the curriculum available to them as the catechism, the Scout Oath, and the pledge of allegiance.

The "Beat the Time" sequences on "Sesame Street" teach the children to "read" television's game shows. The featured stars teach the children to recognize not only names and faces, but also show business categories, such as lead, supporting cast, and extras. The sequences featuring Batman and Robin, Superman, and the rest of television's syndicated heroes, are appreciation courses for beginning watchers of the original programs available on almost every local station in incessant reruns. In addition, they teach the children to "read" the action-adventure and crime-show formulas that advertis-ers use as electronic envelopes, tucking in the commercial "mes-sages" designed to create public attitudes and consumer needs that can be linked to particular products. Indeed, the programs are themselves full-length commercials, hawking over and over again the kind of world view that is compatible with postindustrial, priva-tized, consumer-society, complete with "goodthink."[6]

It's all show-and-tell for the consumer society's version of "the good life"—the cars, the planes, the helicopters, the housing pat-

---

6. In George Orwell's *1984*, the citi-zens are systematically conditioned to think in conformity with the official values and goals of the society. Such nonthinking is called "goodthink" in the telegraphic language of that society.

terns, industrially produced foods and music, to say nothing of the electric refrigerators and blenders and mixers and household equipment, all taken as much for granted as standard props on "Sesame Street" as on any sitcom or variety show, any daytime serial or game show, any action-adventure or crime drama or even any animated series booked into the Saturday-morning children's ghetto. As the children internalize these images, they become captive consumers, wise in the lore associated with the many goods and services loaded into the glamorous showcase whose audience is now the entire globe.

What about all those commercials and the sign-off, heard and seen hundreds of times by now: " 'Sesame Street' has been brought to you through the courtesy of the letter *L*, the letter *U*, and the numbers 4 and 5"? This is a very obvious part of the hidden curriculum; it legitimizes a commercial system of broadcasting that depends for support on purchase of human attention by self-interested people manning institutions with funds enough to afford the expenditure. Practices such as these now determine the culture of childhood to such an extent that when those who are now children reach adulthood, the "normalcy" of this system will be taken for granted. Under such conditions, any future challenge to existing policy is heavily handicapped.

Cultural Neutrality

The creators of "Sesame Street" are as aware as anyone else of the hidden curriculum in all educational materials, their own included. Indeed, they had originally turned to television precisely because they were sensitive to the medium's broadly general and pervasively encompassing power. Equally sensitive to the many cultural differences in the backgrounds of the millions of children who make up their target audience, CTW has tried hard to maintain "cultural neutrality" in the programs. Even so, exceptions abound. For example, "Sesame Street" does not hesitate to indoctrinate children about appropriate male sex roles, "in order to upgrade the black male," explains Joan Ganz Cooney. She goes on to explain further why Children's Television Workshop decided to indoctrinate them about appropriate occupations for women, too:

"Our society doesn't need more babies, we need more doctors." So she pushed for Susan, who is portrayed as also married but childless, to get a job outside the home . . . "The reason we chose public-health nurse," said Mrs. Cooney, "was that the medical services in this country are going to need more and more people. Then, too, we wanted a job with a uniform that little girls could identify." Mrs. Cooney likewise remarked in the same interview, "We talked about making her a doctor, but it didn't seem real, with them living where they live."

In a universe that boasts no perspective-free point, cultural neutrality is a patent impossibility. One can scarcely show and tell something without showing it from a particular angle of vision, telling it in a specific idiom. On the simplest level, all these programs are show-and-tell for family structure and family relations, food and table habits, household arrangements, occupational roles, age- and sex-roles, rural and urban behavior patterns, economic pursuits such as buying and selling and going to work, ecological policy, fashions in vehicles and dress and hair styles, health practices, and . . . well, just about everything. It is a contradiction in terms to assert that these repeated images of culture and social interactions can be divested of cultural content, and the claim that they can be has been challenged by many critics.[7]

The program's hidden curriculum teaches subtler lessons as well. Show-and-tell depends heavily on the language of time and space, and CTW productions are outstanding examples of creative use of movement, rhythm, and pacing. This is a language that communicates a world of significance, especially, perhaps, to preschool children who are still more fluent in body language than in verbal language. One set of spatial relations mutely signals importance or intimacy or consent; another indicates that the relationship is distant or consent is to be withheld, or that the goings-on are unimportant, peripheral to the main event. Children must learn the spatial codes for their own culture and subcultures. Play-acting—their own and dramatizations they watch—is essential to this learning.

Nor is the time-sense that we take so for granted inborn in our young. Children in our culture—at least those raised by educators and television executives—must learn to pace their internal rhythms to mealtimes, playtimes, quiet times, nap times, and bedtimes. Children from every stratum in all social systems must grasp what their culture and subcultures mean by long and short duration, proper synchronization of one's reaction time to others, margins of permissible promptness and tardiness under different conditions—all learned. Music and chants, among other rhythms, help synchronize these cultural rhythms and internalize them. This is only one way in which music is no more culturally neutral than any other kind of language.

In consideration of the Puerto Rican and Chicano children in its

7. Sesame Street, rejected by the BBC in Britain, was bought by their commercial network. * * * In Peru, the Ministry of Education rejected the series. So did the Soviet Union. In each case, the rejection was based on the claim that the programs project a particular set of values appropriate to a particular set of social relations in a particular class within a particular social system. The head of children's programming in Poland, is on record endorsing the programs as culturally neutral, saying * * * "A square is a square both in Poland and the United States and children's cognitive processes are the same the world over." (*The New York Times*, March 20, 1973.) [Goldsen's note].

target audience, "Sesame Street" delivers many musical spots in Latin American style. Guitars are frequently seen and heard; so are *maracas, guiros,* castanets. *Tango, rhumba, mambo, samba, bolero, merengue, danza* rhythms, and so on are frequently heard. American jazz, folk tunes, country-and-western, and rock rhythms and themes are likewise featured, perhaps just a bit more. The ABCs are often sung to the tune of the alphabet melody from Haydn's Variations on an Original Theme of Mozart ("The Alphabet Symphony"). Since no sequence on the show lasts longer than two minutes, the structure simply does not permit introduction of anything more than snatches of music. Thus, the children are ·never given a chance to see operas or hear operatic music (although sequences may caricature opera), or to be introduced to symphonic music or chamber music or choral music or, indeed, any of the music that up to now has helped to nourish imaginations and set the beat of Western culture. The structure is hospitable, however, to mass-produced and mass-distributed music.

The standard measurements of time that we take so for granted —a twenty-four-hour day, a sixty-minute hour, a sixty-second minute—are socially defined and change from culture to culture, from one historic period to another. In the present historic moment, television is introducing massive changes in the way this whole country —especially children—experiences time, even though they are so ever present and widespread that most people hardly have a chance to notice how these rhythms are changing. "Sesame Street" teaches children the fragmented hour and the fifty-four-minute hour. In this it joins with the rest of American television that fractures time and teaches the fifty-and-a-half-minute hour in prime time, the forty-four-minute hour during most of the day. It joins, too, in teaching the sixty-second commercial, even the twenty- and thirty-second commercial as entrenched rhythms and rhythm markers. In that twenty- or thirty-second interval, marked by the new, universal metronome, information and images are so tightly packed that we pay only glancing attention to any specific element, "reading" the whole simultaneously in a single, seemingly timeless instant; and as we do, we scarcely notice the absence of opportunity to reflect and consider intellectually what we have taken in emotionally.

In sum, then, along with letters and numbers and relational concepts, the "Sesame Street" curriculum is teaching the culture of the midway impressed into the service of selling products and ideas. It is a curriculum that has nothing to do with books or with the culture of books and reading. Not one program, not one sequence in any cycle of "Sesame Street" shown in the United States or overseas, has ever starred a book! The daily dramas on the street have never featured anyone absorbed in a book, laughing or crying over a book, or so gripped by a book that he cannot bring himself to set it aside. No sequence has ever shown a child pleading to stay up a little longer to finish a book, or sneaking a flashlight under the covers to keep on reading after lights-out. People caring enough about a book to risk prison for possessing it or to face death for writing it, even for reading a forbidden book—never! The incessant "commercials" sing the praises of the letters and numbers, but never of books and reading. The set itself, the familiar scene on the street, doesn't even give the children a chance to see books. They never appear among the merchandise in Mr. Hooper's store.

Given the stated intentions of "Sesame Street" to push literacy, its failure to push books may seem contradictory. And yet, is it really so paradoxical? All teachers teach who they are, how they think, much more than what they know. It is only natural for show business wedded to advertising and sales to teach the culture of the spectacle.

In a democratic society, literacy is not a legitimate goal in and of itself. There is, after all, more than one kind of literacy. The literacy that goes with books and literature can free the mind, stretch the imagination, liberate the reader from his bondage to the present, linking him back to all of human history, all of human culture, all of human experience. (That's why we still say "*liberal* education," meaning education that liberates.) But there is another kind of literacy that does not have much use for books. A workforce must read to be able to operate equipment in a modern factory. Consumers must read to decipher the instructions on a package of cake mix. The citizenry must read to be able to fill out income-tax forms and use an automated post office. Automobile drivers must read to find the right exits off the throughway. Even a nation of television watchers must be able to read the listings in the local equivalent of *TV Guide* and to follow all the puffery about the stars, to say nothing of deciphering the streamer across the bottom of the screen announcing, "Mature subject matter. Parental guidance suggested."

1977

QUESTIONS
1. According to Goldsen, what are the strengths and weaknesses of "Sesame Street"? What is her thesis? What is her attitude toward the program?
2. In describing what the program teaches, Goldsen must analyze this teaching into various categories: what are her categories? Compare her system of analysis with the one Fredelle Bruser Maynard uses in "The Windless World" (pp. *136–143*), for

another kind of "goodthink," that in the Canadian school readers. Are the differences explained by the fact that different media
are being analyzed? or that they originated in different times and
places?

3. After describing the probable cultural impact of "Sesame Street,"
Goldsen concludes that "any future challenge to existing policy is
heavily handicapped" (p. 162). What are the key assumptions at
this point of her argument? Do Maynard's recollections and analysis make those assumptions seem more plausible, or less so?

4. Goldsen distinguishes between two kinds of literacy (p. 165)
and between hyperbole and fantasy (p. 161); explain these
distinctions.

5. Is Goldsen elitist? Write an essay in which you explain whether
she is and then criticize her or defend her for being what you
decide she is.

RALPH WALDO EMERSON
The Language of the Street

The language of the street is always strong. What can describe
the folly and emptiness of scolding like the word *jawing*? I feel too
the force of the double negative, though clean contrary to our
grammar rules. And I confess to some pleasure from the stinging
rhetoric of a rattling oath in the mouths of truckmen and teamsters.
How laconic and brisk it is by the side of a page of the *North
American Review*. Cut these words and they would bleed; they
are vascular and alive; they walk and run. Moreover they who speak
them have this elegancy, that they do not trip in their speech. It is
a shower of bullets, whilst Cambridge men and Yale men correct
themselves and begin again at every half sentence.

1840   1914

QUESTIONS
In "Style and Meaning (pp. 212–217), Horace M. Kallen, writing ninety years after Emerson, argues the opposite case in this
long-standing dispute. What is each man's strategy? How can
each support his case?

WAYNE C. BOOTH

Boring from Within: The Art of the Freshman Essay[1]

Last week I had for about the hundredth time an experience that always disturbs me. Riding on a train, I found myself talking with my seat-mate, who asked me what I did for a living. "I teach English." Do you have any trouble predicting his response? His face fell, and he groaned, "Oh, dear, I'll have to watch my language." In my experience there are only two other possible reactions. The first is even less inspiriting: "I hated English in school; it was my worst subject." The second, so rare as to make an honest English teacher almost burst into tears of gratitude when it occurs, is an animated conversation about literature, or ideas, or the American language—the kind of conversation that shows a continuing respect for "English" as something more than being sure about *who* and *whom, lie* and *lay.*

Unless the people you meet are a good deal more tactful or better liars than the ones I meet, you've had the two less favorable experiences many times. And it takes no master analyst to figure out why so many of our fellow citizens think of us as unfriendly policemen: it is because too many of us have seen ourselves as unfriendly policemen. I know of a high school English class in Indiana in which the students are explicitly told that their paper grades will not be affected by anything they say; required to write a paper a week, they are graded simply on the number of spelling and grammatical errors. What is more, they are given a standard form for their papers: each paper is to have three paragraphs, a beginning, a middle, and an end —or is it an introduction, a body, and a conclusion? The theory seems to be that if the student is not troubled about having to say anything, or about discovering a good way of saying it, he can then concentrate on the truly important matter of avoiding mistakes.

What's wrong with such assignments? What's wrong with getting the problem of correctness focused sharply enough so that we can really work on it? After all, we do have the job of teaching correct English, don't we? We can't possibly teach our hordes of students to be colorful writers, but by golly, we can beat the bad grammar out of them. Leaving aside the obvious fact that we *can't* beat the bad grammar out of them, not by direct assault, let's think a bit about what that kind of assignment does to the poor teacher who gives it. Those papers must be read, by someone, and unless the teacher has more trained assistance than you and I have, *she's* the victim. She can't

1. Adapted by Mr. Booth from a speech delivered in May 1963 to the Illinois Council of College Teachers of English.

help being bored silly by her own paper-reading, and we all know
what an evening of being bored by a class's papers does to our attitude
toward that class the next day. The old formula of John Dewey was
that any teaching that bores the student is likely to fail. The formula
was subject to abuse, quite obviously, since interest in itself is only
one of many tests of adequate teaching. A safer formula, though
perhaps also subject to abuse, might be: Any teaching that bores the
teacher is sure to fail. And I am haunted by the picture of that poor
woman in Indiana, week after week reading batches of papers written
by students who have been told that nothing they say can possibly
affect her opinion of those papers. Could any hell imagined by Dante
or Jean-Paul Sartre[2] match this self-inflicted futility?

I call it self-inflicted, as if it were a simple matter to avoid receiving
papers that bore us. But unfortunately it is not. It may be a simple
matter to avoid the *total* meaninglessness that the students must give
that Indiana teacher, but we all know that it is no easy matter to
produce interesting papers; our pet cures for boredom never work
as well as they ought to. Every beginning teacher learns quickly and
painfully that nothing works with all students, and that on bad days
even the most promising ideas work with nobody.

As I try to sort out the various possible cures for those batches of
boredom—in ink, double-spaced, on one side of the sheet, only, please
—I find them falling into three groups: efforts to give the students
a sharper sense of writing to an audience, efforts to give them some
substance to express, and efforts to improve their habits of observation and of approach to their task—what might be called improving
their mental personalities.

This classification, both obvious and unoriginal, is a useful one
not only because it covers—at least I hope it does—all of our efforts
to improve what our students can do but also because it reminds us
that no one of the three is likely to work unless it is related to each
of the others. In fact each of the three types of cure—"develop an
awareness of audience," "give them something to say," and "enliven
their writing personalities"—threatens us with characteristic dangers
and distortions; all three together are indispensable to any lasting cure.

Perhaps the most obvious omission in that Indiana teacher's assignments is all sense of an audience to be persuaded, of a serious
rhetorical purpose to be achieved. One tempting cure for this omission is to teach them to put a controversial edge on what they say. So
we ask them to write a three-page paper arguing that China should
be allowed into the UN or that women are superior to men or that
American colleges are failing in their historic task. Then we are sur-

<hr />

2. Booth refers to the elaborately described hell of the *Inferno*, by the fourteenth-century Italian poet Dante Ali-
ghieri, and to the banal locked room in
which the characters of Sartre's *No Exit*
discover that hell is "other people."

prised when the papers turn out to be as boring as ever. The papers on Red China are full of abstract pomposities that the students themselves obviously do not understand or care about, since they have gleaned them in a desperate dash through the most readily available sources listed in the *Readers' Guide*. Except for the rare student who has some political background and awareness, and who thus might have written on the subject anyway, they manage to convey little more than their resentment at the assignment and their boredom in carrying it out. One of the worst batches of papers I ever read came out of a good idea we had at Earlham College for getting the whole student body involved in controversial discussion about world affairs. We required them to read Barbara Ward's *Five Ideas that Change the World*; we even had Lady Jackson[3] come to the campus and talk to everyone about her concern for the backward nations. The papers, to our surprise, were a discouraging business. We found ourselves in desperation collecting the boners that are always a sure sign, when present in great numbers, that students are thoroughly disengaged. "I think altruism is all right, so long as we practice it in our own interest." "I would be willing to die for anything fatal." "It sure is a doggie dog world."

It is obvious what had gone wrong: though we had ostensibly given the student a writing purpose, it had not become *his* purpose, and he was really no better off, perhaps worse, than if we had him writing about, say, piccolos or pizza. We might be tempted in revulsion from such overly ambitious failures to search for controversy in the students' own mundane lives. This may be a good move, but we should not be surprised when the papers on "Let's clean up the campus" or "Why must we have traffic fatalities?" turn out to be just as empty as the papers on the UN or the Congo. They may have more exclamation points and underlined adjectives, but they will not interest any teacher who would like to read papers for his own pleasure or edification. "People often fail to realize that nearly 40,000 people are killed on our highways each year. Must this carnage continue?" Well, I suppose it must, until people who write about it learn to see it with their own eyes, and hearts, instead of through a haze of cliché. The truth is that to make students assume a controversial pose before they have any genuine substance to be controversial about is to encourage dishonesty and slovenliness, and to ensure our own boredom. It may very well lead them into the kind of commercial concern for the audience which makes almost every *Reader's Digest* article intelligible to everyone over the chronological age of ten and boring to everyone over the mental age of fifteen. *Newsweek* magazine recently had a readability survey conducted on itself. It was found to be readable by the

3. Barbara Ward.

average twelfth grader, unlike *Time*, which is readable by the average eleventh grader. The editors were advised, and I understand are taking the advice, that by improving their "readability" by one year they could improve their circulation by several hundred thousand. Whether they will thereby lop off a few thousand adult readers in the process was not reported.

The only protection from this destructive type of concern for the audience is the control of substance, of having something solid to say. Our students bore us, even when they take a seemingly lively controversial tone, because they have nothing to say, to us or to anybody else. If and when they discover something to say, they will no longer bore us, and our comments will no longer bore them. Having something to say, they will be interested in learning how to say it better. Having something to say, they can be taught how to give a properly controversial edge to what will by its nature be controversial—nothing, after all, is worth saying that everybody agrees on already.

When we think of providing substance, we are perhaps tempted first to find some way of filling students' minds with a goodly store of general ideas, available on demand. This temptation is not necessarily a bad one. After all, if we think of the adult writers who interest us, most of them have such a store; they have read and thought about man's major problems, and they have opinions and arguments ready to hand about how men ought to live, how society ought to be run, how literature ought to be written. Edmund Wilson, for example, one of the most consistently interesting men alive, seems to have an inexhaustible flow of reasoned opinions on any subject that comes before him. Obviously our students are not going to interest us until they too have some ideas.

But it is not easy to impart ideas. It is not even easy to impart opinions, though a popular teacher can usually manage to get students to parrot his views. But ideas—that is, opinions backed with genuine reasoning—are extremely difficult to develop. If they were not, we wouldn't have a problem in the first place; we could simply send our students off with an assignment to prove their conviction that God does or does not exist or that the American high school system is the best on God's earth, and the interesting arguments would flow.

There is, in fact, no short cut to the development of reasoned ideas. Years and years of daily contact with the world of ideas are required before the child can be expected to begin formulating his own ideas and his own reasons. And for the most part the capacity to handle abstract ideas comes fairly late. I recently saw a paper of a bright high school sophomore, from a good private school, relating the economic growth of China and India to their political development and relative supply of natural resources. It was a terrible paper; the student's hatred of the subject, his sense of frustration in trying to invent generalizations about processes that were still too big for him, showed in every line. The child's parent told me that when the paper was returned by the geography teacher, he had pencilled on the top of one page, "Why do you mix so many bad ideas with your good ones?" The son was almost in tears, his father told me, with anger and help-lessness. "He talks as if I'd put bad ideas in on purpose. *I* don't know a bad idea from a good one on this subject."

Yet with all this said, I am still convinced that general ideas are not only a resource but also a duty that cannot be dodged just because it is a dangerous one. There is nothing we touch, as English teachers, that is immune to being tainted by our touch; all the difference lies in how we go about it.

Ideas are a resource because adolescents are surprisingly responsive to any real encouragement to think for themselves, *if* methods of forced feeding are avoided. The seventeen-year-old who has been given nothing but commonplaces and clichés all his life and who final-ly discovers a teacher with ideas of his own may have his life changed, and, as I shall say in my final point, when his life is changed his writing is changed. Perhaps some of you can remember, as I can, a first experience with a teacher who could think for himself. I can remember going home from a conversation with my high school chemistry teacher and audibly vowing to myself: "Someday I'm going to be able to think for myself like that." There was nothing especially unconventional about Luther Gidding's ideas—at least I can remem-ber few of them now. But what I cannot forget is the way he had with an idea, the genuine curiosity with which he approached it, the pause while he gave his little thoughtful cough, and then the bulldog tenacity with which he would argue it through. And I am convinced that though he never required me to write a line, he did more to improve my writing during the high school years than all of my English teachers put together. The diary I kept to record my sessions with him, never read by anyone, was the best possible writing prac-tice.

If ideas, in this sense of speculation backed up with an attempt to think about things rigorously and constructively, are a great and often neglected resource, they are also our civic responsibility—a far more serious responsibility than our duty to teach spelling and grammar. It is a commonplace to say that democracy depends for its survival on an informed citizenry, but we all know that mere information is not what we are talking about when we say such things. What we mean is that democracy depends on a citizenry that can reason for themselves, on men who know whether a case has been proved, or at least made probable. Democracy depends, if you will forgive some truisms for a moment, on free choices, and choices cannot be in any sense free if they are made blind: free choice is, in fact, choice that is based on knowledge—not just opinions, but knowledge in the sense of reasoned opinion. And if that half of our population who do not go beyond high school do not learn from us how to put two and two together and how to test the efforts of others to do so, and if the colleges continue to fail with most of the other half, we are doomed to become even more sheeplike, as a nation, than we are already.

Papers about ideas written by sheep are boring; papers written by thinking boys and girls are interesting. The problem is always to find ideas at a level that will allow the student to *reason*, that is, to provide support for his ideas, rather than merely assert them in half-baked form. And this means something that is all too often forgotten by the most ambitious teachers—namely, that whatever ideas the student writes about must somehow be connected with his own experience. Teaching machines will never be able to teach the kind of writing we all want, precisely because no machine can ever know which general ideas relate, for a given student, to some meaningful experience. In the same class we'll have one student for whom philosophical and religious ideas are meaningful, another who can talk with confidence about entropy and the second law of thermodynamics, a third who can write about social justice, and a fourth who can discuss the phony world of Holden Caulfield.[4] Each of them can do a good job on his own subject, because he has as part of his equipment a growing awareness of how conclusions in that subject are related to the steps of argument that support conclusions. Ideally, each of these students ought to have the personal attention of a tutor for an hour or so each week, someone who can help him sharpen those connections, and not force him to write on topics not yet appropriate to his interests or experience. But when these four are in a class of thirty or forty others, taught by a teacher who has three or four other similar sections, we all know what happens: the teacher is forced by his circumstances to provide some sort of mold into which all of the students can be poured. Although he is still better able to adapt to individual differences than a machine, he is unfortunately subject to boredom and fatigue, as a machine would not be. Instead of being the philosopher, scientist, political analyst, and literary critic that these four students require him to be, teaching them and learning from them at the same time, the teacher is almost inevitably tempted to force them all to write about the ideas he himself knows best. The result is that at least three of the four must write out of ignorance.

Now clearly the best way out of this impasse would be for legislatures and school boards and college presidents to recognize the teaching of English for what it is: the most demanding of all teaching jobs, justifying the smallest sections and the lightest course loads. No composition teacher can possibly concentrate on finding special

---

4. The hero of *The Catcher in the Rye*, by J. D. Salinger.

interests, making imaginative assignments, and testing the effectiveness and cogency of papers if he has more than seventy-five students
at a time; the really desirable limit would be about forty-five—three
sections of fifteen students each. Nobody would ever expect a piano
teacher, who has no themes to read, to handle the great masses of
pupils that we handle. Everyone recognizes that for all other technical skills individual attention is required. Yet for this, the most
delicate of all skills, the one requiring the most subtle interrelation-
ships of training, character, and experience, we fling students and
teachers into hopelessly impersonal patterns.

But if I'm not careful I'll find myself saying that our pupils bore us
because the superintendents and college presidents hire us to be
bored. Administrative neglect and misallocation of educational funds
are basic to our problem, and we should let the citizenry know of the
scandal on every occasion. But meanwhile, back at the ranch, we are
faced with the situation as it now is: we must find some way to train
a people to write responsibly even though the people, as represented,
don't want this service sufficiently to pay for it.

The tone of political exhortation into which I have now fallen
leads me to one natural large source of ideas as we try to encourage
writing that is not just lively and controversial but informed and
genuinely persuasive. For many students there is obviously more potential interest in social problems and forces, political controversy,
and the processes of everyday living around them than in more general
ideas. The four students I described a moment ago, students who can
say something about philosophy, science, general political theory, or
literary criticism, are rare. But most students, including these four,
can in theory at least be interested in meaningful argument about
social problems in which they are personally involved.

As a profession we have tried, over the past several decades, a variety of approaches attempting to capitalize on such interests. Papers
on corruption in TV, arguments about race relations, analyses of
distortions in advertising, descriptions of mass communication—these
have been combined in various quantities with traditional subjects
like grammar, rhetoric, and literature. The "communications" movement, which looked so powerful only a few years ago and which now
seems almost dead, had at its heart a perfectly respectable notion, a
notion not much different from the one I'm working with today: get
them to write about something they know about, and make sure that
they see their writing as an act of communication, not as a meaningless exercise. And what better material than other acts of communication.

The dangers of such an approach are by now sufficiently understood. As subject matter for the English course, current "communications media" can at best provide only a supplement to literature
and analysis of ideas. But they can be a valuable supplement. Analysis

in class of the appeals buried in a *New Yorker* or *Life* advertisement followed by a writing assignment requiring similar analyses can be a far more interesting introduction to the intricacies of style than assignments out of a language text on levels of usage or emotion-charged adjectives. Analysis of a *Time* magazine account, purporting to be objective news but in actual fact a highly emotional editorial, can be not only a valuable experience in itself, but it can lead to papers in which the students do say something to us. Stylistic analysis of the treatment of the same news events by two newspapers or weeklies of different editorial policy can lead to an intellectual awakening of great importance, and thus to papers that will not, cannot, bore the teacher. But this will happen only if the students' critical powers are genuinely developed. It will not do simply to teach the instructor's own prejudices.

There was a time in decades not long past when many of the most lively English teachers thought of their job as primarily to serve as handmaids to liberalism. I had one teacher in college who confessed to me that his overriding purpose was to get students to read and believe *The Nation* rather than the editorials of their daily paper. I suppose that his approach was not entirely valueless. It seems preferable to the effort to be noncontroversial that marks too many English teachers in the '60's, and at least it stirred some of us out of our dogmatic slumbers. But unfortunately it did nothing whatever about teaching us to think critically. Though we graduated from his course at least aware—as many college graduates do not seem to be today— that you can't believe anything you read in the daily press until you have analyzed it and related it to your past experience and to other accounts, it failed to teach us that you can't believe what you read in *The Nation* either. It left the job undone of training our ability to think, because it concentrated too heavily on our opinions. The result was, as I remember, that my own papers in that course were generally regurgitated liberalism. I was excited by them, and that was something. But I can't believe that the instructor found reading them anything other than a chore. There was nothing in them that came from my own experience, my own notions of what would constitute evidence for my conclusions. There I was, in Utah in the depths of the depression, writing about the Okies when I could have been writing about the impoverished farmers all around me. I wrote about race relations in the south without ever having talked with a Negro in my life and without recognizing that the bootblack I occasionally saw in Salt Lake City in the Hotel Utah was in any way related to the problem of race relations.

The third element that accounts for our boring papers is the lack of character and personality in the writer. My life, my observations, my insights were not included in those papers on the Okies and race relations and the New Deal. Every opinion was derivative, every observation second-hand. I had no real opinions of my own, and my eyes were not open wide enough for me to make first-hand observations on the world around me. What I wrote was therefore characterless, without true personality, though often full of personal pronouns. My opinions had been changed, my *self* had not. The style was the boy, the opinionated, immature, uninformed boy; whether my teacher knew it or not—and apparently he did not—his real job was to make a man of me if he wanted me to write like a man.

Putting the difficulty in this way naturally leads me to what perhaps many of you have been impatient about from the beginning. Are not the narrative arts, both as encountered in great literature and as practiced by the students themselves, the best road to the infusion of individuality that no good writing can lack? Would not a real look at the life of that bootblack, and an attempt to deal with him in narrative, have led to a more interesting paper than all of my generalized attacks on the prejudiced southerners?

I think it would, but once again I am almost more conscious of the dangers of the cure than of the advantages. As soon as we make our general rule something like, "Have the students write a personal narrative on what they know about, what they can see and feel at first hand," we have opened the floodgates for those dreadful assignments that we all find ourselves using, even though we know better: "My Summer Vacation," "Catching My First Fish," and "Our Trip to the Seattle World's Fair." Here are personal experiences that call for personal observation and narration. What's wrong with them?

Quite simply, they invite triviality, superficiality, puerility. Our students have been writing essays on such non-subjects all their lives, and until they have developed some sort of critical vision, some way of looking at the world they passed through on their vacations or fishing trips, they are going to feed us the same old bromides that have always won their passing grades. "My Summer Vacation" is an invitation to a grocery list of items, because it implies no audience, no point to be made, no point of view, no character in the speaker. A bright student will make something of such an invitation, by dramatizing the comic family quarrel that developed two days out, or by comparing his view of the American motel system with Nabokov's in *Lolita*, or by remembering the types of people seen in the campgrounds. If he had his own eyes and ears open he might have seen, in a men's room in Grand Canyon last summer, a camper with a very thick French accent trying to convert a Brooklyn Jew into believing the story of the Mormon gold plates.[5] Or he could have heard, at Mesa

5. Bearing, according to Mormon tradition, the Book of Mormon, divinely revealed to the prophet Joseph Smith in upstate New York in 1827.

Verde, a young park ranger, left behind toward the end of the season by all of the experienced rangers, struggling ungrammatically through a set speech on the geology of the area and finally breaking down in embarrassment over his lack of education. Such an episode, really *seen*, could be used narratively to say something to other high school students about what education really is,

But mere narration can be in itself just as dull as the most abstract theorizing about the nature of the universe or the most derivative opinion-mongering about politics. Even relatively skilful narration, used too obviously as a gimmick to catch interest, with no real relation to the subject, can be as dull as the most abstract pomposities. We all know the student papers that begin like *Reader's Digest* articles, with stereotyped narration that makes one doubt the event itself: "On a dark night last January, two teen agers were seen etc., etc." One can open any issue of *Time* and find this so-called narrative interest plastered throughout. From the March 29 issue I find, among many others, the following bits of fantasy: #1: "A Bolivian father sadly surveyed his nation's seven universities, then made up his mind. 'I don't want my son mixed up in politics.' . . . So saying, he sent his son off to West Germany to college." So writing, the author sends me into hysterical laughter: the quote is phony, made up for the occasion to disguise the generality of the news item. #2: "Around 12:30 P.M. every Monday and Friday, an aging Cubana Airlines turbo-prop Britannia whistles to a halt at Mexico City's International Airport. Squads of police stand by. All passengers . . . without diplomatic or Mexican passports are photographed and questioned. . . . They always dodge questions. 'Why are you here? Where are you going?' ask the Mexicans. 'None of your business,' answer the secretive travelers." "Why should I go on reading?" ask I. #3: "At 6:30 one morning early this month, a phone shrilled in the small office off the bedroom of Egypt's President. . . Nasser. [All early morning phones "shrill" for *Time*.] Already awake, he lifted the receiver to hear exciting news: a military coup had just been launched against the anti-Nasser government of Syria. The phone rang again. It was the Minister of Culture. . . . How should Radio Cairo handle the Syrian crisis? 'Support the rebels,' snapped Nasser." Oh lucky reporter, I sigh, to have such an efficient wiretapping service. #4: "In South Korea last week, a farmer named Song Kyu Il traveled all the way from the southern provinces to parade before Seoul's Duk Soo Palace with a placard scrawled in his own blood. . . . Farmer Song was thrown in jail, along with some 200 other demonstrators." That's the last we hear of Song, who is invented as an individual for this opening and then dropped. #5: "Defense Secretary Robert McNamara last spring stood beside President Kennedy on the tenth-deck bridge of the nuclear-powered carrier *Enterprise*. For as far as the eye could see, other U. S.

ships deployed over the Atlantic seascape." Well, maybe. But for as far as the eye can see, the narrative clichés are piled, rank on rank. At 12:00 midnight last Thursday a gaunt, harried English professor could be seen hunched over his typewriter, a pile of *Time* magazines beside him on the floor. "What," he murmured to himself, sadly, "Whatever can we do about this trashy imitation of narration?"

Fortunately there is something we can do, and it is directly within our province. We can subject our students to models of genuine narration, with the sharp observation and penetrating critical judgment that underlies all good story telling, whether reportorial or fictional.

It is a truth universally acknowledged, that a single man in possession of a good fortune must be in want of a wife.

However little known the feelings or views of such a man may be on his first entering a neighborhood, this truth is so well fixed in the minds of the surrounding families, that he is considered as the rightful property of someone or other of their daughters.

"My dear Mr. Bennet," said his lady to him one day, "have you heard that Netherfield Park is let at last?"

And already we have a strong personal tone established, a tone of mocking irony which leaves Jane Austen's Mrs. Bennet revealed before us as the grasping, silly gossip she is. Or try this one:

I am an American, Chicago-born—Chicago, that somber city—and go at things as I have taught myself, free-style, and will make the record in my own way: first to knock, first admitted; sometimes an innocent knock, sometimes a not so innocent. But a man's character is his fate, says Heraclitus, and in the end there isn't any way to disguise the nature of the knocks by acoustical work on the door or gloving the knuckles.

Everybody knows there is no fineness or accuracy of suppression; if you hold down one thing you hold down the adjoining.

My own parents were not much to me, though I cared for my mother. She was simple-minded, and what I learned from her was not what she taught. . . .

Do you catch the accent of Saul Bellow here, beneath the accent of his Augie March? You do, of course, but the students, many of them, do not. How do you know, they will ask, that Jane Austen is being ironic? How do you know, they ask again, that Augie is being characterized by his author through what he says? In teaching them how we know, in exposing them to the great narrative voices, ancient and modern, and in teaching them to hear these voices accurately, we are, of course, trying to change their lives, to make them new, to raise their perceptions to a new level altogether. Nobody can really catch these accents who has not grown up sufficiently to see through cheap substitutes. Or, to put it another way, a steady exposure to such voices is the very thing that will produce the maturity that alone can make our students ashamed of beclouded, commercial, borrowed spectacles for viewing the world.

It is true that exposure to good fiction will not in itself transform our students into good writers. Even the best-read student still needs endless hours and years of practice, with rigorous criticism. Fiction will not do the job of discipline in reasoned argument and of practice in developing habits of addressing a living audience. But in the great fiction they will learn what it means to look at something with full attention, what it means to see beneath the surface of society's platitudes. If we then give them practice in writing about things close to the home base of their own honest observations, constantly stretching their powers of generalization and argument but never allowing them to drift into pompous inanities or empty controversiality, we may have that rare but wonderful pleasure of witnessing the miracle: a man and a style where before there was only a bag of wind or a bundle of received opinions. Even when, as with most of our students, no miracles occur, we can hope for papers that we can enjoy reading. And as a final bonus, we might hope that when our students encounter someone on a train who says that he teaches English, their automatic response may be something other than looks of pity or cries of mock alarm.

1963

QUESTIONS

1. *Booth is writing for an audience of English teachers. In what ways might the essay differ if he were writing for an audience of students?*
2. *On page 173 Booth says he has "now fallen" into a "tone of political exhortation." (Tone may be defined as the reflection in language of the attitude a writer takes toward his subject or his audience or both.) What other "tones" are there in the essay? Why does Booth find it necessary to vary the tone?*
3. *What steps are necessary before an "opinion" can become a "reasoned opinion"? Select some subject on which you have a strong opinion and decide whether it is a reasoned opinion.*
4. *Booth characterizes the writing in the Reader's Digest and Time (pp. 176-177). What does he feel the two magazines have in common? Analyze an article from either one of these magazines to see how accurate Booth's characterization is.*

LEWIS THOMAS

Notes on Punctuation

There are no precise rules about punctuation (Fowler[1] lays out some general advice (as best he can under the complex circumstances of English prose (he points out, for example, that we possess only four stops (the comma, the semicolon, the colon and the period (the question mark and exclamation point are not, strictly speaking, stops; they are indicators of tone (oddly enough, the Greeks employed the semicolon for their question mark (it produces a strange sensation to read a Greek sentence which is a straightforward question: Why weepest thou; (instead of Why weepest thou? (and, of course, there are parentheses (which are surely a kind of punctuation making this whole much more complicated by having to count up the left-handed parentheses in order to be sure of closing with the right number (but if the parentheses were left out, with nothing to work with but the stops, we would have considerably more flexibility in the deploying of layers of meaning then if we tried to separate all the clauses by physical barriers (and in the latter case, while we might have more precision and exactitude for our meaning, we would lose the essential flavor of language, which is its wonderful ambiguity))))))))))))).

The commas are the most useful and usable of all the stops. It is highly important to put them in place as you go along. If you try to come back after doing a paragraph and stick them in the various spots that tempt you you will discover that they tend to swarm like minnows into all sorts of crevices whose existence you hadn't realized and before you know it the whole long sentence becomes immobilized and lashed up squirming in commas. Better to use them sparingly, and with affection, precisely when the need for each one arises, nicely, by itself.

I have grown fond of semicolons in recent years. The semicolon tells you that there is still some question about the preceding full sentence; something needs to be added; it reminds you sometimes of the Greek usage. It is almost always a greater pleasure to come across a semicolon than a period. The period tells you that that is that; if you didn't get all the meaning you wanted or expected, anyway you got all the writer intended to parcel out and now you have to move along. But with a semicolon there you get a pleasant little feeling of expectancy; there is more to come; read on; it will get clearer.

1. H. W. Fowler, author of *Modern English Usage* (1926, revised 1965 by Sir Ernest Gowers), a standard reference work.

Colons are a lot less attractive, for several reasons: firstly, they give you the feeling of being rather ordered around, or at least having your nose pointed in a direction you might not be inclined to take if left to yourself, and, secondly, you suspect you're in for one of those sentences that will be labeling the points to be made: firstly, secondly and so forth, with the implication that you haven't sense enough to keep track of a sequence of notions without having them numbered. Also, many writers use this system loosely and incompletely, starting out with number one and number two as though counting off on their fingers but then going on and on without the succession of labels you've been led to expect, leaving you floundering about searching for the ninethly or seventeenthly that ought to be there but isn't.

Exclamation points are the most irritating of all. Look! they say, look at what I just said! How amazing is my thought! It is like being forced to watch someone else's small child jumping up and down crazily in the center of the living room shouting to attract attention. If a sentence really has something of importance to say, something quite remarkable, it doesn't need a mark to point it out. And if it is really, after all, a banal sentence needing more zing, the exclamation point simply emphasizes its banality!

Quotation marks should be used honestly and sparingly, when there is a genuine quotation at hand, and it is necessary to be very rigorous about the words enclosed by the marks. If something is to be quoted, the *exact* words must be used. If part of it must be left out because of space limitations, it is good manners to insert three dots to indicate the omission, but it is unethical to do this if it means connecting two thoughts which the original author did not intend to have tied together. Above all, quotation marks should not be used for ideas that you'd like to disown, things in the air so to speak. Nor should they be put in place around clichés; if you want to use a cliché you must take full responsibility for it yourself and not try to job it off on anon., or on society. The most objectionable misuse of quotation marks, but one which illustrates the dangers of misuse in ordinary prose, is seen in advertising, especially in advertisements for small restaurants, for example "just around the corner," or "a good place to eat." No single, identifiable, citable person ever really said, for the record, "just around the corner," much less "a good place to eat," least likely of all for restaurants of the type that use this type of prose.

The dash is a handy device, informal and essentially playful, telling you that you're about to take off on a different tack but still in some way connected with the present course—only you have to remember that the dash is there, and either put a second dash at the end of the notion to let the reader know that he's back on course, or else end the sentence, as here, with a period.

The greatest danger in punctuation is for poetry. Here it is necessary to be as economical and parsimonious with commas and periods as with the words themselves, and any marks that seem to carry their own subtle meanings, like dashes and little rows of periods, even semicolons and question marks, should be left out altogether rather than inserted to clog up the thing with ambiguity. A single exclamation point in a poem, no matter what else the poem has to say, is enough to destroy the whole work.

The things I like best in T. S. Eliot's poetry, especially in the *Four Quartets*, are the semicolons. You cannot hear them, but they are there, laying out the connections between the images and the ideas. Sometimes you get a glimpse of a semicolon coming, a few lines farther on, and it is like climbing a steep path through woods and seeing a wooden bench just at a bend in the road ahead, a place where you can expect to sit for a moment, catching your breath.

Commas can't do this sort of thing; they can only tell you how the different parts of a complicated thought are to be fitted together, but you can't sit, not even take a breath, just because of a comma,

1979

Guidelines for Equal Treatment of the Sexes in McGraw-Hill Book Company Publications

The word *sexism* was coined, by analogy to *racism*, to denote discrimination based on gender. In its original sense, *sexism* referred to prejudice against the female sex. In a broader sense, the term now indicates any arbitrary stereotyping of males and females on the basis of their gender.

We are endeavoring through these guidelines to eliminate sexist assumptions from McGraw-Hill Book Company publications and to encourage a greater freedom for all individuals to pursue their interests and realize their potentials. Specifically, these guidelines are designed to make McGraw-Hill staff members and McGraw-Hill authors aware of the ways in which males and females have been stereotyped in publications; to show the role language has played in reinforcing inequality; and to indicate positive approaches toward providing fair, accurate, and balanced treatment of both sexes in our publications.

One approach is to recruit more women as authors and contributors in all fields. The writings and viewpoints of women should be represented in quotations and references whenever possible. Anthologies should include a larger proportion of selections by and about women in fields where suitable materials are available but women are currently underrepresented.

Women as well as men have been leaders and heroes, explorers and pioneers, and have made notable contributions to science, medicine, law, business, politics, civics, economics, literature, the arts, sports, and other areas of endeavor. Books dealing with subjects like these, as well as general histories, should acknowledge the achievements of women. The fact that women's rights, opportunities, and accomplishments have been limited by the social customs and conditions of their time should be openly discussed whenever relevant to the topic at hand.

We realize that the language of literature cannot be prescribed. The recommendations in these guidelines, thus, are intended primarily for use in teaching materials, reference works, and nonfiction works in general.

Nonsexist Treatment of Women and Men

Men and women should be treated primarily as people, and not primarily as members of opposite sexes. Their shared humanity and common attributes should be stressed—not their gender difference. Neither sex should be stereotyped or arbitrarily assigned to a leading or secondary role.

1.

a. Though many women will continue to choose traditional occupations such as homemaker or secretary, women should not be type-cast in these roles but shown in a wide variety of professions and trades: as doctors and dentists, not always as nurses; as principals and professors, not always as teachers; as lawyers and judges, not always as social workers; as bank presidents, not always as tellers; as members of Congress, not always as members of the League of Women Voters.

b. Similarly, men should not be shown as constantly subject to the "masculine mystique" in their interests, attitudes, or careers. They should not be made to feel that their self-worth depends entirely upon their income level or the status level of their jobs. They should not be conditioned to believe that a man ought to earn more than a woman or that he ought to be the sole support of a family.

c. An attempt should be made to break job stereotypes for both women and men. No job should be considered sex-typed, and it should never be implied that certain jobs are incompatible with a woman's "femininity" or a man's "masculinity." Thus, women as well as men should be shown as accountants, engineers, pilots, plumbers, bridge-builders, computer operators, TV repairers, and astronauts, while men as well as women should be shown as nurses, grade-school teachers, secretaries, typists, librarians, file clerks, switchboard operators, and baby-sitters.

Women within a profession should be shown at all professional levels, including the top levels. Women should be portrayed in positions of authority over men and over other women, and there should be no implication that a man loses face or that a woman faces difficulty if the employer or supervisor is a woman. All work should be treated as honorable and worthy of respect; no job or job choices should be downgraded. Instead, women and men should be offered more options than were available to them when work was stereotyped by sex.

d. Books designed for children at the pre-school, elementary, and secondary levels should show married women who work outside the home and should treat them favorably. Teaching materials should not assume or imply that most women are wives who are also full-time mothers, but should instead emphasize the fact that women have choices about their marital status, just as men do: that some women choose to stay permanently single and some are in no hurry to marry; that some women marry but do not have children, while others marry, have children, and continue to work outside the home. Thus, a text might say that some married people have children and some do not, and that sometimes *one or both parents* work outside the home. Instructional materials should never imply that all women have a "mother instinct" or that the emotional life of a family suffers because a woman works. Instead they might state that when both parents work outside the home there is usually either greater sharing of the child-rearing activities or reliance on day-care centers, nursery schools, or other help.

According to Labor Department statistics for 1972, over 42 per cent of all mothers with children under 18 worked outside the home, and about a third of these working mothers had children under 6. Publications ought to reflect this reality.

Both men and women should be shown engaged in home maintenance activities, ranging from cooking and housecleaning to washing the car and making household repairs. Sometimes the man should be shown preparing the meals, doing the laundry, or diapering the baby, while the woman builds bookcases or takes out the trash.

e. Girls should be shown as having, and exercising, the same options as boys in their play and career choices. In school materials, girls should be encouraged to show an interest in mathematics, mechanical skills, and active sports, for example, while boys should never be made to feel ashamed of an interest in poetry, art, or music, or an aptitude for cooking, sewing, or child care. Course materials should be addressed to students of both sexes. For example, home economics courses should apply to boys as well as girls, and shop to girls as well as boys. Both males and females should be shown in textbook illustrations depicting career choices.

When as a practical matter it is known that a book will be used primarily by women for the life of the edition (say, the next five years), it is pointless to pretend that the readership is divided equally between males and females. In such cases it may be more beneficial to address the book fully to women and exploit every opportunity (1) to point out to them a broader set of options than they might otherwise have considered, and (2) to encourage them to aspire to a more active, assertive, and policy-making role than they might otherwise have thought of.

f. Women and girls should be portrayed as active participants in the same proportion as men and boys in stories, examples, problems, illustrations, discussion questions, test items, and exercises, regardless of subject matter. Women should not be stereotyped in examples by being spoken of only in connection with cooking, sewing, shopping, and similar activities.

2.

a. Members of both sexes should be represented as whole human beings with *human* strengths and weaknesses, not masculine or feminine ones. Women and girls should be shown as having the same abilities, interests, and ambitions as men and boys. Characteristics that have been traditionally praised in males—such as boldness, initiative, and assertiveness—should also be praised in females. Characteristics that have been praised in females—such as gentleness, compassion, and sensitivity—should also be praised in males.

b. Like men and boys, women and girls should be portrayed as independent, active, strong, courageous, competent, decisive, persistent, serious-minded, and successful. They should appear as logical thinkers, problem-solvers, and decision makers. They should be shown as interested in their work, pursuing a variety of career goals, and both deserving of and receiving public recognition for their accomplishments.

c. Sometimes men should be shown as quiet and passive, or fearful and indecisive, or illogical and immature. Similarly, women should sometimes be shown as tough, aggressive, and insensitive. Stereotypes of the logical, objective male and the emotional, subjective female are to be avoided. In descriptions, the smarter, braver, or more successful person should be a woman or girl as often as a man or boy. In illustrations, the taller, heavier, stronger, or more active person should not always be male, especially when children are portrayed.

3.

Women and men should be treated with the same respect, dignity, and seriousness. Neither should be trivialized or stereotyped, either in text or in illustrations. Women should not be described by physical attributes when men are being described by mental attributes or professional position. Instead, both sexes should be dealt with in the same terms. References to a man's or a woman's appearance, charm, or intuition should be avoided when irrelevant.

no	*yes*
Henry Harris is a shrewd lawyer and his wife Ann is a striking brunette.	The Harrises are an attractive couple. Henry is a handsome blond and Ann is a striking brunette.
	or
	The Harrises are highly respected in their fields. Ann is an accomplished musician and Henry is a shrewd lawyer.
	The Harrises are an interesting couple. Henry is a shrewd lawyer and Ann is very active in community (*or* church *or* civic) affairs.

a. In descriptions of women, a patronizing or girl-watching tone should be avoided, as should sexual innuendoes, jokes, and puns. Examples of practices to be avoided: focusing on physical appearance (a buxom blonde); using special female-gender word forms (poetess, aviatrix, usherette); treating women as sex objects or portraying the typical woman as weak, helpless, or hysterical; making women figures of fun or objects of scorn and treating their issues as humorous or unimportant.

Examples of stereotypes to be avoided: scatterbrained female, fragile flower, goddess on a pedestal, catty gossip, henpecking shrew, apron-wearing mother, frustrated spinster, ladylike little girl. Jokes at women's expense—such as the woman driver or nagging mother-in-law cliches—are to be avoided.

no	yes
the fair sex; the weaker sex	women
the distaff side	*the female side or line*
the girls or the ladies (when adult females are meant)	*the women*
girl, as in: I'll have my *girl* check that.	I'll have my *secretary* (or my *assistant*) check that. (Or use the person's name.)
lady used as a modifier, as in *lady* lawyer	*lawyer* (A woman may be identified simply through the choice of pronouns, as in: *The lawyer made her summation to the jury.* Try to avoid gender modifiers altogether. When you *must* modify, use *woman* or *female*, as in: *a course on women writers*, or *the airline's first female pilot*.)
the little woman; the better half; the ball and chain	wife
female-gender word forms, such as *authoress, poetess, Jewess*	*author, poet, Jew*
female-gender or diminutive word forms, such as *suffragette, usherette, aviatrix*	*suffragist, usher, aviator* (or pilot)
libber (a put-down)	*feminist; liberationist*
sweet young thing	*young woman; girl*

co-ed (as a noun)	*student*

(*Note:* Logically, *co-ed* should refer to any student at a co-educational college or university. Since it does not, it is a sexist term.)

housewife	*homemaker* for a person who works at home, or rephrase with a more precise or more inclusive term
The sound of the drilling disturbed the housewives in the neighborhood.	The sound of the drilling disturbed everyone within earshot (or everyone in the neighborhood).
Housewives are feeling the pinch of higher prices	Consumers (customers or shoppers) are feeling the pinch of higher prices.
career girl or career woman	name the woman's profession: *attorney Ellen Smith; Maria Sanchez, a journalist* or editor or business executive or doctor or lawyer or agent
cleaning woman, cleaning lady, or maid	*housekeeper; house* or *office cleaner*

b. In descriptions of men, especially men in the home, references to general ineptness should be avoided. Men should not be characterized as dependent on women for meals, or clumsy in household maintenance, or as foolish in self-care.

To be avoided: characterizations that stress men's dependence on women for advice on what to wear and what to eat, inability of men to care for themselves in times of illness, and men as objects of fun (the henpecked husband).

c. Women should be treated as part of the rule, not as the exception.

Generic terms, such as doctor and nurse, should be assumed to include both men and women, and modified titles such as "woman doctor" or "male nurse," should be avoided. Work should never be stereotyped as "woman's work" or as "a man-sized job." Writers should avoid showing a "gee-whiz" attitude toward women who perform competently; ("Though a woman, she ran the business as well as any man" or "Though a woman, she ran the business efficiently.")

d. Women should be spoken of as participants in the action, not as possessions of the men. Terms such as *pioneer, farmer,* and *settler* should not be used as though they applied only to adult males.

no	yes
Pioneers moved West, taking their wives and children with them.	Pioneer families moved West.
	Pioneer men and women (*or* pioneer couples) moved West, taking their children with them.

e. Women should not be portrayed as needing male permission in order to act or to exercise rights (except, of course, for historical or factual accuracy).

no	yes
Jim Weiss allows his wife to work part-time.	Judy Weiss works part-time.

4.

Women should be recognized for their own achievements. Intelligent, daring, and innovative women, both in history and in fiction, should be provided as role-models for girls, and leaders in the fight for women's rights should be honored and respected, not mocked or ignored.

5.

In references to humanity at large, language should operate to include women and girls. Terms that tend to exclude females should be avoided whenever possible.

a. The word *man* has long been used not only to denote a person of male gender, but also generically to denote humanity at large. To many people today, however, the word *man* has become so closely associated with the first meaning (a male human being) that they consider it no longer broad enough to be applied to any person or to human beings as a whole. In deference to this position, alternative expressions should be used in place of *man* (or derivative constructions used generically to signify humanity at large) whenever such substitutions can be made without producing an awkward or artificial construction. In cases where *man*-words must be used, special efforts should be made to ensure that pictures and other devices make explicit that such references include women.

Here are some possible substitutions for *man*-words:

no	yes
mankind	humanity, human beings, human race, people

primitive man	primitive people or peoples; primitive human beings; primitive men and women
man's achievements	human achievements
If a man drove 50 miles at 60 mph . . .	If a person (or driver) drove 50 miles at 60 mph . . .
the best man for the job	the best person (or candidate) for the job
manmade	artificial; synthetic, manufactured; constructed; of human origin
manpower	human power; human energy; workers; workforce
grow to manhood	grow to adulthood; grow to manhood or womanhood

b. The English language lacks a generic singular pronoun signifying *he* or *she*, and therefore it has been customary and grammatically sanctioned to use masculine pronouns in expressions such as "one . . . *he*," "anyone . . . *he*," and "each child opens *his* book." Nevertheless, avoid when possible the pronouns *he*, *him*, and *his* in reference to the hypothetical person or humanity in general.

Various alternatives may be considered:

(1) Reword to eliminate unnecessary gender pronouns.

no	*yes*
The average American drinks his coffee black	The average American drinks black coffee.

(2) Recast into the plural.

Most Americans drink their coffee black.

(3) Replace the masculine pronoun with *one, you, he* or *she, her* or *his*, as appropriate. (Use *he* or *she* and its variations sparingly to avoid clumsy prose.)

(4) Alternate male and female expressions and examples.

no	*yes*
I've often heard supervisors say, "He's not the right man for the job," or "He lacks the qualifications for success."	I've often heard supervisors say, "She's not the right person for the job," or "He lacks the qualifications for success."

(5) To avoid severe problems of repetition or inept wording, it may sometimes be best to use the generic *he* freely, but to

add, in the preface and as often as necessary in the text, emphatic statements to the effect that the masculine pronouns are being used for succinctness and are intended to refer to both females and males.

These guidelines can only suggest a few solutions to difficult problems of rewording. The proper solution in any given passage must depend on the context and on the author's intention. For example, it would be wrong to pluralize in contexts stressing a one-to-one relationship, as between teacher and child. In such cases, either using the expression *he or she* or alternating *he* and *she*, as appropriate, will be acceptable.

c. Occupational terms ending in *man* should be replaced whenever possible by terms that can include members of either sex unless they refer to a particular person.

no	*yes*
congressman	member of Congress; representative (but *Congressman* Koch and Congress*woman* Holtzman)
businessman	business executive; business manager
fireman	fire fighter
mailman	mail carrier; letter carrier
salesman	sales representative; salesperson; sales clerk
insurance man	insurance agent
statesman	leader; public servant
chairman	the person presiding at (or chairing) a meeting; the presiding officer; the chair; head leader; coordinator; moderator
cameraman	camera operator
foreman	supervisor

d. Language that assumes all readers are male should be avoided.

no	*yes*
you and your wife	you and your spouse
when you shave in the morning	when you brush your teeth (or wash up) in the morning

6.

The language used to designate and describe females and males should treat the sexes equally.

a. Parallel language should be used for women and men.

no	*yes*
the men and the ladies	the men and the women
	the ladies and the gentlemen
	the girls and the boys
man and wife	husband and wife

> Note that *lady* and *gentleman, wife* and *husband,* and *mother* and *father* are role words. *Ladies* should be used for women only when men are being referred to as *gentlemen.* Similarly, women should be called *wives* and *mothers* only when men are referred to as *husbands* and *fathers.* Like a male shopper, a woman in a grocery store should be called a *customer, not a housewife.*

b. Women should be identified by their own names (e.g., Indira Gandhi). They should not be referred to in terms of their roles as wife, mother, sister, or daughter unless it is in these roles that they are significant in context. Nor should they be identified in terms of their marital relationships (Mrs. Gandhi) unless this brief form is stylistically more convenient (than, say Prime Minister Gandhi) or is paired up with similar references to men.

(1) A woman should be referred to by name in the same way that a man is. Both should be called by their full names, by first or last name only, or by title.

no	*yes*
Bobby Riggs and Billie Jean	Bobby Riggs and Billie Jean King
Billie Jean and Riggs	Billie Jean and Bobby
Mrs. King and Riggs	King and Riggs
	Ms. King (because she prefers Ms.) and Mr. Riggs
Mrs. Meir and Moshe Dayan	Golda Meir and Moshe Dayan or Mrs. Meir and Dr. Dayan

(2) Unnecessary reference to or emphasis on a woman's marital status should be avoided. Whether married or not, a woman may be referred to by the name by which she chooses to be known, whether her name is her original name or her married name.

c. Whenever possible, a term should be used that includes both sexes. Unnecessary references to gender should be avoided.

no	*yes*
college boys and co-eds	students

d. Insofar as possible, job titles should be nonsexist. Different nomenclature should not be used for the same job depending on
whether it is held by a male or by a female. (See also paragraph
5c for additional examples of words ending in *man*.)

no	*yes*
steward or purser or stewardess	flight attendant
policeman and policewoman	police officer
maid and houseboy	house or office cleaner; servant

e. Different pronouns should not be linked with certain work or
occupations on the assumption that the worker is always (or
usually) female or male. Instead either pluralize or use *he or she*
and *she or he*.

no	*yes*
the consumer or shopper . . . she	consumers or shoppers . . . they
the secretary . . . she	secretaries . . . they
the breadwinner . . . his earnings	the breadwinner . . . his or her earnings *or* breadwinners . . . their earnings.

f. Males should not always be first in order of mention. Instead, alternate the order, sometimes using: *women and men, gentlemen
and ladies, she or he, her or his.*

Conclusion

It is hoped that these guidelines have alerted authors and staff
members to the problems of sex discrimination and to various ways
of solving them.

1974

QUESTIONS

1. What assumptions about the powers and functions of language
   underlie these guidelines?
2. Racism and sexism represent discrimination on the basis of race
   or sex. What other kinds of discrimination exist in our society?
   Invent an analogous term for one of these and write a brief
   characterization of it.
3. "Discriminate" and "discrimination" originally had to do simply
   with the act of "distinguishing" or finding "distinguishing features." Explain the relationship between these earlier meanings

and our current one connected with prejudice. Does the perception of distinctions or differences necessarily lead to prejudice?
4. Using the guidelines in the essay, examine a newspaper, a magazine, or a textbook for examples of sexism. Try to determine which examples reflect unconscious prejudice.
5. Study the examples in the guidelines carefully. Will the guidelines lead to greater clarity or precision? Less? Discuss.

ERICH FROMM
The Nature of Symbolic Language

Let us assume you want to tell someone the difference between the taste of white wine and red wine. This may seem quite simple to you. You know the difference very well; why should it not be easy to explain it to someone else? Yet you find the greatest difficulty putting this taste difference into words. And probably you will end up by saying, "Now look here, I can't explain it to you. Just drink red wine and then white wine, and you will know what the difference is." You have no difficulty in finding words to explain the most complicated machine, and yet words seem to be futile to describe a simple taste experience.

Are we not confronted with the same difficulty when we try to explain a feeling experience? Let us take a mood in which you feel lost, deserted, where the world looks gray, a little frightening though not really dangerous. You want to describe this mood to a friend, but again you find yourself groping for words and eventually feel that nothing you have said is an adequate explanation of the many nuances of the mood. The following night you have a dream. You see yourself in the outskirts of a city just before dawn, the streets are empty except for a milk wagon, the houses look poor, the surroundings are unfamiliar, you have no means of accustomed transportation to places familiar to you and where you feel you belong. When you wake up and remember the dream, it occurs to you that the feeling you had in that dream was exactly the feeling of lostness and grayness you tried to describe to your friend the day before. It is just one picture, whose visualization took less than a second. And yet this picture is a more vivid and precise description than you could have given by talking *about* it at length. The picture you see in the dream is a *symbol* of something you felt.

What is a symbol? A symbol is often defined as "something that stands for something else." This definition seems rather disappointing. It becomes more interesting, however, if we concern ourselves with those symbols which are sensory expressions of seeing, hearing, smelling, touching, standing for a "something else" which is an inner experience, a feeling or thought. A symbol of this kind is something outside ourselves; that which it symbolizes is something inside ourselves. Symbolic language is language in which we express inner experience as if it were a sensory experience, as if it were something we were doing or something that was done to us in the world of things. Symbolic language is language in which the world outside is a symbol of the world inside, a symbol for our souls and our minds.

If we define a symbol as "something which stands for something else," the crucial question is: *What is the specific connection between the symbol and that which it symbolizes?*

In answer to this question we can differentiate between three kinds of symbols: the *conventional*, the *accidental* and the *universal* symbol. As will become apparent presently, only the latter two kinds of symbols express inner experiences as if they were sensory experiences, and only they have the elements of symbolic language.

The *conventional* symbol is the best known of the three, since we employ it in everyday language. If we see the word "table" or hear the sound "table," the letters T-A-B-L-E stand for something else. They stand for the thing table that we see, touch and use. What is the connection between the *word* "table" and the *thing* "table"? Is there any inherent relationship between them? Obviously not. The thing table has nothing to do with the sound table, and the only reason the word symbolizes the thing is the convention of calling this particular thing by a particular name. We learn this connection as children by the repeated experience of hearing the word in reference to the thing until a lasting association is formed so that we don't have to think to find the right word.

There are some words, however, where the association is not only conventional. When we say "phooey," for instance, we make with our lips a movement of dispelling the air quickly. It is an expression of disgust in which our mouths participate. By this quick expulsion of air we imitate and thus express our intention to expel something, to get it out of our system. In this case, as in some others, the symbol has an inherent connection with the feeling it symbolizes. But even if we assume that originally many or even all words had their origins in some such inherent connection between symbol and the symbolized, most words no longer have this meaning for us when we learn a language.

Words are not the only illustration for conventional symbols, although they are the most frequent and best-known ones. Pictures also can be conventional symbols. A flag, for instance, may stand for a specific country, and yet there is no connection between the specific colors and the country for which they stand. They have been accepted as denoting that particular country, and we translate the visual impression of the flag into the concept of that country, again on conventional grounds. Some pictorial symbols are not entirely conventional; for example, the cross. The cross can be merely a conventional symbol of the Christian church and in that respect no different from a flag. But the specific content of the cross referring to Jesus' death or, beyond that, to the interpenetration of the material and spiritual planes, puts the connection between the symbol and what it symbolizes beyond the level of mere conventional symbols.

The very opposite to the conventional symbol is the *accidental* symbol, although they have one thing in common: there is no intrinsic relationship between the symbol and that which it symbolizes. Let us assume that someone has had a saddening experience in a certain city; when he hears the name of that city, he will easily connect the name with a mood of sadness, just as he would connect it with a mood of joy had his experience been a happy one. Quite obviously there is nothing in the nature of the city that is either sad or joyful. It is the individual experience connected with the city that makes it a symbol of a mood.

The same reaction could occur in connection with a house, a street, a certain dress, certain scenery, or anything once connected with a specific mood. We might find ourselves dreaming that we are in a certain city. In fact, there may be no particular mood connected with it in the dream; all we see is a street or even simply the name of the city. We ask ourselves why we happened to think of that city in our sleep and may discover that we had fallen asleep in a mood similar to the one symbolized by the city. The picture in the dream represents this mood, the city "stands for" the mood once experienced in it. Here the connection between the symbol and the experience symbolized is entirely accidental.

In contrast to the conventional symbol, the accidental symbol cannot be shared by anyone else except as we relate the events connected with the symbol. For this reason accidental symbols are rarely used in myths, fairy tales, or works of art written in symbolic language because they are not communicable unless the writer adds a lengthy comment to each symbol he uses. In dreams, however, accidental symbols are frequent. * * *

The *universal* symbol is one in which there is an intrinsic relationship between the symbol and that which it represents. We have already given one example, that of the outskirts of the city. The sensory experience of a deserted, strange, poor environment has indeed a significant relationship to a mood of lostness and anxiety. True enough, if we have never been in the outskirts of a city we could not use that symbol, just as the word "table" would be mean-

ingless had we never seen a table. This symbol is meaningful only
to city dwellers and would be meaningless to people living in cultures that have no big cities. Many other universal symbols, however, are rooted in the experience of every human being. Take, for
instance, the symbol of fire. We are fascinated by certain qualities
of fire in a fireplace. First of all, by its aliveness. It changes continuously, it moves all the time, and yet there is constancy in it. It
remains the same without being the same. It gives the impression of
power, of energy, of grace and lightness. It is as if it were dancing
and had an inexhaustible source of energy. When we use fire as a
symbol, we describe the inner experience characterized by the same
elements which we notice in the sensory experience of fire; the
mood of energy, lightness, movement, grace, gaiety—sometimes
one, sometimes another of these elements being predominant in the
feeling.

Similar in some ways and different in others is the symbol of
water—of the ocean or of the stream. Here, too, we find the blending of change and permanence, of constant movement and yet of
permanence. We also feel the quality of aliveness, continuity and
energy. But there is a difference; where fire is adventurous, quick,
exciting, water is quiet, slow and steady. Fire has an element of surprise; water an element of predictability. Water symbolizes the
mood of aliveness, too, but one which is "heavier," "slower," and
more comforting than exciting.

That a phenomenon of the physical world can be the adequate
expression of an inner experience, that the world of things can be a
symbol of the world of the mind, is not surprising. We all know
that our bodies express our minds. Blood rushes to our heads when
we are furious, it rushes away from them when we are afraid; our
hearts beat more quickly when we are angry, and the whole body
has a different tonus if we are happy from the one it has when we
are sad. We express our moods by our facial expressions and our
attitudes and feelings by movements and gestures so precise that
others recognize them more accurately from our gestures than from
our words. Indeed, the body is a symbol—and not an allegory—of
the mind. Deeply and genuinely felt emotion, and even any genuinely felt thought, is expressed in our whole organism. In the case
of the universal symbol, we find the same connection between
mental and physical experience. Certain physical phenomena suggest
by their very nature certain emotional and mental experiences, and
we express emotional experiences in the language of physical experiences, that is to say, symbolically.

The universal symbol is the only one in which the relationship
between the symbol and that which is symbolized is not coincidental but intrinsic. It is rooted in the experience of the affinity

between an emotion or thought, on the one hand, and a sensory experience, on the other. It can be called universal because it is shared by all men, in contrast not only to the accidental symbol, which is by its very nature entirely personal, but also to the conventional symbol, which is restricted to a group of people sharing the same convention. The universal symbol is rooted in the properties of our body, our senses, and our mind, which are common to all men and, therefore, not restricted to individuals or to specific groups. Indeed, the language of the universal symbol is the one common tongue developed by the human race, a language which it forgot before it succeeded in developing a universal conventional language.

There is no need to speak of a racial inheritance in order to explain the universal character of symbols. Every human being who shares the essential features of bodily and mental equipment with the rest of mankind is capable of speaking and understanding the symbolic language that is based upon these common properties. Just as we do not need to learn to cry when we are sad or to get red in the face when we are angry, and just as these reactions are not restricted to any particular race or group of people, symbolic language does not have to be learned and is not restricted to any segment of the human race. Evidence for this is to be found in the fact that symbolic language as it is employed in myths and dreams is found in all cultures—in so-called primitive as well as such highly developed cultures as Egypt and Greece. Furthermore, the symbols used in these various cultures are strikingly similar since they all go back to the basic sensory as well as emotional experiences shared by men of all cultures. Added evidence is to be found in recent experiments in which people who had no knowledge of the theory of dream interpretation were able, under hypnosis, to interpret the symbolism of their dreams without any difficulty. After emerging from the hypnotic state and being asked to interpret the same dreams, they were puzzled and said, "Well, there is no meaning to them—it is just nonsense."

The foregoing statement needs qualification, however. Some symbols differ in meaning according to the difference in their realistic significance in various cultures. For instance, the function and consequently the meaning of the sun is different in northern countries and in tropical countries. In northern countries, where water is plentiful, all growth depends on sufficient sunshine. The sun is the warm, life-giving, protecting, loving power. In the Near East, where the heat of the sun is much more powerful, the sun is a dangerous and even threatening power from which man must protect himself, while water is felt to be the source of all life and the main condition for growth. We may speak of dialects of universal symbolic language, which are determined by those differences in natural conditions which cause certain symbols to have a different meaning in different regions of the earth.

Quite different from these "symbolic dialects" is the fact that many symbols have more than one meaning in accordance with different kinds of experiences which can be connected with one and the same natural phenomenon. Let us take up the symbol of fire again. If we watch fire in the fireplace, which is a source of pleasure and comfort, it is expressive of a mood of aliveness, warmth, and pleasure. But if we see a building or forest on fire, it conveys to us an experience of threat or terror, of the powerlessness of man against the elements of nature. Fire, then, can be the symbolic representation of inner aliveness and happiness as well as of fear, powerlessness, or of one's own destructive tendencies. The same holds true of the symbol water. Water can be a most destructive force when it is whipped up by a storm or when a swollen river floods its banks. Therefore, it can be the symbolic expression of horror and chaos as well as of comfort and peace.

Another illustration of the same principle is a symbol of a valley. The valley enclosed between mountains can arouse in us the feeling of security and comfort, of protection against all dangers from the outside. But the protecting mountains can also mean isolating walls which do not permit us to get out of the valley and thus the valley can become a symbol of imprisonment. The particular meaning of the symbol in any given place can only be determined from the whole context in which the symbol appears, and in terms of the predominant experiences of the person using the symbol. * * *

A good illustration of the function of the universal symbol is a story, written in symbolic language, which is known to almost everyone in Western culture: the Book of Jonah. Jonah has heard God's voice telling him to go to Nineveh and preach to its inhabitants to give up their evil ways lest they be destroyed. Jonah cannot help hearing God's voice and that is why he is a prophet. But he is an unwilling prophet, who, though knowing what he should do, tries to run away from the command of God (or, as we may say, the voice of his conscience). He is a man who does not care for other human beings. He is a man with a strong sense of law and order, but without love.

How does the story express the inner processes in Jonah?

We are told that Jonah went down to Joppa and found a ship which should bring him to Tarshish. In mid-ocean a storm rises and, while everyone else is excited and afraid, Jonah goes into the ship's belly and falls into a deep sleep. The sailors, believing that God must have sent the storm because someone on the ship is to be punished, wake Jonah, who had told them he was trying to flee from God's command. He tells them to take him and cast him forth into the sea and that the sea would then become calm. The sailors (betraying a remarkable sense of humanity by first trying everything else before following his advice) eventually take Jonah and cast him into the sea, which immediately stops raging. Jonah is swallowed by a big fish and stays in the fish's belly three days and three nights. He prays to God to free him from this prison. God makes the fish vomit out Jonah unto the dry land and Jonah goes to Nineveh, fulfills God's command, and thus saves the inhabitants of the city.

The story is told as if these events had actually happened. However, it is written in symbolic language and all the realistic events described are symbols for the inner experiences of the hero. We find a sequence of symbols which follow one another: going into the ship, going into the ship's belly, falling asleep, being in the ocean, and being in the fish's belly. All these symbols stand for the same inner experience: for a condition of being protected and isolated, of safe withdrawal from communication with other human beings. They represent what could be represented in another symbol, the fetus in the mother's womb. Different as the ship's belly, deep sleep, the ocean, and a fish's belly are realistically, they are expressive of the same inner experience, of the blending between protection and isolation.

In the manifest story events happen in space and time: *first*, going into the ship's belly; *then*, falling asleep; *then*, being thrown into the ocean; *then*, being swallowed by the fish. One thing happens after the other and, although some events are obviously unrealistic, the story has its own logical consistency in terms of time and space. But if we understand that the writer did not intend to tell us the story of external events, but of the inner experience of a man torn between his conscience and his wish to escape from his inner voice, it becomes clear that his various actions following one after the other express the same mood in him; and that *sequence in time* is expressive of a *growing intensity* of the same feeling. In his attempt to escape from his obligation to his fellow men Jonah isolates himself more and more until, in the belly of the fish, the protective element has so given way to the imprisoning element that he can stand it no longer and is forced to pray to God to be released from where he had put himself. (This is a mechanism which we find so characteristic of neurosis. An attitude is assumed as a defense against a danger, but then it grows far beyond its original defense function and becomes a neurotic symptom from which the person tries to be relieved.) Thus Jonah's escape into protective isolation ends in the terror of being imprisoned, and he takes up his life at the point where he had tried to escape.

There is another difference between the logic of the manifest and of the latent story. In the manifest story the logical connection is one of causality of external events. Jonah wants to go overseas *because* he wants to flee from God, he falls asleep *because* he is tired, he is thrown overboard *because* he is supposed to be the reason for the storm, and he is swallowed by the fish *because* there are man-eating fish in the ocean. One event occurs because of a previous event. (The last part of the story is unrealistic but not illogical.) But in the latent story the logic is different. The various events are related to each other by their association with the same inner experience. What appears to be a causal sequence of external events stand for a connection of experiences linked with each other by their association in terms of inner events. This is as logical as the manifest story—but it is a logic of a different kind. * * *

1951

GEORGE ORWELL
Politics and the English Language

Most people who bother with the matter at all would admit that the English language is in a bad way, but it is generally assumed that we cannot by conscious action do anything about it. Our civilization is decadent and our language—so the argument runs—must inevitably share in the general collapse. It follows that any struggle against the abuse of language is a sentimental archaism, like preferring candles to electric light or hansom cabs to aeroplanes. Underneath this lies the half-conscious belief that language is a natural growth and not an instrument which we shape for our own purposes.

Now, it is clear that the decline of a language must ultimately have political and economic causes: it is not due simply to the bad influence of this or that individual writer. But an effect can become a cause, reinforcing the original cause and producing the same effect in an intensified form, and so on indefinitely. A man may take to drink because he feels himself to be a failure, and then fail all the more completely because he drinks. It is rather the same thing that is happening to the English language. It becomes ugly and inaccurate because our thoughts are foolish, but the slovenliness of our language makes it easier for us to have foolish thoughts. The point is that the process is reversible. Modern English, especially written English, is full of bad habits which spread by imitation and which can be avoided if one is willing to take the necessary trouble. If one gets rid of these habits one can think more clearly, and to think clearly is a necessary first step towards political regeneration: so that the fight against bad English is not frivolous and is not the exclusive concern of professional writers. I will come back to this presently, and I hope that by that time the meaning of what I have said here will have become clearer. Meanwhile, here are five specimens of the English language as it is now habitually written.

These five passages have not been picked out because they are especially bad—I could have quoted far worse if I had chosen—but because they illustrate various of the mental vices from which we now suffer. They are a little below the average, but are fairly representative samples. I number them so that I can refer back to them when necessary:

"(1) I am not, indeed, sure whether it is not true to say that the Milton who once seemed not unlike a seventeenth-century Shelley had not become, out of an experience ever more bitter in each year, more alien [*sic*] to the founder of that Jesuit sect which nothing could induce him to tolerate."

Professor Harold Laski (Essay in *Freedom of Expression*).

"(2) Above all, we cannot play ducks and drakes with a native battery of idioms which prescribes such egregious collocations of vocables as the Basic *put up with* for *tolerate* or *put at a loss* for *bewilder*."

Professor Lancelot Hogben (*Interglossa*).

"(3) On the one side we have the free personality: by definition it is not neurotic, for it has neither conflict nor dream. Its desires, such as they are, are transparent, for they are just what institutional approval keeps in the forefront of consciousness; another institutional pattern would alter their number and intensity; there is little in them that is natural, irreducible, or culturally dangerous. But *on the other side*, the social bond itself is nothing but the mutual reflection of these self-secure integrities. Recall the definition of love. Is not this the very picture of a small academic? Where is there a place in this hall of mirrors for either personality or fraternity?"

Essay on psychology in *Politics* (New York).

"(4) All the 'best people' from the gentlemen's clubs, and all the frantic fascist captains, united in common hatred of Socialism and bestial horror of the rising tide of the mass revolutionary movement, have turned to acts of provocation, to foul incendiarism, to medieval legends of poisoned wells, to legalize their own destruction of proletarian organizations, and rouse the agitated petty-bourgeoisie to chauvinistic fervour on behalf of the fight against the revolutionary way out of the crisis."

Communist pamphlet.

"(5) If a new spirit *is* to be infused into this old country, there is one thorny and contentious reform which must be tackled, and that is the humanization and galvanization of the B.B.C. Timidity here will bespeak cancer and atrophy of the soul. The heart of Britain may be sound and of strong beat, for instance, but the British lion's roar at present is like that of Bottom in Shakespeare's *Midsummer Night's Dream*—as gentle as any sucking dove. A virile new Britain cannot continue indefinitely to be traduced in the eyes or rather ears, of the world by the effete languors of Langham Place, brazenly masquerading as 'standard English'. When the Voice of Britain is heard at nine o'clock, better far and infinitely less ludicrous to hear aitches honestly dropped than the present priggish, inflated, inhibited, school-ma'amish arch braying of blameless bashful mewing maidens!"

Letter in *Tribune*.

Each of these passages has faults of its own, but, quite apart from avoidable ugliness, two qualities are common to all of them. The first is staleness of imagery: the other is lack of precision. The writer either has a meaning and cannot express it, or he inadvertently says something else, or he is almost indifferent as to whether his words mean anything or not. This mixture of vagueness and sheer incompetence is the most marked characteristic of modern English prose, and especially of any kind of political writing. As soon as certain topics are raised, the concrete melts into the abstract and no one seems able to think of turns of speech that are not hackneyed: prose consists less and less of *words* chosen for the sake of their meaning, and more and more of *phrases* tacked together like the sections of a prefabricated hen-house. I list below, with notes and examples, various of the tricks by means of which the work of prose-construction is habitually dodged:

Dying Metaphors

A newly invented metaphor assists thought by evoking a visual image, while on the other hand a metaphor which is technically "dead" (e.g. *iron resolution*) has in effect reverted to being an ordinary word and can generally be used without loss of vividness. But in between these two classes there is a huge dump of worn-out metaphors which have lost all evocative power and are merely used because they save people the trouble of inventing phrases for themselves. Examples are: *Ring the changes on, take up the cudgels for, toe the line, ride roughshod over, stand shoulder to shoulder with, play into the hands of, no axe to grind, grist to the mill, fishing in troubled waters, on the order of the day, Achilles' heel, swan song, hotbed.* Many of these are used without knowledge of their meaning (what is a "rift", for instance?), and incompatible metaphors are frequently mixed, a sure sign that the writer is not interested in what he is saying. Some metaphors now current have been twisted out of their original meaning without those who use them even being aware of the fact. For example, *toe the line* is sometimes written *tow the line*. Another example is *the hammer and the anvil*, now always used with the implication that the anvil gets the worst of it. In real life it is always the anvil that breaks the hammer, never the other way about: a writer who stopped to think what he was saying would be aware of this, and would avoid perverting the original phrase.

Operators or Verbal False Limbs

These save the trouble of picking out appropriate verbs and nouns, and at the same time pad each sentence with extra syllables which give it an appearance of symmetry. Characteristic phrases are: *render inoperative, militate against, make contact with, be subjected to, give rise to, give grounds for, have the effect of, play a leading part (role) in, make itself felt, take effect, exhibit a tendency to, serve the purpose of, etc., etc.* The keynote is the elimination of simple verbs. Instead of being a single word, such as *break, stop, spoil, mend, kill,* a verb becomes a *phrase,* made up of a noun or adjective tacked on to some general-purposes verb such as *prove, serve, form, play, render.* In addition, the passive voice is wherever possible used in preference to the active, and noun constructions are used instead of gerunds (*by examination of* instead of *by examining*). The range of verbs is further cut down by means of the *-ize* and *de-* formation, and the banal statements are given an appearance of profundity by means of the *not un-* formation. Simple conjunctions and prepositions are replaced by such phrases as *with respect to, having regard to, the fact that, by dint of, in view of, in the interests of, on the hypothesis that;* and the ends of sentences are saved from anticlimax by such resounding commonplaces as *greatly to be desired, cannot be left out of account, a development to be expected in the near future, deserving of serious consideration, brought to a satisfactory conclusion,* and so on and so forth.

Pretentious Diction

Words like *phenomenon, element, individual* (as noun), *objective, categorical, effective, virtual, basic, primary, promote, constitute, exhibit, exploit, utilize, eliminate, liquidate,* are used to dress up simple statements and give an air of scientific impartiality to biased judgments. Adjectives like *epoch-making, epic, historic, unforgettable, triumphant, age-old, inevitable, inexorable, veritable,* are used to dignify the sordid processes of international politics, while writing that aims at glorifying war usually takes on an archaic colour, its characteristic words being: *realm, throne, chariot, mailed fist, trident, sword, shield, buckler, banner, jackboot, clarion.* Foreign words and expressions such as *cul de sac, ancien régime, deus ex machina, mutatis mutandis, status quo, gleichschaltung, weltanschauung,* are used to give an air of culture and elegance. Except for the useful abbreviations *i.e., e.g.,* and *etc.,* there is no real need for any of the hundreds of foreign phrases now current in English. Bad writers, and especially scientific, political and sociological writers, are nearly always haunted by the notion that Latin or Greek words are grander than Saxon ones, and unnecessary words like *expedite, ameliorate, predict, extraneous, deracinated, clandestine, subaqueous* and hundreds of others constantly gain ground from their Anglo-Saxon opposite numbers.[1] The jargon peculiar to Marxist writing (*hyena, hangman, cannibal, petty bourgeois, these gentry, lacquey, flunkey, mad dog, White Guard,* etc.) consists largely of words and phrases translated from Russian, German or French; but the normal way of coining a new word is to use a Latin or Greek root with the appropriate affix and, where necessary, the *-ize* formation. It is often easier to make up words of this kind (*deregionalize, impermissible, extramarital, nonfragmentatory* and so forth) than to think up the English words that will cover one's meaning. The result, in general, is an increase in slovenliness and vagueness.

Meaningless Words

In certain kinds of writing, particularly in art criticism and literary criticism, it is normal to come across long passages which are almost completely lacking in meaning.[2] Words like *romantic, plastic, values, human, dead, sentimental, natural, vitality,* as used in art criticism, are strictly meaningless in the sense that they not only do not point to any discoverable object, but are hardly ever expected to do so by the reader. When one critic writes, "The outstanding feature of Mr. X's work is its living quality", while another writes, "The immediately striking thing about Mr. X's work is its peculiar deadness", the reader accepts this as a simple difference of opinion. If words like *black* and *white* were involved, instead of the jargon words *dead* and *living,* he would see at once that language was being used in an improper way. Many political words are similarly abused. The word *Fascism* has now no meaning except in so far as it signifies "something not desirable". The words *democracy, socialism, freedom, patriotic, realistic, justice,* have each of them several different meanings which cannot be reconciled with one another. In the case of a word like *democracy,* not only is there no agreed definition, but the attempt to make one is resisted from all sides. It is almost universally felt that when we call a country democratic we are praising it: consequently the defenders of every kind of régime

1. An interesting illustration of this is the way in which the English flower names which were in use till very recently are being ousted by Greek ones, *snapdragon* becoming *antirrhinum, forget-me-not* becoming *myosotis,* etc. It is hard to see any practical reason for this change of fashion: it is probably due to an instinctive turning-away from the more homely word and a vague feeling that the Greek word is scientific. [Orwell's note].

2. Example: "Comfort's catholicity of perception and image, strangely Whitmanesque in range, almost the exact opposite in aesthetic compulsion, continues to evoke that trembling atmospheric accumulative hinting at a cruel, an inexorably serene timelessness ... Wrey Gardiner scores by aiming at simple bull's-eyes with precision. Only they are not so simple, and through this contented sadness runs more than the surface bittersweet of resignation" (*Poetry Quarterly*) [Orwell's note].

claim that it is a democracy, and fear that they might have to stop using the word if it were tied down to any one meaning. Words of this kind are often used in a consciously dishonest way. That is, the person who uses them has his own private definition, but allows his hearer to think he means something quite different. Statements like *Marshal Pétain was a true patriot, The Soviet Press is the freest in the world, The Catholic Church is opposed to persecution,* are almost always made with intent to deceive. Other words used in variable meanings, in most cases more or less dishonestly, are: *class, totalitarian, science, progressive, reactionary, bourgeois, equality.*

Now that I have made this catalogue of swindles and perversions, let me give another example of the kind of writing that they lead to. This time it must of its nature be an imaginary one. I am going to translate a passage of good English into modern English of the worst sort. Here is a well-known verse from *Ecclesiastes*:

"I returned and saw under the sun, that the race is not to the swift, nor the battle to the strong, neither yet bread to the wise, nor yet riches to men of understanding, nor yet favour to men of skill; but time and chance happeneth to them all."

Here it is in modern English:

"Objective consideration of contemporary phenomena compels the conclusion that success or failure in competitive activities exhibits no tendency to be commensurate with innate capacity, but that a considerable element of the unpredictable must invariably be taken into account."

This is a parody, but not a very gross one. Exhibit (3), above, for instance, contains several patches of the same kind of English. It will be seen that I have not made a full translation. The beginning and ending of the sentence follow the original meaning fairly closely, but in the middle the concrete illustrations—race, battle, bread—dissolve into the vague phrase "success or failure in competitive activities". This had to be so, because no modern writer of the kind I am discussing—no one capable of using phrases like "objective consideration of contemporary phenomena"—would ever tabulate his thoughts in that precise and detailed way. The whole tendency of modern prose is away from concreteness. Now analyse these two sentences a little more closely. The first contains forty-nine words but only sixty syllables, and all its words are those of everyday life. The second contains thirty-eight words of ninety syllables: eighteen of its words are from Latin roots, and one from Greek. The first sentence contains six vivid images, and only one phrase ("time and chance") that could be called vague. The second contains not a single fresh, arresting phrase, and in spite of its ninety syllables it gives only a shortened version of the meaning contained in the first. Yet without a doubt it is the second kind of sentence that is gaining ground in modern English. I do not want to exaggerate. This kind of writing is not yet universal, and outcrops of simplicity will occur here and there in the worst-written page. Still, if you or I were told to write a few lines on the uncertainty of human fortunes, we should probably come much nearer to my imaginary sentence than to the one from *Ecclesiastes*.

As I have tried to show, modern writing at its worst does not consist in picking out words for the sake of their meaning and inventing images in order to make the meaning clearer. It consists in gumming together long strips of words which have already been set in order by someone else, and making the results presentable by sheer humbug. The attraction of this way of writing is that it is easy. It is easier—even quicker, once you have the habit—to say *In my opinion it is a not unjustifiable assumption that* than to say *I think*. If you use ready-made phrases, you not only don't have to hunt about for words; you also don't have to bother with the rhythms of your sentences, since these phrases are generally so arranged as to be more or less euphonious. When you are composing in a hurry—when you are dictating to a stenographer, for instance, or making a public speech—it is natural to fall into a pretentious, Latinized style. Tags like *a consideration which we should do well to bear in mind* or *a conclusion to which all of us would readily assent* will save many a sentence from coming down with a bump. By using stale metaphors, similes and idioms, you save much mental effort, at the cost of leaving your meaning vague, not only for your reader but for yourself. This is the significance of mixed metaphors. The sole aim of a metaphor is to call up a visual image. When these images clash—as in *The Fascist octopus has sung its swan song, the jackboot is thrown into the melting pot*—it can be taken as certain that the writer is not seeing a mental image of the objects he is naming; in other words he is not really thinking. Look again at the examples I gave at the beginning of this essay. Professor Laski (1) uses five negatives in fifty-three words. One of these is superfluous, making nonsense of the whole passage, and in addition there is the slip *alien* for akin, making further nonsense, and several avoidable pieces of clumsiness which increase the general vagueness. Professor Hogben (2) plays ducks and drakes with a battery which is able to write prescriptions, and, while disapproving of the everyday phrase *put up with*, is unwilling to look *egregious* up in the dictionary and see what it means. (3), if one takes an uncharitable attitude towards it, is simply meaningless: probably one could work out its intended meaning by reading the whole of the article in which it occurs. In (4), the writer knows more or less what he wants to say, but an accumulation of stale phrases chokes him like tea leaves blocking a sink. In (5), words and meaning have almost parted company. People who write in this manner usually have a general emotional meaning—they dislike one thing and want to express solidarity with another—but they are not interested in the detail of what they are saying. A scrupulous writer, in every sentence that he writes, will ask himself at least four questions, thus: What am I trying to say? What words will express it? What image or idiom will make it clearer? Is this image fresh enough to have an effect? And he will probably ask himself two more: Could I put it more shortly? Have I said anything that is avoidably ugly? But you are not obliged to go to all this trouble. You can shirk it by simply throwing your mind open and letting the ready-made phrases come crowding in. They will construct your sentences for you—even think your thoughts for you, to a certain extent—and at need they will perform the important service of partially concealing your meaning even from yourself. It is at this point that the special connection between politics and the debasement of language becomes clear.

In our time it is broadly true that political writing is bad writing. Where it is not true, it will generally be found that the writer is some kind of rebel, expressing his private opinions and not a "party line". Orthodoxy, of whatever colour, seems to demand a lifeless, imitative style. The political dialects to be found in pamphlets, leading articles, manifestos, White Papers and the speeches of under-secretaries do, of course, vary from party to party, but they are all alike in that one almost never finds in them a fresh, vivid, home-made turn of speech. When one watches some tired hack on the platform mechanically repeating the familiar phrases—*bestial atrocities, iron heel, bloodstained tyranny, free peoples of the world, stand shoulder to shoulder*—one often has a curious feeling that one is not watching a live human being but some kind of dummy: a feeling which suddenly becomes stronger at moments when the light catches the speaker's spectacles and turns them into blank discs which seem to have no eyes behind them. And this is not altogether fanciful. A speaker who uses that kind of phraseology has gone some distance towards turning himself into a machine. The appropriate noises are coming out of his larynx, but his brain is not involved as it would be if he were choosing his words for himself. If the speech he is making is one that he is accustomed to make over and over again, he may be almost unconscious of what he is saying, as one is when one utters the responses in church. And this reduced state of consciousness, if not indispensable, is at any rate favourable to political conformity.

In our time, political speech and writing are largely the defence of the indefensible. Things like the continuance of British rule in India, the Russian purges and deportations, the dropping of the atom bombs on Japan, can indeed be defended, but only by arguments which are too brutal for most people to face, and which do not square with the professed aims of political parties. Thus political language has to consist largely of euphemism, question-begging and sheer cloudy vagueness. Defenceless villages are bombarded from the air, the inhabitants driven out into the countryside, the cattle machine-gunned, the huts set on fire with incendiary bullets: this is called *pacification*. Millions of peasants are robbed of their farms and sent trudging along the roads with no more than they can carry: this is called *transfer of population* or *rectification of frontiers*. People are imprisoned for years without trial, or shot in the back of the neck or sent to die of scurvy in Arctic lumber camps: this is called *elimination of unreliable elements*. Such phraseology is needed if one wants to name things without calling up mental pictures of them. Consider for instance some comfortable English professor defending Russian totalitarianism. He cannot say outright, "I believe in killing off your opponents when you can get good results by doing so". Probably, therefore, he will say something like this:

"While freely conceding that the Soviet régime exhibits certain features which the humanitarian may be inclined to deplore, we must, I think, agree that a certain curtailment of the right to political opposition is an unavoidable concomitant of transitional periods, and that the rigours which the Russian people have been called upon to undergo have been amply justified in the sphere of concrete achievement."

The inflated style is itself a kind of euphemism. A mass of Latin words falls upon the facts like soft snow, blurring the outlines and covering up all the details. The great enemy of clear language is insincerity. When there is a gap between one's real and one's declared aims, one turns as it were instinctively to long words and exhausted idioms, like a cuttlefish squirting out ink. In our age there is no such thing as "keeping out of politics". All issues are political issues, and politics itself is a mass of lies, evasions, folly, hatred and schizophrenia. When the general atmosphere is bad, language must suffer. I should expect to find—this is a guess which I have not sufficient knowledge to verify—that the German, Russian and Italian languages have all deteriorated in the last ten or fifteen years, as a result of dictatorship.

But if thought corrupts language, language can also corrupt thought. A bad usage can spread by tradition and imitation, even among people who should and do know better. The debased language that I have been discussing is in some ways very convenient. Phrases like *a not unjustifiable assumption, leaves much to be desired, would serve no good purpose, a consideration which we should do well to bear in mind,* are a continuous temptation, a packet of aspirins always at one's elbow. Look back through this essay, and for certain you will find that I have again and again committed the very faults I am protesting against. By this morning's post I have received a pamphlet dealing with conditions in Germany. The author tells me that he "felt impelled" to write it. I open it at random, and here is almost the first sentence that I see: "(The Allies) have an opportunity not only of achieving a radical transformation of Germany's social and political structure in such a way as to avoid a nationalistic reaction in Germany itself, but at the same time of laying the foundations of a co-operative and unified Europe." You see, he "feels impelled" to write—feels, presumably, that he has something new to say—and yet his words, like cavalry horses answering the bugle, group themselves automatically into the familiar dreary pattern. This invasion of one's mind by ready-made phrases (*lay the foundations, achieve a radical transformation*) can only be prevented if one is constantly on guard against them, and every such phrase anaesthetizes a portion of one's brain.

I said earlier that the decadence of our language is probably curable. Those who deny this would argue, if they produced an argument at all, that language merely reflects existing social conditions, and that we cannot influence its development by any direct tinkering with words and constructions. So far as the general tone or spirit of a language goes, this may be true, but it is not true in detail. Silly words and expressions have often disappeared, not through any evolutionary process but owing to the conscious action of a minority. Two recent examples were *explore every avenue* and *leave no stone unturned*, which were killed by the jeers of a few journalists. There is a long list of flyblown metaphors which could similarly be got rid of if enough people would interest themselves in the job; and it should also be possible to laugh the *not un-* formation out of existence,[3] to reduce the amount of Latin and Greek in the average sentence, to drive out foreign phrases and strayed scientific words, and, in general, to make pretentiousness unfashionable. But all these are minor points. The defence of the English language implies more than this, and perhaps it is best to start by saying what it does *not* imply.

To begin with it has nothing to do with archaism, with the salvaging of obsolete words and turns of speech, or with the setting up of a "standard English" which must never be departed from. On the contrary, it is especially concerned with the scrapping of every word or idiom which has outworn its usefulness. It has nothing to do with correct grammar and syntax, which are of no importance so long as one makes one's meaning clear, or with the avoidance of

---

3. One can cure oneself of the *not un-* formation by memorizing this sentence: *A not unblack dog was chasing a not unsmall rabbit across a not ungreen field* [Orwell's note].

Americanisms, or with having what is called a "good prose style". On the other hand it is not concerned with fake simplicity and the attempt to make written English colloquial. Nor does it even imply in every case preferring the Saxon word to the Latin one, though it does imply using the fewest and shortest words that will cover one's meaning. What is above all needed is to let the meaning choose the word, and not the other way about. In prose, the worst thing one can do with words is to surrender to them. When you think of a concrete object, you think wordlessly, and then, if you want to describe the thing you have been visualizing you probably hunt about till you find the exact words that seem to fit. When you think of something abstract you are more inclined to use words from the start, and unless you make a conscious effort to prevent it, the existing dialect will come rushing in and do the job for you, at the expense of blurring or even changing your meaning. Probably it is better to put off using words as long as possible and get one's meaning as clear as one can through pictures or sensations. Afterwards one can choose—not simply *accept*—the phrases that will best cover the meaning, and then switch round and decide what impression one's words are likely to make on another person. This last effort of the mind cuts out all stale or mixed images, all prefabricated phrases, needless repetitions, and humbug and vagueness generally. But one can often be in doubt about the effect of a word or a phrase, and one needs rules that one can rely on when instinct fails. I think the following rules will cover most cases:

(i) **Never use** a metaphor, simile or other figure of speech which you are used to seeing in print.

(ii) **Never use** a long word where a short one will do.

(iii) If it is possible to cut a word out, always cut it out.

(iv) **Never use** the passive where you can use the active.

(v) **Never use** a foreign phrase, a scientific word or a jargon word if you can think of an everyday English equivalent.

(vi) Break any of these rules sooner than say anything outright barbarous.

These rules sound elementary, and so they are, but they demand a deep change of attitude in anyone who has grown used to writing in the style now fashionable. One could keep all of them and still write bad English, but one could not write the kind of stuff that I quoted in those five specimens at the beginning of this article.

I have not here been considering the literary use of language, but merely language as an instrument for expressing and not for concealing or preventing thought. Stuart Chase and others have come near to claiming that all abstract words are meaningless, and have used this as a pretext for advocating a kind of political quietism. Since you don't know what Fascism is, how can you struggle against

Fascism? One need not swallow such absurdities as this, but one ought to recognize that the present political chaos is connected with the decay of language, and that one can probably bring about some improvement by starting at the verbal end. If you simplify your English, you are freed from the worst follies of orthodoxy. You cannot speak any of the necessary dialects, and when you make a stupid remark its stupidity will be obvious, even to yourself. Political language—and with variations this is true of all political parties, from Conservatives to Anarchists—is designed to make lies sound truthful and murder respectable, and to give an appearance of solidity to pure wind. One cannot change this all in a moment, but one can at least change one's own habits, and from time to time one can even, if one jeers loudly enough, send some worn-out and useless phrase—some *jackboot, Achilles' heel, hotbed, melting pot, acid test, veritable inferno* or other lump of verbal refuse—into the dustbin where it belongs.

1946

QUESTIONS

1. What is Orwell's pivotal point? Where is it best stated?
2. Discuss Orwell's assertion that "the decline of a language must ultimately have political and economic causes." Is this "clear" as he claims?
3. How can you be sure that a metaphor is dying, rather than alive or dead? Is Orwell's test of seeing it often in print a sufficient one? Can you defend any of his examples of dying metaphors as necessary or useful additions to our vocabularies?
4. Orwell gives a list of questions for the writer to ask himself (p. 207) and a list of rules for the writer to follow (p. 210). Why does he consider it necessary to give both kinds of advice? How much do the two overlap? Are both consistent with Orwell's major ideas expressed elsewhere in the essay? Does his injunction to "break any of these rules sooner than say anything outright barbarous" beg the question?
5. Orwell suggests that if you look back through his essay you will find that he has "again and again committed the very faults" he is protesting against. Is this true? If it is, does it affect the validity of his major points?
6. Words create a personality or confer a character. Describe the personality that would be created by following Orwell's six rules; show that character in action.

HORACE M. KALLEN

Style and Meaning

I

My friend is an editor, but he has high ideals. One day we lunched together, and our talk turned upon the matter of literary style. The occasion was a paper of mine in which. I had used some hard technical words that he wanted me to change. He was manifestly diffident about asking the change, but his literary conscience was troubled, and his duty to his readers was plain. Against both his inclination and his duty I had no wish to offer any resistance; he was too whole-souled about the matter, and even momentary wholeness of soul is a rare and beautiful thing. The one phrase which I could not change was, however, just the one he had found most trying. I had written of the span of our human life as a process of "maturation and senescence." "What does that mean," he said with gentle emphasis, "other than growing up and growing old?" He said other things, too, but I have forgotten what they were; I was too full of my retort to hear anything more.

What, in his literary conscience, troubled my friend about that phrase was the feeling that it added nothing and obscured much in the meaning of the words. On behalf of his readers he felt that it augmented the strain of reading and taxed the mind unnecessarily. I think he added also that it was ponderous and harsh. Wasteful, inelegant, dissonant, these are charges sufficient to condemn any phrase to death.

All of them, I think, are conventional charges, and false charges, drawn without thinking because of a false tradition concerning the nature of style and the relation of style to meaning: the tradition of the rhetorician who fixes the outlines of the dead externals of diction and sets them up as measures for the living word; the tradition of a class of men of letters to whom the best way of writing is the way easiest to read, without regard to accuracy in stating intent, or adequacy in giving it form. Accuracy rests upon vocabulary; form is the consequence of logical order unfolding in time. These elements stand out in style, but they are not the fundamentals. The fundamental in every style is the rhythmic idiosyncrasy of its movement. Without that we could not possibly perceive the intent of thought, or get to the total significance of expression. It is to speech exactly what it is to music. It generates and deposits words; *which* words is determined by the thought's own pulse and cadences, that orders them as a magnetic flow orders iron filings or a stream carries leaves. In poetry this is obvious, or should be, particularly in the *vers*

212

libre.[1] In prose it is not so obvious, but it is none the less a fact. Eloquence need have no content; it works by infection, not signification; anybody who has heard a performance by the late Mr. William Jennings Bryan[2] knows that. The written word is even more dependent upon the transmission of the inward pulse for its effect, for it is not carried by a voice. Rhythm is characteristic, individual, the essence of personality in style.

The other element of style is what the rhetoricians call diction. This is the more fixable quality, easier of analysis, easier to talk about. Rhetoric books and editors' minds and writers' dispositions are full of rules about how and what and when and where to choose among words. But I have not noticed that these rules ever helped an aspiring writer, although I have many friends who declare that they have learned by means of them to distinguish between good and bad writing. The rules are, in fact, retrospective; if they help you at all, which is doubtful, they help you to identify excellence after it has been created, but as for creating it—as well accomplish fatherhood by studying anatomy. Editors, critics, reviewers and other middlemen between writers and publics may be well enough aware of this truth. But their own share of the sloth innate to mankind automatically disregards it. They prefer the familiar to the new, the vague to the specific, the similar to the same. Because it is easier, they would rather identify than distinguish. A false clearness attained by short and simple common words is more welcome to them than a true one achieved with correct long and strange ones. Their vocation reënforces their inertia. They are afraid of anything that by challenging a reader's effort may raise his resistance. For them the foremost rule is to choose that word which will tax the mind of the reader least. So, since it requires less effort to understand "growing up" than "maturation," and "growing old" than "senescence," choose "growing up" and "growing old" and throw "maturation" and "sensecence" to the dogs, and call this consequence of laziness and fear good writing.

II

Which goes to show that literary middlemen are quite as wrong about words as rhetoricians, and as innocent of their relation to the spirit as the priests who preach the Word. I should like to change the adage that a man is known by the company he keeps into the adage that a man is known by the vocabulary he keeps. A man can be separated from his company, even if it be that Freudful haunt, his mother. His vocabulary, however, is his very soul; when that

---

1. Free verse, written without rhyme or regular meter.
2. American politician (1860–1925) noted for the power of his oratorical style.

changes, his nature alters; the words he spontaneously and habitually uses are the lasting cores of his thoughts, the furniture of his mind, the framework and order of the world he lives in. But neither rhetoricians nor literary middlemen are more than dimly aware of this. They observe that words have certain vague, elusive overtones of meaning. They call these "connotation," mutter a few generalizations about its rôle in the making of a style, and pass to another thing which they call "denotation." By "denotation" they intend to designate the precise meaning of a word. This, they imagine, being explicit, specific, and tangible, can be measured and defined; and since the aim of prose writing must be the lucid transmission of meaning, the word that sets a given thing easily before the mind, and no more, is the word to use. The denotation of "growing up" is the same as that of "maturation," of "growing old" the same as of "senescence." Why, then, burden the reader's understanding with such heavy weights as "maturation" and "senescence"?

Because, dear editor, there exists no word with a meaning explicit, specific, and tangible. Meanings are as subtle fluids. Words are like barren stream-beds into and out of which the meanings are continuously flowing, stirring them to fruitfulness and life. All words, consequently, are ambiguous. And for this reason a word's denotation is the most unimportant and trivial property it possesses, except for logicians. The import of things lies in what relations they bear to other things. Their dangers and uses, their excellences and defects, their total worth derive from these. A thing is a center through which unnumbered lines of connection pass, as an infinity of lines pass through an identical point in space. The words which designate any given thing do more than merely place and denote and identify it. Each sets in relief one strand of its relationships against all the others, and it is by these relations that the working meaning of the word is defined, not by the thing. Assume, for example, that the denotations of "senescence" and "growing old" are identical, that both designate a seasonal ebbing and depletion of existence, a slowing down and disintegration of the machinery of human life. But "growing old" relates this process to the visible social semblance of a man, to a wrinkling of skin, a whitening and falling out of hair, a stooping of shoulders, a loss of memory and reasonableness, while "senescence" links it with the system of inward physiological changes, deterioration of cell-structure, deposit of mineral salts, and so on. Water and hydroxide, salt and sodium chloride, any group of synonyms you choose, denote precisely the same things, but their *meaning* is the systems of relationships they set these things in. To Spinoza[3] and his followers God and Nature

---

3. Baruch (or Benedict) de **Spinoza**, seventeenth-century Dutch philosopher.

have an identical denotation. But Spinoza himself distinguishes their meanings: God linking all reality with the tradition of conscious supernatural power, Nature with the mathematical order and material mechanisms of the physical world. Identical though these words are in denotation, God relates what it denotes to the aspirations of the heart while Nature relates the same thing to the operations of the intelligence. Words are keys which unlock identical doors on different vistas. Import and importance are due to the vistas alone. Ultimately they define our appreciation of the character and status of those things we mind because we wish, and those we mind because we must. The words that open them to us determine by so doing our theories of life for us. They are the body of our philosophies. People who think of "growing old" as "senescence" and people who think of "senescence" as "growing old" hold, in fact, radically different, if not opposed, *Weltanschauungen.*[4]

III

Nor is this the end. The full, rich meanings which words have at the height of their significational function tend to contract, even as their denotation tends to become irrelevant. The meanings compenetrate upon the point instead of expanding over the view of the point-of-view. They cease to awaken the intelligence to the perception of relationships and serve only to stir the emotion to irrelevant response. Instead of opening the doors of the mind upon visions, they lift the gates of the heart to feeling. Appreciation of them becomes habitual, reflex; their meaning is all in their sound. They touch off joy, depression, pleasantness, discomfort, instantaneously. There exists a distinct class of words affecting us so, feeling-words, to be distinguished sharply from meaning-words. Any word may enter this class or leave it, according to the place its last meaning has held in the folkways of a society. Usage is the arbiter. The head and font of such words is the blessed word Mesopotamia.[5] Philosophy and religion and history abound in them. Many a sounding philosopher has won fame and thanks from mankind for iteration to the point of idiocy of such words as "reality," "spirit," "ideal," "infinite," "eternal," "immortality," "love," "evolution," "superman," "God," "progress," and so on to no end. Think of that balm of Gilead—"in tune with the infinite." Think of the glow which that masterly phrase "Christian Science" evokes, or of the aura of well-being which is shed by the word "Christian" in any connection. Politics has its shibboleths no less—"100% American," "progressive," "socialism," "radical." It was not for nothing that in *Man*

4. Philosophical world views.
5. Land in Asia Minor where the world's first historic civilization, with written documents, began.

and Superman Shaw made the old gentleman tell John Tanner that he was a "radical" before Tanner was born. There resides in such words, value-words, an emotional significance intrinsic to the words themselves, independent of all other meaning. They confer godhead. They create devildom. The things to which they are applied are thereby lifted up or cast down; as in the case of the dog with the bad name, the name, not the dog's the thing. Words which have collapsed from stimuli to perception into stimuli to feeling only, which have become mere value-words, approving or condemning regardless, are the greatest of all conservators, the most effective intrenchments against intelligence and progress. Many a sane and just enterprise has been defeated by the epithet "socialistic"; more than one nefarious scheme advanced by "Christian," "American," "service," and such.

Bacon was wrong. Words are only fools' counters.[6] The wise man realizes that the hope of mankind depends upon the success with which society can be taught to give old things new names. When "growing old" will become generally accepted as "senescence" much of its hardship will vanish. For men will have abandoned the illusion of immortality, they will have acknowledged and learned to rejoice in the order of nature and the cycle of birth and growth and death which governs their being, they will have learned to rob death of its sting and the grave of its victory by going serenely to the end of the passage.

If schooling is habituation in a vocabulary of works and days, education is the continual substitution of one vocabulary for another. The root of style is a theory of life whereby commonplace things are set in a cosmic perspective which is their meaning. And, of all our tools that give perspectives, the most widely used, the most efficacious and enduring, is the living word. Each time and people and person has his own, brought to birth by its characteristic pulse and rhythm, and endowed thereby with its inward beat and outward pattern. For this reason, the style is not alone the man, the style is the age, the society, the civilization. By their styles shall you know them—the Elizabethans from the Georgians, the Victorians from the moderns, the moderns from all. In the measure of their prose and verse, in the vistas of their vocabularies, in the appreciations and condemnations of their value-words, are revealed their secret hearts and public minds, all that they fear and hope for themselves and mankind at work upon an experience they are bring-

---

6. Kallen is apparently recalling a passage not by Francis Bacon, but by the English philosopher Thomas Hobbes (1588–1679), in *Leviathan*: "For words are wise men's counters—they do but reckon by them; but they are the money of fools."

ing to order and excellence by binding with words, by giving it, that is, meanings.

If the beliefs of the rhetoricians and the literary middlemen were true, this could not happen. Repetition, not variety, would be the rule. Edwin Robinson would still be writing like Geoffrey Chaucer, and John Dewey would be rehearsing John of Salisbury.[7] Between these poets and philosophers the difference is not in the denotations of their experiences; it is in the designation of their perspectives. Life and letters themselves repudiate the loose and lazy thinking and writing which goes for excellence among those for whom "least troublesome" is synonym for "best."

1930

7. That is, the poet Edwin Arlington Robinson and the philosopher John Dewey, in the twentieth century, would be writing like their counterparts in much earlier times, such as Geoffrey Chaucer (1340?–1400) and John of Salisbury (1115?–1180).

QUESTIONS

1. On p. 214 Kallen declares, "Meanings are as subtle fluids." Metaphors are usually thought of as uncertain definers; does this one work? What about the "keys" and "doors" mentioned on p. 215?
2. In his concern to stress the plasticity of words and the need for subtle precision, has Kallen gone so far that he would find it hard to acknowledge the everyday efficiency of language, which depends on simple, widely accepted meanings? Does he allow for any criticism of a writer's style? What is his basic position?
3. In "The Language of the Street" (p. 166), Ralph Waldo Emerson, writing ninety years before Kallen, argues the opposite case in this long-standing dispute. What is each man's strategy? How can each support his case?

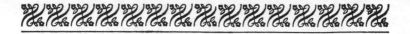

Prose Forms:
An Album of Styles

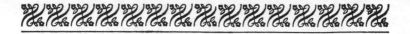

ROGER ASCHAM: The Wind

To see the wind with a man his eyes it is unpossible, the nature of it is so fine and subtile; yet this experience of the wind had I once myself, and that was in the great snow that fell four years ago. I rode in the high way betwixt Topcliff-upon-Swale and Borough-bridge, the way being somewhat trodden before, by wayfaring men; the fields on both sides were plain, and lay almost yard-deep with snow; the night afore had been a little frost, so that the snow was hard and crusted above; that morning the sun shone bright and clear, the wind was whistling aloft, and sharp, according to the time of the year; the snow in the high way lay loose and trodden with horses' feet; so as the wind blew, it took the loose snow with it, and made it so slide upon the snow in the field, which was hard and crusted by reason of the frost over night, that thereby I might see very well the whole nature of the wind as it blew that day. And I had a great delight and pleasure to mark it, which maketh me now far better to remember it. Sometime the wind would be not past two yards broad, and so it would carry the snow as far as I could see. Another time the snow would blow over half the field at once. Sometime the snow would tumble softly; by and by it would fly wonderful fast. And this I perceived also, that the wind goeth by streams, and not whole together. For I should see one stream within a score on me; then the space of two score, no snow would stir; but, after so much quantity of ground, another stream of snow, at the same very time, should be carried likewise, but not equally, for the one would stand still, when the other flew apace and so continue sometime swiftlier, sometime slowlier, sometime broader, sometime narrower, as far as I could see. Nor it flew not straight, but sometime it crooked this way, sometime that way, and sometime it ran round about in a compass. And sometime the snow would be lift clean from the ground up to the air, and by and by it would be all clapt to the ground, as though there had been no wind at all, straightway it would rise and fly again. And that which was the most marvel of all, at one time two drifts of snow flew, the one out of the west into the east, the other out of the north into the east. And I saw two winds, by reason of the snow, the one cross over the other, as it had been two high ways. And, again, I should hear the wind blow in the air, when nothing was stirred at the ground. And when all was still where I rode, not very far from me the snow should be lifted wonderfully. This experience made me more marvel at the nature of the wind, than it made me cunning in the knowledge of the wind; but yet thereby I learned perfectly that it is no marvel at all though men in wind lose their length in shooting, seeing so many ways the wind is so variable in blowing.

1545

FRANCIS BACON: Of Revenge

Revenge is a kind of wild justice; which the more man's nature runs to, the more ought law to weed it out. For as for the first wrong, it doth but offend the law; but the revenge of that wrong putteth the law out of office. Certainly, in taking revenge, a man is but even with his enemy; but in passing it over, he is superior; for it is a prince's part to pardon. And Salomon, I am sure, saith, *It is the glory of a man to pass by an offence.* That which is past is gone, and irrevocable; and wise men have enough to do with things present and to come: therefore they do but trifle with themselves, that labour in past matters. There is no man doth a wrong for the wrong's sake; but thereby to purchase himself profit, or pleasure, or honour, or the like. Therefore why should I be angry with a man for loving himself better than me? And if any man should do wrong merely out of ill nature, why, yet it is but like the thorn or briar, which prick and scratch, because they can do no other. The most tolerable sort of revenge is for those wrongs which there is no law to remedy; but then let a man take heed the revenge be such as there is no law to punish; else a man's enemy is still beforehand, and it is two for one. Some, when they take revenge, are desirous the party should know whence it cometh: this is the more generous. For the delight seemeth to be not so much in doing the hurt as in making the party repent: but base and crafty cowards are like the arrow that flieth in the dark. Cosmus, duke of Florence, had a desperate saying against perfidious or neglecting friends, as if those wrongs were unpardonable: *You shall read* (saith he) *that we are commanded to forgive our enemies; but you never read that we are commanded to forgive our friends.* But yet the spirit of Job was in a better tune: *Shall we* (saith he) *take good at God's hands, and not be content to take evil also*? And so of friends in a proportion. This is certain, that a man that studieth revenge keeps his own wounds green, which otherwise would heal and do well. Public revenges are for the most part fortunate; as that for the death of Caesar; for the death of Pertinax;[1] for the death of Henry the third of France;[2] and many more. But in private revenges it is not so. Nay rather, vindictive persons live the life of witches; who as they are mischievous, so end they infortunate.

1625

1. Publius Helvius Pertinax became Emperor of Rome in 193 and was assassinated three months after his accession to the throne by a soldier in his Prae- torian Guard.
2. King of France 1574–1589; assassi- nated during the Siege of Paris.

JOHN DONNE: Men Are Sleeping Prisoners

We are all conceived in close prison; in our Mothers wombs, we are close prisoners all; when we are born, we are born but to the liberty of the house;[1] prisoners still, though within larger walls; and then all our life is but a going out to the place of execution, to death. Now was there ever any man seen to sleep in the cart, between Newgate, and Tyburn?[2] Between the prison and the place of execution, does any man sleep? And we sleep all the way; from the womb to the grave we are never thoroughly awake; but pass on with such dreams, and imaginations as these, I may live as well, as another, and why should I die, rather than another? But awake, and tell me, says this text *Quis homo*?[3] Who is that other that thou talkest of? *What man is he that liveth, and shall not see death?*

1. Donne distinguishes between a pris- oner confined to a cell and one given somewhat more liberty.
2. London prisoners were taken in
carts from Newgate prison to nearby Ty- burn for execution.
3. "Who [is] the man?"

SAMUEL JOHNSON: The Pyramids

Of the wall [of China] it is very easy to assign the motives. It secured a wealthy and timorous nation from the incursions of Barbarians, whose unskillfulness in arts made it easier for them to supply their wants by rapine than by industry, and who from time to time poured in upon the habitations of peaceful commerce, as vultures descend upon domestic fowl. Their celerity and fierceness made the wall necessary, and their ignorance made it efficacious.

But for the pyramids no reason has ever been given adequate to the cost and labor of the work. The narrowness of the chambers proves that it could afford no retreat from enemies, and treasures might have been reposited at far less expense with equal security. It seems to have been erected only in compliance with that hunger of imagination which preys incessantly upon life, and must be always appeased by some employment. Those who have already all that they can enjoy, must enlarge their desires. He that has built for use, till use is supplied must begin to build for vanity, and extend his plan to the utmost power of human performance, that he may not be soon reduced to form another wish.

I consider this mighty structure as a monument of the insufficiency of human enjoyments. A king, whose power is unlimited, and whose treasures surmount all real and imaginary wants, is compelled to solace, by the erection of a pyramid, the satiety of dominion and tastelessness of pleasures, and to amuse the tediousness of declining life, by seeing thousands laboring without end, and one stone, for no purpose, laid upon another. Whoever thou art, that, not content with a moderate condition, imaginest happiness in royal magnificence, and dreamest that command or riches can feed the appetite of novelty with perpetual gratifications, survey the pyramids, and confess thy folly!

1759

LAURENCE STERNE:

Of Door Hinges and Life in General

Every day for at least ten years together did my father resolve to have it mended—'tis not mended yet: no family but ours would have borne with it an hour—and what is most astonishing, there was not a subject in the world upon which my father was so eloquent, as upon that of door-hinges. And yet at the same time, he was certainly one of the greatest bubbles to them, I think, that history can produce: his rhetoric and conduct were at perpetual handy-cuffs. Never did the parlor-door open—but his philosophy or his principles fell a victim to it; three drops of oyl with a feather, and a smart stroke of a hammer, had saved his honor for ever. Inconsistent soul that man is—languishing under wounds, which he has the power to heal—his whole life a contradiction to his knowledge—his reason, that precious gift of God to him—(instead of pouring in oyl) serving but to sharpen his sensibilities, to multiply his pains and render him more melancholy and uneasy under them—poor unhappy creature, that he should do so! Are not the necessary causes of misery in this life enow, but he must add voluntary ones to his stock of sorrow, struggle against evils which cannot be avoided, and submit to others, which a tenth part of the trouble they create him, would remove from his heart forever?

By all that is good and virtuous! if there are three drops of oyl to be got, and a hammer to be found within ten miles of Shandy-Hall, the parlor-door hinge shall be mended this reign.

1767

CHARLES LAMB: The Two Races of Men

The human species, according to the best theory I can form of it, is composed of two distinct races, *the men who borrow*, and *the men who lend*. To these two original diversities may be reduced all those impertinent classifications of Gothic and Celtic tribes, white men, black men, red men. All the dwellers upon earth, "Parthians, and Medes, and Elamites," flock hither, and do naturally fall in with one or other of these primary distinctions. The infinite superiority of the former, which I choose to designate as the *great race*, is discernible in their figure, port, and a certain instinctive sovereignty. The latter are born degraded. "He shall serve his brethren." There is something in the air of one of this cast, lean and suspicious; contrasting with the open, trusting, generous manners of the other.

Observe who have been the greatest borrowers of all ages—Alcibiades—Falstaff—Sir Richard Steele—our late incomparable Brinsley—what a family likeness in all four!

What a careless, even deportment hath your borrower! what rosy gills! what a beautiful reliance on Providence doth he manifest—taking no more thought than lilies! What contempt for money—accounting it (yours and mine especially) no better than dross. What a liberal confounding of those pedantic distinctions of *meum* and *tuum!* or rather, what a noble simplification of language (beyond Tooke), resolving these supposed opposites into one clear, intelligible pronoun adjective! What near approaches doth he make to the primitive *community*—to the extent of one half of the principle at least!

1823

Literature of Knowledge and Literature of Power

In that great social organ which, collectively, we call literature, there may be distinguished two separate offices that may blend and often do so, but capable, severally, of a severe insulation, and naturally fitted for reciprocal repulsion. There is, first, the literature of *knowledge*, and secondly, the literature of *power*. The function of the first is to *teach*; the function of the second is to *move*; the first is a rudder, the second an oar or a sail. The first speaks to the mere discursive understanding; the second speaks ultimately, it may happen, to the higher understanding or reason, but always through affections of pleasure and sympathy. Remotely, it may travel towards an object seated in what Lord Bacon calls *dry* light; but, proximately, it does and must operate—else it ceases to be a literature of *power*—and on through that *humid* light which clothes itself in the mists and glittering *iris* of human passions, desires, and genial emotions. Men have so little reflected on the higher functions of literature as to find it a paradox if one should describe it as a mean or subordinate purpose of books to give information. But this is a paradox only in the sense which makes it honorable to be paradoxical. Whenever we talk in ordinary language of seeking information or gaining knowledge, we understand the words as connected with something of absolute novelty. But it is the grandeur of all truth which *can* occupy a very high place in human interests that it is never absolutely novel to the meanest of minds: it exists eternally by way of germ or latent principle in the lowest as in the highest, needing to be developed, but never to be planted. To be capable of transplantation is the immediate criterion of a truth that ranges on a lower scale. Besides which, there is a rarer thing than truth—namely, *power*, or deep sympathy with truth. What is the effect, for instance, upon society, of children? By the pity, by the tenderness, and by the peculiar modes of admiration, which connect themselves with the helplessness, with the innocence, and with the simplicity of children, not only are the primal affections strengthened and continually renewed, but the qualities which are dearest in the sight of heaven—the frailty, for instance, which appeals to forbearance, the innocence which symbolizes the heavenly, and the simplicity which is most alien from the worldly—are kept up in perpetual remembrance, and their ideals are continually refreshed. A purpose of the same nature is answered by the high literature, viz., the literature of power. What do you learn from *Paradise Lost*? Nothing at all. What do you learn from a cookery book? Something new, something that you did not know before, in every paragraph. But would you therefore put the wretched cookery book on a higher level of estimation than the divine poem? What you owe to Milton is not any knowledge, of which a million separate items are still but a million of advancing steps on the same earthly level; what you owe is *power*—that is, exercise and expansion to your own latent capacity of sympathy with the infinite, where every pulse and each separate influx is a step upwards, a step ascending as upon a Jacob's ladder from earth to mysterious altitudes above the earth. *All* the steps of knowledge, from first to last, carry you further on the same plane, but could never raise you one foot above your ancient level of earth: whereas the very *first* step in power is a flight—is an ascending movement into another element where earth is forgotten.

1848

JOHN HENRY NEWMAN: Knowledge and Virtue

Knowledge is one thing, virtue is another; good sense is not conscience, refinement is not humility, nor is largeness and justness of view faith. Philosophy, however enlightened, however profound, gives no command over the passions, no influential motives, no vivifying principles. Liberal Education makes not the Christian, not the Catholic, but the gentleman. It is well to be a gentleman, it is well to have a cultivated intellect, a delicate taste, a candid, equitable, dispassionate mind, a noble and courteous bearing in the conduct of life—these are the connatural qualities of a large knowledge; they are the objects of a University; I am advocating, I shall illustrate and insist upon them; but still, I repeat, they are no guarantee for sanctity or even for conscientiousness, they may attach to the man of the world, to the profligate, to the heartless, pleasant, alas, and attractive as he shows when decked out in them. Taken by themselves, they do but seem to be what they are not; they look like virtue at a distance, but they are detected by close observers, and on the long run; and hence it is that they are popularly accused of pretense and hypocrisy, not, I repeat, from their own fault, but because their professors and their admirers persist in taking them for what they are not, and are officious in arrogating for them a praise to which they have no claim. Quarry the granite rock with razors, or moor the vessel with a thread of silk; then may you hope with such keen and delicate instruments as human knowledge and human reason to contend against those giants, the passion and the pride of man.

1852

MATTHEW ARNOLD: Culture

But there is of culture another view, in which not solely the scientific passion, the sheer desire to see things as they are, natural and proper in an intelligent being, appears as the ground of it. There is a view in which all the love of our neighbor, the impulses towards action, help, and beneficence, the desire for removing human error, clearing human confusion, and diminishing human misery, the noble aspiration to leave the world better and happier than we found it—motives eminently such as are called social—come in as part of the grounds of culture, and the main and pre-eminent part. Culture is then properly described not as having its origin in curiosity, but as having its origin in the love of perfection; it is *a study of perfection*. It moves by the force, not merely or primarily of the scientific passion for pure knowledge, but also of the moral and social passion for doing good. As, in the first view of it, we took for its worthy motto Montesquieu's words: "To render an intelligent being yet more intelligent!" so, in the second view of it, there is no better motto which it can have than these words of Bishop Wilson: "To make reason and the will of God prevail!"

Only, whereas the passion for doing good is apt to be overhasty in determining what reason and the will of God say, because its turn is for acting rather than thinking, and it wants to be beginning to act; and whereas it is apt to take its own conceptions, which proceed from its own state of development and share in all the imperfections and immaturities of this, for a basis of action; what distinguishes culture is, that it is possessed by the scientific passion as well as by the passion of doing good; that it demands worthy notions of reason and the will of God, and does not readily suffer its own crude conceptions to substitute themselves for them. And knowing that no action or institution can be salutary and stable which is not based on reason and the will of God, it is not so bent on acting and instituting, even with the great aim of diminishing human error and misery ever before its thoughts, but that it can remember that acting and instituting are of little use, unless we know how and what we ought to act and to institute.

1869

WALTER PATER: The Mona Lisa

The presence that rose thus so strangely beside the waters, is expressive of what in the ways of a thousand years men had come to desire. Hers is the head upon which all "the ends of the world are come," and the eyelids are a little weary. It is a beauty wrought out from within upon the flesh, the deposit, little cell by cell, of strange thoughts and fantastic reveries and exquisite passions. Set it for a moment beside one of those white Greek goddesses or beautiful women of antiquity, and how would they be troubled by this beauty, into which the soul with all its maladies has passed! All the thoughts and experience of the world have etched and molded there, in that which they have of power to refine and make expressive the outward form, the animalism of Greece, the lust of Rome, the mysticism of the middle ages with its spiritual ambition and imaginative loves, the return of the Pagan world, the sins of the Borgias. She is older than the rocks among which she sits; like the vampire, she has been dead many times, and learned the secrets of the grave; and has been a diver in deep seas, and keeps their fallen day about her; and trafficked for strange webs with Eastern merchants: and, as Leda, was the mother of Helen of Troy, and, as Saint Anne, the mother of Mary; and all this has been to her but as the sound of lyres and flutes, and lives only in the delicacy with which it has molded the changing lineaments, and tinged the eyelids and the hands. The fancy of a perpetual life, sweeping together ten-thousand experiences, is an old one; and modern philosophy has conceived the idea of humanity as wrought upon by, and summing up in itself, all modes of thought and life. Certainly Lady Lisa might stand as the embodiment of the old fancy, the symbol of the modern idea.

1868   1873

JAMES THURBER: A Dog's Eye View of Man

If Man has benefited immeasurably by his association with the dog, what, you may ask, has the dog got out of it? His scroll has, of course, been heavily charged with punishments: he has known the muzzle, the leash, and the tether; he has suffered the indignities of the show bench, the tin can on the tail, the ribbon in the hair; his love life with the other sex of his species has been regulated by the frigid hand of authority, his digestion ruined by the macaroons and marshmallows of doting women. The list of his woes could be continued indefinitely. But he has also had his fun, for he has been privileged to live with and study at close range the only creature with reason, the most unreasonable of creatures.

The dog has got more fun out of Man than Man has got out of the dog, for the clearly demonstrable reason that Man is the more laughable of the two animals. The dog has long been bemused by the singular activities and the curious practices of men, cocking his head inquiringly to one side, intently watching and listening to the strangest goings-on in the world. He has seen men sing together and fight one another in the same evening. He has watched them go to bed when it is time to get up, and get up when it is time to go to bed. He has observed them destroying the soil in vast areas, and nurturing it in small patches. He has stood by while men built strong and solid houses for rest and quiet, and then filled them with lights and bells and machinery. His sensitive nose, which can detect what's cooking in the next township, has caught at one and the same time the bewildering smells of the hospital and the munitions factory. He has seen men raise up great cities to heaven and then blow them to hell.

1955

E. B. WHITE: Progress and Change

In resenting progress and change, a man lays himself open to censure. I suppose the explanation of anyone's defending anything as rudimentary and cramped as a Pullman berth is that such things are associated with an earlier period in one's life and that this period in retrospect seems a happy one. People who favor progress and improvements are apt to be people who have had a tough enough time without any extra inconvenience. Reactionaries who pout at innovations are apt to be well-heeled sentimentalists who had the breaks. Yet for all that, there is always a subtle danger in life's refinements, a dim degeneracy in progress. I have just been refining the room in which I sit, yet I sometimes doubt that a writer should refine or improve his workroom by so much as a dictionary: one thing leads to another and the first thing you know he has a stuffed chair and is fast asleep in it. Half a man's life is devoted to what he calls improvements, yet the original had some quality which is lost in the process. There was a fine natural spring of water on this place when I bought it. Our drinking water had to be lugged in a pail, from a wet glade of alder and tamarack. I visited the spring often in those first years, and had friends there—a frog, a woodcock, and an eel which had churned its way all the way up through the pasture creek to enjoy the luxury of pure water. In the normal course of development, the spring was rocked up, fitted with a concrete curb, a copper pipe, and an electric pump. I have visited it only once or twice since. This year my only gesture was the purely perfunctory one of sending a sample to the state bureau of health for analysis. I felt cheap, as though I were smelling an old friend's breath.

1938

VIRGINIA WOOLF: How Should One Read a Book?

It is simple enough to say that since books have classes—fiction, biography, poetry—we should separate them and take from each what it is right that each should give us. Yet few people ask from books what books can give us. Most commonly we come to books with blurred and divided minds, asking of fiction that it shall be true, of poetry that it shall be false, of biography that it shall be flattering, of history that it shall enforce our own prejudices. If we could banish all such preconceptions when we read, that would be an admirable beginning. Do not dictate to your author; try to become him. Be his fellow-worker and accomplice. If you hang back, and reserve and criticise at first, you are preventing yourself from getting the fullest possible value from what you read. But if you open your mind as widely as possible, then signs and hints of almost imperceptible fineness, from the twist and turn of the first sentences, will bring you into the presence of a human being unlike any other. Steep yourself in this, acquaint yourself with this, and soon you will find that your author is giving you, or attempting to give you, something far more definite. The thirty-two chapters of a novel—if we consider how to read a novel first—are an attempt to make something as formed and controlled as a building: but words are more impalpable than bricks; reading is a longer and more complicated process than seeing. Perhaps the quickest way to understand the elements of what a novelist is doing is not to read, but to write; to make your own experiment with the dangers and difficulties of words. Recall, then, some event that has left a distinct impression on you—how at the corner of the street, perhaps, you passed two people talking. A tree shook; an electric light danced; the tone of the talk was comic, but also tragic; a whole vision, an entire conception, seemed contained in that moment.

But when you attempt to reconstruct it in words, you will find that it breaks into a thousand conflicting impressions. Some must be subdued; others emphasised; in the process you will lose, probably, all grasp upon the emotion itself. Then turn from your blurred and littered pages to the opening pages of some great novelist—Defoe, Jane Austen, Hardy. Now you will be better able to appreciate their mastery. It is not merely that we are in the presence of a different person—Defoe, Jane Austen, or Thomas Hardy—but that we are living in a different world. Here, in *Robinson Crusoe*, we are trudging a plain high road; one thing happens after another; the fact and the order of the fact is enough. But if the open air and adventure mean everything to Defoe they mean nothing to Jane Austen. Hers is the drawing-room, and people talking, and by the many mirrors of their talk revealing their characters.

And if, when we have accustomed ourselves to the drawing-room and its reflections, we turn to Hardy, we are once more spun around. The moors are round us and the stars are above our heads. The other side of the mind is now exposed—the dark side that comes uppermost in solitude, not the light side that shows in company. Our relations are not towards people, but towards Nature and destiny. Yet different as these worlds are, each is consistent with itself. The maker of each is careful to observe the laws of his own perspective, and however great a strain they may put upon us they will never confuse us, as lesser writers so frequently do, by introducing two different kinds of reality into the same book. Thus to go from one great novelist to another—from Jane Austen to Hardy, from Peacock to Trollope, from Scott to Meredith—is to be wrenched and uprooted; to be thrown this way and then that. To read a novel is a difficult and complex art. You must be capable not only of great finesse of perception, but of great boldness of imagination if you are going to make use of all that the novelist—the great artist—gives you.

1932

TONI MORRISON: Three Merry Gargoyles

Three merry gargoyles. Three merry harridans. Amused by a long-ago time of ignorance. They did not belong to those generations of prostitutes created in novels, with great and generous hearts, dedicated, because of the horror of circumstance, to ameliorating the luckless, barren life of men, taking money incidentally and humbly for their "understanding." Nor were they from that sensitive breed of young girl, gone wrong at the hands of fate, forced to cultivate an outward brittleness in order to protect her springtime from further shock, but knowing full well she was cut out for better things, and could make the right man happy. Neither were they the sloppy, inadequate whores who, unable to make a living at it alone, turn to drug consumption and traffic or pimps to help complete their scheme of self-destruction, avoiding suicide only to punish the memory of some absent father or to sustain the misery of some silent mother. Except for Marie's fabled love for Dewey Prince, these women hated men, all men, without shame, apology, or discrimination. They abused their visitors with a scorn grown mechanical from use. Black men, white men, Puerto Ricans, Mexicans, Jews, Poles, whatever—all were inadequate and weak, all came under their jaundiced eyes and were the recipients of their disinterested wrath. They took delight in cheating them. On one occasion the town well knew, they lured a Jew up the stairs, pounced on him, all three, held him up by the heels, shook everything out of his pants pockets, and threw him out of the window.

Neither did they have respect for women, who, although not their colleagues, so to speak, nevertheless deceived their husbands —regularly or irregularly, it made no difference. "Sugar-coated whores," they called them, and did not yearn to be in their shoes. Their only respect was for what they would have described as "good Christian colored women." The woman whose reputation was spotless, and who tended to her family, who didn't drink or smoke or run around. These women had their undying, if covert, affection. They would sleep with their husbands, and take their money, but always with a vengeance.

Nor were they protective and solicitous of youthful innocence. They looked back on their own youth as a period of ignorance, and regretted that they had not made more of it. They were not young girls in whores' clothing, or whores regretting their loss of innocence. They were whores in whores' clothing, whores who had never been young and had no word for innocence. With Pecola they were as free as they were with each other. Marie concocted stories for her because she was a child, but the stories were breezy and rough. If Pecola had announced her intention to live the life they did, they would not have tried to dissuade her or voiced any alarm.

1970

JOYCE CARY: Art and Education

A very large number of people cease when quite young to add anything to a limited stock of judgments. After a certain age, say 25, they consider that their education is finished.

It is perhaps natural that having passed through that painful and boring process, called expressly education, they should suppose it over, and that they are equipped for life to label every event as it occurs and drop it into its given pigeonhole. But one who has a label ready for everything does not bother to observe any more, even such ordinary happenings as he has observed for himself, with attention, before he went to school. He merely acts and reacts.

For people who have stopped noticing, the only possible new or renewed experience, and, therefore, new knowledge, is from a work of art. Because that is the only kind of experience which they are prepared to receive on its own terms, they will come out from their shells and expose themselves to music, to a play, to a book, because it is the accepted method of enjoying such things. True, even to plays and books they may bring artistic prejudices which prevent them from seeing *that* play or comprehending *that* book. Their artistic sensibilities may be as crusted over as their minds.

But it is part of an artist's job to break crusts, or let us say rather that artists who work for the public and not merely for themselves are interested in breaking crusts because they want to communicate their intuitions.

1949

JOHN STEINBECK: The Danger of Small Things

I guess it is true that big and strong things are much less dangerous than small soft weak things. Nature (whatever that is) makes the small and weak reproduce faster. And that is not true of course. The ones that did not reproduce faster than they died, disappeared. But how about little faults, little pains, little worries. The cosmic ulcer comes not from great concerns, but from little irritations. And great things can kill a man but if they do not he is stronger and better for them. A man is destroyed by the duck nibblings of nagging, small bills, telephones (wrong number), athlete's foot, ragweed, the common cold, boredom. All of these are the negatives, the tiny frustrations, and no one is stronger for them.

1969

JOHN UPDIKE: Beer Can

This seems to be an era of gratuitous inventions and negative improvements. Consider the beer can. It was beautiful—as beautiful as the clothespin, as inevitable as the wine bottle, as dignified and reassuring as the fire hydrant. A tranquil cylinder of delightfully resonant metal, it could be opened in an instant, requiring only the application of a handy gadget freely dispensed by every grocer. Who can forget the small, symmetrical thrill of those two triangular punctures, the dainty *pffff*, the little crest of suds that foamed eagerly in the exultation of release? Now we are given, instead, a top beetling with an ugly, shmoo-shaped "tab," which, after fiercely resisting the tugging, bleeding fingers of the thirsty man, threatens his lips with a dangerous and hideous hole. However, we have discovered a way to thwart Progress, usually so unthwartable. *Turn the beer can upside down and open the bottom.* The bottom is still the way the top used to be. True, this operation gives the beer an unsettling jolt, and the sight of a consistently inverted beer can might make people edgy, not to say queasy. But the latter difficulty could be eliminated if manufacturers would design cans that looked the same whichever end was up, like playing cards. What we need is Progress with an escape hatch.

1964

TOM WOLFE: The Legend of Junior Johnson

The legend of Junior Johnson! In this legend, here is a country boy, Junior Johnson, who learns to drive by running whiskey for his father, Johnson, Senior, one of the biggest copper-still operators of all time, up in Ingle Hollow, near North Wilkesboro, in northwestern North Carolina, and grows up to be a famous stock car racing driver, rich, grossing $100,000 in 1963, for example, respected, solid, idolized in his hometown and throughout the rural South. There is all this about how good old boys would wake up in the middle of the night in the apple shacks and hear a supercharged Oldsmobile engine roaring over Brushy Mountain and say, "Listen at him—there he goes!" although that part is doubtful, since some nights there were so many good old boys taking off down the road in supercharged automobiles out of Wilkes County, and running loads to Charlotte, Salisbury, Greensboro, Winston-Salem, High Point, or wherever, it would be pretty hard to pick out one. It was Junior Johnson, specifically, however, who was famous for the "bootleg turn" or "about-face," in which, if the Alcohol Tax agents had a roadblock up for you or were too close behind, you threw the car up into second gear, cocked the wheel, stepped on the accelerator and made the car's rear end skid around in a complete 180-degree arc, a complete about-face, and tore on back up the road exactly the way you came from. God! The Alcohol Tax agents used to burn over Junior Johnson. Practically every good old boy in town in Wilkesboro, the county seat, got to know the agents by sight in a very short time. They would rag them practically to their faces on the subject of Junior Johnson, so that it got to be an obsession. Finally, one night they had Junior trapped on the road up toward the bridge around Millersville, there's no way out of there, they had the barricades up and they could hear this souped-up car roaring around the bend, and here it comes—but suddenly they can hear a siren and see a red light flashing in the grille, so they think it's another agent, and boy, they run out like ants and pull those barrels and boards and sawhorses out of the way, and then—Ggghhzzzzzzzhhhhhh-gggggggzzzzzzzeeeeeong!—gawdam! there he goes again, it was him, Junior Johnson! with a gawdam agent's sireen and a red light in his grille!

1965

ROBERT PIRSIG: Concrete, Brick, and Neon

The city closes in on him now, and in his strange perspective it becomes the antithesis of what he believes. The citadel not of Quality, the citadel of form and substance. Substance in the form of steel sheets and girders, substance in the form of concrete piers and roads, in the form of brick, of asphalt, of auto parts, old radios, and rails, dead carcasses of animals that once grazed the prairies. Form and substance without Quality. That is the soul of this place. Blind, huge, sinister and inhuman: seen by the light of fire flaring upward in the night from the blast furnaces in the south, through heavy coal smoke deeper and denser into the neon of BEER and PIZZA and LAUNDROMAT signs and unknown and meaningless signs along meaningless straight streets going off into other straight streets forever.

If it was all bricks and concrete, pure forms of substance, clearly and openly, he might survive. It is the little, pathetic attempts at Quality that kill. The plaster false fireplace in the apartment, shaped and waiting to contain a flame that can never exist. Or the hedge in front of the apartment building with a few square feet of grass behind it. A few square feet of grass, after Montana. If they just left out the hedge and grass it would be all right. Now it serves only to draw attention to what has been lost.

Along the streets that lead away from the apartment he can never see anything through the concrete and brick and neon but he knows that buried within it are grotesque, twisted souls forever trying the manners that will convince themselves they possess Quality, learning strange poses of style and glamour vended by dream magazines and other mass media, and paid for by the vendors of substance. He thinks of them at night alone with their advertised glamorous shoes and stockings and underclothes off, staring through the sooty windows at the grotesque shells revealed beyond them, when the poses weaken and the truth creeps in, the only truth that exists here, crying to heaven, God, there is nothing here but dead neon and cement and brick.

1975

JONATHAN SCHELL: Law in the United States

In the United States, the role of the law in defining the shape of political life is of particular importance. For in the United States, where the national government and the nation itself were brought formally into existence when the states ratified the Constitution, the very being of the government is founded in law. The Founding Fathers' act of creation was a legal act, and the institutions they framed were defined and empowered by law. In the American system, the law is more than a set of restrictions, and more, even, than a universal code of justice; it is to the nation's institutions the breath of the creator. The people decide in elections who will man the institutions, but the law continues to define what the institutions are. It binds them together into a whole that can be seen, understood, and brought to account, and that works. And since, in the United States, customs, communities, and even buildings tend to be rubbed out almost as soon as they appear, there is very little in the way of tradition for the nation to fall back on if legal forms break down. If the controlling, molding influence of the law declines, then the outlines of the political system itself blur and eventually disappear. Institutions, no longer able to grasp firmly what is expected of them and what they are, grow slovenly and misshapen, and wander away from their appointed tasks in the Constitutional scheme. Roles and jurisdictions clash and become confused, power goes to whoever grabs it, and the system warps and sags and heads toward collapse.

1975

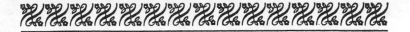

Literature and the Arts

NORTHROP FRYE

The Keys to Dreamland

* * * Suppose you're walking down the street of a North American city. All around you is a highly artificial society, but you don't think of it as artificial: you're so accustomed to it that you think of it as natural. But suppose your imagination plays a little trick on you of a kind that it often does play, and you suddenly feel like a complete outsider, someone who's just blown in from Mars on a flying saucer. Instantly you see how conventionalized every thing is: the clothes, the shop windows, the movement of the cars in traffic, the cropped hair and shaved faces of the men, the red lips and blue eyelids that women put on because they want to conventionalize their faces, or "look nice," as they say, which means the same thing. All this convention is pressing toward uniformity or likeness. To be outside the convention makes a person look queer, or, if he's driving a car, a menace to life and limb. The only exceptions are people who have decided to conform to different conventions, like nuns or beatniks. There's clearly a strong force making toward conformity in society, so strong that it seems to have something to do with the stability of society itself. In ordinary life even the most splendid things we can think of, goodness and truth and beauty, all mean essentially what we're accustomed to. As I hinted just now in speaking of female makeup, most of our ideas of beauty are pure convention, and even truth has been defined as whatever doesn't disturb the pattern of what we already know.

When we move on to literature, we again find conventions, but this time we notice that they are conventions, because we're not so used to them. These conventions seem to have something to do with making literature as unlike life as possible. Chaucer represents people as making up stories in ten-syllable couplets. Shakespeare uses dramatic conventions, which means, for instance, that Iago has to smash Othello's marriage and dreams of future happiness and get him ready to murder his wife in a few minutes. Milton has two nudes in a garden haranguing each other in set speeches beginning with such lines as "Daughter of God and Man, immortal Eve"—Eve being Adam's daughter because she's just been extracted from his ribcase. Almost every story we read demands that we accept as fact something that we know to be nonsense: that good people always win, especially in love; that murders are complicated and ingenious puzzles to be solved by logic, and so on. It isn't only popular literature that demands this: more highbrow stories are apt to be more ironic, but irony has its conventions too. If we go further back into literature, we run into such conventions as the king's rash promise, the enraged cuckold, the cruel mistress of love poetry—never anything that we or any other time would recognize as the normal behavior of adult people, only the maddened ethics of fairyland.

Even the details of literature are equally perverse. Literature is a world where phoenixes and unicorns are quite as important as horses and dogs—and in literature some of the horses talk, like the ones in *Gulliver's Travels*. A random example is calling Shakespeare the "swan of Avon"—he was called that by Ben Jonson. The town of Stratford, Ontario, keeps swans in its river partly as a literary allusion. Poets of Shakespeare's day hated to admit that they were writing words on a page: they always insisted that they were producing music. In pastoral poetry they might be playing a flute (or more accurately an oboe), but every other kind of poetic effort was called song, with a harp, a lyre or a lute in the background, depending on how highbrow the song was. Singing suggests birds, and so for their typical songbird and emblem of themselves, the poets chose the swan, a bird that can't sing. Because it can't sing, they made up a legend that it sang once before death, when nobody was listening. But Shakespeare didn't burst into song before his death: he wrote two plays a year until he'd made enough money to retire, and spent the last five years of his life counting his take.

So however useful literature may be in improving one's imagination or vocabulary, it would be the wildest kind of pedantry to use it directly as a guide to life. Perhaps here we see one reason why the poet is not only very seldom a person one would turn to for insight into the state of the world, but often seems even more gullible and simple-minded than the rest of us. For the poet, the particular literary conventions he adopts are likely to become, for him, facts of life. If he finds that the kind of writing he's best at has a good deal to do with fairies, like Yeats, or a white goddess, like Graves, or a life-force, like Bernard Shaw, or episcopal sermons, like T. S.

Eliot, or bullfights, like Hemingway, or exasperation at social hypo-
crisies, as with the so-called angry school, these things are apt to
take on a reality for him that seems badly out of proportion to his
contemporaries. His life may imitate literature in a way that may
warp or even destroy his social personality, as Byron wore himself
out at thirty-four with the strain of being Byronic. Life and literature, then, are both conventionalized, and of the conventions of literature about all we can say is that they don't much resemble the
conditions of life. It's when two sets of conventions collide that we
realize how different they are.

In fact, whenever literature gets too probable, too much like life,
some self-defeating process, some mysterious law of diminishing
returns, seems to set in. There's a vivid and expertly written novel
by H. G. Wells called *Kipps*, about a lower-middle-class, inarticulate, very likeable Cockney, the kind of character we often find in
Dickens. Kipps is carefully studied: he never says anything that a
man like Kipps wouldn't say; he never sounds the "h" in home or
head; nothing he does is out of line with what we expect such a
person to be like. It's an admirable novel, well worth reading, and
yet I have a nagging feeling that there's some inner secret in bringing him completely to life that Dickens would have and that Wells
doesn't have. All right, then, what would Dickens have done?
Well, one of the things that Dickens often does do is write *badly*.
He might have given Kipps sentimental speeches and false heroics
and all sorts of inappropriate verbiage to say; and some readers
would have clucked and tut-tutted over these passages and
explained to each other how bad Dickens's taste was and how
uncertain his hold on character could be. Perhaps they'd be right
too. But we'd have had Kipps a few times the way he'd look to
himself or the way he'd sometimes wish he could be: that's part of
his reality, and the effect would remain with us however much we
disapproved of it. Whether I'm right about this book or not, and
I'm not at all sure I am, I think my general principle is right.
What we'd never see except in a book is often what we go to books
to find. Whatever is completely lifelike in literature is a bit of a
laboratory specimen there. To bring anything really to life in literature we can't be lifelike: we have to be literaturelike.

The same thing is true even of the use of language. We're often
taught that prose is the language of ordinary speech, which is
usually true in literature. But in ordinary life prose is no more the
language of ordinary speech than one's Sunday suit is a bathing
suit. The people who actually speak prose are highly cultivated and
articulate people, who've read a good many books, and even they
can speak prose only to each other. If you read the beautiful sentences of Elizabeth Bennett's conversation in *Pride and Prejudice*,

you can see how in that book they give a powerfully convincing impression of a sensible and intelligent girl. But any girl who talked as coherently as that on a street car would be stared at as though she had green hair. It isn't only the difference between 1813 and 1962 that's involved either, as you'll see if you compare her speech with her mother's. The poet Emily Dickinson complained that everybody said "What?" to her, until finally she practically gave up trying to talk altogether, and confined herself to writing notes.

All this is involved with the difference between literary and other kinds of writing. If we're writing to convey information, or for any practical reason, our writing is an act of will and intention: we mean what we say, and the words we use represent that meaning directly. It's different in literature, not because the poet doesn't mean what he says too, but because his real effort is one of putting words together. What's important is not what he may have meant to say, but what words themselves say when they get fitted together. With a novelist it's rather the incidents in the story he tells that get fitted together—as D. H. Lawrence says, don't trust the novelist; trust his story. That's why so much of a writer's best writing is or seems to be involuntary. It's involuntary because the forms of literature itself are taking control of it, and these forms are what are embodied in the conventions of literature. Conventions, we see, have the same role in literature that they have in life: they impose certain patterns of order and stability on the writer. Only, if they're such different conventions, it seems clear that the order of words, or the structure of literature, is different from the social order.

The absence of any clear line of connection between literature and life comes out in the issues involved in censorship. Because of the large involuntary element in writing, works of literature can't be treated as embodiments of conscious will or intention, like people, and so no laws can be framed to control their behavior which assume a tendency to do this or an intention of doing that. Works of literature get into legal trouble because they offend some powerful religious or political interest, and this interest in its turn usually acquires or exploits the kind of social hysteria that's always revolving around sex. But it's impossible to give legal definitions of such terms as obscenity in relation to works of literature. What happens to the book depends mainly on the intelligence of the judge. If he's a sensible man we get a sensible decision; if he's an ass we get that sort of decision, but what we don't get is a legal decision, because the basis for one doesn't exist. The best we get is a precedent tending to discourage cranks and pressure groups from attacking serious books. If you read the casebook on the trial of *Lady Chatterley's Lover*, you may remember how bewildered the critics were when they were asked what the moral effect of the book would be. They weren't putting on an act: they didn't know. Novels can only be good or bad in their own categories. There's no such thing as a morally bad novel: its moral effect depends entirely on the moral quality of its reader, and nobody can predict what that will be. And if literature isn't morally bad it isn't morally good either. I suppose one reason why *Lady Chatterley's Lover* dramatized this question so vividly was that it's a rather preachy and self-conscious book: like the Sunday-school novels of my childhood, it bores me a little because it tries so hard to do me good.

So literature has no consistent connection with ordinary life, positive or negative. Here we touch on another important difference between structures of the imagination and structures of practical sense, which include the applied sciences. Imagination is certainly essential to science, applied or pure. Without a constructive power in the mind to make models of experience, get hunches and follow them out, play freely around with hypotheses, and so forth, no scientist could get anywhere. But all imaginative effort in practical fields has to meet the test of practicability, otherwise it's discarded. The imagination in literature has no such test to meet. You don't relate it directly to life or reality: you relate works of literature to each other. Whatever value there is in studying literature, cultural or practical, comes from the total body of our reading, the castle of words we've built, and keep adding new wings to all the time.

So it's natural to swing to the opposite extreme and say that literature is really a refuge or escape from life, a self-contained world like the world of the dream, a world of play or make-believe to balance the world of work. Some literature is like that, and many people tell us that they only read to get away from reality for a bit. And I've suggested myself that the sense of escape, or at least detachment, does come into everybody's literary experience. But the real point of literature can hardly be that. Think of such writers as William Faulkner or François Mauriac, their great moral dignity, the intensity and compassion that they've studied the life around them with. Or think of James Joyce, spending seven years on one book and seventeen on another, and having them ridiculed or abused or banned by the customs when they did get published. Or of the poets Rilke and Valéry, waiting patiently for years in silence until what they had to say was ready to be said. There's a deadly seriousness in all this that even the most refined theories of fantasy or make-believe won't quite cover. Still, let's go along with the idea for a bit, because we're not getting on very fast with the relation of literature of life, or what we could call the horizontal perspective of literature. That seems to block us off on all sides.

The world of literature is a world where there is no reality except that of the human imagination. We see a great deal in it that reminds us vividly of the life we know. But in that very vividness there's something unreal. We can understand this more clearly with pictures, perhaps. There are trick-pictures—*trompe l'oeil*, the French call them—where the resemblance to life is very strong. An American painter of this school played a joke on his bitchy wife by painting one of her best napkins so expertly that she grabbed at the canvas trying to pull it off. But a painting as realistic as that isn't a reality but an illusion: it has the glittering unnatural clarity of a hallucination. The real realities, so to speak, are things that don't remind us directly of our own experience, but are such things as the wrath of Achilles or the jealousy of Othello, which are bigger and more intense experiences than anything we can reach—except in our imagination, which is what we're reaching with. Sometimes, as in the happy endings of comedies, or in the ideal world of romances, we seem to be looking at a pleasanter world than we ordinarily know. Sometimes, as in tragedy and satire, we seem to be looking at a world more devoted to suffering or absurdity than we ordinarily know. In literature we always seem to be looking either up or down. It's the vertical perspective that's important, not the horizontal one that looks out to life. Of course, in the greatest works of literature we get both the up and down views, often at the same time as different aspects of one event.

There are two halves to literary experience, then. Imagination gives us both a better and a worse world than the one we usually live with, and demands that we keep looking steadily at them both. The arts follow the path of the emotions, and of the tendency of the emotions to separate the world into a half that we like and a half that we don't like. Literature is not a world of dreams, but it would be if we had only one half without the other. If we had nothing but romances and comedies with happy endings, literature would express only a wish-fulfilment dream. Some people ask why poets want to write tragedies when the world's so full of them anyway, and suggest that enjoying such things has something morbid or gloating about it. It doesn't, but it might if there were nothing else in literature.

This point is worth spending another minute on. You recall that terrible scene in *King Lear* where Gloucester's eyes are put out on the stage. That's part of a play, and a play is supposed to be entertaining. Now in what sense can a scene like that be entertaining? The fact that it's not really happening is certainly important. It would be degrading to watch a real blinding scene, and far more so to get any pleasure out of watching it. Consequently, the entertainment doesn't consist in its reminding us of a real blinding scene. If it did, one of the great scenes of drama would turn into a piece of repulsive pornography. We couldn't stop anyone from reacting in this way, and it certainly wouldn't cure him, much less help the public, to start blaming or censoring Shakespeare for putting sadistic ideas in his head. But a reaction of that kind has nothing to do with drama. In a dramatic scene of cruelty and hatred we're seeing cruelty and hatred, which we know are permanently real things in human life, from the point of view of the imagination. What the imagination suggests is horror, not the paralyzing sickening horror of a real blinding scene, but an exuberant horror, full of the energy of repudiation. This is as powerful a rendering as we can ever get of life as we don't want it.

So we see that there are moral standards in literature after all, even though they have nothing to do with calling the police when we see a word in a book that's more familiar in sound that in print. One of the things Gloucester says in that scene is: "I am tied to the stake, and I must stand the course." In Shakespeare's day it was a favorite sport to tie a bear to a stake and set dogs on it until they killed it. The Puritans suppressed this sport, according to Macaulay, not because it gave pain to the bear but because it gave pleasure to the spectators. Macaulay may have intended his remark to be a sneer at the Puritans, but surely if the Puritans did feel this way they were one hundred per cent right. What other reason is there for abolishing public hangings? Whatever their motives, the Puritans and Shakespeare were operating in the same direction. Literature keeps presenting the most vicious things to us as entertainment, but what it appeals to is not any pleasure in these things, but the exhilaration of standing apart from them and being able to see them for what they are because they aren't really happening. The more exposed we are to this, the less likely we are to find an unthinking pleasure in cruel or evil things. As the eighteenth century said in a fine mouth-filling phrase, literature refines our sensibilities.

The top half of literature is the world expressed by such words as sublime, inspiring, and the like, where what we feel is not detachment but absorption. This is the world of heroes and gods and titans and Rabelaisian giants, a world of powers and passions and moments of ecstasy far greater than anything we meet outside the imagination. Such forces would not only absorb but annihilate us if they entered ordinary life, but luckily the protecting wall of the imagination is here too. As the German poet Rilke says, we adore them because they disdain to destroy us. We seem to have got quite a long way from our emotions with their division of things into "I like this" and "I don't like this." Literature gives us an experience that stretches us vertically to the heights and depths of what the human mind can conceive, to what corresponds to the conceptions of heaven and hell in religion. In this perspective what I like or don't like disappears, because there's nothing left of me as a separate person: as a reader of literature I exist only as a representative of humanity as a whole.

No matter how much experience we may gather in life, we can never in life get the dimension of experience that the imagination gives us. Only the arts and sciences can do that, and of these, only literature gives us the whole sweep and range of human imagination as it sees itself. It seems to be very difficult for many people to understand the reality and intensity of literary experience. To give an example that you may think a bit irrelevant: why have so many people managed to convince themselves that Shakespeare did not write Shakespeare's plays, when there is not an atom of evidence that anybody else did? Apparently because they feel that poetry must be written out of personal experience, and that Shakespeare didn't have enough experience of the right kind. But Shakespeare's plays weren't produced by his experience: they were produced by his imagination, and the way to develop the imagination is to read a good book or two. As for us, we can't speak or think or comprehend even our own experience except within the limits of our own power over words, and those limits have been established for us by our great writers.

Literature, then, is not a dream-world: it's two dreams, a wish-fulfillment dream and an anxiety dream, that are focused together, like a pair of glasses, and become a fully conscious vision. Art, according to Plato, is a dream for awakened minds, a work of imagination withdrawn from ordinary life, dominated by the same forces that dominate the dream, and yet giving us a perspective and dimension on reality that we don't get from any other approach to reality. So the poet and the dreamer are distinct, as Keats says. Ordinary life forms a community, and literature is among other things an art of communication, so it forms a community too. In ordinary life we fall into a private and separate subconscious every night, where we reshape the world according to a private and separate imagination. Underneath literature there's another kind of subconscious, which is social and not private, a need for forming a community around certain symbols, like the Queen and the flag, or around certain gods that represent order and stability, or becoming and change, or death and rebirth to a new life. This is the myth-making power of the human mind, which throws up and dissolves one civilization after another.

I've taken my title, "The Keys to Dreamland," from what is possibly the greatest single effort of the literary imagination in the twentieth century, Joyce's *Finnegans Wake*. In this book a man goes to sleep and falls, not into the Freudian separate or private subconscious, but into the deeper dream of man that creates and destroys his own societies. The entire book is written in the language of this dream. It's a subconscious language, mainly English, but connected by associations and puns with the eighteen or so other languages that Joyce knew. *Finnegans Wake* is not a book to read, but a book to decipher: as Joyce says, it's about a dreamer, but it's addressed to an ideal reader suffering from an ideal insomnia. The reader or critic, then, has a role complementing the poet's role. We need two powers in literature, a power to create and a power to understand.

In all our literary experience there are two kinds of response. There is the direct experience of the work itself, while we're reading a book or seeing a play, especially for the first time. This experience is uncritical, or rather pre-critical, so it's not infallible. If our experience is limited, we can be roused to enthusiasm or carried away by something that we can later see to have been second-rate or even phony. Then there is the conscious, critical response we make after we've finished reading or left the theatre, where we compare what we've experienced with other things of the same kind, and form a judgment of value and proportion on it. This critical response, with practice, gradually makes our pre-critical responses more sensitive and accurate, or improves our taste, as we say. But behind our responses to individual works, there's a bigger response to our literary experience as a whole, as a total possession.

The critic has always been called a judge of literature, which means, not that he's in a superior position to the poet, but that he ought to know something about literature, just as a judge's right to be on a bench depends on his knowledge of law. If he's up against something the size of Shakespeare, he's the one being judged. The critic's function is to interpret every work of literature in the light of all the literature he knows, to keep constantly struggling to understand what literature as a whole is about. Literature as a whole is not an aggregate of exhibits with red and blue ribbons attached to them, like a cat show, but the range of articulate human imagination as it extends from the height of imaginative heaven to the depth of imaginative hell. Literature is a human apocalypse, man's revelation to man, and criticism is not a body of adjudications, but the awareness of that revelation, the last judgment of mankind.

1964

QUESTIONS

1. Frye uses the word "conventions" a number of times; what meanings does he appear to give the word? Why does he seek to show that life has conventions as does literature? Are they the

same sort of conventions?

2. Early in his essay Frye makes some amusing remarks about poets and their ways. Is he making fun of them? If so, why? Does he suggest that poets are contemptible? If not, what is he trying to do?

3. Toward what sort of audience is Frye addressing his remarks? What can you tell about the audience he has in view from the language he chooses, and from the line of development his essay takes? What conception of the relationship between life and literature does Frye assume his audience might have at the outset? Does Frye seek to persuade his audience to adopt a certain view of literature, perhaps to change a previous view? What devices in his writing (as of tone, diction, figures of speech) are directed toward persuasion?

4. What ideas about literature and its relationship to life does Frye examine and reject? Why does he reject them? What are the main features of his own position? Does he set forth that position in a single thesis sentence anywhere in the essay?

5. What is Frye's view of the moral effect of art and literature? How does his view compare with that of Krutch ("Modern Painting," (pp. 272–278)?

CARL GUSTAV JUNG
The Poet

Creativeness, like the freedom of the will, contains a secret. The psychologist can describe both these manifestations as processes, but he can find no solution of the philosophical problems they offer. Creative man is a riddle that we may try to answer in various ways, but always in vain, a truth that has not prevented modern psychology from turning now and again to the question of the artist and his art. Freud thought that he had found a key in his procedure of deriving the work of art from the personal experiences of the artist. It is true that certain possibilities lay in this direction, for it was conceivable that a work of art, no less than a neurosis, might be traced back to those knots in psychic life that we call the complexes. It was Freud's great discovery that neuroses have a causal origin in the psychic realm—that they take their rise from emotional states and from real or imagined childhood experiences. Certain of his followers, like Rank and Stekel, have taken up related lines of enquiry and have achieved important results. It is undeniable that the poet's psychic disposition permeates his work root and branch. Nor is there anything new in the statement that personal factors largely influence the poet's choice and use of his materials. Credit, however, must certainly be given to the Freudian school for showing how far-reaching this influence is and in what curious ways it comes to expression.

Freud takes the neurosis as a substitute for a direct means of gratification. He therefore regards it as something inappropriate—a mistake, a dodge, an excuse, a voluntary blindness. To him it is essentially a shortcoming that should never have been. Since a neurosis, to all appearances, is nothing but a disturbance that is all the more irritating because it is without sense or meaning, few people will venture to say a good word for it. And a work of art is brought into questionable proximity with the neurosis when it is taken as something which can be analysed in terms of the poet's repressions. In a sense it finds itself in good company, for religion and philosophy are regarded in the same light by Freudian psychology. No objection can be raised if it is admitted that this approach amounts to nothing more than the elucidation of those personal determinants without which a work of art is unthinkable. But should the claim be made that such an analysis accounts for the work of art itself, then a categorical denial is called for. The personal idiosyncrasies that creep into a work of art are not essential; in fact, the more we have to cope with these peculiarities, the less is it a question of art. What is essential in a work of art is that it should rise far above the realm of personal life and speak from the spirit and heart of the poet as man to the spirit and heart of mankind. The personal aspect is a limitation—and even a sin—in the realm of art. When a form of "art" is primarily personal it deserves to be treated as if it were a neurosis. There may be some validity in the idea held by the Freudian school that artists without exception are narcissistic—by which is meant that they are undeveloped persons with infantile and auto-erotic traits. The statement is only valid, however, for the artist as a person, and has nothing to do with the man as an artist. In his capacity of artist he is neither auto-erotic, nor hetero-erotic, nor erotic in any sense. He is objective and impersonal—even inhuman —for as an artist he is his work, and not a human being.

Every creative person is a duality or a synthesis of contradictory aptitudes. On the one side he is a human being with a personal life, while on the other side he is an impersonal, creative process. Since as a human being he may be sound or morbid, we must look at his psychic make-up to find the determinants of his personality. But we can only understand him in his capacity of artist by looking at his creative achievement. We should make a sad mistake if we tried to explain the mode of life of an English gentleman, a Prussian officer, or a cardinal in terms of personal factors. The gentleman, the officer and the cleric function as such in an impersonal role, and their psychic make-up is qualified by a peculiar objectivity. We must grant that the artist does not function in an official capacity—the very opposite is nearer the truth. He nevertheless resembles the types I have named in one respect, for the specifically artistic disposition involves an overweight of collective psychic life as against the personal. Art is a kind of innate drive that seizes a human being and makes him its instrument. The artist is not a person endowed with free will who seeks his own ends, but one who allows art to realize its purposes through him. As a human being he may have moods and a will and personal aims, but as an artist he is "man" in a higher sense—he is "collective man"—one who carries and shapes the unconscious, psychic life of mankind. To perform this difficult office it is sometimes necessary for him to sacrifice happiness and everything that makes life worth living for the ordinary human being.

All this being so, it is not strange that the artist is an especially interesting case for the psychologist who uses an analytical method. The artist's life cannot be otherwise than full of conflicts, for two forces are at war within him—on the one hand the common human longing for happiness, satisfaction and security in life, and on the other a ruthless passion for creation which may go so far as to override every personal desire. The lives of artists are as a rule so highly unsatisfactory—not to say tragic—because of their inferiority on the human and personal side, and not because of a sinister dispensation. There are hardly any exceptions to the rule that a person must pay dearly for the divine gift of the creative fire. It is as though each of us were endowed at birth with a certain capital of energy. The strongest force in our make-up will seize and all but monopolize this energy, leaving so little over that nothing of value can come of it. In this way the creative force can drain the human impulses to such a degree that the personal ego must develop all sorts of bad qualities—ruthlessness, selfishness and vanity (so-called "auto-erotism")—and even every kind of vice, in order to maintain the spark of life and to keep itself from being wholly bereft. The auto-erotism of artists resembles that of illegitimate or neglected children who from their tenderest years must protect themselves from the destructive influence of people who have no love to give them—who develop bad qualities for that very purpose and later maintain an invincible egocentrism by remaining all their lives infantile and helpless or by actively offending against the moral code or the law. How can we doubt that it is his art that explains the artist, and not the insufficiencies and conflicts of his personal life? These are nothing but the regrettable results of the fact that he is an artist—

that is to say, a man who from his very birth has been called to a greater task than the ordinary mortal. A special ability means a heavy expenditure of energy in a particular direction, with a consequent drain from some other side of life.

It makes no difference whether the poet knows that his work is begotten, grows and matures with him, or whether he supposes that by taking thought he produces it out of the void. His opinion of the matter does not change the fact that his own work outgrows him as a child its mother. The creative process has feminine quality, and the creative work arises from unconscious depths—we might say, from the realm of the mothers. Whenever the creative force predominates, human life is ruled and moulded by the unconscious as against the active will, and the conscious ego is swept along on a subterranean current, being nothing more than a helpless observer of events. The work in process becomes the poet's fate and determines his psychic development. It is not Goethe who creates *Faust*, but *Faust* which creates Goethe. And what is *Faust* but a symbol? By this I do not mean an allegory that points to something all too familiar, but an expression that stands for something not clearly known and yet profoundly alive. Here it is something that lives in the soul of every German, and that Goethe has helped to bring to birth. Could we conceive of anyone but a German writing *Faust* or *Also sprach Zarathustra?* Both play upon something that reverberates in the German soul—a "primordial image," as Jacob Burckhardt once called it—the figure of a physician or teacher of mankind. The archetypal image of the wise man, the saviour or redeemer, lies buried and dormant in man's unconscious since the dawn of culture; it is awakened whenever the times are out of joint and a human society is committed to a serious error. When people go astray they feel the need of a guide or teacher or even of the physician. These primordial images are numerous, but do not appear in the dreams of individuals or in works of art until they are called into being by the waywardness of the general outlook. When conscious life is characterized by one-sidedness and by a false attitude, then they are activated—one might say, "instinctively"—and come to light in the dreams of individuals and the visions of artists and seers, thus restoring the psychic equilibrium of the epoch.

In this way the work of the poet comes to meet the spiritual need of the society in which he lives, and for this reason his work means more to him than his personal fate, whether he is aware of this or not. Being essentially the instrument for his work, he is subordinate to it, and we have no reason for expecting him to interpret it for us. He has done the best that in him lies in giving it form, and he must leave the interpretation to others and to the future. A great work of art is like a dream; for all its apparent obviousness it does not explain itself and is never unequivocal. A dream never says: "You ought," or: "This is the truth." It presents an image in much the same way as nature allows a plant to grow, and we must draw our own conclusions. If a person has a nightmare, it means either that he is too much given to fear, or else that he is too exempt from it; and if he dreams of the old wise man it may mean that he is too pedagogical, as also that he stands in need of a teacher. In a subtle way both meanings come to the same thing, as we perceive when we are able to let the work of art act upon us as it acted upon the artist. To grasp its meaning, we must allow it to shape us as it once shaped him. Then we understand the nature of his experience. We see that he has drawn upon the healing and redeeming forces of the collective psyche that underlies consciousness with its isolation and its painful errors; that he has penetrated to that matrix of life in which all men are embedded, which imparts a common rhythm to all human existence, and allows the individual to communicate his feeling and his striving to mankind as a whole.

The secret of artistic creation and of the effectiveness of art is to be found in a return to the state of *participation mystique*—to that level of experience at which it is man who lives, and not the individual, and at which the weal or woe of the single human being does not count, but only human existence. This is why every great work of art is objective and impersonal, but none the less profoundly moves us each and all. And this is also why the personal life of the poet cannot be held essential to his art—but at most a help or a hindrance to his creative task. He may go the way of a Philistine, a good citizen, a neurotic, a fool or a criminal. His personal career may be inevitable and interesting, but it does not explain the poet.

1946

QUESTIONS

1. Jung makes a distinction between the "human being with a personal life" and the "impersonal, creative process." What is the importance of this distinction? How does it help to shape the rest of Jung's argument?

2. Jung says that the "personal idiosyncrasies that creep into a work of art are not essential," since art "should rise far above the realm of personal life and speak from the spirit and heart of the poet as man to the spirit and heart of mankind." Is a contradiction involved here? Can a poet speak from his heart without being personal? Are "personal idiosyncrasies" desirable in a work to give it the flavor of a distinctive style?

3. In "The Keys to Dreamland" (p. 239), Frye says that "litera-

ture has no consistent connection with ordinary life. . . . You don't relate it directly to life or reality: you relate works of literature to each other." Compare Frye's view with Jung's statement that "a great work of art is like a dream: . . . It presents an image in much the same way as nature allows a plant to grow, and we must draw our own conclusions."

4. Consider the following stanzas (69–72) from Byron's "Childe Harold's Pilgrimage." To what extent would Jung feel that psychological considerations were helpful in analyzing these lines?

> To fly from, need not be to hate, mankind:
> All are not fit with them to stir and toil,
> Nor is it discontent to keep the mind
> Deep in its fountain, lest it overboil
> In the hot throng, where we become the spoil
> Of our infection, till too late and long
> We may deplore and struggle with the coil,
> In wretched interchange of wrong for wrong
> Midst a contentious world, striving where none are strong.
>
> There, in a moment we may plunge our years
> In fatal penitence, and in the blight
> Of our own Soul turn all our blood to tears,
> And colour things to come with hues of Night;
> The race of life becomes a hopeless flight
> To those that walk in darkness: on the sea
> The boldest steer but where their ports invite—
> But there are wanderers o'er Eternity
> Whose bark drives on and on, and anchored ne'er shall be.
>
> Is it not better, then, to be alone,
> And love Earth only for its earthly sake?
> By the blue rushing of the arrowy Rhone,
> Or the pure bosom of its nursing Lake,
> Which feeds it as a mother who doth make
> A fair but froward infant her own care,
> Kissing its cries away as these awake;—
> Is it not better thus our lives to wear,
> Than join the crushing crowd, doomed to inflict or bear?
>
> I live not in myself, but I become
> Portion of that around me; and to me
> High mountains are a feeling, but the hum
> Of human cities torture: I can see
> Nothing to loathe in Nature, save to be
> A link reluctant in a fleshly chain,
> Classed among creatures, when the soul can flee,
> And with the sky—the peak—the heaving plain.
> Of ocean, or the stars, mingle—and not in vain.

ROBERT FROST

Education by Poetry: A Meditative Monologue[1]

I am going to urge nothing in my talk. I am not an advocate. I am
going to consider a matter, and commit a description. And I am
going to describe other colleges than Amherst. Or, rather say all
that is good can be taken as about Amherst; all that is bad will be
about other colleges.

I know whole colleges where all American poetry is barred—whole
colleges. I know whole colleges where all contemporary poetry is
barred.

I once heard of a minister who turned his daughter—his poetry-
writing daughter—out on the street to earn a living, because he said
there should be no more books written; God wrote one book, and that
was enough. (My friend George Russell, "Æ", has read no literature,
he protests, since just before Chaucer.)

That all seems sufficiently safe, and you can say one thing for it.
It takes the onus off the poetry of having to be used to teach children
anything. It comes pretty hard on poetry, I sometimes think, what
it has to bear in the teaching process.

Then I know whole colleges where, though they let in older
poetry, they manage to bar all that is poetical in it by treating it as
something other than poetry. It is not so hard to do that. Their reason
I have often hunted for. It may be that these people act from a kind of
modesty. Who are professors that they should attempt to deal with
a thing as high and as fine as poetry? Who are *they*? There is a
certain manly modesty in that.

That is the best general way of settling the problem; treat all
poetry as if it were something else than poetry, as if it were syntax,
language, science. Then you can even come down into the American
and into the contemporary without any special risk.

There is another reason they have, and that is that they are, first
and foremost in life, markers. They have the marking problem to
consider. Now, I stand here a teacher of many years' experience and I
have never complained of having had to mark. I had rather mark
anyone for anything—for his looks, carriage, his ideas, his correctness,
his exactness, anything you please—I would rather give him a mark
in terms of letters, A, B, C, D, than have to use adjectives on him.
We are all being marked by each other all the time, classified,
ranked, put in our place, and I see no escape from that. I am no
sentimentalist. You have got to mark, and you have got to mark,
first of all, for accuracy, for correctness. But if I am going to give a
mark, that is the least part of my marking. The hard part is the
part beyond that, the part where the adventure begins.

1. An address given at Amherst College in 1930.

One other way to rid the curriculum of the poetry nuisance has been considered. More merciful than the others it would neither abolish nor denature the poetry, but only turn it out to disport itself, with the plays and games—in no wise discredited, though given no credit for. Any one who liked to teach poetically could take his subject, whether English, Latin, Greek or French, out into the nowhere along with the poetry. One side of a sharp line would be left to the rigorous and righteous; the other side would be assigned to the flowery where they would know what could be expected of them. Grade marks were more easily given, of course, in the courses concentrating on correctness and exactness as the only forms of honesty recognized by plain people; a general indefinite mark of X in the courses that scatter brains over taste and opinion. On inquiry I have found no teacher willing to take position on either side of the line, either among the rigors or among the flowers. No one is willing to admit that his discipline is not partly in exactness. No one is willing to admit that his discipline is not partly in taste and enthusiasm.

How shall a man go through college without having been marked for taste and judgment? What will become of him? What will his end be? He will have to take continuation courses for college graduates. He will have to go to night schools. They are having night schools now, you know, for college graduates. Why? Because they have not been educated enough to find their way around in contemporary literature. They don't know what they may safely like in the libraries and galleries. They don't know how to judge an editorial when they see one. They don't know how to judge a political campaign. They don't know when they are being fooled by a metaphor, an analogy, a parable. And metaphor is, of course, what we are talking about. Education by poetry is education by metaphor.

Suppose we stop short of imagination, initiative, enthusiasm, inspiration and originality—dread words. Suppose we don't mark in such things at all. There are still two minimal things, that we have got to take care of, taste and judgment. Americans are supposed to have more judgment than taste, but taste is there to be dealt with. That is what poetry, the only art in the colleges of arts, is there for. I for my part would not be afraid to go in for enthusiasm. There is the enthusiasm like a blinding light, or the enthusiasm of the deafening shout, the crude enthusiasm that you get uneducated by poetry, outside of poetry. It is exemplified in what I might call "sunset raving." You look westward toward the sunset, or if you get up early enough, eastward toward the sunrise, and you rave. It is oh's and ah's with you and no more.

But the enthusiasm I mean is taken through the prism of the intellect and spread on the screen in a color, all the way from hyperbole at one end—or overstatement, at one end—to understatement at the other end. It is a long strip of dark lines and many colors. Such enthusiasm is one object of all teaching in poetry. I heard wonderful things said about Virgil yesterday, and many of them seemed to me crude enthusiasm, more like a deafening shout, many of them. But one speech had range, something of overstatement, something of statement, and something of understatement. It had all the colors of an enthusiasm passed through an idea.

I would be willing to throw away everything else but that: enthusiasm tamed by metaphor. Let me rest the case there. Enthusiasm tamed to metaphor, tamed to that much of it. I do not think anybody ever knows the discreet use of metaphor, his own and other people's, the discreet handling of metaphor, unless he has been properly educated in poetry.

Poetry begins in trivial metaphors, petty metaphors, "grace" metaphors, and goes on to the profoundest thinking that we have. Poetry provides the one permissible way of saying one thing and meaning another. People say, "Why don't you say what you mean?" We never do that, do we, being all of us too much poets. We like to talk in parables and in hints and in indirections—whether from diffidence or some other instinct.

I have wanted in late years to go further and further in making metaphor the whole of thinking. I find some one now and then to agree with me that all thinking, except mathematical thinking, is metaphorical, or all thinking except scientific thinking. The mathematical might be difficult for me to bring in, but the scientific is easy enough.

Once on a time all the Greeks were busy telling each other what the All was—or was like unto. All was three elements, air, earth, and water (we once thought it was ninety elements; now we think it is only one). All was substance, said another. All was change, said a third. But best and most fruitful was Pythagoras' comparison of the universe with number. Number of what? Number of feet, pounds, and seconds was the answer, and we had science and all that has followed in science. The metaphor has held and held, breaking down only when it came to the spiritual and psychological or the out of the way places of the physical.

The other day we had a visitor here, a noted scientist, whose latest word to the world has been that the more accurately you know where a thing is, the less accurately you are able to state how fast it is moving. You can see why that would be so, without going back to Zeno's problem of the arrow's flight. In carrying numbers into the realm of space and at the same time into the realm of time you are mixing metaphors, that is all, and you are in trouble. They won't mix. The two don't go together.

Let's take two or three more of the metaphors now in use to live by. I have just spoken of one of the new ones, a charming mixed metaphor right in the realm of higher mathematics and higher physics: that the more accurately you state where a thing is, the less accurately you will be able to tell how fast it is moving. And, of course everything is moving. Everything is an event now. Another metaphor. A thing, they say, is an event. Do you believe it is? Not quite. I believe it is almost an event. But I like the comparison of a thing with an event.

I notice another from the same quarter. "In the neighborhood of matter space is something like curved." Isn't that a good one! It seems to me that that is simply and utterly charming—to say that space is something like curved in the neighborhood of matter. "Something like."

Another amusing one is from—what is the book?—I can't say it now; but here is the metaphor. Its aim is to restore you to your ideas of free will. It wants to give you back your freedom of will. All right, here it is on a platter. You know that you can't tell by name what persons in a certain class will be dead ten years after graduation, but you can tell actuarially how many will be dead. Now, just so this scientist says of the particles of matter flying at a screen, striking a screen; you can't tell what individual particles will come, but you can say in general that a certain number will strike in a given time. It shows, you see, that the individual particle can come freely. I asked Bohr about that particularly, and he said, "Yes, it is so. It can come when it wills and as it wills; and the action of the individual particle is unpredictable. But it is not so of the action of the mass. There you can predict." He says, "That gives the individual atom its freedom, but the mass its necessity."

Another metaphor that has interested us in our time and has done all our thinking for us is the metaphor of evolution. Never mind going into the Latin word. The metaphor is simply the metaphor of the growing plant or of the growing thing. And somebody very brilliantly, quite a while ago, said that the whole universe, the whole of everything, was like unto a growing thing. That is all. I know the metaphor will break down at some point, but it has not failed everywhere. It is a very brilliant metaphor, I acknowledge, though I myself get too tired of the kind of essay that talks about the evolution of candy, we will say, or the evolution of elevators—the evolution of this, that, and the other. Everything is evolution. I emancipate myself by simply saying that I didn't get up the metaphor and so am not much interested in it.

What I am pointing out is that unless you are at home in the metaphor, unless you have had your proper poetical education in the metaphor, you are not safe anywhere. Because you are not at ease with figurative values: you don't know the metaphor in its strength and its weakness. You don't know how far you may expect to ride it and when it may break down with you. You are not safe in science; you are not safe in history. In history, for instance—to show that is the same in history as elsewhere—I heard somebody say yesterday that Aeneas was to be likened unto (those words, "likened unto"!) George Washington. He was that type of national hero, the middle-class man, not thinking of being a hero at all, bent on building the future, bent on his children, his descendants. A good metaphor, as far as it goes, and you must know how far. And then he added that Odysseus should be likened unto Theodore Roosevelt. I don't think that is so good. Someone visiting Gibbon at the point of death, said he was the same Gibbon as of old; still at his parallels.

Take the way we have been led into our present position morally, the world over. It is by a sort of metaphorical gradient. There is a kind of thinking—to speak metaphorically—there is a kind of thinking you might say was endemic in the brothel. It is always there. And every now and then in some mysterious way it becomes epidemic in the world. And how does it do so? By using all the good words that virtue has invented to maintain virtue. It uses honesty, first—frankness, sincerity—those words; picks them up, uses them. "In the name of honesty, let us see what we are." You know. And then it picks up the word joy. "Let us in the name of joy, which is the enemy of our ancestors, the Puritans . . . Let us in the name of joy, which is the enemy of the kill-joy Puritan . . . " You see. "Let us," and so on. And then, "In the name of health . . . " Health is another good word. And that is the metaphor Freudianism trades on, mental health. And the first thing we know, it has us all in up to the top knot. I suppose we may blame the artists a good deal, because they are great people to spread by metaphor. The stage too—the stage is always a good intermediary between the two worlds, the under and the upper, if I may say so without personal prejudice to the stage.

In all this, I have only been saying that the devil can quote Scripture, which simply means that the good words you have lying around the devil can use for his purposes as well as anybody else. Never mind about my morality. I am not here to urge anything. I don't care whether the world is good or bad—not on any particular day.

Let me ask you to watch a metaphor breaking down here before you.

Somebody said to me a little while ago, "It is easy enough for me to think of the universe as a machine, as a mechanism."

I said, "You mean the universe is like a machine?"

He said, "No. I think it is one . . .Well, it is like . . ."

"I think you mean the universe is like a machine."

"All right. Let it go at that."

I asked him, "Did you ever see a machine without a pedal for the foot, or a lever for the hand, or a button for the finger?"

He said "No—no."

I said, "All right. Is the universe like that?"

And he said, "No. I mean it is like a machine, only . . ."

". . . it is different from a machine," I said.

He wanted to go just that far with that metaphor and no further. And so do we all. All metaphor breaks down somewhere. That is the beauty of it. It is touch and go with the metaphor, and until you have lived with it long enough you don't know when it is going. You don't know how much you can get out of it and when it will cease to yield. It is a very living thing. It is as life itself.

I have heard this ever since I can remember, and ever since I have taught: the teacher must teach the pupil to think. I saw a teacher once going around in a great school and snapping pupils' heads with thumb and finger and saying, "Think." That was when thinking was becoming the fashion. The fashion hasn't yet quite gone out.

We still ask boys in college to think, as in the nineties, but we seldom tell them what thinking means; we seldom tell them it is just putting this and that together; it is saying one thing in terms of another. To tell them is to set their feet on the first rung of a ladder the top of which sticks through the sky.

Greatest of all attempts to say one thing in terms of another is the philosophical attempt to say matter in terms of spirit, or spirit in terms of matter, to make the final unity. That is the greatest attempt that ever failed. We stop just short there. But it is the height of poetry, the height of all thinking, the height of all poetic thinking, that attempt to say matter in terms of spirit and spirit in terms of matter. It is wrong to call anybody a materialist simply because he tries to say spirit in terms of matter, as if that were a sin. Materialism is not the attempt to say all in terms of matter. The only materialist —be he poet, teacher, scientist, politician, or statesman—is the man who gets lost in his material without a gathering metaphor to throw it into shape and order. He is the lost soul.

We ask people to think, and we don't show them what thinking is. Somebody says we don't need to show them how to think; bye and bye they will think. We will give them the forms of sentences and, if they have any ideas, then they will know how to write them. But that is preposterous. All there is to writing is having ideas. To learn to write is to learn to have ideas.

The first little metaphor . . . Take some of the trivial ones. I would rather have trivial ones of my own to live by than the big ones of other people.

I remember a boy saying, "He is the kind of person that wounds with his shield." That may be a slender one, of course. It goes a good way in character description. It has poetic grace. "He is the kind that wounds with his shield."

The shield reminds me—just to linger a minute—the shield reminds me of the inverted shield spoken of in one of the books of the *Odyssey*, the book that tells about the longest swim on record. I forget how long it lasted—several days, was it?—but at last as

Odysseus came near the coast of Phoenicia, he saw it on the horizon "like an inverted shield."

There is a better metaphor in the same book. In the end Odysseus comes ashore and crawls up the beach to spend the night under a double olive tree, and it says, as in a lonely farmhouse where it is hard to get fire—I am not quoting exactly—where it is hard to start the fire again if it goes out, they cover the seeds of fire with ashes to preserve it for the night, so Odysseus covered himself with the leaves around him and went to sleep. There you have something that gives you character, something of Odysseus himself. "Seeds of fire." So Odysseus covered the seeds of fire in himself. You get the greatness of his nature.

But these are slighter metaphors than the ones we live by. They have their charm, their passing charm. They are as it were the first steps toward the great thoughts, grave thoughts, thoughts lasting to the end.

The metaphor whose manage we are best taught in poetry—that is all there is of thinking. It may not seem far for the mind to go but it is the mind's furthest. The richest accumulation of the ages is the noble metaphors we have rolled up.

I want to add one thing more that the experience of poetry is to anyone who comes close to poetry. There are two ways of coming close to poetry. One is by writing poetry. And some people think I want people to write poetry, but I don't; that is, I don't necessarily. I only want people to write poetry if they want to write poetry. I have never encouraged anybody to write poetry that did not want to write it, and I have not always encouraged those who did want to write it. That ought to be one's own funeral. It is a hard, hard life, as they say.

(I have just been to a city in the West, a city full of poets, a city they have made safe for poets. The whole city is so lovely that you do not have to write it up to make it poetry; it is ready-made for you. But, I don't know—the poetry written in that city might not seem like poetry if read outside of the city. It would be like the jokes made when you were drunk; you have to get drunk again to appreciate them.)

But as I say, there is another way to come close to poetry, fortunately, and that is in the reading of it, not as linguistics, not as history, not as anything but poetry. It is one of the hard things for a teacher to know how close a man has come in reading poetry. How do I know whether a man has come close to Keats in reading Keats? It is hard for me to know. I have lived with some boys a whole year over some of the poets and I have not felt sure whether they have come near what it was all about. One remark sometimes told me. One remark was their mark for the year; had to be—it was all I got that told me what I wanted to know. And that is enough, if it was the right remark, if it came close enough. I think a man might make twenty fool remarks if he made one good one some time in the year. His mark would depend on that good remark.

The closeness—everything depends on the closeness with which you come, and you ought to be marked for the closeness, for nothing else. And that will have to be estimated by chance remarks, not by question and answer. It is only by accident that you know some day how near a person has come.

The person who gets close enough to poetry, he is going to know more about the word *belief* than anybody else knows, even in religion nowadays. There are two or three places where we know belief outside of religion. One of them is at the age of fifteen to twenty, in our self-belief. A young man knows more about himself than he is able to prove to anybody. He has no knowledge that anybody else will accept as knowledge. In his foreknowledge he has something that is going to believe itself into fulfilment, into acceptance.

There is another belief like that, the belief in someone else, a relationship of two that is going to be believed into fulfilment. That is what we are talking about in our novels, the belief of love. And disillusionment that the novels are full of is simply the disillusionment from disappointment in that belief. That belief can fail, of course.

Then there is a literary belief. Every time a poem is written, every time a short story is written, it is written not by cunning, but by belief. The beauty, the something, the little charm of the thing to be, is more felt than known. There is a common jest, one that always annoys me, on the writers, that they write the last end first, and then work up to it; that they lay a train toward one sentence that they think is pretty nice and have all fixed up to set like a trap to close with. No, it should not be that way at all. No one who has ever come close to the arts has failed to see the difference between things written that way, with cunning and device, and the kind that are believed into existence, that begin in something more felt than known. This you can realize quite as well—not quite as well, perhaps, but nearly as well—in reading as you can in writing. I would undertake to separate short stories on that principle; stories that have been believed into existence and stories that have been cunningly devised. And I could separate the poems still more easily.

Now I think—I happen to think—that those three beliefs that I speak of, the self-belief, the love-belief, and the art-belief, are all closely related to the God-belief, that the belief in God is a relationship you enter into with Him to bring about the future.

There is a national belief like that, too. One feels it. I have been where I came near getting up and walking out on the people who thought that they had to talk against nations, against nationalism, in order to curry favor with internationalism. Their metaphors are all mixed up. They think that because a Frenchman and an American and an Englishman can all sit down on the same platform and receive honors together, it must be that there is no such thing as nations. That kind of bad thinking springs from a source we all know. I should want to say to anyone like that: "Look! First I want to be a person. And I want you to be a person, and then we can be as interpersonal as you please. We can pull each other's noses—do all sorts of things. But, first of all, you have got to have the personality. First of all, you have got to have the nations and then they can be as international as they please with each other."

I should like to use another metaphor on them. I want my palette, if I am a painter, I want my palette on my thumb or on my chair, all clean, pure, separate colors. Then I will do the mixing on the canvas. The canvas is where the work of art is, where we make the conquest. But we want the nations all separate, pure, distinct, things as separate as we can make them; and then in our thoughts, in our arts, and so on, we can do what we please about it.

But I go back. There are four beliefs that I know more about from having lived with poetry. One is the personal belief, which is a knowledge that you don't want to tell other people about because you cannot prove that you know. You are saying nothing about it till you see. The love belief, just the same, has that same shyness. It knows it cannot tell; only the outcome can tell. And the national belief we enter into socially with each other, all together, party of the first part, party of the second part, we enter into that to bring the future of the country. We cannot tell some people what it is we believe, partly, because they are too stupid to understand and partly because we are too proudly vague to explain. And anyway it has got to be fulfilled, and we are not talking until we know more, until we have something to show. And then the literary one in every work of art, not of cunning and craft, mind you, but of real art; that believing the thing into existence, saying as you go more than you even hoped you were going to be able to say, and coming with surprise to an end that you foreknew only with some sort of emotion. And then finally the relationship we enter into with God to believe the future in—to believe the hereafter in.

1930

QUESTIONS

1. In what way does the subtitle describe this essay? Is it rambling? Is it unified?
2. How can the "poetry nuisance" be gotten out of the curriculum? Does Frost think it ought to stay in? Why?
3. What is meant by "enthusiasm passed through an idea" and "enthusiasm tamed to metaphor" (p. 252)? What sort of meta-

phors does Frost use in those phrases, and what do they imply?
4. What does Frost mean when he says "unless you have had your proper poetical education in the metaphor, you are not safe anywhere" (**p.** 253)? Indicate some of the metaphors Frost examines in this essay. From what fields are they drawn? What does he say about each? Nominate some further metaphors—from politics, science, sociology, or anything else—and analyze them. To what extent are they useful? Do they have a breaking point? How might they mislead beyond the breaking point?
5. Frost admires a speech that has "range, something of overstatement, something of statement, and something of understatement." Is this spectrum visible in Frost's own speech? Show where and how.

E. B. WHITE
Some Remarks on Humor

Analysts have had their go at humor, and I have read some of this interpretative literature, but without being greatly instructed. Humor can be dissected, as a frog can, but the thing dies in the process and the innards are discouraging to any but the pure scientific mind.

In a newsreel theatre the other day I saw a picture of a man who had developed the soap bubble to a higher point than it had ever before reached. He had become the ace soap bubble blower of America, had perfected the business of blowing bubbles, refined it, doubled it, squared it, and had even worked himself up into a convenient lather. The effect was not pretty. Some of the bubbles were too big to be beautiful, and the blower was always jumping into them or out of them, or playing some sort of unattractive trick with them. It was, if anything, a rather repulsive sight. Humor is a little like that: it won't stand much blowing up, and it won't stand much poking. It has a certain fragility, an evasiveness, which one had best respect. Essentially, it is a complete mystery. A human frame convulsed with laughter, and the laughter becoming hysterical and uncontrollable, is as far out of balance as one shaken with the hiccoughs or in the throes of a sneezing fit.

One of the things commonly said about humorists is that they are really very sad people—clowns with a breaking heart. There is some truth in it, but it is badly stated. It would be more accurate, I think, to say that there is a deep vein of melancholy running through everyone's life and that the humorist, perhaps more sensible of it than some others, compensates for it actively and positively. Humorists fatten on trouble. They have always made trouble pay. They struggle along with a good will and endure pain cheerfully, knowing how well it will serve them in the sweet by and by. You find them wrestling with foreign languages, fighting folding ironing boards and swollen drainpipes, suffering the terrible discomfort of tight boots (or as Josh Billings[1] wittily called them, "tite" boots). They pour out their sorrows profitably, in a form that is not quite fiction nor quite fact either. Beneath the sparkling surface of these dilemmas flows the strong tide of human woe.

Practically everyone is a manic depressive of sorts, with his up moments and his down moments, and you certainly don't have to be a humorist to taste the sadness of situation and mood. But there is often a rather fine line between laughing and crying, and if a humorous piece of writing brings a person to the point where his emotional responses are untrustworthy and seem likely to break over into the opposite realm, it is because humor, like poetry, has an extra content. It plays close to the big hot fire which is Truth, and sometimes the reader feels the heat.

1954

1. Pseudonym of Henry Wheeler Shaw, nineteenth-century American humorist whose sketches often depended on an exaggerated imitation of the dialect of rural New England or New York.

QUESTIONS

1. White uses a number of concrete details (dissected frog, soap bubbles and bubble blower, clowns with a breaking heart, fighting folding ironing boards and swollen drain pipes, suffering the terrible discomfort of tight boots, big hot fire which is Truth). Which of these are metaphors or analogies (comparisons with a different kind of thing) and which are concrete examples of general statements? Why does White use so many metaphors or analogies in his definition?
2. Rewrite White's definition in abstract or general language, leaving out the analogies or metaphors and the concrete examples. Then compare the rewritten version with the original. Which is clearer? Which is more interesting to read?
3. Compare White's definition of humor with his definition of democracy (p. 518). Is there a recognizable similarity in language or style? In devices used?

X. J. KENNEDY
Who Killed King Kong?

The ordeal and spectacular death of King Kong, the giant ape, undoubtedly have been witnessed by more Americans than have ever seen a performance of *Hamlet, Iphigenia at Aulis,* or even *Tobacco Road.* Since RKO-Radio Pictures first released *King Kong,* a quarter-century has gone by; yet year after year, from prints that grow more rain-beaten, from sound tracks that grow more tinny, ticket-buyers by thousands still pursue Kong's luckless fight against the forces of technology, tabloid journalism, and the DAR. They see him chloroformed to sleep, see him whisked from his jungle isle to New York and placed on show, see him burst his chains to roam the city (lugging a frightened blonde), at last to plunge from the spire of the Empire State Building, machine-gunned by model airplanes.

Though Kong may die, one begins to think his legend unkillable. No clearer proof of his hold upon the popular imagination may be seen than what emerged one catastrophic week in March 1955, when New York WOR-TV programmed *Kong* for seven evenings in a row (a total of sixteen showings). Many a rival network vice-president must have scowled when surveys showed that *Kong*—the 1933 B-picture—had lured away fat segments of the viewing populace from such powerful competitors as Ed Sullivan, Groucho Marx and Bishop Sheen.

But even television has failed to run *King Kong* into oblivion. Coffee-in-the-lobby cinemas still show the old hunk of hokum, with the apology that in its use of composite shots and animated models the film remains technically interesting. And no other monster in movie history has won so devoted a popular audience. None of the plodding mummies, the stultified draculas, the white-coated Lugosis[1] with their shiny pinball-machine laboratories, none of the invisible stranglers, berserk robots, or menaces from Mars has ever enjoyed so many resurrections.

Why does the American public refuse to let King Kong rest in peace? It is true, I'll admit, that *Kong* outdid every monster movie before or since in sheer carnage. Producers Cooper and Schoedsack crammed into it dinosaurs, headhunters, riots, aerial battles, bullets, bombs, bloodletting. Heroine Fay Wray, whose function is mainly to scream, shuts her mouth for hardly one uninterrupted minute from first reel to last. It is also true that *Kong* is larded with good healthy sadism, for those whose joy it is to see the frantic girl

---

1. Bela Lugosi, an actor in many horror movies.

dangled from cliffs and harried by pterodactyls. But it seems to me that the abiding appeal of the giant ape rests on other foundations.

Kong has, first of all, the attraction of being manlike. His simian nature gives him one huge advantage over giant ants and walking vegetables in that an audience may conceivably identify with him. Kong's appeal has the quality that established the Tarzan series as American myth—for what man doesn't secretly image himself a huge hairy howler against whom no other monster has a chance? •If Tarzan recalls the ape in us, then Kong may well appeal to that great-granddaddy primordial brute from whose tribe we have all deteriorated.

Intentionally or not, the producers of *King Kong* encourage this identification by etching the character of Kong with keen sympathy. For the ape is a figure in a tradition familiar to moviegoers: the tradition of the pitiable monster. We think of Lon Chaney in the role of Quasimodo,[2] of Karloff in the original *Frankenstein*. As we watch the Frankenstein monster's fumbling and disastrous attempts to befriend a flower-picking child, our sympathies are enlisted with the monster in his impenetrable loneliness. And so with Kong. As he roars in his chains, while barkers sell tickets to boobs who gape at him, we perhaps feel something more deep than pathos. We begin to sense something of the problem that engaged Eugene O'Neill in *The Hairy Ape*: the dilemma of a displaced animal spirit forced to live in a jungle built by machines.

King Kong, it is true, had special relevance in 1933. Landscapes of the depression are glimpsed early in the film when an impresario, seeking some desperate pretty girl to play the lead in a jungle movie, visits souplines and a Woman's Home Mission. In Fay Wray—who's been caught snitching an apple from a fruitstand—his search is ended. When he gives her a big feed and a movie contract, the girl is magic-carpeted out of the world of the National Recovery Act.[3] And when, in the film's climax, Kong smashes that very Third Avenue landscape in which Fay had wandered hungry, audiences of 1933 may well have felt a personal satisfaction.

What is curious is that audiences of 1960 remain hooked. For in the heart of urban man, one suspects, lurks the impulse to fling a bomb. Though machines speed him to the scene of his daily grind, though IBM comptometers ("freeing the human mind from drudgery") enable him to drudge more efficiently once he arrives, there comes a moment when he wishes to turn upon his machines and kick hell out of them. He wants to hurl his combination radio-alarmclock out the bedroom window and listen to its smash. What

---

2. The title character of Victor Hugo's novel *The Hunchback of Notre Dame*.
3. Legislation intended to bring an end to the Great Depression of the 1930s.

subway commuter wouldn't love—just for once—to see the downtown express smack head-on into the uptown local? Such a wish is
gratified in that memorable scene in *Kong* that opens with a wide-
angle shot: interior of a railway car on the Third Avenue El. Strap-
hangers are nodding, the literate refold their newspapers. Unknown
to them, Kong has torn away a section of trestle toward which the
train now speeds. The motorman spies Kong up ahead, jams on the
brakes. Passengers hurtle together like so many peas in a pail. In a
window of the car appear Kong's bloodshot eyes. Women shriek.
Kong picks up the railway car as if it were a rat, flips it to the street
and ties knots in it, or something. To any commuter the scene must
appear one of the most satisfactory pieces of celluloid ever exposed.

Yet however violent his acts, Kong remains a gentleman. Remarkable is his sense of chivalry. Whenever a fresh boa constrictor threatens Fay, Kong first sees that the lady is safely parked, then man-
fully thrashes her attacker. (And she, the ingrate, runs away every
time his back is turned.) Atop the Empire State Building, ignoring
his pursuers, Kong places Fay on a ledge as tenderly as if she were
a dozen eggs. He fondles her, then turns to face the Army Air
Force. And Kong is perhaps the most disinterested lover since
Cyrano:[4] his attentions to the lady are utterly without hope of
reward. After all, between a five-foot blonde and a fifty-foot ape,
love can hardly be more than an intellectual flirtation. In his simian
way King Kong is the hopelessly yearning lover of Petrarchan convention.[5] His forced exit from his jungle, in chains, results directly
from his single-minded pursuit of Fay. He smashes a Broadway
theater when the notion enters his dull brain that the flashbulbs of
photographers somehow endanger the lady. His perilous shinnying
up a skyscraper to pluck Fay from her boudoir is an act of the
kindliest of hearts. He's impossible to discourage even though the
love of his life can't lay eyes on him without shrieking murder.

The tragedy of King Kong then, is to be the beast who at the
end of the fable fails to turn into the handsome prince. This is the
conviction that the scriptwriters would leave with us in the film's
closing line. As Kong's corpse lies blocking traffic in the street, the
enterpreneur who brought Kong to New York turns to the assembled reporters and proclaims: "That's your story, boys—it was
Beauty killed the Beast!" But greater forces than those of the
screaming Lady have combined to lay Kong low, if you ask me.
Kong lives for a time as one of those persecuted near-animal souls
bewildered in the middle of an industrial order, whose simple
desires are thwarted at every turn. He climbs the Empire State
Building because in all New York it's the closest thing he can find to

---

4. Hero of the romantic drama *Cyrano de Bergerac,* whose extreme sensitivity about his large nose keeps him
from professing his love.

5. The attitude of the lover in the
sonnets of the fourteenth-century Italian
poet Francis Petrarch and his followers.

the clifftop of his jungle isle. He dies, a pitiful dolt, and the army brass and publicity-men cackle over him. His death is the only possible outcome to as neat a tragic dilemma as you can ask for. The machine-guns do him in, while the manicured human hero (a nice clean Dartmouth boy) carries away Kong's sweetheart to the altar. O, the misery of it all. There's far more truth about upper-middle-class American life in *King Kong* than in the last seven dozen novels of John P. Marquand.[6]

A Negro friend from Atlanta tells me that in movie houses in colored neighborhoods throughout the South, *Kong* does a constant business. They show the thing in Atlanta at least every year, presumably to the same audiences. Perhaps this popularity may simply be due to the fact that Kong is one of the most watchable movies ever constructed, but I wonder whether Negro audiences may not find some archetypical appeal in this serio-comic tale of a huge black powerful free spirit whom all the hardworking white policemen are out to kill.

Every day in the week on a screen somewhere in the world, King Kong relives his agony. Again and again he expires on the Empire State Building, as audiences of the devout assist his sacrifice. We watch him die, and by extension kill the ape within our bones, but these little deaths of ours occur in prosaic surroundings. We do not die on a tower, New York before our feet, nor do we give our lives to smash a few flying machines. It is not for us to bring to a momentary standstill the civilization in which we move. King Kong does this for us. And so we kill him again and again, in much-spliced celluloid, while the ape in us expires from day to day, obscure, in desperation.

1960

6. Popular American author of novels of society.

JANET FLANNER

Isadora[1]

In the summer of 1926, like a ghost from the grave, Isadora Duncan began dancing again in Nice. Two decades before, her art, animated by her extraordinary public personality, came as close to founding an aesthetic renaissance as American morality would allow, and the provinces especially had a narrow escape. But in the postwar European years her body, whose Attic[2] splendor once brought Greece to Kansas and Kalamazoo, was approaching its half-century mark. Her spirit was still green as a bay tree, but her

1. Isadora Duncan (1878–1927), American dancer.   2. Classical Greek.

flesh was worn, perhaps by the weight of laurels. She was the last of the trilogy of great female personalities our century cherished. Two of them, Duse and Bernhardt,[3] had already gone to their elaborate national tombs. Only Isadora Duncan, the youngest, the American, remained wandering the foreign earth.

No one had taken Isadora's place in her own country and she was not missed. Of that fervor for the classic dance which she was the first to bring to a land bred on "Turkey in the Straw," beneficial signs remained from which she alone had not benefited. Eurythmic movements[4] were appearing in the curriculums of girls' schools. Vestal virgins formed a frieze about the altar fire of Saint Marks-in-the-Bouwerie on Sabbath afternoons. As a cross between gymnasiums and God, Greek-dance camps flourished in the Catskills, where under the summer spruce, metaphysics and muscles were welded in an Ilissan hocus-pocus for the female young.[5] Lisa, one of her first pupils, was teaching in the studio of the Théâtre des Champs-Elysées. Isadora's sister Elizabeth, to whom Greek might still be Greek if it had not been for Isadora, had a toga school in Berlin. Her brother Raymond, who operated a modern craft school in Paris, wore sandals and Socratic robes as if they were a family coat of arms. Isadora alone had neither sandals nor school. Most grandiose of all her influences, Diaghilev's Russian Ballet—which ironically owed its national rebirth to the inspiration of Isadora, then dancing with new terpsichorean ideals in Moscow was still seasoning as an exotic spectacle in London and Monte Carlo. Only Isadora, animator of all these forces, had become obscure. Only she, with her heroic sculptural movements, had dropped by the wayside, where she lay inert like one of those beautiful battered pagan tombs that still line the Sacred Way between Eleusis and the city of the Parthenon.[6]

As an artist, Isadora made her appearance in our plain and tasteless republic before the era of the half-nude revue, before the discovery of what is now called our Native Literary School, even before the era of the celluloid sophistication of the cinema, which by its ubiquity does so much to unite the cosmopolitanisms of Terre Haute and New York. What America now has, and gorges on in the way of sophistication, it then hungered for. Repressed by generations of Puritanism, it longed for bright, visible, and blatant beauty presented in a public form the simple citizenry could understand. Isadora appeared as a half-clothed Greek. . . .

A Paris *couturier* once said woman's modern freedom in dress is largely due to Isadora. She was the first artist to appear uncinctured,

3. Eleonora Duse and Sarah Bernhardt, celebrated tragic actresses of the generation before Duncan's.
4. Dance movements improvised in harmony with music.
5. Probably an allusion to dancing by the river Ilissus near ancient Athens. Isadora Duncan went to Greece and tried to recreate the kind of ritual or choric dancing that the ancients may have done at Ilissus and elsewhere.
6. That is, from the ancient city fourteen miles west of Athens to Athens itself.

barefooted, and free. She arrived like a glorious bounding Minerva[7] in the midst of a cautious corseted decade. The clergy, hearing of (though supposedly without ever seeing) her bare calf, denounced it as violently as if it had been golden. Despite its longings, for a moment America hesitated, Puritanism rather than poetry coupling lewd with nude in rhyme. But Isadora, originally from California and by then from Berlin, Paris, and other points, arrived bearing her gifts as a Greek. She came like a figure from the Elgin marbles.[8] The world over, and in America particularly, Greek sculpture was recognized to be almost notorious for its purity. The overpowering sentiment for Hellenic culture, even in the unschooled United States, silenced the outcries. Isadora had come as antique art and with such backing she became a cult.

Those were Isadora's great years. Not only in New York and Chicago but in the smaller, harder towns, when she moved across the stage, head reared, eyes mad, scarlet kirtle flying to the music of the "Marseillaise," she lifted from their seats people who had never left theater seats before except to get up and go home. Whatever she danced to, whether it was France's revolutionary hymn, or the pure salon passion of Chopin's waltzes, or the unbearable heat of Brahms' German mode, she conspired to make the atmosphere Greek, fusing *Zeitgeists*[9] and national sounds into one immortal Platonic pantomime.

Thus she inspired people who had never been inspired in their lives before, and to whom inspiration was exhilarating, useless, and unbecoming. Exalted at the concert hall by her display of Greek beauty, limbs, and drapes which though they were two thousand years old she seemed to make excitingly modern, her followers, dazzled, filled with Phidianisms, went home to Fords, big hats, and the theory of Bull Moose,[1] the more real items of their progressive age.

Dancing appeals less to the public than the other two original theatrical forms, drama and opera (unless, like the Russian Ballet, dancing manages to partake of all three). Nevertheless, Isadora not only danced but was demanded all over America and Europe. On the Continent she was more widely known than any other American of that decade, including Woodrow Wilson and excepting only Chaplin and Fairbanks, both of whom, via a strip of celluloid, could penetrate to remote hamlets without ever leaving Hollywood. But Isadora went everywhere in the flesh. She danced before kings

7. Roman goddess of the arts and handicrafts.
8. Sculptures brought by Lord Elgin from the Parthenon to the British Museum, in London.
9. Thoughts and feelings characteristic of the time.

1. The Progressive party, led by Theodore Roosevelt in the 1912 presidential election; *Phidianisms*: poses and gestures modeled on those of the statues of the gods by the great classical Greek sculptor Phidias.

and peasants. She danced from the Pacific to London, from Petrograd to the Black Sea, from Athens to Paris and Berlin.

She penetrated to the Georgian states of the Caucasus, riding third-class amid fleas and disease, performing in obscure halls before yokels and princes whom she left astonished, slightly enlightened, and somehow altered by the vision. For thirty years her life was more exciting and fantastic than anything Zola or Defoe[2] ever fabricated for their heroines. Her companions were the great public talent of our generation—Duse, D'Annunzio, Bakst, Bernhardt, Picabia, Brancusi, Anatole France, Comtesse Anna de Noailles, Sardou, Ellen Terry.[3]

Three of the greatest sculptors of her day at this time took Isadora's body as a permanent model and influence on their work though, alas, left no record in marble. Maillol alone made over five hundred drawings of Isadora dancing to Beethoven's Seventh Symphony; Rodin followed her all over Europe and literally made thousands of drawings, many still in the Musée Rodin in Paris. One of his most beautiful *gouaches*, now in the Metropolitan Museum, is *La Naissance d'un Vase Grecque*,[4] in which he used Isadora's torso as his inspiration. Bourdelle also used Isadora as the main typical figure in his Théâtre des Champs-Elysées frescoes. These artists made the likeness of Isadora's limbs and the loveliness of her small face immortal. This was the great, gay, successful period of life. Her friends ran the gamut from starving poets down to millionaires. She was prodigal of herself, her art, illusions, work, emotions, and everybody's funds. She spent fortunes. After the war was over in France, her Sunday-night suppers in the Rue de la Pompe were banquets where guests strolled in, strolled out, and from low divans supped principally on champagne and strawberry tarts, while Isadora, barely clad in chiffon robes, rose when the spirit moved her to dance exquisitely. Week after week came obscure people whose names she never even knew. They were like moths. She once gave a house party that started in Paris, gathered force in Venice, and culminated weeks later on a houseboat on the Nile. She was a nomad de luxe.

In order to promulgate her pedagogic theories of beauty and education for the young, she legally adopted and supported some thirty or forty children during her life, one group being the little Slavs who afterward danced in Soviet Russia. During her famous season at the New York Century Theatre where she gave a classic Greek

---

2. Émile Zola, nineteenth-century French novelist, and Daniel Defoe, eighteenth-century English novelist; Zola's Thérèse Raquin and Nana, and Defoe's Moll Flanders, outraged their contemporary readers' moral sense.
3. Figures prominent in the literary and visual arts and the theater.
4. *The Birth of a Greek Vase.*

cycle, *Oedipus Rex, Antigone,* and the like, she bought up every Easter lily in Manhattan to decorate the theater the night she opened in Berlioz's *L'Enfance du Christ,*[5] which was her Easter program. The lilies, whose perfume suffocated the spectators, cost two thousand dollars. Isadora had, at the moment, three thousand dollars to her name. And at midnight, long after all good lily-selling florists were in bed, she gave a champagne supper. It cost the other thousand.

Isadora, who had an un-American genius' for art, for organizing love, maternity, politics, and pedagogy on a great personal scale, had also an un-American genius for grandeur.

After the lilies faded, Isadora and her school sat amid their luggage on the pier where the ship was about to sail for France. They had neither tickets nor money. But they had a classic faith in fate and a determination to go back to Europe, where art was understood. Just before the boat sailed, there appeared a schoolteacher. Isadora had never seen her before. The teacher gave Isadora the savings of years and Isadora sailed away. Herself grand, she could inspire grandeur in others, a tragic and tiring gift. There were always schoolteachers and lilies in Isadora's life.

Those three summer programs which Isadora gave in 1926 at her studio in Nice were her last performances on earth. At the end of the next summer she was dead. One of the soirees was given with the concordance of Leo Tecktonius, the pianist, and the other two with Jean Cocteau,[6] who accompanied her dancing with his spoken verse. In all three performances her art was seen to have changed. She treaded the boards but little, she stood almost immobile or in slow splendid steps with slow splendid arms moved to music, seeking, hunting, finding. Across her face, tilting this way and that, fled the mortal looks of tragedy, knowledge, love, scorn, pain. Posing through the works of Wagner, through the tales of Dante, through the touching legend of St. Francis feeding crumbs and wisdom to his birds, Isadora was still great. By an economy (her first) she had arrived at elimination. As if the movements of dancing had become too redundant for her spirit, she had saved from dancing only its shape.

In one of her periodic fits of extravagant poverty and although needing the big sum offered, she once refused to dance in Wanamaker's[7] Auditorium, disdaining for her art such a "scene of suspenders." She refused to appear in certain Continental theaters because they contained restaurants where dining might distract the spectators from her art. She early refused (though she and her family

5. *The Childhood of Christ,* a concert work for singers and orchestra—and an improbable composition for dramatic performance.

6. French poet and dramatist.

7. A large department store.

were starving in Berlin) to dance at the Wintergarten for one thousand gold marks a night because there were animal acts on the bill. During the worst of her final financial predicaments in Paris, when few theaters were offering her anything at all, she refused to dance at the.Théâtre des Champs-Elysées because it was a music hall. Yet her image in sculpture adorned the theater's façade, where Bourdelle had chiseled her likeness for all times and passers-by. She talked vaguely of consenting to dance in Catalonia. To anyone who knew her it seemed natural that Isadora would like to dance in a castle in Spain.

The lack of money, which never worried Isadora as much as it anguished her devoted friends, became more acute during the last years of her life. Nevertheless she refused a legacy of over a quarter of a million francs from the estate of her stormy young husband, Yessenine, the Russian revolutionary poet whom she had married late and unhappily. At the worst of her final picturesque poverty, when, as Isadora gallantly declared, she hardly knew where the next bottle of champagne was coming from (champagne was the only libation she loved), it was decided by her friends that she should write her memoirs. At this time she was living in a small studio hotel in the Rue Delambre, behind the Café du Dôme in Paris. Isadora's handwriting was characteristic; it was large, handsome, illegible, with two or three words to a line and four or five lines to a page. During her authorship the scantly scribbled pages accumulated like white leaves, left to drift over her littered studio floor. Then, as in all the frequent crises in her life, her friends rallied around her with scenes, jealousies, memories, quarrels, recriminations, good cases of wine, fine conversation, threats of farewell, new leases of affection—all the dramatics of loyalty, disillusion, hero worship, duty, fatigue, patience, and devotion which animated even her Platonic associations—all the humorous and painful disorders which genius, as if to prove its exceptional chemistry, catalyzes in commoner lives. The book, called *My Life,* finally appeared posthumously. It was to have furnished money for her to live.

As her autobiography made clear, an integral part of Isadora's nature died young when her two adored little children, Deirdre and Patrick, were tragically drowned in 1913 at Neuilly; the automobile in which they were waiting alone slipped its brakes and plunged into the Seine. The children had been the offspring of free unions, in which Isadora spiritedly believed. She believed, too, in polyandry and that each child thus benefited eugenically by having a different and carefully chosen father. She also attributed the loss of her third child, born the day war was declared, to what she called the curse of the machine. At the wild report that the Germans were advancing by motor on Paris, the old Bois de Boulogne gates were closed, her doctor and his automobile, amidst thousands of cars, were caught behind the grill, and by the time he arrived at her bedside it was too late. The child had been born dead. "Machines have been my enemy," she once said. "They killed my three children. Machines are the opposite of, since they are the invention of, man. Perhaps a machine will one day kill me."

In a moment of melancholy her friend Duse prophesied that Isadora would die like Jocasta.[8] Both prophecies were fulfilled. On August 13, 1927, while driving on the Promenade des Anglais at Nice, Isadora Duncan met her death. She was strangled by her colored shawl, which became tangled in the wheel of the automobile.

A few days later in Paris great good-natured crowds had gathered in the Rue de Rivoli to watch the passing of the American Legion, then holding their initial postwar jollification and parade in France. By a solemn chance, what the crowd saw first, coming down the flag-strewn, gaily decorated thoroughfare, was the little funeral cortege of Isadora Duncan, treading its way to the cemetery of Père-Lachaise. Her coffin was covered by her famous purple dancing cape serving as a pall. On the back of the hearse, her family, though unsympathetic to her radical views, had loyally placed her most imposing floral tribute, a great mauve wreath from the Soviet Union with a banner that read *"Le Coeur de Russie Pleure Isadora."*[9] Though she had once rented the Metropolitan Opera House to plead the cause of France before we went into the war, though she had given her Neuilly château as a hospital, though she had been a warm and active friend to France, the French government sent nothing. Nor did her great French friends, who had once eagerly drunk her fame and champagne, walk behind dead Isadora.

Of all the famous personages she had loved and known and who had hailed her genius and hospitality, only two went to Passy, where she lay in state, to sign the mourners' books—Yvette Guilbert[1] and the actor Lugné-Poë. Hundreds of others scrawled their signatures on the pages, but they were casuals, common, loyal, unknown. Since Isadora was an American, it was regrettable that both the Paris American newspapers, the Paris *Herald* and the Chicago *Tribune*, busy doubtless with the gayer Legion matters, did not send reporters to follow her funeral cortege to its destination. Thus Americans next morning read that Isadora was followed to her grave by a pitiful handful. Only five carriages made up the official procession; but four thousand people—men, women, old, young, and of all nationalities—waited in the rain for the arrival of her body at Père-Lachaise.

---

8. Mother and wife of Oedipus, in Sophocles' tragedy *Oedipus Rex*, whose death is by strangulation.

9. "The heart of Russia weeps for Isadora."

1. A famous cabaret performer.

Of earthly possessions, Isadora had little enough to leave. Still she had made a will—and forgot to sign it.

All her life Isadora had been a practical idealist. She had put into practice certain ideals of art, maternity, and political liberty which people prefer to read as theories on paper. Her ideals of human liberty were not unsimilar to those of Plato, to those of Shelley, to those of Lord Byron, which led him to die dramatically in Greece. All they gained for Isadora were the loss of her passport and the presence of the constabulary on the stage of the Indianapolis Opera House, where the chief of police watched for sedition in the movement of Isadora's knees.

Denounced as a Russian Bolshevik sympathizer, Isadora said she never even received a postal card from the Soviet government to give her news of her school which she housed in its capital. For Isadora had a fancy for facts. As she once told Boston it was tasteless and dull, so, when they were feting her in triumph in Moscow, she told the Communists she found them bourgeois. She had a wayward truthful streak in her and a fancy for paradox. "Everything antique Greek," she once said to an American woman friend, "is supposed to be noble. Did you ever notice how easily the Greeks became Roman?"

Great artists are tragic. Genius is too large, and it may have been grandeur that proved Isadora's undoing—the grandeur of temporary luxury, the grandeur of permanent ideals.

She was too expansive for personal salvation. She had thousands of friends. What she needed was an organized government. She had had checkbooks. Her scope called for a national treasury. It was not for nothing that she was hailed by her first name only, as queens have been, were they great Catherines or Marie Antoinettes.

As she stepped into the machine that was to be her final enemy, Isadora's last spoken words were, by chance, *"Je vais à la gloire!"*[2]

1927

2. "I go to glory!"

QUESTIONS

1. *Isadora Duncan begins her autobiography this way:*

I confess that when it was first proposed to me I had a terror of writing this book. Not that my life has not been more interesting than any novel and more adventurous than any cinema and, if really well written, would not be an epoch-making recital, but there's the rub—the writing of it!

It has taken me years of struggle, hard work and research to learn to make one simple gesture, and I know enough about the Art of writing to realise that it would take me again just so many years of concentrated effort to write one simple, beautiful sentence. How often have I contended that although one man might toil to the Equator and have tremendous exploits with lions and tigers, and try to write about it, yet fail, whereas another, who never left his verandah, might write of the killing of tigers in their jungles in a way to make his readers feel that he was actually there, until they can suffer his agony and apprehension, smell lions and hear the fearful approach of the rattlesnake. Nothing seems to exist save in the imagination, and all the marvellous things that have happened to me may lose their savour because I do not possess the pen of a Cervantes or even of a Casanova.

Then another thing. How can we write the truth about ourselves? Do we even know it? There is the vision our friends have of us; the vision we have of ourselves, and the vision our lover has of us. Also the vision our enemies have of us—and all these visions are different. I have good reason to know this, because I have had served to me with my morning coffee newspaper criticisms that declared I was beautiful as a goddess, and that I was a genius, and hardly had I finished smiling contentedly over this, than I picked up the next paper and read that I was without any talent, badly shaped and a perfect harpy. . . .

So, if at each point of view others see in us a different person how are we to find in ourselves yet another personality of whom to write in this book? Is it to be the Chaste Madonna, or the Messalina, or the Magdalen, or the Blue Stocking? Where can I find the woman of all these adventures? It seems to me there was not one, but hundreds—and my soul soaring aloft, not really affected by any of them.

Isadora Duncan says she was "hundreds" of women. What does she mean? (Look up in an encyclopedia the examples she mentions, if you are not familiar with them). Which does Flanner present? Which emerges from this section of her autobiography? raphy?

2. *Write two brief contrasting character sketches, each with a different point of view. You could take someone you know personally or some public figure about whom you can gather sufficient information.*

JOSEPH WOOD KRUTCH

Modern Painting

I am, I hope, not insensitive to any of the arts. I have spent happy hours in museums, and I listen with pleasure to Bach, Mozart, and Beethoven. But I have more confidence in my ability to understand what is said in words than I have in my understanding of anything that dispenses with them. Such opinions as I hold concerning modern music or modern painting are as tentative as those I once expressed about modern architecture.

Nevertheless, as I said on that occasion, it is one of the privileges of the essayist to hold forth on subjects he doesn't know much about. Because he does not pretend to any expertness, those who know better than he what he is talking about need be no more than mildly exasperated. His misconceptions may give valuable hints to those who would set him right. If he didn't expose his obtuseness, his would-be mentors wouldn't know so well just what the misconceptions are and how they arose. An honest philistinism is easier to educate than the conscious or unconscious hypocrisy of those who admire whatever they are told that they should.

In the case of modern painting, the very fact that I can take pleasure in some of the works of yesterday's *avant-garde* but little in that of my own day suggests, even to me, that I may be merely the victim of a cultural lag. But there is no use in pretending that I am delighted by what delights me not, and I find that much serious criticism of the most recent painting is no help. Those who write it are talking over my head; they just don't start far enough back.

For instance, I read in the *Nation* that what a certain painter I had never heard of had accomplished during the war might be summarized as "an unstructured painterliness—neither expressionist nor surrealist in character, and therefore out of keeping with available alternatives." Shortly after the war "he followed through with an intimation of the picture facade as its own reason for being, preferring a unitary sensation, by being irregularly blotted out by masses that kept on pushing at, and disappearing past, the perimeters. Executed on a vastness of scale quite unprecedented in easel painting (which he was in any event attacking), these paintings sidestep drawing and the illusion of spatial recession without ever giving the impression of evasiveness. The result was a sense of the picture surface—now extraordinarily flattened—as a kind of wall whereby constricted elements no longer had any exclusive formal relationship with one another."

When I read things like that my first impulse is to exclaim, "If that young man expresses himself in terms too deep for me..."[1] But then I realize the possibility that the words do say something to those whose visual perceptions are better trained than mine. I am at best a second grader, still struggling with the multiplication table, who has wandered into a seminar at the Institute for Advanced Studies.

When, therefore, I happened to see an advertisement of the Book-of-the-Month Club explaining that the Metropolitan Museum of Art had been persuaded to prepare a twelve-part seminar on art, which could be subscribed to for "only $60," I had the feeling that this might very well be getting down to my level. The advertisement was adorned by reproductions of two contrasting

---

1. " * * * Why, what a most particularly deep young man that deep young man must be." So the aesthete Bunthorne sings admiringly of himself in Gilbert and Sullivan's *Patience*.

pictures: one of the Metropolitan's own "Storm" (or "Paul and Virginia") by Pierre Cot, and the other of a swirling abstraction. "Which of these is a good painting?" demanded the headline. My immediate answer "Neither." And I was not too much discouraged by the fact that I was pretty sure this was not the right answer.

I think I know at least some of the reasons why "The Storm" is not one of the great masterpieces—even though some supposedly competent expert must have once paid a whopping price for it. On the other hand, I had not the slightest idea why the abstraction was good or even just not quite as bad as the supposedly horrid example facing it.

I confess that I did not subscribe to the seminars. But I did borrow a set from an acquaintance who had done so, and I must report that I did understand what the Metropolitan people were saying as I had not understood the *Nation* critic. But I was not by any means wholly convinced. Many years ago I read Roger Fry on "Significant Form" and the terrible-tempered Albert Barnes on *The Art in Painting*. I found nothing in the Metropolitan seminar that was not this doctrine somewhat updated, and I was no more convinced than I had been by the earlier critics that what they were talking about was indeed the only thing in painting worth talking about, or that significant form by itself (if that is possible) was as good as, if not better than, classical paintings in which equally significant form had been imposed upon subject matters themselves interesting or moving in one way or another. In that problem lies the real crux of the matter. Granted that "composition," "significant form," or whatever you want to call it is a *sine qua non* of great painting, is it also the one thing necessary? Is it *the* art in painting or only *an* art in painting? My mentors from the Metropolitan are by no means fanatical. They never themselves insist that subject matter, or the communication of an emotion in connection with it, is irrelevant in judging a picture. But unless my memory fails me, they never really face the question of the extent to which the painter who abandons the suggestion of a subject matter is to that extent lesser than one who at the same time tells a story, reveals a character, or communicates an attitude.

The hopeful student is confronted at the very beginning with what seems to me this unanswered question. He is warned that "Whistler's Mother" was called by the artist "Arrangement in Grey and Black"—and let that be a lesson to you. You may think that your enjoyment of the picture derives from its "appealing likeness of the author's mother and from sentimental associations with old age," but "the *real* [italics in the original] subject is something else . . . We may ask whether the picture would be just as effective if we omitted the subject altogether . . . the abstract school of contemporary painting argues that subject matter is only something that gets in the way. It confuses the issue—the issue being pure expression by means of color, texture, line, and shape existing in their own right and representing nothing at all."

Throughout the course, stress is laid again and again on the comparison between two seemingly very different pictures said to be similar, although I don't think they are ever said to be identical. For instance, Vermeer's "The Artist and His Studio" is compared with Picasso's "The Studio." "Picasso," I am told, "had sacrificed . . . the interest inherent in the objects comprising the picture . . . the fascination and variety of natural textures . . . the harmonies of flowing light, the satisfaction of building solid forms out of light and shape. What has he gained? . . . Complete freedom to manipulate the forms of his picture . . . The abstractionist would argue that the enjoyment of a picture like Picasso's 'The Studio' is more intense because it is purer than the enjoyment we take in Vermeer."

Is "purer" the right adjective? Is it purer or merely thinner? To me the answer is quite plain and the same as that given to the proponents of pure poetry who argued that poetry is essentially only sound so that the most beautiful single line in French literature is Racine's "*La fille de Minos et de Pasiphaé*," [2] not because the genealogy of Phèdre was interesting but just because the sound of the words is delightful. The sound of "O frabjous day! Callooh! Callay!" is also delightful but I don't think it as good as, for instance, "No spring, nor summer beauty hath such grace,/ As I have seen in one autumnal face."

It is all very well to say that two pictures as different as those by Vermeer and Picasso are somewhat similar in composition and that to this extent they produce a somewhat similar effect. But to say that the total experience of the two is not vastly different is, so it seems to me, pure nonsense and so is the statement that the two experiences are equally rich.

The author of the seminar session just quoted seems himself to think so when he writes: "But we also contend that a painting is a projection of the personality of the man who painted it, and a statement of the philosophy of the age that produced it."

If that is true, then the painter who claims to be "painting nothing but paint" is either a very deficient painter or is, perhaps without knowing it, projecting his personality and making a statement of a philosophy of the age that produced it. He is doing that just as

2. "The daughter of Minos and Pasiphaé"—that is, Phèdre, title character of a tragedy by the seventeenth-century French dramatist Jean Racine.

truly and just as inevitably as Whistler was doing more than an arrangement in black and grey. And if that also is true, then the way to understand what is most meaningful and significant in any modern painting is to ask what it is that the painter, consciously or not, is revealing about his personality and about the age that finds his philosophy and his personality congenial.

At least that much seems often to be admitted by admiring critics of certain painters not fully abstract but who seem to be interested primarily in pure form. Take, for instance, the case of Ferdinand Léger and his reduction of the whole visible world, including human beings, to what looks like mechanical drawings. Are they examples of pure form meaning nothing but themselves? Certainly they are not always so considered by admirers. When the painter died in 1955 the distinguished critic André Chastel wrote:

> From 1910 on, his views of cities with smoke-like zinc, his country scenes inspired as if by a woodchopper, his still lifes made as if of metal, clearly showed what always remained his inspiration: the maximum hardening of a world of objects, which he made firmer and more articulate than they are in reality. Sacrifice of color and nuance was total and line was defined with severity and a well-meaning aggressiveness, projecting his violent, cold Norman temperament. This revolution he consecrated himself to seemed rather simple—the exaltation of the machine age, which after 1920 dominated the western world.

To me it seems equally plain that even those who profess to paint nothing but paint are in fact doing a great deal more because they would not find anything of the sort to be the real aim of painting unless they had certain attitudes toward nature, toward society, and toward man. What that attitude is cannot, I think, be very well defined without recourse to two words that I hate to use because they have become so fashionable and are so loosely tossed about. What these painters are expressing is the alienation of the existentialist. They no longer represent anything in the external world because they no longer believe that the world that exists outside of man in any way shares or supports human aspirations and values or has any meaning for him. They are determined, like the existential moralist, to go it alone. They do not believe that in nature there is anything inherently beautiful, just as the existentialist moralizer refuses to believe that there is any suggestion of moral values in the external universe. The great literature and painting of the past have almost invariably been founded upon assumptions the exact opposite of these. They expressed man's attempt to find beauty and meaning in an external world from which he was not alienated because he believed that both his aesthetic and his moral sense corresponded to something outside himself.

Salvador Dali (whom, in general, I do not greatly admire) once made the remark that Picasso's greatness consisted in the fact that he had destroyed one by one all the historical styles of painting. I am not sure that there is not something in that remark, and if there is, then it suggests that in many important respects Picasso is much like the workers in several branches of literature whose aim is to destroy the novel with the antinovel, the theater with the anti-theater, and philosophy by philosophies that consist, like logical positivism and linguistic analysis, in a refusal to philosophize. They are all determined, as the surrealist André Breton once said he was, to "wring the neck of literature."

Having now convinced myself of all these things, I will crawl farther out on a limb and confess that I have often wondered if the new styles created by modern painters—pointillism, cubism, surrealism, and the mechanism of Léger (to say nothing of op and pop)—ought not be regarded as gimmicks rather than actual styles. And to my own great astonishment I have discovered that Picasso himself believes, or did once believe, exactly that.

The luxurious French monthly *Jardin des Arts* published (March 1964) a long and laudatory article on Picasso in the course of which it cited "a text of Picasso on himself" which had been reproduced at various times but most recently in a periodical called *Le Spectacle du Monde* (November 1962). I translate as follows:

When I was young I was possessed by the religion of great art. But, as the years passed, I realized that art as one conceived it up to the end of the 1880's was, from then on, dying, condemned, and finished and that the pretended artistic activity of today, despite all its superabundance, was nothing but a manifestation of its agony . . . Despite appearances our contemporaries have given their heart to the machine, to scientific discovery, to wealth, to the control of natural forces, and of the world . . . From that moment when art became no longer the food of the superior, the artist was able to exteriorize his talent in various sorts of experiments, in new formulae, in all kinds of caprices and fantasies, and in all the varieties of intellectual charlatanism . . .

As for me, from cubism on I have satisfied these gentlemen [rich people who are looking for something extravagant] and the critics also with all the many bizarre notions which have come into my head and the less they understood the more they admired them . . . Today, as you know, I am famous and rich. But when I am alone with my soul, I haven't the courage to consider myself as an artist. In the great and ancient sense of that word, Greco, Titian, Rembrandt, and Goya were great painters. I am only the entertainer of a public which understands its age.

Chirico is another modern painter who has said something very much like this. But enough of quotations. And to me it seems that Picasso said all that I have been trying to say, namely, that a picture somehow involved with the world of reality outside man is more valuable than one that has nothing to say about anything except the painter himself. What he calls painters "in the great and ancient sense of that word" were able to be such only because they were not alienated existentialists.

1967

QUESTIONS

1. Indicate particular details that show what Krutch suggests to be the proper business of an essayist.
2. What is this essay's thesis? What assumptions underlie the thesis?
3. What relationship does Krutch see between modern painting and "the philosophy of the age"? How does he attempt to demonstrate, or illustrate, that relationship? Is this view persuasive? Why, or why not?
4. Does Krutch assume that his audience is disposed at the outset to think of modern painting very much as he does, or very differently? to think as he does in some particulars, and not in others? Show, by specific details of his manner, what attitudes he seems to expect, what responses he anticipates.
5. Why does Krutch quote (p. 273) a passage he has read about a certain painter? What can be learned from the quotation? Would it help to know the identity of the painter? Why doesn't Krutch name him?
6. What effect does Krutch achieve by referring twice, in two separate connections, to Picasso?

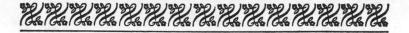

Signs of the Times

FRAN LEBOWITZ

The Sound of Music: Enough Already

First off, I want to say that as far as I am concerned, in instances where I have not personally and deliberately sought it out, the only difference between music and Muzak is the spelling. Pablo Casals[1] practicing across the hall with the door open—being trapped in an elevator, the ceiling of which is broadcasting "Parsley, Sage, Rosemary, and Thyme"—it's all the same to me. Harsh words? Perhaps. But then again these are not gentle times we live in. And they are being made no more gentle by this incessant melody that was once real life.

There was a time when music knew its place. No longer. Possibly this is not music's fault. It may be that music fell in with a bad crowd and lost its sense of common decency. I am willing to consider this. I am willing even to try and help. I would like to do my bit to set music straight in order that it might shape up and leave the mainstream of society. The first thing that music must understand is that there are two kinds of music—good music and bad music. Good music is music that I want to hear. Bad music is music that I don't want to hear.

So that music might more clearly see the error of its ways I offer the following. If you are music and you recognize yourself on this list, you are bad music.

1. *Music in Other People's Clock Radios*

There are times when I find myself spending the night in the home of another. Frequently the other is in a more reasonable line of work than I and must arise at a specific hour. Ofttimes the other, unbeknownst to me, manipulates an appliance in such a way that I am awakened by Stevie Wonder. On such occasions I announce that if I wished to be awakened by Stevie Wonder I

---

1. Great Spanish cellist.

would sleep with Stevie Wonder. I do not, however, wish to be awakened by Stevie Wonder and that is why God invented alarm clocks. Sometimes the other realizes that I am right. Sometimes the other does not. And that is why God invented *many* others.

2. Music Residing in the Hold Buttons of Other People's Business Telephones

I do not under any circumstances enjoy hold buttons. But I am a woman of reason. I can accept reality. I can face the facts. What I cannot face is the music. Just as there are two kinds of music—good and bad—so there are two kinds of hold buttons—good and bad. Good hold buttons are hold buttons that hold one silently. Bad hold buttons are hold buttons that hold one musically. When I hold I want to hold silently. That is the way it was meant to be, for that is what God was talking about when he said, "Forever hold your peace." He would have added, "and quiet," but he thought you were smarter.

3. Music in the Streets

The past few years have seen a steady increase in the number of people playing music in the streets. The past few years have also seen a steady increase in the number of malignant diseases. Are these two facts related? One wonders. But even if they are not— and, as I have pointed out, one cannot be sure—music in the streets has definitely taken its toll. For it is at the very least disorienting. When one is walking down Fifth Avenue, one does not expect to hear a string quartet playing a Strauss waltz. What one expects to hear while walking down Fifth Avenue is traffic. When one does indeed hear a string quartet playing a Strauss waltz while one is walking down Fifth Avenue, one is apt to become confused and imagine that one is not walking down Fifth Avenue at all but rather that one has somehow wound up in Old Vienna. Should one imagine that one is in Old Vienna one is likely to become quite upset when one realizes that in Old Vienna there is no sale at Charles Jourdan.[2] And that is why when I walk down Fifth Avenue I want to hear traffic.

4. Music in the Movies

I'm not talking about musicals. Musicals are movies that warn you by saying, "Lots of music here. Take it or leave it." I'm talking about regular movies that extend no such courtesy but allow unsus-

2. A shoe store in New York City.

pecting people to come to see them and then assault them with a barrage of unasked-for tunes. There are two major offenders in this category: black movies and movies set in the fifties. Both types of movies are afflicted with the same misconception. They don't know that movies are supposed to be movies. They think that movies are supposed to be records with pictures. They have failed to understand that if God had wanted records to have pictures, he would not have invented television.

5. Music in Public Places Such as Restaurants, Supermarkets, Hotel Lobbies, Airports, Etc.

When I am in any of the above-mentioned places I am not there to hear music. I am there for whatever reason is appropriate to the respective place. I am no more interested in hearing "Mack the Knife" while waiting for the shuttle to Boston than someone sitting ringside at the Sands Hotel[3] is interested in being forced to choose between sixteen varieties of cottage cheese. If God had meant for everything to happen at once, he would not have invented desk calendars.

Epilogue

Some people talk to themselves. Some people sing to themselves. Is one group better than the other? Did not God create all people equal? Yes, God created all people equal. Only to some he gave the ability to make up their own words.

1978

3. *shuttle to Boston*: an hourly airline service from New York; *ringside at the* *Sands Hotel*: near the stage in a famous Las Vegas resort hotel.

QUESTIONS

1. What is the point of Lebowitz's epilogue?
2. How would you describe the personality Lebowitz presents? Maintaining a humorous tone is not easy; how does she do it, or try to do it? What sort of reader would you expect to find her amusing? annoying?
3. Lebowitz sometimes employs a device that might be called pseudo-logic—a series of statements that implies a comic conclusion. Pick an example and explain the connections in the reasoning upon which the success of the device depends.
4. Many a true word is spoken in jest. What is the serious substance of Lebowitz's discussion? Outline a straightforward serious paper on the same subject.

ART BUCHWALD

Hurts Rent-A-Gun

The Senate recently passed a new gun-control bill, which some observers consider worse than no bill at all. Any serious attempt at handgun registration was gutted, and Senate gun lovers even managed to repeal a 1968 gun law controlling the purchase of .22 rimfire ammunition.

After the Senate got finished with its work on the gun-control bill, I received a telephone call from my friend Bromley Hurts, who told me he had a business proposition to discuss with me. I met him for lunch at a pistol range in Maryland.

"I think I've got a fantastic idea," he said, "I want to start a new business called Hurts Rent-A-Gun."

"What on earth for?" I asked.

"There are a lot of people in this country who only use a handgun once or twice a year, and they don't want to go to all the expense of buying one. So we'll rent them a gun for a day or two. By leasing a firearm from us, they won't have to tie up all their money."

"That makes sense," I admitted.

"Say a guy is away from home on a trip, and he doesn't want to carry his own gun with him. He can rent a gun from us and then return it when he's finished with his business."

"You could set up rent-a-gun counters at gas stations," I said excitedly.

"And we could have stores in town where someone could rent a gun to settle a bet," Hurts said.

"A lot of people would want to rent a gun for a domestic quarrel," I said.

"Right. Say a jealous husband suspects there is someone at home with his wife. He rents a pistol from us and tries to catch them in the act. If he discovers his wife is alone, he isn't out the eighty dollars it would have cost him to buy a gun."

"Don't forget about kids who want to play Russian roulette. They could pool their allowances and rent a gun for a couple of hours," I said.

"Our market surveys indicate," Hurts said, "that there are also a lot of kids who claim their parents don't listen to them. If they could rent a gun, they feel they could arrive at an understanding with their folks in no time."

"There's no end to the business," I said. "How would you charge for Hurts Rent-A-Gun?"

"There would be hourly rates, day rates, and weekly rates, plus ten cents for each bullet fired. Our guns would be the latest models, and we would guarantee clean barrels and the latest safety devices. If a gun malfunctions through no fault of the user, we will give him another gun absolutely free."

"For many Americans it's a dream come true," I said.

"We've also made it possible for people to return the gun in another town. For example, if you rent the gun in Chicago and want to use it in Salt Lake City, you can drop it off there at no extra charge."

"Why didn't you start this before?"

"We wanted to see what happened with the gun-control legislation. We were pretty sure the Senate and the White House would not do anything about strong gun control, especially during an election year. But we didn't want to invest a lot of money until we were certain they would all chicken out."

"I'd like the franchise for Washington's National Airport," I said.

"You've got it. It's a great location," Hurts said. "You'll make a fortune in hijackings alone."

1973

Americans on guns

EDWARD BUNKER

Let's End the Dope War:
A Junkie's View of the Quagmire

The United States has no choice but eventually to abandon its "war" on heroin addiction and adopt the so-called English system, which allows designated physicians to prescribe, under careful regulation and monitoring, maintenance doses of any narcotic except heroin, usually morphine or methadone, to registered addicts. Until a few years ago, physicians also prescribed heroin, but a slight rise in figures (it turned out to be false) changed that; now the heroin is dispensed from clinics. England isn't alone; nearly all Western European nations allow doctors to treat addicts with narcotics. None has a social problem with addiction; none has a crime rate gone berserk because of narcotics. European authorities believe that the United States created its own problem and tenaciously exacerbates it through collective delusions.

At the turn of the century, when opium, morphine and heroin were cheaper than aspirin and sold in more places, and when every male alcoholic was matched by a female drug addict, it was cause for a few clucks of sympathy when a family member was hooked, but no stigma was involved. We had 200,000 addicts in a population of 78 million, all of them living normally. Physicians gave opium and its derivatives for every sickness and every symptom. Even the temperance fanatics saw little wrong with it, by comparison to the demon rum.

Had anyone suddenly announced that henceforth addicts would be denied narcotics, there would have been public uproar. We stumbled into our present situation a little at a time. A Hague conference on international affairs, a precursor to the League of Nations and United Nations, drafted an agreement among nations to regulate and reduce the unrestrained international traffic of opium and its derivatives. This had nothing to do with addiction in Europe or the United States; it had to do with England flooding China with Indian opium that the Chinese didn't want. As an outgrowth of that, governments decided that narcotics should no longer be sold like gumdrops.

It was at that point that England and the United States diverged. We planted the seed of the tree of disaster that we are now harvesting, whereas England realized that trying to eradicate addiction would just create illegal traffic. The British had the benefit of having watched similar attempts in Asia in the nineteenth century. They also didn't want to make criminals of citizens who had a sickness. So the opium-laced patent medicines were taken away, morphine and heroin no longer sold to anyone, but there was never any question of depriving addicts of a supply—especially after the British saw what was happening in the United States. Strict laws against smuggling and trafficking were put in force, but these haven't been used very often. Registered addicts got their supply of pharmaceutical quality narcotics as they would any other routine, inexpensive medicine. Way back then England had, proportionate to its population, slightly fewer addicts than the United States. The figures held steady for a decade, and then slowly fell as older addicts died without contaminating others. Now England has about 3,000, 70 percent of whom are employed, pay taxes, and live at least as normally as diabetics on insulin. The streets of London are safe to walk at night.

The United States went the other way. We would not merely stop the spread of addiction to future generations, we would stamp it out forthwith. The first shot of the "war" was the Harrison Narcotic Act of 1914, which on its face curtails open distribution but seems to leave the question of treating addicts to doctors. The medical profession, which had and still has the highest rate of addiction of any profession, began to care for addicts in their sickness. Clinics

were opened, private physicians wrote prescriptions. Then the
United States Supreme Court, handing down the decision that has
caused all the trouble, ruled that physicians could not give addicts
any narcotics. Instantly the illicit traffic sprang up, though for several years the price was such that an addict could maintain his habit
by working. The international and domestic racketeers didn't visualize what the traffic would bear, so where a legal daily dose had cost
15¢ it now cost 50¢. Throughout the 1930s the number of addicts
remained about the same in both England and the United States. It
has never been a big thing to be an addict in England. The most
the English feel is slight pity; more stigma is attached to being an
alcoholic. By the same token, there's no mystique, no sense of flirt-
ing with danger, which is an element that attracts youth here.

Addiction began to rise slightly in New York City in the years
just before World War II, but during the war years the problem
nearly disappeared. International routes were closed and synthetic
narcotics were not yet being produced—the Germans were developing them—in sufficient quantity to reach the underground market.
In 1946 addiction in the United States reached its lowest point in
recent decades: 20,000 junkies, most of them in New York. There,
too, was where the postwar traffic got its first hold.

By the time Dwight Eisenhower took office in 1953 the number
of addicts had increased to 50,000 and another "war" was declared.
Congress passed the Jones-Miller law, requiring mandatory minimum sentences of ten years (no probation, no parole) for possession, sale, transporting of any amount of heroin, cocaine or mari-
juana. It was all the same in those days. Sentences of fifty years (no
parole) were common. In the decades since Jones-Miller became
law, addiction has increased geometrically: 50,000 addicts in 1953,
150,000 in 1965, 560,000 in 1975. California, especially in Los
Angeles, has always had a few addicts because of its proximity to
the Mexican border. The 1950 estimate was 1,000, and when it
started to rise soon thereafter the legislature began writing tougher
laws. In the next decade the statutes were changed several times,
culminating in 1961 with sentences whereby anyone with a prior
conviction (one joint was enough) who was caught with any usable
amount of heroin (even half a gram) received a mandatory fifteen-
year-to-life sentence—fifteen years before being eligible for parole.
Addiction in Los Angeles is now 60,000.

When he was appointed President, Gerald Ford declared his war
on dope, asking for three-year minimum terms for traffickers.
Clearly, penalties are not the answer, but we don't seem to learn
very fast.

There's a parable about lilies in a pond that double every day, but nobody notices the danger that they will cover everything because the pond is still half clear on the last day. With drug addiction we are nearing the last day: it has increased by a factor of twenty-eight—from 20,000 to 560,000—in thirty years. This wildfire growth has been in the face of relentless attack and Draconian sentences.[1] Yet a Drug Enforcement Agency official in California, when asked his opinion of heroin maintenance, deplored it, saying that all we need is tougher penalties and more money for enforcement.

Everyone recognizes that 90 percent of addicts are forced to commit crimes to maintain their expensive habits. Street crime *is* addict crime. The actual cost of manufacturing a gram of pure heroin—enough to maintain an addict for at least one day, perhaps two or three—is around 10¢. That's the cost if it were dispensed by a physician and if nobody made a profit. The illicit price is $100, for which the junkie must steal $300 in merchandise, one-third of retail value being par for hot goods. At least 50 percent of property crimes are committed by addicts, and the recent spread of crime to suburbs and small towns seems to correspond with heroin addiction leaping the tracks from the ghetto and barrio. Now such places as Eugene and Medford, Ore., Tacoma, Wash., and Redding, Calif. have heroin addicts—and their crimes. Twenty years ago Seattle had no addicts; now it has 16,000. Santa Barbara, Calif. once jailed all its known addicts for a couple of months. It was probably unlawful, but burglaries dropped 55 percent. Upon the arrival of limited methadone maintenance in San Francisco, property crimes went down 20 percent. The *Los Angeles Times* recently reported the arrest of a young junkie who admitted 250 residence burglaries in fifteen months to pay for a $200 a day habit, crimes committed not to live regally without work but to keep away from sweating, stomach cramps, vomiting, diarrhea and worse. According to outdated figures (pre-inflation) the average addict spends $8,000 a year on heroin; he also must eat and sleep. Multiply that by 560,000, add billions in law enforcement, institutions and lost taxes. Finally, look ahead to what the crime rate will be in ten years if addiction keeps spreading at even a fraction of the present rate.

That's just the economics; it doesn't include human misery beyond reckoning—not because of addiction per se but because of the life our twentieth-century leper is forced to live. The United States and the addict are locked in a weird dance of flagellation,[2]

---

1. After Draco, an Athenian lawgiver of the seventh century B.C., whose code of laws was extremely harsh. His name means "the dragon."

2. The practice of averting divine vengeance through self-punishment by whipping.

one through helplessness, the other because it clings to the concept of a "war." As in any war, demagogic propaganda drives out detached thought. The myths of drug addiction have become accepted reality. Even the Supreme Court, citadel of reason, has succumbed. In a case dealing with criminal sanctions to be levied merely for the *status* of being an addict, the Court called addicts "living dead" and "zombies." When you know that the only way to tell if someone is using heroin is by urinalysis it's hard to visualize a zombie. One of the "living dead" was a founder of Johns Hopkins. An addict from his 20s to his death, he was the greatest surgeon of the era (he fixed before putting on his gloves) and developed asepsis[3] in surgical technique. He didn't become emaciated, sunken-eyed and sallow because he was a doctor and had morphine available. Hermann Goering was a monster but hardly a zombie even after twenty years of morphine.

The medical reality of narcotic addiction is that fifty years of the heaviest imaginable habit will have no deleterious effect whatsoever on heart, liver, lungs, kidneys, cardiovascular or respiratory systems. It *might* affect calcium balance; so does milk. It might even contribute to longevity because it's the ultimate tranquilizer. The image of the scarecrow is appropriate, but that's because of the awful life society forces the addict to live. An addict is indeed enslaved. Nothing else matters when his habit must be satisfied, and his are the labors of Sisyphus.[4] When he gets his drug he is "normal," though probably less ambitious and driving than is thought ideal in the Protestant ethic.

The enslavement alone would justify the relentless war—if war could cure the addict or stop the traffic. Alas, half a century of this conflict has had precisely the opposite result. War has made selling narcotics in the United States the most lucrative business in the world. With so much money being made both from the traffic and the battle against it, wealthy and ruthless men have a vested interest in maintaining the status quo. To the big trafficker each invested dollar returns a hundred overnight—and the growth rate is faster than IBM's, because the frenzied street junkie wants to reduce the pressure, and the one way to do it is to get a couple of customers and become a pusher. Nobody could push dope in Europe. Why should an addict buy from a pusher when he can get a prescription and go to a drugstore?

The "war" has been on two fronts for a long time, and a third has been recently added. The first has been the campaign to cure

3. The boiling of surgical instruments to prevent infection from germs.
4. A mythical Greek figure condemned to the unending task of rolling a huge boulder up a hill.

the addict, usually while he's confined, but in the last decade with community programs as well. All are total failures, so much so that the bureaucrats administering them cannot allow thorough follow-up studies, lest the public scream at the gross waste of money. Synanon, the famed therapeutic community, claims just 10 percent success among those who stay two years, and they are but a fraction of those who enter. And Synanon deals with motivated persons. New York conducted a three-year follow-up on 247 adolescent addicts who had been treated in a heavily staffed, extremely expensive program. The young junkies were given group and private therapy and counseling, remedial education, vocational training and aid on release. The failure rate was 100 percent. Of the 247, eight were out of jail and drug-free—but when interviewed each claimed never to have been an addict. They'd been busted with dope on them and sent for treatment, which was better than jail.

Civil commitment programs in California and New York are expensive and useless. Ten years ago Congress established the Narcotic Addict Rehabilitation Act, and the Bureau of Prisons has NARA programs in many of its institutions. Under NARA, addicts convicted of nonviolent federal crimes are committed for treatment. All NARA does is provide a lot of $20,000-a-year jobs for sociologists. The NARA director at Terminal Island, Calif. has not produced one cured junkie after ten years and 1,000 commitments. On the other hand, it's easy to produce scores who have become addicts at Terminal Island. Indeed, wardens at Terminal Island, McNeil Island, Atlanta and elsewhere have declared the drug problem in prison insoluble. That raises an interesting question: if the federal government cannot control narcotics in federal prisons, how can it be controlled in the whole United States?

Addicts call themselves "dope fiends," and it fits. They live unimaginably mean lives, on the whole. They call it "running," and that, too, fits. A frantic cycle of stealing something, selling it, finding the connection and finally getting fixed. If they are lucky there's enough for a day or two, but usually in an hour they're running again. Unless they can become dealers the Damoclean sword[5] of getting sick hangs perpetually overhead, and the stays of execution are but a few hours at a time. Often they hit the street during withdrawals, ready to do anything to relieve the agony.

Sooner or later—and often—a junkie goes to jail, where he usually has to kick cold turkey. "Kick" because that's what he does, jerking his legs for sleepless days; "cold turkey" because waves of goose bumps torment his body. After he kicks. he may spend

---

5. Damocles, a Syracusan courtier of the fourth century B.C., found himself at a sumptuous banquet seated under a naked sword suspended from a single thread, symbolizing the precariousness of power.

months or years in jail or prison. Nonetheless, within hours, days or weeks of release he'll be inexorably drawn back to sticking a needle in his arm, knowing what his life is going to be, knowing he'll again find himself puking and shitting on himself on a jail floor.

Why do they do it? Theories are abundant, mostly psychological, but I believe that once a person has been fully hooked a permanent biochemical change takes place, and that once a body adapts, it is never again normal without narcotics. Though studies on that aspect of the problem are few, it's well known that a nonaddict can be given liberal doses of narcotics for ten days or longer with no discomfort when the medication is stopped, whereas an addict suffers mild symptoms after two days, and after a week will be fully sick. His body chemistry has changed. Whatever the cause, there is no cure. For all statistical purposes, once a junkie always a junkie.

If anything in this war has proven a greater failure than curing addicts, it is the second campaign of stopping the traffic. Half a century of unrelenting crackdown has achieved nothing. Every President since Truman has declared a new jihad[6] on the dealers of death, but all street pushers are dope fiends and nothing will dissuade them. They can't help themselves. The middle level of the distribution network is hard to penetrate, and so much money can be made that there will never be a shortage of persons eager to try their luck, no matter what the penalties. I know a 23-year-old ex-G.I. who flew into Hong Kong with $1,400 in his pocket. He bought a pound of #4 White Dragon Pearl heroin, broke it into tiny lumps and wrapped them in three layers of condom, tying them into little balls. These he swallowed. He put the rest in his colon. He failed the "smuggler profile" at customs, but the rigorous search revealed nothing. Would you advocate stomach pumps and enemas for anyone who *might* be a smuggler? He sold the load for $22,000. He could have made $150,000 if he'd diluted it to street quality and retailed it. He repeated the journey several times, taking another G.I. with him. In one year he had made enough to live like a prince forever in Mexico. That's where he is now.

The criminal syndicates, national and international (especially the latter), are invulnerable to arrest and prosecution. In some places the kingpin traffickers and the rulers are one and the same. We look foolish to the world as we struggle in the net that tightens just because we struggle.

As for stopping the smuggling, a half-minute of thought about what that entails should get it crossed off the list of possibilities. Moreover, when customs boasts of seizing 5 kilos of pure heroin

6. A religious war.

worth, say, $3 million, the impression conveyed is that somewhere Fu Manchu[7] is gnashing his teeth at this tremendous loss, or that somewhere addicts are falling into convulsions because the supply is cut off (why should that make anyone happy?). But $1 million was street value; Fu Manchu lost, perhaps, $15,000 and is in no danger of going bankrupt. The addict, it is true, may pay a little more, since dealers will take advantage of the alleged "shortage."

The third and newest campaign of the war is the attempt to curtail the growth of opium. Last December, President Ford announced that he'd consulted with the Chiefs of State of Colombia, Turkey and Mexico on the matter and elicited promises of cooperation in return for financing. Rep. Peter Rodino (D., N.J.) followed up the President's announcement with a proposal that we cut off aid to all noncooperative countries. Both men were either making political hay (narcotics is always good for that) or they don't understand the realities. Colombia grows no opium. Turkey had an agreement to stop raising it, but reneged after a year (during which there was no heroin shortage) because our compensation wasn't enough to repay the Turkish opium farmers for abandoning the crop. We let it go without a whimper.

As for Mexico, the central government is willing to help as long as we give enough millions to subsidize the effort, but Mexico isn't like the United States; Mexico City has only limited control in the hinterland, where the attitude is that our approach to drug addiction is hilariously stupid and that selling narcotics for U.S. consumption is no sin. In the mountains of Sinaloa where the opium grows, as soon as you leave the cities conditions have changed little since Pancho Villa.[8] When the government wants to go into the mountains it has to send troops. According to some Mexican dealers that's what the government has been doing recently. Opium fields are being burned and dealers arrested or killed. Virtually all of Mexico's crude brown heroin is for the U.S. market, where the wholesale price has gone up 40 percent since August 1975.

Before rejoicing, note that Mexico's production is picayune, perhaps 1 percent of the world supply. Ford neglected to mention the so-called Golden Triangle of Burma, Laos and Thailand, where 70 percent of the world's illicit opium grows, enough to supply 15 million addicts. In those jungle mountains the clans and tribes that grow opium neither know nor care what country they are in. They do know that they have all the guns in the area. Growing and selling opium is their way of life.

7. Fictional Oriental villain.   8. Mexican bandit leader (1877–1923).

Afghanistan and Pakistan also grow a lot of opium, though so far it hasn't been needed in the illicit pipeline. In fact, there's a lot of opium to curtail. Just 3 square miles of poppies can supply the U.S. market nicely. And even if there's a worldwide shortage, the American market will be the last to feel it because we pay 100 times more than anyone else.

Finally, matters would change only for the worse if every opium poppy in the world keeled over and died. Too many fortunes are at stake not to have contingency plans, and those are to manufacture the synthetics, such as dolphine, blue-morphan and dilaudid, which are more addictive than the real thing. Dilaudid, the oldest synthetic, is preferred to heroin by many addicts, and except for its stronger "rush" when injected is hard to differentiate from heroin. The chemical process is no more difficult than that of converting morphine base into heroin, or making LSD or speed. The base of the synthetic opiates is coal tar. Do we next try to curtail the world's supply of coal tar?

We cannot cure addicts and we cannot stop the traffic. Sooner or later, now or when the 560,000 junkies become 2 million, we are going to change our system and allow addicts to have regulated doses of narcotics, including heroin. Methadone has paved the way, showing that the world won't collapse if addicts are allowed what they need as critically as diabetics need insulin. Methadone programs are not without their own problems but, for those on them, they are the most effective therapy thus far attempted. Addicts who have spent years stealing or in jail suddenly get jobs and pay taxes because they can drink a glass of methadone and Tang every day. More than 80 percent are employed. True, some are still criminals, and a few sell part of their ration, but methadone is a viable program—or would be if the bureaucrats hadn't gotten in. It reaches only a minuscule percentage; in Los Angeles, for example, 2,000 out of 60,000, and even that is threatened because taxpayers rightfully resent spending $7 a day to give narcotics to a dope fiend. When you consider that methadone costs 10¢ per dose, plus 15¢ for the glass of Tang, it looks as though someone is doing nicely. The markup isn't nearly that of illicit heroin—6¢ to $100—but it's too much for the taxpayer and too much for the majority of addicts. We need a cheaper method of distribution.

Nor will methadone alone do the job. Too many addicts dislike it. Younger addicts still want the "rush" of a fix. And some people gain excessive weight on methadone, 40 or 50 pounds, while others become so somnolent that they can't do anything but doze in front of the television. Some are afraid of methadone because the withdrawal is much worse than that of heroin. Its main good points are that it can be taken orally, eliminating hepatitis and infection, and requires just one dose a day, compared to heroin's three or four.

What we must do, and will do despite the screams of law-enforcement officers and others, is register all addicts, determine the daily maintenance dose for each individual (some addicts in England use both methadone and heroin) and issue ration cards that allow the individual to buy that much each day in drugstores. Methadone clinics already allow most patients to take home enough for several days. Some if it will be resold, but no junkie is going to cut himself short. Pushers will disappear. We'd still have a lot of addict-citizens, but not many addict-criminals. You might even be able to walk in Central Park at night. The cost would be virtually nothing—and would save billions.

What can we lose by trying it for a year? Nothing else has worked. It would do nothing for today's addicts, except allow them to live normal lives. It might save the children.

1977

HERB GOLDBERG

In Harness: The Male Condition

Most men live in harness. Richard was one of them. Typically he had no awareness of how his male harness was choking him until his personal and professional life and his body had nearly fallen apart.

Up to that time he had experienced only occasional short bouts of depression that a drink would bring him out of. For Richard it all crashed at an early age, when he was thirty-three. He came for psychotherapy with resistance, but at the instruction of his physician. He had a bad ulcer, was losing weight, and, in spite of repeated warnings that it could kill him, he was drinking heavily.

His personal life was also in serious trouble. He had recently lost his job as a disc jockey on a major radio station because he'd been arrested for drunk driving. He had totaled his car against a tree and the newspapers had a picture of it on the front page. Shortly thereafter his wife moved out, taking with her their eight-year-old daughter. She left at the advice of friends who knew that he had become violent twice that year while drunk.

As he began to talk about himself it became clear that he had been securely fitted into his male harness early in his teens. In high school he was already quite tall and stronger than most. He was therefore urged to go out for basketball, which he did, and he got lots of attention for it.

He had a deep, resonant voice that he had carefully cultivated. He was told that he should go into radio announcing and dramatics, so he got into all the high school plays. In college he majored in theater arts.

In his senior year in college he dated one of the most beautiful and sought-after girls in the junior class. His peer group envied him, which reassured Richard that he had a good thing going. So he married Joanna a year after graduating and took a job with a small radio station in Fresno, California. During the next ten years he played out the male role; he fathered a child and fought his way up in a very competitive profession.

It wasn't until things had fallen apart that he even let himself know that he had any feelings of his own, and in therapy he began to see why it had been so necessary to keep his feelings buried. They were confusing and frightening.

More than anything else, there was a hypersensitive concern over what others thought about him as a "man." As other suppressed feelings began to surface they surprised him. He realized how he had hated the pressures of being a college basketball player. The preoccupation with being good and winning had distorted his life in college.

Though he had been to bed with many girls before marriage and even a few afterward, he acknowledged that rarely was it a genuine turn-on for him. He liked the feeling of being able to seduce a girl but the experience itself was rarely satisfying, so he would begin the hunt for another as soon as he succeeded with one. "Some of those girls were a nightmare," he said, "I would have been much happier without them. But I was caught in the bag of proving myself and I couldn't seem to control it."

The obsessive preoccupation in high school and college with cultivating a deep, resonant "masculine" voice he realized was similar to the obsession some women have with their figures. Though he thought he had enjoyed the attention he got being on stage, he acknowledged that he had really disliked being an entertainer, or "court jester," as he put it.

When he thought about how he had gotten married he became particularly uncomfortable. "I was really bored with Joanna after the first month of dating but I couldn't admit it to myself because I thought I had a great thing going. I married her because I figured if I didn't one of the other guys would. I couldn't let that happen."

Richard had to get sick in his harness and nearly be destroyed by role-playing masculinity before he could allow himself to be a person with his own feelings, rather than just a hollow male image.

Had it not been for a bleeding ulcer he might have postponed looking at himself for many years more.

Like many men. Richard had been a zombie, a daytime sleep-
walker. Worse still, he had been a highly "successful" zombie,
which made it so difficult for him to risk change. Our culture is saturated with successful male zombies, businessmen zombies, golf
zombies, sports car zombies, playboy zombies, etc. They are playing
by the rules of the male game plan. They have lost touch with, or
are running away from, their feelings and awareness of themselves
as people. They have confused their social masks for their essence
and they are destroying themselves while fulfilling the traditional
definitions of masculine-appropriate behavior. They set their life
sails by these role definitions. They are the heroes, the studs, the
providers, the warriors, the empire builders, the fearless ones.
Their reality is always approached through these veils of gender
expectations.

When something goes seriously wrong, they discover that they
are shadows to themselves as well as to others. They are unknown
because they have been so busy manipulating and masking themselves in order to maintain and garner more status that a genuine
encounter with another person would threaten them, causing them
to flee or to react with extreme defensiveness.

Men evaluate each other and are evaluated by many women
largely by the degree to which they approximate the ideal masculine
model. Women have rightfully lashed out against being placed into
a mold and being related to as a sex object. Many women have
described their roles in marriage as a form of socially approved pros-
titution. They assert that they are selling themselves out for an
unfulfilling portion of supposed security. For psychologically defensive reasons the male has not yet come to see himself as a
prostitute, day in and day out, both in and out of the marriage
relationship.

The male's inherent survival instincts have been stunted by the
seemingly more powerful drive to maintain his masculine image. He
would, for example, rather die in the battle than risk living in a different way and being called a "coward" or "not a man." He would
rather die at his desk prematurely than free himself from his compulsive patterns and pursuits. As a recently published study concluded, "A surprising number of men approaching senior citizenship
say they would rather die than be buried in retirement."

The male in our culture is at a growth impasse. He won't move
—not because he is protecting his cherished central place in the
sun, but because he *can't* move. He is a cardboard Goliath precari-
ously balanced and on the verge of toppling over if he is pushed

even ever so slightly out of his well-worn path. He lacks the fluidity of the female who can readily move between the traditional definitions of male or female behavior and roles. She can be wife and mother or a business executive. She can dress in typically feminine fashion or adopt the male styles. She will be loved for having "feminine" interests such as needlework or cooking, or she will be admired for sharing with the male in his "masculine" interests. That will make her a "man's woman." She can be sexually assertive or sexually passive. Meanwhile, the male is rigidly caught in his masculine pose and, in many subtle and direct ways, he is severely punished when he steps out of it.

Unlike some of the problems of women, the problems of men are not readily changed through legislation. The male has no apparent and clearly defined targets against which he can vent his rage. Yet he is oppressed by the cultural pressures that have denied him his feelings, by the mythology of the woman and the distorted and self-destructive way he sees and relates to her, by the urgency for him to "act like a man" which blocks his ability to respond to his inner promptings both emotionally and physiologically, and by a generalized self-hate that causes him to feel comfortable only when he is functioning well in harness, or when he lives for joy and for personal growth.

The prevalent "enlightened" male's reaction to the women's liberation movement bears testimony to his inability to mobilize himself on his own behalf. He has responded to feminist assertions by donning sack cloth, sprinkling himself with ashes, and flagellating himself—accusing himself of the very things she is accusing him of. An article entitled, "You've Come a Long Way, Buddy," perhaps best illustrates the male self-hating attitude. In it, the writer said,

The members of the men's liberation movement are . . . a kind of embarrassing vanguard, the first men anywhere on record to take a political stand based on the idea that what the women are saying is right—men are a bunch of lazy, selfish, horny, unhappy oppressors.

Many other undoubtedly well-intentioned writers on the male condition have also taken a basically guilt- and shame-oriented approach to the male, alternately scolding him, warning him, and preaching to him that he better change and not be a male chauvinist pig anymore. During many years of practice as a psychotherapist, I have never seen a person grow or change in a self-constructive, meaningful way when he was motivated by guilt, shame, or self-hate. That manner of approach smacks of old-time religion and degrades the male by ignoring the complexity of the binds and repressions that are his emotional heritage.

Precisely because the tenor and mood of the male liberation

efforts so far have been one of self-accusation, self-hate, and a repetition of feminist assertions, I believe it is doomed to failure in its present form. It is buying the myth that the male is culturally favored—a notion that is clung to despite the fact that every critical statistic in the area of longevity, disease, suicide, crime, accidents, childhood emotional disorders, alcoholism, and drug addiction shows a disproportionately higher male rate.

Many men who join male liberation groups do so to please or impress their women or to learn how to deal with and hold onto their recently liberated wives or girlfriends. Once in a male liberation group they intellectualize their feelings and reactions into lifelessness. In addition, the men tend to put each other down for thinking like "typical male chauvinists" or using words like "broad," "chick," "dike," etc. They have introjected the voices of their feminist accusers and the result is an atmosphere that is joyless, self-righteous, cautious, and lacking in a vitalizing energy. A new, more subtle kind of competitiveness pervades the atmosphere: the competition to be the least competitive and most free of the stereotyped version of male chauvinism.

The women's liberation movement did not effect its astounding impact via self-hate, guilt, or the desire to placate the male. Instead it has been energized by anger and outrage. Neither will the male change in any meaningful way until he experiences his underlying rage toward the endless, impossible binds under which he lives, the rigid definitions of his role, the endless pressure to be all things to all people, and the guilt-oriented, self-denying way he has traditionally related to women, to his feelings, and to his needs.

Because it is so heavily repressed, male rage only manifests itself indirectly and in hidden ways. Presently it is taking the form of emotional detachment, interpersonal withdrawal, and passivity in relationship to women. The male has pulled himself inward in order to deny his anger and to protect himself and others from his buried cascade of resentment and fury. Pathetic, intellectualized attempts not to be a male chauvinist pig will *never* do the job.

There is also a commonly expressed notion that men will somehow be freed as a by-product of the feminist movement. This is a comforting fantasy for the male but I see no basis for it becoming a reality. It simply disguises the fear of actively determining his own change. Indeed, by responding inertly and passively, the male will be moved, but not in a meaningful and productive direction. If there is to be a constructive change for the male he will have to chart his own way, develop his own style and experience his own anxieties, fear, and rage because *this time mommy won't do it!*

Recently, I asked a number of men to write to me about how they see their condition and what liberation would mean to them. A sense of suffocation and confusion was almost always present.

A forty-six-year-old businessman wrote: "From what do I need to be liberated? I'm too old and tired to worry about myself. I know that I'm only a high-grade mediocrity. I've come to accept a life where the dreams are now all revealed as unreality. I don't know how my role or my son's role should change. If I knew I suppose it would be in any way that would make my wife happier and less of a shrew."

A thirty-nine-year-old carpenter discussing the "joys" of working responded: "I contend that the times in which it is fun and rewarding in a healthy way have been fairly limited. Most of the time it has been a question of running in fear of failure." Referring to his relationships, he continued. "There is another aspect of women's and men's lib that I haven't experienced extensively. This is the creation of close friendships outside of the marriage. My past experiences have been stressful to the point where I am very careful to limit any such contact. What's the fear? I didn't like the sense of insecurity developed by my wife and the internal stresses that I felt. It created guilt feelings."

A fifty-seven-year-old college professor expressed it this way: "Yes, there's a need for male lib and hardly anyone writes about it the way it really is, though a few make jokes. My gut reaction, which is what you asked for, is that men—the famous male chauvinist pigs who neglect their wives, underpay their women employees, and rule the world—are literally slaves. They're out there picking that cotton, sweating, swearing, taking lashes from the boss, working fifty hours a week to support themselves and the plantation, only then to come back to the house to do another twenty hours a week rinsing dishes, toting trash bags, writing checks, and acting as butlers at the parties. It's true of young husbands and middle-aged husbands. Young bachelors may have a nice deal for a couple of years after graduating, but I've forgotten, and I'll never again be young! Old men. Some have it sweet, some have it sour.

"Man's role—how has it affected my life? At thirty-five, I chose to emphasize family togetherness and income and neglect my profession if necessary. At fifty-seven, I see no reward for time spent with and for the family, in terms of love or appreciation. I see a thousand punishments for neglecting my profession. I'm just tired and have come close to just walking away from it and starting over; just research, publish, teach, administer, play tennis, and travel. Why haven't I? Guilt. And love. And fear of loneliness. How should the man's role in my family change? I really don't know how it can, but I'd like a lot more time to do my thing."

The most remarkable and significant aspect of the feminist movement to date has been woman's daring willingness to own up to her resistances and resentment toward her time-honored, sanctified roles of wife and even mother. The male, however, has yet to fully realize, acknowledge, and rebel against the distress and stifling aspects of many of the roles he plays—from good husband, to good daddy, to good provider, to good lover, etc. Because of the inner pressure to constantly affirm his dominance and masculinity, he continues to act as if he can stand up under, fulfill, and even enjoy all the expectations placed on him no matter how contradictory and devitalizing they are.

It's time to remove the disguises of privilege and reveal the male condition for what it really is.

1976

QUESTIONS

1. From what sort of evidence or experience does Goldberg draw his conclusions? Do the men who seek help from a psychotherapist represent a good cross section of all males? What biases might be encountered in such a group of subjects?

2. Compare Goldberg's conception of the male in harness with S. J. Perelman's idea of machismo (pp. 311–316). Are the two talking about similar things? Is it true, as Goldberg states, that "the male in our culture is at a growth impasse" (p. 294)?

3. Describing what happens to men who try to understand women's liberation by joining a group of their own, Goldberg says that "once in a male liberation group [men] intellectualize their feelings and reactions into lifelessness" (p. 296). What other paths to understanding do men have open to them? Do liberated women pose a threat to men and their images?

4. Betty Rollin, in "Motherhood: Who Needs It?" (pp. 301–311), talks about extinguishing the "Motherhood Myth" to encourage women to discover and be themselves. What does Goldberg imply about extinguishing Fatherhood? How do these two ideas differ? Which would have a greater impact on society?

5. Compare the approach to human personality taken by Goldberg with that of Willard Gaylin, also a psychotherapist, in "What You See Is the Real You" (pp. 438–440). Do they seem to agree on the nature of human personality? Explain.

6. Construct a dialogue in which Goldberg's "harnessed" man and a liberated woman discuss birth control, the proper role of parents, platonic relationships between men and women, or some similar topic.

LINDA BIRD FRANCKE

The Body Count in the Battle of the Sexes

It was the kind of party where everyone knew everyone else, except no one knew me. Deciding to utilize my assertiveness training, I clenched my muscles and aimed for a tanned, mustachioed blue-eyed man, whose T-shirt alligator rippled on a most beguiling ridge of muscle. We hit it off immediately, bantering, laughing, cracking entre-nous[1] jokes before we even had an entre-nous.

My popularity ego, whose pendulum swing can flash from "nobody loves me" to "everybody loves me" in the time it takes to say "white wine," soared to a new high when we were joined by an even more attractive man, whose white-milk teeth and sun-wrinkled brown eyes positively enveloped me in warmth and interest. Heady with proof of my alluring femininity, I left the party reluctantly, determined to unearth the phone numbers of my new-found swains. The next day I discovered why they had been so warm and cozy. For some time the two had been a couple and that very day they had just bought their first house together.

I have almost come to the conclusion that there just aren't any men left these days that are worth the salt to put on a pigeon's tail. In more incidences then I care to remember, the men to whom I've been irresistibly attracted would have been more attracted to my brother, had I had one. The reason is obvious. I am drawn to them because of the absence of sexual tension, a cease-fire in the war between the sexes. They are attracted to me for the exact same reason—which all adds up, in an ongoing relationship, to absolute zero.

A woman can't look for peace in a relationship with a man because if she finds it, she doesn't have a man. And vice versa. The trick is to organize the war games so that the body count is minimal.

In some cases, the war is undeclared, and like Vietnam, the outcome indecisive.

In the early morning sunshine last week, I overheard a conversation on the tennis court between two married women who apparently hadn't seen each other in a while. Knowing it was not only insensitive but out of it to say "How's Ralph?," the server asked instead, "Are you still married?" "I don't know," the receiver replied. "What about you?" "Well, sort of, I guess," the server said

1. Between ourselves; that is, suggesting intimacy.

before double-faulting. Though the divorce rate has spiraled, the number of semi-marriages that don't fit anywhere on the statisticians' charts has probably passed the undiagnosed plague level of the Middle Ages.

Where the rules of the war games are articulated, if not the strategies, the men appear to have left the bargaining table altogether. As women have come bursting out of their kitchens, armed with determination, degrees and Title IX[2] to protect them against discrimination, men seem to be climbing over each other's backs to get out of the way.

My old friend Sally, who has made a name for herself in educational films in New York, had dinner in Los Angeles recently with another old friend, who has made a much bigger name for himself in television. Settling down over late-night brandies, she was stunned when he turned to her and said, "You know, I can't imagine being married to you. I'd panic and run." Why, Sally asked, hurt that their friendship, which had never even touched on the subject of marriage, seemed suddenly flawed. "You're a star," he said. But, Sally pointed out, he was the one getting quoted in *Time* and *Newsweek* and was probably earning $100,000 a year to her $20,000. "Maybe so," he said declaratively, "but underneath it all I think you're smarter than I am."

What lurking terrors possess men when their women achieve success on their own? Oh, we've read to a newsprint fault about Bella and Martin and Mary and Harding and Farrah and Lee,[3] but what about my pal Lucy, who has achieved considerable stature in publishing and whose equally successful husband has retreated to bed in a seemingly terminal state of depression?

And then there is Maggie, of whom I am very fond, who got along just fine with her executive husband until, with his support, she went back to work and quickly ascended the corporate ladder. Her husband, though he appeared to be proud of his Galatea[4] in public, was evidently quite the opposite in private, and for the last three years of their marriage had not slept with her. "It was fine until I got my expense account," said a still puzzled and recently separated Maggie. "He couldn't stand it when I took him and some of my clients out to dinner. He said he felt like my wife."

The truth of the matter is, that in spite of Virginia Slims, we haven't come such a long way, babies. Oh, on the surface things

---

2. **Of the United States Legal Code.**

3. Bella Abzug, New York politician, and her husband; Mary Wells Lawrence, advertising-agency executive, and her airline-executive husband; and Farrah Fawcett-Majors and her husband, both in show business.

4. Statue created by the legendary sculptor Pygmalion and so loved by him that the goddess Aphrodite brought it to life; hence, a woman who has been in some sense "created" by a man.

have changed with D-day speed. There are girls in the Little League and the Boys' Club, and women welders working on twelve-story steel skeletons. But when these women come home to their men, there is a lurking unease and things haven't changed so much. Scratch almost any man, and you'll find wistful memories of his mother darning socks and cooking Sunday lunch and sending his father off in the morning with swept lapels and always, but always, being there to support and encourage her family. Women are still doing most of those things, but they are leaving the problem of lapel lint to the suit-wearers and racing for the front door themselves.

It's a brave new world and the rules have changed, if not the participants. "Independent" and "assertive" have become threatening words in this new war, where the body count is mounting. "Linda," my mother worried me when I told her I'd been promoted at *Newsweek*, "you've got to learn to be more dependent."

It's no wonder, really, that so many men have turned to other men for solace and sport, becoming conscientious objectors in a war they prefer not to enter. But what is puzzling is why so many heterosexual men—successful and highly visible men—are opting out of the skirmish as well, when presumably the liberation of women was to be their own liberation, too. Humpty Dumpty has had a great fall. And neither the king's women nor the king's men can figure out how to put Humpty together again.

1977

BETTY ROLLIN

Motherhood: Who Needs It?

Motherhood is in trouble, and it ought to be. A rude question is long overdue: Who needs it? The answer used to be (1) society and (2) women. But now, with the impending horrors of overpopulation, society desperately *doesn't* need it. And women don't need it either. Thanks to the Motherhood Myth—the idea that having babies is something that all normal women instinctively want and need and will enjoy doing—they just *think* they do.

The notion that the maternal wish and the activity of mothering are instinctive or biologically predestined is baloney. Try asking most sociologists, psychologists, psychoanalysts, biologists—many of whom are mothers—about motherhood being instinctive: it's like asking department store presidents if their Santa Clauses are real.

"Motherhood—instinctive?" shouts distinguished sociologist/author Dr. Jessie Bernard. "Biological destiny? Forget biology! If it were biology, people would die from not doing it."

"Women don't need to be mothers any more than they need spaghetti," says Dr. Dichard Rabkin, a New York psychiatrist. "But if you're in a world where everyone is eating spaghetti, thinking they need it and want it, you will think so too. Romance has really contaminated science. So-called instincts have to do with stimulation. They are not things that well up inside of you."

"When a woman says with feeling that she craved her baby from within, she is putting into biological language what is psychological," says University of Michigan psychoanalyst and motherhood-researcher Dr. Frederick Wyatt. "There are no instincts," says Dr. William Goode, president-elect of the American Sociological Association. "There are reflexes, like eye-blinking, and drives, like sex. There is no innate drive for children. Otherwise, the enormous cultural pressures that there are to reproduce wouldn't exist. There are no cultural pressures to sell you on getting your hand out of the fire."

There are, to be sure, biologists and others who go on about biological destiny, that is, the innate or instinctive goal of motherhood. (At the turn of the century, even good old capitalism was explained by a theorist as "the *instinct* of acquisitiveness.") And many psychoanalysts will hold the Freudian view that women feel so rotten about not having a penis that they are necessarily propelled into the child-wish to replace the missing organ. Psychoanalysts also make much of the psychological need to repeat what one's parent of the same sex has done. Since every woman has a mother, it is considered normal to wish to imitate one's mother by being a mother.

There is, surely, a wish to pass on love if one has received it, but to insist women must pass it on in the same way is like insisting that every man whose father is a gardener has to be a gardener. One dissenting psychoanalyst says, simply, "There is a wish to comply with one's biology, yes, but we needn't and sometimes we shouldn't." (Interestingly, the woman who has been the greatest contributor to child therapy and who has probably given more to children than anyone alive is Dr. Anna Freud, Freud's magnificent daughter, who is not a mother.)

Anyway, what an expert cast of hundreds is telling us is, simply, that biological *possibility* and desire are not the same as biological *need*. Women have childbearing equipment. To choose not to use the equipment is no more blocking what is instinctive than it is for a man who, muscles or no, chooses not to be a weight lifter.

So much for the wish. What about the "instinctive" *activity* of mothering? One animal study shows that when a young member of a species is put in a cage, say, with an older member of the same species, the latter will act in a protective, "maternal" way. But that goes for both males and females who have been "mothered" themselves. And studies indicate that a human baby will also respond to whoever is around playing mother—even if it's father. Margaret Mead and many others frequently point out that mothering can be a fine occupation; if you want it, for either sex. Another experiment with monkeys who were brought up without mothers found them lacking in maternal behavior toward their own offspring. A similar study showed that monkeys brought up without other monkeys of the opposite sex had no interest in .mating—all of which suggests that both mothering and mating behavior are learned, not instinctual. And, to turn the cart (or the baby carriage) around, baby ducks who lovingly follow their mothers seemed, in the mother's absence, to just as lovingly follow wooden ducks or even vacuum cleaners.

If motherhood isn't instinctive, when and why, then, was the Motherhood Myth born? Until recently, the entire question of maternal motivation was academic. Sex, like it or not, meant babies. Not that there haven't always been a lot of interesting contraceptive tries. But until the creation of the diaphragm in the 1880's, the birth of babies was largely unavoidable. And, generally speaking, nobody really seemed to mind. For one thing, people tend to be sort of good sports about what seems to be inevitable. For another, in the past, the population needed beefing up. Mortality rates were high, and agricultural cultures, particularly, have always needed children to help out. So because it "just happened" and because it was needed, motherhood was assumed to be innate.

Originally, it was the word of God that got the ball rolling with "Be fruitful and multiply," a practical suggestion, since the only people around then were Adam and Eve. But in no time, supermoralists like St. Augustine changed the tone of the message: "Intercourse, even with one's legitimate wife, is unlawful and wicked where the conception of the offspring is prevented," he, we assume, thundered. And the Roman Catholic position was thus cemented. So then and now, procreation took on a curious value among people who viewed (and view) the pleasures of sex as sinful. One could partake in the sinful pleasure, but feel vindicated by the ensuing birth. Motherhood cleaned up sex. Also, it cleaned up women, who have always been considered somewhat evil, because of Eve's transgression (". . . but the woman was deceived and became a transgressor. Yet woman will be saved through bearing children . . . ," I Timothy, 2:14–15), and somewhat dirty because of menstruation.

And so, based on need, inevitability, and pragmatic fantasy—the Myth *worked*, from society's point of view—the Myth grew like corn in Kansas. And society reinforced it with both laws and propaganda—laws that made woman a chattel, denied her education and personal mobility, and madonna propaganda that she was beautiful and wonderful doing it and it was all beautiful and wonderful to do. (One rarely sees a madonna washing dishes.)

In fact, the Myth persisted—breaking some kind of record for long-lasting fallacies—until something like yesterday. For as the truth about the Myth trickled in—as women's rights increased, as women gradually got the message that it was certainly possible for them to do most things that men did, that they live longer, that their brains were not tinier—then, finally, when the really big news rolled in, that they could *choose* whether or not to be mothers—what happened? The Motherhood Myth soared higher than ever. As Betty Friedan made oh-so-clear in *The Feminine Mystique*, the '40's and '50's produced a group of ladies who not only had babies as if they were going out of style (maybe they were) but, as never before, they turned motherhood into a cult. First, they wallowed in the aesthetics of it all—natural childbirth and nursing became maternal musts. Like heavy-bellied ostriches, they grounded their heads in the sands of motherhood, only coming up for air to say how utterly happy and fulfilled they were. But, as Mrs. Friedan says only too plainly, they weren't. The Myth galloped on, moreover, long after making babies had turned from practical asset to liability for both individual parents *and* society. With the average cost of a middle-class child figured conservatively at $30,000 (not including college), any parent knows that the only people who benefit economically from children are manufacturers of consumer goods. Hence all those gooey motherhood commercials. And the Myth gathered momentum long after sheer numbers, while not yet extinguishing us, have made us intensely uncomfortable. Almost all of our societal problems, from minor discomforts like traffic to major ones like hunger, the population people keep reminding us, have to do with there being too many people. And who suffers most? The kids who have been so mindlessly brought into the world, that's who. They are the ones who have to cope with all of the difficult and dehumanizing conditions brought on by overpopulation. They are the ones who have to cope with the psychological nausea of feeling unneeded by society. That's not the only reason for drugs, but, surely, it's a leading contender.

Unfortunately, the population curbers are tripped up by a romantic, stubborn, ideological hurdle. How can birth-control programs really be effective as long as the concept of glorious motherhood remains unchanged? (Even poor old Planned Parenthood has to euphemize—why not Planned Unparenthood?) Particularly among the poor, motherhood is one of the few inherently positive institutions that are accessible. As Berkeley demographer Judith Blake points out, "Poverty-oriented birth control programs do not make sense as a welfare measure . . . as long as existing pronatalist policies . . . encourage mating, pregnancy, and the care, support, and rearing of children." Or, she might have added, as long as the less-than-idyllic child-rearing part of motherhood remains "in small print."

Sure, motherhood gets dumped on sometimes: Philip Wylie's Momism[1] got going in the '40's and Philip Roth's *Portnoy's Complaint* did its best to turn rancid the chicken-soup concept of Jewish motherhood. But these are viewed as the sour cries of a black humorist here, a malcontent there. Everyone shudders, laughs, but it's like the mouse and the elephant joke. Still, the Myth persists. Last April, a Brooklyn woman was indicted on charges of manslaughter and negligent homicide—eleven children died in a fire in a building she owned and criminally neglected—"But," sputtered her lawyer, "my client, Mrs. Breslow, is a mother, a grandmother, and a great-grandmother!"

Most remarkably, the Motherhood Myth persists in the face of the most overwhelming maternal unhappiness and incompetence. If reproduction were merely superfluous and expensive, if the experience were as rich and rewarding as the cliché would have us believe, if it were a predominantly joyous trip for everyone riding—mother, father, child—then the going everybody-should-have-two-children plan would suffice. Certainly, there are a lot of joyous mothers, and their children and (sometimes, not necessarily) their husbands reflect their joy. But a lot of evidence suggests that for more women than anyone wants to admit, motherhood can be miserable. ("If it weren't," says one psychiatrist wryly, "the world wouldn't be in the mess it's in.")

There is a remarkable statistical finding from a recent study of Dr. Bernard's, comparing the mental illness and unhappiness of married mothers and single women. The latter group, it turned out, was both markedly less sick and overtly more happy. Of course, it's not easy to measure slippery attitudes like happiness. "Many women have achieved a kind of reconciliation—a conformity," says Dr. Bernard,

that they interpret as happiness. Since feminine happiness is supposed to lie in devoting one's life to one's husband and children, they do that; so *ipso facto*, they assume they are happy. And for many women, untrained for independence and "processed" for motherhood, they find their state far preferable to the alternatives, which don't really exist.

Also, unhappy mothers are often loath to admit it. For one thing, if in society's view not to be a mother is to be a freak, not to be a *blissful* mother, is to be a witch. Besides, unlike a disappointing mar-

1. Philip Wylie's *A Generation of Vipers* (1942) blamed many of the ills of American society on dominating mothers.

riage, disappointing motherhood cannot be terminated by divorce. Of course, none of that stops such a woman from expressing her dissatisfaction in a variety of ways. Again, it is not only she who suffers but her husband and children as well. Enter the harridan housewife, the carping shrew. The realities of motherhood can turn women into terrible people. And, judging from the 50,000 cases of child abuse in the U.S. each year, some are worse than terrible.

In some cases, the unpleasing realities of motherhood begin even before the beginning. In *Her Infinite Variety*, Morton Hunt describes young married women pregnant for the first time as "very likely to be frightened and depressed, masking these feelings in order not to be considered contemptible. The arrival of pregnancy interrupts a pleasant dream of motherhood and awakens them to the realization that they have too little money, or not enough space, or unresolved marital problems. . . ."

The following are random quotes from interviews with some mothers in Ann Arbor, Mich., who described themselves as reasonably happy. They all had positive things to say about their children, although when asked about the best moment of their day, they *all* confessed it was when the children were in bed. Here is the rest:

Suddenly I had to devote myself to the child totally. I was under the illusion that the baby was going to fit into my life, and I found that I had to switch my life and my schedule to fit *him*. You think, "I'm in love, I'll get married, and we'll have a baby." First there's two, then three, it's simple and romantic. You don't even think about the work. . . .

You never get away from the responsibility. Even when you leave the children with a sitter, you are not out from under the pressure of the responsibility. . . .

I hate ironing their pants and doing their underwear, and they never put their clothes in the laundry basket. . . . As they get older, they make less demands on our time because they're in school, but the demands are greater in forming their values. . . . Best moment of the day is when all the children are in bed. . . . The worst time of the day is 4 P.M., when you have to get dinner started, the kids are tired, hungry and crabby—everybody wants to talk to you about *their* day . . . your day is only half over.

Once a mother, the responsibility and concern for my children became so encompassing. . . . It took a great deal of will to keep up other parts of my personality. . . . To me, motherhood gets harder as they get older because you have less control. . . . In an abstract sense, I'd have several. . . . In the non-abstract, I would not have any. . . .

I had anticipated that the baby would sleep and eat, sleep and eat. Instead, the experience was overwhelming. I really had not thought particularly about what motherhood would mean in a realistic sense. I want to do *other* things, like to become involved in things that are worthwhile

—I don't mean women's clubs—but I don't have the physical energy to go out in the evenings. I feel like I'm missing something . . . the experience of being somewhere with people and having them talking about something—something that's going on in the world.

Every grownup person expects to pay a price for his pleasures, but seldom is the price as vast as the one endured "however happily" by most mothers. We have mentioned the literal cost factor. But what does that mean? For middle-class American women, it means a life style with severe and usually unimagined limitations; i.e., life in the suburbs, because who can afford three bedrooms in the city? And what do suburbs mean? For women, suburbs mean other women and children and leftover peanut-butter sandwiches and car pools and seldom-seen husbands. Even the Feminine Mystiqueniks—the housewives who finally admitted that their lives behind brooms (OK, electric brooms) were driving them crazy— were loath to trace their predicament to their children. But it is simply a fact that a childless married woman has no child-work and little housework. She can live in a city, or, if she still chooses the suburbs or the country, she can leave on the commuter train with her husband if she wants to. Even the most ardent job-seeking mother will find little in the way of great opportunities in Scarsdale.[2] Besides, by the time she wakes up, she usually lacks both the preparation for the outside world and the self-confidence to get it. You will say there are plenty of city-dwelling working mothers. But most of those women do additional-funds-for-the-family kind of work, not the interesting career kind that takes plugging during childbearing years.

Nor is it a bed of petunias for the mother who does make it professionally. Says writer critic Marya Mannes:

If the creative woman has children, she must pay for this indulgence with a long burden of guilt, for her life will be split three ways between them and her husband and her work. . . . No woman with any heart can compose a paragraph when her child is in trouble. . . . The creative woman has no wife to protect her from intrusion. A man at his desk in a room with closed door is a man at work. A woman at a desk in any room is available.

Speaking of jobs, do remember that mothering, salary or not, is a job. Even those who can afford nurses to handle the nitty-gritty still need to put out emotionally. "Well-cared-for" neurotic rich kids are not exactly unknown in our society. One of the more absurd aspects of the Myth is the underlying assumption that, since most women are biologically equipped to bear children, they are

A **wealthy** suburb of New York City.

psychologically, mentally, emotionally, and technically equipped (or interested) to rear them. Never mind happiness. To assume that such an exacting, consuming, and important task is something almost all women are equipped to do is far more dangerous and ridiculous than assuming that everyone with vocal chords should seek a career in the opera.

A major expectation of the Myth is that children make a not-so-hot marriage hotter, or a hot marriage, hotter still. Yet almost every available study indicates that childless marriages are far happier. One of the biggest, of 850 couples, was conducted by Dr. Harold Feldman of Cornell University, who states his finding in no uncertain terms: "Those couples with children had a significantly lower level of marital satisfaction than did those without children." Some of the reasons are obvious. Even the most adorable children make for additional demands, complications, and hardships in the lives of even the most loving parents. If a woman feels disappointed and trapped in her mother role, it is bound to affect her marriage in any number of ways: she may take out her frustrations directly on her husband, or she may count on him too heavily for what she feels she is missing in her daily life.

". . . You begin to grow away from your husband," says one of the Michigan ladies. "He's working on his career and you're working on your family. But you both must gear your lives to the children. You do things the children enjoy, more than things you might enjoy." More subtle and possibly more serious is what motherhood may do to a woman's sexuality. Often when the stork flies in, sexuality flies out. Both in the emotional minds of some women *and* in the minds of their husbands, when a woman becomes a mother, she stops being a woman. It's not only that motherhood may destroy her physical attractiveness, but its madonna concept may destroy her *feelings* of sexuality.

And what of the payoff? Usually, even the most self-sacrificing of maternal self-sacrificers expects a little something back. Gratified parents are not unknown to the Western world, but there are probably at least just as many who feel, to put it crudely, shortchanged. The experiment mentioned earlier—where the baby ducks followed vacuum cleaners instead of their mothers—indicates that what passes for love from baby to mother is merely a rudimentary kind of object attachment. Without necessarily feeling like a Hoover, a lot of women become disheartened because babies and children are not only not interesting to talk to (not everyone thrills at the wonders of da-da-ma-ma talk) but they are generally not empathetic, considerate people. Even the nicest children are not capable of empathy, surely a major ingredient of love, until they are much older. Sometimes they're never capable of it. Dr. Wyatt says that often, in later years particularly, when most of the "returns" are in, it is the "good mother" who suffers most of all. It is then she must face a reality: The child—the appendage with her genes—is not an appendage, but a separate person. What's more, he or she may be a separate person who doesn't even like her—or whom she doesn't really like.

So if the music is lousy, how come everyone's dancing? Because the motherhood minuet is taught freely from birth, and whether or not she has rhythm or likes the music, every woman is expected to do it. Indeed, she *wants* to do it. Little girls start learning what to want—and what to be—when they are still in their cribs. Dr. Miriam Keiffer, a young social psychologist at Bensalem, the Experimental College of Fordham University, points to studies showing that

at six months of age, mothers are already treating their baby girls and boys quite differently. For instance, mothers have been found to touch, comfort, and talk to their females more. If these differences can be found at such an early stage, it's not surprising that the end product is as different as it is. What is surprising is that men and women are, in so many ways, similar.

Some people point to the way little girls play with dolls as proof of their innate motherliness. But remember, little girls are *given* dolls. When Margaret Mead presented some dolls to New Guinea children, it was the boys, not the girls, who wanted to play with them, which they did by crooning lullabies and rocking them in the most maternal fashion.

By the time they reach adolescence, most girls, unconsciously or not, have learned enough about role definition to qualify for a master's degree. In general, the lesson has been that no matter what kind of career thoughts one may entertain, one must, first and foremost, be a wife and mother. A girl's mother is usually her first teacher. As Dr. Goode says, "A woman is not only taught by society to have a child; she is taught to have a child who will have a child." A woman who has hung her life on the Motherhood Myth will almost always reinforce her young married daughter's early training by pushing for grandchildren. Prospective grandmothers are not the only ones. Husbands, too, can be effective sellers. After all, they have the Fatherhood Myth to cope with. A married man is *supposed* to have children. Often, particularly among Latins, children are a sign of potency. They help him assure the world—and himself —that he is the big man he is supposed to be. Plus, children give him both immortality (whatever that means) and possibly the chance to become more in his lifetime through the accomplishments of his children, particularly his son. (Sometimes it's important, however, for the son to do better, but not *too* much better.)

Friends, too, can be counted on as myth-pushers. Naturally one wants to do what one's friends do. One study, by the way, found a correlation between a woman's fertility and that of her three closest friends. The negative sell comes into play here, too. We have seen what the concept of non-mother means (cold, selfish, unwomanly, abnormal). In practice, particuarly in the suburbs, it can mean, simply, exclusion—both from child-centered activities (that is, most activities) and child-centered conversations (that is, most conversations). It can also mean being the butt of a lot of unfunny jokes. ("Whaddya waiting for? An immaculate conception? Ha ha.") Worst of all, it can mean being an object of pity.

In case she's escaped all those pressures (that is, if she was brought up in a cave), a young married woman often wants a baby just so that she'll (1) have something to do (motherhood is better than clerk/typist, which is often the only kind of job she can get, since little more has been expected of her and, besides, her boss also expects her to leave and be a mother); (2) have something to hug and possess, to be needed by and have power over; and (3) have something to *be*—e.g., a baby's mother. Motherhood affords an instant identity. First, through wifehood, you are somebody's wife; then you are somebody's mother. Both give not only identity and activity, but status and stardom of a kind. During pregnancy, a woman can look forward to the kind of attention and pampering she may not ever have gotten or may never otherwise get. Some women consider birth the biggest accomplishment of their lives, which may be interpreted as saying not much for the rest of their lives. As Dr. Goode says, "It's like the gambler who may know the roulette wheel is crooked, but it's the only game in town." Also, with motherhood, the feeling of accomplishment is immediate. It is really much faster and easier to make a baby than paint a painting, or write a book, or get to the point of accomplishment in a job. It is also easier in a way to shift focus from self-development to child development—particularly since, for women, self-development is considered selfish. Even unwed mothers may achieve a feeling of this kind. (As we have seen, little thought is given to the aftermath.) And, again, since so many women are underdeveloped as people, they feel that, besides children, they have little else to give —to themselves, their husbands, to their world.

You may ask why then, when the realities do start pouring in, does a woman want to have a second, third, even fourth child? OK, (1) just because reality is pouring in doesn't mean she wants to *face* it. A new baby can help bring back some of the old illusions. Says psychoanalyst Dr. Natalie Shainess, "She may view each successive child as a knight in armor that will rescue her from being a 'bad unhappy mother.'" (2) Next on the horror list of having no children, is having one. It suffices to say that only children are not only OK, they even have a high rate of exceptionality. (3) Both parents usually want at least one child of each sex. The husband, for reasons discussed earlier, probably wants a son. (4) The more children one has, the more of an excuse one has not to develop in any other way.

What's the point? A world without children? Of course not. Nothing could be worse or more unlikely. No matter what anyone *Discus* says in *Look* or anywhere else, motherhood isn't about to go out like a blown bulb, and who says it should? Only the Myth must go out, and now it seems to be dimming.

The younger-generation females who have been reared on the Myth have not rejected it totally, but at least they recognize it can be more loving to children not to have them. And at least they speak of adopting children instead of bearing them. Moreover, since the new nonbreeders are "less hung-up" on ownership, they seem to recognize that if you dig loving children, you don't necessarily have to own one. The end of the Motherhood Myth might make available more loving women (and men!) for those children who already exist.

When motherhood is no longer culturally compulsory, there will, certainly, be less of it. Women are now beginning to think and do more about development of self, of their individual resources. Far from being selfish, such development is probably our only hope. That means more alternatives for women. And more alternatives mean more selective, better, happier, motherhood—and childhood and husbandhood (or manhood) and peoplehood. It is not a question of whether or not children are sweet and marvelous to have and rear; the question is, even if that's so, whether or not one wants to pay the price for it. It doesn't make sense any more to pretend that women need babies, when what they really need is themselves. If God were still speaking to us in a voice we could hear, even He would probably say, "Be fruitful. Don't multiply."

1970

S. J. PERELMAN

The Machismo Mystique

It was 3 P.M., that climactic midafternoon moment toward which every gallant worthy of the name bends his energies, and I'd done all the preparatory work time and an unencumbered credit card could accomplish. I had stoked my Chilean vis-à-vis with three vodka martinis, half a gallon of Sancerre, and two balloons of Armagnac until her eyes were veritable liquid pools. Under my bold, not to say outrageous, compliments her damask skin and the alabaster column of her throat glowed like a lovely pink pearl; her hair, black as the raven's wing, shimmered in the reflection of the boudoir lamp shading our discreet banquette; and every now and again as my knee nudged hers under the table, my affinity's magnificent bosom· heaved uncontrollably. I had glissed through all those earnest confidences that begin, "You know, I've never said this to anyone before," to, "Look, I'm not very articulate, but I feel that in these parlous times, it behooves us all to reach out, to cling to another lonely person—do you know what I mean?" Suddenly I had the feeling that she knew what I meant, all right. In a swift glance, I encompassed the small chic restaurant whence all but we had fled—its idle barman and the maître d'hôtel stifling a yawn— and I struck.

"Listen," I said as if inspired. "This friend of mine, the Marquis de Cad, who has a wonderful collection of African sculpture, was called away to Cleveland, and I promised to stop by his flat and dust it. Why don't we pick up a bottle of lemon oil . . ."

Inamorata threw back her sleek head and shouted with laughter. "Stop, *querido*,"[1] she implored. "You're ruining my mascara. Such *machismo*—who would have expected it from a shrimp like you?"

Quicker than any hidalgo of Old Spain to erase an insult, I sprang up prepared to plunge my poniard into her bosom (a striking demonstration of the maxim that man kills that which he most loves). Unfortunately, I had left my poniard at home on the bureau and was wearing only a tie-tack that could never penetrate anyone so thick-skinned. Nonetheless, I made the hussy smart for her insolence. "Let me tell you something, Chubby," I rasped. "Never underestimate the American male. I may not dance the mambo or reek of garlic, but I'm just as feisty as those caballeros of yours below the Rio Grande. Remember that our first colonial flag in Kentucky, the Dark and Bloody Ground, portrayed a coiled rattlesnake over the legend, 'Don't Tread on Me.' "

"Big deal," she scoffed. "Do you want an example of real *machismo*—the kind of masculinity Latin-American men are capable of? Tell them to bring me another Armagnac."

Downcast at the realization that our matinee had blown out the back, I sullenly acceded. The story as she related it dealt with a bar in Guatemala City called *Mi apuesta* (The Wager) after a bet once made there. Two young bloods or *machos*, it appeared, had

1. Beloved.

swaggered in one evening, stiff with conceit and supremely self-confident, arrogant as a pair of fighting cocks. Lounging at the bar over a glass of manzanilla, one of them remarked to the other, "*Te apuesto que no eres bastante macho para matar al primero que entre*" (I wager you're not man enough to kill the first hombre who comes in).

The other sneered thinly. "No?" he said. "I bet you fifty *centavos* I will."

The bet was covered, whereupon the challenged party extracted a Beretta from his waistband, and a moment later, as a totally inoffensive stranger stepped through the saloon door, a bullet drilled him through the heart.

"*Madre de Dios*," I exclaimed, shocked. "What happened to the assassin?"

"*Niente*," said Inamorata calmly. "The judge gave him a three months' suspended sentence on the ground that the crime was in no way premeditated."

Needless to say, whenever Inamorata rang up after our abortive meeting and besought me to lunch her again, I showed her a clean pair of heels. (They were two fellows who dispensed towels at the Luxor Baths; they pursued her madly, and I hope with more success than I had.) At any rate, in pondering the whole business of *machismo*, of male bravado and excessive manliness, it occurred to me that I had met quite a few *machos* in my time, both in the entertainment world and belles-lettres. The one I remember most vividly in the former was a Hollywood screenwriter—a big redheaded blowhard I'll call Rick Ferret. A Montanan who claimed to have grown up on the range, Ferret was forever beating his gums about his amatory exploits; by his own blushing admission, he was Casanova reborn, the swordsman supreme, the reincarnation of Don Juan. According to him, women in every walk of life—society leaders and shopgirls, leading ladies and vendeuses—fell in windrows in his path, and though it was obvious to his auditors at the Brown Derby that he dealt in quantity rather than quality, the references he dropped to his nuclear power and durability left us pale with jealousy.

One evening, I attended a party at his house in Laurel Canyon. Living with him at the time was a lady named Susie, quite well-endowed and with a rather sharp tongue. So late was the hour when the bash ended that the two insisted I stay over, and the next morning, while I was adjusting my false lashes, Ferret entered the bathroom and proceeded to take a shower. Just as he was snorting and puffing like a grampus, I chanced to observe a quite formidable scar on his *Sitzfleisch*. With an apology for the personal nature of the question, I asked if it was a war wound of some kind.

"Yes, in a way," he said carelessly, turning off the taps. "There's quite a story attached to it." He opened the door of the bathroom to disperse the steam, and I glimpsed his Susie breakfasting in bed a few feet distant. "The fact is," he went on, "it happened some years ago down on the south fork of the Brazos while I was rounding up some mavericks. This gang of rustlers from Durango way cut into the herd, and I took after them hell for leather. Well, the greasers were spoiling for action, and they got it." He chuckled. "Before I could yank out my six-guns, they creased me here, but I managed to rub out the whole dad-blamed lot."

"Oh, for God's sake, Ferret," I heard Susie's voice croak from the bedroom. "You know perfectly well you had a boil lanced on your tail only last Tuesday."

The two most celebrated *machos* I ever knew, I suppose, were Ernest Hemingway—unquestionably the holder of the black belt in the Anglo-Saxon world—and Mike Todd, who, to pilfer a phrase from Marcel Proust, might aptly be termed the Sweet Cheat Gone. My go-around with Hemingway took place in the winter of 1954, directly after his two widely publicized plane crashes in East Africa. He was borne into the New Stanley Hotel in Nairobi in a somewhat disoriented state, suffering a double concussion, a smashed kidney, and alarming symptoms of *folie de grandeur*.[2] I turned up there two days later from Uganda with fourteen women comprising the first American all-girl safari (quite another story), and since my room was adjacent to his, saw a good bit of him thereafter. What with his tribulations and frequent infusions of hooch, Papa was inclined to ramble somewhat, and it was not always easy to follow the thread of his discourse. Once in a while, though, the clouds dissipated, and we were able to chat about mutual friends in the Montparnasse of the 'twenties. It was on such an occasion, one night, that he told me an anecdote that stunningly dramatized his *machismo*.

It concerned a period when he used to box at Stillman's Gymnasium in New York, a favorite haunt of enthusiasts of what is termed the manly art. His adversaries, Hemingway blushingly admitted, never matched his own speed and strength, but one of them improved so under his tutelage that occasionally the pair had a tolerable scrimmage. Thinking to intensify it, Hemingway suggested they discard their gloves and fight bareknuckle. This, too, while diverting, soon palled, but at last he had an inspiration.

"The room we boxed in," Hemingway explained, "had these rows of pipes running along the walls—you know, like backstage in a

2. Delusions of grandeur.

theater? Well, we flooded the place with steam, so thickly that it looked like a pea-soup fog in London. Then we started charging each other like a couple of rhinos. Butting our heads together and roaring like crazy. God, it was terrific—you could hear the impact of bone on bone, and we bled like stuck pigs. Of course, that made the footwork a bit more difficult, slipping and sliding all over, but it sure heightened the fun. Man, those were the days. You had to have real *cojones*[3] to stand up to it."

The same hormonal doodads were imperative in order to cope with Mike Todd and his vagaries. Todd's *machismo* was that common form that afflicts all undersized men—megalomania. He freely identified himself with Napoleon, P. T. Barnum, and Carl Laemmle, Junior, not to mention the Roman emperors of the decline. Whereas the latter, however, believed in giving the populace bread and circuses, Todd gave them circuses and kept the bread. Rarely if ever has there been anyone more unwilling to fork over what he owed to those actors, writers, and technicians who aided him in his grandiloquent projects of stage and screen. The little corpuscle, in short, believed in flaunting money where it made the most impression—at Deauville, Monaco, and the gaming tables of Las Vegas. In this respect, he was a true *mucho*. My sole souvenir of our frenetic association is a replica of the carpetbag Phileas Fogg carried on his celebrated journey, a thousand of which Todd distributed in lordly fashion to Broadway companions, investors, accountants, dentists, and other sycophants. But surely, his admirers have since queried me, I must have been awed by his tremendous vitality; Only in part, I respond: *Moi-même*, I prefer the anthropoid apes. The gibbon swings farther, the chimpanzee's reflexes, are quicker, the orangutan can scratch faster, and the gorilla—my particular love object—has been known to crunch a Stillson wrench in his teeth.

Of such literary *machos* was the late Robert Ruark, who of course patterned himself on Hemingway. Their careers afford ample demonstration of my two favorite maxims: a) that the gaudier the patter, the cheaper the scribe, and b) that easy writing makes hard reading. The legend of Ruark's fatal charisma with women still gives one a pain in the posterior when recounted, and his press interviews, studded with reference to the millions of words he merchandised, act as a tourniquet on bleeders like myself who labor over a postcard. Even John O'Hara, somewhat more talented, was not above buttonholing acquaintances and boasting that he had

3. **Testicles.**

written this or that deathless vignette in three quarters of an hour. It is interesting, by the way, that Scott Fitzgerald, with whom O'Hara was given to comparing himself, never made any claims to his own facility when I knew him in Hollywood. On the contrary, both he and Nathanael West were continually obsessed by delusions of their inadequacy with sex and their small literary output.

Looking back over a long and mottled career, I think the best illustration of real *machismo* I ever beheld took place on the terrace of the Café du Dôme in Paris in 1927. I was seated there at dusk one day with a fellow journalist when an enormous yellow Hispano-Suiza landaulet driven by a chauffeur drew up at the curb. From it emerged a tall and beautiful, exquisitely clad lady, followed by another even more photogenic—both clearly high-fashion mannequins. Reaching into the tonneau, they brought forth a wizened homunculus with a yellow face resembling Earl Sande, the celebrated jockey. Hooking their arms through his, they assisted him to a table farther down the terrace. I turned to my *copain* with my eyebrows raised, searching for some explanation of the phenomenon. A slow smile overspread his countenance, and he held his hands apart as does one when asked to steady a skein of wool.

That's *machismo*, sweetheart.

1975

QUESTIONS

1. Write your own definition of machismo, basing it on Perelman's examples.
2. Perelman says his next-to-last paragraph contains his "best illustration of real machismo." Explain why you agree or disagree.
3. Toward the end of his essay Perelman talks about writers who boast about how fast and how much they write. Why do you think Perelman includes these examples? Explain whether they are a part of his definition of machismo or merely analogous to it.
4. Describe an incident (either actual or invented) which illustrates machismo. Then change the incident so that it no longer illustrates machismo. Explain whether the changes involved (1) changes in people, (2) changes in circumstances or social customs, or (3) changes in both. What conclusions can you draw about whether machismo is a part of human nature or is culturally conditioned?
5. Perelman has a very distinctive style. Try to determine what its characteristics are by rewriting one of his paragraphs in a more neutral style.
6. Read the McGraw-Hill "Guidelines for Equal Treatment of the Sexes" (pp. 181–192). In what ways are machismo attitudes reflected in language?

PETER C. NEWMAN

Home Country

In the early and middle sixties, when I was working out of the Parliamentary Press Gallery in Ottawa reporting on the vagaries of the Diefenbaker-Pearson years,[1] I would occasionally get a hearty phone call frome someone in the American embassy there, asking me "as a personal favor" to talk to "this friend of mine, a great guy, really sold on Canada, up here researching a big take-out on the undefended border, all that jazz, you know."

The friend would generally turn out to be some young producer from NBC or a hardened old hand from the St. Louis *Post-Dispatch*, baffled by the lassitude of our life-style, impatient with the size of our snowdrifts, and frustrated by his inability to find a strong focus for the big take-out. (There is, after all, only so much you can do with an undefended border, even if you are a great guy.)

When we met, he would greet me a shade too jovially, and five sentences into the conversation it would become obvious that in the American embassy's catalogue of reliable spokesmen, interesting characters, and harmless kooks, my name represented a small fringe element; I was known as a Canadian nationalist. The itinerant luminary and the embassy official obviously thought this an innocuous pastime, like lepidopterology or ice-fishing, and I would obligingly mumble my nationalist's set piece over drinks, pointing out as mildly as I could that Canada as a nation was in danger of drowning in American dollars, American culture, American know-how, and the American dream.

Eventually, the visitor would take his leave, looking a little glassy of eye, and when his take-out or program finally appeared, my nationalistic ideas would be reduced to half a paragraph or two minutes on the screen, the kind of obligatory glimpse that gyrating witch doctors used to command in documentaries about emerging African states.

But times have changed. The American embassy has long since stopped phoning me; all those great guys are reporting on less benign expressions of our nationalism; and along with that small band of Canadians who were nationalists a decade ago, I find myself a moderate voice in a rising chorus of anti-American sentiment. This attitude seems so foreign to the habitual Canadian cast of mind that it almost amounts to a denial of our national charac-

1. John Diefenbaker, a Progressive Conservative, and Lester B. Pearson, a Liberal, held the office of prime minister, respectively, from 1957 to 1963 and from 1963 to 1968.

ter. After displaying for so long the emotional responses of a fearful, immature twenty-year-old who has not yet resolved his adolescent identity crisis, we are experiencing a mood of surging self-assertion. This new aggressive nationalism is strongest among the radical young and the activist intellectuals, but in the past year it has become an issue that even the old-line liberal internationalists, who still form the country's political establishment, have been unable to avoid. It is as though we have come to realize for the first time the true implications of our dependency on the United States. "Little by little," writes James Eayrs, a University of Toronto professor who has come very lately to the nationalist cause, "our independence is seeping southward. It takes place so painlessly that the victim does not notice. But one day he tries to exercise his independence and finds it isn't there—like the decapitated swordsman in the Thurber cartoon who, protesting he's fit to carry on dueling, is told to try and blow his nose."

During the past few years we have been displaying our determination to hold on to our heads in various ways, but nationalism in Canada is still a cause in search of a leader, an issue yet to be joined.

Its historic roots go far deeper than these recent manifestations would suggest. A self-governing colony may sound like a contradiction in terms; yet this has been the underlying theme of our history. Canada moved directly from being a colony of Great Britain to becoming an economic satellite of the United States. Originally, the Canadian nation was a fusion, or rather a living-together, of French-Canadians (following their defeat by the British) and those united Empire Loyalists who left the thirteen colonies after the Revolutionary War because they opted for England and King George. They were joined by waves of Scottish, Irish, and European immigrants fleeing various tyrannies. Born out of many defeats, Canada achieved a form of independence in 1867 (i.e., dominion status within the British Empire), which left its foreign policies to be dictated by Whitehall.[2] Full freedom in international dealings came only in 1931, and it wasn't until 1949 that the judicial committee of the Privy Council[3] in London ceased to be the final appeal from Canadian courts. This prolonged dependence on the mother country caused an impatient generation of Canadian patriots of Lester Pearson's vintage to believe that the umbilical cord with England could be cut only if Canada were aligned with the United States through closer military, economic, and social ties.

2. That is, the British Government. Whitehall is the street in London on which the main government offices are located.

3. An advisory body to the British monarch, composed of the highest dignitaries and officials of the land.

And so we went directly from being bastard Englishmen to being bastard Americans.

The conquest of the Canadian economy by American business-men has reduced Canadians to being minority shareholders in their own country. For example, more than 90 percent of all factories in Canada important enough to have at least five thousand names on their payrolls are controlled by parent corporations in the United States. In addition, some 99 percent of oil refining, 85 percent of primary metal smelting, 78 percent of chemical production, and 77 percent of the electrical apparatus industry are American-owned. The cliché is that when the American economy catches a cold, we sneeze; the fact is that we develop pneumonia.

When you point out the extent of American economic domina-tion to Americans living in Canada, they become intensely upset, hurt by our failure to remember that American capital has under-written most of the country's development risks, reducing from gen-erations to years the time required to attain our high standards of living. They had come to regard Canadians as the dullish denizens of their northernmost "state" and are baffled by all of the recent uproar. What they do not realize, and what it has taken us so long to comprehend, is that in exchange for our borrowed American affluence we have been selling out our way of life. In our naïve, northern way, we had no idea that allowing the Americans to develop our natural resources implied we were willing to have them pollute our environment, direct our trade unions, deluge our media, bookstores, magazine racks, moviehouses, and even school texts with American ideas and values so that we are in real danger of forget-ting who we are and why we are here.

Until recently, any concern with perpetuating the Canadian iden tity was considered fairly absurd and old-fashioned, since the admired attitude was internationalism and the only real mark of acceptance in every field of endeavor came from the United States. I bought it on Fifth Avenue; he studied at Harvard; she had her hysterectomy at the Mayo; we got our tan in Palm Beach—these were the meaninful accolades. We were the country cousins awed by the new Roman Empire and understood perfectly what Anthony Burgess meant when he wrote: "John Kenneth Galbraith and Marshall McLuhan are the two greatest modern Canadians the United States has produced." All that has changed. The American experience we so envied has become too precious to be entrusted to the new, disturbing America that emerged in the sixties—the Amer-ica of the Kennedy assassinations, Kent State, and Vietnam.

By the very act of confronting our problems of domination from without and dissension from within, Canadians may be able to rework the miracle of their existence. In any case, having survived for a century as an irrelevant hunk of geography—a kind of gullible Gulliver of the North—we have now joined the mainstream of history at last.

1971

ANTHONY BURGESS
Is America Falling Apart?

I am back in Bracciano, a castellated town about 13 miles north of Rome, after a year in New Jersey. I find the Italian Government still unstable, gasoline more expensive than anywhere in the world, butchers and bank clerks and tobacconists (which also means salt-sellers) ready to go on strike at the drop of a *cappello*,[1] neo-Fascists at their dirty work, the hammer and sickle painted on the rumps of public statues, a thousand-lire note (officially worth about $1.63) shrunk to the slightness of a dollar bill.

Nevertheless, it's delightful to be back. People are underpaid but they go through an act of liking their work, the open markets are luscious with esculent color, the community is more important than the state, the human condition is humorously accepted. The *tramontana* blows viciously today, and there's no central heating to turn on, but it will be pleasant when the wind drops. The two television channels are inadequate, but next Wednesday's rerun of an old Western, with Gary Cooper coming into a saloon saying "*Ciao, ragazzi*,"[2] is something to look forward to. Manifold consumption isn't important here. The quality of life has nothing to do with the quantity of brand names. What matters is talk, family, cheap wine in the open air, the wresting of minimal sweetness out of the long-known bitterness of living. I was spoiled in New Jersey. The Italian for *spoiled* is *viziato*, cognate with *vitiated*, which has to do with vice.

Spoiled? Well, yes. I never had to shiver by a fire that wouldn't draw, or go without canned kraut juice or wild rice. America made me develop new appetites in order to make proper use of the supermarket. A character in Evelyn Waugh's *Put Out More Flags* said that the difference between prewar and postwar life was that, prewar, if one thing went wrong the day was ruined; postwar, if one thing went right the day would be made. America is a prewar country, psychologically unprepared for one thing to go wrong. Now

---

1. Hat.
2. "*Ciao, ragazzi*": "Howdy, boys,"   in Italian; *tramontana*: north wind.

everything seems to be going wrong. Hence the neurosis, despair, the Kafka feeling that the whole marvelous fabric of American life is coming apart at the seams. Italy is used to everything going wrong. This is what the human condition is about.

Let me stay for a while on this subject of consumption. American individualism, on the face of it an admirable philosophy, wishes to manifest itself in independence of the community. You don't share things in common; you have your own things. A family's strength is signalized by its possessions. Herein lies a paradox. For the desire for possessions must eventually mean dependence on possessions. Freedom is slavery. Once let the acquisitive instinct burgeon (enough flour for the winter, not just for the week), and there are ruggedly individual forces only too ready to make it come to full and monstrous blossom. New appetites are invented; what to the European are bizarre luxuries become, to the American, plain necessities.

During my year's stay in New Jersey I let my appetites flower into full Americanism except for one thing. I did not possess an automobile. This self-elected deprivation was a way into the nastier side of the consumer society. Where private ownership prevails, public amenities decay or are prevented from coming into being. The wretched run-down rail services of America are something I try, vainly, to forget. The nightmare of filth, outside and in, that enfolds the trip from Springfield, Mass., to Grand Central Station would not be accepted in backward Europe. But far worse is the nightmare of travel in and around Los Angeles, where public transport does not exist and people are literally choking to death in their exhaust fumes. This is part of the price of the metaphysic of individual ownership.

But if the car owner can ignore the lack of public transport, he can hardly ignore the decay of services in general. His car needs mechanics, and mechanics grow more expensive and less efficient. The gadgets in the home are cheaper to replace than repair. The more efficiently self-contained the home, primary fortress of independence, seems to be, the more dependent it is on the great impersonal corporations, as well as a diminishing army of servitors. Skills at the lowest level have to be wooed slavishly and exorbitantly rewarded. Plumbers will not come. Nor, at the higher level, will doctors. And doctors and dentists, in a nation committed to maiming itself with sugar and cholesterol, know their scarcity value and behave accordingly.

Americans are at last realizing that the acquisition of goods is not the whole of life. Consumption, on one level, is turning insipid, especially as the quality of the artifacts themselves seems to be deteriorating. Planned obsolescence is not conducive to pride in workmanship. On another level, consumption is turning sour. There is a growing guilt about the masses of discarded junk—rusting automobiles and refrigerators and washing machines and dehumidifiers—that it is uneconomical to recycle. Indestructible plastic hasn't even the grace to undergo chemical change. America, the world's biggest consumer, is the world's biggest polluter. Awareness of this is a kind of redemptive grace, but it doesn't appreciably lead to repentance and a revolution in consumer habits. Citizens of Los Angeles are horrified by that daily pall of golden smog, but they don't noticeably clamor for a decrease in the number of owner-vehicles. There is no worse neurosis than that which derives from a consciousness of guilt and an inability to reform.

America is anachronistic in so many ways, and not least in its clinging to a belief—now known to be unviable—in the capacity of the individual citizen to do everything for himself. Americans are admirable in their distrust of the corporate state—they have fought both Fascism and Communism—but they forget that there is a use for everything, even the loathesome bureaucratic machine. America needs a measure of socialization, as Britain needed it. Things—especially those we need most—don't always pay their way, and it is here that the state must enter, dismissing the profit element. Part of the present American neurosis, again, springs from awareness of this but inability to do anything about practical implementation. Perhaps only a country full of bombed cities feels capable of this kind of social revolution.

It would be supererogatory for me to list those areas in which thoughtful Americans feel that collapse is coming. It is enough for me to concentrate on what, during my New Jersey stay, impinged on my own life. Education, for instance, since I have a 6-year-old son to be brought up. America has always despised its teachers and, as a consequence, it has been granted the teachers it deserves. The quality of first-grade education that my son received, in a New Jersey town noted for the excellence of its public schools, could not, I suppose, be faulted on the level of dogged conscientiousness. The principal had read all the right pedagogic books, and was ready to quote these in the footnotes to his circular exhortations to parents. The teachers worked rigidly from the approved rigidly programed primers, ensuring that school textbook publication remains the big business it is.

But there seemed to be no spark; no daring, no madness, no readiness to engage the individual child's mind as anything other than raw material for statistical reductions. The fear of being unorthodox is rooted in the American teacher's soul: you can be fired for treading the path of experimental enterprise. In England, teachers cannot be fired, except for raping girl students and getting boy students drunk. In consequence, there is the kind of security that breeds eccentric genius, the capacity for firing mad enthusiasms.

I know that American technical genius, and most of all the moon landings, seems to give the lie to too summary a condemnation of the educational system, but there is more to education than the segmental equipping of the mind. There is that transmission of the value of the past as a force still miraculously fertile and moving— mostly absent from American education at all levels.

Of course, America was built on a rejection of the past. Even the basic Christianity which was brought to the continent in 1620 was of a novel and bizarre kind that would have nothing to do with the great rank river of belief that produced Dante and Michelangelo. America as a nation has never been able to settle to a common belief more sophisticated than the dangerous naiveté of the Declaration of Independence. "Life, liberty and the pursuit of happiness," indeed. And now America, filling in the vacuum left by the liquefied British Empire, has the task of telling the rest of the world that there's something better than Communism. The something better can only be money-making and consumption for its own sake. In the name of this ghastly creed the jungles must be defoliated.[3]

No wonder the guilt of the thoughtful Americans I met in Princeton and New York and, indeed, all over the Union tended to express itself as an extravagant masochism, a desire for flagellation. Americans want to take on all the blame they can find, gluttons for punishment. "What do Europeans really think of us?" is a common question at parties. The expected answer is: "They think you're a load of decadent, gross-lipped, potbellied, callous, overbearing neoimperialists." Then the head can be bowed and the chest smitten: "*Nostra culpa, nostra maxima culpa.* . . ."[4] But the fact is that such an answer, however much desired, would not be an honest one. Europeans think more highly of Americans now than they ever did. Let me try to explain why.

When Europe, after millennia of war, rapine, slavery, famine, intolerance, had sunk to the level of a sewer, America became the golden dream, the Eden where innocence could be recovered. Original sin was the monopoly of that dirty continent over there; in America man could glow in an aura of natural goodness, driven along his shining path by divine reason. The Declaration of Inde-

---

3. That is, in order to deny the enemy protective cover—a part of American strategy during the Vietnam war.
4. "Through our fault, through our most grievous fault," a modification of *Mea culpa, mea maxima culpa* ("Through my fault . . ."), part of the act of confession in the Roman Catholic church.

pendence itself is a monument to reason. Progress was possible, and the wrongs committed against the Indians, the wildlife, the land itself, could be explained away in terms of the rational control of environment necessary for the building of a New Jerusalem.[5] Right and wrong made up the moral dichotomy; evil—that great eternal inextirpable entity—had no place in America.

At last, with the Vietnam war and especially the Mylai horror,[6] Americans are beginning to realize that they are subject to original sin as much as Europeans are. Some things—the massive crime figures, for instance—can now be explained only in terms of absolute evil. Europe, which has long known about evil and learned to live with it (*live* is *evil* spelled backwards), is now grimly pleased to find that America is becoming like Europe. America is no longer Europe's daughter nor her rich stepmother: she is Europe's sister. The agony that America is undergoing is not to be associated with breakdown so much as with the parturition of self-knowledge.

It has been assumed by many that the youth of America has been in the vanguard of the discovery of both the disease and the cure. The various copping-out movements, however, from the Beats on, have committed the gross error of assuming that original sin rested with their elders, their rulers, and that they themselves could manifest their essential innocence by building little neo-Edens. The drug culture could confirm that the paradisal vision was available to all who sought it. But instant ecstasy has to be purchased, like any other commodity, and, in economic terms, that passive life of pure being involves parasitism. Practically all of the crime I encountered in New York—directly or through report—was a preying of the opium-eaters on the working community. There has to be a snake in paradise. You can't escape the heritage of human evil by building communes, usually on an agronomic ignorance that, intended to be a rejection of inherited knowledge, that suspect property of the elders, does violence to life. The American young are well-meaning but misguided, and must not themselves be taken as guides.

The guides, as always, lie among the writers and artists. And Americans ought to note that, however things may seem to be falling apart, arts and the humane scholarship are flourishing here, as they are not, for instance, in England. I'm not suggesting that Bellow, Mailer, Roth and the rest have the task of finding a solution to the American mess, but they can at least clarify its nature and show how it relates to the human condition in general. Literature, that most directly human of the arts, often reacts magnificently to an ambience of unease or apparent breakdown. The Eliza-

---

5. The holy city described by John in Revelation xxi, here a figurative expression for a perfected society.

6. A massacre by American troops of over a hundred Vietnamese civilians in the village of Mylai.

bethans,[7] to whose era we look back as to an irrecoverable Golden Age, were far more conscious than modern Americans of the chaos and corruption and incompetence of the state. Shakespeare's period was one of poverty, unemployment, ghastly inflation, violence in the streets. Twenty-six years after his death there was a bloody civil war, followed by a dictatorship of religious fanatics, followed by a calm respite in which the seeds of a revolution were sown. England survived. America will survive.

I'm not suggesting that Americans sit back and wait for a transient period of mistrust and despair to resolve itself, like a disease, through the unconscious healing forces which lie deep in organic nature. Man, as Thornton Wilder showed in *The Skin of Our Teeth*,[8] always comes through—though sometimes only just. Americans living here and now have a right to an improvement in the quality of their lives, and they themselves, not the remote governors, must do something about it. It is not right that men and women should fear to go on the streets at night, and that they should sometimes fear the police as much as the criminals, both of whom sometimes look like mirror images of each other. I have had too much evidence, in my year in New Jersey, of the police behaving like the "Fascist pigs" of the revolutionary press. There are too many guns about, and the disarming of the police should be a natural aspect of the disarming of the entire citizenry.

American politics, at both the state and the Federal levels, is too much concerned with the protection of large fortunes, America being the only example in history of a genuine timocracy. The wealth qualification for the aspiring politician is taken for granted; a governmental system dedicated to the promotion of personal wealth in a few selected areas will never act for the public good. The time has come, nevertheless, for citizens to demand, from their government, a measure of socialization—the provision of amenities for the many, of which adequate state pensions and sickness benefits, as well as nationalized transport, should be priorities.

As for those remoter solutions to the American nightmare—only an aspect, after all, of the human nightmare—an Englishman must be diffident about suggesting that America made her biggest mistake in becoming America—meaning a revolutionary republic based on a romantic view of human nature. To reject a limited monarchy in favor of an absolute one (which is, after all, what the American Presidency is) argues a trust in the disinterestedness of an elected

7. The British during the reign of Elizabeth I, 1558–1603.
8. American play depicting man's tragicomic struggle for survival from prehistoric times to the present.

ruler which is, of course, no more than a reflection of belief in the innate goodness of man—so long as he happens to be American man. The American Constitution is out of date. Republics tend to corruption. Canada and Australia have their own problems, but they are happier countries than America.

This *Angst*[9] about America coming apart at the seams, which apparently is shared by nearly 50 per cent of the entire American population, is something to rejoice about. A sense of sin is always admirable, though it must not be allowed to become neurotic. If electric systems break down and gadgets disintegrate, it doesn't matter much. There is always wine to be drunk by candlelight, uniced. If America's position as a world power collapses, and the Union dissolves into independent states, there is still the life of the family or the individual to be lived. England has survived her own dissolution as an imperial power, and Englishmen seem to be happy enough. But I ask the reader to note that I, an Englishman, no longer live in England, and I can't spend more than six months at a stretch in Italy—or any other European country, for that matter. I home to America as to a country more stimulating than depressing. The future of mankind is being worked out there on a scale typically American—vast, dramatic, almost apocalyptical. I brave the brutality and the guilt in order to be in on the scene. I shall be back.

1971

9. Anxiety.

QUESTIONS

1. What would Burgess say of the Whole Earth Catalogue: is it a rejection of consumerism or a surrender to it?
2. Burgess' observation about the Italian word for spoiled implies a concern for etymology and precision of language. Is there evidence of that concern in his choice of English words?

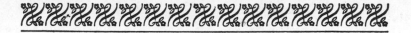

People, Places

THOMAS JEFFERSON
George Washington[1]

I think I knew General Washington intimately and thoroughly; and were I called on to delineate his character, it should be in terms like these.

His mind was great and powerful, without being of the very first order; his penetration strong, though not so acute as that of a Newton, Bacon, or Locke; and as far as he saw, no judgment was ever sounder. It was slow in operation, being little aided by invention or imagination, but sure in conclusion. Hence the common remark of his officers, of the advantage he derived from councils of war, where hearing all suggestions, he selected whatever was best; and certainly no general ever planned his battles more judiciously. But if deranged during the course of the action, if any member of his plan was dislocated by sudden circumstances, he was slow in re-adjustment. The consequence was, that he often failed in the field, and rarely against an enemy in station, as at Boston and York. He was incapable of fear, meeting personal dangers with the calmest unconcern. Perhaps the strongest feature in his character was prudence, never acting until every circumstance, every consideration, was maturely weighed; refraining if he saw a doubt, but, when once decided, going through with his purpose, whatever obstacles opposed. His integrity was most pure, his justice the most inflexible I have ever known, no motives of interest or consanguinity, of friendship or hatred, being able to bias his decision. He was, indeed, in every sense of the words, a wise, a good, and a great man. His temper was naturally irritable and high toned; but reflection and resolution had obtained a firm and habitual ascendency over it. If

---

1. From a letter written in 1814 to a Doctor Jones, who was writing a history and wanted to know about Washington's role in the Federalist-Republican controversy.

ever, however, it broke its bonds, he was most tremendous in his wrath. In his expenses he was honorable, but exact; liberal in contributions to whatever promised utility; but frowning and unyielding on all visionary projects, and all unworthy calls on his charity. His heart was not warm in its affections; but he exactly calculated every man's value, and gave him a solid esteem proportioned to it. His person, you know, was fine, his stature exactly what one would wish, his deportment easy, erect and noble; the best horseman of his age, and the most graceful figure that could be seen on horseback. Although in the circle of his friends, where he might be unreserved with safety, he took a free share in conversation, his colloquial talents were not above mediocrity, possessing neither copiousness of ideas, nor fluency of words. In public, when called on for a sudden opinion, he was unready, short and embarrassed. Yet he wrote readily, rather diffusely, in an easy and correct style. This he had acquired by conversation with the world, for his education was merely reading, writing and common arithmetic, to which he added surveying at a later day. His time was employed in action chiefly, reading little, and that only in agriculture and English history. His correspondence became necessarily extensive, and, with journalizing his agricultural proceedings, occupied most of his leisure hours within doors. On the whole, his character was, in its mass, perfect, in nothing bad, in few points indifferent; and it may truly be said, that never did nature and fortune combine more perfectly to make a man great, and to place him in the same constellation with whatever worthies have meritied from man an everlasting remembrance. For his was the singular destiny and merit, of leading the armies of his country successfully through an arduous war, for the establishment of its independence; of conducting its councils through the birth of a government, new in its forms and principles, until it had settled down into a quiet and orderly train; and of scrupulously obeying the laws through the whole of his career, civil and military, of which the history of the world furnishes no other example.

* * * I am satisfied the great body of republicans think of him as I do. We were, indeed, dissatisfied with him on his ratification of the British treaty. But this was short lived. We knew his honesty, the wiles with which he was encompassed, and that age had already begun to relax the firmness of his purposes; and I am convinced he is more deeply seated in the love and gratitude of the republicans, than in the Pharisaical homage of the federal monarchists.[2] For he was no monarchist from preference of his judgment. The soundness of that gave him correct views of the rights of man, and his severe justice

---

2. Jefferson here compares those who sought to make the new United States a kingdom, with Washington as king, to the biblical Pharisees, the haughty sect of ancient Israel.

devoted him to them. He has often declared to me that he considered our new Constitution as an experiment on the practicability of republican government, and with what dose of liberty man could be trusted for his own good; that he was determined the experiment should have a fair trial, and would lose the last drop of his blood in support of it. And these declarations he repeated to me the oftener and more pointedly, because he knew my suspicions of Colonel Hamilton's views,[3] and probably had heard from him the same declarations which I had, to wit, "that the British constitution, with its unequal representation, corruption and other existing abuses, was the most perfect government which had ever been established on earth, and that a reformation of those abuses would make it an impracticable government." I do believe that General Washington had not a firm confidence in the durability of our government. He was naturally distrustful of men, and inclined to gloomy apprehensions; and I was ever persuaded that a belief that we must at length end in something like a British constitution, had some weight in his adoption of the ceremonies of levees,[4] birthdays, pompous meetings with Congress, and other forms of the same character, calculated to prepare us gradually for a change which he believed possible, and to let it come on with as little shock as might be to the public mind.

These are my opinions of General Washington which I would vouch at the judgment seat of God, having been formed on an acquaintance of thirty years. I served with him in the Virginia legislature from 1769 to the Revolutionary war, and again, a short time in Congress, until he left us to take command of the army. During the war and after it we corresponded occasionally, and in the four years of my continuance in the office of Secretary of State, our intercourse was daily, confidential and cordial. After I retired from that office, great and malignant pains were taken by our federal monarchists, and not entirely without effect, to make him view me as a theorist, holding French principles of government,[5] which would lead infallibly to licentiousness and anarchy. And to this he listened the more easily, from my known disapprobation of the British treaty. I never saw him afterwards, or these malignant insinuations should have been. dissipated before his just judgment, as mists before the sun. I felt on his death, with my countrymen, that "verily a great man hath fallen this day in Israel."

1814

3. Alexander Hamilton (1757–1804) advocated a strong central federal government, led by the "wealthy, good, and wise." His views were opposed by the relatively more democratic views of Jefferson.

4. Morning receptions held by a head of state to enable him to attend to public affairs while rising and dressing. The form was characteristic of European monarchs.

5. Radical political views advanced by extreme democrats in the course of the French Revolution.

NATHANIEL HAWTHORNE
Abraham Lincoln

Of course, there was one other personage, in the class of statesmen, whom I should have been truly mortified to leave Washington without seeing; since (temporarily, at least, and by force of circumstances) he was the man of men. But a private grief had built up a barrier about him, impeding the customary free intercourse of Americans with their chief magistrate; so that I might have come away without a glimpse of his very remarkable physiognomy, save for a semi-official opportunity of which I was glad to take advantage. The fact is, we were invited to annex ourselves, as supernumeraries, to a deputation that was about to wait upon the President, from a Massachusetts whip factory, with a present of a splendid whip.

Our immediate party consisted only of four or five (including Major Ben Perley Poore,[1] with his note-book and pencil), but we were joined by several other persons, who seemed to have been lounging about the precincts of the White House, under the spacious porch, or within the hall, and who swarmed in with us to take the chances of a presentation. Nine o'clock had been appointed as the time for receiving the deputation, and we were punctual to the moment; but not so the President, who sent us word that he was eating his breakfast, and would come as soon as he could. His appetite, we were glad to think, must have been a pretty fair one; for we waited about half an hour in one of the antechambers, and then were ushered into a reception-room, in one corner of which sat the Secretaries of War and of the Treasury, expecting, like ourselves, the termination of the Presidential breakfast. During this interval there were several new additions to our group, one or two of whom were in a working-garb, so that we formed a very miscellaneous collection of people, mostly unknown to each other, and without any common sponsor, but all with an equal right to look our head servant in the face.

By and by there was a little stir on the staircase and in the passage-way, and in lounged a tall, loose-jointed figure, of an exaggerated Yankee port and demeanor, whom (as being about the homeliest man I ever saw, yet by no means repulsive or disagreeable) it was impossible not to recognize as Uncle Abe.

Unquestionably, Western man though he be, and Kentuckian by birth, President Lincoln is the essential representative of all Yankees, and the veritable specimen, physically, of what the world seems determined to regard as our characteristic qualities. It is the

1. American journalist and biographer.

strangest and yet the fittest thing in the jumble of human vicissitudes, that he, out of so many millions, unlooked for, unselected by any intelligible process that could be based upon his genuine qualities, unknown to those who chose him, and unsuspected of what endowments may adapt him for his tremendous responsibility, should have found the way open for him to fling his lank personality into the chair of state—where, I presume, it was his first impulse to throw his legs on the council-table, and tell the Cabinet Ministers a story. There is no describing his lengthy awkwardness, nor the uncouthness of his movement; and yet it seemed as if I had been in the habit of seeing him daily, and had shaken hands with him a thousand times in some village street; so true was he to the aspect of the pattern American, though with a certain extravagance which, possibly, I exaggerated still further by the delighted eagerness with which I took it in. If put to guess his calling and livelihood, I should have taken him for a country school-master as soon as anything else. He was dressed in a rusty black frock coat and pantaloons, unbrushed, and worn so faithfully that the suit had adapted itself to the curves and angularities of his figure, and had grown to be an outer skin of the man. His hair was black, still unmixed with gray, stiff, somewhat bushy, and had apparently been acquainted with neither brush nor comb that morning, after the disarrangement of the pillow; and as to a nightcap, Uncle Abe probably knows nothing of such effeminacies. His complexion is dark and sallow, betokening, I fear, a insalubrious atmosphere around the White House; he has thick black eyebrows and an impending brow; his nose is large, and the lines about his mouth are very strongly defined.

The whole physiognomy is as coarse a one as you would meet anywhere in the length and breadth of the States; but, withal, it is redeemed, illuminated, softened, and brightened by a kindly though serious look out of his eyes, and an expression of homely sagacity, that seems weighted with rich results of village experience. A great deal of native sense; no bookish cultivation, no refinement; honest at heart, and thoroughly so, and yet, in some sort, sly—at least, endowed with a sort of tact and wisdom that are akin to craft, and would impel him, I think, to take an antagonist in flank, rather than to make a bull-run at him right in front. But, on the whole, I like this sallow, queer, sagacious visage, with the homely human sympathies that warmed it; and, for my small share in the matter, would as lief have Uncle Abe for a ruler as any man whom it would have been practicable to put in his place.

Immediately on his entrance the President accosted our member of Congress, who had us in charge, and, with a comical twist of his face, made some jocular remark about the length of his breakfast. He then greeted us all round, not waiting for an introduction, but shaking and squeezing everybody's hand with the utmost cordiality, whether the individual's name was announced to him or not. His manner towards us was wholly without pretence, but yet had a kind of natural dignity, quite sufficient to keep the forwardest of us from clapping him on the shoulder and asking him for a story. A mutual acquaintance being established, our leader took the whip out of its case, and began to read the address of presentation. The whip was an exceedingly long one, its handle wrought in ivory (by some artist in the Massachusetts State Prison, I believe), and ornamented with a medallion of the President, and other equally beautiful devices; and along its whole length there was a succession of golden bands and ferrules. The address was shorter than the whip, but equally well made, consisting chiefly of an explanatory description of these artistic designs, and closing with a hint that the gift was a suggestive and emblematic one, and that the President would recognize the use to which such an instrument should be put.

This suggestion gave Uncle Abe rather a delicate task in his reply, because, slight as the matter seemed, it apparently called for some declaration, or intimation, or faint foreshadowing of policy in reference to the conduct of the war, and the final treatment of the Rebels. But the President's Yankee aptness and not-to-be-caughtness stood him in good stead, and he jerked or wiggled himself out of the dilemma with an uncouth dexterity that was entirely in character; although, without his gesticulation of eye and mouth—and especially the flourish of the whip, with which he imagined himself touching up a pair of fat horses—I doubt whether his words would be worth recording, even if I could remember them. The gist of the reply was, that he accepted the whip as an emblem of peace, not punishment; and, this great 'affair over, we retired out of the presence in high good humor, only regretting that we could not have seen the President sit down and fold up his legs (which is said to be a most extraordinary spectacle), or have heard him tell one of those delectable stories for which he is so celebrated. A good many of them are afloat upon the common talk of Washington, and are certainly the aptest, pithiest, and funniest little things imaginable; though, to be sure, they smack of the frontier freedom, and would not always bear repetition in a drawing-room, or on the immaculate page of the *Atlantic*.[2]

Good Heavens! what liberties have I been taking with one of the potentates of the earth, and the man on whose conduct more impor-

2. This passage was one of those omitted from the article as originally published, and the following note was appended to explain the omission, which had been indicated by a line of points:

"We are compelled to omit two or three pages, in which the author describes the interview, and gives his idea of the personal appearance and deportment of the President. The sketch appears to have been written in a benign spirit, and perhaps conveys a not inaccurate impression of its august subject; but it lacks *reverence*, and it pains us to see a gentleman of ripe age, and who has spent years under the corrective influence of foreign institutions, falling into the characteristic and most ominous fault of Young America."

tant consequences depend than on that of any other historical personage of the century! But with whom is an American citizen entitled to
take a liberty, if not with his own chief magistrate? However, lest the
above allusions to President Lincoln's little peculiarities (already well
known to the country and to the world) should be misinterpreted, I
deem it proper to say a word or two in regard to him, of unfeigned
respect and measurable confidence. He is evidently a man of keen
faculties, and, what is still more to the purpose, of powerful character. As to his integrity, the people have that intuition of it which
is never deceived. Before he actually entered upon his great office,
and for a considerable time afterwards, there is no reason to suppose
that he adequately estimated the gigantic task about to be imposed
on him, or, at least, had any distinct idea how it was to be managed;
and I presume there may have been more than one veteran politician who proposed to himself to take the power out of President
Lincoln's hands into his own, leaving our honest friend only the public responsibility for the good or ill success of the career. The
extremely imperfect development of his statesmanly qualities, at that
period, may have justified such designs. But the President is teach-
able by events, and has now spent a year in a very arduous course of
education; he has a flexible mind, capable of much expansion, and
convertible towards far loftier studies and activities than those of his
early life; and if he came to Washington a backwoods humorist, he
has already transformed himself into as good a statesman (to speak
moderately) as his prime minister.[3]

1862

3. Presumably the Secretary of State, William H. Seward.

QUESTIONS

1. In one sentence summarize Hawthorne's attitude toward Lincoln in the first seven paragraphs.
2. What is the basic pattern of the opening sentence of the fifth
   paragraph? Find other examples of this pattern. What is their
   total impact on Hawthorne's description?
3. In his final paragraph Hawthorne seeks to prevent misunderstanding by stressing his respect for and confidence in Lincoln.
   Is there anything in the paragraph which runs counter to that
   expression? To what effect?
4. In the footnote to the seventh paragraph the editor of The
   Atlantic Monthly explains his omission of the first seven
   paragraphs. On the evidence of this statement what sort of a
   person does the editor seem to be? Is there anything in the omitted paragraphs that would tend to justify his decision? Is the full
   description superior to the last paragraph printed alone? Explain.
5. Describe someone you know with a strong personality that has
   contrasting characteristics.

N. SCOTT MOMADAY

The Way to Rainy Mountain

A single knoll rises out of the plain in Oklahoma, north and west of the Wichita Range. For my people, the Kiowas, it is an old landmark, and they gave it the name Rainy Mountain. The hardest weather in the world is there. Winter brings blizzards, hot tornadic winds arise in the spring, and in summer the prairie is an anvil's edge. The grass turns brittle and brown, and it cracks beneath your feet. There are green belts along the rivers and creeks, linear groves of hickory and pecan, willow and witch hazel. At a distance in July or August the steaming foliage seems almost to writhe in fire. Great green and yellow grasshoppers are everywhere in the tall grass, popping up like corn to sting the flesh, and tortoises crawl about on the red earth, going nowhere in the plenty of time. Loneliness is an aspect of the land. All things in the plain are isolate; there is no confusion of objects in the eye, but *one* hill or *one* tree or *one* man. To look upon that landscape in the early morning, with the sun at your back, is to lose the sense of proportion. Your imagination comes to life, and this, you think, is where Creation was begun.

I returned to Rainy Mountain in July. My grandmother had died in the spring, and I wanted to be at her grave. She had lived to be very old and at last infirm. Her only living daughter was with her when she died, and I was told that in death her face was that of a child.

I like to think of her as a child. When she was born, the Kiowas were living the last great moment of their history. For more than a hundred years they had controlled the open range from the Smoky Hill River to the Red, from the headwaters of the Canadian to the fork of the Arkansas and Cimarron. In alliance with the Comanches, they had ruled the whole of the southern Plains. War was their sacred business, and they were among the finest horsemen the world has ever known. But warfare for the Kiowas was preeminently a matter of disposition rather than of survival, and they never understood the grim, unrelenting advance of the U.S. Cavalry. When at last, divided and ill-provisioned, they were driven onto the Staked Plains in the cold rains of autumn, they fell into panic. In Palo Duro Canyon they abandoned their crucial stores to pillage and had nothing then but their lives. In order to save themselves, they surrendered to the soldiers at Fort Sill and were imprisoned in the old stone corral that now stands as a military museum. My grandmother was spared the humiliation of those high gray walls by eight or ten years, but she must have known from birth the affliction of defeat, the dark brooding of old warriors.

Her name was Aho, and she belonged to the last culture to evolve in North America. Her forebears came down from the high country in western Montana nearly three centuries ago. They were a mountain people, a mysterious tribe of hunters whose language has never been positively classified in any major group. In the late seventeenth century they began a long migration to the south and east. It was a journey toward the dawn, and it led to a golden age. Along the way the Kiowas were befriended by the Crows, who gave them the culture and religion of the Plains. They acquired horses, and their ancient nomadic spirit was suddenly free of the ground. They acquired Tai-me, the sacred Sun Dance doll, from that moment the object and symbol of their worship, and so shared in the divinity of the sun. Not least, they acquired the sense of destiny, therefore courage and pride. When they entered upon the southern Plains they had been transformed. No longer were they slaves to the simple necessity of survival; they were a lordly and dangerous society of fighters and thieves, hunters and priests of the sun. According to their origin myth, they entered the world through a hollow log. From one point of view, their migration was the fruit of an old prophecy, for indeed they emerged from a sunless world.

Although my grandmother lived out her long life in the shadow of Rainy Mountain, the immense landscape of the continental interior lay like memory in her blood. She could tell of the Crows, whom she had never seen, and of the Black Hills, where she had never been. I wanted to see in reality what she had seen more perfectly in the mind's eye, and traveled fifteen hundred miles to begin my pilgrimage.

Yellowstone, it seemed to me, was the top of the world, a region of deep lakes and dark timber, canyons and waterfalls. But, beautiful as it is, one might have the sense of confinement there. The skyline in all directions is close at hand, the high wall of the woods and deep cleavages of shade. There is a perfect freedom in the mountains, but it belongs to the eagle and the elk, the badger and the bear. The Kiowas reckoned their stature by the distance they could see, and they were bent and blind in the wilderness.

Descending eastward, the highland meadows are a stairway to the plain. In July the inland slope of the Rockies is luxuriant with flax and buckwheat, stonecrop and larkspur. The earth unfolds and the limit of the land recedes. Clusters of trees, and animals grazing far in the distance, cause the vision to reach away and wonder to build upon the mind. The sun follows a longer course in the day, and the sky is immense beyond all comparison. The great billowing clouds that sail upon it are the shadows that move upon the grain like water, dividing light. Farther down, in the land of the Crows and Blackfeet, the plain is yellow. Sweet clover takes hold of the hills and bends upon itself to cover and seal the soil. There the Kiowas paused on their way; they had come to the place where they must change their lives. The sun is at home on the plains. Precisely there does it have the certain character of a god. When the Kiowas came to the land of the Crows, they could see the dark lees of the hills at dawn across the Bighorn River, the profusion of light on the grain shelves, the oldest deity ranging after the solstices. Not yet would they veer southward to the caldron of the land that lay below; they must wean their blood from the northern winter and hold the mountains a while longer in their view. They bore Tai-me in procession to the east.

A dark mist lay over the Black Hills, and the land was like iron. At the top of a ridge I caught sight of Devil's Tower upthrust against the gray sky as if in the birth of time the core of the earth had broken through its crust and the motion of the world was begun. There are things in nature that engender an awful quiet in the heart of man; Devil's Tower is one of them. Two centuries ago, because they could not do otherwise, the Kiowas made a legend at the base of the rock. My grandmother said:

Eight children were there at play, seven sisters and their brother. Suddenly the boy was struck dumb; he trembled and began to run upon his hands and feet. His fingers became claws, and his body was covered with fur. Directly there was a bear where the boy had been. The sisters were terrified; they ran, and the bear after them. They came to the stump of a great tree, and the tree spoke to them. It bade them climb upon it, and as they did so it began to rise into the air. The bear came to kill them, but they were just beyond its reach. It reared against the tree and scored the bark all around with its claws. The seven sisters were borne into the sky, and they became the stars of the Big Dipper.

From that moment, and so long as the legend lives, the Kiowas have kinsmen in the night sky. Whatever they were in the mountains, they could be no more. However tenuous their well-being, however much they had suffered and would suffer again, they had found a way out of the wilderness.

My grandmother had a reverence for the sun, a holy regard that now is all but gone out of mankind. There was a wariness in her, and an ancient awe. She was a Christian in her later years, but she had come a long way about, and she never forgot her birthright. As a child she had been to the Sun Dances; she had taken part in those annual rites, and by them she had learned the restoration of her people in the presence of Tai-me. She was about seven when the last Kiowa Sun Dance was held in 1887 on the Washita River above Rainy Mountain Creek. The buffalo were gone. In order to consummate the ancient sacrifice—to impale the head of a buffalo bull upon the medicine tree—a delegation of old men journeyed into Texas, there to beg and barter for an animal from the Goodnight herd. She was ten when the Kiowas came together for the last time as a living Sun Dance culture. They could find no buffalo; they had to hang an old hide from the sacred tree. Before the dance could begin, a company of soldiers rode out from Fort Sill under orders to disperse the tribe. Forbidden without cause the essential act of their faith, having seen the wild herds slaughtered and left to rot upon the ground, the Kiowas backed away forever from the medicine tree. That was July 20, 1890, at the great bend of the Washita. My grandmother was there. Without bitterness, and for as long as she lived, she bore a vision of deicide.

Now that I can have her only in memory, I see my grandmother in the several postures that were peculiar to her: standing at the wood stove on a winter morning and turning meat in a great iron skillet; sitting at the south window, bent above her beadwork, and afterwards, when her vision failed, looking down for a long time into the fold of her hands; going out upon a cane, very slowly as she did when the weight of age came upon her; praying. I remember her most often at prayer. She made long, rambling prayers out of suffering and hope, having seen many things. I was never sure that I had the right to hear, so exclusive where they of all mere custom and company. The last time I saw her she prayed standing by the side of her bed at night, naked to the waist, the light of a kerosene lamp moving upon her dark skin. Her long, black hair, always drawn and braided in the day, lay upon her shoulders and against her breasts like a shawl. I do not speak Kiowa, and I never understood her prayers, but there was something inherently sad in the sound, some merest hesitation upon the syllables of sorrow. She began in a high and descending pitch, exhausting her breath to silence; then again and again—and always the same intensity of effort, of something that is, and is not, like urgency in the human voice. Transported so in the dancing light among the shadows of her room, she seemed beyond the reach of time. But that was illusion; I think I knew then that I should not see her again.

Houses are like sentinels in the plain, old keepers of the weather watch. There, in a very little while, wood takes on the appearance of great age. All colors wear soon away in the wind and rain, and then the wood is burned gray and the grain appears and the nails turn red with rust. The windowpanes are black and opaque; you imagine there is nothing within, and indeed there are many ghosts, bones given up to the land. They stand here and there against the sky, and you approach them for a longer time than you expect. They belong in the distance; it is their domain.

Once there was a lot of sound in my grandmother's house, a lot of coming and going, feasting and talk. The summers there were full of excitement and reunion. The Kiowas are a summer people; they abide the cold and keep to themselves, but when the season turns and the land becomes warm and vital they cannot hold still; an old love of going returns upon them. The aged visitors who came to my grandmother's house when I was a child were made of lean and leather, and they bore themselves upright. They wore great black hats and bright ample shirts that shook in the wind. They rubbed fat upon their hair and wound their braids with strips of colored cloth. Some of them painted their faces and carried the scars of old and cherished enmities. They were an old council of warlords, come to remind and be reminded of who they were. Their wives and daughters served them well. The women might indulge themselves; gossip was at once the mark and compensation of their servitude. They made loud and elaborate talk among themselves, full of jest and gesture, fright and false alarm. They went abroad in fringed and flowered shawls, bright beadwork and German silver. They were at home in the kitchen, and they prepared meals that were banquets.

There were frequent prayer meetings, and great nocturnal feasts. When I was a child I played with my cousins outside, where the lamplight fell upon the ground and the singing of the old people rose up around us and carried away into the darkness. There were a lot of good things to eat, a lot of laughter and surprise. And afterwards, when the quiet returned, I lay down with my grandmother and could hear the frogs away by the river and feel the motion of the air.

Now there is a funeral silence in the rooms, the endless wake of some final word. The walls have closed in upon my grandmother's house. When I returned to it in mourning, I saw for the first time in my life how small it was. It was late at night, and there was a white moon, nearly full. I sat for a long time on the stone steps by the kitchen door. From there I could see out across the land; I could see the long row of trees by the creek, the low light upon the rolling plains, and the stars of the Big Dipper. Once I looked at the moon and caught sight of a strange thing. A cricket had perched upon the handrail, only a few inches away from me. My line of vision was such that the creature filled the moon like a fossil. It had gone there, I thought, to live and die, for there, of all places, was its small definition made whole and eternal. A warm wind rose up and purled like the longing within me.

The next morning I awoke at dawn and went out on the dirt road to Rainy Mountain. It was already hot, and the grasshoppers began to fill the air. Still, it was early in the morning, and the birds sang out of the shadows. The long yellow grass on the mountain shone in the bright light, and a scissortail hied above the land. There, where it ought to be, at the end of a long and legendary way, was my grandmother's grave. Here and there on the dark stones were ancestral names. Looking back once, I saw the mountain and came away.

1969

VIRGINIA WOOLF

My Father: Leslie Stephen

By the time that his children were growing up, the great days of my father's life were over. His feats on the river and on the mountains had been won before they were born. Relics of them were to be found lying about the house—the silver cup on the study mantelpiece; the rusty alpenstocks that leaned against the bookcase in the corner; and to the end of his days he would speak of great climbers and explorers with a peculiar mixture of admiration and envy. But his own years of activity were over, and my father had to content himself with pottering about the Swiss valleys or taking a stroll across the Cornish moors.

That to potter and to stroll meant more on his lips than on other people's is becoming obvious now that some of his friends have given their own version of those expeditions. He would start off after breakfast alone, or with one companion. Shortly after dinner he would return. If the walk had been successful, he would have out his great map and commemorate a new short cut in red ink. And he was quite capable, it appears, of striding all day across the moors without speaking more than a word or two to his companion. By that time, too, he had written the *History of English Thought in the Eighteenth Century*, which is said by some to be his masterpiece; and the *Science of Ethics*—the book which interested him most; and *The Playground of Europe*, in which is to be found "The Sunset on Mont Blanc"—in his opinion the best thing he ever wrote. He still wrote daily and methodically, though never for long at a time.

In London he wrote in the large room with three long windows at the top of the house. He wrote lying almost recumbent in a low rocking chair which he tipped to and fro as he wrote, like a cradle, and as he wrote he smoked a short clay pipe, and he scattered books round him in a circle. The thud of a book dropped on the floor could be heard in the room beneath. And often as he mounted the stairs to his study with his firm, regular tread he would burst, not into song, for he was entirely unmusical, but into a strange rhythmical chant, for verse of all kinds, both "utter trash," as he called it, and the most sublime words of Milton and Wordsworth, stuck in his memory, and the act of walking or climbing seemed to inspire him to recite whichever it was that came uppermost or suited his mood.

But it was his dexterity with his fingers that delighted his children before they could potter along the lanes at his heels or read his books. He would twist a sheet of paper beneath a pair of scissors and out would drop an elephant, a stag, or a monkey, with trunks, horns, and tails delicately and exactly formed. Or, taking a pencil, he would draw beast after beast—an art that he practiced almost unconsciously as he read, so that the flyleaves of his books swarm with owls and donkeys as if to illustrate the "Oh, you ass!" or "Conceited dunce" that he was wont to scribble impatiently in the margin. Such brief comments, in which one may find the germ of the more temperate statements of his essays, recall some of the characteristics of his talk. He could be very silent, as his friends have testified. But his remarks, made suddenly in a low voice between the puffs of his pipe, were extremely effective. Sometimes with one word—but his one word was accompanied by a gesture of the hand—he would dispose of the tissue of exaggerations which his own sobriety seemed to provoke. "There are 40,000,000 unmarried women in London alone!" Lady Ritchie once informed him. "Oh, Annie, Annie!" my father exclaimed in tones of horrified but affectionate rebuke. But Lady Ritchie, as if she enjoyed being rebuked, would pile it up even higher next time she came.

The stories he told to amuse his children of adventures in the Alps—but accidents only happened, he would explain, if you were so foolish as to disobey your guides—or of those long walks, after one of which, from Cambridge to London on a hot day, "I drank, I am sorry to say, rather more than was good for me," were told very briefly, but with a curious power to impress the scene. The things that he did not say were always there in the background. So, too, though he seldom told anecdotes, and his memory for facts was bad, when he described a person—and he had known many people, both famous and obscure—he would convey exactly what he thought of him in two or three words. And what he thought might be the opposite of what other people thought. He had a way of upsetting established reputations and disregarding conventional values that could be disconcerting, and sometimes perhaps wounding, though no one was more respectful of any feeling that seemed to him genuine. But when, suddenly opening his bright blue eyes and rousing himself from what had seemed complete abstraction, he gave his opinion, it was difficult to disregard it. It was a habit, especially when deafness made him unaware that this opinion could be heard, that had its inconveniences.

"I am the most easily bored of men," he wrote, truthfully as usual; and when, as was inevitable in a large family, some visitor threatened to stay not merely for tea but also for dinner, my father would express his anguish at first by twisting and untwisting a certain lock of hair. Then he would burst out, half to himself, half to the powers above, but quite audibly, "Why can't he go? Why can't he go?" Yet such is the charm of simplicity—and did he not say, also truthfully, that "bores are the salt of the earth"?—that the bores seldom went, or, if they did, forgave him and came again.

Too much, perhaps, has been said of his silence; too much stress has been laid upon his reserve. He loved clear thinking; he hated sentimentality and gush; but this by no means meant that he was cold and unemotional, perpetually critical and condemnatory in daily life. On the contrary, it was his power of feeling strongly and of expressing his feeling with vigor that made him sometimes so alarming as a companion. A lady, for instance, complained of the wet summer that was spoiling her tour in Cornwall. But to my father, though he never called himself a democrat, the rain meant that the corn was being laid; some poor man was being ruined; and the energy with which he expressed his sympathy—not with the lady—left her discomfited. He had something of the same respect for farmers and fishermen that he had for climbers and explorers. So, too, he talked little of patriotism, but during the South African War—and all wars were hateful to him—he lay awake thinking that he heard the guns on the battlefield. Again, neither his reason nor his cold common sense helped to convince him that a child could be late for dinner without having been maimed or killed in an accident. And not all his mathematics together with a bank balance which he insisted must be ample in the extreme could persuade him, when it came to signing a check, that the whole family was not "shooting Niagara to ruin,"[1] as he put it. The pictures that he would draw of old age and the bankruptcy court, of ruined men of letters who have to support large families in small houses at Wimbledon (he owned a very small house at Wimbledon), might have convinced those who complain of his understatements that hyperbole was well within his reach had he chosen.

Yet the unreasonable mood was superficial, as the rapidity with which it vanished would prove. The checkbook was shut; Wimbledon and the workhouse were forgotten. Some thought of a humor-

---

1. The reference is to going over Niagara Falls in a boat.

ous kind made him chuckle. Taking his hat and his stick, calling for his dog and his daughter, he would stride off into Kensington Gardens, where he had walked as a little boy, where his brother Fitzjames and he had made beautiful bows to young Queen Victoria and she had swept them a curtsy; and so, round the Serpentine, to Hyde Park Corner, where he had once saluted the great Duke himself; and so home. He was not then in the least "alarming"; he was very simple, very confiding; and his silence, though one might last unbroken from the Round Pond to the Marble Arch, was curiously full of meaning, as if he were thinking half aloud, about poetry and philosophy and people he had known.

He himself was the most abstemious of men. He smoked a pipe perpetually, but never a cigar. He wore his clothes until they were too shabby to be tolerable; and he held old-fashioned and rather puritanical views as to the vice of luxury and the sin of idleness. The relations between parents and children today have a freedom that would have been impossible with my father. He expected a certain standard of behavior, even of ceremony, in family life. Yet if freedom means the right to think one's own thoughts and to follow one's own pursuits, then no one respected and indeed insisted upon freedom more completely than he did. His sons, with the exception of the Army and Navy, should follow whatever professions they chose; his daughters, though he cared little enough for the higher education of women, should have the same liberty. If at one moment he rebuked a daughter sharply for smoking a cigarette— smoking was not in his opinion a nice habit in the other sex—she had only to ask him if she might become a painter, and he assured her that so long as she took her work seriously he would give her all the help he could. He had no special love for painting; but he kept his word. Freedom of that sort was worth thousands of cigarettes.

It was the same with the perhaps more difficult problem of literature. Even today there may be parents who would doubt the wisdom of allowing a girl of fifteen the free run of a large and quite unexpurgated library. But my father allowed it. There were certain facts—very briefly, very shyly he referred to them. Yet "Read what you like," he said, and all his books, "mangy and worthless," as he called them, but certainly they were many and various, were to be had without asking. To read what one liked because one liked it, never to pretend to admire what one did not—that was his only lesson in the art of reading. To write in the fewest possible words, as clearly as possible, exactly what one meant—that was his only lesson in the art of writing. All the rest must be learned for oneself. Yet a child must have been childish in the extreme not to feel that such was the teaching of a man of great learning and wide experience, though he would never impose his own views or parade his own knowledge. For, as his tailor remarked when he saw my father walk past his shop up Bond Street, "There goes a gentleman that wears good clothes without knowing it."

In those last years, grown solitary and very deaf, he would sometimes call himself a failure as a writer; he had been "jack of all trades, and master of none." But whether he failed or succeeded as a writer, it is permissible to believe that he left a distinct impression of himself on the minds of his friends. Meredith[2] saw him as "Phoebus Apollo turned fasting friar" in his earlier days; Thomas Hardy, years later, looked at the "spare and desolate figure" of the Schreckhorn[3] and thought of

> him,
> Who scaled its horn with ventured life and limb,
> Drawn on by vague imaginings, maybe,
> Of semblance to his personality
> In its quaint glooms, keen lights, and rugged trim.

But the praise he would have valued most, for though he was an agnostic nobody believed more profoundly in the worth of human relationships, was Meredith's tribute after his death: "He was the one man to my knowledge worthy to have married your mother." And Lowell,[4] when he called him "L.S., the most lovable of men," has best described the quality that makes him, after all these years, unforgettable.

1950[5]

2. George Meredith (1882–1909), English novelist and poet.
3. One of the peaks in the Swiss Alps.
4. James Russell Lowell, nineteenth-century American poet, essayist, and editor.
5. Published posthumously.

QUESTIONS

1. What are the basic qualities Woolf admires, as revealed in this selection?
2. Giving praise can be a difficult rhetorical and social undertaking. How does Woolf avoid the pitfalls, or try to? Compare Doris Lessing, in "My Father" (pp. 344–351). Does she take similar risks? Or compare Nathaniel Hawthorne, in "Abraham Lincoln" (pp. 330–333).
3. What are the main currents of the Stephens' family life as revealed here? Any such description must be selective; what does Woolf leave out? Do the omissions detract from her essay? If you think so, say why.
4. In some of her other work Woolf shows a deep and sensitive concern for women's experience and awareness. Do you find a feminist awareness here? In what way?

DORIS LESSING

My Father

We use our parents like recurring dreams, to be entered into when needed; they are always there for love or for hate; but it occurs to me that I was not always there for my father. I've written about him before, but novels, stories, don't have to be "true." Writing this article is difficult because it has to be "true." I knew him when his best years were over.

There are photographs of him. The largest is of an officer in the 1914–18 war. A new uniform—buttoned, badged, strapped, tabbed —confines a handsome, dark young man who holds himself stiffly to confront what he certainly thought of as his duty. His eyes are steady, serious, and responsible, and show no signs of what he became later. A photograph at sixteen is of a dark, introspective youth with the same intent eyes. But it is his mouth you notice—a heavily-jutting upper lip contradicts the rest of a regular face. His moustache was to hide it: "Had to do something—a damned fleshy mouth. Always made me uncomfortable, that mouth of mine."

Earlier a baby (eyes already alert) appears in a lace waterfall that cascades from the pillowy bosom of a fat, plain woman to her feet. It is the face of a head cook. "Lord, but my mother was a practical female—almost as bad as you!" as he used to say, or throw at my mother in moments of exasperation. Beside her stands, or droops, arms dangling, his father, the source of the dark, arresting eyes, but otherwise masked by a long beard.

The birth certificate says: Born 3rd August, 1886, Walton Villa, Creffield Road, S. Mary at the Wall, R.S.D. Name, Alfred Cook. Name and surname of Father: Alfred Cook Tayler. Name and maiden name of Mother: Caroline May Batley. Rank or Profession: Bank Clerk. Colchester, Essex.

They were very poor. Clothes and boots were a problem. They "made their own amusements." Books were mostly the Bible and *The Pilgrim's Progress.*[1] Every Saturday night they bathed in a hip-bath in front of the kitchen fire. No servants. Church three times on Sundays. "Lord, when I think of those Sundays! I dreaded them all week, like a nightmare coming at you full tilt and no escape." But he rabbited with ferrets along the lanes and fields, bird-nested, stole fruit, picked nuts and mushrooms, paid visits to the black-smith and the mill and rode a farmer's carthorse.

They ate economically, but when he got diabetes in his forties

1. An allegory of Christian's progress toward heaven through a world filled with tempters, by the seventeenth-century writer John Bunyan.

and subsisted on lean meat and lettuce leaves, he remembered suet puddings, treacle puddings, raisin and currant puddings, steak and kidney puddings, bread and butter pudding, "batter cooked in the gravy with the meat," potato cake, plum cake, butter cake, porridge with treacle, fruit tarts and pies, brawn, pig's trotters and pig's cheek and home-smoked ham and sausages. And "lashings of fresh butter and cream and eggs." He wondered if this diet had produced the diabetes, but said it was worth it.

There was an elder brother described by my father as: "Too damned clever by half. One of those quick, clever brains. Now I've always had a slow brain, but I get there in the end, damn it!"

The brothers went to a local school and the elder did well, but my father was beaten for being slow. They both became bank clerks in, I think, the Westminster Bank, and one must have found it congenial, for he became a manager, the "rich brother," who had cars and even a yacht. But my father did not like it, though he was conscientious. For instance, he changed his writing, letter by letter, because a senior criticised it. I never saw his unregenerate hand, but the one he created was elegant, spiky, careful. Did this mean he created a new personality for himself, hiding one he did not like, as he hid his "damned fleshy mouth"? I don't know.

Nor do I know when he left home to live in Luton, or why. He found family life too narrow? A safe guess—he found everything too narrow. His mother was too down-to-earth? He had to get away from his clever elder brother?

Being a young man in Luton was the best part of his life. It ended in 1914, so he had a decade of happiness. His reminiscences of it were all of pleasure, the delight of physical movement, of dancing in particular. All his girls were "a beautiful dancer, light as a feather." He played billiards and ping-pong (both for his country); he swam, boated, played cricket and football,[2] went to picnics and horse races, sang at musical evenings. One family of a mother and two daughters treated him "like a son only better. I didn't know whether I was in love with the mother or the daughters, but oh I did love going there; we had such good times." He was engaged to one daughter, then, for a time, to the other. An engagement was broken off because she was rude to a waiter. "I could not marry a woman who allowed herself to insult someone who was defenceless." He used to say to my wryly smiling mother: "Just as well I didn't marry either of *them*; they would never have stuck it out the way you have, old girl."

Just before he died he told me he had dreamed he was standing in a kitchen on a very high mountain holding X in his arms. "Ah,

2. Soccer.

yes, that's what I've missed in my life. Now don't you let yourself
be cheated out of life by the old dears. They take all the colour out
of everything if you let them."

But in that decade—"I'd walk 10, 15 miles to a dance two or three
times a week and think nothing of it. Then I'd dance every dance
and walk home again over the fields. Sometimes it was moonlight,
but I liked the snow best, all crisp and fresh. I loved walking back
and getting into my digs³ just as the sun was rising. My little dog
was so happy to see me, and I'd feed her, and make myself porridge
and tea, then I'd wash and shave and go off to work."

The boy who was beaten at school, who went too much to
church, who carried the fear of poverty all his life, but who nevertheless was filled with the memories of country pleasures; the young
bank clerk who worked such long hours for so little money, but who
danced, sang, played, flirted—this naturally vigorous, sensuous being
was killed in 1914, 1915, 1916. I think the best of my father died
in that war, that his spirit was crippled by it. The people I've met,
particularly the women, who knew him young, speak of his high
spirits, his energy, his enjoyment of life. Also of his kindness, his
compassion and—a word that keeps recurring—his wisdom. "Even
when he was just a boy he understood things that you'd think even
an old man would find it easy to condemn." I do not think these
people would have easily recognised the ill, irritable, abstracted,
hypochondriac man I knew.

He "joined up" as an ordinary soldier out of a characteristically
quirky scruple: it wasn't right to enjoy officers' privileges when the
Tommies⁴ had such a bad time. But he could not stick the communal
latrines, the obligatory drinking, the collective visits to brothels, the
jokes about girls. So next time he was offered a commission he took it.

His childhood and young man's memories, kept fluid, were added
to, grew, as living memories do. But his war memories were congealed in stories that he told again and again, with the same words
and gestures, in stereotyped phrases. They were anonymous, general,
as if they had come out of a communal war memoir. He met a
German in no-man's-land, but both slowly lowered their rifles and
smiled and walked away. The Tommies were the salt of the earth,
the British fighting men the best in the world. He had never known
such comradeship. A certain brutal officer was shot in a sortie by his
men, but the other officers, recognising rough justice, said nothing.
He had known men intimately who saw the Angels at Mons.⁵ He
wished he could force all the generals on both sides into the
trenches for just one day, to see what the common soldiers endured
—*that* would have ended the war at once.

3. Lodgings.
4. Foot soldiers.
5. An apparition that appeared during
a World War I battle.

There was an undercurrent of memories, dreams, and emotions much deeper, more personal. This dark region in him, fate-ruled, where nothing was true but horror, was expressed inarticulately, in brief, bitter exclamations or phrases of rage, incredulity, betrayal. The men who went to fight in that war believed it when they said it was to end war. My father believed it. And he was never able to reconcile his belief in his country with his anger at the cynicism of its leaders. And the anger, the sense of betrayal, strengthened as he grew old and ill.

But in 1914 he was naïve, the German atrocities in Belgium inflamed him, and he enlisted out of idealism, although he knew he would have a hard time. He knew because a fortuneteller told him. (He could be described as uncritically superstitious or as psychically gifted.) He would be in great danger twice, yet not die—he was being protected by a famous soldier who was his ancestor. "And sure enough, later I heard from the Little Aunties that the church records showed we were descended the backstairs way from the Duke of Wellington, or was it Marlborough? Damn it, I forget. But one of them would be beside me all through the war, she said." (He was romantic, not only about this solicitous ghost, but also about being a descendant of the Huguenots, on the strength of the "e" in Tayler; and about "the wild blood" in his veins from a great uncle who, sent unjustly to prison for smuggling, came out of a ten-year sentence and earned it, very efficiently, along the coasts of Cornwall until he died.)

The luckiest thing that ever happened to my father, he said, was getting his leg shattered by shrapnel ten days before Passchendaele.[6] His whole company was killed. He knew he was going to be wounded because of the fortuneteller, who had said he would know. "I did not understand what she meant, but both times in the trenches, first when my appendix burst and I nearly died, and then just before Passchendaele, I felt for some days as if a thick, black velvet pall was settled over me. I can't tell you what it was like. Oh, it was awful, awful, and the second time it was so bad I wrote to the old people and told them I was going to be killed."

His leg was cut off at mid-thigh, he was shell-shocked, he was very ill for many months, with a prolonged depression afterwards. "You should always remember that sometimes people are all seething underneath. You don't know what terrible things people have to fight against. You should look at a person's eyes, that's how you tell. . . . When I was like that, after I lost my leg, I went to a nice doctor man and said I was going mad, but he said, don't worry, everyone locks up things like that. You don't know—horrible, horri-

---

6. A prolonged and futile battle of World War I, in which British and Com- monwealth forces sustained massive casualties.

ble, awful things. I was afraid of myself, of what I used to dream. I wasn't myself at all."

In the Royal Free Hospital was my mother, Sister McVeagh. He married his nurse which, as they both said often enough (though in different tones of voice), was just as well. That was 1919. He could not face being a bank clerk in England, he said, not after the trenches. Besides, England was too narrow and conventional. Besides, the civilians did not know what the soldiers had suffered, they didn't want to know, and now it wasn't done even to remember "The Great Unmentionable." He went off to the Imperial Bank of Persia, in which country I was born.

The house was beautiful, with great stone-floored high-ceilinged rooms whose windows showed ranges of snow-streaked mountains. The gardens were full of roses, jasmine, pomegranates, walnuts. Kermanshah he spoke of with liking, but soon they went to Teheran, populous with "Embassy people," and my gregarious mother created a lively social life about which he was irritable even in recollection.

Irritableness—that note was first struck here, about Persia. He did not like, he said, "the graft and the corruption." But here it is time to try and describe something difficult—how a man's good qualities can also be his bad ones, or if not bad, a danger to him.

My father was honourable—he always knew exactly what that word meant. He had integrity. His "one does not do that sort of thing," his "no, it is *not* right," sounded throughout my childhood and were final for all of us. I am sure it was true he wanted to leave Persia because of "the corruption." But it was also because he was already unconsciously longing for something freer, because as a bank official he could not let go into the dream-logged personality that was waiting for him. And later in Rhodesia, too, what was best in him was also what prevented him from shaking away the shadows: it was always in the name of honesty or decency that he refused to take this step or that out of the slow decay of the family's fortunes.

In 1925 there was leave from Persia. That year in London there was an Empire Exhibition, and on the Southern Rhodesian stand some very fine maize cobs and a poster saying that fortunes could be made on maize at 25/-[7] a bag. So on an impulse, turning his back forever on England, washing his hands of the corruption of the East, my father collected all his capital, £800, I think, while my mother packed curtains from Liberty's, clothes from Harrods, visiting cards, a piano, Persian rugs, a governess and two small children.

Soon, there was my father in a cigar-shaped house of thatch and

7. Twenty-five shillings. A shilling was then worth about twenty-five cents.

mud on the top of a kopje[8] that overlooked in all directions a great system of mountains, rivers, valleys, while overhead the sky arched from horizon to empty horizon. This was a couple of hundred miles south from the Zambesi, a hundred or so west from Mozambique, in the district of Banket, so called because certain of its reefs were of the same formation as those called *banket* on the Rand. Loma-gundi—gold country, tobacco country, maize country—wild, almost empty. (The Africans had been turned off it into reserves.) Our neighbours were four, five, seven miles off. In front of the house . . . no neighbours, nothing; no farms, just wild bush with two rivers but no fences to the mountains seven miles away. And beyond these mountains and bush again to the Portuguese border,[9] over which "our boys" used to escape when wanted by the police for pass or other offences.

And then? There was bad luck. For instance, the price of maize dropped from 25/- to 9/- a bag. The seasons were bad, prices bad, crops failed. This was the sort of thing that made it impossible for him ever to "get off the farm," which, he agreed with my mother, was what he most wanted to do.

It was an absurd country, he said. A man could "own" a farm for years that was totally mortgaged to the Government and run from the Land Bank, meanwhile employing half-a-hundred Africans at 12/- a month and none of them knew how to do a day's work. Why, two farm labourers from Europe could do in a day what twenty of these ignorant black savages would take a week to do. (Yet he was proud that he had a name as a just employer, that he gave "a square deal.") Things got worse. A fortuneteller had told him that her heart ached when she saw the misery ahead for my father: this was the misery.

But it was my mother who suffered. After a period of neurotic ill-ness, which was a protest against her situation, she became brave and resourceful. But she never saw that her husband was not living in a real world, that he had made a captive of her common sense. We were always about to "get off the farm." A miracle would do it —a sweepstake, a goldmine, a legacy. And then? What a question! We would go to England where life would be normal with people coming in for musical evenings and nice supper parties at the Tro-cadero after a show. Poor woman, for the twenty years we were on the farm, she waited for when life would begin for her and for her children, for she never understood that what was a calamity for her was for them a blessing.

Meanwhile my father sank towards his death (at 61). Everything

---

8. Small hill. The term is South Afri-can Dutch.

9. That is, the border of Mozambique, then a Portuguese possession.

changed in him. He had been a dandy and fastidious, now he hated to change out of shabby khaki. He had been sociable, now he was misanthropic. His body's disorders—soon diabetes and all kinds of stomach ailments—dominated him. He was brave about his wooden leg, and even went down mine shafts and climbed trees with it, but he walked clumsily and it irked him badly. He greyed fast, and slept more in the day, but would be awake half the night pondering about. . . .

It could be gold divining. For ten years he experimented on private theories to do with the attractions and repulsions of metals. His whole soul went into it but his theories were wrong or he was *unlucky*—after all, if he had found a mine he would have had to leave the farm. It could be the relation between the minerals of the earth and of the moon; his decision to make infusions of all the plants on the farm and drink them himself in the interests of science; the criminal folly of the British Government in not realising that the Germans and the Russians were conspiring as Anti-Christ to . . . the inevitability of war because no one would listen to Churchill, but it would be all right because God (by then he was a British Israelite[1]) had destined Britain to rule the world; a prophecy said 10 million dead would surround Jerusalem—how would the corpses be cleared away?; people who wished to abolish flogging should be flogged; the natives understood nothing but a good beating; hanging must not be abolished because the Old Testament said "an eye for an eye and a tooth for a tooth. . . ."

Yet, as this side of him darkened, so that it seemed all his thoughts were of violence, illness, war, still no one dared to make an unkind comment in his presence or to gossip. Criticism of people, particularly of women, made him more and more uncomfortable till at last he burst out with: "It's all very well, but no one has the right to say that about another person."

In Africa, when the sun goes down, the stars spring up, all of them in their expected places, glittering and moving. In the rainy season, the sky flashed and thundered. In the dry season, the great dark hollow of night was lit by veld fires: the mountains burned through September and October in chains of red fire. Every night my father took out his chair to watch the sky and the mountains, smoking, silent, a thin shabby fly-away figure under the stars. "Makes you think—there are so many worlds up there, wouldn't really matter if we did blow ourselves up—plenty more where we came from."

The Second World War, so long foreseen by him, was a bad

1. A reference to the contention that the English-speaking peoples are the descendants of the "ten tribes" of Israel, deported by Sargon of Assyria on the fall of Samaria in 721 B.C.

time. His son was in the Navy and in danger, and his daughter a sorrow to him. He became very ill. More and more often it was necessary to drive him into Salisbury with him in a coma, or in danger of one, on the back seat. My mother moved him into a pretty little suburban house in town near the hospitals, where he took to his bed and a couple of years later died. For the most part he was unconscious under drugs. When awake he talked obsessively (a tongue licking a nagging sore place) about "the old war." Or he remembered his youth. "I've been dreaming—Lord, to see those horses come lickety-split down the course with their necks stretched out and the sun on their coats and everyone shouting. . . . I've been dreaming how I walked along the river in the mist as the sun was rising. . . . Lord, lord, lord, what a time that was, what good times we all had then, before the old war."

1974

QUESTIONS

1. Lessing says that "writing this article is difficult because it has to be 'true'." Why does she put quotation marks around "true"? Why would it be more difficult to write something that has to be "true" than, as she says, stories that "don't have to be 'true'?" How has she tried to make this sketch "true"? How well do you think she has succeeded?
2. Find facts about Lessing's father that are repeated or referred to more than once. Why does she repeat them?
3. Lessing says that it was difficult for her to write about her father because she "knew him when his best years were over." What other things about those "best years" might she have wanted to know that she apparently didn't?
4. If a stranger were writing about Lessing's father but had the same facts available, might the account differ in any ways? Explain.

LINDA LANE[1]

Over the Counter: A Conversation with a Saleswoman

I went as far as the sixth grade in school. I'm 57 now. I was 16 and didn't want to be 16 in the seventh grade so I quit. I was out of school a year and a half with blood poisoning and one teacher I had left me back twice. When I walked into her classroom the first day, she told me to get to the last row last seat and that's the

---

1. A pseudonym for the subject of this interview, a woman who works at a five- and-ten-cent store.

way it was all year. She just didn't like me. I got her as a teacher twice and it was the same thing again.

After getting married and having a baby at sixteen I became a maid because my mother was a maid. Most jobs I got $35 a month plus room and board. $30 went to board my baby. My husband was a seaman and didn't support us. My mother used to make $8 a month when she came to this country so I thought I was doing pretty good. I was proud I could work and felt better off than most people. This was in the Depression. The nicest maid job I had was with a bootlegger. I could eat and talk with the family. We all ate in the kitchen. I had my own room with my baby and $10 a month. The rich people I worked for I couldn't have my baby and most of the time I didn't have my own room. One rich person I was a maid for took money out of my pay for a water glass I broke and a window that was already broken so I quit and she accused me of stealing. Anyway I didn't have anything in common with those people and ate in the kitchen alone so I was very lonely. That's one of the reasons I like my job at the 5 & 10 better than being a maid. Here I talk to people and no one tells me I'm doing something wrong.

My job is marking the prices on the items and I only spend two hours on the counters and no one watches over me. Five kids and another husband later I'm doing well taking home from $65.12 from $82.50 a week gross. I started working for this store around Easter time 16 years ago. I made Easter baskets for $1.00 an hour. Then they offered me a full time job at $48 a week.

Once they didn't pay me for a day I stayed home sick so I walked out. It was the first rebellious thing I ever did and it felt so good—I was never the same again. The reason I had walked out was that the girl on the bird counter was out for eight days and she got paid for all eight days. She had such a bad job that the manager knew he couldn't get anyone else so fast so he paid her. I had to take care of her counter when she was out and it was a terrible job.

Then my boss offered me $60 a week to stay. It was upsetting in a way—I told him that Jean worked there for 25 years and she was getting $48 so why should I get $60? He told me not to fight other people's battles.

All the women get $82.50 now except part-time and floorgirls. When women leave or are fired the boss doesn't replace them—we have eight women less than we had five years ago but we have to get the same work done. The woman on hardware has three counters to take care of now.

The manager has so many gimmicks to get the salesgirls to work harder. Each girl gets a "campaign button" with her name on it and the customers "vote" for the girls. The salesgirl with the most votes gets $10 in merchandise and a customer's name is taken from a jar and she gets $10 in merchandise too. This makes the girls super-polite to customers—they're not usually because it's a hectic job. It also pits the women against each other. They even had this contest on television and they hired a model to be a typical 5&10 salesgirl. We were thinking, "Why not one of us?"

The manager tells the salesgirls they can raise the prices on their counters as much as they think people will pay. The girls like that—they want to feel they have some control over their jobs. I guess it makes them feel important to be on the boss's side. He gets a commission from the profits of the store.

A few years ago I talked to the other women about starting a union, but their lives depend on the job. They wanted to organize but they were afraid of getting fired. Most of them didn't get far in school and they have to work because their husbands don't make enough. A year ago there was talk of a union, so the office raised everyone $.10 an hour. Big deal. I tell the women to threaten to quit cause then the boss gets panicked and gives them a raise, but the women are too scared.

The women chip in for everything. I don't mind chipping in for another girl but the brown-nosers start collecting for the manager every Christmas—they buy him a shirt which he doesn't need and give him the leftover money too. These "choice" women give him the gift on the side and none of the other women see him get the gift. All the gifts are bought in the 5&10 except the manager's. The assistant manager changes every year and the women chip in for his leaving too. I refuse to chip in for them with some other women and the brown-nosers get mad at us. We all get a Christmas bonus—$15 for one-year's service and $5 for each year after that, and they take off taxes too.

I like the high-school girls who work at night. We get along good. Only, once one of them told me to get flowers from the basement to fill up the counter so I said to her, "What? No more Indians, all chiefs?"

The prices go up every day and it's depressing. Now you can buy anything at the 5&10, from refrigerators to pencils, and you can probably get it cheaper someplace else. They have less help than years ago and they blame it on our "wage increases." The manager comments every Christmas that people would buy horseshit if it was on the counter with a price on it. Jean, who is working over thirty years now, got seven shares of the company's stock as a bonus for twenty-five years' service—she got a $2 dividend every three months—it just went up to $2.50. If she wanted 10 shares, she would have had to pay $90 in taxes right away, so she only took seven—she got a bill for taxes anyway. When she got the shares I went out and bought the *Wall Street Journal*—we had a good laugh.

She once tried to get another job. But if you work at a 5&10 other stores don't consider it a good reference because they think the women are dishonest and it's just like having no reference at all. The salesgirls that work here are very honest—I don't believe any of them steal. The other day my boss (the manager) was going up the stairs and one of the salesgirls was in front of him. He told her to get out of the way, she was going too slow for him. She had her hands in her pockets and he asked her why does she always have her hands in her pockets and then mentioned he was "working on getting rid of the pockets." What does he think, she can put one of the store's TVs in her pocket?

The store has a problem of shoplifting. The first shoplifter I saw was a well-dressed woman and she had a prayer book in her hands. I wouldn't steal cause I wouldn't want my kids to. I don't want them to be dishonest. Some people steal in front of their kids and they can afford to pay for it because they are made to pay for it when they are caught. Sometimes the manager and the floorgirl go to hell with it. Once the floorgirl followed a man in his seventies all around the store. He had a rolled-up newspaper under his arm and she accused him of stealing—he shook out the newspaper and showed he had nothing in it. Many times they'll throw kids out of the store—usually black kids. If a black person comes into the store they say, "Watch that one."

If you're working and you're not getting the right pay you want to steal cause you feel you're getting even with the boss. As a maid you steal what you can cause you're not getting paid enough. They give you a feeling you're no good so you steal from them to make them suffer. I did this once but some of my friends did it a lot. Sometimes the people you work for leave a penny or a nickel around to see if you would take it. Everybody that's got money got it some way and they got it by crooking people under them. That's how they got rich.

There's a real Hitler behind the lunch counter. She yells at the girls in front of the customers. She's the boss behind there and sometimes the customers complain about her. I feel sorry for her when I'm not mad at her. I know she has a hard life at home and needs to be "somebody." There aren't enough girls at the fountain so they are all pretty irritable. Right now, on top of all that, there's a gimmick of the boss's that drives the girls crazy. There's a sign on the fountain that says, "If your waitress doesn't ask if you want dessert, you get a free dessert." So people say the waitress didn't ask them when she did. Never eat at any 5&10—they have to use the food up from previous days before they make a new batch. Some of the stuff looks horrible—especially when the jelly apples get a week old, sometimes they get re-dipped.

Each girl that works behind the lunch counter has her own tip box. At the end of the day they have to take it to the office and the office personnel count it and take out the tax money from the tips. It's none of their business how much tips the girls get so they shouldn't take tax money off. Countergirls get less pay than the rest of us, too.

The whole story in a nutshell is we work hard. We keep the store clean and stocked but the company is trying to trick us and cheat us in little ways all the time. It's always the little person that gets hurt. It's about time that something happens so it's the rich people that hurt for a change. I'm not anyone's enemy unless they're an enemy to me and it seems to me people aren't seeing who their real friends are.

Two of my daughters and one son worked at this store. If you ask my nine-year-old granddaughter what she wants to be when she grows up she'll tell you a salesgirl at the 5&10. I think it's the best position she's ever seen a woman in, since her mother's on welfare. She likes the colors of the items and she likes to visit me at work. That would be the third generation to work there—but her grandmother wants her to be President of the U.S.

1971

QUESTIONS

1. This interview has the looseness of conversation. What are the major points that Linda Lane makes? Choose one of these points and determine which parts of the interview help to support it. Then write an essay, using that material to support the point you have selected. Will you want to include any seemingly irrelevant material? Why, or why not?
2. Imagine an interview with you or with a character of your invention on a subject like the choice of a career, the advantages and disadvantages of a certain job, or the like. Write for thirty minutes without letting your pencil rest. Then analyze your "interview" to determine its major points and the major kinds of support for them.
3. Construct a dialogue between Linda Lane and either Herb Goldberg, author of "In Harness: The Male Condition" (pp. 292–298), or Betty Rollin, author of "Motherhood: Who Needs It?" (pp. 301–311).

BENJAMIN STEIN

Whatever Happened to Small-Town America?

Jim Rockford, private detective in NBC-TV's popular *The Rockford Files*, is in trouble. He is driving along in rural northern California on routine detective business, when his car suddenly hits a big bump and is incapacitated. Rockford, who is used to life in Los Angeles, is frantic. There he is, in the middle of nowhere, without any means of getting out: no taxicabs, no rental cars, no buses, no limousine service, nothing.

Then salvation comes, in the form of a towtruck operator who just happens to be passing by. He offers to tow Rockford into the nearest town for repairs. By chance, the town is named "New Pastoria." Rockford grins with delight; he is back in the driver's seat. But then he gets a jolt—the towtruck driver wants $100 just to tow Rockford a few miles. There is no alternative, so Rockford agrees; at least he'll be able to leave soon. But while he is having lunch and waiting for the car to be fixed, Rockford learns that the repairs, which he thought would be minor, are going to cost over $1,500. Again, that jolt—he isn't in Los Angeles now, so he can't just go to Aamco and get another estimate. The situation is starting to become painful to Rockford—and to look familiar to veteran television viewers as well.

Naturally, the car can't be fixed until the next day. So Rockford is consigned to the local motel, where he soon finds himself in the arms of a seemingly confused but seductive teenybopper. Suddenly, someone bursts in and takes a compromising photograph; then while Rockford is still holding the supposedly shaken girl, a deputy sheriff comes roaring up, gun drawn, and threatens him. The deputy turns out to be the girl's fiancé, and he suspects that Rockford has been messing with his girl. Now hardened television watchers know for sure that they are about to see one of the few formula scenarios of the movies and television today—the nightmare descent of the innocent city dweller into the incomprehensibly wicked and evil depths of the countryside. It has been seen a hundred times before, with slight variations, and it is a story as familiar as the one about the rookie cop teamed up with the tough twenty-year veteran, or the murdered prostitute with the heart of gold.

This characterization of the small town as evil and threatening to innocent city dwellers is now a staple of contemporary American mass culture. But the small town wasn't always seen that way. Over a relatively brief time, cultural attitudes toward small towns have changed virtually 180 degrees, from the old view of the small town as the bastion of everything good about America to the current view of the small town as everything frightening and corrupt about America. The change has been so complete that when we see a vestige of the old view appear, we are startled.

Yet last summer, when New York City was having such severe fiscal troubles, the old view surfaced. In a column in the *Wall Street Journal*, Arthur Schlesinger, Jr., said that President Ford's reluctance to help New York could be explained entirely by the traditional American antipathy toward the big city, and love for the small town. (Professor Schlesinger has obviously not been watching enough television.) Schlesinger quoted at great length from a book by Morton and Lucia White, *The Intellectual versus the City— From Thomas Jefferson to Frank Lloyd Wright.* The authors' thesis is that the greatest American thinkers have had a strong animus toward their cities. The Whites say that they can find no unifying theme for this dislike. Some, like Jefferson and William Dean Howells, disliked the American city because it was too commercialized, too filled with the extremes of wealth and poverty. Some, like Henry Adams, disliked the city because it was crowded with large numbers of non-Anglo-Saxon residents. Others, like Jane Addams and Henry James, faulted the American city for lacking the grace and charm of the older, more settled cities of Europe.

At least until the 1920s, many American intellectuals regarded their cities as "too big, too noisy, too dirty, too smelly, too commercial, too crowded, too full of immigrants, too full of Jews," and on and on. Small towns, on the other hand, were thought to be America's salvation. Jefferson summed up the small-town virtues that would make America great: "Crime is scarcely heard of, breaches of order are rare, and our societies, if not refined, are rational, moral, and affectionate, at least."

Somehow, between the age of Monticello and the age of Malibu, things have become turned around. In the televised and filmed literature of America, small towns are now the places where bad things happen; the innocent wayfarer returns to the city for protection. It is more or less routine on television for naïve families to have a tire blowout outside a small town and completely disappear into the maw of a town-wide criminal conspiracy. The small towns of the movies are no better. Innocent youths ride through them only to be driven off mountain roads, or blown to pieces by crazed local sheriffs. Even the really tough guys—Mannix or Cannon or Baretta or Tarry Orwell or poor Jim Rockford—take their lumps in small towns.

Big-City Fear and Loathing

To understand what has brought about such a remarkable change in cultural attitudes, it is instructive to see what else happens to Rockford in New Pastoria. He has already been rendered symbolically impotent—what can a man do without a car? Moreover, the very milieu that has left him powerless is the same one that can alone return his power to him—by fixing his car. The dependence that Rockford feels toward his tormentors is like something out of the Patty Hearst trial;[1] it is pitiful. And it reveals the rage that people who cannot fix things feel toward people who can, which is basically the rage of the city dweller toward the small-town dewller. And this provides a clue to the attitude of the media toward the small town. Many writers for the media feel that small towns have some power over them, which they resent enormously.

In fact, the small town has offended against television and movie writers in a number of ways. Not only can small-town people repair things—which puts them immensely more in control of their lives than most writers ever will be—but they are also resistant to the political currents which move writers. For these are the small towns that have cars with bumper stickers reading "This is Wallace Country." These are the small towns that voted for Goldwater. People ride around in pickup trucks with rifles hanging in the rear window. They don't protest United States imperialism or refuse to eat grapes. In such small towns, presumably, under every gingham dress is the robe of the women's auxiliary to the Ku Klux Klan.

It is not coincidental that after Rockford is rendered impotent by the forces of the small town, he is then confronted with a teenaged seductress. This dramatizes his impotence and suggests that people in those small towns are not just politically, but also morally, insane. Finally, Rockford's brush with a lawman who is clearly acting against the law is also perfectly true to form. When the political moral climate is so completely bizarre, what can be expected of law enforcement officials?

After the brush with the deputy, Rockford meets the mayor of New Pastoria, who is also the mother of the juvenile seductress. It turns out that the mayor is trying to lead the formerly economically depressed town to prosperity, through unspecified means. After Rockford returns to his room to sleep, he is plunged into a literal nightmare. Thugs break into his room, claim he is a drug dealer, threaten to kill him, and practically scare him to death. He is then betrayed by a seemingly kind old ex-sheriff, thrown into jail on trumped-up drug charges. and offered his release in exchange for a huge bribe. The story resembles a televised version of one of Kafka's more representative works.[2]

Finally, while out on bail, Rockford breaks into the district attorney's office and finds evidence that the town has been systematically preying on traveling city folk, breaking their cars, charging outrageous repair bills, framing them on various charges, and then black-

1. Against the charge of joining her kidnapers in a bank robbery, Patricia Hearst's defense was that the isolation and stress of her captivity produced so great a dependence on her captors that her conversion to their cause was involuntary.

2. Franz Kafka (1883–1924) was the Czech author of, among other works, *The Trial*, a novel whose protagonist is destroyed in a labyrinth of legalistic frustration and persecution.

mailing them—the source of the income for New Pastoria's economic renaissance. Rockford eventually breaks the scheme wide open, but only with the help of authorities from the city. New Pastoria, the quintessence of the small town of television and the movies, comes in for a hell of a beating.

Cultural Politics and the Media

But the reasons that small towns came to have such a bad image in the "industry" involve more than merely political differences and have even deeper roots.

Even while Jefferson was writing about how wonderful life was in rural Virginia, early abolitionists were noticing that in those idyllic Southern towns, some human beings owned other human beings. That in itself was terrible, and the owners often did terrible things to the people they owned. The idea gained strength, especially after the Civil War, that small Southern towns were places where the mask of law was used to hide horrifying crimes against law and morality.

Some early silent and talking pictures picked up the theme. The most notable example was *I Am a Fugitive from a Chain Gang*, in 1932, which marked a turning point of sorts because its message was that small Southern towns were so evil and corrupt that they unjustly oppressed white people, too.

At about the same time, small towns were being scorned by many great American novelists of the 1920s who—from Baltimore or New York or Paris—saw the American small town as the lair of the "booboisie," that dreaded American species named by H. L. Mencken. Small towns were not only stupid, but terribly unfashionable as well.

The classic example of a small-town conspiracy against the outside work was not revealed, however, until after World War II. A film called *Bad Day at Black Rock* told the story of a small town in the Southwest that went amok after Pearl Harbor and murdered a local Japanese-American farmer, whose son was fighting with the Nisei forces in Italy. Spencer Tracy, who had been with the Nisei soldier when he was killed, brings the son's medal to his family after the end of the war. All the people in the small town participate in the coverup, and when Tracy gets too inquisitive, they try to kill him. It is in all ways a prototypical story—there is the same bewildering solidarity, the same lawless police officials, and the same lazy cunning that were to be copied again and again by television and the movies. It was no coincidence, as the saying goes, that *Bad Day at Black Rock* came out in 1955, a time when virtually the entire American mass media were arranging themselves into a political and cultural style which still persists to this day, although some weakening is evident.

It is obviously problematic to move from analyzing media prototypes to analyzing the sociological reality of the creators of such images. Yet writers for television and films have political and cultural points of view, just like everyone else. And they are predominantly liberal and antiestablishment (without realizing, of course, that they *are* the "establishment," show-business intellectuals maintain one of the most delightful routines of "doublethink" anywhere). It is no accident that George McGovern and Tom Hayden found many large donors in Hollywood. The people who are now writing were shaped intellectually at a time when most intellectual respectability, so it seemed, belonged to left-wing thought. Many idolized Franklin D. Roosevelt and hated Joe McCarthy. In Hollywood, finding a writer who is a Republican is almost like seeing a woman without painted toenails at the Beverly Hills Hotel swimming pool. When the presidential elections come around, the longest lists of writers and directors will always be found on the stationery of the most liberal Democratic candidates.

To such people, small towns are the enemy. Small towns did not support Adlai Stevenson; some of them didn't even like Roosevelt. These writers' formative years were spent reading about lynchings in small towns and rural areas. They know that once they leave New York or Los Angeles, they are in political *terra incognita*,[3] and that scares them. When they depict a small town as frightening, they are really telling us that they are frightened.

But they are more than frightened; they are angry, too. By consistently casting conservative votes, the small towns have blocked them politically from creating the kind of America they would like to create. Small towns now have lots of people who didn't like big cities in the past because big cities had too many Jews, and a truly great number of the people who write movies and television shows are Jewish. It is hardly surprising that many of these writers should not be enamored of small towns.

Not that there is any religious animus involved—far from it. These writers do not care one bit about the religious practices of the people in the small towns. If they are religious, that is one more piece of hypocrisy, but piled on top of so much hypocrisy, it doesn't matter much. What is at work is an ethnic/cultural polarity. The typical Hollywood writer, from my experience, is of an ethnic background from a large Eastern city—usually from Brooklyn. He grew up being taught that people in small towns hated him, were different from him, and were out to get him. As a result, when he gets

3. The Latin label used on old maps for unexplored land.

the chance, he attacks the small town on television or in the movies.

No matter that statistics show that living in a small town is about seven times safer than living in a large city. A person whose sole source of knowledge about America came from watching television detective shows would think that driving outside a big city is comparable to jumping off a tall building. Any number of movies —*Deliverance, Macon County Line, The California Kid*—make the same point. The television shows and movies are not telling it "like it is"; instead they are giving us the point of view of a small and extremely powerful section of the American intellectual community —those who write for the mass visual media.

The Cultural Civil War

What is happening, as a consequence, is something unusual and remarkable. A national culture is making war upon a way of life that is still powerfully attractive and widely practiced in the safe country. To be specific, about half of all Americans still live in small towns and rural areas, and, more interestingly, about three out of four Americans sampled in a 1975 Gallup poll said they would prefer to live in a suburb or a small town, or on a farm. (Almost 25 percent chose a farm!) Thus feelings of affection for small towns run deep in America, and small-town life is treasured by millions of people. But in the mass culture of the country, a hatred for the small town is spewed out on television screens and movie screens every day.

So far as I know, this is a historical first. In many earlier societies, there had been a literature which belittled and criticized the small town and the rural way of life. But it was confined to small groups of the population. For the masses of the people, there was a folk tradition which glorified the rural and small-town way of life. Now that situation is turned around. Television and the movies are America's folk culture, and they have nothing but contempt for the way of life of a very large part of the folk.

In no time before the advent of television has a writer been able to reach so many people so quickly. Similarly, before the age of television, writers as a group were never able to circulate their opinions so widely in so short a space of time. What happened was the coincidence of a cultural event and an electronic event. The cultural event was rather complicated. It involved the emergence among television and movie writers of a predominantly left-wing, antiestablishment style of thought and view of the world—the result of a whole series of events that are too lengthy to enumerate (and which I do not fully understand), but are clearly apparent. Part of that

worldview is an animus against small-town America. The electronic
event was the growth of television; and entry to its ranks of writers,
as for the movies, was decided on a strictly meritocratic basis. The
result was that aggressive, striving people with a modicum of talent
could become television and movie writers. Thus the medium and
the message came together around the mid-1950s, although the two
had been converging for some time before.

The consequence of this merger has been that the American
people are told falsehoods about their country—untruths that those
in control of writing for the media believe, or at any rate refuse to
disbelieve. And the falsehoods have consequences.

The anti-small-town show makes the point clearly. Poll after poll
has shown that Americans in cities fear crime more than anything
else—even more than inflation. Statistics also show that the most
frequently committed crime is simple mugging, and that the typical
mugger is a teenage, minority-group male. And what people fear
when they leave their cars and houses are precisely teenaged, minority-group youths.

But most writers of America cannot cope intellectually with the
idea that some of those pitiful minorities, whom they were taught
were oppressed and tormented, are now themselves tormenting
others in turn. Many therefore take their own free-floating anxiety
about crime and violence and move it to a place that is more comfortable for them—the small town, which they were taught to hate
and fear. It is a complete reversal of reality to make the small town
more dangerous than the big city, but it accords perfectly with
these writers' view of reality—or what reality should be. (There are
other examples of this inverted depiction of crime on television. For
instance, if a crime is committed in the city, it is usually by a
person who is either rich or insane. The real world, in which violent
crimes are committed by people who are poor, vicious, and quite
sane, rarely shows its head.)

The simple consequence of this distortion of reality is that people
are misinformed. Far more serious and dangerous, however, is that
people are taught to hate and fear their own culture. They are given
additional reasons to detest a fundamental social unit of their country—the small town. This detestation leads like a stream, among
many such streams that such writers and intellectuals have fashioned, into a mighty confluence of doubt of America by Americans.
People are told that their culture is, at its root, sick, violent, and
depraved, and this message gives them little confidence in the
future of that culture. It also leads them to feel ashamed of their
country and to believe that if their society is in decline, it deserves
to be.

It is simply inconceivable that a medium capable of making a
brand new deodorant number one in sales in only six months ("Try

it under your own two arms—we're Sure") could not, after years of trying, make Americans feel ambivalent about small towns.

A Small-Town Revival?

And yet, the polls still show a strong attachment to the concept of small-town life. That, perhaps, is the result of some reality penetrating into the minds of people who watch television. Those people have been to small towns. The small towns are often pretty, clean, and quiet. No one hurt them or threatened them there. So the television shows make them feel ambivalent about the small town, but cannot destroy all feelings of affection. What the television shows and movies can do is create self-doubt and confusion. What would be terribly interesting would be the reactions of Americans to small towns if their views had not been affected by television shows and movies that are filled with negative images.

We may get to see just that. There are signs of a change in the attitude of the media toward small towns and rural America. Somewhere along the line, someone discovered that the hatred of small towns collided with the environmental issue. Suddenly, for the groups whose parents were taught that everything outside the city was the domain of the Klansman, the city and its pollution now became the enemy.

A new generation of ad men and women and music hucksters have come along who realized that when you call something "country" or "farm-fresh" or "natural," people think of it as lacking poisonous pollutants and additives. On the same shows where the small town is cruelly trapping the innocent city dweller, the commercials are showing how wonderful it is to live on a farm and get fresh food and have a fresh complexion, and how healthful it is to live in a small town where there is plenty of fresh air and hard work. People have begun to think that out in the country, there are not only fewer sulphur-dioxide emissions, but less meanness and tension. Television documentaries now tell about city people who are leading new lives in Vermont and Maine.

A generational clash is developing in the media. The people most in tune with the generation of the 1960s and 1970s know that, despite all the television shows, Ralph Nader has authoritatively told them that big cities are disgusting, unhealthy places—and they believe him. Such people are resuscitating the country image in those media forms which most quickly adapt to changing trends, music and advertising. On the radio air waves, country music expands to new stations at an almost geometric rate. It is customarily only a matter of time before such trends move to prime time and the silver screen.

But the writers who grew up without the environmental issue are still around, and are still powerful. Their world view has not changed and they are still grinding out the melodramas which make the small town eat dirt.

So a struggle in the media continues in which ground is gained and lost. The signs of how it will turn out are unclear, but they seem to indicate a small-town renascence. A recent phenomenon is the sudden emergence of pictures about small towns, particularly in the South, which are not slanderous and which are making big money, even in suburban markets. Think of Burt Reynolds and you can think of the cinematic genre referred to. The emergence of Nashville as a powerful media center is another sign of the regeneration of the image of the small town. It grows daily more powerful in both records and films, and it is the capital of small-town America (a fact which earned it an astonishingly crude slam in the movie which bears its name). Several new television shows are set in small towns—*Sara, The Bionic Woman,* and *Mary Hartman, Mary Hartman*—and the small towns are treated affectionately. Even a recent made-for-television movie adapted from the works of John O'Hara took a compassionate view of small-town life.

Still, these are just straws in the wind. The predominant theme in prime time and at the theater is still that small towns are places where bad things happen to innocent people. It is a view that is neither realistic nor helpful to America or to anyone in particular, but it reveals something about how the media and our culture are shaped.

1976

QUESTIONS

Benjamin Stein's article was challenged by the following letter. Stein's response to the letter is also given.

Benjamin Stein's "Whatever Happened to Small-Town America?" [is] remarkable in its many inaccuracies—about Hollywood and its portrayal of small towns, and about small towns themselves. The conclusion of the article, that left-wing and liberal Jewish writers in Hollywood are subverting innocent (non-Jewish) moviegoers and television watchers, reminded me of similar charges made fifty years ago by the right-wind opponents of Weimar democracy.[1]

Admittedly, Mr. Stein never quite raises the religious issue; he says only that the "typical Hollywood writer, from my experience, is of an ethnic background from a large Eastern city—usually from Brooklyn." Perhaps he is right. Still, this does not prove the writers are liberal or left-wing, that they were large donors to the McGovern and Hayden campaigns, or for that matter, that they are against small towns. More important, my impression (based on an inveterate reading of film and television credits) is that the Westerns, crime dramas, and adventure sto-

1. In other words, the Nazi party.

ries from which Mr. Stein draws most of his evidence are generally written by people whose names suggest they are neither ethnics nor from Brooklyn.

Mr. Stein is correct on one point: The media's love affair with the small-town pastoral has died down since World War II, even if it was never quite as passionate as Mr. Stein thinks. Still, the pastoral remains very much alive in television news features—for example, in Charles Kuralt's CBS news series, "On the Road."

Television's portrayal of small-town criminality, however, is more complex than Mr. Stein suggests. Hollywood writers are saying that crime is sometimes carried out and sometimes covered up by the power holders in small towns, and this process is immeasurably aided by the fact that they are friends, and often relatives. To me, these stories are mainly warnings against the pastoral myth, depicting the dark side of Gemeinschaft,[2] and suggesting that it can breed lawlessness and conspiracy as well as cohesion and warmth.

This theme is old as the hills, even in Hollywood, and it was probably first imported by the writers of Western movies, who were usually not from Brooklyn. Mr. Stein himself mentions the 1956 film *Bad Day at Black Rock*, but Will Wright's recent *Sixguns and Society* (University of California Press, 1975) indicates that the small-town society of the Western was almost always depicted as weak, thus creating the need for the outlaw-hero. In some films, such as *High Noon* (1952) and *Broken Arrow* (1950), the leaders of the small town even tried to have the hero killed because he was endangering its stability or other interests in his single-minded pursuit of morality.

Now that Westerns are passé, at least for the moment, their critique of small-town Gemeinschaft has been transferred to other television dramas and to contemporary hamlets—including "Fernwood, Ohio," where Mary Hartman lives and suffers. Although Mr. Stein sees *Mary Hartman, Mary Hartman* as a sign of a newly favorable attitude toward small towns on television, he evidently has not watched the series regularly. Otherwise he would know that while Mary Hartman may be a traditional small-town innocent, most of the townspeople—who cause suffering to her, her family, and her friends—are depicted as corrupt. Even so, "Fernwood, Ohio," is hardly a typical hamlet, since its major male characters all work on an assembly line.

Nor is television's current image of the small town pure fiction. Hollywood exaggerates empirical reality, as it exaggerates everything else, but the small towns are not as crime-free as Mr. Stein would like to believe. According to FBI Crime Reports, which divide America into "metropolitan areas," "other cities," and "rural areas," the "rural areas" have almost as high a violent-crime rate as "other cities," and keep up with them in rates of murder and rape. To be sure, the rates are lower than those of large cities, and there is no street crime and mugging, but small town America is hardly peaceful. Moreover, a long list of journalistic and sociological studies, as well as naturalistic novels, have shown that the familial and friendship ties that typically characterize small-town life have cemented economic and political alliances that breed corruption and other forms of white-collar crime, and occasionally even murder.

---

2. Community; the word was used by the Nazis to characterize the cultural and racial German elite, as opposed to minorities such as the Jews who were excluded from the community.

Rural political machines, for example, predated and have outlived their urban counterparts, and while the news media have not paid much attention to them, their deviations from legality differ little. In short, the media do not "detest a fundamental social unit," as Mr. Stein would have us believe, but only one of its faults.

I am also surprised that a viewer as experienced as Mr. Stein still believes that media fiction can alter basic attitudes and values. He admits himself that the media's portrayal of small-town criminality has not diminished the fondness many Americans feel toward the small town, but then goes on to say that "it is simply inconceivable that a medium capable of making a brand new deodorant number one in sales in only six months . . . could not, after years of trying, make Americans feel ambivalent about small towns." In fact, there is no evidence that the media are capable of making Americans feel such ambivalence—the ability to hype up deodorant sales proves nothing about attitudes. After all, when you sell patent medicines that at best offer symptomatic relief, it is not very difficult to persuade people to try a new one every so often with a catchy commercial.

In the end, Mr. Stein has the same view of the American public, whom he sees as being subverted by Hollywood, as that which he accuses the left-wing and liberal writers of having, those whom he imagines dominate television. He sees the television audience as a gullible mass whose culture is shaped by the media; consequently, he suggests that the continued fondness for small-town life "is, perhaps, the result of some reality penetrating into the minds of people who watch television." A curious phrase, but since Mr. Stein is out to expose a previously unrecognized menace, he must also invent a thickheaded populace for whom reality is only a sometime thing.

—Herbert J. Gans

Benjamin Stein's reply:

In my article, I tried to raise two points: 1) Movies and television programs typically picture small towns as evil, dangerous places; and 2) creative people involved in the making of these shows dislike and fear small towns, for largely political reasons.

Professor Gans apparently recognizes the first point, but believes that the trend began earlier than I said. That is possible, but his example, *High Noon* (1952), does not support his contention, since it was made twenty years after *I Am a Fugitive from a Chain Gang* (1932), which I cited as the first of the anti-small-town films.

That is a small point, however. If Professor Gans does not recognize that the animus against small towns has become a staple ingredient of television adventure dramas, he simply has not been watching television. If he does not acknowledge the movies' maltreatment of small towns, he simply has not been going to the movies.

The second point was, if anything, understated in my article. Since coming to Los Angeles I have interviewed many producers, directors, and writers concerning their political feelings. Without exception, they are fearful and worried about small towns, mainly because of the political views they see represented there.

Two examples make the point clearly. I asked Meta Rosenberg, an extremely intelligent woman who produces *The Rockford Files*, how she felt about small towns. She answered that they had some good points, but that they could easily become thoroughly corrupt, because there were no forces to dissipate corruption once it started. When I asked her if small towns were frightening, she thought for a moment and said, without prompting, "Jesus Christ, they did vote for Nixon."

When asked about small towns, Stanley Kramer, a producer-director with impressive credits (including *High Noon*), said, "Of course, they're reactionary, extremely reactionary. They pursue the clichés of America so strictly that they endanger America."

These comments are unusually succinct, but highly representative. I think it might be instructive for Professor Gans to spend some time in the dream factories to see how what goes in influences what comes out.

1. *Gans and Stein are obviously in disagreement. Exactly what is in dispute? Is it important? Who best states the issue(s)? What sort of evidence is called for? Do these authors provide it? What else do you need to know to decide between the two?*
2. *In "Literacy Without Books: Sesame Street" (pp. 157–165) Rose K. Goldsen also speaks of the impact of television. Is her position (as revealed in her unstated assumptions and as well as her explicit assertions) closer to that of one or the other of these two disputants?*
3. *Write an essay explaining which of the disputants you agree with, or why you can't decide between them, or why the issue doesn't matter.*

LEWIS H. LAPHAM

A Nation of Dreamers

*Heard melodies are sweet, but those unheard
Are sweeter.*

—John Keats
"Ode on a Grecian Urn"

The American preference for the invisible never ceases to astonish me. Just when I begin to think that I live in a materialist society, I find myself surrounded by people who choose to believe in what isn't there.

My observations do not conform to the official portraits of the American character. The American is said to be a practical man who believes in what he can see and measure. The United States supposedly inherited not only the earth but also the traditions of the eighteenth century mind—skeptical, inquiring, and given to experiment. This assumption receives the support of the many lobbyists for the idea of American pragmatism, who, despite their political and regional differences, agree on the triumph of reason and the scientific method. The artistic interests talk about the prevailing indifference to the ineffable; businessmen say that maybe they don't know the difference between Beethoven and Molière, but they sure as hell know the difference between profit and loss; politicians mention "hard realities"; and the lost tribe of the counterculture speaks of philistines squandering a third of the world's resources on the manufacture of gaudy baubles. All the witnesses testify to the preeminence of facts.

Not so. The United States is a nation of dreamers, captivated by the power of metaphor. Whenever possible the American substitutes the symbol for whatever it is that the symbol represents. Social critics sometimes deplore the rapaciousness with which Americans consume the goods and services of a spendthrift economy. The critics fail to notice that the objects mean nothing in themselves, that the material acquisitions serve as tedious preliminaries to the desired immateriality.

This point was made plain on the Fourth of July in New York Harbor, in the words of a sign propped against a fence at the southern end of Manhattan Island. Facing the sea and directed toward the largest flotilla of ships assembled anywhere in the world in more than 100 years,[1] the sign read: "Welcome to Battery Park City." This was a fine sentiment but entirely abstract. Battery Park City is an empty lot, a barren mound of mud and sand.

The transcendental bias of the American mind can turn the whole world into metaphor. Consider the Mafia, or the domino theory. The best available evidence suggests that there is no such thing as a Mafia, that American business simply undertakes both legitimate and illegitimate enterprises, and that sometimes people get killed. But nobody likes that interpretation. Too many people have too much of a vested interest in the preservation of the dark romance. What would become of television police dramas, or the prizes for investigative reporting? The domino theory[2] described an imaginary mechanism on a map. To protect the integrity of the metaphor, the United States sent an army to Asia. Further examples can be extended through an appropriately infinite sequence. Nobody wants to know the name of Deep Throat, the invisible source of the information that led to the Watergate spectacle and a President's abdication. If the man acquired an identity, complete with motives and a house in the suburbs, he no longer could be imaged as omniscient. Entire vocabularies of symbolic jargon—academic, bureaucratic, scientific—describe the entire kingdoms of nonexistent thought. Modern art depends on abstract theories that explain the absence of paint. American restaurants substitute the hyperbole of their menus for the taste of their food; so also do por-

---

1. The Tall Ships, a gathering of square-rigged sailing vessels from many nations that visited the United States in 1976 to celebrate the Bicentennial.

2. The idea that one country's falling to Communism would cause others to fall, like a line of dominoes set on end.

nographic magazines publish literary essays that hardly anybody bothers to read. They appear as symbols of an imaginary conversation. The television image, which is intself a metaphor, goes forth to an invisible audience. Jimmy Carter succeeds as a political candidate because he presents the voters with an emptiness they can fill with images of their own.

Or consider the metaphor of New York City. By any material standard (comparison with Paris, say, or even with London) the city must be judged deficient. From a height or a distance it can be seen as beautiful, but the texture of the streets consists of fear, noise, ugliness, and anger. It is the metaphysical promise, the sense of the unseen but imminent possibility, that gives the city its character. Walking around beggars lying in the street, the citizens carry on fierce discussions of social injustice: they speculate about the interior dialogue of politicians whom they have never seen, about the chance of war in countries in which they have never traveled. The less they know about the subject in question, the more easily they can escape the coils of specific fact and float into the sphere of abstraction.

The unheard melodies on John Keats's Grecian urn fill out the implied harmonies in almost the whole of American literature. The writers remembered, for their communion with the unknowable, among them Thoreau, Melville, Whitman, and Fitzgerald, lose themselves in what Irving Howe recently described as "a sacred emptiness of space," in which each man becomes both performer and pioneer, inventing himself as he clears the wilderness of his mortality. The modern school of writing, much praised by the critics who teach theories of imagination, follows the tradition into the thin atmosphere of surrealism. In the novels of Robert Coover, Donald Barthelme, and Thomas Pynchon, the narrative exists only to be discarded. Like the hulk of a first-stage rocket, it carries the author's circus of ideas into the metaphor of space. Except in a figurative way, as representatives of abstraction, the people in the novels have neither meaning or substance.

The eloquent theories of politicians and professors of sociology seldom withstand the judgment of practical result because, more often than not, they are meant to be appreciated as symbols. The politicians have no choice in this because they seldom see the things their laws describe. They talk about housing and federal health insurance, about poverty levels and public transportation, but they do not ride in subways or wait in lines for food stamps. Like the view of New York City from a helicopter, the idea of racial equality is beautiful as an abstraction. If somebody interprets it in a literal-minded way, mistaking the symbolic for the real, well, then, obviously the thing won't work. The race riots in Boston result from an error in translation. When Tom Wicker spoke encouragingly to the prisoners at Attica[3] about the "inequities of the system," he offered them a metaphor instead of information. A number of them died because nobody told them that journalism is a form of fiction.

An obsession with metaphor also governs the conduct of American business. I have noticed that few highly placed executives understand money as a commodity. Perhaps this is because they almost never see it. The transfer of huge sums takes place as a sequence of abstractions projected on a screen. Making their way upward through the company hierarchy, once-knowledgeable engineers learn to speak the ritual language of hierophants. On the highest tiers of organizations that resemble Babylonian ziggurats,[4] the officials walk solemnly to and fro, bowing to one another in their circumambulations and making grave gestures of consensus. Every now and then they pause to examine the sky through the modern equivalents of the astrolabe[5]—computer print-outs, projections of oil reserves, summaries of the consumer-price index, et cetera. The technology furnishes them with metaphors.

Even the American approach to sex proceeds along the lines of religious pilgrimage. The confessional testimony, most of it in the form of best-selling disappointment, suggests that not many people (at least not those who write about it) find much pleasure in the act of love. Quite often they would rather be in Philadelphia,[6] but they have been sent forth to find meaning and success. Like all the other toys in the department-store window, the sexual object must be acquired as proof of something else. Nobody knows quite what; but, presumably (see the manuals, clinics, advisories to the lovelorn), something beyond the merely human. Together with the Holy Grail, the ideal orgasm remains just over the horizon of their experience. Both men and women talk about their liaisons in the way that explorers used to write about their voyaging in unknown seas. By keeping logs and chronologies, they plot their positions in the world.

The tendency to think in symbols also accounts for the otherwise baffling American perception of time. It has often been demonstrated that Americans retain little more than a dim notion of the past. The universities continue to report a lack of interest in anything that took place as long ago as last week: a Gallup poll pub-

3. A prison in New York State, scene of a bloody riot in 1971. Tom Wicker is an American journalist.
4. Massive pyramid-like buildings in ancient imperial Babylon.
5. Medieval instrument for examining the relations of stars and planets, often used for astrological calculations.
6. Proverbial expression of willingness to accept something dreary to avoid something worse.

lished early this year showed that only 50 percent of the respondents could remember what was the significance of the year 1776. People who cannot imagine the past cannot envision the future. The sense of time falls in upon itself, collapsing like an accordion into the evangelical present. The effect is greatly magnified by the symbolic nature of the television image, in which the visible part stands for the invisible whole. If three or four black men carrying signs can be made to represent the discontent of the Negro race, then they have been raised to the power of metaphor. The confinement in the present imposes a necessary preoccupation with what isn't there. Nothing can exist, because anything so foolish as to make itself visible must submit to the passage of time. To live always at the point of becoming makes it difficult to enjoy, much less to sustain, the sense of being.

I cannot imagine a state of mind less consistent with the orthodox definitions of materialism. If dissatisfaction becomes imbued with the significance of a religious quest, then the satisfied man stands condemned as a heretic. To admit being satisfied is to confess the squalor of one's aspirations. Which is why the traditional disappointment with success follows. Having acquired the object of what he thought was his desire, the young man cannot feel the emotional correlative he had previously assigned to the grasping of that object. In the midst of his possessions he mourns the loss of innocence. Anybody who neglects to offer the conventional denials risks alliance with the Evil One, i.e., with people who know or have what they want. God forbid that a man should enjoy the things of the world, that he should delight in its fruitfulness and surround himself with friends, works, and families.

In its courageous aspects, the longing for the invisible expresses the spirit of the American frontier. The *Mayflower* sails in search of the unknown Thomas Jefferson: Orville Wright imagines the flight of the unseen SST. But, at least for the time being, the dreaming American mind appears to have retreated into the caves of the supernatural. The crowds gathered in the tent shows of wandering evangelicals remind me of the crowds shuffling through the neon markets of sexual illusion. The preacher and the whore promise the transcendent moment of an escape from time. It is an escape that even Houdini found impossible to perform.

1976

KILDARE DOBBS

Canada's Regions

The truth is that the thought "Canada" is impossible to think all at once. Love of country is difficult when, like Aristotle's "creature of vast size,"[1] its unity and wholeness are lost to imagination. And so the patriotism of Canadians tends to be—in a perfectly respectable and human sense—provincial, and even parochial.

The people of each region have their own character.

Maritimers are a seafaring race whose roots are deep in history. Canada is sometimes thought of (quite wrongly) as a "new" country. The Maritime provinces belong essentially to the Old World. The things that surprise, enchant, and sometimes distress North American travelers in Europe are also to be found here: craftsmanship, tradition, cheerful poverty. A sense of history clings about the silvery weathered shingles of fishermen's huts; the vivid colors of boats and lobster floats—red, blue, ocher, green—and the black-and-white dazzle of painted wooden houses are affirmations of life and vigor against the hard gray weather and the dangerous ocean. Men have been here a long time; they have come to terms with the forests, the rocks, the tides. It was in 1605 that Samuel de Champlain planted Canada's first settlement at Port Royal—now Annapolis Royal, Nova Scotia. Not far away, at Pubnico, there are some eight hundred French-speaking Nova Scotians named D'Entremont. Most of them have the ascetic features of the family face: they are all descended from the Sieur D'Entremont who landed here in 1650. St. John's, Newfoundland, was first settled in 1613: its people retain the Jacobean[2] turns of phrase, the ballads, the hearty manners of their ancestors.

Maritimers, many of them with the quick pride of Scots Highland descent, are touchy about the chronic depression of their region. Aware that their economy is to some extent subsidized from Central Canada, they resent "Upper Canadians" and are fond of denouncing the frantic pace of life in Ontario compared with the pleasant, lethargic tempo of their own existence.

French Canadians cherish their own mythology and defensive folklore. "*Je me souviens*,"[3] their motto, recalls the national trauma

---

1. In Aristotle's illustration (in Chapter 7 of the *Poetics*) of the relation between magnitude and unity of plot: "Beauty is a matter of size and order, and therefore impossible either (1) in a very minute creature, since our perception becomes indistinct as it approaches instantaneity; or (2) in a creature of vast size—one, say, a thousand miles long—as in that case, instead of the object being seen all at once, the unity and wholeness of it is lost to the beholder."

2. Relating to the reign (1603–1625) of James I of England.

3. "I remember," motto of the province of Quebec.

—the conquest of New France upon the Plains of Abraham before the walled city of Quebec. Since that fatal day, September 13, 1759, they have seen themselves as beleaguered champions of the Catholic faith and its guardian the French tongue in a continent predominantly American and Protestant. Henri Bourassa, most eloquent of Canadian orators, spoke for his nation when he cried out passionately at the Montreal Eucharistic Congress on September 6, 1910: "Providence has willed that the principal group of this French and Catholic colonization should constitute in America a separate corner of the earth, where the social, religious, and political situation most closely approximates to that which the Church teaches us to be the ideal state of society. . . . But, it is said, you are only a handful; you are fatally destined to disappear; why persist in the struggle? We are only a handful, it is true; but in the school of Christ I did not learn to estimate right and moral forces by number and wealth. We are only a handful; but we count for what we are; and we have the right to live. . . ."

More than fifty years later the "ideal state of society" of the devout *habitants* has disappeared and the French Canadians have become an urban proletariat. While the fragrant spirit of John XXIII has sweetened their faith, they have discovered their political strength and a new sense of purpose. By a paradox they have become most sharply aware of their distinctness at the very moment when they are becoming most "American."

The crooked streets of Quebec City cast their old spell, delightfully French-provincial in the shade of old trees in summer, antique as a Christmas card under the winter snow. In the citadel, redcoats of the 22nd Foot[4] wheel and stamp to orders shouted in the curiously nasal French of the province. *Monsieur le Président* (Mr. Speaker) sits under the crucifix in the legislative assembly. A spectacled nun appears at the grille through which visitors are interviewed at the ancient Couvent des Ursulines, a moment later she returns to display with shy pride the skull of General Montcalm.[5] But such impressions can be deceptive. The dark-haired girls, demure in their little black dresses, are North American women, capable, energetic, adventurous. And under the sober jacket of the young *séparatiste* hurrying to early Mass beats the heart of an automobile salesman.

All this is much more obvious in Montreal, the world's second

4. Soldiers of the Royal 22nd Regiment who carry out ceremonial duties at the Citadel.

5. *Couvent des Ursulines*: Convent of the Ursuline Sisters, founded in 1639, one of the oldest educational institutions for women in North America; Louis Joseph de Montcalm, French general who in 1759 defended Quebec unsuccessfully against the British army under General James Wolfe. Both Montcalm and Wolfe died in battle on the Plains of Abraham, and Montcalm's body was buried in the Ursulines' chapel.

biggest French-speaking city. This is the city which, above all others, has seized the affection of Canadians. Novel after novel has explored the intricate life of its streets and parks. Despite the bilingual signs and the brooding presence of huge, prison-like religious institutions, Montreal is plainly a New World city. Everyone here is cheerfully on the make. There is that sense (strong too in Toronto) that nothing is permanent. Buildings are constantly being torn down to be replaced by taller and richer ones, streets being ripped open for new sewers or subways, ambulances racing to the rescue of accident victims, sirens screaming, signs dazzling, merchandise being sacrificed to make way for the new line, the new model, the new chain-store—the whole exciting circus of planned obsolescence and competitive selling.

French Canadians are awakening to the knowledge that this is their world and their country. They have recognized their enemy in the "Anglo-Saxon" *élite* who dominate Canada's economy. This *élite*, though stoutly entrenched in Montreal, whose commercial life it controls, has its spiritual home in Toronto.

One of the few shared sentiments of all regions of Canada is an unreasoning dislike of Toronto. Unreasoning, because the Toronto loathed throughout Canada has pretty well ceased to exist. The dour, philistine Orangemen[6] who earned the city its unpleasant reputation have long been outnumbered by swarms of immigrants from Europe and from other parts of Canada. True, there's still a great parade down University Avenue on the glorious Twelfth of July, with drums and bands and orange sashes and even King Billy[7] on his white charger. But the crowds who turn out to cheer are mostly Italians—everyone, after all, loves a band. For if Montreal is bicultural, Toronto is multicultural—an expanding, expansive metropolis which will soon have a population of two million. As Montreal is the center of French-speaking Canadian life, Toronto is the hub of English Canada. Here are centered its publishing and communication industries, its commercial and financial empires, music, art, and theater. Heavy industry is close by in Hamilton, and a third of Canada's population is concentrated in the rich farmlands and small cities of southern Ontario within a radius of three hundred miles.

Ontario people are sober, hard-working, orderly; as if to insist on their difference from the Americans they resemble so closely, they are strong for the Queen. The men tend to be serious about their work to the point of solemnity; at the same time they cherish the image of Huck Finn and are boyishly eager to head out for the bush. They are decent people, if—as they often complain themselves—a bit dull. And they are not nearly so hostile to French

6. Descendants of Protestant immigrants from Northern Ireland.
7. A figure representing William III, also known as William of Orange, who was king of England from 1689 to 1702.

Canadians as the latter imagine: their reaction to Separatist agita-
tion is to organize classes in French. Normally, of course, they do
not think about Quebec; it simply doesn't impinge on their consciousness any more than Canada itself does on the mind of a New
Yorker. For the only evidence of French Canada in Ontario (outside a few border communities) is the bilingual food-package:
"snap, crackle, pop" on one side of the cereal carton becomes "*cric,
crac, croc*" on the other. It's hard to build understanding on evidence as flimsy as that.

The West begins at Winnipeg, a mystique of white Stetsons,
"man-size" beefsteaks, and back-slapping hospitality. There is a
tendency, too, for the necktie to atrophy into a sort of halter of
bootlaces. Ontario and Quebec and the Maritimes suddenly recede
to a great distance not only in space but in time. Here they are "the
East." The cities of Central Canada, which seem to the people who
live in them so new and raw, from here take on the aspect of
ancient centers of privilege and decorum, crusted with culture and
learning. Wide, empty landscapes of bald prairie, oppressed by the
enormous sky, wait at the limits of prairie cities. The company of
fellow-men becomes vital. And in Alberta, as the flat prairie begins
to undulate in ever shorter and steeper waves to the foothills of the
Rockies, the company of God himself is sought by the people of the
"Bible belt"; not only in theocratic colonies of bearded, black-clad
Hutterites,[8] but in small, bleak churches and conventicles of innumerable fundamentalist sects.

British Columbia, cut off from the rest of Canada by range
beyond range of enormous, uninhabitable mountains, lives its own
life. British Columbians are the most American Canadians, farthest
removed from bicultural compromises; they are also the most British. Life is pleasant in the mild green climate of the Coast. The
mist comes down on the mountains and silent forests, the Pacific
glimmers below—who needs Canada? "As far as I'm concerned," a
British Columbian told me not long ago, "the Atlantic Ocean
might just as well be washing at the foot of the Rockies." In the
remote valleys of the Interior—as the hinterland of Vancouver is
gallantly called—a few pilgrim souls, the last puritans, live by the
light of conscience: Quakers, anarchists, pacifists, the unhappy
Doukhobor Sons of Freedom.[9] Cowboys ride the range on the high,

8. Members of a religious, communis-
tic group founded in Moravia in the sixteenth century by Jacob Hutter. Some of
the sect settled at Tabor, South Dakota,
in 1874, and thereafter eventually
migrated to Canada.

9. The sect of the Doukhobors—literally, "spirit-wrestlers"—originated among
Russian peasants in the seventeenth century. The members believe in the absolute equality of all men and resist all
authority, whether civil or ecclesiastic. In
the 1890s most of them migrated to Saskatchewan, Canada. Since then, their
civil-disobedience techniques, including
the removal of all their clothes when
apprehended by law officers, have led
them into trouble with Canadian authorities.

semi-arid plateau of the Cariboo country. Loggers, miners, and fishermen earn the provincial income. But a good two-thirds of British Columbians are concentrated in the cities of Vancouver and Victoria where the living is easy, summer and winter.

People who do not know Canada sometimes think of it, as Voltaire[1] did, as a few acres of snow.

It is, of course, a northern country. Over most of it the climate is one of violent extremes—swelteringly hot summers and Siberian winters. Arctic Canada—the true North—is almost uninhabited. There are only some eleven thousand Eskimoes. The other people of a few small, scattered communities like Churchill, Inuvik, and Aklavik live a frontier life with, at Inuvik, every modern convenience, including heated sewage. (Because of permafrost, drainpipes are above the surface, and have to be heated to avoid freezing.) Northerners regard the rest of Canada and indeed the rest of the world as "Outside."

There is still a powerful myth of the North. Against all evidence, Canadians sometimes like to think of themselves as a hardy, frugal race of *hommes du nord*. For the farther north one goes, the farther one is from the United States and from supermarkets, superhighways, and advertising men in crew-cuts and two-button suits. One must suffer to be a Canadian (says the myth): here incomes are lower and prices higher than in the republic to the south: go north, young man. Canadians may not be particularly hardy, but they are hard-headed. They indulge this dream only at election time and when they are on vacation.

1964

1. French philosopher and author; the   Enlightenment.
leading figure of the eighteenth-century

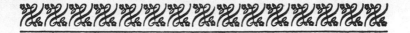

Human Nature

B. F. SKINNER
What Is Man?

As a science of behavior follows the strategy of physics and biology, the autonomous agent to which we have traditionally attributed behavior is replaced by the environment—the environment in which the species evolved and in which the behavior of the individual is shaped and maintained.

Take, for example, a "cognitive" activity, *attention*. A person responds to only a small part of the stimuli impinging upon him. The traditional view is that he himself determines which stimuli are to be effective—by paying attention to them. Some kind of inner gatekeeper allows some stimuli to enter and keeps all others out. A sudden or strong stimulus may break through and "attract" attention, but the person himself is otherwise in control. An analysis of the environmental circumstances reverses the relation. The kinds of stimuli that break through by "attracting attention" do so because they have been associated in the evolutionary history of the species or the personal history of the individual with important—e.g., dangerous—things. Less forceful stimuli attract attention only to the extent that they have figured in contingencies of reinforcement.

We can arrange contingencies that insure that an organism—even such a simple organism as a pigeon—will attend to one object and not to another, or to one property of an object, such as its color, and not to another, such as its shape. The inner gatekeeper is replaced by the contingencies that the person has been exposed to and that select the stimuli he reacts to.

Face

In the traditional view a person perceives the world around him and acts upon it to make it known to him. It has even been argued that the world would not exist if no one perceived it. The action is exactly reversed in an environmental analysis. There would, of course, be no perception if there were no world to perceive, but we would not perceive an existing world if there were no appropriate contingencies.

We say that a baby perceives his mother's face and knows it. Our evidence is that the baby responds in one way to his mother's face and in other ways to other faces or other things. He makes this distinction not through some mental act of perception but because of prior contingencies. Some of these may be contingencies of survival. The face and facial expressions of the human mother have been associated with security, warmth, food and other important things during both the evolution of the species and the life of the child.

The role of the environment is particularly subtle when what is known is the knower himself. If there is no external world to initiate knowing, must we not then say that the knower himself acts first? This is, of course, the field of consciousness or awareness which a scientific analysis of behavior is often accused of ignoring. The charge is a serious one and should be taken seriously.

Man is said to differ from the other animals mainly because he is "aware of his own existence." He knows what he is doing; he knows that he has had a past and will have a future; he alone follows the classical injunction, "Know thyself." Any analysis of human behavior that neglected these facts would be defective indeed. And some analyses do. "Methodological behaviorism" limits itself to what can be observed publicly; mental processes may exist, but their nature rules them out of scientific consideration. The "behaviorists" in political science and many logical positivists in philosophy have followed a similar line. But we can study self-observation, and we must include it in any reasonably complete account of human behavior. Rather than ignore consciousness, an experimental analysis of behavior has put much emphasis on certain crucial issues. The question is not whether a man can know himself but what he knows when he does so.

Skin

The problem arises in part from the indisputable fact of privacy: a small part of the universe is enclosed within a human skin. It would be foolish to deny the existence of that private world, but it is also foolish to assert that because it is private its nature is different from the world outside. The difference is not in the stuff that composes the private world but in its accessibility. There is an exclusive intimacy about a headache or heartache that has seemed to support the doctrine that knowing is a kind of possession.

The difficulty is that although privacy may bring the knower closer to what he knows, it interferes with the process through which he comes to know anything. As we have seen, contingencies under which a child learns to describe his feelings are necessarily defective; the verbal community cannot use the same procedures for this that it uses to teach a child to describe objects. There are, of course, natural contingencies under which we learn to respond to private stimuli, and they generate behavior of great precision; we could not walk if we were not stimulated by parts of our own body. But very little awareness is associated with this kind of behavior and, in fact, we behave in these ways most of the time without being aware of the stimuli to which we are responding. We do not attribute awareness to other species that obviously use similar private stimuli. To "know" private stimuli is more than to respond to them.

Help

The verbal community specializes in self-descriptive contingencies. It asks: What did you do yesterday? Why did you do that? How do you feel about that? The answers help persons adjust to each other effectively. And it is because such questions are asked that a person responds to himself and his behavior in the special way called knowing or being aware. Without the help of a verbal community all behavior would be unconscious. Consciousness is a social product. It is not only *not* the special field of autonomous man, it is not within the range of a solitary man.

And it is not within the range of accuracy of anyone. The privacy that seems to confer intimacy upon self-knowledge makes it impossible for the verbal community to maintain precise contingencies. Introspective vocabularies are by nature inaccurate, and that is one reason why they have varied so widely among schools of philosophy and psychology. Even a carefully trained observer runs into trouble when he studies new private stimuli.

Aware

Theories of psychotherapy that emphasize awareness assign a role to autonomous man that is the function of contingencies of reinforcement. Awareness may help if the problem is in part a lack of awareness, and "insight" into one's condition may help if one then takes remedial action. But awareness or insight alone is not always enough, and may be too much. One need not be aware of one's behavior or the conditions controlling it in order to behave effectively—or ineffectively.

The extent to which a man *should* be aware of himself depends upon the importance of self-observation for effective behavior. Self-knowledge is valuable only to the extent that it helps to meet the contingencies under which it has arisen.

Think

Perhaps the last stronghold of autonomous man is the complex "cognitive" activity called thinking. Because it is complex, it has yielded only slowly to explanation in terms of contingencies of reinforcement. We say that a person *forms a concept or an abstraction,* but all we see is that certain kinds of contingencies of reinforcement have brought a response under the control of a single property of a stimulus. We say that a person *recalls* or *remembers* what he has seen or heard but all we see is that the present occasion evokes a response, possibly in weakened or altered form, acquired on another occasion. We say that a person *associates* one word with another, but all we observe is that one verbal stimulus evokes the response previously made to another. Rather than suppose that it is therefore autonomous man who forms concepts or abstractions, recalls or remembers, and associates, we can put matters in good order simply by noting that these terms do not refer to forms of behavior.

A person may take explicit action, however, when he solves a problem. The creative artist may manipulate a medium until something of interest turns up. Much of this can be done covertly, and we are then likely to assign it to a different dimensional system; but it can always be done overtly, perhaps more slowly but also often more effectively, and with rare exceptions it must have been learned in overt form. The culture constructs special contingencies to promote thinking. It teaches a person to make fine discriminations by making differential reinforcement more precise. It teaches techniques to use in solving problems. It provides rules that make it unnecessary to expose a person to the contingencies from which the rules derive, and it provides rules for finding rules.

Self-control or self-management is a special kind of problem-solving that, like self-knowledge, raises all the issues associated with privacy. It is always the environment that builds the behavior with which we solve problems, even when the problems are found in the private world inside the skin. We have not investigated the matter of self-control in a very productive way, but the inadequacy of our analysis is no reason to fall back on a miracle-working mind. If our understanding of contingencies of reinforcement is not yet sufficient to explain all kinds of thinking, we must remember that the appeal to mind explains nothing at all.

Inside

In shifting control from autonomous man to the observable environment we do not leave an empty organism. A great deal goes on inside the skin, and physiology will eventually be able to tell us more about it. It will explain why behavior indeed relates to the antecedent events of which we can show it to be a function.

People do not always correctly understand the assignment. Many physiologists regard themselves as looking for the "physiological correlates" of mental events. They regard physiological research as simply a more scientific version of introspection. But physiological techniques are not, of course, designed to detect or measure personalities, feelings, or thoughts. At the moment neither introspection nor physiology supplies very adequate information about what is going on inside a man as he behaves, and since they are both directed inward they have the same effect of diverting attention from the external environment.

Much of the misunderstanding about an inner man comes from the metaphor of storage. Evolutionary and environmental histories change an organism, but they are not stored within it. Thus we observe that babies suck their mothers' breasts and can easily imagine that a strong tendency to do so has survival value, but much more is implied by a "sucking instinct" regarded as something a baby possesses that enables it to suck. The concept of "human nature" or "genetic endowment" is dangerous when we take it in that sense. We are closer to human nature in a baby than in an adult, or in a primitive culture than in an advanced one, in the sense that environmental contingencies are less likely to have obscured the genetic endowment, and it is tempting to dramatize that endowment by implying that earlier stages have survived in concealed form: man is a naked ape. But anatomists and physiologists will not find an ape, or for that matter, instincts. They will find anatomical and physiological features that are the product of an evolutionary history.

Sin

It is often said too that the personal history of the individual is stored within him as a "habit." The cigarette habit is talked of as being something more than the behavior said to show that a person possesses it. But the only other information we have is about the reinforcers and the schedules of reinforcement that make a person smoke a great deal. The contingencies are not stored; they simply leave a person changed.

The issue has had a curious place in theology. Does man sin because he is sinful, or is he sinful because he sins? Neither question points to anything very useful. To say that a man is sinful because he sins is to give an operational definition of sin. To say that he sins because he is sinful is to trace his behavior to a supposed inner trait. But whether a person engages in the kind of behavior called sinful depends upon circumstances not mentioned in either question. The sin assigned as an inner possession (the sin a person "knows") is to be found in a history of reinforcement.

Self

It is the nature of an experimental analysis of human behavior to strip away the functions previously assigned to autonomous man and transfer them one by one to the controlling environment. The analysis leaves less and less for autonomous man to do. But what about man himself? Is there not something about a person—a self —that is more than a living body?

A self is a repertoire of behavior appropriate to a given set of contingencies, and a substantial part of the conditions to which a person is exposed may play a dominant role. Under other conditions a person may sometimes report, "I'm not myself today" or "I couldn't have done what you said I did, because that's not like me." The identity conferred upon a self arises from the contingencies responsible for the behavior.

Split

Two or more repertoires generated by different sets of contingencies compose two or more selves. A person possesses one repertoire appropriate to his life with his friends and another appropriate to his life with his family. A problem of identity arises when a person finds himself with family and friends at the same time.

Self-knowledge and self-control imply two selves in this sense. The self-knower is almost always a product of social contingencies, but the self that is known may come from other sources. The controlling self (the conscience or superego) is of social origin, but the controlled self is more likely to be the product of genetic susceptibilities to reinforcement (the id or the Old Adam). The controlling self generally represents the interests of others; the controlled self the interests of the individual.

Stranger

The picture that emerges from a scientific analysis is not of a body with a person inside but of a body that *is* a person in the sense that it displays a complex repertoire of behavior. The picture is, of course, unfamiliar. The man we thus portray is a stranger, and from the traditional point of view he may not seem to be a man at all.

C. S. Lewis put it bluntly: "Man is being abolished."

There is clearly some difficulty in identifying the man to whom

Lewis referred. He cannot have meant the human species; far from being abolished, it is filling the earth. Nor are individual men growing less effective or productive. What is being abolished is autonomous man—the inner man, the homunculus, the possessing demon, the man defended by the literatures of freedom and dignity.

His abolition is long overdue. Autonomous man is a device we use to explain what we cannot explain in any other way. We constructed him from our ignorance, and as our understanding increases, the very stuff of which he is composed vanishes. Science does not dehumanize man, it de-homunculizes him, and it must do so if it is to prevent the abolition of the human species.

To man *qua* man we readily say good riddance. Only by dispossessing autonomous man can we turn to the real causes of human behavior—from the inferred to the observed, from the miraculous to the natural, from the inaccessible to the manipulable.

Purpose

It is often said that in doing so we must treat the man who survives as a mere animal. "Animal" is a pejorative term—but only because "man" has been made spuriously honorific. Joseph Wood Krutch argued that the traditional view supports Hamlet's exclamation "How like a god!" while Pavlov emphasized "How like a dog!" But that was a step forward. A god is the archetypal pattern of an explanatory fiction, of a miracle-working mind, of the metaphysical. Man is much more than a dog, but like a dog he is within range of a scientific analysis.

An important role of autonomous man has been to give direction to human behavior, and it is often said that in dispossessing an inner agent we leave man without a purpose: "Since a scientific psychology must regard human behavior objectively, as determined by necessary laws, it must represent human behavior as unintentional." But "necessary laws" would have this effect only if they referred exclusively to antecedent conditions. Intention and purpose refer to selective consequences, the effects of which we can formulate in "necessary laws." Has life, in all the forms in which it exists on the surface of the earth, a purpose? And is this evidence of intentional design? The primate hand evolved *in order that* the primate could more successfully manipulate things, but its purpose was to be found not in a prior design but rather in the process of selection. Similarly, in operant conditioning—when a pianist acquires the behavior of playing a smooth scale, for example—we find the purpose of the skilled movement of the hand in the consequences that follow it. In neither the evolution of the human hand nor in the acquired use of the hand is any prior intention or purpose at issue.

There is a difference between biological and individual purpose in that the latter can be felt. No one could have felt the purpose in the development of the human hand, but a person can in a sense feel the purpose with which he plays a smooth scale. But he does not play a smooth scale *because* he feels the purpose of doing so; what he feels is a by-product of his behavior and of its consequences. The relation of the human hand to the contingencies of survival under which it evolved is, of course, out of reach of personal observation; the relation of the behavior to contingencies of reinforcement that have generated it is not.

Control

As a scientific analysis of behavior dispossesses autonomous man and turns the control he has been said to exert over to the environment, the individual may seem particularly vulnerable. He is henceforth to be controlled by the world around him, and in large part by other men. Is he not then simply a victim? Certainly men have been victims, as they have been victimizers, but the word is too strong. It implies despoliation, which is by no means an essential consequence of interpersonal control. But even under benevolent control is the individual not helpless—"at a dead end in his long struggle to control his own destiny"?

It is only autonomous man who has reached a dead end. Man himself may be controlled by his environment, but it is an environment almost wholly of his own making. The physical environment of most persons is largely man-made—the walls that shelter them, the tools they use, the surfaces they walk on—and the social environment is obviously man-made. It generates the language a person speaks, the customs he follows, and the behavior he exhibits with respect to the ethical, religious, governmental, economic, educational and psychotherapeutic institutions that control him.

The evolution of a culture is in fact a kind of gigantic exercise in self-control. As the individual controls himself by manipulating the world he lives in, so the human species has constructed an environment in which its members behave in a highly effective way. Mistakes have been made, and we have no assurance that the environment man has constructed will continue to provide gains that outstrip the losses. But man as we know him, for better or for worse, is what man has made of man.

Roles

This will not satisfy those who cry "Victim!" C. S. Lewis protested: ". . . the power of man to make himself what he pleases . . . means . . . the power of some men to make other men what they please." This is inevitable in the nature of cultural evolution. We must distinguish the controlling self from the controlled self even when they are both inside the same skin, and when control is exercised through the design of an external environment, the selves are, with minor exceptions, distinct.

The person who, purposely or not, introduces a new cultural practice is only one among possibly billions it will affect. If this does not seem like an act of self-control, it is only because we have misunderstood the nature of self-control in the individual.

When a person changes his physical or social environment "intentionally"—that is, in order to change human behavior, possibly including his own—he plays two roles: one as a controller, as the designer of a controlling culture, and another as the controlled, as the product of a culture. There is nothing inconsistent about this; it follows from the nature of the evolution of a culture, with or without intentional design.

The human species probably has undergone little genetic change in recorded time. We have only to go back a thousand generations to reach the artists of the caves of Lascaux.[1] Features bearing directly on survival (such as resistance to disease) change substantially in a thousand generations, but the child of one of the Lascaux artists transplanted to the world of today might be almost indistinguishable from a modern child.

Man has improved himself enormously in the same period of time by changing the world he lives in. Modern religious practices developed over a hundred generations and modern government and law developed in fewer than a hundred. Perhaps no more than 20 generations have been needed to produce modern economic practices, and possibly no more than four or five to produce modern education, psychotherapy, and the physical and biological technologies that have increased man's sensitivity to the world around him and his power to change that world.

Change

Man has "controlled his own destiny," if that expression means anything at all. The man that man has made is the product of the culture man has devised. He has emerged from two quite different processes of evolution: biological and cultural. Both may now accelerate because both are subject to intentional design. Men have already changed their genetic endowment by breeding selectively and by changing contingencies of survival, and for a long time they have introduced cultural practices as cultural mutations. They may now begin to do both with a clearer eye to the consequences.

1. The reference is to the prehistoric paintings of animals on the walls of caves at Lascaux, in southern France.

Stage

The individual is the carrier of both his species and his culture. Cultural practices like genetic traits are transmitted from individual to individual. Even within the most regimented culture every personal history is unique. But the individual remains merely a stage in a process that began long before he came into existence and will long outlast him. He has no ultimate responsibility for a species trait or a cultural practice, even though it was he who underwent the mutation or introduced the practice that became part of the species or culture.

Even if Lamarck had been right in supposing that the individual could change his genetic structure through personal effort, we should have to point to the environmental circumstances responsible for the effort, as we shall have to do when geneticists begin to change the human endowment. And when an individual engages in the intentional design of a cultural practice, we must turn to the culture that induces him to do so and supplies the art or science he uses.

End

One of the great problems of individualism, seldom recognized as such, is death—the inescapable fate of the individual, the final assault on freedom and dignity. Death is one of those remote events that are brought to bear on behavior only with the aid of cultural practices. What we see is the death of others, as in Pascal's famous metaphor: "Imagine a number of men in chains, all under sentence of death, some of whom are each day butchered in the sight of others; those remaining see their own condition in that of their fellows, and looking at each other with grief and despair await their turn. This is an image of the human condition."

Some religions have made death more important by picturing a future existence in heaven or hell, but the individualist has a special reason to fear death: it is the prospect of personal annihilation. The individualist can find no solace in reflecting upon any contribution that will survive him. He has refused to be concerned for the survival of his culture and is not reinforced by the fact that the culture will long survive him. In the defense of his own freedom and dignity he has denied the contributions of the past and must therefore relinquish all claim upon the future.

Pictures

Science probably has never demanded a more sweeping change in a traditional way of thinking about a subject, nor has there ever been a more important subject. In the traditional picture a person perceives the world around him, selects features to be perceived, discriminates among them, judges them good or bad, changes them to make them better (or worse), and may be held responsible for his action and justly rewarded or punished for its consequences. In the scientific picture a person is a member of a species shaped by evolutionary contingencies of survival, displaying behavioral processes that bring him under the control of the environment in which he lives, and largely under the control of a social environment that he and millions of others like him have constructed and maintained during the evolution of a culture. The direction of the controlling relation is reserved: a person does not act upon the world; the world acts upon him.

It is difficult to accept such a change simply on intellectual grounds and nearly impossible to accept its implications. The reaction of the traditionalist is usually described in terms of feelings. One of these, to which the Freudians have appealed in explaining the resistance to psychoanalysis, is wounded vanity. Freud himself expounded, as Ernest Jones said, "the three heavy blows which narcissism or self-love of mankind has suffered at the hands of science. The first was cosmological and was dealt by Copernicus; the second was biological and was dealt by Darwin; the third was psychological and was dealt by Freud."

But what are the signs or symptoms of wounded vanity, and how shall we explain them? What people do about a scientific picture of man is to call it wrong, demeaning and dangerous, to argue against it, and to attack those who propose or defend it. These are signs of wounded vanity only to the extent that the scientific formulation destroys accustomed reinforcers. If a person can no longer take credit or be admired for what he does, then he seems to suffer a loss of dignity or worth, and behavior previously reinforced by credit or admiration will undergo extinction. Extinction often leads to aggressive attack.

Futility

Another effect of the scientific picture has been described as a loss of faith or "nerve," as a sense of doubt or powerlessness, or as discouragement, depression, or despondency. A person is said to feel that he can do nothing about his own destiny, but what he feels is a weakening of old responses that are no longer reinforced.

Another effect is a kind of nostalgia. Old repertoires break through as traditionalists seize upon and exaggerate similarities between present and past. They call the old days the good old days, when people recognized the inherent dignity of man and the importance of spiritual values. These fragments of outmoded behavior tend to be wistful—that is, they have the character of increasingly unsuccessful behavior.

Rainbow

These reactions to a scientific conception of man are, of course, unfortunate. They immobilize men of good will, and anyone concerned with the future of his culture will do what he can to correct them. No theory changes what it is a theory about. We change nothing because we look at it, talk about it, or analyze it in a new way. Keats drank confusion to Newton for analyzing the rainbow, but the rainbow remained as beautiful as ever and became for many even more beautiful.

Man has not changed because we look at him, talk about him, and analyze him scientifically. His achievements in science, government, religion, art and literature remain as they have always been, to be admired as one admires a storm at sea or autumn foliage or a mountain peak, quite apart from their origins and untouched by a scientific analysis. What does change is our chance of doing something about the subject of a theory. Newton's analysis of the light in a rainbow was a step in the direction of the laser.

Perils

The traditional conception of man is flattering; it confers reinforcing privileges. It is therefore easy to defend and difficult to change. It was designed to build up the individual as an instrument of countercontrol, and it did so effectively, but in such a way as to limit future progress.

We have seen how the literatures of freedom and dignity, with their concern for autonomous man, have perpetuated the use of punishment and condoned the use of only weak nonpunitive techniques. It is not difficult to demonstrate a connection between the unlimited right of the individual to pursue happiness and the catastrophes threatened by unchecked breeding, the unrestrained affluence that exhausts resources and pollutes the environment, and the imminence of nuclear war.

Physical and biological technologies have alleviated pestilence and famine and the painful, dangerous and exhausting features of daily life, and a behavioral technology can begin to alleviate other kinds of ills. In the analysis of human behavior it is just possible that we are slightly beyond Newton's position in the analysis of light, for we are beginning to make technological applications, and there are wonderful possibilities—all the more wonderful because traditional approaches have been so ineffective.

It is hard to imagine a world in which people live together without quarreling, maintain themselves by producing the food, shelter and clothing they need, enjoy themselves and contribute to the enjoyment of others in art, music, literature and games, consume only a reasonable part of the resources of the world and add as little as possible to its pollution, bear no more children than they can raise decently, continue to explore the world around them and discover better ways of dealing with it, and come to know themselves and the world around them accurately and comprehensively. Yet all this is possible. We have not yet seen what man can make of man.

1971

QUESTIONS

1. *What does Skinner say to indicate that he expects disagreement? Does he make any concessions in his address to his readers that would suggest an effort to win over those who disagree with him?*
2. *Is Skinner an optimist or a pessimist?*
3. *Is Skinner hard to read because his ideas are strange and disturbing or is his writing bad? Does Orwell's "Politics and the English Language" (pp. 200–211) offer any help in answering this question?*

JEROME S. BRUNER
Freud and the Image of Man

By the dawn of the sixth century before Christ, the Greek physicist-philosophers had formulated a bold conception of the physical world as a unitary material phenomenon. The Ionians had set forth a conception of matter as fundamental substance, transformation of which accounted for the myriad forms and substances of the physical world. Anaximander was subtle enough to recognize that matter must be viewed as a generalized substance, free of any particular sensuous properties. Air, iron, water or bone were only elaborated forms, derived from a more general stuff. Since that time, the phenomena of the physical world have been conceived as continuous and monistic, as governed by the common laws of matter. The view was a bold one, bold in the sense of running counter to the immediate testimony of the senses. It has served as an axiomatic basis of physics for more than two millennia. The bold view eventually became the obvious view, and it gave shape to our common understanding of the physical world. Even the alchemists rested their case upon this doctrine of material continuity and, indeed, had they known about neutron bombardment, they might even have hit upon the proper philosopher's stone.

The good fortune of the physicist—and these matters are always relative, for the material monism of physics may have impeded nineteenth-century thinking and delayed insights into the nature of complementarity in modern physical theory—this early good fortune or happy insight has no counterpart in the sciences of man. Lawful continuity between man and the animal kingdom, between dreams and unreason on one side and waking rationality on the other, between madness and sanity, between consciousness and unconsciousness, between the mind of the child and the adult mind, between primitive and civilized man—each of these has been a cherished discontinuity preserved in doctrinal canons. There were voices in each generation, to be sure, urging the exploration of continuities. Anaximander had a passing good approximation to a theory of evolution based on natural selection; Cornelius Agrippa offered a plausible theory of the continuity of mental health and disease in terms of bottled-up sexuality. But Anaximander did not prevail against Greek conceptions of man's creation nor did Cornelius Agrippa against the demonopathy of the *Malleus Maleficarum*.[1] Neither in establishing the continuity between the varied states of man nor in pursuing the continuity between man and animal was there conspicuous success until the nineteenth century.

I need not insist upon the social, ethical, and political significance of an age's image of man, for it is patent that the view one takes of man affects profoundly one's standard of dignity and the humanly possible. And it is in the light of such a standard that we establish our laws, set our aspirations for learning, and judge the fitness of men's acts. Those who govern, then, must perforce be jealous guardians of man's ideas about man, for the structure of government rests upon an uneasy consensus about human nature and human wants. Since the idea of man is of the order of *res publica*,[2] it is an idea not subject to change without public debate. Nor is it simply a matter of public concern. For man as individual has a deep and emotional investment in his image of himself. If we have learned anything in the last half-century of psychology, it is that man has powerful and exquisite capacities for defending himself against violation of his cherished self-image. This is not to say that Western man has not persistently asked: "What is man that thou art mindful of him?" It is only that the question, when pressed, brings us to the edge of anxiety where inquiry is no longer free.

Two figures stand out massively as the architects of our present-day conception of man: Darwin and Freud. Freud's was the more daring, the more revolutionary, and in a deep sense, the more poetic insight. But Freud is inconceivable without Darwin. It is both timely and perhaps historically just to center our inquiry on Freud's contribution to the modern image of man. Darwin I shall treat as a

---

1. *The Hammer for Evil Doers*, a notorious medieval book about demons and witchcraft.

2. The state.

necessary condition for Freud and for his success, recognizing, of course, that this is a form of psychological license. Not only is it the centenary of Freud's birth; it is also a year in which the current of popular thought expressed in commemoration of the date quickens one's awareness of Freud's impact on our times.

Rear-guard fundamentalism did not require a Darwin to slay it in an age of technology. He helped, but this contribution was trivial in comparison with another. What Darwin had done was to propose a set of principles unified around the conception that all organic species had their origins and took their form from a common set of circumstances—the requirements of biological survival. All living creatures were on a common footing. When the post-Darwin era of exaggeration had passed and religious literalism had abated into a new nominalism, what remained was a broad, orderly, and unitary conception of organic nature, a vast continuity from the monocellular protozoans to man. Biology had at last found its unifying principle in the doctrine of evolution. Man was not unique but the inheritor of an organic legacy.

As the summit of an evolutionary process, man could still view himself with smug satisfaction, indeed proclaim that God or Nature had shown a persistent wisdom in its effort to produce a final, perfect product. It remained for Freud to present the image of man as the unfinished product of nature: struggling against unreason, impelled by driving inner vicissitudes and urges that had to be contained if man were to live in society, host alike to seeds of madness and majesty, never fully free from an infancy anything but innocent. What Freud was proposing was that man at his best and man at his worst is subject to a common set of explanations: that good and evil grow from a common process.

Freud was strangely yet appropriately fitted for his role as architect of a new conception of man. We must pause to examine his qualifications, for the image of man that he created was in no small measure founded on his painfully achieved image of himself and of his times. We are concerned not so much with his psychodynamics, as with the intellectual traditions he embodies. A child of his century's materialism, he was wedded to the determinism and the classical physicalism of nineteenth-century physiology so boldly represented by Helmholtz. Indeed, the young Freud's devotion to the exploration of anatomical structures was a measure of the strength of this inheritance. But at the same time, as both Lionel Trilling and W. H. Auden have recognized with much sensitivity, there was a deep current of romanticism in Freud—a sense of the role of impulse, of the drama of life, of the power of symbolism, of ways of knowing that were more poetic than rational in spirit, of the poet's cultural alienation. It was perhaps this romantic's sense of drama that led to his gullibility about parental seduction and to his generous susceptibility to the fallacy of the dramatic instance.

Freud also embodies two traditions almost as antithetical as romanticism and nineteenth-century scientism. He was profoundly a Jew, not in a doctrinal sense but in his conception of morality, in his love of the skeptical play of reason, in his distrust of illusion, in the form of his prophetic talent, even in his conception of mature eroticism. His prophetic talent was antithetic to a Utopianism either of innocence or of social control. Nor did it lead to a counsel of renunciation. Free oneself of illusion, of neurotic infantilism, and "the soft voice of intellect" would prevail. Wisdom for Freud was neither doctrine nor formula, but the achievement of maturity. The patient who is cured is the one who is now free enough of neurosis to decide intelligently about his own destiny. As for his conception of mature love, it has always seemed to me that its blend of tenderness and sensuality combined the uxorious imagery of the Chassidic tradition[3] and the sensual quality of the Song of Songs. And might it not have been Freud rather than a commentator of the Haftorahs[4] who said, "In children, it was taught, God gives humanity a chance to make good its mistakes." For the modern trend of permissiveness toward children is surely a feature of the Freudian legacy.

But for all the Hebraic quality, Freud is also in the classical tradition—combining the Stoics and the great Greek dramatists. For Freud as for the Stoics, there is no possibility of man disobeying the laws of nature. And yet, it is in this lawfulness that for him the human drama inheres. His love for Greek drama and his use of it in his formulation are patent. The sense of the human tragedy, the inevitable working out of the human plight—these are the hallmarks of Freud's case histories. When Freud, the tragic dramatist, becomes a therapist, it is not to intervene as a directive authority. The therapist enters the drama of the patient's life, makes possible a play within a play, the transference, and when the patient has "worked through" and understood the drama, he has achieved the wisdom necessary for freedom. Again, like the Stoics, it is in the recognition of one's own nature and in the acceptance of the laws that govern it that the good life is to be found.

Freud's contribution lies in the continuities of which he made us aware. The first of these is the continuity of organic lawfulness. Accident in human affairs was no more to be brooked as "explanation" than accident in nature. The basis for accepting such an "obvious" proposition had, of course, been well prepared by a bur-

---

3. Or Hasidic; the reference is to a Jewish sect devoted to mystical rather than secular study.

4. The Old Testament Prophets.

geoning nineteenth-century scientific naturalism. It remained for Freud to extend naturalistic explanation to the heart of human affairs. The *Psychopathology of Everyday Life* is not one of Freud's deeper works, but "the Freudian slip" has contributed more to the common acceptance of lawfulness in human behavior than perhaps any of the more rigorous and academic formulations from Wundt to the present day. The forgotten lunch engagement, the slip of the tongue, the barked shin could no longer be dismissed as accident. Why Freud should have succeeded where the novelists, philosophers, and academic psychologists had failed we will consider in a moment.

Freud's extension of Darwinian doctrine beyond Haeckel's theorem that ontogeny recapitulates phylogeny[5] is another contribution to continuity. It is the conception that in the human mind, the primitive, infantile, and archaic exist side-by-side with the civilized and evolved.

Where animals are concerned we hold the view that the most highly developed have arisen from the lowest. . . . In the realm of mind, on the other hand, the primitive type is so commonly preserved alongside the transformations which have developed out of it that it is superfluous to give instances in proof of it. When this happens, it is usually the result of a bifurcation in development. One quantitative part of an attitude or an impulse has survived unchanged while another has undergone further development. This brings us very close to the more general problem of conservation in the mind. . . . Since the time when we recognized the error of supposing that ordinary forgetting signified destruction or annihilation of the memory-trace, we have been inclined to the opposite view that nothing once formed in the mind could ever perish, that everything survives in some way or other, and is capable under certain conditions of being brought to light again . . . (Freud, *Civilization and Its Discontents*, pp. 14–15).

What has now come to be common sense is that in everyman there is the potentiality for criminality, and that these are neither accidents nor visitations of degeneracy, but products of a delicate balance of forces that, under different circumstances, might have produced normality or even saintliness. Good and evil, in short, grow from a common root.

Freud's genius was in his resolution of polarities. The distinction of child and adult was one such. It did not suffice to reiterate that the child was father to the man. The theory of infantile sexuality and the stages of psychosexual development were an effort to fill the gap, the latter clumsy, the former elegant. Though the alleged progression of sexual expression from the oral, to the anal, to the phal-

5. That is, the evolution of the fetus into an independent organism parallels the evolutionary development of that species.

lic, and finally to the genital has not found a secure place either in common sense or in general psychology, the developmental continuity of sexuality has been recognized by both. Common sense honors the continuity in the baby-books and in the permissiveness with which young parents of today resolve their doubts. And the research of Beach and others has shown the profound effects of infantile experience on adult sexual behavior—even in lower organisms.

If today people are reluctant to report their dreams with the innocence once attached to such recitals, it is again because Freud brought into common question the discontinuity between the rational purposefulness of waking life and the seemingly irrational purposelessness of fantasy and dream. While the crude symbolism of Freud's early efforts at dream interpretation has come increasingly to be abandoned—that telephone poles and tunnels have an invariant sexual reference—the conception of the dream as representing disguised wishes and fears has become common coin. And Freud's recognition of deep unconscious processes in the creative act, let it also be said, has gone far toward enriching our understanding of the kinship between the artist, the humanist, and the man of science.

Finally, it is our heritage from Freud that the all-or-none distinction between mental illness and mental health has been replaced by a more humane conception of the continuity of these states. The view that neurosis is a severe reaction to human trouble is as revolutionary in its implications for social practice as it is daring in formulation. The "bad seed" theories, the nosologies of the nineteenth century, the demonologies and doctrines of divine punishment—none of these provided a basis for compassion toward human suffering comparable to that of our time.

One may argue, at last, that Freud's sense of the continuity of human conditions, of the likeness of the human plight, has made possible a deeper sense of the brotherhood of man. It has in any case tempered the spirit of punitiveness toward what once we took as evil and what we now see as sick. We have not yet resolved the dilemma posed by these two ways of viewing. Its resolution is one of the great moral challenges of our age.

Why, after such initial resistance, were Freud's views so phenomenally successful in transforming common conceptions of man?

One reason we have already considered: the readiness of the Western world to accept a naturalistic explanation of organic phenomena and, concurrently, to be readier for such explanation in the mental sphere. There had been at least four centuries of uninterrupted scientific progress, recently capped by a theory of evolution that brought man into continuity with the rest of the animal kingdom. The rise of naturalism as a way of understanding nature and man witnessed a corresponding decline in the explanatory aspirations of religion. By the close of the nineteenth century, religion, to use Morton White's phrase, "too often agreed to accept the role of a non-scientific spiritual grab-bag, or an ideological know-nothing." The elucidation of the human plight had been abandoned by religion and not yet adopted by science.

It was the inspired imagery, the proto-theory of Freud that was to fill the gap. Its success in transforming the common conception of man was not simply its recourse to the "cause-and-effect" discourse of science. Rather it is Freud's imagery, I think, that provides the clue to this ideological power. It is an imagery of necessity, one that combines the dramatic, the tragic, and the scientific views of necessity. It is here that Freud's intellectual heritage matters so deeply. Freud's is a theory or a proto-theory peopled with actors. The characters are from life: the blind, energic, pleasure-seeking id; the priggish and punitive super-ego; the ego, battling for its being by diverting the energy of the others to its own use. The drama has an economy and a terseness. The ego develops canny mechanisms for dealing with the threat of id impulses: denial, projection,[6] and the rest. Balances are struck between the actors, and in the balance is character and neurosis. Freud was using the dramatic technique of decomposition, the play whose actors are parts of a single life. It is a technique that he himself had recognized in fantasies and dreams, one he honored in "The Poet and the Daydream."

The imagery of the theory, moreover, has an immediate resonance with the dialectic of experience. True, it is not the stuff of superficial conscious experience. But it fits the human plight, its conflictedness, its private torment, its impulsiveness, its secret and frightening urges, its tragic quality.

Concerning its scientific imagery, it is marked by the necessity of the classical mechanics. At times the imagery is hydraulic: suppress this stream of impulses, and perforce it breaks out in a displacement elsewhere. The system is a closed and mechanical one. At times it is electrical, as when cathexes are formed and withdrawn like electrical charges. The way of thought fitted well the common-sense physics of its age.

Finally, the image of man presented was thoroughly secular; its ideal type was the mature man free of infantile neuroticism, capable of finding his own way. This freedom from both Utopianism and asceticism has earned Freud the contempt of ideological totalitarians of the Right and the Left. But the image has found a ready home in the rising, liberal intellectual middle class. For them, the Freudian ideal type has become a rallying point in the struggle against spiritual regimentation.

I have said virtually nothing about Freud's equation of sexuality

---

6. The attribution to others of one's own feelings.

and impulse. It was surely and still is a stimulus to resistance. But to say that Freud's success lay in forcing a reluctant Victorian world to accept the importance of sexuality is as empty as hailing Darwin for his victory over fundamentalism. Each had a far more profound effect.

Can Freud's contribution to the common understanding of man in the twentieth century be likened to the impact of such great physical and biological theories as Newtonian physics and Darwin's conception of evolution? The question is an empty one. Freud's mode of thought is not a theory in the conventional sense, it is a metaphor, an analogy, a way of conceiving man, a drama. I would propose that Anaximander is the proper parallel: his view of the connectedness of physical nature was also an analogy—and a powerful one. Freud is the ground from which theory will grow, and he has prepared the twentieth century to nurture the growth. But far more important, he has provided an image of man that has made him comprehensible without at the same time making him contemptible.

1956

EDWARD O. WILSON

Sex

Sex is central to human biology and a protean phenomenon that permeates every aspect of our existence and takes new forms through each step in the life cycle. Its complexity and ambiguity are due to the fact that sex is not designed primarily for reproduction. Evolution has devised much more efficient ways for creatures to multiply than the complicated procedures of mating and fertilization. Bacteria simply divide in two (in many species, every twenty minutes), fungi shed immense numbers of spores, and hydras bud offspring directly from their trunks. Each fragment of a shattered sponge grows into an entire new organism. If multiplication were the only purpose of reproductive behavior, our mammalian ancestors could have evolved without sex. Every human being might be asexual and sprout new offspring from the surface cells of a neutered womb. Even now, a swift, bacterium-like method of asexual reproduction occurs on the rare occasions when identical twins are created by a single division of an already fertilized egg.

Nor is the primary function of sex the giving and receiving of pleasure. The vast majority of animal species perform the sexual act

mechanically and with minimal foreplay. Pairs of bacteria and protozoans form sexual unions without the benefit of a nervous system,
while corals, clams, and many other invertebrate animals simply
shed their sex cells into the surrounding water—literally without
giving the matter a thought, since they lack a proper brain. Pleasure
is at best an enabling device for animals that copulate, a means for
inducing creatures with versatile nervous systems to make the heavy
investment of time and energy required for courtship, sexual intercourse, and parenting.

Moreover, sex is in every sense a gratuitously consuming and risky
activity. The reproductive organs of human beings are anatomically
complex in ways that make them subject to lethal malfunctions,
such as ectopic pregnancy and venereal disease. Courtship activities
are prolonged beyond the minimal needs of signaling. They are energetically expensive and even dangerous, to the degree that the more
ardent are put at greater risk of being killed by rivals or predators.
At the microscopic level, the genetic devices by which sex is determined are finely tuned and easily disturbed. In human beings one
sex chromosome too few or too many, or a subtle shift in the hormone balance of a developing fetus, creates abnormalities in physiology and behavior.

Thus sex by itself lends no straightforward Darwinian advantage.
Moreover, sexual reproduction automatically imposes a genetic
deficit. If an organism multiplies without sex, all of its offspring will
be identical to itself. If, on the other hand, an organism accepts
sexual partnership with another, unrelated individual, half the genes
in each of its offspring will be of alien origin. With each generation
thereafter, the investment in genes per descendant will be cut in
half.

So there are good reasons for reproduction to be nonsexual: It
can be made private, direct, safe, energetically cheap, and selfish.
Why, then, has sex evolved?

The principal answer is that sex creates diversity. And diversity is
the way a parent hedges its bets against an unpredictably changing
environment. Imagine a case of two animal species, both of which
consist entirely of individuals carrying two genes. Let us arbitrarily
label one gene A and the other a. For instance, these genes might
be for brown (A) versus blue (a) eye color, or right-handedness
(A) versus left-handedness (a). Each individual is Aa because it
possesses both genes. Suppose that one species reproduces without
sex. Then all the offspring of every parent will be Aa.

The other population uses sex for reproduction; it produces sex
cells, each of which contains only one of the genes, A or a. When
two individuals mate they combine their sex cells, and since each
adult contributes sex cells bearing either A or a, three kinds of

offspring are possible: AA, Aa, and aa. So, from a starting popula-tion of Aa individuals, asexual parents can produce only Aa offspring, while sexual parents can produce AA, Aa, and aa offspring. Now let the environment change—say a hard winter, a flood, or the invasion of a dangerous predator—so that aa individu-als are favored. In the next generation, the sexually reproducing population will have the advantage and will consist predominantly of aa organisms until conditions change to favor, perhaps, AA or Aa individuals.

Diversity, and thus adaptability, explains why so many kinds of organisms bother with sexual reproduction. They vastly outnumber the species that rely on the direct and simple but, in the long run, less prudent modes of sexless multiplication.

Then why are there usually just two sexes? It is theoretically pos-sible to evolve a sexual system based on one sex—anatomically uni-form individuals who produce identically shaped reproductive cells and combine them indiscriminately. Some lower plants do just that. It is also possible to have hundreds of sexes, which is the mode among some fungi. But a two-sex system prevails through most of the living world. This system appears to permit the most efficient possible division of labor.

The quintessential female is an individual specialized for making eggs. The large size of the egg enables it to resist drying, to survive adverse periods by consuming stored yolk, to be moved to safety by the parent, and to divide at least a few times after fertilization before needing to ingest nutrients from the outside. The male is defined as the manufacturer of the sperm, the little gamete. A sperm is a minimum cellular unit, stripped down to a head packed with DNA and powered by a tail containing just enough stored energy to carry the vehicle to the egg.

When the two gametes unite in fertilization they create an instant mixture of genes surrounded by the durable housing of the egg. By cooperating to create zygotes, the female and male make it more likely that at least some of their offspring will survive in the event of a changing environment. A fertilized egg differs from an asexually reproducing cell in one fundamental respect: it contains a newly assembled mixture of genes.

The anatomical difference between the two kinds of sex cell is often extreme. In particular, the human egg is eighty-five thousand times larger than the human sperm. The consequences of this gametic dimorphism ramify throughout the biology and psychology of human sex. The most important immediate result is that the female places a greater investment in each of her sex cells. A woman can expect to produce only about four hundred eggs in her lifetime. Of these a maximum of about twenty can be converted into healthy infants. The costs of bringing an infant to term and caring for it afterward are relatively enormous. In contrast, a man releases 100 million sperm with each ejaculation. Once he has achieved fertilization his purely physical commitment has ended. His genes will benefit equally with those of the female, but his investment will be far less than hers unless she can induce him to contribute to the care of the offspring. If a man were given total freedom to act, he could theoretically inseminate thousands of women in his lifetime.

The resulting conflict of interest between the sexes is a property of not only human beings but also the majority of animal species. Males are characteristically aggressive, especially toward one another and most intensely during the breeding season. In most species, assertiveness is the most profitable male strategy. During the full period of time it takes to bring a fetus to term, from the fertilization of the egg to the birth of the infant, one male can fertilize many females but a female can be fertilized by only one male. Thus if males are able to court one female after another, some will be big winners and others will be absolute losers, while virtually all healthy females will succeed in being fertilized. It pays males to be aggressive, hasty, fickle, and undiscriminating. In theory it is more profitable for females to be coy, to hold back until they can identify males with the best genes. In species that rear young, it is also important for the females to select males who are more likely to stay with them after insemination.

Human beings obey this biological principle faithfully. It is true that the thousands of existing societies are enormously variable in the details of their sexual mores and the division of labor between the sexes. This variation is based on culture. Societies mold their customs to the requirements of the environment and in so doing duplicate in totality a large fraction of the arrangements encountered throughout the remainder of the animal kingdom: from strict monogamy to extreme forms of polygamy, and from a close approach to unisex to extreme differences between men and women in behavior and dress. People change their attitudes consciously and at will; the reigning fashion of a society can shift within a generation. Nevertheless, this flexibility is not endless, and beneath it all lie general features that conform closely to the expectations from evolutionary theory. So let us concentrate initially on the biologically significant generalities and defer, for the moment, consideration of the undeniably important plasticity controlled by culture.

We are, first of all, moderately polygynous, with males initiating most of the changes in sexual partnership. About three-fourths of all human societies permit the taking of multiple wives, and most of them encourage the practice by law and custom. In contrast, marriage to multiple husbands is sanctioned in less than one percent of societies. The remaining monogamous societies usually fit that category in a legal sense only, with concubinage and other extramarital stratagems being added to allow de facto polygyny.

Because women are commonly treated by men as a limited resource and hence as valued property, they are the beneficiaries of hypergamy, the practice of marrying upward in social position. Polygyny and hypergamy are essentially complementary strategies. In diverse cultures men pursue and acquire, while women are protected and bartered. Sons sow wild oats and daughters risk being ruined. When sex is sold, men are usually the buyers. It is to be expected that prostitutes are the despised members of society; they have abandoned their valuable reproductive investment to strangers. In the twelfth century, Maimonides[1] neatly expressed this biological logic as follows:

For fraternal sentiments and mutual love and mutual help can be found in their perfect form only among those who are related by their ancestry. Accordingly a single tribe that is united through a common ancestor —even if he is remote—because of this, love one another, help one another, and have pity on one another; and the attainment of these things is the greatest purpose of the Law. Hence *harlots* are prohibited, because through them lines of ancestry are destroyed. For a child born of them is a stranger to the people; no one knows to what family group he belongs, and no one in his family group knows him; and this is the worst of conditions for him and his father.

Anatomy bears the imprint of the sexual division of labor. Men are on the average 20 to 30 percent heavier than women. Pound for pound, they are stronger and quicker in most categories of sport. The proportion of their limbs, their skeletal torsion, and the density of their muscles are particularly suited for running and throwing, the archaic specialties of the ancestral hunter-gatherer males. The world track records reflect the disparity. Male champions are always between 5 and 20 percent faster than women champions: in 1974 the difference was 8 percent in the 100 meters, 11 percent in the 400 meters, 15 percent in the mile, 10 percent in the 10,000 meters, and so on through every distance. Even in the marathon, where size and brute strength count least, the difference was 13 percent. Women marathoners have comparable endurance, but men are faster—their champions run twenty-six five-minute miles one after another. The gap cannot be attributed to a lack of incentive and training. The great women runners of East Germany and the Soviet Union are the products of nationwide recruitment and scientifically planned training programs. Yet their champions, who con-

1. Twelfth-century rabbi and philosopher.

sistently set Olympic and world records, could not place in an average men's regional track meet. The overlap in performances between all men and women is of course great; the best women athletes are better than most male athletes, and women's track and field is an exciting competitive world of its own. But there is a substantial difference between average and best performances. The leading woman marathon runner in the United States in 1975, for example, would have ranked 752d in the national men's listing. Size is not the determinant. The smaller male runners, at 125 to 130 pounds, perform as well relative to women as do their taller and heavier competitors.

It is of equal importance that women match or surpass men in a few other sports, and these are among the ones furthest removed from the primitive techniques of hunting and aggression: long-distance swimming, the more acrobatic events of gymnastics, precision (but not distance) archery, and small-bore rifle shooting. As sports and sport-like activities evolve into more sophisticated channels dependent on skill and agility, the overall achievements of men and women can be expected to converge more closely.

The average temperamental differences between the human sexes are also consistent with the generalities of mammalian biology. Women as a group are less assertive and physically aggressive. The magnitude of the distinction depends on the culture. It ranges from a tenuous, merely statistical difference in egalitarian settings to the virtual enslavement of women in some extreme polygynous societies. But the variation in degree is not nearly so important as the fact that women differ consistently in this qualitative manner regardless of the degree. The fundamental average difference in personality traits is seldom if ever transposed.

The physical and temperamental differences between men and women have been amplified by culture into universal male dominance. History records not a single society in which women have controlled the political and economic lives of men. Even when queens and empresses ruled, their intermediaries remained primarily male. At the present writing not a single country has a woman as head of state, although Golda Meir of Israel and Indira Gandhi of India were, until recently, assertive, charismatic leaders of their countries. In about 75 percent of societies studied by anthropologists, the bride is expected to move from the location of her own family to that of her husband, while only 10 percent require the reverse exchange. Lineage is reckoned exclusively through the male line at least five times more frequently than it is through the female line. Men have traditionally assumed the positions of chieftains, shamans, judges, and warriors. Their modern technocratic counterparts rule the industrial states and head the corporations and churches.

These differences are a simple matter of record—but what is their significance for the future? How easily can they be altered?

It is obviously of vital social importance to try to make a value-free assessment of the relative contributions of heredity and environment to the differentiation of behavioral roles between the sexes. Here is what I believe the evidence shows: modest genetic differences exist between the sexes; the behavioral genes interact with virtually all existing environments to create a noticeable divergence in early psychological development; and the divergence is almost always widened in later psychological development by cultural sanctions and training. Societies can probably cancel the modest genetic differences entirely by careful planning and training, but the convergence will require a conscious decision based on fuller and more exact knowledge than is now available.

The evidence for a genetic difference in behavior is varied and substantial. In general, girls are predisposed to be more intimately sociable and less physically venturesome. From the time of birth, for example, they smile more than boys. This trait may be especially revealing, since * * * the infant smile, of all human behaviors, is most fully innate in that its form and function are virtually invariant. Several independent studies have shown that newborn females respond more frequently than males with eyes-closed, reflexive smiling. The habit is soon replaced by deliberate, communicative smiling that persists into the second year of life. Frequent smiling then becomes one of the more persistent of female traits and endures through adolescence and maturity. By the age of six months, girls also pay closer attention to sights and sounds used in communication than they do to nonsocial stimuli. Boys of the same age make no such distinction. The ontogeny then proceeds as follows: one-year-old girls react with greater fright and inhibition to clay faces, and they are more reluctant to leave their mothers' sides in novel situations. Older girls remain more affiliative and less physically venturesome than boys of the same age.

In her study of the !Kung San, Patricia Draper found no difference in the way young boys and girls are reared. All are supervised closely but unobtrusively and are seldom given any work. Yet boys wander out of view and earshot more frequently than girls, and older boys appear to be slightly more prone to join the men hunters than are the girls to join the women gatherers. In still closer studies, N. G. Blurton Jones and Melvin J. Konner found that boys also engage more frequently in rough-and-tumble play and overt aggression. They also associate less with adults than do girls. From these subtle differences the characteristic strong sexual division of labor in !Kung encampments emerges by small steps.

In Western cultures boys are also more venturesome than girls and more physically aggressive on the average. Eleanor Maccoby and Carol Jacklin, in their review *The Psychology of Sex Differences*, concluded that this male trait is deeply rooted and could have a genetic origin. From the earliest moments of social play, at age 2 to 2½ years, boys are more aggressive in both words and actions. They have a larger number of hostile fantasies and engage more often in mock fighting, overt threats, and physical attacks, which are directed preferentially at other boys during efforts to acquire dominance status. Other studies, summarized by Ronald P. Rohner, indicate that the differences exist in many cultures.

The skeptic favoring a totally environmental explanation might still argue that the early divergence in role playing has no biological component but is merely a response to biased training practices during very early childhood. If it occurs, the training would have to be subtle, at least partly unconscious in application, and practiced by parents around the world. The hypothesis of total environmentalism is made more improbable by recent evidence concerning the biology of hermaphrodites, who are genetically female but acquire varying degrees of masculine anatomy during the early stages of fetal development. The anomaly occurs in one of two ways.

The first is a rare hereditary condition caused by a change in a single gene site and known as the female adrenogenital syndrome. In either sex, possession of two of the altered genes—hence, a complete lack of the normal gene in each cell of the body—prevents the adrenal glands from manufacturing their proper hormone, cortisol. In its place the adrenal glands secrete a precursor substance which has an action similar to that of the male sex hormone. If the individual is genetically male, the hormonal boost has no significant effect on sexual development. If the fetus is female, the abnormal level of male hormone alters the external genitalia in the direction of maleness. Sometimes the clitoris of such an individual is enlarged to resemble a small penis, and the labia majora are closed. In extreme cases a full penis and empty scrotum are developed.

The second means of producing the effect is by artificial hormone treatment. During the 1950s women were often given progestins, a class of artificial substances that act like progesterone, the normal hormone of pregnancy, to help them prevent miscarriages. It was discovered that in a few cases progestins, by exerting a masculinizing effect on female fetuses, transformed them into hermaphrodites of the same kind caused by the female adrenogenital syndrome.

By sheer accident the hormone-induced hermaphrodites approach a properly controlled scientific experiment designed to estimate the influence of heredity on sex differences. The experiment is not perfect, but it is as good as any other we are likely to encounter. The hermaphrodites are genetically female, and their internal sexual organs are fully female. In most of the cases studied in the United States, the external genitalia were altered surgically to an entirely female condition during infancy, and the individuals were then reared as girls. These children were subjected during fetal development to male hormones or to substances that mimic them but then "trained" to be ordinary girls until maturity. In such cases it is possible to dissect the effects of learning from the effects of deeper biological alterations, which in some cases stem directly from a known gene mutation. Behavioral maleness would almost certainly have to be ascribed to the effect of the hormones on development of the brain.

Did the girls show behavioral changes connected with their hormonal and anatomical masculinization? As John Money and Anke Ehrhardt discovered, the changes were both quite marked and correlated with the physical changes. Compared with unaffected girls of otherwise similar social backgrounds, the hormonally altered girls were more commonly regarded as tomboys while they were growing up. They had a greater interest in athletic skills, were readier to play with boys, preferred slacks to dresses and toy guns to dolls. The group with the adrenogenital syndrome was more likely to show dissatisfaction with being assigned to a female role. The evaluation of this latter group is flawed by the fact that cortisone had to be administered to the girls to offset their genetic defect. It is possible that hormone treatment alone could somehow have biased the girls toward masculine behavior. If the effect occurred it was still biological in nature, although not as deep as fetal masculinization. And of course, the effect could not have occurred in the progestin-altered girls.

So at birth the twig is already bent a little bit—what are we to make of that? It suggests that the universal existence of sexual division of labor is not entirely an accident of cultural evolution. But it also supports the conventional view that the enormous variation among societies in the degree of that division is due to cultural evolution. Demonstrating a slight biological component delineates the options that future societies may consciously select. Here the second dilemma of human nature presents itself. In full recognition of the struggle for women's rights that is now spreading throughout the world, each society must make one or the other of the three following choices:

Condition its members so as to exaggerate sexual differences in behavior. This is the pattern in almost all cultures. It results more often than not in domination of women by men and exclusion of women from many professions and activities. But this need not be the case. In theory at least, a carefully designed society with strong sexual divisions could be richer in spirit, more diversified, and even more productive than a unisex society. Such a society might safe-guard human rights even while channeling men and women into different occupations. Still, some amount of social injustice would be inevitable, and it could easily expand to disastrous proportions.

Train its members so as to eliminate all sexual differences in behavior. By the use of quotas and sex-biased education it should be possible to create a society in which men and women *as groups* share equally in all professions, cultural activities, and even, to take the absurd extreme, athletic competition. Although the early predispositions that characterize sex would have to be blunted, the biological differences are not so large as to make the undertaking impossible. Such control would offer the great advantage of eliminating even the hint of group prejudice (in addition to individual prejudice) based on sex. It could result in a much more harmonious and productive society. Yet the amount of regulation required would certainly place some personal freedoms in jeopardy, and at least a few individuals would not be allowed to reach their full potential.

Provide equal opportunities and access but take no further action. To make no choice at all is of course the third choice open to all cultures. Laissez-faire[2] on first thought might seem to be the course most congenial to personal liberty and development, but this is not necessarily true. Even with identical education for men and women and equal access to all professions, men are likely to maintain disproportionate representation in political life, business, and science. Many would fail to participate fully in the equally important, formative aspects of child rearing. The result might be legitimately viewed as restrictive on the complete emotional development of individuals. Just such a divergence and restriction has occurred in the Israeli kibbutzim, which represent one of the most powerful experiments in egalitarianism conducted in modern times.

From the time of the greatest upsurge of the kibbutz movement, in the 1940s and 1950s, its leaders promoted a policy of complete sexual equality, of encouraging women to enter roles previously reserved for men. In the early years it almost worked. The first generation of women were ideologically committed, and they shifted in large numbers to politics, management, and labor. But they and their daughters have regressed somewhat toward traditional roles, despite being trained from birth in the new culture. Furthermore, the daughters have gone further than the mothers. They now demand and receive a longer period of time each day with their children, time significantly entitled "the hour of love." Some of the most gifted have resisted recruitment into the higher levels of commercial and political leadership so that the representation in these

2. Nonintervention.

roles is far below that enjoyed by the same generation of men. It has been argued that this reversion merely represents the influence of the strong patriarchal tradition that persists in the remainder of Israeli society, even though the role division is now greater inside the kibbutzim than outside. The Israeli experience shows how difficult it is to predict the consequences and assess the meaning of changes in behavior based on either heredity or ideology.

From this troubling ambiguity concerning sex roles one firm conclusion can be drawn: the evidences of biological constraint alone cannot prescribe an ideal course of action. However, they can help us to define the options and to assess the price of each. The price is to be measured in the added energy required for education and reinforcement and in the attrition of individual freedom and potential. And let us face the real issue squarely: since every option has a cost, and concrete ethical principles will rarely find universal acceptance, the choice cannot be made easily. In such cases we could do well to consider the wise counsel of Hans Morgenthau: "In the combination of political wisdom, moral courage and moral judgment, man reconciles his political nature with his moral destiny. That this conciliation is nothing more than a *modus vivendi*,[3] uneasy, precarious, and even paradoxical, can disappoint only those who prefer to gloss over and to distort the tragic contradictions of human existence with the soothing logic of a specious concord." I am suggesting that the contradictions are rooted in the surviving relics of our prior genetic history, and that one of the most inconvenient and senseless, but nevertheless unavoidable of these residues is the modest predisposition toward sex role differences.

*　*　*

1978

3. Way of living; compromise.

QUESTIONS

1. Wilson points to both genetic differences and cultural conditioning as factors in determining differences between the sexes. Which does he decide is more important? How does this decision affect the rest of what he has to say?
2. Why does Wilson begin his essay with a discussion of some misconceptions about sex?
3. On pp. 404–405 Wilson describes the three choices he believes are open to societies today in view of the spread of the women's rights movement. Discuss the relative merits of each of these choices. Then write an essay in which you support one of them, or an alternative choice which Wilson does not discuss, as the best.

KAYLA F. BERNHEIM and
RICHARD R. J. LEWINE

Schizophrenia

At a cocktail party two strangers are introduced. They shake hands and say they are pleased to meet each other. Quickly they search for and find an area of common interest they can discuss. During their brief conversation, they look at each other frequently, smile, and nod. Within a short time, one of them sees a friend, ends the conversation politely, and moves away. The other turns and joins a nearby discussion.

Human behavior is, in general, quite predictable. We know a great deal about how strangers will behave—at a party, at a movie, in a classroom, on the street. As we get to know somebody well, we are able to predict how he or she will behave in many more situations. The extent to which we are comfortable with other people depends, in part on how predictable we perceive them to be.

Even when people behave in unexpected ways, we are comfortable if we can create a scenario in which their behavior makes sense. Gregarious John is quiet tonight because he's tired. Mary is wearing a dress today instead of jeans because she wants to impress her companion. Jerry is shouting because he feels unfairly treated by Bob.

Occasionally, however, we come across people whose behavior is neither predictable nor comprehensible. Acting as if they live in a radically different world, they make us feel uncomfortable and even frightened. A man stops in the middle of the street to yell at unseen oppressors; a woman smiles vacuously and begins to hum when asked for her ticket in a train. We, as observers, search for an explanation for these behaviors, and, finding none, we say these people are "crazy" or "mentally ill."

As far as we know, there have been people in all cultures at all times who behaved in bizarre, unpredictable, inexplicable ways. Today, such behaviors are seen as evidence of schizophrenia, a disorder in which mental and emotional processes are seriously disturbed. However, even now understanding schizophrenia is no easy matter. Public misconceptions abound, and even professionals are not yet in complete agreement about what schizophrenia looks like, let alone what causes it. Still, we now understand much about schizophrenia. We have a general idea about how and why the disordered behaviors develop, and we know something about how to change them. In the future we will know how to prevent them from occurring.

* * *

[A Brief Description]

Each of us has had periods in which we were unable to "think straight." Fatigue, overwork, and emotional stress can impair concentration and cause thoughts to race. The schizophrenic individual appears more susceptible to this problem than other people. Thinking may be confused and disjointed a great deal of the time, and for no apparent reason. In addition, most of us engage in fantasizing some of the time. Both enjoyable and frightening fantasies occur to us from time to time, but we are able to separate fantasy from reality fairly easily. The schizophrenic may be overwhelmed by fantasy, unable to distinguish between what is real and what is not. The thinking disturbance in schizophrenia can range from mild confusion with fleeting, unrealistic ideas to an almost complete inability to understand and respond appropriately to events in the environment.

The ability to feel normal emotions is disturbed in schizophrenic people. Emotions may be *dulled*, resulting in an apparent indifference to situations and events to which most of us would react strongly. Life frequently seems boring and empty to the schizophrenic. Sometimes, however, schizophrenics react intensely, but in an *inappropriate* way. They may laugh, cry, or become enraged for no apparent reason. Not only do these feelings appear unrelated to the situations in which they occur, they may be unrelated to the thoughts the person is having as well. So a schizophrenic person is likely to think about events in an abnormal way and to respond emotionally to situations in an abnormal way.

The ability to engage in social relationships is also impaired. Again, many of the experiences of the schizophrenic are ones all of us have had at some time or another: a desire to be alone, a need for social withdrawal, ambivalence regarding intimate relationships, difficulty in making life decisions, existential boredom, and feelings of passivity and of living lives beyond our own control. The schizophrenic differs, however, both in the pervasiveness and intensity of these feelings. Whereas most of us continue to love, play, and work in the face of these feelings, the schizophrenic frequently withdraws from many areas of life. At his core, the schizophrenic is socially isolated. We do not mean this in a physical sense. Rather a schizophrenic may be surrounded by people yet feel lonely, misunderstood, and all alone in the world; there are no "intimates," no shared secrets or joys.

Perhaps as a result of these difficulties in thinking, feeling, and relating, self-esteem is very low. The schizophrenic's self-perception may include feelings of disgust and failure. Turned primarily inward to a world of fantasies and dreams, the schizophrenic will often withdraw from others and from reality.

* * *

Schizophrenia refers to a chronic disorder in which thinking, feeling, and relating tend to be disturbed in characteristic ways. Before going on to discuss the causes of schizophrenia, let's be clear about what schizophrenia does not mean.

[*Misconceptions about Schizophrenia*]

Perhaps the most widespread misconception is that schizophrenia means a split personality: Dr. Jekyll and Mr. Hyde, "the three faces of Eve,"[1] the mild-mannered man who suddenly murders his wife. While such behavior does occur (and is called a "dissociative reaction") it is *not* what is meant by schizophrenia. While the root of the term *schizophrenia* does mean "split mind," the split refers to a breakup of the personality components (thinking, feeling, and relating) rather than a split into two or more separate, coherent personalities.

In particular, the "split" refers to two phenomena. First of all, the schizophrenic is "split from reality." While the professional term for this condition is "psychotic," such lay terms as "crazy," "out of one's mind," or "out of touch" describe the same state. When psychotic, a person's perceptions of and feelings about his world are at marked variance with those of other people. He may hear voices when no one is speaking; he may think he is a famous scientist; he may feel that the radio is sending him special messages; he may perceive that parts of his body do not belong to him. Our world, the world we all agree on, has changed for him in mysterious, often frightening and occasionally beautiful ways. However, schizophrenics are not constantly psychotic, nor do they perceive everything about them in a psychotic way. The word *psychotic* refers to a temporary state in which various aspects of the environment are falsely perceived or interpreted. It does *not* refer to a stable personality trait, like the word *shy*. Thus, schizophrenics may be psychotic at times and "sane" (in proper touch with the environment) at others. Nonetheless, it is the behavior resulting from their psychotic perceptions that is usually most upsetting to those around them.

The second "split" experienced by the schizophrenic is between the thinking processes and the emotional processes. For most of us,

---

1. A famous case of multiple personality in the 1950s, the subject of a book and a movie.

thinking and feeling are consistent with each other most of the time. When sad, we usually wear a sad expression, have sad thoughts, tend to move slowly and with effort, and cry. People tend to think, feel, and act "all of a piece." In schizophrenia, thinking, feeling, and acting become fragmented in relation to each other and in relation to the events of the world. The schizophrenic individual may feel sad when thinking happy thoughts. Or he may feel nothing at all.

Hence, the "split" in schizophrenia refers not to a transformation into separate people, but rather to the dissolution of the functions of a single person. "Split personality" is, therefore, a misnomer and really refers to a separate disorder.

A second widely held misconception is that schizophrenics are invariably unpredictable, aggressive, and dangerous. This is not so. While schizophrenics are sometimes dangerous, due to the psychotic ways in which they misperceive their environment, they are much more often withdrawn, apathetic, and frightened. Indeed, the public is in less danger from mental patients, as a group, than from the "normal" people in our environment.

As with normal people, the best predictor of future behavior is past behavior (other things being equal). One would have good reason to be wary of a nonschizophrenic person who has been aggressive in the past. Likewise, if a schizophrenic has been aggressive at times when he was particularly disturbed, there is a reasonable probability that he could become so again if his illness worsened. However, schizophrenics who are not aggressive (the large majority) are not likely to become so unpredictably.

Part of the confusion about this point probably stems from the interchangeable use of the words *psychotic* and *psychopathic* in the mass media. A "psychopathic killer" is a killer who has no conscience. He is not irrational, not disorganized as the psychotic is. Rather, he does not feel that killing is wrong. While it is possible to be schizophrenic *and* psychopathic, the great majority of schizophrenics have learned to make normal moral judgments. If they hurt someone, it is usually because of their misperception of environmental events or the meaning of those events. Schizophrenic aggressiveness tends to be motivated by fear that one is being threatened in some way, rather than by a desire to hurt another person. Indeed, they are most often horrified by such acts when they regain normal perceptions. In summary, while schizophrenics may, at times, behave aggressively, they are, as a group, *less* aggressive than the general population.

A misconception rarely stated but often acted upon is that schizophrenia is contagious. People are frightened of contact with schizophrenics, not only because the person's behavior is sometimes bizarre and unpredictable, but because they feel it might somehow "rub off." This is understandable in light of how precarious our own hold on reality sometimes seems to us to be at moments of stress. But, the fear is groundless. One *cannot* become schizophrenic simply through contact, however extensive, with someone who is disturbed. Families and friends need not be wary that contact with the patient will, of itself, make them ill.

One other misconception ought to be laid to rest—the notion that schizophrenics are totally unable to function and must be consigned to an institution for life. While this conception had some validity in the past, when untreated schizophrenia often resulted in progressive mental deterioration and institutional care was commonly a necessity for those seriously afflicted, it has little validity now. Recent advances in treatment procedures have made life-long incarceration a rarity. While not presently a *curable* condition, schizophrenia is a highly *treatable* one. Patients who become ill at this time can expect, by and large, to lead their lives outside of institutions. Indeed, many schizophrenics have made, and maintained, a high level of adjustment to their own and their community's expectations. While the level of maximal adjustment varies from individual to individual, total disability is the exception rather than the rule.

Models of Madness

These myths and misconceptions interfere with the ability to provide an environment that is conducive to recovery. To the extent that one holds these false beliefs, one will be frightened and suspicious of schizophrenic people. One would be unwilling to offer a schizophrenic person a job, to live next door to him, to interact with him socially. The effect of this social ostracism is to make return to the community a difficult and fearful prospect.

What causes schizophrenia? It is common to discuss the various descriptions and explanations of schizophrenia in terms of models —that is the system of beliefs within which one ascribes causation. In the Middle Ages, for example, the religious model was used to account for mental illness. All mental illness was explained by the presence of demons. The sufferer was said to be "possessed," and the goal of treatment was to drive out, or exorcise, the evil spirit. The physically less distressing treatments involved insulting the devil. This might be done in the following way: "Thou lustful and stupid one, . . . thou lean sow, famine-stricken and most impure, . . . thou wrinkled beast, thou mangy beast, thou beast of all beasts the most beastly." This went on until either the demon or the patient gave up.

It was not until the early 1800s, when people began to look at the brain rather than at the soul as the site of disturbance, that the concept of disease replaced the concept of possession as the presumed cause of behavioral and emotional disorders. Through the medical treatments of the 1800s and early 1900s might appear inhumane by current standards, this was a critical turning point in the history of psychiatric disorders. Since a physical disorder was thought to underlie mental illness, abnormal behavior was subject to careful observation and clinical investigation. The science of psychiatry and our understanding of psychiatric disorders is, therefore, less than two hundred years old. Schizophrenia itself has been studied for fewer than one hundred years. Today, there are many models from which to choose.

At one extreme is the medical model, by which schizophrenia is labeled as a disease caused by an, as yet, unknown physical process. The schizophrenic individual is seen as sick. Behaviors occurring as a function of his illness are presumed to be out of his control. He is not held responsible for them. He is, however, held responsible for accepting the appropriate social role—that of patient. He is expected to seek medical help and to cooperate with the physician's attempts to cure or control the illness. Researchers working within this model search for biological causes of schizophrenia while clinicians prescribe biological treatments.

This view has led to important advances in our understanding and treatment of schizophrenia. But, in its pure form, it neglects the ways in which psychological, social, and cultural factors interact with physiology to produce behavior. Its unmodified application often produces helpless, dependent, passive behavior which may be antithetical to recovery.

At another extreme are those who maintain that schizophrenia is merely a myth created by the labeling of patients. It has been argued that mental illness—and schizophrenia in particular—reflects a misapplication of the medical model to social and interpersonal problems. It is said that different human beings, because of different values, ideologies, needs, and styles, will necessarily come into conflict with each other. Some people handle these conflicts well; others do poorly. Within this model "mental illness" is an inappropriate label for incompetent handling of problems in living. It describes people with faulty judgment who make mistakes with reference to how they should behave and who are responsible for those mistakes. The label, then, essentially refers to a moral failing, and schizophrenics are simply behaving irresponsibly. Society reinforces their irresponsibility by imputing their behavior to an "illness" that is outside of their control. Indeed, it has been argued that the "cure" for such difficulties involves admission of guilt and repayment of damages. The schizophrenic ought to take responsibility for his misbehavior, admit that it is wrong, change it, and attempt to make amends for whatever suffering he has caused others.

There is little doubt that schizophrenic behavior proves burdensome for those with whom the disturbed person interacts. Families may be embarrassed, frightened, and upset by such behavior. They typically accept financial responsibility for the support and treatment of the schizophrenic person who may not hold a job or develop a secure peer group or live independently. However, the difficulties inherent in the moral model are analogous to the difficulties involved in blaming a blind man for bumping into someone. That is, physical impairments do exist. Further, they often affect behavior. The inability to demonstrate a specific physical basis for a given behavior doesn't mean that one doesn't exist. In fact, research in the area of schizophrenia yields strong evidence that a physiological basis for at least some schizophrenic symptoms is highly probable.

Why should a society label someone as ill, if indeed, he is not ill? According to one view, the label is used to shut out and lock up people whose behavior society finds offensive. The label thus serves the same political purpose as the label "witch" did during the Inquisition. This argument is part of a wider view according to which the fabric of society is held together by laws and by social mores, including manners and customs. People who break laws are called criminals, and people who violate mores are called mentally ill. Both groups are treated in much the same way: society attempts to "rehabilitate" them through coercive control. Indeed, the distinction between "criminal" and "mentally ill" becomes more and more blurred as criminal behavior is accounted for in terms of childhood rearing, responses to poverty, and even to genetic predispositions.

One cannot deny the plausibility of this argument, nor is it possible to deny the fact that the label "schizophrenia" has been used for political purposes in some instances and has been inaccurate in others. However, it is illogical to argue that because a label can be misapplied it has no value. Racial and religious labels are analogous. The label "Jewish," for example, refers to a person with a certain set of religious beliefs and cultural values and traditions or whose parents are Jewish. However, some people think that Jews are sneaky and greedy, just as some people think that schizophrenics are invariably dangerous. In Hitler's Germany, the label "Jewish" was used to scapegoat people. Some people were made to bear the label inappropriately, for political purposes, in much the same way that some people have borne the label "schizophrenic" for the family's or society's purposes.

If the label "schizophrenia" has some important implications for the person to whom it applies, the fact that the community responds to these individuals in one way or another is a separate issue and should not be confused with what is going on within the individual.

According to another extreme view, sometimes called "anti-psychiatry," schizophrenic behavior is seen as an island of sanity in a society that sets "crazy" standards of behavior:

The condition of alienation, of being asleep, of being unconscious, of being out of one's mind, is the condition of normal man.

And

social adaptation to a dysfunctional society may be very dangerous. The perfectly adjusted bomber pilot may be a greater threat to species survival than the hospitalized schizophrenic deluded that the Bomb is inside him. Our society may itself have become biologically dysfunctional, and some forms of schizophrenic alienation from the alienation of society may have a sociobiological function that we have not recognized.[2]

The schizophrenic is thus seen as a prophet, whose heightened state of awareness represents "true" sanity.

The behavioral symptoms of schizophrenia have remained remarkably constant across time and across cultures. If schizophrenia is, indeed, a "sane response to an insane world," different cultures ought to produce varying amounts and kinds of responses. This has not been the case.

However, since this argument is essentially a definitional one, it can't be refuted on grounds of logic or evidence. If a person uses the word *table* to mean "a container for holding liquids," we can only insist that, for us, the word has a different meaning. The same is true of the words *sane* and *insane*. They are used here in the way they are commonly used, but we cannot prevent someone from using them in a different way.

Most professionals would agree that an adequate explanation of the complex phenomenon called schizophrenia involves aspects of many models. The role of heredity, constitution, learning, motivation, social conditions, and societal expectations in determining one's mental health are all acknowledged. Schizophrenia results from the interaction between factors inside the individual (his

2. The quotations are from R. D. (1967). Laing, *The Politics of Experience*

biochemistry and his personality traits) and factors outside (environmental stress).

[*Contributing Factors*]

Schizophrenia probably has its roots in a biochemical abnormality within the body. While there are those who dispute this view, the evidence at this point appears highly persuasive and comes primarily from two sources. First, a large body of research data indicates that schizophrenia has a genetic component. That is to say, the tendency to manifest schizophrenic symptoms under stress is, in large part, genetically based. While it has been known for many years that schizophrenia tends to run in families (and, indeed, this knowledge has been causal in the suspicion that faulty family rearing practices cause schizophrenia), it is only recently that adoption studies and twin studies have helped to tease apart the genetic and environmental contributions to the illness. While the genetic contribution is clear, nongenetic factors have also been implicated by these same studies. Nonetheless, insofar as genes provide us with our basic physical equipment, a genetic predisposition toward schizophrenia means that some part of the body is malfunctioning or likely to malfunction under a certain set of circumstances. Analogies with other medical diseases are common. Both diabetes and hypertension run in families. They are not *solely* genetically determined. Rather, what is inherited is a *predisposition* to become ill in this way, given the right set of factors.

The other major source of evidence for a biological predisposition to schizophrenia comes from a recent treatment innovation. In 1955, clinicians in the United States began using chlorpromazine (Thorazine®) to treat schizophrenia. The results were overwhelmingly positive. Many patients who had been withdrawn became communicative; many patients who had been assaultive became calm; many patients who had lost touch with reality regained it. Both recent clinical experience and controlled scientific studies have confirmed the initial impression that the symptoms of schizophrenia are markedly and lastingly reduced in many patients through the use of chlorpromazine and other related drugs. We need only compare Census figures of mental hospitals over the last two decades to become convinced of the importance of medication in the treatment of schizophrenia. The number of inpatients in state and county mental hospitals (the majority of whom were diagnosed schizophrenics) in the U.S.A. climbed steadily for several decades to a peak of 559,000 in 1955. Then, for nineteen consecutive years the number fell until, in 1974, fewer then 216,000 people inhabited these institutions. While the mechanism of the drugs' effect is still unclear and while many problems with their use remain, the way has been paved toward a biochemical explanation for at least some of the phenomena we call schizophrenia.

Thus, while much research remains to be done, it is reasonable to expect that schizophrenia has, as one of its components, a biochemical abnormality. We can also be sure that this approach will not yield the *whole* answer.

Each individual is different—in intelligence, in upbringing, in values, in adaptability. Thus, each individual responds to and copes with illness in a different way. This may well account for the wide variety of ways in which schizophrenia is manifested, and is certainly related to the relative success each individual has in overcoming the effects of the illness.

By way of example, consider Sam and John, both middle-aged men who have recently had a heart attack. Sam's life has been single-minded. His career has been his only interest. While he has a wife and two children, he has related to them only superficially for many years. He is proud that he has been able to provide them with a comfortable, even luxurious, life style, but he has never taken much interest in giving or receiving, emotional support. Rather, he has always seen himself as "strong" and has tried to raise his children to be strong as well. He hasn't cried since he was an adolescent, and he has always minimized or ignored pain or physical impairment in himself and in his family. Sam has many business acquaintances with whom he is on excellent terms. They see him as an extremely capable businessman.

Sam's heart attack comes as a massive shock to his self-image. Unable to communicate his very real fears to anyone or to accept them himself, he works hard to convince himself that they do not exist. As usual, he is successful. He is so successful that he cannot take his physician's advice seriously. His values, attitudes,' and coping style all dictate that he go back to work quickly and that he work at least as hard as he did before.

John has also worked very hard and has been financially successful, and he is also proud of himself. But he has always been more invested in relationships with people than with his career. He sees himself as fallible, and at times a weak, person who depends on his wife and other family members for help when he is in emotional or physical pain. He has accepted his weaknesses as well as his strengths and has attempted to teach his children that they need not be perfect. John does not have a large number of acquaintances. He spends much of his time with a small group of friends whom he has known many years. Together they make music (John plays the violin), play cards, or discuss their feelings about personal or community issues. John's friends see him as a warm, affectionate person.

John's heart attack also comes as quite a shock. He becomes quite depressed and discusses his fear of dying with his wife and with one of his close friends. When the doctor tells him that he can expect to live a long and comfortable life if he will slow down a bit at work and take certain other precautions, he agrees readily, even though the reduced family income will mean no more summer trips. His wife doesn't seem to mind about that, and John begins to think, with pleasure, of the additional time he will be able to spend with family and friends.

Sam and John are very different people. They respond to the same event quite differently. The outcomes of that event will be predictably different, and will depend as much on *how* they respond as on *what* they are responding to.

Both clinical experience and research have indicated that environmental events may be quite important with respect to the timing and frequency of schizophrenic "episodes." Stress can take many forms. For most of us, a death in the family is perceived as stressful. But the birth of a child or promotion to a better job, like other happy events, can produce stress too. In fact, any change in life circumstances requires some adjustment in the individual, and people vary in their capacity to adjust.

The role of stress in the development of schizophrenic symptoms is particularly hard to study since what is 'stressful for one person may not be stressful for another. Nonetheless, two conclusions can be drawn. First, the biological predisposition to become mentally disorganized lowers a schizophrenic's resistance to stress in general, although some people who are so predisposed can tolerate more stress than others. Second, the issue of becoming independent from one's family of origin appears to pose special difficulties for individuals predisposed to schizophrenia. This is not surprising in view of the fact that mental, emotional, and social competence are requirements of successful competion of this task. The predisposed individual may be impaired in each of these areas.

Schizophrenia occurs as a result of three factors: internal physiological and psychological predispositions, and environmental stress. Whether or not a person who has no genetic predisposition for schizophrenia can become schizophrenic (versus experiencing an acute psychotic episode) due to stress alone is still a disputable point. In such cases where no genetic evidence is apparent, it is more likely that familial schizophrenia went undiagnosed for a variety of reasons or that family members carried a predisposition without showing symptoms themselves. The latter situation is analogous to the one in which two short parents have a tall offspring. These arguments form the basis of the "diathesis-stress" model. The "diathesis" refers to the biochemical predisposition toward the illness (schizophrenia) which *must* be present in order for the illness to manifest itself. However, the diathesis alone is not enough. It must be activated by a stressor. Thus, while a person with no diathesis for schizophrenia can become disturbed under severe stress—with anxiety, with ulcers, with neurotic manifestations—he will not become schizophrenic. Further, while a person *with* a schizophrenic diathesis (which may or may not include overtly schizophrenic family members) may enjoy good health, he carries a *tendency* to become schizophrenic under the right set of circumstances. At present, we have no way to measure the strength of his tendency to become ill.

At the same time, having a schizophrenic relative *does not* mean that one is necessarily carrying the predisposition for the illness. The family inheritance patterns indicate that schizophrenia may well be a multigenic phenomenon, with many family members carrying no "schizophrenic genes," some family members carrying a small number, and a few unlucky family members carrying a significant number.

Schizophrenia refers to characteristically disturbed ways of thinking, feeling, and relating that develop in biologically predisposed individuals under certain personal and environmental circumstances. Schizophrenia is a complex phenomenon that has existed in all cultures at all times. It is not a purely medical disorder, nor is it a purely social, or political phenomenon. Rather, it evolves through an interaction between genetic, personal, environmental and cultural factors.

1979

RICHARD B. SEWALL

A Sense of the Ending[1]

The last time I appeared on this stage[2] was in a minor part in a Cap and Bells production of *Much Ado About Nothing*. I was Friar Francis. I had nine speeches—six one-liners and two big juicy ones. The two big ones were full of wisdom and sound advice, as befits a friar—or, indeed, a convocation speaker. I read the Friar's part through the other day, to get myself in the spirit of this platform

---

1. From a convocation address delivered at Williams College, Williamstown, Massachussetts.

2. As an undergraduate at Williams College.

again and perhaps to recall a little bit of the old undergraduate glory. As a matter of fact, for me, it was anything but glorious. My timing was bad on the one-liners, and the big speeches fell curiously flat. Frankly, I don't think I understood them then. But I know more about Shakespeare (and a few other things) now; and, as I read those lines over, they hit me at 67 as they never did at 17. Listen to Friar Francis trying to get his listeners to accept something he feels deeply—in this case, his belief in the innocence of a slandered young lady. One can feel his frustration in every word:

> Call me a fool;
> Trust not my reading nor my observations,
> Which with experimental seal doth warrant
> The tenour of my book; trust not my age,
> My reverence, calling, nor divinity,
> If this sweet lady lie not guiltless here
> Under some biting error.

Fifty years (between 17 and 67) make a lot of difference, and now at last I know what the Friar felt: the frustration of trying to convey something you feel deeply to an audience that is either skeptical or uninvolved. The Friar put my difficulty plainly, even if it is not quite the same as his. I want to talk to you today about matters which cannot be to you as intensely personal as they are to me; I'm involved as you cannot be, and I cannot bridge the gap by the triumphant march of logic, by statistics, by hard evidence. I want to share with you, simply, a bit of experience I've picked up on the way.

Oh, there are lots of "biting errors" I could expose, were my mood so inclined: educational fallacies rampant in my own beloved New Haven and right here in Williamstown; the sinister drift of our national culture and politics and economy; the global threats to our environment and our peace. I could scare you to death! Or, changing the tune, as appropriate to this day, I could talk about the library as the beating heart of this or any other educational institution. I could talk about Jack Sawyer and all he did for this college. But although all these possibilities are close to my mind and heart, they are not closest, and I decided I must talk about what is closest or I'd better not talk at all. What is closest? Just two things, intimately bound, almost inseparable: love and death.

Shortly after I came to this decision, I ran across a remark by William Butler Yeats. "I am still of the opinion," he wrote, "that only two topics can be of the least interest to a serious and studious mind—sex and death." My first thought was: What a stuffy way to put it! And my second was: Why be so glandular? Why sex and death? I prefer my way of putting it, and Woody Allen's: love and death. I don't intend to be clinical about either, and I am not addressing the "serious and studious mind." I am talking to you as fellow pilgrims—old, middle-aged and young—in this vale of tears and laughter. And I want to share with you a little of what I've learned this past year—I would say the most educational year of my life, the high-water mark of my experience as a human being.

I guess you'll have to know the facts: My wife, Mathilde, died of cancer of the pancreas last November, and my brother John (Williams '28) was killed in a car accident last March. With all the tragedy in the world, you may wonder at my bringing up these two personal losses. It may seem a little impudent of me, even a little embarrassing. "They talk of hallowed things aloud," said Emily Dickinson, trying to explain her aversion to society, "and embarrass my dog." But she was young when she said that. She clammed up, and she was wrong. She was too easily embarrassed.

So here's the first and perhaps simplest thing I've learned this past year: Never be embarrassed to talk about hallowed things, like love and death. We Americans are a little finicky about both. We reduce love to sex and talk about it clinically as in Kinsey and the sex books, or grossly as in *Playboy* and *Penthouse*, or sentimentally as in the popular songs. There's very little talk about the tragic side of love, the comic side of love, love as a discipline, love as a means of education, love as the end and aim of education, the very reason we're here today.

And as for death, we hide from it, pretty it up, pack it away in hospitals, spend millions every year on lavish funerals, or get so glutted with it over the media that we hear or read, with hardly a tremor, about hundreds of thousands dying in Vietnam, or Africa, or Bangladesh. The result is that death is hardly real at all to us. It's a forbidden subject except at funerals and in sermons that aim to take away its sting. I think we'd be better able to cope with it if we talked about it more, if we shared our experience of it more frankly. And so I'm facing you with it—ironically, on this festive occasion, this day of a new beginning when the last thing you want to hear about is the old, old ending.

Which leads me to the second thing I've learned this past year: It's a sense of the ending that makes the beginning, and all that follows therefrom, so much more meaningful. Why deny a reality that, paradoxically, can be so life-giving, so enriching?

I heard the other day of a great-great-grandmother who—this was generations ago—amazed her family by announcing one morning: "I want to die in that rocking chair, and I'm going to close my own eyes." She did both. Her name was Experience Bardwell Lyman. The young people called her "Aunt Speedie," and a hundred years later her descendants are still talking and laughing about her and living a little more fully because of her. I wonder if this is what

Wallace Stevens had in mind when he wrote, "Death is the mother of beauty."

Her great-grandchildren still point to that rocker. Aunt Speedie knew how to die and how to talk about it. She had a sense of her ending—clear-eyed, frank, unabashed, humorous. My friend Emily Dickinson knew how to talk about it, too—in her poetry:

> By a departing light
> We see acuter, quite,
> Than by a wick that stays.
> There's something in the flight
> That clarifies the sight
> And decks the rays.

"There's something in the flight/That clarifies the sight . . ." or, in the words of the old hymn, takes "The dimness of our souls away." Why do things get so dim and unclear? Going along in the old routine, we get in a kind of acquiescent numbness, we get used to things, we don't see sharply or hear clearly or feel intensely.

I had a teacher of creative writing once who told our class, "You must look at things not only as if you were seeing them for the first time but as if you were seeing them for the last time, as if you were never to see them again and had to take them all in and remember them forever." Keep that in mind the next time you look around at these hills. Never, never get used to them!

We need to be jolted out of our numbness, often not so gently as my teacher did it. "Such men as I," cried Dmitri Karamazov, "need a blow . . ." and he spoke for the whole human race. Sometimes nothing but death will remind us that we are alive. That's a terrible thing to say, but it's true.

Love and death . . . What has tortured me these past ten months since Mathilde died are the things I didn't say, the love I didn't express. Why was I so dim, so finicky, so inhibited, so embarrassed? Or were the look in the eyes enough, the squeeze of the hand, the kiss on the brow? I hope to God they were. Heaven knows she was up to anything. She had nerve for both of us. She and Aunt Speedie would have gotten along fine. A week before she died, I came in her room wearing a new dark-green shirt under an old greenish tweed jacket. "They were made for each other," she said. "You could wear them anywhere—even my funeral." Which I did.

The evening of the night she died, she was hilarious, never wittier, and (as always) a bit of a rascal. She ribbed her doctor about what a lousy skier he was. When a friend asked her why she couldn't eat a bit of the lovely cheese cake she'd brought her, she replied, "Because, my dear, I have a touch of cancer."

It was at the time those three doctors went to examine Nixon in San Clemente to see if he was well enough to testify. In my then state of compassion, I averred as how it was tough on the poor man to have to go through all that examination again. Our cheese-cake friend, a veteran Nixon-hater, said, "Nonsense! Nothing is bad enough for that man," etc., etc. "No," said Mathilde, looking quite saintly on her sickbed, "you're wrong. I'm so full of love I can't wish harm on any one." And with a twinkle she added, "You know, if I should get well, I think I'd be rather nice." ("Death is the mother of beauty.")

Then another friend said, "Tillie, when you get well, I want you to make me one of those saints." (Til was a potter, I should tell you, and did ceramic sculpture. One of her favorite themes was St. Francis and the birds.) "Evaline," she answered, "if I get well, I'll make nothing but saints." Six hours later she was dead. Aunt Speedie was one up on her: Mathilde didn't close her own eyes. Will it shock you—it shouldn't by now—when I tell you that I closed them? It was very simple, very sad and very beautiful.

Love and death . . . . It's clear to me that the closer she came to death, the more she learned to love and the more she learned *about* love—and the more she taught us both *to love* and *about love*. The departing light clarified the sight—in all of us. She knew where she was going, and she knew what she was learning, and she talked about it. "These last three months," she told her doctor a few weeks before the end, "have been the best of my life. I wouldn't have missed them for anything."

To understand more fully this remarkable statement, you must hear the last letter she ever wrote. It was to a friend, Holly Tuttle of New Haven, who lost her husband some years ago. The letter says more about love and death than I could in a week of convocation addresses. It's more than just a letter; it's a document. And I read it to you with no embarrassment at all. Remember: "There's something in the flight/That clarifies the sight." All things—individual lives, colleges, libraries, college educations—take on new meaning in the light of their endings—or when they end for you, as they must. *Love them while you can*, and never, never be embarrassed.

And now here's the letter, and I'm done:

DEAR HOLLY—You sent me such a good letter—I do want to answer—The problem of dealing with this fellow Death has been interesting (funny—what would woman's lib. say to my making Death masculine—surely I can't think of myself being swept up by a lady). In the first place—when I saw him come striding up to my house—garbed in all his strange garments that we humans have wished on him—I wasn't in the least spooked. I opened the door and we had a nice little chat. Subsequent chats have been reassuring and I know he's my good friend. I'm sure you too have a nodding acquaintance with him so you have the same feelings.

Then there's LOVE. I feel I'd never have known its endless horizons had I lived out my full span. Somehow in a smooth life we take each other for granted and now even with someone like Richard new little vistas open up—and with casual acquaintances—whole worlds. My plumber—Tommy Citerella—stopped in to see me after he'd attended to my drips and leaks—sat down and looked out at the view I have from my bed—a valley—a mill house—a waterfall—a lake—all hung in the most sensational color—

"Missus" he said—"you have to have faith. You have to pray. God's never failed me. He's saved me three times."

"Tommy," I said, "I don't know where to aim my prayers. God is such a mystery."

"Missus," he said, "don't worry. I'll take over all the praying"—and he took my two hands and leaned down and kissed me on the brow.

So now—what do I have to worry about?

LOVE, TIL

Death is the mother of beauty . . . a sense of the ending. Do you see what I mean?

1975

ELISABETH KÜBLER-ROSS

On the Fear of Death

Let me not pray to be sheltered from
dangers but to be fearless in facing
them.
  Let me not beg for the stilling of
my pain but for the heart to conquer it.
  Let me not look for allies in life's
battlefield but to my own strength.
  Let me not crave in anxious fear to
be saved but hope for the patience to
win my freedom.
  Grant me that I may not be a
coward, feeling your mercy in my
success alone; but let me find the grasp
of your hand in my failure.

RABINDRANATH TAGORE,
Fruit-Gathering

Epidemics have taken a great toll of lives in past generations. Death in infancy and early childhood was frequent and there were few families who didn't lose a member of the family at an early age. Medicine has changed greatly in the last decades. Widespread vaccinations have practically eradicated many illnesses, at least in western Europe and the United States. The use of chemotherapy, especially the antibiotics, has contributed to an ever decreasing number of fatalities in infectious diseases. Better child care and education has effected a low morbidity and mortality among children. The many diseases that have taken an impressive toll among the young and middle-aged have been conquered. The number of old people is on the rise, and with this fact come the number of people with malignancies and chronic diseases associated more with old age.

Pediatricians have less work with acute and life-threatening situations as they have an ever increasing number of patients with psychosomatic disturbances and adjustment and behavior problems. Physicians have more people in their waiting rooms with emotional problems than they have ever had before, but they also have more elderly patients who not only try to live with their decreased physical abilities and limitations but who also face loneliness and isolation with all its pains and anguish. The majority of these people are not seen by a psychiatrist. Their needs have to be elicited and gratified by other professional people, for instance, chaplains and social workers. It is for them that I am trying to outline the changes that have taken place in the last few decades, changes that are ultimately responsible for the increased fear of death, the rising number of emotional problems, and the greater need for understanding of and coping with the problems of death and dying.

When we look back in time and study old cultures and people, we are impressed that death has always been distasteful to man and will probably always be. From a psychiatrist's point of view this is very understandable and can perhaps best be explained by our basic knowledge that, in our unconscious, death is never possible in regard to ourselves. It is inconceivable for our unconscious to imagine an actual ending of our own life here on earth, and if this life of ours has to end, the ending is always attributed to a malicious intervention from the outside by someone else. In simple terms, in our unconscious mind we can only be killed; it is inconceivable to die of a natural cause or of old age. Therefore death in itself is associated with a bad act, a frightening happening, something that in itself calls for retribution and punishment.

One is wise to remember these fundamental facts as they are essential in understanding some of the most important, otherwise unintelligible communications of our patients.

The second fact that we have to comprehend is that in our unconscious mind we cannot distinguish between a wish and a deed. We are all aware of some of our illogical dreams in which two completely opposite statements can exist side by side—very acceptable in our dreams but unthinkable and illogical in our wakening state. Just as our unconscious mind cannot differentiate between the wish to kill somebody in anger and the act of having done so, the young child is unable to make this distinction. The child who angrily wishes his mother to drop dead for not having gratified his needs will be traumatized greatly by the actual death of his mother —even if this event is not linked closely in time with his destructive wishes. He will always take part or the whole blame for the loss of his mother. He will always say to himself—rarely to others—"I did it, I am responsible, I was bad, therefore Mommy left me." It is well to remember that the child will react in the same manner if he loses a parent by divorce, separation, or desertion. Death is often seen by a child as an impermanent thing and has therefore little distinction from a divorce in which he may have an opportunity to see a parent again.

Many a parent will remember remarks of their children such as, "I will bury my doggy now and next spring when the flowers come up again, he will get up." Maybe it was the same wish that motivated the ancient Egyptians to supply their dead with food and goods to keep them happy and the old American Indians to bury their relatives with their belongings.

When we grow older and begin to realize that our omnipotence is really not so omnipotent, that our strongest wishes are not powerful enough to make the impossible possible, the fear that we have contributed to the death of a loved one diminishes—and with it the guilt. The fear remains diminished, however, only so long as it is not challenged too strongly. Its vestiges can be seen daily in hospital corridors and in people associated with the bereaved.

A husband and wife may have been fighting for years, but when the partner dies, the survivor will pull his hair, whine and cry louder and beat his chest in regret, fear and anguish, and will hence fear his own death more than before, still believing in the law of talion —an eye for an eye, a tooth for a tooth—"I am responsible for her death, I will have to die a pitiful death in retribution."

Maybe this knowledge will help us understand many of the old customs and rituals which have lasted over the centuries and whose purpose is to diminish the anger of the gods or the people as the case may be, thus decreasing the anticipated punishment. I am thinking of the ashes, the torn clothes, the veil, the *Klage Weiber*[1] of the old days—they are all means to ask you to take pity on them, the mourners, and are expressions of sorrow, grief, and shame. If someone grieves, beats his chest, tears his hair, or refuses to eat, it is an attempt at self-punishment to avoid or reduce the anticipated punishment for the blame that he takes on the death of a loved one.

This grief, shame, and guilt are not very far removed from feel-

1. **Wailing wives.**

ings of anger and rage. The process of grief always includes some qualities of anger. Since none of us likes to admit anger at a deceased person, these emotions are often disguised or repressed and prolong the period of grief or show up in other ways. It is well to remember that it is not up to us to judge such feelings as bad or shameful but to understand their true meaning and origin as something very human. In order to illustrate this I will again use the example of the child—and the child in us. The five-year-old who loses his mother is both blaming himself for her disappearance and being angry at her for having deserted him and for no longer gratifying his needs. The dead person then turns into something the child loves and wants very much but also hates with equal intensity for this severe deprivation.

The ancient Hebrews regarded the body of a dead person as something unclean and not to be touched. The early American Indians talked about the evil spirits and shot arrows in the air to drive the spirits away. Many other cultures have rituals to take care of the "bad" dead person, and they all originate in this feeling of anger which still exists in all of us, though we dislike admitting it. The tradition of the tombstone may originate in this wish to keep the bad spirits deep down in the ground, and the pebbles that many mourners put on the grave are left-over symbols of the same wish. Though we call the firing of guns at military funerals a last salute, it is the same symbolic ritual as the Indian used when he shot his spears and arrows into the skies.

I give these examples to emphasize that man has not basically changed. Death is still a fearful, frightening happening, and the fear of death is a universal fear even if we think we have mastered it on many levels.

What has changed is our way of coping and dealing with death and dying and our dying patients.

Having been raised in a country in Europe where science is not so advanced, where modern techniques have just started to find their way into medicine, and where people still live as they did in this country half a century ago, I may have had an opportunity to study a part of the evolution of mankind in a shorter period.

I remember as a child the death of a farmer. He fell from a tree and was not expected to live. He asked simply to die at home, a wish that was granted without questioning. He called his daughters into the bedroom and spoke with each one of them alone for a few moments. He arranged his affairs quietly, though he was in great pain, and distributed his belongings and his land, none of which was to be split until his wife should follow him in death. He also asked each of his children to share in the work, duties, and tasks that he had carried on until the time of the accident. He asked his friends to visit him once more, to bid good-bye to them. Although I was a small child at the time, he did not exclude me or my siblings. We were allowed to share in the preparations of the family just as we were permitted to grieve with them until he died. When he did die, he was left at home, in his own beloved home which he had built, and among his friends and neighbors who went to take a last look at him where he lay in the midst of flowers in the place he had lived in and loved so much. In that country today there is still no make-believe slumber room, no embalming, no false makeup to pretend sleep. Only the signs of very disfiguring illnesses are covered up with bandages and only infectious cases are removed from the home prior to the burial.

Why do I describe such "old-fashioned" customs? I think they are an indication of our acceptance of a fatal outcome, and they help the dying patient as well as his family to accept the loss of a loved one. If a patient is allowed to terminate his life in the familiar and beloved environment, it requires less adjustment for him. His own family knows him well enough to replace a sedative with a glass of his favorite wine; or the smell of a home-cooked soup may give him the appetite to sip a few spoons of fluid which, I think is still more enjoyable than an infusion. I will not minimize the need for sedatives and infusions and realize full well from my own experience as a country doctor that they are sometimes life-saving and often unavoidable. But I also know that patience and familiar people and foods could replace many a bottle of intravenous fluids given for the simple reason that it fulfills the physiological need without involving too many people and/or individual nursing care.

The fact that children are allowed to stay at home where a fatality has stricken and are included in the talk, discussions, and fears gives them the feeling that they are not alone in the grief and gives them the comfort of shared responsibility and shared mourning. It prepares them gradually and helps them view death as part of life, an experience which may help them grow and mature.

This is in great contrast to a society in which death is viewed as taboo, discussion of it is regarded as morbid, and children are excluded with the presumption and pretext that it would be "too much" for them. They are then sent off to relatives, often accompanied with some unconvincing lies of "Mother has gone on a long trip" or other unbelievable stories. The child senses that something is wrong, and his distrust in adults will only multiply if other relatives add new variations of the story, avoid his questions or suspicions, shower him with gifts as a meager substitute for a loss he is not permitted to deal with. Sooner or later the child will become aware of the changed family situation and, depending on the age and personality of the child, will have an unresolved grief and regard this incident as a frightening, mysterious, in any case very traumatic experience with untrustworthy grownups, which he has no way to cope with.

It is equally unwise to tell a little child who lost her brother that God loved little boys so much that he took little Johnny to heaven. When this little girl grew up to be a woman she never solved her anger at God, which resulted in a psychotic depression when she lost her own little son three decades later.

We would think that our great emancipation, our knowledge of science and of man, has given us better ways and means to prepare ourselves and our families for this inevitable happening. Instead the days are gone when a man was allowed to die in peace and dignity in his own home.

The more we are making advancements in science, the more we seem to fear and deny the reality of death. How is this possible?

We use euphemisms, we made the dead look as if they were asleep, we ship the children off to protect them from the anxiety and turmoil around the house if the patient is fortunate enough to die at home, we don't allow children to visit their dying parents in the hospitals, we have long and controversial discussions about whether patients should be told the truth—a question that rarely arises when the dying person is tended by the family physician who has known him from delivery to death and who knows the weaknesses and strengths of each member of the family.

I think there are many reasons for this flight away from facing death calmly. One of the most important facts is that dying nowadays is more gruesome in many ways, namely, more lonely, mechanical, and dehumanized; at times it is even difficult to determine technically when the time of death has occurred.

Dying becomes lonely and impersonal because the patient is often taken out of his familiar environment and rushed to an emergency room. Whoever has been very sick and has required rest and comfort especially may recall his experience of being put on a stretcher and enduring the noise of the ambulance siren and hectic rush until the hospital gates open. Only those who have lived through this may appreciate the discomfort and cold necessity of such transportation which is only the beginning of a long ordeal— hard to endure when you are well, difficult to express in words when noise, light, pumps, and voices are all too much to put up with. It may well be that we might consider more the patient under the sheets and blankets and perhaps stop our well-meant efficiency and rush in order to hold the patient's hand, to smile, or to listen to a question. I include the trip to the hospital as the first episode in dying, as it is for many. I am putting it exaggeratedly in contrast to the sick man who is left at home—not to say that lives should not be saved if they can be saved by a hospitalization but to keep the focus on the patient's experience, his needs and his reactions.

When a patient is severely ill, he is often treated like a person with no right to an opinion. It is often someone else who makes the decision if and when and where a patient should be hospitalized. It would take so little to remember that the sick person too has feelings, has wishes and opinions, and has—most important of all—the right to be heard.

Well, our presumed patient has now reached the emergency room. He will be surrounded by busy nurses, orderlies, interns, residents, a lab technician perhaps who will take some blood, an electrocardiogram technician who takes the cardiogram. He may be moved to X-ray and he will overhear opinions of his condition and discussions and questions to members of the family. He slowly but surely is beginning to be treated like a thing. He is no longer a person. Decisions are made often without his opinion. If he tries to rebel he will be sedated and after hours of waiting and wondering whether he has the strength, he will be wheeled into the operating room or intensive treatment unit and become an object of great concern and great financial investment.

He may cry for rest, peace, and dignity, but he will get infusions, transfusions, a heart machine, or tracheostomy[2] if necessary. He may want one single person to stop for one single minute so that he can ask one single question—but he will get a dozen people around the clock, all busily preoccupied with his heart rate, pulse, electrocardiogram or pulmonary functions, his secretions or excretions but not with him as a human being. He may wish to fight it all but it is going to be a useless fight since all this is done in the fight for his life, and if they can save his life they can consider the person afterwards. Those who consider the person first may lose precious time to save his life! At least this seems to be the rationale or justification behind all this—or is it? Is the reason for this increasingly mechanical, depersonalized approach our own defensiveness? Is this approach our own way to cope with and repress the anxieties that a terminally or critically ill patient evokes in us? Is our concentration on equipment, on blood pressure our desperate attempt to deny the impending death which is so frightening and discomforting to us that we displace all our knowledge onto machines, since they are less close to us than the suffering face of another human being which would remind us once more of our lack of omnipotence, our own limits and failures, and last but not least perhaps our own mortality?

---

2. The surgical opening of a passage through the neck into the trachea.

Maybe the question has to be raised: Are we becoming less human or more human? * * * [I]t is clear that whatever the answer may be, the patient is suffering more—not physically, perhaps, but emotionally. And his needs have not changed over the centuries, only our ability to gratify them.

1969

QUESTIONS
1. How is Kübler-Ross' essay organized? What difference does it make that she postpones presenting generalizations about her subject until late in her discussion?
2. To speak of rights, as Kübler-Ross does in the last pages of her essay, is to raise the question of where they come from; for example, the Declaration of Independence (pp. 514–517) implies that the rights it asserts come from God; from what source would you expect Kübler-Ross to derive the rights she speaks of?
3. Kübler-Ross doubts the rationale for efficiency in medical care, but at the same time recognizes the life-saving results of this efficiency. There is obviously a dilemma here: what are the extreme opposite positions that define the dilemma? What is the best intermediate or compromise position?
4. Richard B. Sewall in "A Sense of the Ending" (pp. 418–423) also speaks of dying. To what extent is he in harmony with Kübler-Ross? What differences do you find? What is the special contribution of each author?
5. Kübler-Ross opens her discussion with a quotation. Read Shakespeare's Sonnet 73 and Hopkins' "Spring and Fall: To a Young Child." Would these poems be appropriate for introducing her essay? Why, or why not?

73

That time of year thou mayst in me behold
When yellow leaves, or none, or few, do hang
Upon those boughs which shake against the cold,
Bare ruined choirs, where late the sweet birds sang.
In me thou see'st the twilight of such day
As after sunset fadeth in the west;
Which by and by black night doth take away,
Death's second self, that seals up all in rest.
In me thou see'st the glowing of such fire,
That on the ashes of his youth doth lie,
As the deathbed whereon it must expire,
Consumed with that which it was nourished by.
This thou perceiv'st, which makes thy love more strong,
To love that well which thou must leave ere long.

—William Shakespeare

SPRING AND FALL

TO A YOUNG CHILD

Margaret, are you grieving
Over Goldengrove unleaving?
Leaves, like the things of man, you
With your fresh thoughts care for, can you?
Ah! as the heart grows older
It will come to such sights colder
By and by, nor spare a sigh
Though worlds of wanwood leafmeal lie;
And yet you *will* weep and know why.
Now no matter, child, the name:
Sorrow's springs are the same.
Nor mouth had, no nor mind, expressed
What heart heard of, ghost [soul] guessed:
It is the blight man was born for,
It is Margaret you mourn for.

—Gerard Manley Hopkins

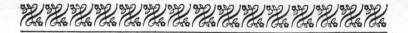

Ethics

JAMES THURBER
The Bear Who Let It Alone

In the words of the Far West there once lived a brown bear who could take it or let it alone. He would go into a bar where they sold mead, a fermented drink made of honey, and he would have just two drinks. Then he would put some money on the bar and say, "See what the bears in the back room will have," and he would go home. But finally he took to drinking by himself most of the day. He would reel home at night, kick over the umbrella stand, knock down the bridge lamps, and ram his elbows through the windows. Then he would collapse on the floor and lie there until he went to sleep. His wife was greatly distressed and his children were very frightened.

At length the bear saw the error of his ways and began to reform. In the end he became a famous teetotaller and a persistent temperance lecturer. He would tell everybody that came to his house about the awful effects of drink, and he would boast about how strong and well he had become since he gave up touching' the stuff. To demonstrate this, he would stand on his head and on his hands and he would turn cartwheels in the house, kicking over the umbrella stand, knocking down the bridge lamps, and ramming his elbows through the windows. Then he would lie down on the floor, tired by his healthful exercise, and go to sleep. His wife was greatly distressed and his children were very frightened.

Moral: You might as well fall flat on your face as lean over too far backward.

1955

LORD CHESTERFIELD
Letter to His Son

London, October 16, O.S. 1747

DEAR BOY

The art of pleasing is a very necessary one to possess, but a very difficult one to acquire. It can hardly be reduced to rules; and your own good sense and observation will teach you more of it than I can. "Do as you would be done by," is the surest method that I know of pleasing. Observe carefully what pleases you in others, and probably the same things in you will please others. If you are pleased with the complaisance and attention of others to your humors, your tastes, or your weaknesses, depend upon it, the same complaisance and attention on your part to theirs will equally please them. Take the tone of the company that you are in, and do not pretend to give it; be serious, gay, or even trifling, as you find the present humor of the company; this is an attention due from every individual to the majority. Do not tell stories in company; there is nothing more tedious and disagreeable; if by chance you know a very short story, and exceedingly applicable to the present subject of conversation, tell it in as few words as possible; and even then, throw out that you do not love to tell stories, but that the shortness of it tempted you.

Of all things banish the egotism out of your conversation, and never think of entertaining people with your own personal concerns or private affairs; though they are interesting to you, they are tedious and impertinent to everybody else; besides that, one cannot keep one's own private affairs too secret. Whatever you think your own excellencies may be, do not affectedly display them in company; nor labor, as many people do, to give that turn to the conversation, which may supply you with an opportunity of exhibiting them. If they are real, they will infallibly be discovered, without your pointing them out yourself, and with much more advantage. Never maintain an argument with heat and clamor, though you think or know yourself to be in the right; but give your opinion modestly and coolly, which is the only way to convince; and, if that does not do, try to change the conversation, by saying, with good-humor, "We shall hardly convince one another; nor is it necessary that we should, so let us talk of something else."

Remember that there is a local propriety to be observed in all companies; and that what is extremely proper in one company may be, and often is, highly improper in another.

The jokes, the *bon-mots*, the little adventures, which may do very well in one company, will seem flat and tedious, when related in another. The particular characters, the habits, the cant of one company may give merit to a word, or a gesture, which would have none at all if divested of those accidental circumstances. Here people very commonly err; and fond of something that has entertained them in one company, and in certain circumstances, repeat it with emphasis in another, where it is either insipid, or, it may be, offensive, by being ill-timed or misplaced. Nay, they often do it with this silly preamble: "I will tell you an excellent thing," or, "I will tell you the best thing in the world." This raises expectations, which, when absolutely disappointed, make the relator of this excellent thing look, very deservedly, like a fool.

If you would particularly gain the affection and friendship of particular people, whether men or women, endeavor to find out their predominant excellency, if they have one, and their prevailing weakness, which everybody has; and do justice to the one, and something more than justice to the other. Men have various objects in which they may excel, or at least would be thought to excel; and, though they love to hear justice done to them, where they know that they excel, yet they are most and best flattered upon those points where they wish to excel, and yet are doubtful whether they do or not. As for example: Cardinal Richelieu, who was undoubtedly the ablest statesman of his time, or perhaps of any other, had the idle vanity of being thought the best poet too; he envied the great Corneille his reputation, and ordered a criticism to be written upon the *Cid*.[1] Those, therefore, who flattered skillfully, said little to him of his abilities in state affairs, or at least but *en passant*, and as it might naturally occur. But the incense which they gave him, the smoke of which they knew would turn his head in their favor, was as a *bel esprit* and a poet. Why? Because he was sure of one excellency, and distrustful as to the other.

You will easily discover every man's prevailing vanity by observing his favorite topic of conversation; for every man talks most of what he has most a mind to be thought to excel in. Touch him but there, and you touch him to the quick. The late Sir Robert Walpole[2] (who was certainly an able man) was little open to flattery upon that head, for he was in no doubt himself about it; but his prevailing weakness was, to be thought to have a polite and happy turn to gallantry— of which he had undoubtedly less than any man living. It was his favorite and frequent subject of conversation, which proved to those who had any penetration that it was his prevailing weakness, and they applied to it with success.

Women have, in general, but one object, which is their beauty;

1. When the French classic tragedy *The Cid*, founded upon the legendary exploits of the medieval Castilian warrior-hero, was published in 1636 by its author Pierre Corneille (1606–1684), it was the subject of violent criticism, led by the French minister of state Richelieu (1585–1642).

2. For two decades a powerful prime minister, Robert Walpole (1676–1745) was also a patron of the arts and prided himself upon his taste.

upon which scarce any flattery is too gross for them to follow. Nature has hardly formed a woman ugly enough to be insensible to flattery upon her person; if her face is so shocking that she must, in some degree, be conscious of it, her figure and air, she trusts, make ample amends for it. If her figure is deformed, her face, she thinks, counterbalances it. If they are both bad, she comforts herself that she has graces, a certain manner, a *je ne sais quoi*[3] still more engaging than beauty. This truth is evident from the studied and elaborate dress of the ugliest woman in the world. An undoubted, uncontested, conscious beauty is, of all women, the least sensible of flattery upon that head; she knows it is her due, and is therefore obliged to nobody for giving it her. She must be flattered upon her understanding; which, though she may possibly not doubt of herself, yet she suspects that men may distrust.

Do not mistake me, and think that I mean to recommend to you abject and criminal flattery: no; flatter nobody's vices or crimes: on the contrary, abhor and discourage them. But there is no living in the world without a complaisant indulgence for people's weaknesses, and innocent, though ridiculous vanities. If a man has a mind to be thought wiser, and a woman handsomer, than they really are, their error is a comfortable one to themselves, and an innocent one with regard to other people; and I would rather make them my friends by indulging them in it, than my enemies by endeavoring (and that to no purpose) to undeceive them.

There are little attentions, likewise, which are infinitely engaging, and which sensibly affect that degree of pride and self-love, which is inseparable from human nature, as they are unquestionable proofs of the regard and consideration which we have for the persons to whom we pay them. As, for example, to observe the little habits, the likings, the antipathies, and the tastes of those whom we would gain; and then take care to provide them with the one, and to secure them from the other; giving them, genteelly, to understand, that you had observed they liked such a dish, or such a room, for which reason you had prepared it: or, on the contrary, that having observed they had an aversion to such a dish, a dislike to such a person, etc., you had taken care to avoid presenting them. Such attention to such trifles flatters self-love much more then greater things, as it makes people think themselves almost the only objects of your thoughts and care.

These are some of the arcana[4] necessary for your initiation in the great society of the world. I wish I had known them better at your age; I have paid the price of three and fifty years for them, and shall not grudge it if you reap the advantage. Adieu.

1747

3. A certain inexpressible quality.   4. Secret things.

SAMUEL L. CLEMENS

Advice to Youth

Being told I would be expected to talk here, I inquired what sort of a talk I ought to make. They said it should be something suitable to youth—something didactic, instructive, or something in the nature of good advice. Very well. I have a few things in my mind which I have often longed to say for the instruction of the young; for it is in one's tender early years that such things will best take root and be most enduring and most valuable. First, then, I will say to you, my young friends—and I say it beseechingly, urgingly—

Always obey your parents, when they are present. This is the best policy in the long run, because if you don't they will make you. Most parents think they know better than you do, and you can generally make more by humoring that superstition than you can by acting on your own better judgment.

Be respectful to your superiors, if you have any, also to strangers, and sometimes to others. If a person offend you, and you are in doubt as to whether it was intentional or not, do not resort to extreme measures; simply watch your chance and hit him with a brick. That will be sufficient. If you shall find that he had not intended any offense, come out frankly and confess yourself in the wrong when you struck him; acknowledge it like a man and say you didn't mean to. Yes, always avoid violence; in this age of charity and kindliness, the time has gone by for such things. Leave dynamite to the low and unrefined.

Go to bed early, get up early—this is wise. Some authorities say get up with the sun; some others say get up with one thing, some with another. But a lark is really the best thing to get up with. It gives you a splendid reputation with everybody to know that you get up with the lark; and if you get the right kind of a lark, and work at him right, you can easily train him to get up at half past nine, every time—it is no trick at all.

Now as to the matter of lying. You want to be very careful about lying; otherwise you are nearly sure to get caught. Once caught, you can never again be, in the eyes of the good and the pure, what you were before. Many a young person has injured himself permanently through a single clumsy and illfinished lie, the result of carelessness born of incomplete training. Some authorities hold that the young ought not to lie at all. That, of course, is putting it rather stronger than necessary; still, while I cannot go quite so far as that, I do maintain, and I believe I am right, that the young ought to be temperate in the use of this great art until practice and experience shall give them that confidence, elegance, and precision which alone can

436

make the accomplishment graceful and profitable. Patience, diligence, painstaking attention to detail—these are the requirements; these, in time, will make the student perfect; upon these, and upon these only, may he rely as the sure foundation for future eminence. Think what tedious years of study, thought, practice, experience, went to the equipment of that peerless old master who was able to impose upon the whole world the lofty and sounding maxim that "truth is mighty and will prevail"—the most majestic compound fracture of fact which any of woman born has yet achieved. For the history of our race, and each individual's experience, are sown thick with evidence that a truth is not hard to kill and that a lie told well is immortal. There is in Boston a monument of the man who discovered anaesthesia; many people are aware, in these latter days, that that man didn't discover it at all, but stole the discovery from another man. Is this truth mighty, and will it prevail? Ah no, my hearers, the monument is made of hardy material, but the lie it tells will outlast it a million years. An awkward, feeble, leaky lie is a thing which you ought to make it your unceasing study to avoid; such a lie as that has no more real permanence than an average truth. Why, you might as well tell the truth at once and be done with it. A feeble, stupid, preposterous lie will not live two years—except it be a slander upon somebody. It is indestructible, then, of course, but that is no merit of yours. A final word: begin your practice of this gracious and beautiful art early—begin now. If I had begun earlier, I could have learned how.

Never handle firearms carelessly. The sorrow and suffering that have been caused through the innocent but heedless handling of firearms by the young! Only four days ago, right in the next farm-house to the one where I am spending the summer, a grandmother, old and gray and sweet, one of the loveliest spirits in the land, was sitting at her work, when her young grandson crept in and got down an old, battered, rusty gun which had not been touched for many years and was supposed not to be loaded, and pointed it at her, laughing and threatening to shoot. In her fright she ran screaming and pleading toward the door on the other side of the room; but as she passed him he placed the gun almost against her very breast and pulled the trigger! He had supposed it was not loaded. And he was right—it wasn't. So there wasn't any harm done. It is the only case of that kind I ever heard of. Therefore, just the same, don't you meddle with old unloaded firearms; they are the most deadly and unerring things that have ever been created by man. You don't have to take any pains at all with them; you don't have to have a rest, you don't have to have any sights on the gun, you don't have to take aim, even. No, you just pick out a relative and bang away, and you are sure to get him. A youth who can't hit a cathedral at thirty yards with a Gatling gun in three-quarters of an hour, can take up an old empty musket and bag his grandmother every time, at a hundred. Think what Waterloo[1] would have been if one of the armies had been boys armed with old muskets supposed not to be loaded, and the other army had been composed of their female relations. The very thought of it makes one shudder.

There are many sorts of books; but good ones are the sort for the young to read. Remember that. They are a great, an inestimable, an unspeakable means of improvement. Therefore be careful in your selection, my young friends; be very careful; confine yourselves exclusively to Robertson's Sermons, Baxter's *Saint's Rest, The Innocents Abroad*, and works of that kind.[2]

But I have said enough. I hope you will treasure up the instructions which I have given you, and make them a guide to your feet and a light to your understanding. Build your character thoughtfully and painstakingly upon these precepts, and by and by, when you have got it built, you will be surprised and gratified to see how nicely and sharply it resembles everybody else's.

1882   1923

1. The bloody battle (1815) in which Napoleon suffered his final defeat at the hands of English and German troops under the Duke of Wellington.
2. The five volumes of sermons by Frederick William Robertson (1816–

1853), an English clergyman, and Richard Baxter's *Saints' Everlasting Rest* (1650) were once well-known religious works. *The Innocents Abroad* is Clemens's own collection of humorous travel sketches.

QUESTIONS

1. Is this piece unified? Does it have a thesis sentence? If you think it is unified, in what does the unity consist? If you think it is not unified, where are the breaks? Would it have seemed more unified when it was given as a speech?
2. What "image" or "personality" does Clemens project or assume? What does he do that creates his image or personality?
3. How much of his advice applies only to the young? How much of it is to be taken seriously?
4. What does Clemens assume about his audience? How many of these assumptions would hold true today?

WILLARD GAYLIN

What You See Is the Real You

It was, I believe, the distinguished Nebraska financier Father Edward J. Flanagan[1] who professed to having "never met a bad

1. Founder (1917) of Boys Town, a self-governing community for homeless and abandoned boys, for which he was also an energetic fund raiser.

boy." Having, myself, met a remarkable number of bad boys, it might seem that either our experiences were drastically different or we were using the word "bad" differently. I suspect neither is true, but rather that the Father was appraising the "inner man," while I, in fact, do not acknowlege the existence of inner people.

Since we psychoanalysts have unwittingly contributed to this confusion, let one, at least, attempt a small rectifying effort. Psychoanalytic data—which should be viewed as supplementary information —is, unfortunately, often viewed as alternative (and superior) explanation. This has led to the prevalent tendency to think of the "inner" man as the real man and the outer man as an illusion or pretender.

While psychoanalysis supplies us with an incredibly useful tool for explaining the motives and purposes underlying human behavior, most of this has little bearing on the moral nature of that behavior.

Like roentgenology, psychoanalysis is a fascinating, but relatively new, means of illuminating the person. But few of us are prepared to substitute an X-ray of Grandfather's head for the portrait that hangs in the parlor. The inside of the man represents another view, not a truer one. A man may not always be what he appears to be, but what he appears to be is always a significant part of what he is. A man is the sum total of *all* his behavior. To probe for unconscious determinants of behavior and then define *him* in their terms exclusively, ignoring his overt behavior altogether, is a greater distortion than ignoring the unconscious completely.

Kurt Vonnegut has said, "You are what you pretend to be," which is simply another way of saying, you are what we (all of us) perceive you to be, not what you think you are.

Consider for a moment the case of the ninety-year-old man on his deathbed (surely the Talmud must deal with this?) joyous and relieved over the success of his deception. For ninety years he has shielded his evil nature from publc observation. For ninety years he has affected courtesy, kindness, and generosity—suppressing all the malice he knew was within him while he calculatedly and artificially substituted grace and charity. All his life he had been fooling the world into believing he was a good man. This "evil" man will, I predict, be welcomed into the Kingdom of Heaven.

Similarly, I will not be told that the young man who earns his pocket money by mugging old ladies is "really" a good boy. Even my generous and expansive definition of goodness will not accommodate that particular form of self-advancement.

It does not count that beneath the rough exterior he has a heart —or, for that matter, an entire innards—of purest gold, locked away from human perception. You are for the most part what you seem to be, not what you would wish to be, nor, indeed, what you believe yourself to be.

Spare me, therefore, your good intentions, your inner sensitivities, your unarticulated and unexpressed love. And spare me also those tedious psychohistories which—by exposing the goodness inside the bad man, and the evil in the good—invariably establish a vulgar and perverse egalitarianism, as if the arrangement of what is outside and what inside makes no moral difference.

Saint Francis[2] may, in his unconscious, indeed have been compensating for, and denying, destructive, unconscious Oedipal impulses identical to those which Atilla projected and acted on. But the similarity of the unconscious constellations in the two men matters precious little, if it does not distinguish between them.

I do not care to learn that Hitler's heart was in the right place. A knowledge of the unconscious life of the man may be an adjunct to understanding his behavior. It is *not* a substitute for his behavior in describing him.

The inner man is a fantasy. If it helps you to identify with one, by all means, do so; preserve it, cherish it, embrace it, but do not present it to others for evaluation or consideration, for excuse or exculpation, or, for that matter, for punishment or disapproval.

Like any fantasy, it serves your purposes alone. It has no standing in the real world which we share with each other. Those character traits, those attitudes, that behavior—that strange and alien stuff sticking out all over you—*that's the real you!*

1977

2. Saint Francis of Assisi, who early in the thirteenth century renounced parental wealth, entered on a life of poverty, and founded the Franciscan order of begging friars.

QUESTIONS

1. Gaylin makes a key distinction between the inner and the outer man. Why is it necessary for him to start with this distinction?
2. Gaylin finds in the relation between an X-ray and a portrait an analogy for the relation between the inner man and the outer man. How accurate is this analogy?
3. Compare the approach to human personality taken by Gaylin with that of Herb Goldberg, also a psychotherapist, in "In Harness: The Male Condition" (pp. 292–298). Do they seem to agree on the nature of human personality? Explain.
4. Discuss the effectiveness of the examples in the essay and suggest others that Gaylin might have used.
5. Comment on the appropriateness of Gaylin's title.
6. Gaylin says in his first paragraph that he does "not acknowledge the existence of inner people," while in his fourth paragraph he

says that "the inside of the man represents another view, not a truer one." How can you account for this seeming contradiction?

7. Erving Goffman's "Reality and Contrivance" (pp. 441–445) deals with some of the same ideas as Gaylin's essay. Compare the two selections with respect to their ways of arguing, points of emphasis, conclusions, and effectiveness.

ERVING GOFFMAN

Reality and Contrivance

In our own Anglo-American culture there seem to be two common-sense models according to which we formulate our conceptions of behavior: the real, sincere, or honest performance; and the false one that thorough fabricators assemble for us, whether meant to be taken unseriously, as in the work of stage actors, or seriously, as in the work of confidence men. We tend to see real performances as something not purposely put together at all, being an unintentional product of the individual's unselfconscious response to the facts in his situation. And contrived performances we tend to see as something painstakingly pasted together, one false item on another, since there is no reality to which the items of behavior could be a direct response. It will be necessary to see now that these dichotomous conceptions are by way of being the ideology of honest performers, providing strength to the show they put on, but a poor analysis of it.

First, let it be said that there are many individuals who sincerely believe that the definition of the situation they habitually project is the real reality. In this report I do not mean to question their proportion in the population but rather the structural relation of their sincerity to the performances they offer. If a performance is to come off, the witnesses by and large must be able to believe that the performers are sincere. This is the structural place of sincerity in the drama of events. Performers may be sincere—or be insincere but sincerely convinced of their own sincerity—but this kind of affection for one's part is not necessary for its convincing performance. There are not many French cooks who are really Russian spies, and perhaps there are not many women who play the part of wife to one man and mistress to another; but these duplicities do occur, often being sustained successfully for long periods of time. This suggests that while persons usually are what they appear to be, such appearances could still have been managed. There is, then, a statistical relation between appearances and reality, not an intrinsic or necessary one. In fact, given the unanticipated threats that play upon a performance, and given the need (later to be discussed) to maintain solidarity with one's fellow performers and some distance from the witnesses, we find that a rigid incapacity to depart from one's inward view of reality may at times endanger one's performance. Some performances are carried off successfully with complete dishonesty, others with complete honesty; but for performances in general neither of these extremes is essential and neither, perhaps, is dramaturgically advisable.

The implication here is that an honest, sincere, serious performance is less firmly connected with the solid world than one might first assume. And this implication will be strengthened if we look again at the distance usually placed between quite honest performances and quite contrived ones. In this connection take, for example, the remarkable phenomenon of stage acting. It does take deep skill, long training, and psychological capacity to become a good stage actor. But this fact should not blind us to another one: that almost anyone can quickly learn a script well enough to give a charitable audience some sense of realness in what is being contrived before them. And it seems this is so because ordinary social intercourse is itself put together as a scene is put together, by the exchange of dramatically inflated actions, counteractions, and terminating replies. Scripts even in the hands of unpracticed players can come to life because life itself is a dramatically enacted thing. All the world is not, of course, a stage, but the crucial ways in which it isn't are not easy to specify.

The recent use of "psychodrama" as a therapeutic technique illustrates a further point in this regard. In these psychiatrically staged scenes patients not only act out parts with some effectiveness, but employ no script in doing so. Their own past is available to them in a form which allows them to stage a recapitulation of it. Apparently a part once played honestly and in earnest leaves the performer in a position to contrive a showing of it later. Further, the parts that significant others played to him in the past also seem to be available, allowing him to switch from being the person that he was to being the persons that others were for him. This capacity to switch enacted roles when obliged to do so could have been predicted; everyone apparently can do it. For in learning to perform our parts in real life we guide our own productions by not too consciously maintaining an incipient familiarity with the routine of those to whom we will address ourselves. And when we come to be able properly to manage a real routine we are able to do this in part because of "anticipatory socialization," having already been schooled in the reality that is just coming to be real for us.

When the individual does move into a new position in society and obtains a new part to perform, he is not likely to be told in full detail how to conduct himself, nor will the facts of his new situation press sufficiently on him from the start to determine his conduct without his further giving thought to it. Ordinarily he will be given only a few cues, hints, and stage directions, and it will be assumed that he already has in his repertoire a large number of bits and pieces of performances that will be required in the new setting. The individual will already have a fair idea of what modesty, deference, or righteous indignation looks like, and can make a pass at playing these bits when necessary. He may even be able to play out the part of a hypnotic subject or commit a "compulsive" crime on the basis of models for these activities that he is already familiar with.

A theatrical performance or a staged confidence game requires a thorough scripting of the spoken content of the routine; but the vast part involving "expression given off" is often determined by meager stage directions. It is expected that the performer of illusions will already know a good deal about how to manage his voice, his face, and his body, although he—as well as any person who directs him—may find it difficult indeed to provide a detailed verbal statement of this kind of knowledge. And in this, of course, we approach the situation of the straightforward man in the street. Socialization may not so much involve a learning of the many specific details of a single concrete part—often there could not be enough time or energy for this. What does seem to be required of the individual is that he learn enough pieces of expression to be able to "fill in" and manage, more or less, any part that he is likely to be given. The legitimate performances of everyday life are not "acted" or "put on" in the sense that the performer knows in advance just what he is going to do, and does this solely because of the effect it is likely to have. The expressions it is felt he is giving off will be especially "inaccessible" to him. But as in the case of less legitimate performers, the incapacity of the ordinary individual to formulate in advance the movements of his eyes and body does not mean that he will not express himself through these devices in a way that is dramatized and pre-formed in his repertoire of actions. In short, we will act better than we know how.

When we watch a television wrestler gouge, foul, and snarl at his opponent we are quite ready to see that, in spite of the dust, he is, and knows he is, merely playing at being the "heavy," and that in another match he may be given the other role, that of clean-cut wrestler, and perform this with equal verve and proficiency. We seem less ready to see, however, that while such details as the number and character of the falls may be fixed beforehand, the

details of the expressions and movements used do not come from a
script but from command of an idiom, a command that is exercised
from moment to moment with little calculation or forethought.

In reading of persons in the West Indies who become the
"horse" or the one possessed of a voodoo spirit, it is enlightening to
learn that the person possessed will be able to provide a correct portrayal of the god that has entered him because of "the knowledge
and memories accumulated in a life spent visiting congregations of
the cult"; that the person possessed will be in just the right social
relation to those who are watching; that possession occurs at just
the right moment in the ceremonial undertakings, the possessed one
carrying out his ritual obligations to the point of participating in a
kind of skit with persons possessed at the time with other spirits.
But in learning this, it is important to see that this contextual struc-
turing of the horse's role still allows participants in the cult to
believe that possession is a real thing and that persons are possessed
at random by gods whom they cannot select.

And when we observe a young American middle-class girl playing
dumb for the benefit of her boy friend, we are ready to point to
items of guile and contrivance in her behavior. But like herself and
her boy friend, we accept as an unperformed fact that this performer *is* a young American middle-class girl. But surely here we
neglect the greater part of the performance. It is commonplace to
say that different social groupings express in different ways such
attributes as age, sex, territory, and class status, and that in each
case these bare attributes are elaborated by means of a distinctive
complex cultural configuration of proper ways of conducting oneself. To *be* a given kind of person, then, is not merely to possess the
required attributes, but also to sustain the standards of conduct and
appearance that one's social grouping attaches thereto. The
unthinking ease with which performers consistently carry off such
standard-maintaining routines does not deny that a performance has
occurred, merely that the participants have been aware of it.

A status, a position, a social place is not a material thing, to be
possessed and then displayed; it is a pattern of appropriate conduct,
coherent, embellished, and well articulated. Performed with ease or
clumsiness, awareness or not, guile or good faith, it is none the less
something that must be enacted and portrayed, something that
must be realized. Sartre, here, provides a good illustration:

Let us consider this waiter in the café. His movement is quick and forward, a little too precise, a little too rapid. He comes toward the patrons
with a step a little too quick. He bends forward a little too eagerly; his
voice, his eyes express an interest a little too solicitous for the order of
the customer. Finally there he returns, trying to imitate in his walk the
inflexible stiffness of some kind of automaton while carrying his tray

with the recklessness of a tightrope-walker by putting it in a perpetually unstable, perpetually broken equilibrium which he perpetually re-establishes by a light movement of the arm and hand. All his behavior seems to us a game. He applies himself to chaining his movements as if they were mechanisms, the one regulating the other; his gestures and even his voice seem to be mechanisms; he gives himself the quickness and pitiless rapidity of things. He is playing, he is amusing himself. But what is he playing? We need not watch long before we can explain it: he is playing at being a waiter in a café. There is nothing there to surprise us. The game is a kind of marking out and investigation. The child plays with his body in order to explore it, to take inventory of it; the waiter in the café plays with his condition in order to realize it. This obligation is not different from that which is imposed on all tradesmen. Their condition is wholly one of ceremony. The public demands of them that they realize it as a ceremony; there is the dance of the grocer, of the tailor, of the auctioneer, by which they endeavor to persuade their clientele that they are nothing but a grocer, an auctioneer, a tailor. A grocer who dreams is offensive to the buyer, because such a grocer is not wholly a grocer. Society demands that he limit himself to his function as a grocer, just as the soldier at attention makes himself into a soldier, a thing with a direct regard which does not see at all, which is no longer meant to see, since it is the rule and not the interest of the moment which determines the point he must fix his eyes on (the sight "fixed at ten paces"). There are indeed many precautions to imprison a man in what he is, as if we lived in perpetual fear that he might escape from it, that he might break away and suddenly elude his condition.

1959

NORMAN PODHORETZ

My Negro Problem—And Ours

If we—and . . . I mean the relatively conscious whites and the relatively conscious blacks, who must, like lovers, insist on, or create, the consciousness of the others—do not falter in our duty now, we may be able, handful that we are, to end the racial nightmare, and achieve our country, and change the history of the world.

—JAMES BALDWIN[1]

Two ideas puzzled me deeply as a child growing up in Brooklyn during the 1930's in what today would be called an integrated neighborhood. One of them was that all Jews were rich; the other was that all Negroes were persecuted. These ideas has appeared in

---

1. The quotation is from the conclusion of Baldwin's *The Fire Next Time*.

print; therefore they must be true. My own experience and the evidence of my senses told they were not true, but that only confirmed what a day-dreaming boy in the provinces—for the lower-class neighborhoods of New York belong as surely to the provinces as any rural town in North Dakota—discovers very early: *his* experience is unreal and the evidence of his senses is not to be trusted. Yet even a boy with a head full of fantasies incongruously synthesized out of Hollywood movies and English novels cannot altogether deny the reality of his own experience—especially when there is so much deprivation in that experience. Nor can he altogether gainsay the evidence of his own senses—especially such evidence of the senses as comes from being repeatedly beaten up, robbed, and in general hated, terrorized, and humiliated.

And so for a long time I was puzzled to think that Jews were supposed to be rich when the only Jews I knew were poor, and that Negroes were supposed to be persecuted when it was the Negroes who were doing the only persecuting I knew about—and doing it, moreover, to *me*. During the early years of the war, when my older sister joined a left-wing youth organization, I remember my astonishment at hearing her passionately denounce my father for thinking that Jews were worse off than Negroes. To me, at the age of twelve, it seemed very clear that Negroes were better off than Jews —indeed, than *all* whites. A city boy's world is contained within three or four square blocks, and in my world it was the whites, the Italians and Jews, who feared the Negroes, not the other way around. The Negroes were tougher than we were, more ruthless, and on the whole they were better athletes. What could it mean, then, to say that they were badly off and that we were more fortunate? Yet my sister's opinions, like print, were sacred, and when she told me about exploitation and economic forces I believed her. I believed her, but I was still afraid of Negroes. And I still hated them with all my heart.

It had not always been so—that much I can recall from early childhood. When did it start, this fear and this hatred? There was a kindergarten in the local public school, and given the character of the neighborhood, at least half of the children in my class must have been Negroes. Yet I have no memory of being aware of color differences at that age, and I know from observing my own children that they attribute no significance to such differences even when they begin noticing them. I think there was a day—first grade? second grade?—when my best friend Carl hit me on the way home from school and announced that he wouldn't play with me any more because I had killed Jesus. When I ran home to my mother crying for an explanation, she told me not to pay any attention to such foolishness, and then in Yiddish she cursed the *goyim* and the *schwartzes*, the *schwartzes* and the *goyim*.[2] Carl, it turned out, was a *schwartze*, and so was added a third to the categories into which people were mysteriously divided.

Sometimes I wonder whether this is a true memory at all. It is blazingly vivid, but perhaps it never happened: can anyone really remember back to the age of six? There is no uncertainty in my mind, however, about the years that followed. Carl and I hardly ever spoke, though we met in school every day up through the eighth or ninth grade. There would be embarrassed moments of catching his eye or of his catching mine—for whatever it was that had attracted us to one another as very small children remained alive in spite of the fantastic barrier of hostility that had grown up between us, suddenly and out of nowhere. Nevertheless, friendship would have been impossible, and even if it had been possible, it would have been unthinkable. About that, there was nothing anyone could do by the time we were eight years old.

Item: The orphanage across the street is torn down, a city housing project begins to rise in its place, and on the marvelous vacant lot next to the old orphange they are building a playground. Much excitement and anticipation as Opening Day draws near. Mayor LaGuardia himself comes to dedicate this great gesture of public benevolence. He speaks of neighborliness and borrowing cups of sugar, and of the playground he says that children of all races, colors, and creeds will learn to live together in harmony. A week later, some of us are swatting flies on the playground's inadequate little ball field. A gang of Negro kids, pretty much our own age, enter from the other side and order us out of the park. We refuse, proudly and indignantly, with superb masculine fervor. There is a fight, they win, and we retreat, half whimpering, half with bravado. My first nauseating experience of cowardice. And my first appalled realization that there are people in the world who do not seem to be afraid of anything, who act as though they have nothing to lose. Thereafter the playground becomes a battleground, sometimes quiet, sometimes the scene of athletic competition between Them and Us. But rocks are thrown as often as baseballs. Gradually we abandon the place and use the streets instead. The streets are safer, though we do not admit this to ourselves. We are not, after all, sissies—that most dreaded epithet of an American boyhood.

Item: I am standing alone in front of the building in which I live. It is late afternoon and getting dark. That day in school the teacher had asked a surly Negro boy named Quentin a question he

---

2. The Yiddish words *goyim* (Gentiles or white non-Jews) and *schwartzes* (blacks) are both partially derogatory terms.

was unable to answer. As usual I had waved my arm eagerly ("Be a good boy, get good marks, be smart, go to college, become a doctor") and, the right answer bursting from my lips, I was held up lovingly by the teacher as an example to the class. I had seen Quentin's face—a very dark, very cruel, very Oriental-looking face—harden, and there had been enough threat in his eyes to make me run all the way home for fear that he might catch me outside.

Now, standing idly in front of my own house, I see him approaching from the project accompanied by his little brother who is carrying a baseball bat and wearing a grin of malicious anticipation. As in a nightmare, I am trapped. The surroundings are secure and familiar, but terror is suddenly present and there is no one around to help. I am locked to the spot. I will not cry out or run away like a sissy, and I stand there, my heart wild, my throat clogged. He walks up, hurls the familiar epithet ("Hey, mo' f——r"), and to my surprise only pushes me. It is a violent push, but not a punch. Maybe I can still back out without entirely losing my dignity. Maybe I can still say, "Hey, c'mon Quentin, whaddya wanna do *that* for? I dint do nothin' to *you*," and walk away, not too rapidly. Instead, before I can stop myself, I push him back—a token gesture—and I say, "Cut that out, I don't wanna fight, I ain't got nothin' to fight about." As I turn to walk back into the building, the corner of my eye catches the motion of the bat his little brother has handed him. I try to duck, but the bat crashes colored lights into my head.

The next thing I know, my mother and sister are standing over me, both of them hysterical. My sister—she who was later to join the "progressive" youth organization—is shouting for the police and screaming imprecations at those dirty little black bastards. They take me upstairs, the doctor comes, the police come. I tell them that the boy who did it was a stranger, that he had been trying to get money from me. They do not believe me, but I am too scared to give them Quentin's name. When I return to school a few days later, Quentin avoids my eyes. He knows that I have not squealed, and he is ashamed. I try to feel proud, but in my heart I know that it was fear of what his friends might do to me that had kept me silent, and not the code of the street.

Item: There is an athletic meet in which the whole of our junior high school is participating. I am in one of the seventh-grade rapid-advance classes, and "segregation" has now set in with a vengeance. In the last three or four years of the elementary school from which we have just graduated, each grade had been divided into three classes, according to "intelligence." (In the earlier grades the divisions had either been arbitrary or else unrecognized by us as having anything to do with brains.) These divisions by IQ, or however it was arranged, had resulted in a preponderance of Jews in the "1" classes and a corresponding preponderance of Negroes in the "3's," with the Italians split unevenly along the spectrum. At least a few Negroes had always made the "1's," just as there had always been a few Jewish kids among the "3's" and more among the "2's" (where Italians dominated). But the junior high's rapid-advance class of which I am now a member is overwhelmingly Jewish and entirely white—except for a shy lonely Negro girl with light skin and reddish hair.

The athletic meet takes place in a city-owned stadium far from the school. It is an important event to which a whole day is given over. The winners are to get those precious little medallions stamped with the New York City emblem that can be screwed into a belt and that prove the wearer to be a distinguished personage. I am a fast runner, and so I am assigned the position of anchor man on my class's team in the relay race. There are three other seventh-grade teams in the race, two of them all Negro, as ours is all white. One of the all-Negro teams is very tall—their anchor man waiting silently next to me on the line looks years older than I am, and I do not recognize him. He is the first to get the baton and crosses the finishing line in a walk. Our team comes in second, but a few minutes later we are declared the winners, for it has been discovered that the anchor man on the first-place team is not a member of the class. We are awarded the medallions, and the following day our homeroom teacher makes a speech about how proud she is of us for being superior athletes as well as superior students. We want to believe that we deserve the praise, but we know that we could not have won even if the other class had not cheated.

That afternoon, walking home, I am waylaid and surrounded by five Negroes, among whom is the anchor man of the disqualified team. "Gimme my medal, mo'f——r," he grunts. I do not have it with me and I tell him so. "Anyway, it ain't yours," I say foolishly. He calls me a liar on both counts and pushes me up against the wall on which we sometimes play handball. "Gimmie my mo'f——n' medal," he says again. I repeat that I have left it home. "Le's search the li'l mo'f——r," one of them suggests, "he prolly got it *hid* in his mo'f——n' *pants*." My panic is now unmanageable. (How many times had I been surrounded like this and asked in soft tones, "Len' me a nickel, boy." How many times had I been called a liar for pleading poverty and pushed around, or searched, or beaten up, unless there happened to be someone in the marauding gang like Carl who liked me across that enormous divide of hatred and who would therefore say, "Aaah, c'mon, le's git someone else, *this* boy ain't got no money on 'im.") I scream at them through tears of rage and self-contempt, "Keep your f———n' filthy lousy black hands offa me! I swear I'll get the cops." This is all they need to hear, and the five of them set upon me. They bang me around, mostly in the stomach and on the arms and shoulders, and when several adults loitering near the candy store down the block notice what is going on and begin to shout, they run off and away.

I do not tell my parents about the incident. My team-mates, who have also been waylaid, each by a gang led by his opposite number from the disqualified team, have had their medallions taken from them, and they never squeal either. For days, I walk home in terror, expecting to be caught again, but nothing happens. The medallion is put away into a drawer, never to be worn by anyone.

Obviously experiences like these have always been a common feature of childhood life in working-class and immigrant neighborhoods, and Negroes do not necessarily figure in them. Wherever, and in whatever combination, they have lived together in the cities, kids of different groups have been at war, beating up and being beaten up: micks against kikes against wops against spicks against polacks. And even relatively homogeneous areas have not been spared the warring of the young: one block against another, one gang (called in my day, in a pathetic effort at gentility, an "S.A.C.," or social-athletic club) against another. But the Negro-white conflict had—and no doubt still has—a special intensity and was conducted with a ferocity unmatched by intramural white battling.

In my own neighborhood, a good deal of animosity existed between the Italian kids (most of whose parents were immigrants from Sicily) and the Jewish kids (who came largely from East European immigrant families). Yet everyone had friends, sometimes close friends, in the other "camp," and we often visited one another's strange-smelling houses, if not for meals, then for glasses of milk, and occasionally for some special event like a wedding or a wake. If it happened that we divided into warring factions and did battle, it would invariably be half-hearted and soon patched up. Our parents, to be sure, had nothing to do with one another and were mutually suspicious and hostile. But we, the kids, who all spoke Yiddish or Italian at home, were Americans, or New Yorkers, or Brooklyn boys: we shared a culture, the culture of the street, and at least for a while this culture proved to be more powerful than the opposing cultures of the home.

Why, why should it have been so different as between the Negroes and us? How was it borne in upon us so early, white and black alike, that we were enemies beyond any possibility of reconciliation? Why did we hate one another so?

I suppose if I tried, I could answer those questions more or less adequately from the perspective of what I have since learned. I could draw upon James Baldwin—what better witness is there?—to describe the sense of entrapment that poisons the soul of the Negro with hatred for the white man whom he knows to be his jailer. On the other side, if I wanted to understand how the white man comes to hate the Negro, I could call upon the psychologists who have spoken of the guilt that white Americans feel toward Negroes and that turns into hatred for lack of acknowledging itself as guilt. These are plausible answers and certainly there is truth in them, Yet when I think back upon my own experience of the Negro and his of me, I find myself troubled and puzzled, much as I was as a child when I heard that all Jews were rich and all Negroes persecuted. How could the Negroes in my neighborhood have regarded the whites across the street and around the corner as jailers? On the whole, the whites were not so poor as the Negroes, but they were quite poor enough, and the years were years of Depression. As for white hatred of the Negro, how could guilt have had anything to do with it? What share had these Italian and Jewish immigrants in the enslavement of the Negro? What share had they—downtrodden people themselves breaking their own necks to eke out a living—in the exploitation of the Negro?

No, I cannot believe that we hated each other back there in Brooklyn because they thought of us as jailers and we felt guilty toward them. But does it matter, given the fact that we all went through an unrepresentative confrontation? I think it matters profoundly, for if we managed the job of hating each other so well without benefit of the aids to hatred that are supposedly at the root of this madness everywhere else, it must mean that the madness is not yet properly understood. I am far from pretending that I understand it, but I would insist that no view of the problem will begin to approach the truth unless it can account for a case like the one I have been trying to describe. Are the elements of any such view available to us?

At least two, I would say, are. One of them is a point we frequently come upon in the work of James Baldwin, and the other is a related point always stressed by psychologists who have studied the mechanisms of prejudice. Baldwin tells us that one of the reasons Negroes hate the white man is that the white man refuses to *look* at him: the Negro knows that in white eyes all Negroes are alike; they are faceless and therefore not altogether human. The psychologists, in their turn, tell us that the white man hates the Negro because he tends to project those wild impulses that he fears in himself onto an alien group which he then punishes with his contempt. What Baldwin does *not* tell us, however, is that the principle of facelessness is a two-way street and can operate in both directions with no difficulty at all. Thus, in my neighborhood in Brooklyn, I was as faceless to the Negroes as they were to me, and if they hated me because I never looked at them, I must also have hated them for never looking at *me*. To the Negroes, my white skin was enough to define me as the enemy, and in a war it is only the uniform that counts and not the person.

So with the mechanism of projection that the psychologists talk about: it too works in both directions at once. There is no question that the psychologists are right about what the Negro represents symbolically to the white man. For me as a child the life lived on the other side of the playground and down the block on Ralph Avenue seemed the very embodiment of the values of the street— free, independent, reckless, brave, masculine, erotic. I put the word "erotic" last, though it is usually stressed above all others, because in fact it came last, in consciousness as in importance. What mainly counted for me about Negro kids of my own age was that they were "bad boys." There were plenty of bad boys among the whites—this was, after all, a neighborhood with a long tradition of crime as a career open to aspiring talents—but the Negroes were *really* bad, bad in a way that beckoned to one, and made one feel inadequate. We all went home every day for a lunch of spinach-and-potatoes; *they* roamed around during lunch hour, munching on candy bars. In winter *we* had to wear itchy woolen hats and mittens and cumbersome galoshes; *they* were bareheaded and loose as they pleased. We rarely played hookey, or got into serious trouble in school, for all our street-corner bravado; *they* were defiant, forever staying out (to do what delicious things?), forever making disturbances in class and in the halls, forever being sent to the principal and returning uncowed. But most important of all, they were *tough*; beautifully, enviably tough, not giving a damn for anyone or anything. To hell with the teacher, the truant officer, the cop; to hell with the whole of the adult world that held *us* in its grip and that we never had the courage to rebel against except sporadically and in petty ways.

This is what I saw and envied and feared in the Negro: this is what finally made him faceless to me, though some of it, of course, was actually there. (The psychologists also tell us that the alien group which becomes the object of a projection will tend to respond by trying to live up to what is expected of them.) But what, on his side, did the Negro see in me that made me faceless to *him*? Did he envy me my lunches of spinach-and-potatoes and my itchy woolen caps and my prudent behavior in the face of authority, as I envied him his noon-time candy bars and his bare head in winter and his magnificent rebelliousness? Did those lunches and caps spell for him the prospect of power and riches in the future? Did they mean that there were possibilities open to me that were denied to him? Very likely they did. But if so, one also supposes that he feared the impulses within himself toward submission to authority no less powerfully than I feared the impulses in myself toward defiance. If I represented the jailer to him, it was not because I was oppressing him or keeping him down: it was because I symbolized for him the dangerous and probably pointless temptation toward greater repression, just as he symbolized for me the equally perilous tug toward greater freedom. I personally was to be rewarded for this repression with a new and better life in the future, but how many of my friends paid an even higher price and were given only gall in return.

We have it on the authority of James Baldwin that all Negroes hate whites. I am trying to suggest that on their side all whites—all American whites, that is—are sick in their feelings about Negroes. There are Negroes, no doubt, who would say that Baldwin is wrong, but I suspect them of being less honest than he is, just as I suspect whites of self-deception who tell me they have no special feeling toward Negroes. Special feelings about color are a contagion to which white Americans seem susceptible even when there is nothing in their background to account for the susceptibility. Thus everywhere we look today in the North we find the curious phenomenon of white middle-class liberals with no previous personal experience of Negroes—people to whom Negroes have always been faceless in virtue rather than faceless in vice—discovering that their abstract commitment to the cause of Negro rights will not stand the test of a direct confrontation. We find such people fleeing in droves to the suburbs as the Negro population in the inner city grows; and when they stay in the city we find them sending their children to private school rather than to the "integrated" public school in the neighborhood. We find them resisting the demand that gerrymandered school districts be re-zoned for the purpose of overcoming de facto segregation; we find them judiciously considering whether the Negroes (for their own good, of course) are not perhaps pushing too hard; we find them clucking their tongues over Negro militancy; we find them speculating on the question of whether there may not, after all, be something in the theory that the races are biologically different; we find them saying that it will take a very long time for Negroes to achieve full equality, no matter what anyone does; we find them deploring the rise of black nationalism and expressing the solemn hope that the leaders of the Negro community will discover ways of containing the impatience and incipient violence within the Negro ghettos.

But that is by no means the whole story; there is also the phenomenon of what Kenneth Rexroth once called "crow-jimism."

There are the broken-down white boys like Vivaldo Moore in Baldwin's *Another Country* who go to Harlem in search of sex or simply to brush up against something that looks like primitive vitality, and who are so often punished by the Negroes they meet for crimes that they would have been the last ever to commit and of which they themselves have been as sorry victims as any of the Negroes who take it out on them. There are the writers and intellectuals and artists who romanticize Negroes and pander to them, assuming a guilt that is not properly theirs. And there are all the white liberals who permit Negroes to blackmail them into adopting a double standard of moral judgment, and who lend themselves—again assuming the responsibility for crimes they never committed—to cunning and contemptuous exploitation by Negroes they employ or try to befriend.

And what about me? What kind of feelings do I have about Negroes today? What happened to me, from Brooklyn, who grew up fearing and envying and hating Negroes? Now that Brooklyn is behind me, do I fear them and envy them and hate them still? The answer is yes, but not in the same proportions and certainly not in the same way. I now live on the upper west side of Manhattan, where there are many Negroes and many Puerto Ricans, and there are nights when I experience the old apprehensiveness again, and there are streets that I avoid when I am walking in the dark, as there were streets that I avoided when I was a child. I find that I am not afraid of Puerto Ricans, but I cannot restrain my nervousness whenever I pass a group of Negroes standing in front of a bar or sauntering down the street. I know now, as I did not know when I was a child, that power is on my side, that the police are working for me and not for them. And knowing this I feel ashamed and guilty, like the good liberal I have grown up to be. Yet the twinges of fear and the resentment they bring and the self-contempt they arouse are not to be gainsaid.

But envy? Why envy? And hatred? Why hatred? Here again the intensities have lessened and everything has been complicated and qualified by the guilts and the resulting over-compensations that are the heritage of the enlightened middle-class world of which I am now a member. Yet just as in childhood I envied Negroes for what seemed to me their superior masculinity, so I envy them today for what seems to me their superior physical grace and beauty. I have come to value physical grace very highly, and I am now capable of aching with all my being when I watch a Negro couple on the dance floor, or a Negro playing baseball or basketball. They are on the kind of terms with their own bodies that I should like to be on with mine, and for that precious quality they seemed blessed to me.

The hatred I still feel for Negroes is the hardest of all the old feelings to face or admit, and it is the most hidden and the most overlarded by the conscious attitudes into which I have succeeded in willing myself. It no longer has, as for me it once did, any cause or justification (except, perhaps, that I am constantly being denied my right to an honest expression of the things I earned the right as a child to feel). How, then, do I know that this hatred has never entirely disappeared? I know it from the insane rage that can stir in me at the thought of Negro anti-Semitism; I know it from the disgusting prurience that can stir in me at the sight of a mixed couple; and I know it from the violence that can stir in me whenever I encounter that special brand of paranoid touchiness to which many Negroes are prone.

This, then, is where I am; it is not exactly where I think all other white liberals are, but it cannot be so very far away either. And it is because I am convinced that we white Americans are—for whatever reason, it no longer matters—so twisted and sick in our feelings about Negroes that I despair of the present push toward integration. If the pace of progress were not a factor here, there would perhaps be no cause for despair: time and the law and even the international political situation are on the side of the Negroes, and ultimately, therefore, victory—of a sort, anyway—must come. But from everything we have learned from observers who ought to know, pace has become as important to the Negroes as substance. They want equality and they want it *now*, and the white world is yielding to their demand only as much and as fast as it is absolutely being compelled to do. The Negroes know this in the most concrete terms imaginable, and it is thus becoming increasingly difficult to buy them off with rhetoric and promises and pious assurances of support. And so within the Negro community we find more and more people declaring—as Harold R. Isaacs recently put it in an article in *Commentary*—that they want *out*: people who say that integration will never come, or that it will take a hundred or a thousand years to come, or that it will come at too high a price in suffering and struggle for the pallid and sodden life of the American middle class that at the very best it may bring.

The most numerous, influential, and dangerous movement that has grown out of Negro despair with the goal of integration is, of course, the Black Muslims. This movement, whatever else we may say about it, must be credited with one enduring achievement: it inspired James Baldwin to write an essay which deserves to be placed among the classics of our language. Everything Baldwin has ever been trying to tell us is distilled in *The Fire Next Time* into a statement of overwhelming persuasiveness and prophetic magnificence. Baldwin's message is and always has been simple. It is this:

"Color is not a human or personal reality; it is a political reality." And Baldwin's demand is correspondingly simple; color must be forgotten, lest we all be smited with a vengeance "that does not really depend on, and cannot really be executed by, any person or organization, and that cannot be prevented by any police force or army: historical vengeance, a cosmic vengeance based on the law that we recognize when we say, 'Whatever goes up must come down.' " The Black Muslims Baldwin portrays as a sign and a warning to the intransigent white world. They come to proclaim how deep is the Negro's disaffection with the white world and all its works, and Baldwin implies that no American Negro can fail to respond somewhere in his being to their message: that the white man is the devil, that Allah has doomed him to destruction, and that the black man is about to inherit the earth. Baldwin of course knows that this nightmare inversion of the racism from which the black man has suffered can neither win nor even point to the neighborhood in which victory might be located. For in his view the neighborhood of victory lies in exactly the opposite direction: the transcendence of color through love.

Yet the tragic fact is that love is not the answer to hate—not in the world of politics, at any rate. Color is indeed a political rather than a human or a personal reality and if politics (which is to say power) has made it into a human and personal reality, then only politics (which is to say power) can unmake it once again. But the way of politics is slow and bitter, and as impatience on the one side is matched by a setting of the jaw on the other, we move closer and closer to an explosion and blood may yet run in the streets.

Will this madness in which we are all caught never find a resting-place? Is there never to be an end to it? In thinking about the Jews I have often wondered whether their survival as a distinct group was worth one hair on the head of a single infant. Did the Jews have to survive so that six million innocent people should one day be burned in the ovens of Auschwitz? It is a terrible question and no one, not God himself, could ever answer it to my satisfaction. And when I think about the Negroes in America and about the image of integration as a state in which the Negroes would take their rightful place as another of the protected minorities in a pluralistic society, I wonder whether they really believe in their hearts that such a state can actually be attained, and if so *why* they should wish to survive as a distinct group. I think I know why the Jews once wished to survive (though I am less certain as to why we still do): they not only believed that God had given them no choice, but they were tied to a memory of past glory and a dream of imminent redemption. What does the American Negro have that might correspond to this? His past is a stigma, his color is a stigma, and his vision of the future is the hope of erasing the stigma by making color irrelevant, by making it disappear as a fact of consciousness.

I share this hope, but I cannot see how it will ever be realized unless color does *in fact* disappear: and that means not integration, it means assimilation, it means—let the brutal word come out—miscegenation. The Black Muslims, like their racist counterparts in the white world, accuse the "so-called Negro leaders" of secretly pursuing miscegenation as a goal. The racists are wrong, but I wish they were right, for I believe that the wholesale merger of the two races is the most desirable alternative for everyone concerned. I am not claiming that this alternative can be pursued programmatically or that it is immediately feasible as a solution; obviously there are even greater barriers to its achievement than to the achievement of integration. What I am saying, however, is that in my opinion the Negro problem can be solved in this country in no other way.

I have told the story of my own twisted feelings about Negroes here, and of how they conflict with the moral convictions I have since developed, in order to assert that such feelings must be acknowledged as honestly as possible so that they can be controlled and ultimately disregarded in favor of the convictions. It is *wrong* for a man to suffer because of the color of his skin. Beside that clichéd proposition of liberal thought, what argument can stand and be respected? If the arguments are the arguments of feeling, they must be made to yield; and one's own soul is not the worst place to begin working a huge social transformation. Not so long ago, it used to be asked of white liberals, "Would you like your sister to marry one?" When I was a boy and my sister was still unmarried I would certainly have said no to that question. But now I am a man, my sister is already married, and I have daughters. If I were to be asked today whether I would like a daughter of mine "to marry one," I would have to answer: "No, I wouldn't *like* it at all. I would rail and rave and rant and tear my hair. And then I hope I would have the courage to curse myself for raving and ranting, and to give her my blessing. How dare I withhold it at the behest of the child I once was and against the man I now have a duty to be?"

1964

DESMOND MORRIS

Altruistic Behavior

Altruism is the performance of an unselfish act. As a pattern of behavior this act must have two properties: it must benefit someone else, and it must do so to the disadvantage of the benefactor. It is not merely a matter of being helpful, it is helpfulness at a cost to yourself.

This simple definition conceals a difficult biological problem. If I harm myself to help you, then I am increasing your chances of success relative to mine. In broad evolutionary terms, if I do this, your offspring (or potential offspring) will have better prospects than mine. Because I have been altruistic, your genetic line will stand a better chance of survival than mine. Over a period of time, my unselfish line will die out and your selfish line will survive. So altruism will not be a viable proposition in evolutionary terms.

Since human beings are animals whose ancestors have won the long struggle for survival during their evolutionary history, they cannot be genetically programmed to display true altruism. Evolution theory suggests that they must, like all other animals, be entirely selfish in their actions, even when they appear to be at their most self-sacrificing and philanthropic.

This is the biological, evolutionary argument and it is completely convincing as far as it goes, but it does not seem to explain many of mankind's "finer moments." If a man sees a burning house and inside it his small daughter, an old friend, a complete stranger, or even a screaming kitten, he may, without pausing to think, rush headlong into the building and be badly burned in a desperate attempt to save a life. How can actions of this sort be described as selfish? The fact is that they can, but it requires a special definition of the term "self."

When you think of your "self," you probably think of your living body, complete, as it is at this moment. But biologically it is more correct to think of yourself as merely a temporary housing, a disposable container, for your genes. Your genes—the genetic material that you inherited from your parents and which you will pass on to your children—are in a sense immortal. Our bodies are merely the carriers which they use to transport themselves from one generation to the next. It is they, not we, who are the basic units of evolution. We are only their guardians, protecting them from destruction as best we can, for the brief span of our lives.

Religion pictures man as having an immortal soul which leaves his body at death and floats off to heaven (or hell, as the case may be), but the more useful image is to visualize a man's immortal soul as sperm-shaped and a woman's as egg-shaped, and to think of them as leaving the body during the breeding process rather than at death. Following this line of thought through, there is, of course, an afterlife, but it is not in some mysterious "other world," it is right here in the heaven (or hell) of the nursery and the playground, where our genes continue their immortal journey down the tunnel of time, re-housed now in the brand-new flesh-containers we call children.

So, genetically speaking, our children are us—or, rather, half of us, since our mate has a half share of the genes of each child. This makes our devoted and apparently selfless parental care nothing more than *genetic self-care*. The man who risks death to save his small daughter from a fire is in reality saving his own genes in their new body-package. And in saving his genes, his act becomes biologically selfish, rather than altruistic.

But supposing the man leaping into the fire is trying to save, not his daughter, but an old friend? How can this be selfish? The answer here lies in the ancient history of mankind. For more than a million years, man was a simple tribal being, living in small groups where everyone knew everyone else and everyone was closely genetically related to everyone else. Despite a certain amount of outbreeding, the chances were that every member of your own tribe was a relative of some kind, even if a rather remote one. A certain degree of altruism was therefore appropriate where all the other members of your tribe were concerned. You would be helping copies of your own genes, and although you might not respond so intensely to their calls for help as you would do with your own children, you would nevertheless give them a degree of help, again on a basis of genetic selfishness.

This is not, of course, a calculated process. It operates unconsciously and is based on an emotion we call "love." Our love for our children is what we say we are obeying when we act "selflessly" for them, and our love of our fellow-men is what we feel when we come to the aid of our friends. These are inborn tendencies and when we are faced with calls for help we feel ourselves obeying these deep-seated urges unquestioningly and unanalytically. It is only because we see ourselves as "persons" rather than as "gene machines" that we think of these acts of love as unselfish rather than selfish.

So far, so good, but what about the man who rushes headlong into the fire to save a complete stranger? The stranger is probably *not* genetically related to the man who helps him, so this act must surely be truly unselfish and altruistic? The answer is Yes, but only by accident. The accident is caused by the rapid growth of human populations in the last few thousand years. Previously, for millions of years, man was tribal and any inborn urge to help his fellow-men would have meant automatically that he was helping gene-sharing relatives, even if only remote ones. There was no need for this urge to be selective, because there were no strangers around to create problems. But with the urban explosion, man rapidly found himself in huge communities, surrounded by strangers, and with no time for his genetic constitution to alter to fit the startlingly new circumstances. So his altruism inevitably spread to include all his new fellow-citizens, even though many of them may have been genetically quite unrelated to him.

Politicians, exploiting this ancient urge, were easily able to spread the aid-system even further, to a national level called patriotism, so that men would go and die for their country as if it were their ancient tribe or their family.

The man who leaps into the fire to save a small kitten is a special case. To many people, animals are child-substitutes and receive the same care and love as real children. The kitten-saver is explicable as a man who is going to the aid of his symbolic child. This process of symbolizing, of seeing one thing as a metaphorical equivalent of another, is a powerful tendency of the human animal and it accounts for a great deal of the spread of helpfulness across the human environment.

In particular it explains the phenomenon of dying for a cause. This always gives the appearance of the ultimate in altruistic behavior, but a careful examination of the nature of each cause reveals that there is some basic symbolism at work. A nun who gives her life for Christ is already technically a "bride" of Christ and looks upon all people as the "children" of God. Her symbolism has brought the whole of humanity into her "family circle" and her altruism is for her symbolic family, which to her can become as real as other people's natural families.

In this manner it is possible to explain the biological bases for man's seemingly altruistic behavior. This is in no way intended to belittle such activities, but merely to point out that the more usual, alternative explanations are not necessary. For example, it is often stated that man is fundamentally wicked and that his kind acts are largely the result of the teachings of moralists, philosophers and priests; that if he is left to his own devices he will become increasingly savage, violent and cruel. The confidence trick involved here is that if we accept this viewpoint we will attribute all society's good qualities to the brilliant work of these great teachers. The biological truth appears to be rather different. Since selfishness is genetic rather than personal, we will have a natural tendency to help our blood-relatives and hence our whole tribe. Since our tribes have swollen into nations, our helpfulness becomes stretched further and further, aided and abetted by our tendency toward accepting symbolic substitutes for the real thing. Altogether this means that we are now, by nature, a remarkably helpful species. If there are breakdowns in this helpfulness, they are probably due, not to our "savage nature" reasserting itself, but to the unbearable tensions under which people so often find themselves in the strained and overcrowded world of today.

It would be a mistake, nevertheless, to overstate man's angelic helpfulness. He is also intensely competitive. But under normal circumstances these rival tendencies balance each other out, and this balance accounts for a great deal of human intercourse, in the form of *transactional behavior*. This is behavior of the "I'll-scratch-your-back-if-you'll-scratch-mine" type. We do deals with one another. My actions help you, but they are not altruistic because they also help me at the same time. This co-operative behavior is perhaps the dominant feature of day-to-day social interaction. It is the basis of trade and commerce and it explains why such activities do not become more ruthless. If the competitive element were not tempered by the basic urge to help one another, business practices would rapidly become much more savage and brutal than they are, even today.

An important extension of this two-way co-operative behavior is embodied in the phrase: "one good turn now deserves another later." This is delayed, or nonspecific co-operation. I give help to you now, even though you cannot help me in return. I do this daily to many people I meet. One day I will need help and then, as part of a "long-term deal," they will return my help. I do not keep a check on what I am owed or by whom. Indeed, the person who finally helps me may not be one of the ones I have helped. But a whole network of social debts will have built up in a community and, as there is a great division of labor and skills in our species today, such a system will be beneficial to all the members of the society. This has been called "reciprocal altruism." But once again it is not true altruism because sooner or later, one way or another, I will be rewarded for my acts of helpfulness.

Anticipation of a delayed-reward of this kind is often the hidden motive for a great deal of what is claimed to be purely altruistic behavior. Many countries hand out official awards to their citizens for "services to the community," but frequently these services have been deliberately undertaken in the anticipation that they are award-worthy. Comparatively few public honors ever come as a surprise. And many other "good works" are undertaken with later social (or heavenly) rewards in mind. This does not necessarily make the "works" any less good, of course, it merely explains the motives involved.

The following table sums up the relationship between competitiveness and helpfulness, and their intermediates:

1	Self-assertive behavior	Helps me	Harms you	Mild competitiveness to full criminality
2	Self-indulgent behavior	Helps me	No effect on you	The private, non-social pleasures
3	Co-operative behavior	Helps me	Helps you	Transaction, trade, barter, and negotiation
4	Courteous behavior	No effect on me	Helps you	Kindness and generosity
5	"Altruistic" behavior	Harms me	Helps you	Loving devotion, philanthropy, self-sacrifice, and patriotism

1977

QUESTIONS

1. Morris defines a number of terms, including "altruism," "self," and "immortal soul." What is the method of these definitions? What is their importance?
2. How does Morris construct his argument? Is it convincing? Why, or why not?
3. Morris writes from a biological point of view. What alternative approaches to his subject are possible? How would they differ from Morris'?
4. Could the chart at the end of the essay be extended to include other kinds of behavior? Do you believe the distinctions in its various categories are sufficiently fine? Why, or why not?

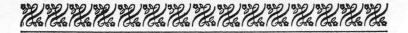

Politics
and Government

GEORGE ORWELL

Shooting an Elephant

In Moulmein, in Lower Burma, I was hated by large numbers of people—the only time in my life that I have been important enough for this to happen to me. I was sub-divisional police officer of the town, and in an aimless, petty kind of way anti-European feeling was very bitter. No one had the guts to raise a riot, but if a European woman went through the bazaars alone somebody would probably spit betel juice over her dress. As a police officer I was an obvious target and was baited whenever it seemed safe to do so. When a nimble Burman tripped me up on the football field and the referee (another Burman) looked the other way, the crowd yelled with hideous laughter. This happened more than once. In the end the sneering yellow faces of young men that met me everywhere, the insults hooted after me when I was at a safe distance, got badly on my nerves. The young Buddhist priests were the worst of all. There were several thousands of them in the town and none of them seemed to have anything to do except stand on street corners and jeer at Europeans.

All this was perplexing and upsetting. For at that time I had already made up my mind that imperialism was an evil thing and the sooner I chucked up my job and got out of it the better. Theoretically—and secretly, of course—I was all for the Burmese and all against their oppressors, the British. As for the job I was doing, I hated it more bitterly than I can perhaps make clear. In a job like that you see the dirty work of Empire at close quarters. The wretched prisoners huddling in the stinking cages of the lock-ups, the grey, cowed faces of the long-term convicts, the scarred buttocks of the men who had been flogged with bamboos—all these oppressed me with an intolerable sense of guilt. But I could get

463

nothing into perspective. I was young and ill-educated and I had had to think out my problems in the utter silence that is imposed on every Englishman in the East. I did not even know that the British Empire is dying, still less did I know that it is a great deal better than the younger empires that are going to supplant it. All I knew was that I was stuck between my hatred of the empire I served and my rage against the evil-spirited little beasts who tried to make my job impossible. With one part of my mind I thought of the British Raj as an unbreakable tyranny, as something clamped down, in *saecula saeculorum*,[1] upon the will of prostrate peoples; with another part I thought that the greatest joy in the world would be to drive a bayonet into a Buddhist priest's guts. Feelings like these are the normal by-products of imperialism; ask any Anglo-Indian official, if you can catch him off duty.

One day something happened which in a roundabout way was enlightening. It was a tiny incident in itself, but it gave me a better glimpse than I had had before of the real nature of imperialism—the real motives for which despotic governments act. Early one morning the sub-inspector at a police station the other end of the town rang me up on the 'phone and said that an elephant was ravaging the bazaar. Would I please come and do something about it? I did not know what I could do, but I wanted to see what was happening and I got on to a pony and started out. I took my rifle, an old .44 Winchester and much too small to kill an elephant, but I thought the noise might be useful *in terrorem*. Various Burmans stopped me on the way and told me about the elephant's doings. It was not, of course, a wild elephant, but a tame one which had gone "must." It had been chained up, as tame elephants always are when their attack of "must" is due, but on the previous night it had broken its chain and escaped. Its mahout, the only person who could manage it when it was in that state, had set out in pursuit, but had taken the wrong direction and was now twelve hours' journey away, and in the morning the elephant had suddenly reappeared in the town. The Burmese population had no weapons and were quite helpless against it. It had already destroyed somebody's bamboo hut, killed a cow and raided some fruit-stalls and devoured the stock; also it had met the municipal rubbish van and, when the driver jumped out and took to his heels, had turned the van over and inflicted violences upon it.

The Burmese sub-inspector and some Indian constables were waiting for me in the quarter where the elephant had been seen. It was a very poor quarter, a labyrinth of squalid bamboo huts, thatched with palm-leaf, winding all over a steep hillside. I remem-

---

1. In ancient times; *the British Raj*: the imperial government of British In-   dia and Burma.

ber that it was a cloudy, stuffy morning at the beginning of the rains. We began questioning the people as to where the elephant had gone and, as usual, failed to get any definite information. That is invariably the case in the East; a story always sounds clear enough at a distance, but the nearer you get to the scene of events the vaguer it becomes. Some of the people said that the elephant had gone in one direction, some said that he had gone in another, some professed not even to have heard of any elephant. I had almost made up my mind that the whole story was a pack of lies, when we heard yells a little distance away. There was a loud, scandalized cry of "Go away, child! Go away this instant!" and an old woman with a switch in her hand came round the corner of a hut, violently shooing away a crowd of naked children. Some more women followed, clicking their tongues and exclaiming; evidently there was something that the children ought not to have seen. I rounded the hut and saw a man's dead body sprawling in the mud. He was an Indian, a black Dravidian coolie, almost naked, and he could not have been dead many minutes. The people said that the elephant had come suddenly upon him round the corner of the hut, caught him with its trunk, put its foot on his back and ground him into the earth. This was the rainy season and the ground was soft, and his face had scored a trench a foot deep and a couple of yards long. He was lying on his belly with arms crucified and head sharply twisted to one side. His face was coated with mud, the eyes wide open, the teeth bared and grinning with an expression of unendurable agony. (Never tell me, by the way, that the dead look peaceful. Most of the corpses I have seen looked devilish.) The friction of the great beast's foot had stripped the skin from his back as neatly as one skins a rabbit. As soon as I saw the dead man I sent an orderly to a friend's house nearby to borrow an elephant rifle. I had already sent back the pony, not wanting it to go mad with fright and throw me if it smelt the elephant.

The orderly came back in a few minutes with a rifle and five cartridges, and meanwhile some Burmans had arrived and told us that the elephant was in the paddy fields below, only a few hundred yards away. As I started forward practically the whole population of the quarter flocked out of the houses and followed me. They had seen the rifle and were all shouting excitedly that I was going to shoot the elephant. They had not shown much interest in the elephant when he was merely ravaging their homes, but it was different now that he was going to be shot. It was a bit of fun to them, as it would be to an English crowd; besides they wanted the meat. It made me vaguely uneasy. I had no intention of shooting the elephant—I had merely sent for the rifle to defend myself if necessary —and it is always unnerving to have a crowd following you. I marched down the hill, looking and feeling a fool, with the rifle over my shoulder and an ever-growing army of people jostling at my heels. At the bottom, when you got away from the huts, there was a metalled road and beyond that a miry waste of paddy fields a thousand yards across, not yet ploughed but soggy from the first rains and dotted with coarse grass. The elephant was standing eight yards from the road, his left side towards us. He took not the slightest notice of the crowd's approach. He was tearing up bunches of grass, beating them against his knees to clean them and stuffing them into his mouth.

I had halted on the road. As soon as I saw the elephant I knew with perfect certainty that I ought not to shoot him. It is a serious matter to shoot a working elephant—it is comparable to destroying a huge and costly piece of machinery—and obviously one ought not to do it if it can possibly be avoided. And at that distance, peacefully eating, the elephant looked no more dangerous than a cow. I thought then and I think now that his attack of "must" was already passing off; in which case he would merely wander harmlessly about until the mahout came back and caught him. Moreover, I did not in the least want to shoot him. I decided that I would watch him for a little while to make sure that he did not turn savage again, and then go home.

But at that moment I glanced round at the crowd that had followed me. It was an immense crowd, two thousand at the least and growing every minute. It blocked the road for a long distance on either side. I looked at the sea of yellow faces above the garish clothes—faces all happy and excited over this bit of fun, all certain that the elephant was going to be shot. They were watching me as they would watch a conjurer about to perform a trick. They did not like me, but with the magical rifle in my hands I was momentarily worth watching. And suddenly I realized that I should have to shoot the elephant after all. The people expected it of me and I had got to do it; I could feel their two thousand wills pressing me forward, irresistibly. And it was at this moment, as I stood there with the rifle in my hands, that I first grasped the hollowness, the futility of the white man's dominion in the East. Here was I, the white man with his gun, standing in front of the unarmed native crowd —seemingly the leading actor of the piece; but in reality I was only an absurd puppet pushed to and fro by the will of those yellow faces behind. I perceived in this moment that when the white man turns tyrant it is his own freedom that he destroys. He becomes a sort of hollow, posing dummy, the conventionalized figure of a sahib. For it is the condition of his rule that he shall spend his life in trying to impress the "natives," and so in every crisis he has got to do what the "natives" expect of him. He wears a mask, and his face grows to fit it. I had got to shoot the elephant. I had committed myself to doing it when I sent for the rifle. A sahib has got to act like a sahib; he has got to appear resolute, to know his own mind and do definite things. To come all that way, rifle in hand, with two thousand people marching at my heels, and then to trail feebly away, having done nothing—no, that was impossible. The crowd would laugh at me. And my whole life, every white man's life in the East, was one long struggle not to be laughed at.

But I did not want to shoot the elephant. I watched him beating his bunch of grass against his knees, with that preoccupied grandmotherly air that elephants have. It seemed to me that it would be murder to shoot him. At that age I was not squeamish about killing animals, but I had never shot an elephant and never wanted to. (Somehow it always seems worse to kill a *large* animal.) Besides, there was the beast's owner to be considered. Alive, the elephant was worth at least a hundred pounds; dead, he would only be worth the value of his tusks, five pounds, possibly. But I had got to act quickly. I turned to some experienced-looking Burmans who had been there when we arrived, and asked them how the elephant had been behaving. They all said the same thing: he took no notice of you if you left him alone, but he might charge if you went too close to him.

It was perfectly clear to me what I ought to do. I ought to walk up to within, say, twenty-five yards of the elephant and test his behavior. If he charged, I could shoot; if he took no notice of me, it would be safe to leave him until the mahout came back. But also I knew that I was going to do no such thing. I was a poor shot with a rifle and the ground was soft mud into which one would sink at every step. If the elephant charged and I missed him, I should have about as much chance as a toad under a steam-roller. But even then I was not thinking particularly of my own skin, only of the watchful yellow faces behind. For at that moment, with the crowd watching me, I was not afraid in the ordinary sense, as I would have been if I had been alone. A white man mustn't be frightened in front of "natives"; and so, in general, he isn't frightened. The sole thought in my mind was that if anything went wrong those two thousand Burmans would see me pursued, caught, trampled on and reduced to a grinning corpse like that Indian up the hill. And if that happened it was quite probable that some of them would laugh. That would never do. There was only one alternative. I shoved the cartridges into the magazine and lay down on the road to get a better aim.

The crowd grew very still, and a deep, low, happy sigh, as of people who see the theatre curtain go up at last, breathed from innumerable throats. They were going to have their bit of fun after all. The rifle was a beautiful German thing with cross-hair sights. I did not then know that in shooting an elephant one would shoot to cut an imaginary bar running from ear-hole to ear-hole. I ought, therefore, as the elephant was sideways on, to have aimed straight at his ear-hole; actually I aimed several inches in front of this, thinking the brain would be further forward.

When I pulled the trigger I did not hear the bang or feel the kick—one never does when a shot goes home—but I heard the devilish roar of glee that went up from the crowd. In that instant, in too short a time, one would have thought, even for the bullet to get there, a mysterious, terrible change had come over the elephant. He neither stirred nor fell, but every line of his body had altered. He looked suddenly stricken, shrunken, immensely old, as though the frightful impact of the bullet had paralysed him without knocking him down. At last, after what seemed a long time—it might have been five seconds, I dare say—he sagged flabbily to his knees. His mouth slobbered. An enormous senility seemed to have settled upon him. One could have imagined him thousands of years old. I fired again into the same spot. At the second shot he did not collapse but climbed with desperate slowness to his feet and stood weakly upright, with legs sagging and head drooping. I fired a third time. That was the shot that did for him. You could see the agony of it jolt his whole body and knock the last remnant of strength from his legs. But in falling he seemed for a moment to rise, for as his hind legs collapsed beneath him he seemed to tower upward like a huge rock toppling, his trunk reaching skywards like a tree. He trumpeted, for the first and only time. And then down he came, his belly towards me, with a crash that seemed to shake the ground even where I lay.

I got up. The Burmans were already racing past me across the mud. It was obvious that the elephant would never rise again, but he was not dead. He was breathing very rhythmically with long rattling gasps, his great mound of a side painfully rising and falling. His mouth was wide open—I could see far down into caverns of pale pink throat. I waited a long time for him to die, but his breathing did not weaken. Finally I fired my two remaining shots into the spot where I thought his heart must be. The thick blood welled out of him like red velvet, but still he did not die. His body did not even jerk when the shots hit him, the tortured breathing continued without a pause. He was dying, very slowly and in great agony, but in some world remote from me where not even a bullet could damage him further. I felt that I had got to put an end to that dreadful noise. It seemed dreadful to see the great beast lying there, powerless to move and yet powerless to die, and not even to be able to finish him. I sent back for my small rifle and poured shot after shot into his heart and down his throat. They seemed to make no impression. The tortured gasps continued as steadily as the ticking of a clock.

In the end I could not stand it any longer and went away. I

heard later that it took him half an hour to die. Burmans were bringing dahs² and baskets even before I left, and I was told they had stripped his body almost to the bones by the afternoon.

Afterwards, of course, there were endless discussions about the shooting of the elephant. The owner was furious, but he was only an Indian and could do nothing. Besides, legally I had done the right thing, for a mad elephant has to be killed, like a mad dog, if its owner fails to control it. Among the Europeans opinion was divided. The older men said I was right, the younger men said it was a damn shame to shoot an elephant for killing a coolie, because an elephant was worth more than any damn Coringhee coolie. And afterwards I was very glad that the coolie had been killed; it put me legally in the right and it gave me a sufficient pretext for shooting the elephant. I often wondered whether any of the others grasped that I had done it solely to avoid looking a fool.

1936

2. Butcher knives.

QUESTIONS

1. The proportion of this essay devoted to narrative is relatively high. What effect(s) does Orwell aim at? How does he organize his essay? Where does he state his thesis? Would he have done better to argue his thesis directly, rather than mainly by example? Why, or why not?
2. What issue does Orwell address and what kind of evidence is proper to it? Does he actually prove anything?
3. The following is a sketch from The Graphic (London) of January 21, 1888, written by a Major-General H. G. Robley.

Shooting a Man-Eating Crocodile

It is tedious work waiting for the man-eater to come out of the water, but a fat native child as a lure will make the monster speedily walk out of his aqueous lair. Contracting the loan of a chubby infant, however, is a matter of some negotiation, and it is perhaps not to be wondered at that mammas occasionally object to their offspring being pegged down as food for a great crocodile; but there are always some parents to be found whose confidence in the skill of the British sportsman is unlimited. My sketch [omitted here] gives a view of the collapse of the man-eater, who, after viewing the tempting morsel tethered carefully to a bamboo near the water's edge, makes a rush through the sedges. The sportsman, hidden behind a bed of reeds, then fires, the bullet penetrates the heart, and the monster is dead in a moment. The little bait, whose only alarm has been caused by the report of the rifle, is now taken home by its doting mother for its matutinal banana. The natives wait to get the musky flesh of the animal, and the sportsman secures the scaly skin and the massive head of porous bone as a trophy.

There are probably educational and social similarities between Robley and Orwell and, of course, both were imperial Englishmen in a colonial setting. However, the differences between the two men are far more striking; briefly and basically, what are they? How are these similarities and differences reflected in the essays' style?

4. Does Robley show any sign that he recognizes what Orwell calls "the futility of the white man's dominion in the East" (p. 466)? Could it be that this dominion was not futile for Robley, or in his day?

5. Compare this sketch with Jonathan Swift's "A Modest Proposal" (pp. 485–493). How can you tell that Robley is not ironic and that Swift is? If you can't tell, what does your uncertainty suggest about the nature of irony?

MARTIN LUTHER KING, JR.
Letter from Birmingham Jail[1]

MY DEAR FELLOW CLERGYMEN:

While confined here in the Birmingham city jail, I came across your recent statement calling my present activities "unwise and untimely." Seldom do I pause to answer criticism of my work and ideas. If I sought to answer all the criticisms that cross my desk, my secretaries would have little time for anything other than such correspondence in the course of the day, and I would have no time for constructive work. But since I feel that you are men of genuine good will and that your criticisms are sincerely set forth, I want to try to answer your statement in what I hope will be patient and reasonable terms.

I think I should indicate why I am here in Birmingham, since you have been influenced by the view which argues against "outsiders coming in." I have the honor of serving as president of the

1. This response to a published statement by eight fellow clergymen from Alabama (Bishop C. C. J. Carpenter, Bishop Joseph A. Durick, Rabbi Hilton L. Grafman, Bishop Paul Hardin, Bishop Holan B. Harmon, the Reverend George M. Murray, the Reverend Edward V. Ramage and the Reverend Earl Stallings) was composed under somewhat constricting circumstances. Begun on the margins of the newspaper in which the statement appeared while I was in jail, the letter was continued on scraps of writing paper supplied by a friendly Negro trusty, and concluded on a pad my attorneys were eventually permitted to leave me. Although the text remains in substance unaltered, I have indulged in the author's prerogative of polishing it for publication [King's note].

Southern Christian Leadership Conference, an organization operating in every southern state, with headquarters in Atlanta, Georgia. We have some eighty-five affiliated organizations across the South, and one of them is the Alabama Christian Movement for Human Rights. Frequently we share staff, educational, and financial resources with our affiliates. Several months ago the affiliate here in Birmingham asked us to be on call to engage in a nonviolent direct-action program if such were deemed necessary. We readily consented, and when the hour came we lived up to our promise. So I, along with several members of my staff, am here because I was invited here. I am here because I have organizational ties here.

But more basically, I am in Birmingham because injustice is here. Just as the prophets of the eighth century B.C. left their villages and carried their "thus saith the Lord" far beyond the boundaries of their home towns, and just as the Apostle Paul left his village of Tarsus and carried the gospel of Jesus Christ to the far corners of the Greco-Roman world, so am I compelled to carry the gospel of freedom beyond my own home town. Like Paul, I must constantly respond to the Macedonian call for aid.

Moreover, I am cognizant of the interrelatedness of all communities and states. I cannot sit idly by in Atlanta and not be concerned about what happens in Birmingham. Injustice anywhere is a threat to justice everywhere. We are caught in an inescapable network of mutuality, tied in a single garment of destiny. Whatever affects one directly, affects all indirectly. Never again can we afford to live with the narrow, provincial "outside agitator" idea. Anyone who lives inside the United States can never be considered an outsider anywhere within its bounds.

You deplore the demonstrations taking place in Birmingham. But your statement, I am sorry to say, fails to express a similar concern for the conditions that brought about the demonstrations. I am sure that none of you would want to rest content with the superficial kind of social analysis that deals merely with effects and does not grapple with underlying causes. It is unfortunate that demonstrations are taking place in Birmingham, but it is even more unfortunate that the city's white power structure left the Negro community with no alternative.

In any nonviolent campaign there are four basic steps: collection of the facts to determine whether injustices exist; negotiation; self-purification; and direct action. We have gone through all these steps in Birmingham. There can be no gainsaying the fact that racial injustice engulfs this community. Birmingham is probably the most thoroughly segregated city in the United States. Its ugly record of brutality is widely known. Negroes have experienced grossly unjust treatment in the courts. There have been more unsolved bombings of Negro homes and churches in Birmingham than in any other city in the nation. These are the hard, brutal facts of the case. On the basis of these conditions, Negro leaders sought to negotiate with the city fathers. But the latter consistently refused to engage in good-faith negotiation.

Then, last September, came the opportunity to talk with leaders of Birmingham's economic community. In the course of the negotiations, certain promises were made by the merchants—for example, to remove the stores' humiliating racial signs. On the basis of these promises, the Reverend Fred Shuttlesworth and the leaders of the Alabama Christian Movement for Human Rights agreed to a moratorium on all demonstrations. As the weeks and months went by, we realized that we were the victims of a broken promise. A few signs, briefly removed, returned; the others remained.

As in so many past experiences, our hopes had been blasted, and the shadow of deep disappointment settled upon us. We had no alternative except to prepare for direct action, whereby we would present our very bodies as a means of laying our case before the conscience of the local and the national community. Mindful of the difficulties involved, we decided to undertake a process of self-purification. We began a series of workshops on nonviolence, and we repeatedly asked ourselves: "Are you able to accept blows without retaliating?" "Are you able to endure the ordeal of jail?" We decided to schedule our direct-action program for the Easter season, realizing that except for Christmas, this is the main shopping period of the year. Knowing that a strong economic-withdrawal program would be the by-product of direct action, we felt that this would be the best time to bring pressure to bear on the merchants for the needed change.

Then it occurred to us that Birmingham's mayoral election was coming up in March, and we speedily decided to postpone action until after election day. When we discovered that the Commissioner of Public Safety, Eugene "Bull" Connor, had piled up enough votes to be in the run-off, we decided again to postpone action until the day after the run-off so that the demonstrations could not be used to cloud the issues. Like many others, we wanted to see Mr. Connor defeated, and to this end we endured postponement after postponement. Having aided in this community need, we felt that our direct-action program could be delayed no longer.

You may well ask, "Why direct action? Why sit-ins, marches, and so forth? Isn't negotiation a better path?" You are quite right in calling for negotiation. Indeed, this is the very purpose of direct action. Nonviolent direct action seeks to create such a crisis and foster such a tension that a community which has constantly refused to negotiate is forced to confront the issue. It seeks so to dramatize the issue that it can no longer be ignored. My citing the creation of tension as part of the work of the nonviolent-resister may sound rather shocking. But I must confess that I am not afraid of the word "tension." I have earnestly opposed violent tension, but there is a type of constructive, nonviolent tension which is necessary for growth. Just as Socrates felt that it was necessary to create a tension in the mind so that individuals could rise from the bondage of myths and half-truths to the unfettered realm of creative analysis and objective appraisal, so must we see the need for nonviolent gadflies to create the kind of tension in society that will help men rise from the dark depths of prejudice and racism to the majestic heights of understanding and brotherhood.

The purpose of our direct-action program is to create a situation so crisis-packed that it will inevitably open the door to negotiation. I therefore concur with you in your call for negotiation. Too long has our beloved Southland been bogged down in a tragic effort to live in monologue rather than dialogue.

One of the basic points in your statement is that the action that I and my associates have taken in Birmingham is untimely. Some have asked: "Why didn't you give the new city administration time to act?" The only answer that I can give to this query is that the new Birmingham administration must be prodded about as much as the outgoing one, before it will act. We are sadly mistaken if we feel that the election of Albert Boutwell as mayor will bring the millennium to Birmingham. While Mr. Boutwell is a much more gentle person than Mr. Connor, they are both segregationists, dedicated to maintenance of the status quo. I have hoped that Mr. Boutwell will be reasonable enough to see the futility of massive resistance to desegregation. But he will not see this without pressure from devotees of civil rights. My friends, I must say to you that we have not made a single gain in civil rights without determined legal and nonviolent pressure. Lamentably, it is an historical fact that privileged groups seldom give up their privileges voluntarily. Individuals may see the moral light and voluntarily give up their unjust posture; but, as Reinhold Niebuhr has reminded us, groups tend to be more immoral than individuals.

We know through painful experience that freedom is never voluntarily given by the oppressor; it must be demanded by the oppressed. Frankly, I have yet to engage in a direct-action campaign that was "well timed" in the view of those who have not suffered unduly from the disease of segregation. For years now I have heard the word "Wait!" It rings in the ear of every Negro with piercing familiarity. This "Wait" has almost always meant "Never." We must come to see, with one of our distinguished jurists, that "justice too long delayed is justice denied."

We have waited for more than 340 years for our constitutional and God-given rights. The nations of Asia and Africa are moving with jetlike speed toward gaining political independence, but we still creep at horse-and-buggy pace toward gaining a cup of coffee at a lunch counter. Perhaps it is easy for those who have never felt the stinging darts of segregation to say, "Wait." But when you have seen vicious mobs lynch your mothers and fathers at will and drown your sisters and brothers at whim; when you have seen hate-filled policemen curse, kick, and even kill your black brothers and sisters; when you see the vast majority of your twenty million Negro brothers smothering in an airtight cage of poverty in the midst of an affluent society; when you suddenly find your tongue twisted and your speech stammering as you seek to explain to your six-year-old daughter why she can't go to the public amusement park that has just been advertised on television, and see tears welling up in her eyes when she is told that Funtown is closed to colored children, and see ominous clouds of inferiority beginning to form in her little mental sky, and see her beginning to distort her personality by developing an unconscious bitterness toward white people; when you have to concoct an answer for a five-year-old son who is asking, "Daddy, why do white people treat colored people so mean?"; when you take a cross-country drive and find it necessary to sleep night after night in the uncomfortable corners of your automobile because no motel will accept you; when you are humiliated day in and day out by nagging signs reading "white" and "colored"; when your first name becomes "nigger," your middle name becomes "boy" (however old you are) and your last name becomes "John," and your wife and mother are never given the respected title "Mrs."; when you are harried by day and haunted by night by the fact that you are a Negro, living constantly at tiptoe stance, never quite knowing what to expect next, and are plagued with inner fears and outer resentments; when you are forever fighting a degenerating sense of "nobodiness"—then you will understand why we find it difficult to wait. There comes a time when the cup of endurance runs over, and men are no longer willing to be plunged into the abyss of despair. I hope, sirs, you can understand our legitimate and unavoidable impatience.

You express a great deal of anxiety over our willingness to break laws. This is certainly a legitimate concern. Since we so diligently urge people to obey the Supreme Court's decision of 1954 outlawing segregation in the public schools, at first glance it may seem rather paradoxical for us consciously to break laws. One may well ask: "How can you advocate breaking some laws and obeying others?" The answer lies in the fact that there are two types of laws: just and unjust. I would be the first to advocate obeying just laws. One has not only a legal but a moral responsibility to obey just laws. Conversely, one has a moral responsibility to disobey unjust laws. I would agree with St. Augustine that "an unjust law is no law at all."

Now, what is the difference between the two? How does one determine whether a law is just or unjust? A just law is a man-made code that squares with the moral law or the law of God. An unjust law is a code that is out of harmony with the moral law. To put it in the terms of St. Thomas Aquinas: An unjust law is a human law that is not rooted in eternal law and natural law. Any law that uplifts human personality is just. Any law that degrades human personality is unjust. All segregation statutes are unjust because segregation distorts the soul and damages the personality. It gives the segregator a false sense of superiority and the segregated a false sense of inferiority. Segregation, to use the terminology of the Jewish philosopher Martin Buber, substitutes an "I-it" relationship for an "I-thou" relationship and ends up relegating persons to the status of things. Hence segregation is not only politically, economically, and sociologically unsound, it is morally wrong and sinful. Paul Tillich has said that sin is separation. Is not segregation an existential expression of man's tragic separation, his awful estrangement, his terrible sinfulness? Thus it is that I can urge men to obey the 1954 decision of the Supreme Court, for it is morally right; and I can urge them to disobey segregation ordinances, for they are morally wrong.

Let us consider a more concrete example of just and unjust laws. An unjust law is a code that a numerical or power majority group compels a minority group to obey but does not make binding on itself. This is *difference* made legal. By the same token, a just law is a code that a majority compels a minority to follow and that it is willing to follow itself. This is *sameness* made legal.

Let me give another explanation. A law is unjust if it is inflicted on a minority that, as a result of being denied the right to vote, had no part in enacting or devising the law. Who can say that the legislature of Alabama which set up that state's segregation laws was democratically elected? Throughout Alabama all sorts of devious methods are used to prevent Negroes from becoming registered voters, and there are some counties in which, even though Negroes constitute a majority of the population, not a single Negro is registered. Can any law enacted under such circumstances be considered democratically structured?

Sometimes a law is just on its face and unjust in its application. For instance, I have been arrested on a charge of parading without a permit. Now, there is nothing wrong in having an ordinance which requires a permit for a parade. But such an ordinance becomes unjust when it is used to maintain segregation and to deny citizens the First-Amendment privilege of peaceful assembly and protest.

I hope you are able to see the distinction I am trying to point out. In no sense do I advocate evading or defying the law, as would the rabid segregationist. That would lead to anarchy. One who breaks an unjust law must do so openly, lovingly, and with a willingness to accept the penalty. I submit that an individual who breaks a law that conscience tells him is unjust, and who willingly accepts the penalty of imprisonment in order to arouse the conscience of the community over its injustice, is in reality expressing the highest respect for law.

Of course, there is nothing new about this kind of civil disobedience. It was evidenced sublimely in the refusal of Shadrach, Meshach, and Abednego to obey the laws of Nebuchadnezzar, on the ground that a higher moral law was at stake. It was practiced superbly by the early Christians, who were willing to face hungry lions and the excruciating pain of chopping blocks rather than submit to certain unjust laws of the Roman Empire. To a degree, academic freedom is a reality today because Socrates practiced civil disobedience.[2] In our own nation, the Boston Tea Party represented a massive act of civil disobedience.

We should never forget that everything Adolf Hitler did in Germany was "legal" and everything the Hungarian freedom fighters[3] did in Hungary was "illegal." It was "illegal" to aid and comfort a Jew in Hitler's Germany. Even so, I am sure that, had I lived in Germany at the time, I would have aided and comforted my Jewish brothers. If today I lived in a Communist country where certain principles dear to the Christian faith are suppressed, I would openly advocate disobeying that country's anti-religious laws.

I must make two honest confessions to you, my Christian and Jewish brothers. First, I must confess that over the past few years I have been gravely disappointed with the white moderate. I have almost reached the regrettable conclusion that the Negro's great stumbling block in his stride toward freedom is not the White Citizen's Counciler or the Ku Klux Klanner, but the white moderate, who is more devoted to "order" than to justice; who prefers a negative peace which is the absence of tension to a positive peace which is the presence of justice; who constantly says, "I agree with you in the goal you seek, but I cannot agree with your methods of direct action"; who paternalistically believes he can set the timetable for another man's freedom; who lives by a mythical concept of time and who constantly advises the Negro to wait for a "more convenient season." Shallow understanding from people of good will is more frustrating than absolute misunderstanding from people of ill will. Lukewarm acceptance is much more bewildering than outright rejection.

2. The ancient Greek philosopher Socrates was tried by the Athenians for corrupting their youth through his skeptical, questioning manner of teaching. He refused to change his ways, and was condemned to death.

3. In the anti-Communist revolution of 1956, which was quickly put down by the Russian army.

I had hoped that the white moderate would understand that law and order exist for the purpose of establishing justice and that when they fail in this purpose they become the dangerously structured dams that block the flow of social progress. I had hoped that the white moderate would understand that the present tension in the South is a necessary phase of the transition from an obnoxious negative peace, in which the Negro passively accepted his unjust plight, to a substantive and positive peace, in which all men will respect the dignity and worth of human personality. Actually, we who engage in nonviolent direct action are not the creators of tension. We merely bring to the surface the hidden tension that is already alive. We bring it out in the open, where it can be seen and dealt with. Like a boil that can never be cured so long as it is covered up but must be opened with all its ugliness to the natural medicines of air and light, injustice must be exposed, with all the tension its exposure creates, to the light of human conscience and the air of national opinion, before it can be cured.

In your statement you assert that our actions, even though peaceful, must be condemned because they precipitate violence. But is this a logical assertion? Isn't this like condemning a robbed man because his possession of money precipitated the evil act of robbery? Isn't this like condemning Socrates because his unswerving commitment to truth and his philosophical inquiries precipitated the act by the misguided populace in which they made him drink hemlock? Isn't this like condemning Jesus because his unique God-consciousness and never-ceasing devotion to God's will precipitated the evil act of crucifixion? We must come to see that, as the federal courts have consistently affirmed, it is wrong to urge an individual to cease his efforts to gain his basic constitutional rights because the quest may precipitate violence. Society must protect the robbed and punish the robber.

I had also hoped that the white moderate would reject the myth concerning time in relation to the struggle for freedom. I have just received a letter from a white brother in Texas. He writes: "All Christians know that the colored people will receive equal rights eventually, but it is possible that you are in too great a religious hurry. It has taken Christianity almost two thousand years to accomplish what it has. The teachings of Christ take time to come to earth." Such an attitude stems from a tragic misconception of time, from the strangely irrational notion that there is something in the very flow of time that will inevitably cure all ills. Actually, time itself is neutral; it can be used either destructively or constructively. More and more I feel that the people of ill will have used time much more effectively than have the people of good will. We will have to repent in this generation not merely for the hateful words and actions of the bad people, but for the appalling silence of the good people. Human progress never rolls in on wheels of inevitability; it comes through the tireless efforts of men willing to be co-workers with God, and without this hard work, time itself becomes an ally of the forces of social stagnation. We must use time creatively, in the knowledge that the time is always ripe to do right. Now is the time to make real the promise of democracy and transform our pending national elegy into a creative psalm of brotherhood. Now is the time to lift our national policy from the quicksand of racial injustice to the solid rock of human dignity.

You speak of our activity in Birmingham as extreme. At first I was rather disappointed that fellow clergymen would see my nonviolent efforts as those of an extremist. I began thinking about the fact that I stand in the middle of two opposing forces in the Negro community. One is a force of complacency, made up in part of Negroes who, as a result of long years of oppression, are so drained of self-respect and a sense of "somebodiness" that they have adjusted to segregation; and in part of a few middle-class Negroes who, because of a degree of academic and economic security and because in some ways they profit by segregation, have become insensitive to the problems of the masses. The other force is one of bitterness and hatred, and it comes perilously close to advocating violence. It is expressed in the various black nationalist groups that are springing up across the nation, the largest and best-known being Elijah Muhammad's Muslim movement. Nourished by the Negro's frustration over the continued existence of racial discrimination, this movement is made up of people who have lost faith in America, who have absolutely repudiated Christianity, and who have concluded that the white man is an incorrigible "devil."

I have tried to stand between these two forces, saying that we need emulate neither the "do-nothingism" of the complacent nor the hatred and despair of the black nationalist. For there is the more excellent way of love and nonviolent protest. I am grateful to God that, through the influence of the Negro church, the way of nonviolence became an integral part of our struggle.

If this philosophy had not emerged, by now many streets of the South would, I am convinced, be flowing with blood. And I am further convinced that if our white brothers dismiss as "rabble-rousers" and "outside agitators" those of us who employ nonviolent direct action, and if they refuse to support our nonviolent efforts, millions of Negroes will, out of frustration and despair, seek solace and security in black-nationalist ideologies—a development that would inevitably lead to a frightening racial nightmare.

Oppressed people cannot remain oppressed forever. The yearning for freedom eventually manifests itself, and that is what has happened to the American Negro. Something within has reminded him of his birthright of freedom, and something without has reminded him that it can be gained. Consciously or unconsciously, he has been caught up by the *Zeitgeist*,[4] and with his black brothers of Africa and his brown and yellow brothers of Asia, South America, and the Caribbean, the United States Negro is moving with a sense of great urgency toward the promised land of racial justice. If one recognizes this vital urge that has engulfed the Negro community, one should readily understand why public demonstrations are taking place. The Negro has many pent-up resentments and latent frustrations, and he must release them. So let him march; let him make prayer pilgrimages to the city hall; let him go on freedom rides—and try to understand why he must do so. If his repressed emotions are not released in nonviolent ways, they will seek expression through violence; this is not a threat but a fact of history. So I have not said to my people, "Get rid of your discontent." Rather, I have tried to say that this normal and healthy discontent can be channeled into the creative outlet of nonviolent direct action. And now this approach is being termed extremist.

But though I was initially disappointed at being categorized as an extremist, as I continued to think about the matter I gradually gained a measure of satisfaction from the label. Was not Jesus an extremist for love: "Love your enemies, bless them that curse you, do good to them that hate you, and pray for them which despitefully use you, and persecute you." Was not Amos an extremist for justice: "Let justice roll down like waters and righteousness like an ever-flowing stream." Was not Paul an extremist for the Christian gospel: "I bear in my body the marks of the Lord Jesus." Was not Martin Luther an extremist: "Here I stand; I cannot do otherwise, so help me God." And John Bunyan: "I will stay in jail to the end of my days before I make a butchery of my conscience." And Abraham Lincoln: "This nation cannot survive half slave and half free." And Thomas Jefferson: "We hold these truths to be self-evident, that all men are created equal. . . ." So the question is not whether we will be extremists, but what kind of extremists we will be. Will we be extremists for hate or for love? Will we be extremists for the preservation of injustice or for the extension of justice? In that dramatic scene on Calvary's hill three men were crucified. We must never forget that all three were crucified for the same crime—the crime of extremism. Two were extremists for immorality, and thus fell below their environment. The other, Jesus Christ, was an extremist for love, truth, and goodness, and thereby rose above his environment. Perhaps the South, the nation, and the world are in dire need of creative extremists.

I had hoped that the white moderate would see this need. Per-

---

4. The spirit of the times.

haps I was too optimistic; perhaps I expected too much. I suppose I should have realized that few members of the oppressor race can understand the deep groans and passionate yearnings of the oppressed race, and still fewer have the vision to see that injustice must be rooted out by strong, persistent, and determined action. I am thankful, however, that some of our white brothers in the South have grasped the meaning of this social revolution and committed themselves to it. They are still all too few in quantity, but they are big in quality. Some—such as Ralph McGill, Lillian Smith, Harry Golden, James McBride Dabbs, Ann Braden, and Sarah Patton Boyle—have written about our struggle in eloquent and prophetic terms. Others have marched with us down nameless streets of the South. They have languished in filthy, roach-infested jails, suffering the abuse and brutality of policemen who view them as "dirty nigger-lovers." Unlike so many of their moderate brothers and sisters, they have recognized the urgency of the moment and sensed the need for powerful "action" antidotes to combat the disease of segregation.

Let me take note of my other major disappointment. I have been so greatly disappointed with the white church and its leadership. Of course, there are some notable exceptions. I am not unmindful of the fact that each of you has taken some significant stands on this issue. I commend you, Reverend Stallings, for your Christian stand on this past Sunday, in welcoming Negroes to your worship service on a nonsegregated basis. I commend the Catholic leaders of this state for integrating Spring Hill College several years ago.

But despite these notable exceptions, I must honestly reiterate that I have been disappointed with the church. I do not say this as one of those negative critics who can always find something wrong with the church. I say this as a minister of the gospel, who loves the church; who was nurtured in its bosom; who has been sustained by its spiritual blessings and who will remain true to it as long as the cord of life shall lengthen.

When I was suddenly catapulted into the leadership of the bus protest in Montgomery, Alabama, a few years ago, I felt we would be supported by the white church. I felt that the white ministers, priests, and rabbis of the South would be among our strongest allies. Instead, some have been outright opponents, refusing to understand the freedom movement and misrepresenting its leaders; all too many others have been more cautious than courageous and have remained silent behind the anesthetizing security of stained-glass windows.

In spite of my shattered dreams, I came to Birmingham with the hope that the white religious leadership of this community would see the justice of our cause and, with deep moral concern, would serve as the channel through which our just grievances could reach the power structure. I had hoped that each of you would understand. But again I have been disappointed.

I have heard numerous southern religious leaders admonish their worshipers to comply with a desegregation decision because it is the law, but I have longed to hear white ministers declare: "Follow this decree because integration is morally right and because the Negro is your brother." In the midst of blatant injustices inflicted upon the Negro, I have watched white churchmen stand on the sideline and mouth pious irrelevancies and sanctimonious trivialities. In the midst of a mighty struggle to rid our nation of racial and economic injustice, I have heard many ministers say: "Those are social issues, with which the gospel has no real concern." And I have watched many churches commit themselves to a completely otherworldly religion which makes a strange, un-Biblical distinction between body and soul, between the sacred and the secular.

I have traveled the length and breadth of Alabama, Mississippi, and all the other southern states. On sweltering summer days and crisp autumn mornings I have looked at the South's beautiful churches with their lofty spires pointing heavenward. I have beheld the impressive outlines of her massive religious-education buildings. Over and over I have found myself asking: "What kind of people worship here? Who is their God? Where were their voices when the lips of Governor Barnett dripped with words of interposition and nullification? Where were they when Governor Wallace gave a clarion call for defiance and hatred? Where were their voices of support when bruised and weary Negro men and women decided to rise from the dark dungeons of complacency to the bright hills of creative protest?"

Yes, these questions are still in my mind. In deep disappointment I have wept over the laxity of the church. But be assured that my tears have been tears of love. There can be no deep disappointment where there is not deep love. Yes, I love the church. How could I do otherwise? I am in the rather unique position of being the son, the grandson, and the great-grandson of preachers. Yes, I see the church as the body of Christ. But, oh! How we have blemished and scarred that body through social neglect and through fear of being nonconformists.

There was a time when the church was very powerful—in the time when the early Christians rejoiced at being deemed worthy to suffer for what they believed. In those days the church was not merely a thermometer that recorded the ideas and principles of popular opinion; it was a thermostat that transformed the mores of society. Whenever the early Christians entered a town, the people in power became disturbed and immediately sought to convict the

Christians for being "disturbers of the peace" and "outside agitators." But the Christians pressed on, in the conviction that they were "a colony of heaven," called to obey God rather than man. Small in number, they were big in commitment. They were too God-intoxicated to be "astronomically intimidated." By their effort and example they brought an end to such ancient evils as infanticide and gladiatorial contests.

Things are different now. So often the contemporary church is a weak, ineffectual voice with an uncertain sound. So often it is an archdefender of the status quo. Far from being disturbed by the presence of the church, the power structure of the average community is consoled by the church's silent—and often even vocal—sanction of things as they are.

But the judgment of God is upon the church as never before. If today's church does not recapture the sacrificial spirit of the early church, it will lose its authenticity, forfeit the loyalty of millions, and be dismissed as an irrelevant social club with no meaning for the twentieth century. Every day I meet young people whose disappointment with the church has turned into outright disgust.

Perhaps I have once again been too optimistic. Is organized religion too inextricably bound to the status quo to save our nation and the world? Perhaps I must turn my faith to the inner spiritual church, the church within the church, as the true *ekklesia*[5] and the hope of the world. But again I am thankful to God that some noble souls from the ranks of organized religion have broken loose from the paralyzing chains of conformity and joined us as active partners in the struggle for freedom. They have left their secure congregations and walked the streets of Albany, Georgia, with us. They have gone down the highways of the South on tortuous rides for freedom. Yes, they have gone to jail with us. Some have been dismissed from their churches, have lost the support of their bishops and fellow ministers. But they have acted in the faith that right defeated is stronger than evil triumphant. Their witness has been the spiritual salt that has preserved the true meaning of the gospel in these troubled times. They have carved a tunnel of hope through the dark mountain of disappointment.

I hope the church as a whole will meet the challenge of this decisive hour. But even if the church does not come to the aid of justice, I have no despair about the future. I have no fear about the outcome of our struggle in Birmingham, even if our motives are at present misunderstood. We will reach the goal of freedom in Birmingham and all over the nation, because the goal of America is freedom. Abused and scorned though we may be, our destiny is tied up with America's destiny. Before the pilgrims landed at Plym-

5. The Greek New Testament word for the early Christian church.

outh, we were here. Before the pen of Jefferson etched the majestic words of the Declaration of Independence across the pages of history, we were here. For more than two centuries our forebears labored in this country without wages; they made cotton king; they built the homes of their masters while suffering gross injustice and shameful humiliation—and yet out of a bottomless vitality they continued to thrive and develop. If the inexpressible cruelties of slavery could not stop us, the opposition we now face will surely fail. We will win our freedom because the sacred heritage of our nation and the eternal will of God are embodied in our echoing demands.

Before closing I feel impelled to mention one other point in your statement that has troubled me profoundly. You warmly commended the Birmingham police force for keeping "order" and "preventing violence." I doubt that you would have so warmly commended the police force if you had seen its dogs sinking their teeth into unarmed, nonviolent Negroes. I doubt that you would so quickly commend the policemen if you were to observe their ugly and inhumane treatment of Negroes here in the city jail; if you were to watch them push and curse old Negro women and young Negro girls; if you were to see them slap and kick old Negro men and young boys; if you were to observe them, as they did on two occasions, refuse to give us food because we wanted to sing our grace together. I cannot join you in your praise of the Birmingham police department.

It is true that the police have exercised a degree of discipline in handling the demonstrators. In this sense they have conducted themselves rather "nonviolently" in public. But for what purpose? To preserve the evil system of segregation. Over the past few years I have consistently preached that nonviolence demands that the means we use must be as pure as the ends we seek. I have tried to make clear that it is wrong to use immoral means to attain moral ends. But now I must affirm that it is just as wrong, or perhaps even more so, to use moral means to preserve immoral ends. Perhaps Mr. Connor and his policemen have been rather nonviolent in public, as was Chief Pritchett in Albany, Georgia, but they have used the moral means of nonviolence to maintain the immoral end of racial injustice. As T. S. Eliot has said, "The last temptation is the greatest treason: To do the right deed for the wrong reason."

I wish you had commended the Negro sit-inners and demonstrators of Birmingham for their sublime courage, their willingness to suffer, and their amazing discipline in the midst of great provocation. One day the South will recognize its real heroes. They will be the James Merediths,[6] with the noble sense of purpose that enables

---

6. Meredith was the first black to enroll at the University of Mississippi.

them to face jeering and hostile mobs, and with the agonizing loneliness that characterizes the life of the pioneer. They will be old,
oppressed, battered Negro women, symbolized in a seventy-
two-year-old woman in Montgomery, Alabama, who rose up with a
sense of dignity and with her people decided not to ride segregated
buses, and who responded with ungrammatical profundity to one
who inquired about her weariness: "My feets is tired, but my soul
is at rest." They will be the young high school and college students,
the young ministers of the gospel and a host of their elders, coura-
geously and nonviolently sitting in at lunch counters and willingly
going to jail for conscience' sake. One day the South will know that
when these disinherited children of God sat down at lunch counters, they were in reality standing up for what is best in the American dream and for the most sacred values in our Judaeo-Christian
heritage, thereby bringing our nation back to those great wells of
democracy which were dug deep by the founding fathers in their
formulation of the Constitution and the Declaration of Independence.

Never before have I written so long a letter. I'm afraid it is much
too long to take your precious time. I can assure you that it would
have been much shorter if I had been writing from a comfortable
desk, but what else can one do when he is alone in a narrow jail
cell, other than write long letters, think long thoughts, and pray
long prayers?

If I have said anything in this letter that overstates the truth and
indicates an unreasonable impatience, I beg you to forgive me. If I
have said anything that understates the truth and indicates my
having a patience that allows me to settle for anything less than
brotherhood, I beg God to forgive me.

I hope this letter finds you strong in the faith. I also hope that
circumstances will soon make it possible for me to meet each of
you, not as an integrationist or a civil-rights leader but as a fellow
clergyman and a Christian brother. Let us all hope that the dark
clouds of racial prejudice will soon pass away and the deep fog of
misunderstanding will be lifted from our fear-drenched communities, and in some not too distant tomorrow the radiant stars of love
and brotherhood will shine over our great nation with all their scin-
tillating beauty.

> Yours for the cause of Peace and Brotherhood,
> MARTIN LUTHER KING, JR.

1963

JAMES THURBER
The Rabbits Who Caused All the Trouble

Within the memory of the youngest child there was a family of rabbits who lived near a pack of wolves. The wolves announced that they did not like the way the rabbits were living. (The wolves were crazy about the way they themselves were living, because it was the only way to live.) One night several wolves were killed in an earthquake and this was blamed on the rabbits, for it is well known that rabbits pound on the ground with their hind legs and cause earthquakes. On another night one of the wolves was killed by a bolt of lightning and this was also blamed on the rabbits, for it is well known that lettuce-eaters cause lightning. The wolves threatened to civilize the rabbits if they didn't behave, and the rabbits decided to run away to a desert island. But the other animals, who lived at a great distance, shamed them, saying, "You must stay where you are and be brave. This is no world for escapists. If the wolves attack you, we will come to your aid, in all probability." So the rabbits continued to live near the wolves and one day there was a terrible flood which drowned a great many wolves. This was blamed on the rabbits, for it is well known that carrot-nibblers with long ears cause floods. The wolves descended on the rabbits, for their own good, and imprisoned them in a dark cave, for their own protection.

When nothing was heard about the rabbits for some weeks, the other animals demanded to know what had happened to them. The wolves replied that the rabbits had been eaten and since they had been eaten the affair was a purely internal matter. But the other animals warned that they might possibly unite against the wolves unless some reason was given for the destruction of the rabbits. So the wolves gave them one. "They were trying to escape," said the wolves, "and, as you know, this is no world for escapists."

Moral: Run, don't walk, to the nearest desert island.

1955

JONATHAN SWIFT

A Modest Proposal

How does Swift get his ideas across

Tone of

For Preventing the Children of Poor People in Ireland from Being a Burden to Their Parents or Country, and for Making Them Beneficial to the Public

It is a melancholy object to those who walk through this great town[1] or travel in the country, when they see the streets, the roads, and cabin doors, crowded with beggars of the female-sex, followed by three, four, or six children, all in rags and importuning every passenger for an alms. These mothers, instead of being able to work for their honest livelihood, are forced to employ all their time

1. Dublin.

in strolling to beg sustenance for their helpless infants, who, as they grow up, either turn thieves for want of work, or leave their dear native country to fight for the Pretender in Spain, or sell themselves to the Barbadoes.[2]

I think it is agreed by all parties that this prodigious number of children in the arms, or on the backs, or at the heels of their mothers, and frequently of their fathers, is in the present deplorable state of the kingdom a very great additional grievance; and therefore whoever could find out a fair, cheap, and easy method of making these children sound, useful members of the commonwealth would deserve so well of the public as to have his statue set up for a preserver of the nation.

But my intention is very far from being confined to provide only for the children of professed beggars; it is of a much greater extent, and shall take in the whole number of infants at a certain age who are born of parents in effect as little able to support them as those who demand our charity in the streets.

As to my own part, having turned my thoughts for many years upon this important subject, and maturely weighed the several schemes of other projectors,[3] I have always found them grossly mistaken in their computation. It is true, a child just dropped from its dam may be supported by her milk for a solar year, with little other nourishment; at most not above the value of two shillings,[4] which the mother may certainly get, or the value in scraps, by her lawful occupation of begging; and it is exactly at one year old that I propose to provide for them in such a manner as instead of being a charge upon their parents or the parish, or wanting food and raiment for the rest of their lives, they shall on the contrary contribute to the feeding, and partly to the clothing, of many thousands.

There is likewise another great advantage in my scheme, that it will prevent those voluntary abortions, and that horrid practice of women murdering their bastard children, alas, too frequent among us, sacrificing the poor innocent babes, I doubt, more to avoid the expense than the shame, which would move tears and pity in the most savage and inhuman breast.

The number of souls in this kingdom being usually reckoned one million and a half, of these I calculate there may be about two hundred thousand couple whose wives are breeders; from which number I subtract thirty thousand couples who are able to maintain

---

2. Many poor Irish sought to escape poverty by emigrating to the Barbadoes and other western English colonies, paying for transport by binding themselves to work for a landowner there for a period of years. The Pretender, claimant to the English throne, was barred from succession after his father, King James II, was deposed in a Protestant revolution; thereafter, many Irish Catholics joined the Pretender in his exile in France and Spain, and in his unsuccessful attempts at counterrevolution.

3. People with projects; schemers.

4. A shilling used to be worth about twenty-five cents.

their own children, although I apprehend there cannot be so many under the present distresses of the kingdom; but this being granted, there will remain an hundred and seventy thousand breeders. I again subtract fifty thousand for those women who miscarry, or whose children die by accident or disease within the year. There only remain an hundred and twenty thousand children of poor parents annually born. The question therefore is, how this number shall be reared and provided for, which, as I have already said, under the present situation of affairs, is utterly impossible by all the methods hitherto proposed. For we can neither employ them in handicraft or agriculture; we neither build houses (I mean in the country) nor cultivate land. They can very seldom pick up a livelihood by stealing till they arrive at six years old, except where they are of towardly[5] parts; although I confess they learn the rudiments much earlier, during which time they can however be looked upon only as probationers, as I have been informed by a principal gentleman in the county of Cavan, who protested to me that he never knew above one or two instances under the age of six, even in a part of the kingdom so renowned for the quickest proficiency in that art.

I am assured by our merchants that a boy or a girl before twelve years old is no salable commodity; and even when they come to this age they will not yield above three pounds, or three pounds and half a crown[6] at most on the Exchange; which cannot turn to account either to the parents or the kingdom, the charge of nutriment and rags having been at least four times that value.

I shall now therefore humbly propose my own thoughts, which I hope will not be liable to the least objection.

I have been assured by a very knowing American of my acquaintance in London, that a young healthy child well nursed is at a year old a most delicious, nourishing, and wholesome food, whether stewed, roasted, baked, or boiled; and I make no doubt that it will equally serve in a fricassee or a ragout.

I do therefore humbly offer it to public consideration that of the hundred and twenty thousand children, already computed, twenty thousand may be reserved for breed, whereof only one fourth part to be males, which is more than we allow to sheep, black cattle, or swine; and my reason is that these children are seldom the fruits of marriage, a circumstance not much regarded by our savages, therefore one male will be sufficient to serve four females. That the remaining hundred thousand may at a year old be offered in sale to the persons of quality and fortune through the kingdom, always advising the mother to let them suck plentifully in the last month,

---

5. Obedient.
6. A pound was twenty shillings; a   crown, five shillings.

so as to render them plump and fat for a good table. A child will make two dishes at an entertainment for friends; and when the family dines alone, the fore or hind quarter will make a reasonable dish, and seasoned with a little pepper or salt will be very good boiled on the fourth day, especially in winter.

I have reckoned upon a medium that a child just born will weigh twelve pounds, and in a solar year if tolerably nursed increaseth to twenty-eight pounds.

I grant this food will be somewhat dear, and therefore very proper for landlords, who, as they have already devoured most of the parents, seem to have the best title to the children.

Infant's flesh will be in season throughout the year, but more plentiful in March, and a little before and after. For we are told by a grave author, an eminent French physician,[7] that fish being a prolific diet, there are more children born in Roman Catholic countries about nine months after Lent than at any other season; therefore, reckoning a year after Lent, the markets will be more glutted than usual, because the number of popish infants is at least three to one in this kingdom; and therefore it will have one other collateral advantage, by lessening the number of Papists among us.[8]

I have already computed the charge of nursing a beggar's child (in which list I reckon all cottagers, laborers, and four fifths of the farmers) to be about two shillings per annum, rags included; and I believe no gentleman would repine to give ten shillings for the carcass of a good fat child, which, as I have said, will make four dishes of excellent nutritive meat, when he hath only some particular friend or his own family to dine with him. Thus the squire will learn to be a good landlord, and grow popular among the tenants; the mother will have eight shillings net profit, and be fit for work till she produces another child.

Those who are more thrifty (as I must confess the times require) may flay the carcass; the skin of which artificially[9] dressed will make admirable gloves for ladies, and summer boots for fine gentlemen.

As to our city of Dublin, shambles[1] may be appointed for this purpose in the most convenient parts of it, and butchers we may be assured will not be wanting; although I rather recommend buying the children alive, and dressing them hot from the knife as we do roasting pigs.

A very worthy person, a true lover of his country, and whose virtues I highly esteem, was lately pleased in discoursing on this matter to offer a refinement upon my scheme. He said that many

7. The sixteenth-century comic writer François Rabelais.
8. The speaker is addressing Protestant Anglo-Irish, who were the chief landowners and administrators, and his views of Catholicism in Ireland and abroad echo theirs.
9. Skillfully.
1. Slaughterhouses.

gentlemen of this kingdom, having of late destroyed their deer, he conceived that the want of venison might be well supplied by the bodies of young lads and maidens, not exceeding fourteen years of age nor under twelve, so great a number of both sexes in every county being now ready to starve for want of work and service; and these to be disposed of by their parents, if alive, or otherwise by their nearest relations. But with due deference to so excellent a friend and so deserving a patriot, I cannot be altogether in his sentiments; for as to the males, my American acquaintance assured me from frequent experience that their flesh was generally tough and lean, like that of our schoolboys, by continual exercise, and their taste disagreeable; and to fatten them would not answer the charge. Then as to the females, it would, I think with humble submission, be a loss to the public, because they soon would become breeders themselves: and besides, it is not improbable that some scrupulous people might be apt to censure such a practice (although indeed very unjustly) as a little bordering upon cruelty; which, I confess, hath always been with me the strongest objection against any project, how well soever intended.

But in order to justify my friend, he confessed that this expedient was put into his head by the famous Psalmanazar, a native of the island Formosa,[2] who came from thence to London above twenty years ago, and in conversation told my friend that in his country when any young person happened to be put to death, the executioner sold the carcass to persons of quality as a prime dainty; and that in his time the body of a plump girl of fifteen, who was crucified for an attempt to poison the emperor, was sold to his Imperial Majesty's prime minister of state, and other great mandarins of the court, in joints from the gibbet, at four hundred crowns. Neither indeed can I deny that if the same use were made of several plump young girls in this town, who without one single groat to their fortunes cannot stir abroad without a chair,[3] and appear at the playhouse and assemblies in foreign fineries which they never will pay for, the kingdom would not be the worse.

Some persons of a desponding spirit are in great concern about that vast number of poor people who are aged, diseased, or maimed, and I have been desired to employ my thoughts what course may be taken to ease the nation of so grievous an encumbrance. But I am not in the least pain upon that matter, because it is very well known that they are every day dying and rotting by cold and famine, and filth and vermin, as fast as can be reasonably expected. And

---

2. Actually a Frenchman, George Psalmanazar had passed himself off as from Formosa (now Taiwan) and had written a fictitious book about his "homeland,"

with descriptions of human sacrifice and cannibalism.

3. A sedan chair; *groat*: an English coin worth about four pennies.

as to the younger laborers, they are now in almost as hopeful a condition. They cannot get work, and consequently pine away for want of nourishment to a degree that if at any time they are accidentally hired to common labor, they have not strength to perform it; and thus the country and themselves are happily delivered from the evils to come.

I have too long digressed, and therefore shall return to my subject. I think the advantages by the proposal which I have made are obvious and many, as well as of the highest importance.

For first, as I have already observed, it would greatly lessen the number of Papists with whom we are yearly overrun, being the principal breeders of the nation as well as our most dangerous enemies; and who stay at home on purpose to deliver the kingdom to the Pretender, hoping to take their advantage by the absence of so many good Protestants, who have chosen rather to leave their country than to stay at home and pay tithes against their conscience to an Episcopal curate.

Secondly, the poorer tenants will have something valuable of their own, which by law may be made liable to distress,[4] and help to pay their landlord's rent, their corn and cattle being already seized and money a thing unknown.

Thirdly, whereas the maintenance of an hundred thousand children, from two years old and upwards, cannot be computed at less than ten shillings a piece per annum, the nation's stock will be thereby increased fifty thousand pounds per annum, besides the profit of a new dish introduced to the tables of all gentlemen of fortune in the kingdom who have any refinement in taste. And the money will circulate among ourselves, the goods being entirely of our own growth and manufacture.

Fourthly, the constant breeders, besides the gain of eight shillings sterling per annum by the sale of their children, will be rid of the charge of maintaining them after the first year.

Fifthly, this food would likewise bring great custom to taverns, where the vintners will certainly be so prudent as to procure the best receipts for dressing it to perfection, and consequently have their houses frequented by all the fine gentlemen, who justly value themselves upon their knowledge in good eating; and a skillful cook, who understands how to oblige his guests, will contrive to make it as expensive as they please.

Sixthly, this would be a great inducement to marriage, which all wise nations have either encouraged by rewards or enforced by laws and penalties. It would increase the care and tenderness of mothers toward their children, when they were sure of a settlement for life

4. Seizure for the payment of debts.

to the poor babes, provided in some sort by the public, to their annual profit instead of expense. We should see an honest emulation among the married women, which of them could bring the fattest child to the market. Men would become as fond of their wives during the time of their pregnancy as they are now of their mares in foal, their cows in calf, or sows when they are ready to farrow; nor offer to beat or kick them (as is too frequent a practice) for fear of a miscarriage.

Many other advantages might be enumerated. For instance, the addition of some thousand carcasses in our exportation of barreled beef, the propagation of swine's flesh, and improvement in the art of making good bacon, so much wanted among us by the great destruction of pigs, too frequent at our tables, which are no way comparable in taste or magnificence to a well-grown, fat, yearling child, which roasted whole will make a considerable figure at a lord mayor's feast or any other public entertainment. But this and many others I omit, being studious of brevity.

Supposing that one thousand families in this city would be constant customers for infants' flesh, besides others who might have it at merry meetings, particularly weddings and christenings, I compute that Dublin would take off annually about twenty thousand carcasses, and the rest of the kingdom (where probably they will be sold somewhat cheaper) the remaining eighty thousand.

I can think of no one objection that will possibly be raised against this proposal, unless it should be urged that the number of people will be thereby much lessened in the kingdom. This I freely own, and it was indeed one principal design in offering it to the world. I desire the reader will observe, that I calculate my remedy for this one individual kingdom of Ireland and for no other that ever was, is, or I think ever can be upon earth. Therefore let no man talk to me of other expedients: of taxing our absentees at five shillings a pound: of using neither clothes nor household furniture except what is of our own growth and manufacture: of utterly rejecting the materials and instruments that promote foreign luxury: of curing the expensiveness of pride, vanity, idleness, and gaming in our women: of introducing a vein of parsimony, prudence, and temperance: of learning to love our country, in the want of which we differ even from Laplanders and the inhabitants of Topinamboo[5]: of quitting our animosities and factions, nor acting any longer like the Jews, who were murdering one another at the very moment their city was taken: of being a little cautious not to sell our country and conscience for nothing: of teaching landlords to have at least one degree of mercy toward their tenants: lastly, of putting a

5. A district in Brazil.

spirit of honesty, industry, and skill into our shopkeepers; who, if a resolution could now be taken to buy only our native goods, would immediately unite to cheat and exact upon us in the price, the measure, and the goodness, nor could ever yet be brought to make one fair proposal of just dealing, though often and earnestly invited to it.[6]

Therefore I repeat, let no man talk to me of these and the like expedients, till he hath at least some glimpse of hope that there will ever be some hearty and sincere attempt to put them in practice.

But as to myself, having been wearied out for many years with offering vain, idle, visionary thoughts, and at length utterly despairing of success, I fortunately fell upon this proposal, which, as it is wholly new, so it hath something solid and real, of no expense and little trouble, full in our own power, and whereby we can incur no danger in disobliging England. For this kind of commodity will not bear exportation, the flesh being of too tender a consistence to admit a long continuance in salt, although perhaps I could name a country[7] which would be glad to eat up our whole nation without it.

After all, I am not so violently bent upon my own opinion as to reject any offer proposed by wise men, which shall be found equally innocent, cheap, easy, and effectual. But before something of that kind shall be advanced in contradiction to my scheme, and offering a better, I desire the author or authors will be pleased maturely to consider two points. First, as things now stand, how they will be able to find food and raiment for an hundred thousand useless mouths and backs. And secondly, there being a round million of creatures in human figure throughout this kingdom, whose sole subsistence put into a common stock would leave them in debt two millions of pounds sterling, adding those who are beggars by profession to the bulk of farmers, cottagers, and laborers, with their wives and children who are beggars in effect; I desire those politicians who dislike my overture, and may perhaps be so bold to attempt an answer, that they will first ask the parents of these mortals whether they would not at this day think it a great happiness to have been sold for food at a year old in the manner I prescribe, and thereby have avoided such a perpetual scene of misfortunes as they have since gone through by the oppression of landlords, the impossibility of paying rent without money or trade, the want of common sustenance, with neither house nor clothes to cover them from the inclemencies of the weather, and the most inevitable prospect of entailing the like or greater miseries upon their breed forever.

I profess, in the sincerity of my heart, that I have not the least personal interest in endeavoring to promote this necessary work,

6. Swift himself had made these proposals seriously in various previous works.

7. England.

having no other motive than the public good of my country, by advancing our trade, providing for infants, relieving the poor, and giving some pleasure to the rich. I have no children by which I can propose to get a single penny; the youngest being nine years old, and my wife past childbearing.

1729

QUESTIONS

1. This essay has been called one of the best examples of sustained irony in the English language. Irony is difficult to handle because there is always the danger that the reader will miss the irony and take what is said literally. What does Swift do to try to prevent this? In answering this question, consider such matters as these: Is the first sentence of the essay ironic? At what point do you begin to suspect that Swift is using irony? What further evidence accumulates to make you certain that Swift is being ironic?
2. What is the speaker like? How are his views and character different from Swift's? Is the character of the speaker consistent? What is the purpose of the essay's final sentence?
3. Why does Swift use such phrases as "just dropt from its dam," "whose wives are breeders," "one fourth part to be males"?
4. Does the essay shock you? Was it Swift's purpose to shock you?
5. What is the main target of Swift's attack? What subsidiary targets are there? Does Swift offer any serious solutions for the problems and conditions he is describing?
6. What devices of argument, apart from the use of irony, does Swift use that could be successfully applied to other subjects?
7. In the study questions for George Orwell's "Shooting an Elephant" (p. 469), there is a brief sketch from The Graphic of 1888, "Shooting a Man-Eating Crocodile." How can you tell that this sketch is not ironic and that "A Modest Proposal" is? If you can't tell, what does your uncertainty suggest about the nature of irony?

JOHN KENNETH GALBRAITH

Inflation

I

Through most of man's history, the counterpart of war, civil disorder, famine or other cosmic disaster has been inflation. In recent times, inflation has acquired new habits; it persists in periods of peace, in periods of decline and stagnation and in periods of high and rising prosperity. This tendency has been strongly manifest in the United States. Except for a few years in the early sixties and, more debatably, in the early seventies inflation has been a continuing feature of American life since World War II. The later experience, that of the mid-seventies in particular, made the earlier inflation seem mild.

The public response to this recurrent inflation has been interesting. It has been widely deplored and condemned. Politicians of both parties have taken a strong position against it. Conservatives, anciently the self-designated custodians of the "honest dollar," have continued to stress this tenet of their faith. Businessmen, bankers, insurance executives and nearly every type of professional public spokesman at one time or another have warned of the dangers of continued inflation. Meanwhile, liberals have deplored failure to take effective action while often proposing none themselves. Next only to the virtues of competition, there is nothing on which the conventional wisdom is more completely agreed than on the importance of stable prices. Yet this conviction leads to remarkably little effort and, indeed, to remarkably few suggestions for specific action. Where inflation is concerned, nearly everyone finds it convenient to confine himself to conversation. All branches of the conventional wisdom are equally agreed on the undesirability of any remedies that are effective.

II

There are several reasons for this barren position. First, to be sure, some reap material benefit from inflation. They too oppose it, for reasons of respectability, but their opposition is less than impassioned. Of importance also is the influence of inaction—or postponement—as a policy. This does not reflect mere negativism, as is often supposed and even more frequently charged. In the nineteenth-century model of the competitive society, a rhythmic sequence of expansion and contraction in economic activity was assumed. The expansion was accompanied by rising prices; in the contracting phase, these gave way to falling prices. The movements in either direction were thought to be self-limiting. Thus, if prices were rising, one had only to wait. Presently they would reverse themselves and begin to fall.

In the course of time, confidence in the self-limiting character of these movements was seriously weakened. This was especially true as regards the period of contraction or depression, and the Great Depression dealt a decisive blow. Although as late as the early thirties it was a tenet of the conventional wisdom that in depressions the appropriate course of action was a severe "hands-off" policy, government intervention against depression came eventually to be regarded as inevitable.

However, there was never any equally dramatic assault on the older confidence that rising prices and inflation would cure themselves. Keynes[1] led the attack on the conviction that depressions were self-correcting by picturing the possibility, indeed the probability, that the economy would find its equilibrium with an unspecified amount of unemployment. Dozens seized his point and sought to persuade the politicians and the public. The notion that, in peacetime, prices might as a normal thing rise continuously and persistently has had no Keynes.

Thus the conviction, or more precisely the hope, has remained that peacetime inflation might somehow be self-correcting. This is not a hope in which even conservatives repose very great confidence. But in combination with the belief, so common in recent years, that the behavior of the economic system is bound to be favorable if only earnest and God-fearing men are in command of its destinies, it provides a strong reason for always waiting to see if prices won't turn down by themselves. Even liberals, who are required to advocate although not to specify action to prevent inflation, are in practice tempted to wait and see.

This disposition to inaction is reinforced by the belief, powerful ever since the thirties, that the most grievous threat to the American economy is a depression. If this danger lurks, however obscurely, around the corner, then there is all the less reason to act to control inflation. For inflation may any day come to an end in the thunder of economic collapse or the lesser misery of a few million unemployed. These eventualities are much more grave than rising prices. We are especially hesitant, knowingly at least, to invoke measures which might precipitate them. Some inflation remedies might do so or, at any rate, be blamed.

However, the forces which act to make inflation a peculiarly unmanageable problem in our time are imbedded much more deeply in the fabric of our social life. We are impelled, for reasons of economic security, to operate the economy at a level of output where it is not stable—where persistent advances in prices are not only probable but normal. The remedies that would be effective collide with the urgencies of production for purposes of economic security. Or they are in conflict with attitudes which emphasize the importance of economic growth and of unhampered markets for the efficient use of resources. This conflict has been further complicated by what is in part a belief, in part a hope, and in part a faith that the conflict can be evaded. A principal means to this evasion is the manipulation of the monetary supply—what economists have come to call monetary policy.

* * *

1. John Maynard Keynes (1883–1946), English economist.

III

Understanding of the problem of the modern inflation begins with a basic distinction between two parts of the economy and the differences in price behavior therein. In that part of the economy where, as with agriculture, there are many producers and an approach to what economists term pure competition, no individual seller controls or influences prices. There prices will move up automatically in response to increased demand. In the typical industrial market—steel, machinery, oil, automobiles, most nonferrous metals, chemicals—a relatively small number of large firms enjoy, in one way or another, a considerable discretion in setting prices. In these markets—the ones characterized by what economists call oligopoly —as capacity operation is approached, it becomes possible to mark up prices. The word approached is emphasized. The possibility exists before capacity operation is reached. The fact that all firms are nearing capacity is assurance that no firm, by holding back, will capture an increased share of the market. It cannot supply it. Nor, under these circumstances, is there danger that there will be extra stocks lurking around at a lower price.

At this point, it is necessary to foreclose on what is perhaps the commonest error in contemporary attitudes toward inflation, although the point is well understood by economists. This is the almost inevitable temptation to regard increased production as a remedy for inflation. It is the most natural of errors; the first thoughts on the matter are wonderfully simple and forthright. If inflation is caused by output pressing generally on capacity, then one need only get more capacity and more output and thus ensure that this tension no longer exists. But as just a moment's further thought will suggest, additional all-round production, even when it can be readily obtained from existing capacity, will pay out, in wages and other costs, the income by which it is bought. Moreover, wants do not have an origin that is independent of production. They are nurtured by the same process by which production is increased. Accordingly, the effect of increased production from existing plant capacity is to increase also the purchasing power to buy that production and the desires which ensure that the purchasing power will be used.

But there is worse to come. If production is nearing capacity, a considerably increased output will require an increase in capacity. The increased investment that this implies will, in the form of wages, payments for materials, returns to capital and profits, add to purchasing power and the current demand for goods. It does so before the added capacity resulting from the investment is in place to meet the demand. Thus the effort to increase production adds to the pressure on current capacity—and to the prospect for inflationary price increases.

A cat chasing its own tail may, by an extraordinary act of feline dexterity, succeed on occasion in catching it. To overcome inflation by increasing production, while superficially similar, will not so often be successful.

IV

The response of the economy, when it is operating near capacity, to an increase in demand will not be uniform for all industries. As just observed, in the competitive industries, i.e., those where prices are set impersonally by the market, any increase in demand when supply can no longer be readily expanded will, predictably, raise prices. Similarly, a reduction in demand will reduce prices. However, in the characteristic industrial markets—those of oligopoly and administered prices—the effect of the increase in demand must be implemented by a specific decision by the firm to change its price. This decision may, on occasion, be delayed and for a variety of reasons: Inertia; the need to establish a consensus on the extent of the increase under circumstances where the antitrust laws forbid formal communication between firms; the fear of a durably adverse public reaction to the advance; the fear that, over a longer span of time, the price increases will be damaging to the competitive position of the firm or industry; and the possibility of attracting the attention of the union and stimulating wage demands all may lead to delay. (It is worth repeating that this kind of price behavior can occur only in that part of the economy where producers are sufficiently few and are otherwise so situated as to have power over their own prices. Such behavior is not vouchsafed to the farmer or to the businessman who is one of many in the market.) For many of the same reasons, price increases, when they occur, will not bring prices to the point where they maximize the short-run or current returns of the company. It is the long-run that the corporation likes. If the prices that maximize profits at the moment will bring wage demands that will threaten the cost position of the company over time; or if there promises to be long-run damage to the competitive position of the company; or if the public reputation will be hurt, then short-run maximization of return does not accord with self-interest even when this is defined in the narrowest of pecuniary terms. The firm will not proceed to maximize its current return unless something happens—an important point—to make this possible without damaging the longer-run interest.

Two things follow. In a period of high and rising demand, short-run possibilities for increasing prices are likely to run ahead of the long-run assessment of where prices should be. Therefore, firms in the typical industrial market are likely to have what amounts to a reserve of unliquidated gains from unmade price advances. Unlike the farmer or other competitive producer, who is effectively isolated from any such opportunity, firms in these markets could exact higher prices than they do. They will do so if circumstances so change as to make short-run maximization more nearly consistent with the firm's view of its long-run interest.

As a result, price increases in these industries are not tied tightly to capacity operations or, as in competitive industries, to rising demand. Demand in, say, the steel industry may fall to something less than capacity levels, but if there is an unliquidated gain, and something alters the relation between short- and long-run maximization so as to make the former more feasible, prices will still be increased. As just stated, this can happen when demand is falling. Indeed, falling profits may make price increases inevitable. In the competitive industries, output being given, prices will never go up except by reason of an increase in demand. When demand falls, prices predictably will fall.[2]

While prices in the administered-price industries may rise in face of some excess capacity and fall in face of falling demand, the scope for such movements should not be exaggerated. Excess capacity, if it is considerable, will increase the danger that some firm will fail to go along or, at a later date, resort to surreptitious price-cutting. These dangers will act to enhance the doubts about the wisdom of raising prices to maximize short-run gains and increase the reluctance to do so. There will be similar and perhaps stronger fear of the longer-run consequences of such price increases when demand is falling. The action may have to be reversed. Perhaps meanwhile wages will have moved up partly because of the price increase. The important point is only that in industries characterized by oligopoly, the relation between demand, capacity and price has a degree of play. Prices are not restricted immediately when demand is curbed or excess capacity appears.

v

In the inflation drama, it remains only to introduce Hamlet. That, by common consent, is the union. It is the instigator presumptive of that most familiar of economic phenomena, the wage-price spiral.

The role of wages in relation to inflation has long been a troublesome matter for economists. Obviously wages, through marginal cost effects, have something to do with price increases. Yet a firm that advances its prices after a wage increase could have done so

---

2. These movements will be affected, also, by differential movements in demand and also differences in the rate at which different industries adapt their plant to changes in demand [Galbraith's note].

before. At the previous lower costs and the higher prices, it would have made more money. The wage increase did nothing to enable it to get the higher price. An advance in steel wages adds only infinitesimally to the demand for steel mill products and only after a time. In any event, this is not something which steel firms take into consideration in their typically prompt response to a wage increase.[3]

The explanation lies in the existence of the margin of unliquidated gain and in the further fact that the wage advance, of itself, promptly increases the opportunity for short-run maximization in relation to long-run maximization. This is most obviously the case when the firm has been unwilling to advance its prices because of fear that it would attract the attention of the union which would press for wage increases. Now the union's attention has manifestly been attracted, and there need no longer be any reluctance on this score. The danger of an adverse public reaction is also least at such times. The public will ordinarily attribute the advance in prices to the union. In steel and other industries, there is now a well-established policy of making the occasion of a wage increase the opportunity for a rather large increase in prices and company revenues.

This is the core of the relation of wages to prices but not quite all of it. It would be wrong to suggest that the initiative to the whole movement lies with the wage demand of the unions. Living costs rise, eroding the last wage gains and stimulating efforts to recoup. And when demand and responding production are at capacity levels, profits will ordinarily be good. These in turn act as the lodestone to union demands. In the appropriate industries, the unexploited opportunity for price increases can now be seized. So it goes. One cannot single out a particular spoke in a wheel, paint it black (or red) and say that it shoves all the others. However, this does not prevent the effort. Its futility as a subject of social controversy notwithstanding, few subjects are more debated than the relative responsibility of workers and employers for the price advances which inflation comprises.

VI

As stated, the wage, price and profit spiral originates in the part of the economy where firms with a strong (or oligopolistic) market position bargain with strong unions. These price movements work themselves through the economy with a highly diverse effect on different groups. Where firms are strong in their markets and unions

3. It is, of course, a part of the progressive expansion of money incomes which sustains the inflationary movement. But it is still true that the price increase precedes and does not follow the expansion in income [Galbraith's note].

are effective, no one is much hurt, if at all, by inflation. Concern over the problem will be marked by the fortitude with which we all are able to contemplate the sorrows of others. Elsewhere, the effect will be highly mixed. Those individuals and groups will suffer most which have least control over their prices or wages and hence the least capacity to protect themselves by increasing their own return. Or if such control, as in the case of agriculture, is slight, then the effect will depend on whether the income elasticity of the demand for the particular product—roughly the effect of increased incomes on the demand for the product—is small or great. And something will depend also on whether the particular producer's costs are affected promptly or belatedly by the increase in prices.

Thus, by way of illustration, farmers have little or no control over the prices at which they sell their products. Inflation reaches them by way of impersonal market movements. For the wheat or potato farmer, the income elasticity is very low—as wage incomes rise, individuals spend no more for bread or potatoes and, on occasion, spend less. Meanwhile, the farmer's costs of fuel, fertilizer and other factors from the oligopolistic sector of the economy will have risen. For the beef-cattle producer, by contrast, income elasticity is rather higher. He is the beneficiary of the well-known and statistically quite demonstrable tendency of people who have an increase in pay to celebrate with red meat. Other things equal, and in the cattle business they frequently are not, his position will be happier than that of the producer of bread grains or potatoes.

Such discrimination is pervasive. The individual or firm which, either in line of business or as the result of speculative acumen, holds large unhedged inventories, benefits from the increased demand for these and from the consequent increase in price.

At the other extreme are those who experience the rising costs but whose own prices remain largely unaffected because they are fixed by law or custom or, at a minimum, by someone else. This is the position, during inflation, of the teacher, preacher and other of the white-collar community and of those who are reaping the reward of past services to society in the form of pensions or other such payments. The result of rising costs and comparatively fixed returns for all of these groups is much too familiar to require exegesis. Those on pensions suffer severely. Those who depend for their pay on the public treasury, especially of state and local governments, are also likely to suffer during inflation. Like all others, they experience the increase in prices. Their income is likely to lag. This lag is of considerable social consequence.

Not all venders of professional services do suffer. Occasional groups have discretion over their prices and are able to take prompt advantage of the general increase in money wages and demand, to raise their own charges and revenues. Lawyers and doctors normally fall in such a category. There have been others. In the early days of World War II, a grateful and very anxious citizenry rewarded its soldiers, sailors and airmen with a substantial increase in pay. In the teeming city of Honolulu, in prompt response to this advance in wage income, the prostitutes raised the prices of their services. This was at a time when, if anything, increased volume was causing a reduction in their average unit costs. However, in this instance, the high military authorities, deeply angered by what they deemed improper, immoral and indecent profiteering, ordered a return to the previous scale.[4]

In a free market, in an age of endemic inflation, it is unquestionably more rewarding, in purely pecuniary terms, to be a speculator or a prostitute than a teacher, preacher or policeman. Such is what conventional wisdom calls the structure of incentives.

VII

In basic outline, the requirements for inflation control will now be clear. When the economy is at or near capacity, firms in the concentrated sector can advance their prices and will have inducement from advancing wages to do so. Such price increases, with their further effects, will be prevented only if there is slack in the economy. Then various restraints begin to operate on the price advances, on the firms in granting wage advances, and on unions in asking for them. But, since firms may have unliquidated gains when operating at rather less than capacity, this slack in the absence of other measures may have to be considerable. In recent years, prices have continued to rise in much of the oligopolistic sector of the economy (where strong unions bargain with strong firms) right through recessions.

Were it possible to prevent wages from reacting on prices, and vice versa, then it would be possible to have price stability with production a good deal closer to current capacity and full employment. Wage movements would not then serve as a reason for raising prices and as a justification, or cover, for adding to profits. The derived effect of these increases on other sectors would be eliminated. It would thus be possible to have higher output and employment without inflation.

4. This was accomplished under authority delegated to the military authorities by the Office of Price Administration (or, more precisely, its predecessor) in which I held the responsible authority. The step, for which I assumed I would be held to account, greatly worried me. Uniquely among acts of public insanity with which I have been associated, it never became a matter of public knowledge [Galbraith's note].

In the past, there has been much argument whether, in the strategy of inflation control, one should seek to come to grips with the level of demand (in relation to the capacity of the economy and the labor force) or whether one should seek to deal with the wage-price spiral. Economists have generally emphasized the importance of the level of demand; to the layman, the wage-price spiral has always seemed the phenomenon that most obviously required attention. The proper answer, it will be seen, is that both are important. Inflation can be controlled by a sufficiently heavy reduction in the level of demand. It can be controlled with a less drastic reduction if something could be done to arrest the interaction of wages and prices or, to speak more precisely, of wages, profits and prices.

The conflicts here will be evident. The introduction of slack, especially if it must be considerable, is in conflict with the imperatives of economic security. And the use of controls is in conflict with the ancient conviction that resources must be allocated efficiently among their various employments and that the free market is the most efficient and possibly even the only satisfactory instrument of such allocation. Setting the store that we do by the production of goods, we have here a seemingly decisive argument against the use of controls.

1958, 1976

QUESTIONS

1. Galbraith divides his discussion into numbered sections; can you provide titles for some or all of these sections? What is the logical progression of his argument? What is his point?
2. In the Notes on Composition (pp. 670–672) the means of developing a thesis are discussed as responses to a pair of questions: "What do you mean?" and "How do you know?" What are Galbraith's responses to these questions?
3. In the Declaration of Independence (pp. 514–517) the underlying political assumptions are made explicit. Galbraith's are not. What does he assume? How does he seem to regard the relation between the economic system and the political system?
4. On p. 497 Galbraith uses the analogy of a cat chasing its tail. How effectively does this analogy serve its purpose?
5. What sort of person does Galbraith seem to be in this discussion? Several times (on p. 494, for example), he speaks of "the conventional wisdom." What does he mean? How does his use of this phrase affect the image or personality he projects?

NICCOLÒ MACHIAVELLI

The Morals of the Prince[1]

On the Reasons Why Men Are Praised or Blamed—Especially Princes

It remains now to be seen what style and principles a prince ought to adopt in dealing with his subjects and friends. I know the subject has been treated frequently before, and I'm afraid people will think me rash for trying to do so again, especially since I intend to differ in this discussion from what others have said. But since I intend to write something useful to an understanding reader, it seemed better to go after the real truth of the matter than to repeat what people have imagined. A great many men have imagined states and princedoms such as nobody ever saw or knew in the real world, for there's such a difference between the way we really live and the way we ought to live that the man who neglects the real to study the ideal will learn how to accomplish his ruin, not his salvation. Any man who tries to be good all the time is bound to come to ruin among the great number who are not good. Hence a prince who wants to keep his post must learn how not to be good, and use that knowledge, or refrain from using it, as necessity requires.

Putting aside, then, all the imaginary things that are said about princes, and getting down to the truth, let me say that whenever men are discussed (and especially princes because they are prominent), there are certain qualities that bring them either praise or blame. Thus some are considered generous, others stingy (I use a Tuscan term, since "greedy" in our speech means a man who wants to take other people's goods. we call a man "stingy" who clings to his own); some are givers, others grabbers; some cruel, others merciful; one man is treacherous, another faithful; one is feeble and effeminate, another fierce and spirited; one humane, another proud; one lustful, another chaste; one straightforward, another sly; one harsh, another gentle; one serious, another playful; one religious, another skeptical, and so on. I know everyone will agree that among these many qualities a prince certainly ought to have all those that are considered good. But since it is impossible to have and exercise them all, because the conditions of human life simply do not allow

1. From *The Prince,* a book on state-craft written for Giuliano de' Medici (1479–1516), a member of one of the most famous and powerful families of Renaissance Italy.

it, a prince must be shrewd enough to avoid the public disgrace of those vices that would lose him his state. If he possibly can, he should also guard against vices that will not lose him his state; but if he cannot prevent them, he should not be too worried about indulging them. And furthermore, he should not be too worried about incurring blame for any vice without which he would find it hard to save his state. For if you look at matters carefully, you will see that something resembling virtue, if you follow it, may be your ruin, while something else resembling vice will lead, if you follow it, to your security and well-being.

On Liberality and Stinginess

Let me begin, then, with the first of the qualities mentioned above, by saying that a reputation for liberality is doubtless very fine; but the generosity that earns you that reputation can do you great harm. For if you exercise your generosity in a really virtuous way, as you should, nobody will know of it, and you cannot escape the odium of the opposite vice. Hence if you wish to be widely known as a generous man, you must seize every opportunity to make a big display of your giving. A prince of this character is bound to use up his entire revenue in works of ostentation. Thus, in the end, if he wants to keep a name for generosity, he will have to load his people with exorbitant taxes and squeeze money out of them in every way he can. This is the first step in making him odious to his subjects; for when he is poor, nobody will respect him. Then, when his generosity has angered many and brought rewards to a few, the slightest difficulty will trouble him, and at the first approach of danger, down he goes. If by chance he foresees this, and tries to change his ways, he will immediately be labeled a miser.

Since a prince cannot use this virtue of liberality in such a way as to become known for it unless he harms his own security, he won't mind, if he judges prudently of things, being known as a miser. In due course he will be thought the more liberal man, when people see that his parsimony enables him to live on his income, to defend himself against his enemies, and to undertake major projects without burdening his people with taxes. Thus he will be acting liberally toward all those people from whom he takes nothing (and there are an immense number of them), and in a stingy way toward those people on whom he bestows nothing (and they are very few). In our times, we have seen great things being accomplished only by men who have had the name of misers; all the others have gone under. Pope Julius II, though he used his reputation as a generous man to gain the papacy, sacrificed it in order to be able to make war; the present king of France has waged many wars without levying a single extra tax on his people, simply because he could take care of the extra expenses out of the savings from his long parsimony. If the present king of Spain had a reputation for generosity, he would never have been able to undertake so many campaigns, or win so many of them.

Hence a prince who prefers not to rob his subjects, who wants to be able to defend himself, who wants to avoid poverty and contempt, and who doesn't want to become a plunderer, should not mind in the least if people consider him a miser; this is simply one of the vices that enable him to reign. Someone may object that Caesar used a reputation for generosity to become emperor, and many other people have also risen in the world, because they were generous or were supposed to be so. Well, I answer, either you are a prince already, or you are in the process of becoming one; in the first case, this reputation for generosity is harmful to you, in the second case it is very necessary. Caesar was one of those who wanted to become ruler in Rome; but after he had reached his goal, if he had lived, and had not cut down on his expenses, he would have ruined the empire itself. Someone may say: there have been plenty of princes, very successful in warfare, who have had a reputation for generosity. But I answer: either the prince is spending his own money and that of his subjects, or he is spending someone else's. In the first case, he ought to be sparing; in the second case, he ought to spend money like water. Any prince at the head of his army, which lives on loot, extortion, and plunder, disposes of other people's property, and is bound to be very generous; otherwise, his soldiers would desert him. You can always be a more generous giver when what you give is not yours or your subjects'; Cyrus, Caesar, and Alexander[2] were generous in this way. Spending what belongs to other people does no harm to your reputation, rather it enhances it; only spending your own substance harms you. And there is nothing that wears out faster than generosity; even as you practice it, you lose the means of practicing it, and you become either poor and contemptible or (in the course of escaping poverty) rapacious and hateful. The thing above all against which a prince must protect himself is being contemptible and hateful; generosity leads to both. Thus, it's much wiser to put up with the reputation of being a miser, which brings you shame without hate, than to be forced— just because you want to appear generous—into a reputation for rapacity, which brings shame on you and hate along with it.

2. Persian, Roman, and Macedonian conquerors and rulers in ancient times.

On Cruelty and Clemency: Whether It Is Better to Be Loved or Feared

Continuing now with our list of qualities, let me say that every prince should prefer to be considered merciful rather than cruel, yet he should be careful not to mismanage this clemency of his. People thought Cesare Borgia[3] was cruel, but that cruelty of his reorganized the Romagna, united it, and established it in peace and loyalty. Anyone who views the matter realistically will see that this prince was much more merciful than the people of Florence, who, to avoid the reputation of cruelty, allowed Pistoia to be destroyed.[4] Thus, no prince should mind being called cruel for what he does to keep his subjects united and loyal; he may make examples of a very few, but he will be more merciful in reality than those who, in their tenderheartedness, allow disorders to occur, with their attendant murders and lootings. Such turbulence brings harm to an entire community, while the executions ordered by a prince affect only one individual at a time. A new prince, above all others, cannot possibly avoid a name for cruelty, since new states are always in danger. And Virgil, speaking through the mouth of Dido,[5] says:

> My cruel fate
> And doubts attending an unsettled state
> Force me to guard my coast from foreign foes.

Yet a prince should be slow to believe rumors and to commit himself to action on the basis of them. He should not be afraid of his own thoughts; he ought to proceed cautiously, moderating his conduct with prudence and humanity, allowing neither overconfidence to make him careless, nor overtimidity to make him intolerable.

Here the question arises: is it better to be loved than feared, or vice versa? I don't doubt that every prince would like to be both; but since it is hard to accommodate these qualities, if you have to make a choice, to be feared is much safer than to be loved. For it is a good general rule about men, that they are ungrateful, fickle, liars and deceivers, fearful of danger and greedy for gain. While you serve their welfare, they are all yours, offering their blood, their belongings, their lives, and their children's lives, as we noted above —so long as the danger is remote. But when the danger is close at hand, they turn against you. Then, any prince who has relied on their words and has made no other preparations will come to grief;

3. The son of Pope Alexander VI (referred to later) and duke of Romagna, which he subjugated in 1499–1502.
4. By unchecked rioting between opposing factions (1502).
5. Queen of Carthage and tragic heroine of Virgil's epic, *The Aeneid*.

because friendships that are bought at a price, and not with greatness and nobility of soul, may be paid for but they are not acquired, and they cannot be used in time of need. People are less concerned with offending a man who makes himself loved than one who makes himself feared: the reason is that love is a link of obligation which men, because they are rotten, will break any time they think doing so serves their advantage; but fear involves dread of punishment, from which they can never escape.

Still, a prince should make himself feared in such a way that, even if he gets no love, he gets no hate either; because it is perfectly possible to be feared and not hated, and this will be the result if only the prince will keep his hands off the property of his subjects or citizens, and off their women. When he does have to shed blood, he should be sure to have a strong justification and manifest cause; but above all, he should not confiscate people's property, because men are quicker to forget the death of a father than the loss of a patrimony. Besides, pretexts for confiscation are always plentiful, it never fails that a prince who starts living by plunder can find reasons to rob someone else. Excuses for proceeding against someone's life are much rarer and more quickly exhausted.

But a prince at the head of his armies and commanding a multitude of soldiers should not care a bit if he is considered cruel; without such a reputation, he could never hold his army together and ready for action. Among the marvelous deeds of Hannibal,[6] this was prime: that, having an immense army, which included men of many different races and nations, and which he led to battle in distant countries, he never allowed them to fight among themselves or to rise against him, whether his fortune was good or bad. The reason for this could only be his inhuman cruelty, which, along with his countless other talents, made him an object of awe and terror to his soldiers; and without the cruelty, his other qualities would never have sufficed. The historians who pass snap judgments on these matters admire his accomplishments and at the same time condemn the cruelty which was their main cause.

When I say, "His other qualities would never have sufficed," we can see that this is true from the example of Scipio,[7] an outstanding man not only among those of his own time, but in all recorded history; yet his armies revolted in Spain, for no other reason than his excessive leniency in allowing his soldiers more freedom than military discipline permits. Fabius Maximus rebuked him in the

---

6. Carthaginian general who led a massive but unsuccessful invasion of Rome in 218–203 B.C.

7. The Roman general whose successful invasion of Carthage in 203 B.C. caused Hannibal's army to be recalled from Rome. The episode described here occurred in 206 B.C.

senate for this failing, calling him the corrupter of the Roman armies. When a lieutenant of Scipio's plundered the Locrians,[8] he took no action in behalf of the people, and did nothing to discipline that insolent lieutenant; again, this was the result of his easygoing nature. Indeed, when someone in the senate wanted to excuse him on this occasion, he said there are many men who knew better how to avoid error themselves than how to correct error in others. Such a soft temper would in time have tarnished the fame and glory of Scipio, had he brought it to the office of emperor; but as he lived under the control of the senate, this harmful quality of his not only remained hidden but was considered creditable.

Returning to the question of being feared or loved, I conclude that since men love at their own inclination but can be made to fear at the inclination of the prince, a shrewd prince will lay his foundations on what is under his own control, not on what is controlled by others. He should simply take pains not to be hated, as I said.

The Way Princes Should Keep Their Word

How praiseworthy it is for a prince to keep his word and live with integrity rather than by craftiness, everyone understands; yet we see from recent experience that those princes have accomplished most who paid little heed to keeping their promises, but who knew how craftily to manipulate the minds of men. In the end, they won out over those who tried to act honestly.

You should consider then, that there are two ways of fighting, one with laws and the other with force. The first is properly a human method, the second belongs to beasts. But as the first method does not always suffice, you sometimes have to turn to the second. Thus a prince must know how to make good use of both the beast and the man. Ancient writers made subtle note of this fact when they wrote that Achilles and many other princes of antiquity were sent to be reared by Chiron the centaur,[9] who trained them in his discipline. Having a teacher who is half man and half beast can only mean that a prince must know how to use both these two natures, and that one without the other has no lasting effect.

Since a prince must know how to use the character of beasts, he should pick for imitation the fox and the lion. As the lion cannot protect himself from traps, and the fox cannot defend himself from

8. A people of Sicily, defeated by Scipio in 205 B.C. and placed under Q. Pleminius; *Fabius Maximus*: not only a senator but a high public official and general who had fought against Hannibal in Italy.

9. Half man and half horse, the mythical Chiron was said to have taught the arts of war and peace, including hunting, medicine, music, and prophecy; *Achilles*: foremost among the Greek heroes in the Trojan War.

wolves, you have to be a fox in order to be wary of traps, and a lion to overawe the wolves. Those who try to live by the lion alone are badly mistaken. Thus a prudent prince cannot and should not keep his word when to do so would go against his interest, or when the reasons that made him pledge it no longer apply. Doubtless if all men were good, this rule would be bad; but since they are a sad lot, and keep no faith with you, you in your turn are under no obligation to keep it with them.

Besides, a prince will never lack for legitimate excuses to explain away his breaches of faith. Modern history will furnish innumerable examples of this behavior, showing how many treaties and promises have been made null and void by the faithlessness of princes, and how the man succeeded best who knew best how to play the fox. But it is a necessary part of this nature that you must conceal it carefully; you must be a great liar and hypocrite. Men are so simple of mind, and so much dominated by their immediate needs, that a deceitful man will always find plenty who are ready to be deceived. One of many recent examples calls for mention. Alexander VI[1] never did anything else, never had another thought, except to deceive men, and he always found fresh material to work on. Never was there a man more convincing in his assertions, who sealed his promises with more solemn oaths, and who observed them less. Yet his deceptions were always successful, because he knew exactly how to manage this sort of business.

In actual fact, a prince may not have all the admirable qualities we listed, but it is very necessary that he should seem to have them. Indeed, I will venture to say that when you have them and exercise them all the time, they are harmful to you; when you just seem to have them, they are useful. It is good to appear merciful, truthful, humane, sincere, and religious; it is good to be so in reality. But you must keep your mind so disposed that, in case of need, you can turn to the exact contrary. This has to be understood: a prince, and especially a new prince, cannot possibly exercise all those virtues for which men are called "good." To preserve the state, he often has to do things against his word, against charity, against humanity, against religion. Thus he has to have a mind ready to shift as the winds of fortune and the varying circumstances of life may dictate. And as I said above, he should not depart from the good if he can hold to it, but he should be ready to enter on evil if he has to.

Hence a prince should take great care never to drop a word that does not seem imbued with the five good qualities noted above; to anyone who sees or hears him, he should appear all compassion, all honor, all humanity, all integrity, all religion. Nothing is more nec-

1. Pope from 1492 to 1503.

essary than to seem to have this last virtue. Men in general judge more by the sense of sight than by the sense of touch, because everyone can see but only a few can test by feeling. Everyone sees what you seem to be, few know what you really are; and those few do not dare take a stand against the general opinion, supported by the majesty of the government. In the actions of all men, and especially of princes who are not subject to a court of appeal, we must always look to the end. Let a prince, therefore, win victories and uphold his state; his methods will always be considered worthy, and everyone will praise them, because the masses are always impressed by the superficial appearance of things, and by the outcome of an enterprise. And the world consists of nothing but the masses; the few who have no influence when the many feel secure. A certain prince of our own time, whom it's just as well not to name,[2] preaches nothing but peace and mutual trust, yet he is the determined enemy of both; and if on several different occasions he had observed either, he would have lost both his reputation and his throne.

1513

2. Probably Ferdinand of Spain, then allied with the house of Medici.

THOMAS JEFFERSON
Original Draft of the Declaration of Independence

A DECLARATION OF THE REPRESENTATIVES OF THE UNITED STATES OF AMERICA, IN GENERAL CONGRESS ASSEMBLED.

When in the course of human events it becomes necessary for a people to advance from that subordination in which they have hitherto remained, & to assume among the powers of the earth the equal & independant station to which the laws of nature & of nature's god entitle them, a decent respect to the opinions of mankind requires that they should declare the causes which impel them to the change.

We hold these truths to be sacred & undeniable; that all men are created equal & independant, that from that equal creation they derive rights inherent & inalienable, among which are the preservation of life, & liberty, & the spirit of happiness; that to secure these ends, governments are instituted among men, deriving their just powers from the consent of the governed; that whenever any form of government shall become destructive of these ends, it is the right of the people to alter or to abolish it, & to institute new government, laying it's foundation on such principles & organising it's powers in such form, as to them shall seem most likely to effect their safety & happiness. prudence indeed will dictate that governments long established should not be changed for light & transient causes: and accordingly all experience hath shewn that mankind are more disposed to suffer while evils are sufferable, than to right themselves by abolishing the forms to which they are accustomed. but when a long train of abuses & usurpations, begun at a distinguished period, & pursuing invariably the same object, evinces a design to subject them to arbitrary power, it is their right, it is their duty, to throw off such government & to provide new guards for their future security. such has been the patient sufferance of these colonies; & such is now the necessity which constrains them to expunge their former systems of government. the history of his present majesty, is a history of unremitting injuries and usurpations, among which no one fact stands single or solitary to contradict the uniform tenor of the rest, all of which have in direct object the establishment of an absolute tyranny over these states. to prove this, let facts be submited to a candid world, for the truth of which we pledge a faith yet unsullied by falsehood.

he has refused his assent to laws the most wholesome and necessary for the public good:

he has forbidden his governors to pass laws of immediate & pressing importance, unless suspended in their operation till his assent should be obtained; and when so suspended, he has neglected utterly to attend to them.

he has refused to pass other laws for the accommodation of large districts of people unless those people would relinquish the right of representation, a right inestimable to them, & formidable to tyrants alone:[1]

he has dissolved Representative houses repeatedly & continually, for opposing with manly firmness his invasions on the rights of the people:

he has refused for a long space of time to cause others to be elected, whereby the legislative powers, incapable of annihilation, have returned to the people at large for their exercise, the state remaining in the mean time exposed to all the dangers of invasion from without, &, convulsions within:

1. At this point in the manuscript a strip containing the following clause is inserted: "He called together legislative bodies. at places unusual, unco[mforta-ble, & distant from] the depository of their public records for the sole purpose of fatiguing [them into compliance] with his measures:" Missing parts in the Library of Congress text are supplied from the copy made by Jefferson for George Wythe. This copy is in the New York Public Library. The fact that this passage was omitted from John Adams's transcript suggests that it was not a part of Jefferson's original rough draft.

he has suffered the administration of justice totally to cease in some of these colonies, refusing his assent to laws for establishing judiciary powers:

he has made our judges dependant on his will alone, for the tenure of their offices, and amount of their salaries:

he has erected a multitude of new offices by a self-assumed power, & sent hither swarms of officers to harrass our people & eat out their substance:

he has kept among us in times of peace standing armies & ships of war:

he has affected[2] to render the military, independent of & superior to the civil power:

he has combined with others to subject us to a jurisdiction foreign to our constitutions and unacknowledged by our laws; giving his assent to their pretended acts of legislation, for quartering large bodies of armed troops among us;

> for protecting them by a mock-trial from punishment for any murders they should commit on the inhabitants of these states;

> for cutting off our trade with all parts of the world;

> for imposing taxes on us without our consent;

> for depriving us of the benefits of trial by jury

he has endeavored to prevent the population of these states; for that purpose obstructing the laws for naturalization of foreigners; refusing to pass others to encourage their migrations hither; & raising the conditions of new appropriations of lands;

> for transporting us beyond seas to be tried for pretended offences:

> for taking away our charters & altering fundamentally the forms of our governments;

> for suspending our own legislatures & declaring themselves invested with power to legislate for us in all cases whatsoever:

he has abdicated government here, withdrawing his governors, & declaring us out of his allegiance & protection:

he has plundered our seas, ravaged our coasts, burnt our towns & destroyed the lives of our people:

he is at this time transporting large armies of foreign mercenaries to compleat the works of death, desolation & tyranny, already begun with circumstances of cruelty & perfidy unworthy the head of a civilized nation:

he has endeavored to bring on the inhabitants of our frontiers the merciless Indian savages, whose known rule of warfare

---

2. Tried.

is an undistinguished destruction of all ages, sexes, & conditions of existence:

he has incited treasonable insurrections of our fellow-citizens,
with the allurements of forfeiture & confiscation of our property:

he has waged cruel war against human nature itself, violating
it's most sacred rights of life & liberty in the persons of a distant
people who never offended him, captivating & carrying them
into slavery in another hemisphere, or to incur miserable death
in their transportion thither. this piratical warfare, the
opprobrium of *infidel* powers, is the warfare of the CHRIS-
TIAN king of Great Britain. determined to keep open
a market where MEN should be bought & sold; he has pros-
tituted his negative for suppressing every legislative attempt
to prohibit or to restrain this execrable commerce: and that
this assemblage of horrors might want no fact of distinguished
die, he is now exciting those very people to rise in arms among
us, and to purchase that liberty of which *he* has deprived them,
by murdering the people upon whom *he* also obtruded them;
thus paying off former crimes committed against the *liberties*
of one people, with crimes which he urges them to commit
against the *lives* of another.

in every stage of these oppressions we have petitioned for redress
in the most humble terms; our repeated petitions have been answered
by repeated injury. a prince whose character is thus marked by every
act which may define a tyrant, is unfit to be the ruler of a people
who mean to be free. future ages will scarce believe that the hardi-
ness of one man, adventured within the short compass of twelve
years only, on so many acts of tyranny without a mask, over a people
fostered & fixed in principles of liberty.

Nor have we been wanting in attentions to our British brethren.
we have warned them from time to time of attempts by their legislature to extend a jurisdiction over these our states. we have reminded them of the circumstances of our emigration & settlement
here, no one of which could warrant so strange a pretension: that
these were effected at the expence of our own blood & treasure, unas-
sisted by the wealth or the strength of Great Britain: that in con-
stituting indeed our several forms of government, we had adopted
one common king, thereby laying a foundation for perpetual league
& amity with them; but that submission to their [Parliament, was
no Part of our Constitution, nor ever in Idea, if History may be][3]
credited: and we appealed to their native justice & magnanimity, as
to the ties of our common kindred to disavow these usurpations

---

3. An illegible passage is supplied from John Adams's transcription.

which were likely to interrupt our correspondence & connection. they too have been deaf to the voice of justice & of consanguinity, & when occasions have been given them, by the regular course of their laws, of removing from their councils the disturbers of our harmony, they have by their free election re-established them in power. at this very time too they are permitting their chief magistrate to send over not only soldiers of our common blood, but Scotch & foreign mercenaries to invade & deluge us in blood. these facts have given the last stab to agonizing affection, and manly spirit bids us to renounce for ever these unfeeling 'brethren. we must endeavor to forget our former love for them, and to hold them as we hold the rest of mankind, enemies in war, in peace friends. we might have been a free & a great people together; but a communication of grandeur & of freedom it seems is below their dignity. be it so, since they will have it: the road to glory & happiness is open to us too; we will climb it in a separate state, and acquiesce in the necessity which pronounces our everlasting Adieu!

We therefore the representatives of the United States of America in General Congress assembled do, in the name & by authority of the good people of these states, reject and renounce all allegiance & subjection to the kings of Great Britain & all others who may hereafter claim by, through, or under them; we utterly dissolve & break off all political connection which may have heretofore subsisted between us & the people or parliament of Great Britain; and finally we do assert and declare these colonies to be free and independant states, and that as free & independant states they shall hereafter have power to levy war, conclude peace, contract alliances, establish commerce, & to do all other acts and things which independant states may of right do. And for the support of this declaration we mutually pledge to each other our lives, our fortunes, & our sacred honour.

1776

THOMAS JEFFERSON and OTHERS
The Declaration of Independence

In Congress, July 4, 1776
The unanimous Declaration of the
thirteen united States of America

When in the Course of human events it becomes necessary for one people to dissolve the political bands which have connected them with another, and to assume among the powers of the earth, the separate and equal station to which the Laws of Nature and of Nature's God entitle them, a decent respect to the opinions of mankind requires that they should declare the causes which impel them to the separation.

We hold these truths to be self-evident, that all men are created equal, that they are endowed by their Creator with certain unalienable Rights, that among these are Life, Liberty and the pursuit of Happiness. That to secure these rights, Governments are instituted among Men, deriving their just powers from the consent of the governed, That whenever any Form of Government becomes destructive of these ends, it is the Right of the People to alter or to abolish it, and to institute new Government, laying its foundation on such principles and organizing its powers in such form, as to them shall seem most likely to affect their Safety and Happiness. Prudence, indeed, will dictate that Governments long established should not be changed for light and transient causes; and accordingly all experience hath shewn that mankind are more disposed to suffer, while evils are sufferable, than to right themselves by abolishing the forms to which they are accustomed. But when a long train of abuses and usurpations, pursuing invariably the same Object evinces a design to reduce them under absolute Despotism, it is their right, it is their duty, to throw off such Government, and to provide new Guards for their future security. Such has been the patient sufferance of these Colonies; and such is now the necessity which constrains them to alter their former Systems of Government. The history of the present King of Great Britain is a history of repeated injuries and usurpations, all having in direct object the establishment of an absolute Tyranny over these States. To prove this, let Facts be submitted to a candid world.

He has refused his Assent to Laws, the most wholesome and necessary for the public good.

He has forbidden his Governors to pass laws of immediate and pressing importance, unless suspended in their operation till his Assent should be obtained; and when so suspended, he has utterly neglected to attend to them.

He has refused to pass other Laws for the accommodation of large districts of people, unless those people would relinquish the right of Representation in the Legislature, a right inestimable to them and formidable to tyrants only.

He has called together legislative bodies at places unusual, uncomfortable, and distant from the depository of their Public Records, for the sole purpose of fatiguing them into compliance with his measures.

He has dissolved Representative Houses repeatedly, for opposing with manly firmness his invasions on the rights of the people.

He has refused for a long time, after such dissolutions, to cause others to be elected; whereby the Legislative Powers, incapable of Annihilation, have returned to the People at large for their exercise; the State remaining in the mean time exposed to all the dangers of invasion from without, and convulsions within.

He has endeavored to prevent the population of these States; for that purpose obstructing the Laws for Naturalization of Foreigners; refusing to pass others to encourage their migration hither, and raising the conditions of new Appropriations of Lands.

He has obstructed the Administration of Justice, by refusing his Assent to Laws for establishing Judiciary Powers.

He has made Judges dependent on his Will alone, for the tenure of their offices, and the amount and payment of their salaries.

He has erected a multitude of New Offices, and sent hither swarms of Officers to harass our people, and eat out their substance.

He has kept among us, in times of peace, Standing Armies without the Consent of our legislatures.

He has affected to render the Military independent of and superior to the Civil Power.

He has combined with others to subject us to a jurisdiction foreign to our constitution, and unacknowledged by our laws; giving his Assent to their Acts of pretended Legislation: For quartering large bodies of armed troops among us: For protecting them, by a mock Trial, from punishment for any Murders which they should commit on the Inhabitants of these States: For cutting off our Trade with all parts of the world: For imposing Taxes on us without our Consent: For depriving us in many cases, of the benefits of Trial by Jury; For transporting us beyond Seas to be tried for pretended offenses: for abolishing the free System of English Laws in a neighboring Province, establishing therein an Arbitrary government, and enlarging its Boundaries so as to render it at once an example and fit instrument for introducing the same absolute rule into these Colonies: For taking away our Charters, abolishing our most valuable Laws and altering fundamentally the Forms of our Governments: For suspending our own Legislatures, and declaring themselves invested with power to legislate for us in all cases whatsoever.

He has abdicated Government here, by declaring us out of his Protection and waging War against us.

He has plundered our seas, ravaged our Coasts, burnt our towns, and destroyed the lives of our people.

He is at this time transporting large Armies of foreign Mercenaries to complete the works of death, desolation and tyranny, already begun with circumstances of Cruelty & Perfidy scarcely paralleled in the most barbarous ages, and totally unworthy the Head of a civilized nation.

He has constrained our fellow Citizens taken Captive on the high Seas to bear Arms against their Country, to become the executioners of their friends and Brethren, or to fall themselves by their Hands.

He has excited domestic insurrections amongst us, and has endeavored to bring on the inhabitants of our frontiers, the merciless Indian Savages, whose known rule of warfare, is an undistinguished destruction of all ages, sexes, and conditions.

In every stage of these Oppressions We have Petitioned for Redress in the most humble terms: Our repeated Petitions have been answered only by repeated injury. A Prince, whose character is thus marked by every act which may define a Tyrant, is unfit to be the ruler of a free people.

Nor have We been wanting in attention to our British brethren. We have warned them from time to time of attempts by their legislature to extend an unwarrantable jurisdiction over us. We have reminded them of the circumstances of our emigration and settlement here. We have appealed to their native justice and magnanimity, and we have conjured them by the ties of our common kindred to disavow these usurpations, which would inevitably interrupt our connections and correspondence. They too have been deaf to the voice of justice and of consanguinity. We must, therefore, acquiesce in the necessity, which denounces our Separation, and hold them, as we hold the rest of mankind, Enemies in War, in Peace Friends.

We, THEREFORE, the Representatives of the UNITED STATES OF AMERICA, in General Congress, Assembled, appealing to the Supreme Judge of the world for the rectitude of our intentions, do, in the Name, and by Authority of the good People of these Colonies, solemnly publish and declare, That these United Colonies are, and of Right ought to be FREE AND INDEPENDENT STATES; that they are Absolved from all Allegiance to the British Crown, and that all political connection between them and the State of Great Britain, is and ought to be totally dissolved; and that as Free and Independent States, they have full Power to levy War, conclude Peace, contract Alliances, establish Commerce, and to do all other Acts and Things which Independent States may of right do. And for the support of this Declaration, with a firm reliance on the protection of Divine Providence, we mutually pledge to each other our Lives, our Fortunes, and our sacred Honor.

1776

QUESTIONS

1. The Declaration of Independence was addressed to several audiences: the king of Great Britain, the people of Great Britain, the

people of America, and the world at large. Show ways in which the final draft was adapted for its several audiences.

2. Examine the second paragraph of each version closely. How have the revisions in the final version increased its effectiveness over the first draft?

3. The Declaration has often been called a classic example of deductive argument: setting up general statements, relating particular cases to them, and drawing conclusions. Trace this pattern through the document, noting the way each part is developed. Would the document have been as effective if the long middle part had either come first or been left out entirely? Explain.

4. Find the key terms and phrases of the Declaration (such as "these truths . . . self-evident," "created equal," "unalienable rights," and so on) and determine how fully they are defined by the contexts in which they occur. Why are no formal definitions given for them?

5. The signers of the Declaration appeal both to general principles and to factual evidence in presenting their case. Which of the appeals to principle could still legitimately be made today by a nation eager to achieve independence? In other words, how far does the Declaration reflect unique events of history and how far does it reflect universal aspirations and ideals?

E. B. WHITE

Democracy

We received a letter from the Writers' War Board the other day asking for a statement on "The Meaning of Democracy." It presumably is our duty to comply with such a request, and it is certainly our pleasure.

Surely the Board knows what democracy is. It is the line that forms on the right. It is the don't in don't shove. It is the hole in the stuffed shirt through which the sawdust slowly trickles; it is the dent in the high hat. Democracy is the recurrent suspicion that more than half of the people are right more than half of the time. It is the feeling of privacy in the voting booths, the feeling of communion in the libraries, the feeling of vitality everywhere. Democracy is a letter to the editor. Democracy is the score at the beginning of the ninth. It is an idea which hasn't been disproved yet, a song the words of which have not gone bad. It's the mustard on the hot dog and the cream in the rationed coffee. Democracy is a request from a War Board, in the middle of a morning in the middle of a war, wanting to know what democracy is.

1943

QUESTIONS

1. White's piece is dated July 3, 1943, the middle of World War II. How did the occasion shape what White says about democracy?

2. Look up "democracy" in a standard desk dictionary. Of the several meanings given, which one best applies to White's definition? Does more than one apply?

3. Translate White's definition into non-metaphorical language. (For example, "It is the line that forms on the right" might be translated by "It has no special privileges.") Determine what is lost in the translation, or, in other words, what White has gained by using figurative language.

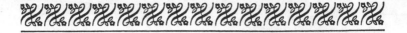

Prose Forms: Apothegms

At the beginning of Bacon's essay "Of Truth," jesting Pilate asks, "What is truth?" and does not stay for an answer. Perhaps Pilate asked in jest because he thought the question foolish; perhaps because he thought an answer impossible. Something of Pilate's skepticism is in most of us, but something too of a belief that there is truth, even if—as the history of philosophy teaches us—determining its nature may be enormously difficult. We readily assume some things to be true even if we hesitate to say what ultimately is Truth.

The test of truth most often is an appeal to the observed facts of experience. The observation of experience yields knowledge; the generalized statement of that knowledge yields a concept of the experience; the concise, descriptive form in which that concept is expressed we call variously, apothegm, proverb, maxim, or aphorism. Thus Sir James Mackintosh can speak of apothegms as "the condensed good sense of nations," because the apothegm conveys the distilled observations of people about their own persistent conduct. To hear the familiar "Absence makes the heart grow fonder" is to be reminded of a general truth which you and the world acknowledge. It does not matter that the equally familiar "Out of sight, out of mind" seems to contradict the other saying; both are true but applicable to different situations. Both statements are immediately recognizable as true and neither requires to be argued for, representing as they do the collective experience of mankind intelligently observed.

Aphoristic statements often occur within the context of more extended pieces of writing, and while not apothegms in the strictest sense, but rather propositions, they have the force of apothegms. For example, Percy Shelley's Defence of Poetry (1821) concludes that "Poets are the unacknowledged legislators of the world." Seventy years later in his Preface to The Picture of Dorian Gray Oscar Wilde asserts that "All art is quite useless." Although these statements seem contradictory, each is unarguable within its own context.

Not everyone is as astute an observer as the writer of apothegms and maxims, of course, but everyone is presumably capable of perceiving their rightness. What we perceive first is the facts to which the saying applies. When Franklin says "An empty bag cannot stand upright" (in 1740 he obviously had in mind a cloth bag), we acknowledge that this is the condition of the empty bag—and of ourselves when we are empty. Or when La Rochefoucauld says "We are all strong enough to endure the misfortunes of others," he too observes a condition that exists among people.

Many aphoristic assertions claim their validity primarily in descriptive terms. But the descriptive "is" in most apothegms and maxims is joined to a normative "ought" and the sayings therefore convey admonitions about and judgments of the conditions they describe. "Waste not, want not" is a simple illustration of this use of fact to admonish. Samuel Butler briefly gives us the presumed fact that "the world will always be governed by self-interest." Then he quickly advises: "We should not try to stop this, we should try to make the self-interest of cads a little more consistent with that of decent people." The condition of "ought" need not always be admonitory; it may be the implied judgment in La Rochefoucauld's assertion that "It is the habit of mediocre minds to condemn all that is beyond their grasp." The judgment is explicit in Franklin's "Fish and visitors stink in three days." And Bierce's definitions of ordinary words are not specifications of meanings in the way of ordinary dictionaries, but critical concepts of the experiences to which the words point.

"Wisdom" or "good sense," then, is the heart of the apothegm or maxim, the conjunction of "is" and "ought" in an assertion of universal truth. Unlike ordinary assertions of fact or opinion usually concerned with particular rather than universal experience, the wise saying is complete in its brevity. Before the ordinary assertion is allowed to hold, we require that the assumptions on which it rests, the implications it carries, the critical concepts and terms it contains, be examined closely and explored or justified. If someone says that the modern college student wants most to succeed materially in life, we want to be satisfied about what constitutes "modern," which college students (and where) are referred to, what else is involved in the comparative "most," what specifically is meant by "materially." But the apothegm assumes facts widely known and accepted, and in its judgments invokes values or attitudes readily intelligible to the great majority. It is the truth as most people experience it.

In a sense, every writer's concern is ultimately with truth. Certainly the essayist is directly concerned, in defining and ordering ideas, to say what is true and, somehow, to say it "new." Much of what he or she says is of the nature of assertion about particular experience; he or she must therefore be at pains to handle such matters as assumptions and logical proofs carefully and deliberately. But one cannot always be starting from scratch, not daring to assume anything, trusting no certain knowledge or experience or beliefs held in common with other people. Careful one must be, but also aware that there is available, in addition to methods of logical analysis and proof, rules of evidence, and the other means to effective exposition, the whole memory and record of the vast experience of the race contained in a people's apothegms and aphorisms. In them is a treasury of truths useful to many demands of clarity and precision. And in them, too, is a valuable lesson in the way a significantly large body of experience—direct, in a person's day-to-day encounters; indirect, in the study of all forms of history—can be observed, conceptualized, and then expressed in an economy of language brief in form, comprehensive in meaning, and satisfyingly true.

Light purse, heavy heart.   1733
He's a fool that makes his doctor his heir.
Love well, whip well.
Hunger never saw bad bread.
Fools make feasts, and wise men eat 'em.
He that lies down with dogs, shall rise up with fleas.
He is ill clothed, who is bare of virtue.
There is no little enemy.

Without justice courage is weak.   1734
Where there's marriage without love, there will be love without
marriage.
Do good to thy friend to keep him, to thy enemy to gain him.
He that cannot obey, cannot command.
Marry your son when you will, but your daughter when you can.

Approve not of him who commends all you say.   1735
Necessity never made a good bargain.
Be slow in chusing a friend, slower in changing.
Three may keep a secret, if two of them are dead.
Deny self for self's sake.
To be humble to superiors is duty, to equals courtesy, to inferiors
nobleness.

Fish and visitors stink in three days.   1736
Do not do that which you would not have known.
Bargaining has neither friends nor relations.
Now I've a sheep and a cow, every body bids me good morrow.
God helps them that help themselves.
He that speaks much, is much mistaken.
God heals, and the doctor takes the fees.

There are no ugly loves, nor handsome prisons.   1737
Three good meals a day is bad living.

Who has deceiv'd thee so oft as thyself?   1738
Read much, but not many books.
Let thy vices die before thee.

He that falls in love with himself, will have no rivals.   1739
Sin is not hurtful because it is forbidden, but it is forbidden
because it's hurtful.

An empty bag cannot stand upright.   1740

Learn of the skilful: he that teaches himself, hath a fool for his
master.   1741

Death takes no bribes. 1742

An old man in a house is a good sign. 1744
Fear God, and your enemies will fear you.

He's a fool that cannot conceal his wisdom. 1745
Many complain of their memory, few of their judgment.

When the well's dry, we know the worth of water. 1746
The sting of a reproach is the truth of it.

Write injuries in dust, benefits in marble. 1747

Nine men in *ten* are suicides. 1749
A man in a passion rides a mad horse.

He is a governor that governs his passions, and he is a servant
that serves them. 1750
Sorrow is good for nothing but sin.

Calamity and prosperity are the touchstones of integrity. 1752
Generous minds are all of kin.

Haste makes waste. 1753

The doors of wisdom are never shut. 1755

The way to be safe, is never to be secure. 1757

WILLIAM BLAKE: Proverbs of Hell

In seed time learn, in harvest teach, in winter enjoy.
Drive your cart and your plough over the bones of the dead.
The road of excess leads to the palace of wisdom.
Prudence is a rich, ugly old maid courted by Incapacity.
He who desires but acts not, breeds pestilence.
The cut worm forgives the plough.
Dip him in the river who loves water.
A fool sees not the same tree that a wise man sees.
He whose face gives no light, shall never become a star.
Eternity is in love with the productions of time.
The busy bee has no time for sorrow.
The hours of folly are measur'd by the clock; but of wisdom, no
    clock can measure.
All wholesome food is caught without a net or a trap.
Bring out number, weight, and measure in a year of dearth.
No bird soars too high, if he soars with his own wings.

A dead body revenges not injuries.

The most sublime act is to set another before you.

If the fool would persist in his folly he would become wise.

Folly is the cloak of knavery.

Shame is Pride's cloak.

Prisons are built with stones of Law, brothels with bricks of Religion.

The pride of the peacock is the glory of God.

The lust of the goat is the bounty of God.

The wrath of the lion is the wisdom of God.

The nakedness of woman is the work of God.

Excess of sorrow laughs. Excess of joy weeps.

The roaring of lions, the howling of wolves, the raging of the stormy sea, and the destructive sword are portions of eternity too great for the eye of man.

The fox condemns the trap, not himself.

Joys impregnate. Sorrows bring forth.

Let man wear the fell of the lion, woman the fleece of the sheep.

The bird a nest, the spider a web, man friendship.

The selfish, smiling fool, and the sullen, frowning fool shall be both thought wise, that they may be a rod.

What is now proved was once only imagin'd.

The rat, the mouse, the fox, the rabbit watch the roots; the lion, the tiger, the horse, the elephant watch the fruits.

The cistern contains: the fountain overflows.

One thought fills immensity.

Always be ready to speak your mind, and a base man will avoid you.

Everything possible to be believ'd is an image of truth.

The eagle never lost so much time as when he submitted to learn of the crow.

The fox provides for himself; but God provides for the lion.

Think in the morning. Act in the noon. Eat in the evening. Sleep in the night.

He who has suffer'd you to impose on him, knows you.

As the plough follows words, so God rewards prayers.

The tigers of wrath are wiser than the horses of instruction.

Expect poison from the standing water.

You never know what is enough unless you know what is more than enough.

Listen to the fool's reproach! it is a kingly title!

The eyes of fire, the nostrils of air, the mouth of water, the beard of earth.

The weak in courage is strong in cunning.

The apple tree never asks the beech how he shall grow; nor the lion, the horse, how he shall take his prey.

The thankful receiver bears a plentiful harvest.

If others had not been foolish, we should be so.

The soul of sweet delight can never be defil'd.

When thou seest an eagle, thou seest a portion of Genius; lift up thy head!

As the caterpillar chooses the fairest leaves to lay her eggs on, so the priest lays his curse on the fairest joys.

To create a little flower is the labor of ages.

Damn braces. Bless relaxes.

The best wine is the oldest, the best water the newest.

Prayers plough not! Praises reap not!

Joys laugh not! Sorrows weep not!

The head Sublime, the heart Pathos, the genitals Beauty, the hands and feet Proportion.

As the air to a bird or the sea to a fish, so is contempt to the contemptible.

The crow wish'd everything was black, the owl that everything was white.

Exuberance is Beauty.

If the lion was advised by the fox, he would be cunning.

Improvement makes straight roads; but the crooked roads without improvement are roads of Genius.

Sooner murder an infant in its cradle than nurse unacted desires.

Where man is not, nature is barren.

Truth can never be told so as to be understood, and not be believ'd.

Enough! or Too much.

1790

AMBROSE BIERCE: *from* The Devil's Dictionary

abdication, *n.* An act whereby a sovereign attests his sense of the high temperature of the throne.

abscond, *v.i.* To "move in a mysterious way," commonly with the property of another.

absent, *adj.* Peculiarly exposed to the tooth of detraction; vilified; hopelessly in the wrong; superseded in the consideration and affection of another.

accident, *n.* An inevitable occurrence due to the action of immutable natural laws.

accordion, *n.* An instrument in harmony with the sentiments of an assassin.

achievement, *n.* The death of endeavor and the birth of disgust.

admiration, *n.* Our polite recognition of another's resemblance to ourselves.

alone, *adj.* In bad company.

applause, *n.* The echo of a platitude.

ardor, *n.* The quality that distinguishes love without knowledge.

bore, *n.* A person who talks when you wish him to listen.

cemetery, *n.* An isolated suburban spot where mourners match lies, poets write at a target and stone-cutters spell for a wager. The inscription following will serve to illustrate the success attained in these Olympian games:

> His virtues were so conspicuous that his enemies, unable to overlook them, denied them, and his friends, to whose loose lives they were a rebuke, represented them as vices. They are here commemorated by his family, who shared them.

childhood, *n.* The period of human life intermediate between the idiocy of infancy and the folly of youth—two removes from the sin of manhood and three from the remorse of age.

Christian, *n.* One who believes that the New Testament is a divinely inspired book admirably suited to the spiritual needs of his neighbor. One who follows the teachings of Christ in so far as they are not inconsistent with a life of sin.

compulsion, *n.* The eloquence of power.

congratulation, *n.* The civility of envy.

conservative, *n.* A statesman who is enamored of existing evils, as distinguished from the Liberal, who wishes to replace them with others.

consult, *v.t.* To seek another's approval of a course already decided on.

contempt, *n.* The feeling of a prudent man for an enemy who is too formidable safely to be opposed.

coward, *n.* One who in a perilous emergency thinks with his legs.

debauchee, *n.* One who has so earnestly pursued pleasure that he has had the misfortune to overtake it.

destiny, *n.* A tyrant's authority for crime and a fool's excuse for failure.

diplomacy, *n.* The patriotic art of lying for one's country.

distance, *n.* The only thing that the rich are willing for the poor to call theirs and keep.

duty, *n.* That which sternly impels us in the direction of profit, along the line of desire.

education, *n.* That which discloses to the wise and disguises from the foolish their lack of understanding.

erudition, *n.* Dust shaken out of a book into an empty skull.

extinction, *n.* The raw material out of which theology created the future state.

faith, *n.* Belief without evidence in what is told by one who speaks without knowledge, of things without parallel.

genealogy, *n.* An account of one's descent from an ancestor who did not particularly care to trace his own.

ghost, *n.* The outward and visible sign of an inward fear.

habit, *n.* A shackle for the free.

heaven, *n.* A place where the wicked cease from troubling you with talk of their personal affairs, and the good listen with attention while you expound your own.

historian, *n.* A broad-gauge gossip.

hope, *n.* Desire and expectation rolled into one.

hypocrite, *n.* One who, professing virtues that he does not respect, secures the advantage of seeming to be what he despises.

impiety, *n.* Your irreverence toward my deity.

impunity, *n.* Wealth.

language, *n.* The music with which we charm the serpents guarding another's treasure.

logic, *n.* The art of thinking and reasoning in strict accordance with the limitations and incapacities of the human misunderstanding. The basis of logic is the syllogism, consisting of a major and a minor premise and a conclusion—thus:

Major Premise: Sixty men can do a piece of work sixty times as quickly as one man.

Minor Premise: One man can dig a post-hole in sixty seconds; therefore—

Conclusion: Sixty men can dig a post-hole in one second.

This may be called the syllogism arithmetical, in which, by combining logic and mathematics, we obtain a double certainty and are twice blessed.

love, *n.* A temporary insanity curable by marriage or by removal of the patient from the influences under which he incurred the disorder. This disease, like *caries* and many other ailments, is prevalent only among civilized races living under artificial conditions; barbarous nations breathing pure air and eating simple food enjoy immunity from its ravages. It is sometimes fatal, but more frequently to the physician than to the patient.

miracle, *n.* An act or event out of the order of nature and unaccountable, as beating a normal hand of four kings and an ace with four aces and a king.

monkey, *n.* An arboreal animal which makes itself at home in genealogical trees.

mouth, *n.* In man, the gateway to the soul; in woman, the outlet of the heart.

non-combatant, *n.* A dead Quaker.

platitude, *n.* The fundamental element and special glory of popular literature. A thought that snores in words that smoke. The wisdom of a million fools in the diction of a dullard. A fossil sentiment in artificial rock. A moral without the fable. All that is mortal of a departed truth. A demi-tasse of milk-and-morality. The

Pope's-nose of a featherless peacock. A jelly-fish withering on the shore of the sea of thought. The cackle surviving the egg. A dessicated epigram.

pray, *v.* To ask that the laws of the universe be annulled in behalf of a single petitioner confessedly unworthy.

presidency, *n.* The greased pig in the field game of American politics.

prude, *n.* A bawd hiding behind the back of her demeanor.

rapacity, *n.* Providence without industry. The thrift of power.

reason, *v.i.* To weigh probabilities in the scales of desire.

religion, *n.* A daughter of Hope and Fear, explaining to Ignorance the nature of the Unknowable.

resolute, *adj.* Obstinate in a course that we approve.

retaliation, *n.* The natural rock upon which is reared the Temple of Law.

saint, *n.* A dead sinner revised and edited.

> The Duchess of Orleans relates that the irreverent old calumniator, Marshal Villeroi, who in his youth had known St. Francis de Sales, said, on hearing him called saint: "I am delighted to hear that Monsieur de Sales is a saint. He was fond of saying indelicate things, and used to cheat at cards. In other respects he was a perfect gentleman, though a fool."

valor, *n.* A soldierly compound of vanity, duty and the gambler's hope:

> "Why have you halted?" roared the commander of a division at Chickamauga, who had ordered a charge; "move forward, sir, at once."
>
> "General," said the commander of the delinquent brigade, "I am persuaded that any further display of valor by my troops will bring them into collision with the enemy."

1906

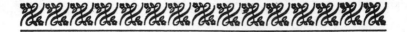

History

HENRY DAVID THOREAU
The Battle of the Ants

One day when I went out to my wood-pile, or rather my pile of stumps, I observed two large ants, the one red, the other much larger, nearly half an inch long, and black, fiercely contending with one another. Having once got hold they never let go, but struggled and wrestled and rolled on the chips incessantly. Looking farther, I was surprised to find that the chips were covered with such combatants, that it was not a *duellum*, but a *bellum*, a war between two races of ants, the red always pitted against the black, and frequently two red ones to one black. The legions of these Myrmidons[1] covered all the hills and vales in my wood-yard, and the ground was already strewn with the dead and dying, both red and black. It was the only battle which I have ever witnessed, the only battle-field I ever trod while the battle was raging; internecine war; the red republicans on the one hand, and the black imperialists on the other. On every side they were engaged in deadly combat, yet without any noise that I could hear, and human soldiers never fought so resolutely. I watched a couple that were fast locked in each other's embraces, in a little sunny valley amid the chips, now at noonday prepared to fight till the sun went down, or life went out. The smaller red champion had fastened himself like a vice to his adversary's front, and through all the tumblings on that field never for an instant ceased to gnaw at one of his feelers near the root, having already caused the other to go by the board; while the stronger black one dashed him from side to side, and, as I saw on looking nearer, had already divested him of several of his members. They fought with more pertinacity than bulldogs. Neither manifested the least disposition to retreat. It was evident that their battle-cry was "Conquer or die." In the meanwhile there came along a single red ant on the

---

1. The reference is to the powerful soldiers of Achilles in Homer's *Iliad*.

hillside of this valley, evidently full of excitement, who either had despatched his foe, or had not yet taken part in the battle; probably the latter, for he had lost none of his limbs; whose mother had charged him to return with his shield or upon it. Or perchance he was some Achilles, who had nourished his wrath apart, and had now come to avenge or rescue his Patroclus.[2] He saw this unequal combat from afar—for the blacks were nearly twice the size of the red—he drew near with rapid pace till he stood on his guard within half an inch of the combatants; then, watching his opportunity, he sprang upon the black warrior, and commenced his operations near the root of his right fore leg, leaving the foe to select among his own members; and so there were three united for life, as if a new kind of attraction had been invented which put all other locks and cements to shame. I should not have wondered by this time to find that they had their respective musical bands stationed on some eminent chip, and playing their national airs the while, to excite the slow and cheer the dying combatants. I was myself excited somewhat even as if they had been men. The more you think of it, the less the difference. And certainly there is not the fight recorded in Concord history, at least, if in the history of America, that will bear a moment's comparison with this, whether for the numbers engaged in it, or for the patriotism and heroism displayed. For numbers and for carnage it was an Austerlitz or Dresden.[3] Concord Fight! Two killed on the patriots' side, and Luther Blanchard wounded! Why here every ant was a Buttrick—"Fire! for God's sake fire!"—and thousands shared the fate of Davis and Hosmer. There was not one hireling there. I have no doubt that it was a principle they fought for, as much as our ancestors, and not to avoid a three-penny tax on their tea; and the results of this battle will be as important and memorable to those whom it concerns as those of the battle of Bunker Hill, at least.

I took up the chip on which the three I have particularly described were struggling, carried into my house, and placed it under a tumbler on my window-sill, in order to see the issue. Holding a microscope to the first-mentioned red ant, I saw that, though he was assiduously gnawing at the near fore leg of his enemy, having severed his remaining feeler, his own breast was all torn away, exposing what vitals he had there to the jaws of the black warrior, whose breastplate was apparently too thick for him to pierce; and the dark carbuncles of the sufferer's eyes shone with ferocity such as war only could excite. They struggled half an hour longer under the tumbler, and when I looked again the black soldier had severed the heads of his foes from their bodies, and the still living heads were hanging on

2. A Greek warrior in the *Iliad*, whose death Achilles avenges.

3. Bloody Napoleonic victories.

either side of him like ghastly trophies at his saddle-bow, still apparently as firmly fastened as ever, and he was endeavoring with feeble struggles, being without feelers, and with only the remnant of a leg, and I know not how many other wounds, to divest himself of them; which at length, after half an hour more, he accomplished. I raised the glass, and he went off over the window-sill in that crippled state. Whether he finally survived that combat, and spent the remainder of his days in some Hôtel des Invalides,[4] I do not know; but I thought that his industry would not be worth much thereafter. I never learned which party was victorious, nor the cause of the war, but I felt for the rest of that day as if I had my feelings excited and harrowed by witnessing the struggle, the ferocity and carnage, of a human battle before my door.

Kirby and Spence tell us that the battles of ants have long been celebrated and the date of them recorded, though they say that Huber[5] is the only modern author who appears to have witnessed them. "Aeneas Sylvius," say they, "after giving a very circumstantial account of one contested with great obstinacy by a great and small species on the trunk of a pear tree," adds that " 'this action was fought in the pontificate of Eugenius the Fourth, in the presence of Nicholas Pistoriensis, an eminent lawyer, who related the whole history of the battle with the greatest fidelity.' A similar engagement between great and small ants is recorded by Olaus Magnus, in which the small ones, being victorious, are said to have buried the bodies of their own soldiers, but left those of their giant enemies a prey to the birds. This event happened previous to the expulsion of the tyrant Christiern the Second from Sweden." The battle which I witnessed took place in the Presidency of Polk, five years before the passage of Webster's Fugitive-Slave Bill.[6]

1854

4. The famous French hospital for wounded soldiers and sailors.
5. Kirby and Spence were nineteenth-century American entomologists; Huber was a great Swiss entomologist.
6. Passed in 1851.

QUESTIONS

1. Thoreau uses the Latin word bellum to describe the battle of the ants and he quickly follows this with a reference to the Myrmidons of Achilles. What comparison is implicit here? Find further examples of it. This passage comes from a chapter entitled "Brute Neighbors"; how does this comparison amplify the meaning of that title?

2. Describe the life, or part of the life, of an animal so that, while remaining faithful to the facts as you understand them, your description opens outward as does Thoreau's, and speaks not only of the animal but also of man, society, or nature.

JOHN LIVINGSTON LOWES
Time in the Middle Ages

We live in terms of *time*. And so pervasive is that element of our consciousness that we have to stand, as it were, outside it for a moment to realize how completely it controls our lives. For we think and act perpetually, we mortals who look before and after, in relation to hours and days and weeks and months and years. Yesterday and to-morrow, next week, a month from now, a year ago, in twenty minutes—those are the terms in which, wittingly or automatically, we act and plan and think. And to orient ourselves at any moment in that streaming continuum we carry watches on our wrists, and put clocks about our houses and on our public towers, and somewhere in our eye keep calendars, and scan time-tables when we would go abroad. And all this is so utterly familiar that it has ceased to be a matter of conscious thought or inference at all. And—to come to the heart of the business—unless we are mariners or woodsmen or astronomers or simple folk in lonely places, we never any longer reckon with the *sky*. Except for its bearing on the weather or upon our moods, or for contemplation of its depths of blue or fleets of white, or of the nightly splendor of its stars, we are oblivious of its influence. And therein lies the great gulf fixed between Chaucer's century[1] and ours.

For Chaucer and his contemporaries, being likewise human, also lived in terms of time. But their calendar and time-piece was that sky through which moved immutably along predestined tracks the planets and the constellations. And no change, perhaps, wrought by the five centuries between us is more revealing of material differences than that shift of attitude towards "this brave o'erhanging firmament," the sky. And it is that change, first of all, that I wish, if I can, to make clear.

There could be, I suspect, no sharper contrast than that between the "mysterious universe" of modern science, as interpreters like Eddington and Jeans have made even laymen dimly perceive it, and the nest of closed, concentric spheres in terms of which Chaucer and his coevals thought. The structure of that universe may be stated simply enough. Its intricacies need not concern us here. About the earth, as the fixed center, revolved the spheres of the seven then known planets, of which the sun and the moon were two. Beyond these seven planetary spheres lay the sphere of the fixed stars. Beyond that in turn, and carrying along with it in its "diurnal sway"

---

1. The fourteenth; the reference is to the great Middle English poet Geoffrey Chaucer.

the eight spheres which lay within it, moved the *primum mobile,* a ninth sphere with which, to account for certain planetary eccentricities, the Middle Ages had supplemented the Ptolemaic system.[2] We must think, in a word, of Chaucer's universe as geocentric— the "litel erthe," encompassed by "thilke speres thryes three." As an interesting fact which we have learned, we know it; to conceive it as reality demands an exercise of the imagination. And only with that mental *volte-face*[3] accomplished can we realize the cosmos as Chaucer thought of it.

Now the order of succession of the planetary spheres had far-reaching implications. Starting from the earth, which was their center, that succession was as follows: Moon, Mercury, Venus, Sun, Mars, Jupiter, Saturn. And implicit in that order were two fundamental consequences—the astrological status of the successive hours of the day, and the sequence of the days of the week. The two phenomena stood in intimate relation, and some apprehension of each is fundamental to an understanding of the framework of conceptions within which Chaucer thought, and in terms of which he often wrote.

There were, then, in the first place—and this is strange to us— two sorts of *hours,* with both of which everybody reckoned. There were the hours from midnight to midnight, which constituted the "day natural"—the hours, that is, with which we are familiar—and these, in Chaucer's phrase, were "hours equal," or "hours of the *clock.*" But there were also the hours which were reckoned from sunrise to sunset (which made up "day artificial"), and on from sunset to sunrise again. And these, which will most concern us, were termed "hours inequal," or "hours of the *planets.*" And they were the hours of peculiar significance, bound up far more closely with human affairs than the "hours of the clock." It is worth, then, a moment's time to get them clear.

They were termed "inequal" for an obvious reason. For the periods between sunrise and sunset, and sunset and sunrise, respectively, change in length with the annual course of the sun, and the length of their twelfths, or hours, must of necessity change too. Between the equinoxes, then, it is clear that the inequal hours will now be longer by day than by night, now longer by night than by day. And only twice in the year, at the equinoxes, will the equal hours and the inequal hours—the hours of the clock and the hours of the planets—be identical. Moreover, each of the inequal hours (and this is of the first importance) was "ruled" by one of the seven planets, and it was as "hours of the planets" that the "hours inequal" touched most intimately human life. And that brings us at once to

---

2. The ancient view of the cosmos, with the earth at its center.

3. About-face; *thilke speres thryes three*: "those spheres thrice three."

the days of the week, and their now almost forgotten implications. Why, to be explicit, is to-day Saturday? And why to-morrow Sunday? To answer those two questions is to arrive at one of the determining concepts of Chaucer's world.

Let me first arrange the seven planets in their order, starting (to simplify what follows) with the outermost. Their succession will then be this: Saturn, Jupiter, Mars, Sun, Venus, Mercury, Moon. Now Saturn will rule the first hour of the day which, for that reason, bears his name, and which we still call *Saturday*. Of that day Jupiter will rule the second hour, Mars the third, the Sun the fourth, Venus the fifth, Mercury the sixth, the Moon the seventh, and Saturn again, in due order, the eighth. Without carrying the computation farther around the clock it is obvious that Saturn will also rule the fifteenth and the twenty-second hours of the twenty-four which belong to his day. The twenty-third hour will then be ruled by Jupiter, the twenty-fourth by Mars, and the twenty-fifth by the Sun. But the twenty-fifth hour of one day is the first hour of the next, and accordingly the day after Saturn's day will be the Sun's day. And so, through starry compulsion, the next day after Saturday *must* be Sunday. In precisely the same fashion—accomplished most quickly by remembering that each planet must rule the twenty-second hour of its own day—the ruling planet of the first hour of each of the succeeding days may readily be found. And their order, so found, including Saturn and the Sun, is this: Saturn, Sun, Moon, Mars, Mercury, Jupiter, Venus—then Saturn again, and so on *ad libitum*.[4] And the days of the week will accordingly be the days of the seven planets in that fixed order.

Now Saturn's day, the Sun's day, and the Moon's day are clearly recognizable in their English names of Saturday, Sunday, and Monday. But what of the remaining four—to wit, the days of Mars, Mercury, Jupiter, and Venus, which we call Tuesday, Wednesday, Thursday, and Friday? French has preserved, as also in Lundi, the planetary designations: Mardi (*Martis dies*), Mercredi (*Mercurii dies*), Jeudi (*Jovis dies*), and Vendredi (*Veneris dies*). The shift of the names in English is due to the ousting, in those four instances, of the Roman pantheon by the Germanic. Tiw, Woden, Thor, and Frig (or Freya) have usurped the seats of Mars, Mercury, Jupiter, and Venus, and given their barbarous names to the days. And in France a fourth, even more significant substitution has taken place. For the sun's day is in French *dimanche*, and *dimanche* is *dominica dies*, the Lord's day. And so between Saturn's planet and Diana's moon is memorialized, along with Mercury and Jupiter and Venus and Mars, the second Person of the Christian Trinity. The

4. As you wish.

ancient world has crumbled, and its detritus has been remoulded into almost unrecognizable shapes. But half the history of Europe and of its early formative ideas is written in the nomenclature of the week. And that nomenclature depends in turn upon the succession of the planetary hours. And it was in terms of those hours that Chaucer and his contemporaries thought.

In the *Knight's Tale*,[5] to be specific, Palamon, Emily, and Arcite go to pray, each for the granting of his own desire, to the temples respectively of Venus, Diana, and Mars. And each goes, as in due observance of ceremonial propriety he must, in the hour of the planet associated with the god to whom he prays. Palamon goes to the temple of Venus, "And *in hir houre* he walketh forth." A few lines earlier that hour has been stated in everyday terms: it was "The Sonday night, er day bigan to springe . . . Although it nere nat day by houres two"—two hours, that is, before sunrise. The day that was springing after Sunday night was Monday, and the hour of Monday's sunrise is the hour of the Moon. And the hour two hours earlier, in which Palamon walked forth, was the hour ruled by Venus, to whose temple he was on the way. And Emily and Arcite, as the tale goes on, performed their pilgrimages at similarly reckoned hours. To Chaucer and his readers all this was familiar matter of the day, as instantly comprehensible as are now to us the hours which we reckon by the clock. For us alas! it has become a theme for cumbrous exposition, because the hours of the planets have vanished, with the gods whose names they bore. All that is left of them is the time-worn and wonted sequence of the seven designations of the days.

Nothing, indeed, is more characteristic of the period in which Chaucer wrote than the strange, twisted mythology, transmogrified and confused, which emerged from the association of the planets and the gods. Not even Ovid had conceived such metamorphoses.[6] For the gods were invested with the attributes of planets, and as such became accountable for the most bizarre occurrences, and kept amazing company. Under the aegis of Mars, to take one instance only, were enrolled the butchers, hangmen, tailors, barbers, cooks, cutlers, carpenters, smiths, physicians, and apothecaries—a band about as "martial" as Falstaff's Thomas Wart and Francis Feeble.[7] And so, in "the temple of mighty Mars the rede" in the *Knight's Tale*, there were depicted, together with the "open werre"[8] which was his by virtue of his godhead, the disastrous chances proceeding from his malign ascendancy as planet—the corpse in the bushes

5. One of the stories in Chaucer's *Canterbury Tales*.

6. Ovid's *Metamorphoses* includes poetical renderings of myths dealing with the transformation of men and women into birds, flowers, trees, etc.

7. Recruits in Shakespeare's *Henry IV, Part 2*.

8. Open war; *rede*: red.

with cut throat, the nail driven, like Jael's, into the temple,[9] the sow eating the child in the cradle, the cook scalded in spite of his long ladle. And from among the members of what Chaucer twice calls Mars' "divisioun" there were present—together with the pick-purse, and "the smyler with the knyf under the cloke"—the barber and the butcher and the smith. And in the next paragraph Mars becomes again "this god of armes"—god of war and wicked planet inextricably interfused.

Moreover, as the day and week were conceived in terms of planetary sequence, so the year stood in intricate relation to the *stars*. The sun, with the other planets, moved annually along the vast starry track across the sky which then, as now, was called the zodiac —so called, as Chaucer lucidly explains to "litel Lowis" in the *Treatise on the Astrolabe*, because (and his etymology is sound) "*zodia* in langage of Greek sowneth [signifies] 'bestes' . . . and in the zodiak ben the twelve signes that han names of bestes." These twelve signs, as everybody knows, are Aries, Taurus, Gemini, Cancer, Leo, Virgo, Libra, Scorpio, Sagittarius, Capricornus, Aquarius, Pisces—or, to follow Chaucer's praiseworthy example and translate, Ram, Bull, Twins, Crab, Lion, Virgin, Scales, Scorpion, Archer, Goat, Water-carrier, Fishes. There they were, "eyrish bestes,"[1] as Chaucer calls them in a delightful passage that will meet us later, and along their celestial highway passed, from one sign to another, and from house to house, the seven eternal wanderers. To us who read this—though not to countless thousands even yet—the twelve constellations of the zodiac are accidental groupings, to the eye, of infinitely distant suns. To Chaucer's century they were strangely living potencies, and the earth, in the words of a greater than Chaucer,[2] was "this huge stage . . . whereon the stars in secret influence comment." Each sign, with its constellation, had its own individual efficacy or quality—Aries, "the colerik hote signe"; Taurus, cold and dry; and so on through the other ten. Each planet likewise had its own pecular nature—Mars, like Aries, hot and dry; Venus hot and moist; and so on through the other five. And as each planet passed from sign to sign, through the agency of the successive constellations its character and influence underwent change. Chaucer in the *Astrolabe* put the matter in its simplest terms: "Whan an hot planete cometh in-to an hot signe, then encresseth his hete; and yif a planete be cold, thanne amenuseth [diminshes] his coldnesse, by -cause of the hote signe." But there was far more to it than that. For these complex planetary changes exercised a determining influence upon human beings and their affairs. Arcite behind prison bars cries out:

9. The reference is to Judges iv.17–22, in which Jael offers shelter to Sisera, gives him her cloak, and quenches his thirst, and then while he is asleep kills him by driving a nail into his temple.
1. Beasts of the air.
2. Shakespeare.

> Som wikke aspect or disposicioun
> Of Saturne, *by sum constellacioun*,
> Hath yeven us this.

And "the olde colde Saturnus" names the constellation:

> Myn is the prison in the derke cote...
> *Whyl I dwelle in the signe of the Leoun.*

The tragedy of Constance, as the Man of Law conceived it, comes about because Mars, at the crucial moment, was in his "derkest hous." Mars gave, on the other hand, the Wife of Bath,[3] as she avers, her "sturdy hardinesse," because Mars, at her birth, was in the constellation Taurus, which was, in astrological terminology, her own "ascendent." And since the constellation Taurus was also the "night house" of Venus, certain other propensities which the wife displayed had been thrust upon her, as she cheerfully averred, by the temporary sojourn of Mars in Venus's house, when she was born.

But the march of the signs along the zodiac touched human life in yet another way. "Everich of thise twelve signes," Chaucer wrote again to his little Lewis, "hath respecte to a certein parcelle of the body of a man and hath it in governance; as Aries hath thyn heved, and Taurus thy nekke and thy throte. Gemini thyn armholes and thyn armes, and so forth." And at once one recalls Sir Toby Belch and Sir Andrew Aguecheek in *Twelfth Night*. "Shall we not set about some revels?" asks Sir Andrew. "What shall we do else?" replies Sir Toby. "Were we not born under Taurus?" "Taurus!" exclaims Sir Andrews, "that's sides and heart." "No, sir," retorts Sir Toby, "it is legs and thighs." And you may still pick up, in the shops of apothecaries here and there, cheaply printed almanacs, designed to advertise quack remedies, in which the naked human figure is displayed with lines drawn from each of the pictured zodiacal signs—Ram, Bull, Crab, Scorpion—to the limbs or organs, legs, thighs, sides, or heart, which that particular sign (in Chaucerian phrase) "hath in governance." It is not only in worn stone and faded parchments that strange fragments of the elder world survive.

1934

3. The forthright and lusty teller of "The Wife of Bath's Tale" in Chaucer's *Canterbury Tales*.

QUESTIONS

1. Arrange the steps of Lowes' explanation of medieval time in a different order. Is your order superior to Lowes' or inferior? By what criteria?
2. When the advertising man and the engineer from the electronics laboratory become suburban gardeners, why may they have to reckon with the sky and neglect their watches and calendars?

3. List some ways in which the abstractions of watch and calendar
(and time table) "rule" our lives. This list will be a selection from
the particulars of daily life. What generalizations about our
society will these particulars justify? Does our society, as focused
in these generalizations, have a mythology—a set of hypothetical
or typical characters going through hypothetical or typical experiences?

DOROTHY GIES McGUIGAN

To Be a Woman and a Scholar

On a Saturday morning in June exactly three hundred years ago
this year, the first woman in the world to receive a doctoral degree
mounted a pulpit in the cathedral of Padua to be examined in Aristotelian dialectics.

Her name was Elena Lucrezia Cornaro Piscopia. She was thirty-
two years old, single, daughter of one of the wealthiest families in
Venice. Precociously brilliant, she had begun to study Aristotle at
the age of seven. Her father had backed her studies and supplied
the best of tutors; by the time she enrolled in the University of
Padua, she knew not only Latin and Greek, French, English, and
Spanish, but also Hebrew, Arabic, and Chaldaic.

News of the unique phenomenon of a woman scholar had drawn
such throngs to witness her doctoral trial that it had to be moved
from the hall of the University of Padua into the cathedral. Elena
had first applied to take her doctorate in theology, but the Chancel-
lor of the university's Theological Faculty, Cardinal Gregorio Barbarigo, Bishop of Padua, had refused indignantly. "Never," he replied.
"Woman is made for motherhood, not for learning." He wrote later
of the incident, "I talked with a French cardinal about it and he
broke out in laughter." Reluctantly Barbarigo agreed that she be
allowed to take the doctoral examination in philosophy. A modest,
deeply religious young woman, Elena Cornaro had quailed before
the prospect of the public examination; it was her proud, ambitious
father who had insisted. A half hour before the solemn program
began, Elena expressed such anguish and reluctance that her confes-
sor had to speak very sternly to persuade her to go through with it.
Her examiners were not lenient because of her sex, for the prestige
of the university was at stake. But Elena's replies—in Latin, of
course—were so brilliant that the judges declared the doctorate in
philosophy was "hardly an honor for so towering an intellect." The
doctoral ring was placed on Elena's finger, the ermine cape of

teacher laid about her shoulders, and the laurel crown of poet placed on her dark curly head. The entire assembly rose and chanted a Te Deum.[1]

What was it like to be a gifted woman, an Elena Cornaro, three hundred years ago? What happened to a bright woman in the past who wanted to study another culture, examine the roots of a language, master the intricacies of higher mathematics, write a book— or prevent or cure a terrible disease?

To begin with, for a woman to acquire anything that amounted to real learning, she needed four basics.

She needed to survive. In the seventeenth century women's life expectancy had risen only to thirty-two; not until 1750 did it begin to rise appreciably and reach, in mid-nineteenth century, age forty-two. A woman ambitious for learning would do well to choose a life of celibacy, not only to avoid the hazards of childbirth but because there was no room for a scholar's life within the confines of marriage and childbearing. Elena Cornaro had taken a vow of chastity at the age of eleven, turned down proposals of marriage to become an oblate of the Benedictine Order.

Secondly, to aspire to learning a woman needed basic literacy; she had to be one of the fortunate few who learned at least to read and write. Although literacy studies in earlier centuries are still very incomplete and comparative data on men's and women's literacy are meager, it appears that before 1650 a bare 10 percent of women in the city of London could sign their names. What is most striking about this particular study is that when men are divided by occupation—with clergy and the professions at the top, 100 percent literate, and male laborers at the bottom of the scale, about 15 percent literate—women as a group fell below even unskilled male laborers in their rate of literacy. By about 1700 half the women in London could sign their names; in the provinces women's literacy remained much lower.

The third fundamental a woman needed if she aspired to learning was, of course, an economic base. It was best to be born, like Elena Cornaro, to a family of wealth who owned a well-stocked library and could afford private tutors. For girls of poor families the chance of learning the bare minimum of reading and writing was small. Even such endowed charity schools as Christ's Hospital in London were attended mostly by boys; poor girls in charity schools were apt to have their literacy skills slighted in favor of catechism, needlework, knitting, and lace-making in preparation for a life in domestic service.

The fourth fundamental a woman scholar needed was simply a

1. **Festival hymn of rejoicing and praise of God.**

very tough skin, for she was a deviant in a society where the learned woman, far from being valued, was likely to hear herself preached against in the pulpit and made fun of on the public stage. Elena Cornaro was fortunate to have been born in Italy where an array of learned women had flourished during the Renaissance and where the woman scholar seems to have found a more hospitable ambiance than in the northern countries.

In eighteenth-century England the gifted writer Lady Mary Wortley Montagu, writing in 1753 about proposed plans for a little granddaughter's education, admonished her daughter with some bitterness "to conceal whatever Learning [the child] attains, with as much solicitude as she would hide crookedness or lameness."

In post-Renaissance Europe two overriding fears dominated thinking on women's education: the fear that learning would unfit women for their social role, defined as service to husband and children and obedience to the church; and, a corollary of the first, that open access to education would endanger women's sexual purity. For while humanist philosophy taught that education led to virtue, writers on education were at once conflicted when they applied the premise to women. Nearly all, beginning with the influential sixteenth-century Juan Luis Vives, opted for restricting women's learning. Only a few radical thinkers—some men, such as Richard Mulcaster in Tudor England and the extraordinary Poullain de la Barre in seventeenth-century France, some women, like the feisty Bathsua Makin and revolutionary Mary Wollstonecraft—spoke out for the full development of women's intellectual potential.

In any case, since institutions of higher learning were designed for young men entering the professions—the church, the law, government service—from which women were excluded, they were excluded too from the universities that prepared for them. And, just as importantly, they were excluded from the grammar or preparatory schools, whose curriculum was based on Latin, the code language of the male intellectual elite. Since most scholarly texts were written in Latin, ignorance of that language prevented women from reading scholarly literature in most fields—which only gradually and belatedly became available in translation.

Richard Hyrde, a tutor in the household of Sir Thomas More and himself a defender of learning in women, cited the common opinion:

. . . that the frail kind of women, being inclined of their own courage unto vice, and mutable at every newelty [*sic*], if they should have skill in many things that must be written in the Latin and Greek tongue . . . it would of likelihood both inflame their stomachs a great deal the more to that vice, that men say they be too much given unto of their own nature already and instruct them also with more subtility and conveyance, to set forward and accomplish their froward intent and purpose.

And yet, despite all the hurdles, some bright women did manage to make a mark as scholars and writers. Sometimes girls listened in on their brothers' tutored lessons. A fortunate few, like Elena Cornaro, had parents willing and able to educate daughters equally with sons. The daughters of Sir Thomas More, of the Earl of Arundel, and of Sir Anthony Cooke in Tudor England were given excellent educations. Arundel's daughter, Lady Joanna Lumley, produced the earliest known English translation of a Greek drama.

But by far the largest number of women scholars in the past were almost totally self-educated. Through sheer intellectual curiosity, self-discipline, often grinding hard work, they taught themselves what they wanted to know. Such self-teaching may well be the only truly joyous form of learning. Yet it has its drawbacks: it may also be haphazard and superficial. Without access to laboratory, lecture, and dissecting table, it was all but impossible for women to train themselves in higher mathematics, for instance, in science, in anatomy.

Mary Wollstonecraft wrote in 1792 that most women who have acted like rational creatures or shown any vigor of intellect have accidentally been allowed "to run wild," and running wild in the family library was the usual way intellectually ambitious women educated themselves. Such a self-taught scholar was Elizabeth Tanfield, Viscountess Cary, who as a girl in Elizabethan England, taught herself French, Spanish, Italian, Latin, and added Hebrew "with very little teaching." Her unsympathetic mother refused to allow her candles to read at night, so Elizabeth bribed the servants, and by her wedding day—she was married at fifteen—she had run up a candle debt of a hundred pounds. She wrote numerous translations, poetry—most of which she destroyed—and at least one play, *Mariam, the Faire Queen of Jewry.*

Very often the critical phase of women's intellectual development took place at a different period in their lives from the normal time of men's greatest development. Gifted women often came to a period of intellectual crisis and of intense self-teaching during adulthood.

When Christine de Pisane, daughter of the Italian astrologer and physician at the court of Charles V of France, found herself widowed at twenty-five with three children to support, she turned to writing—certainly one of the first, if not the first, woman in Europe to support herself through a literary career. But Christine found her education wholly inadequate, and at the age of thirty-four she laid down a complete course of study for herself, teaching herself Latin, history, philosophy, literature. She used her pen later on to urge better educational opportunities for women, to defend her sex from the charges of such misogynistic writers as Jean de Meung.[2] In her book, *The City of Ladies*, Christine imagined talented women building a town for themselves where they could lead peaceful and creative lives—an existence impossible, she considered, in fifteenth-century France.

Like Christine de Pisane, the Dutch scholar Anna van Schurman of Utrecht, a contemporary of Elena Cornaro, found her early education superficial and unsatisfying. Like most upper middle class girls of the seventeenth century, Anna, precocious though she was, had been taught chiefly to sing nicely, to play musical instruments, to carve portraits in boxwood and wax, to do needlework and tapestry and cut paperwork. At the age of twenty-eight, frustrated by the lack of intellectual stimulation in her life, Anna turned her brilliant mind to serious studies, became one of the finest Latinists of her day, learned Hebrew, Syriac, Chaldaic, wrote an Ethiopian grammar that was the marvel of Dutch scholars, carried on an international correspondence—in Latin, of course—with all the leading scholars of continental Europe. When a professor of theology at Leyden wrote that women were barred from equality with men "by the sacred laws of nature," Anna wrote a Latin treatise in reply in 1641, defending the intellectual capacity of women and urging, as Christine de Pisane had, much greater educational opportunities. Her work was widely translated and made Anna van Schurman a model for women scholars all over Europe.

In France, during the lifetime of Anna van Schurman, a group of bright, intellectually malnourished women—most of them convent-educated—developed one of the most ingenious devices for women's lifelong learning. Bored with the dearth of cultivated conversation at the French court, the Marquise de Rambouillet, Mlle de Scudéry, Mme de Lafayette, and a host of others opened their town houses in Paris, invited men and women of talent and taste to hone their wits and talk of science and philosophy, literature and language, love and friendship. The salon has been described as "an informal university for women." Not only did it contribute to adult women's education, but it shaped standards of speaking and writing for generations in France and profoundly influenced French culture as a whole.

An offshoot of the salons were the special lecture courses offered by eminent scholars in chemistry, etymology and other subjects—lectures largely attended by women. Fontenelle wrote his popular

---

2. Medieval French author of the satirical antifeminist portion of the influ- ential poem *The Romance of the Rose*.

book on astronomy, *The Plurality of Worlds*, specifically for a female readership, and Descartes declared he had written his *Discourse on Method* in French rather than Latin so that women too would be able to read it.

There was, rather quickly, a backlash. Molière's satires on learned women did much to discredit the ladies who presided at salons— and who might at times be given to a bit of overelegance in speech and manner. When Abbé Fénélon wrote his influential treatise, *On the Education of Girls*, in 1686—just eight years after Elena Cornaro had won her doctorate—he mentioned neither Elena Cornaro nor Anna van Schurman nor Christine de Pisane. He inveighed against the pernicious effect of the salons. Declaring that "A woman's intellect is normally more feeble and her curiosity greater than those of men, it is undesirable to set her to studies which may turn her head. A girl," admonished that worthy French cleric, "must learn to obey without respite, to hold her peace and allow others to do the talking. Everything is lost if she obstinately tries to be clever and to get a distaste for domestic duties. The virtuous woman spins, confines herself to her home, keeps quiet, believes and obeys."

So much for the encouragement of women scholars in late seventeenth century France.

Across the Channel in England in the second half of the seventeenth century, bright ambitious women were studying not only the classics and languages but learning to use the newly perfected telescope and microscope, and to write on scientific subjects. Margaret Cavendish, Duchess of Newcastle, a remarkable woman with a wide-ranging mind and imagination, wrote not only biography, autobiography, and romance, but also popular science—she called it "natural philosophy"—directed especially to women readers. The versatile and talented writer Aphra Behn—the first woman in England to make her living by her pen—translated Fontenelle's *Plurality of Worlds* into English in 1688. In the preface she declared she would have preferred to write an original work on astronomy but had "neither health nor leisure" for such a project; it was, in fact, the year before her death and she was already ailing. But she defended the Copernican system vigorously against the recent attack by a Jesuit priest, did not hesitate to criticize the author, Fontenelle, and to correct an error in the text on the height of the earth's atmosphere.

But the learned lady in England as in France found herself criticized from the pulpit and satirized on the stage. Margaret Cavendish was dubbed "Mad Madge of Newcastle." Jonathan Swift poked fun at Mary Astell for her proposal to found a women's college. Thomas Wright in *The Female Virtuosos*, the anonymous authors of *The Humours of Oxford* and *Female Wits*, Shadwell, Congreve, and others lampooned the would-be woman scholar. The shy poet, Anne, Countess of Winchilsea, who had only reluctantly identified herself as author of a published volume of verse, was cruelly pilloried by Pope and Gay in their play *Three Hours after Marriage*. And Aphra Behn, author of a phenomenal array of plays, poems, novels, and translations, could read this published verse about herself and her work at about the same time she was translating Fontenelle:

> Yet hackney writers, when their verse did fail
> To get 'em brandy, bread and cheese, and ale,
> Their wants by prostitution were supplied;
> Show but a tester [sixpence] you might up and ride;
> For punk and poetess agree so pat
> You cannot well be this, and not be that.

So if one asks what it was like to be a gifted woman, to aspire to learning at the time of Elena Cornaro, the answer must be that it was a difficult and demanding choice, requiring not merely intellectual gifts but extraordinary physical and mental stamina, and only a rare few women succeeded in becoming contributing scholars and writers. All the usual scholarly careers were closed to women, so that even for women who succeeded in educating themselves to the level of their male colleagues, the opportunities to support themselves were meager.

In a day when it was considered impermissible for a woman to speak in public, it was also considered inappropriate and unfeminine to draw attention to herself by publishing a work under her own name. Many—perhaps most—women scholars and writers—from Anne, Countess of Winchilsea, Lady Mary Wortley Montagu down to Fanny Burney and Jane Austen—published their works at first either anonymously or pseudonymously. Nor was Elizabeth Tanfield the only woman scholar who destroyed her own writings before they were published.

And what of Elena Cornaro's life after she won her doctorate in 1678? During the six years she lived after that event, she divided her time between scholarly pursuits and service to the poor, sick and needy. Baroque Italy paid honor to its unique woman scholar. Certainly Elena Cornaro aroused no antagonisms, but rather filled with discretion the approved nunlike role designated for the woman in Catholic countries who chose not to marry. Scholars and statesmen from several countries made a point of visiting her in Padua, and she was invited to join fellow scholars in the Academy of Ricovrati in Padua. When she died of tuberculosis in 1684 at the age of thirty-eight—a disease that was in a measure responsible for her eminence, for she had been sent to Padua partly to escape the damp air of Venice—her funeral attracted a greater throng than her doctoral examination. A delegation of distinguished university faculty accompanied the procession through the streets of Padua, and on her coffin were heaped books in the languages she had mastered and the sciences she had studied. She was buried in the Chapel of St. Luke among the Benedictine monks, having carefully instructed her maid to sew her robe together at the hem so that even in death her modesty would be preserved.

Of her writings very little has survived. She had arranged to have her correspondence and many of her manuscripts destroyed before she died, and the remainder of her writings were disseminated as souvenirs among family and friends.

After Elena Cornaro's death a half century passed before a second woman, again Italian, Laura Maria Catherina Bassi, was awarded a doctorate at the University of Bologna. Not until 150 years later did American universities admit women for degrees, and two centuries passed before Oxford and Cambridge conferred degrees on women. Only in our own decade, in 1970, did the Catholic Church finally award the degree of Doctor of Theology that had been denied Elena Cornaro to two women: one to the seventeenth century Spanish saint, Teresa of Avila, the other to thirteenth century St. Catherine of Siena, who had in fact never learned to read and write. One hopes that in some academic elysium those two saintly ladies are proudly showing off their belated scholarly credentials.

1978

QUESTIONS

1. What obstacles stood in the way of a woman seeking learning in the past, and what did she need in order to overcome them? Which of these obstacles and needs still exist? Are there any new difficulties today?

2. What do you imagine were Elena Cornaro's thoughts and feelings in the hour before the public examination for the doctorate? Write an essay exploring this question. You might like to try placing yourself in her position and writing from her point of view.

CHIEF SEATTLE

Address[1]

The Governor made a fine speech, but he was outranged and out-classed that day. Chief Seattle, who answered on behalf of the Indians, towered a foot above the Governor. He wore his blanket like the toga of a Roman senator, and he did not have to strain his famous voice, which everyone agreed was audible and distinct at a distance of half a mile.

Seattle's oration was in Duwamish. Doctor Smith, who had learned the language, wrote it down; under the flowery garlands of his translation the speech rolls like an articulate iron engine, grim with meanings that outlasted his generation and may outlast all the generations of men. As the amiable follies of the white race become less amiable, the iron rumble of old Seattle's speech sounds louder and more ominous.

Standing in front of Doctor Maynard's office in the stumpy clearing, with his hand on the little Governor's head, the white invaders about him and his people before him, Chief Seattle said:

"Yonder sky that has wept tears of compassion upon my people for centuries untold, and which to us appears changeless and eternal, may change. Today is fair. Tomorrow may be overcast with clouds. My words are like the stars that never change. Whatever Seattle says the great chief at Washington can rely upon with as much certainty as he can upon the return of the sun or the seasons. The White Chief says that Big Chief at Washington sends us greetings of friendship and goodwill. That is kind of him for we know he has little need of our friendship in return. His people are many. They are like the grass that covers vast prairies. My people are few. They resemble the scattering trees of a storm-swept plain. The great, and—I presume—good, White Chief sends us word that he wishes to buy our lands but is willing to allow us enough to live comfortably. This indeed appears just, even generous, for the Red Man no longer has rights that he need respect, and the offer may be wise also, as we are no longer in need of an extensive country.... I will not dwell on, nor mourn over, our untimely decay, nor reproach our paleface brothers with hastening it, as we too may have been somewhat to blame.

"Youth is impulsive. When our young men grow angry at some real or imaginary wrong, and disfigure their faces with black paint,

1. In 1854, Governor Isaac Stevens, Commissioner of Indian Affairs for the Washington Territory, proffered a treaty to the Indians providing for the sale of two million acres of their land to the federal government. This address is the reply of Chief Seattle of the Duwampo tribe. The translator was Henry A. Smith.

it denotes that their hearts are black, and then they are often cruel and relentless, and our old men and old women are unable to restrain them. Thus it has ever been. Thus it was when the white men first began to push our forefathers further westward. But let us hope that the hostilities between us may never return. We would have everything to lose and nothing to gain. Revenge by young men is considered gain, even at the cost of their own lives, but old men who stay at home in times of war, and mothers who have sons to lose, know better.

"Our good father at Washington—for I presume he is now our father as well as yours, since King George has moved his boundaries further north—our great good father, I say, sends us word that if we do as he desires he will protect us. His brave warriors will be to us a bristling wall of strength, and his wonderful ships of war will fill our harbors so that our ancient enemies far to the northward—the Hydas and Tsimpsians—will cease to frighten our women, children, and old men. Then in reality will he be our father and we his children. But can that ever be? Your God is not our God! Your God loves your people and hates mine. He folds his strong and protecting arms lovingly about the paleface and leads him by the hand as a father leads his infant son—but He has forsaken His red children —if they really are his. Our God, the Great Spirit, seems also to have forsaken us. Your God makes your people wax strong every day. Soon they will fill the land. Our people are ebbing away like a rapidly receding tide that will never return. The white man's God cannot love our people or He would protect them. They seem to be orphans who can look nowhere for help. How then can we be brothers? How can your God become our God and renew our prosperity and awaken in us dreams of returning greatness? If we have a common heavenly father He must be partial—for He came to his paleface children. We never saw Him. He gave you laws but He had no word for His red children whose teeming multitudes once filled this vast continent as stars fill the firmament. No; we are two distinct races with separate origins and separate destinies. There is little in common between us.

"To us the ashes of our ancestors are sacred and their resting place is hallowed ground. You wander far from the graves of your ancestors and seemingly without regret. Your religion was written upon tables of stone by the iron finger of your God so that you could not forget. The Red Man could never comprehend nor remember it. Our religion is the traditions of our ancestors—the dreams of our old men, given them in solemn hours of night by the Great Spirit; and the visions of our sachems; and it is written in the hearts of our people.

"Your dead cease to love you and the land of their nativity as soon as they pass the portals of the tomb and wander way beyond the stars. They are soon forgotten and never return. Our dead never forget the beautiful world that gave them being.

"Day and night cannot dwell together. The. Red Man has ever fled the approach of the White Man, as the morning mist flees before the morning sun. However, your proposition seems fair and I think that my people will accept it and will retire to the reservation you offer them. Then we will dwell apart in peace, for the words of the Great White Chief seem to be the words of nature speaking to my people out of dense darkness.

"It matters little where we pass the remnant of our days. They will not be many. A few more moons; a few more winters—and not one of the descendants of the mighty hosts that once moved over this broad land or lived in happy homes, protected by the Great Spirit, will remain to mourn over the graves of a people once more powerful and hopeful than yours. But why should I mourn at the untimely fate of my people? Tribe follows tribe, and nation follows nation, like the waves of the sea. It is the order of nature, and regret is useless. Your time of decay may be distant, but it will surely come, for even the White Man whose God walked and talked with him as friend with friend, cannot be exempt from the common destiny. We may be brothers after all. We will see.

"We will ponder your proposition, and when we decide we will let you know. But should we accept it, I here and now make this condition that we will not be denied the privilege without molestation of visiting at any time the tombs of our ancestors, friends and children. Every part of this soil is sacred in the estimation of my people. Every hillside, every valley, every plain and grove, has been hallowed by some sad or happy event in days long vanished. . . . The very dust upon which you now stand responds more lovingly to their footsteps than to yours, because it is rich with the blood of our ancestors and our bare feet are conscious of the sympathetic touch. . . . Even the little children who lived here and rejoiced here for a brief season will love these somber solitudes and at eventide they greet shadowy returning spirits. And when the last Red Man shall have perished, and the memory of my tribe shall have become a myth among the White Men, these shores will swarm with the invisible dead of my tribe, and when your children's children think themselves alone in the field, the store, the shop, upon the highway, or in the silence of the pathless woods, they will not be alone. . . . At night when the streets of your cities and villages are silent and you think them deserted, they will throng with the returning hosts that once filled and still love this beautiful land. The White Man will never be alone.

"Let him be just and deal kindly with my people, for the dead are not powerless. Dead, did I say? There is no death, only a change of worlds."

1854

HANNAH ARENDT
Denmark and the Jews

At the Wannsee Conference,[1] Martin Luther, of the Foreign Office, warned of great difficulties in the Scandinavian countries, notably in Norway and Denmark. (Sweden was never occupied, and Finland, though in the war on the side of the Axis, was one country the Nazis never even approached on the Jewish question. This surprising exception of Finland, with some two thousand Jews, may have been due to Hitler's great esteem for the Finns, whom perhaps he did not want to subject to threats and humiliating blackmail.) Luther proposed postponing evacuations from Scandinavia for the time being, and as far as Denmark was concerned, this really went without saying, since the country retained its independent government, and was respected as a neutral state, until the fall of 1943, although it, along with Norway, had been invaded by the German Army in April, 1940. There existed no Fascist or Nazi movement in Denmark worth mentioning, and therefore no collaborators. In Norway, however, the Germans had been able to find enthusiastic supporters; indeed, Vidkun Quisling, leader of the pro-Nazi and anti-Semitic Norwegian party, gave his name to what later became known as a "quisling government." The bulk of Norway's seventeen hundred Jews were stateless, refugees from Germany; they were seized and interned in a few lightning operations in October and November, 1942. When Eichmann's office ordered their deportation to Auschwitz, some of Quisling's own men resigned their government posts. This may not have come as a surprise to Mr. Luther and the Foreign Office, but what was much more serious, and certainly totally unexpected, was that Sweden immediately offered asylum, and even Swedish nationality, to all who were persecuted. Dr. Ernst von Weizsäcker, Undersecretary of State of the Foreign Office, who received the proposal, refused to discuss it, but the offer helped nevertheless. It is always relatively easy to get out of a country illegally, whereas it is nearly impossible to enter the place of refuge without permission and to dodge the immigration authorities. Hence, about nine hundred people, slightly more than half of the small Norwegian community, could be smuggled into Sweden.

1. A meeting of German officials on "the Jewish question."

It was in Denmark, however, that the Germans found out how fully justified the Foreign Offices's apprehensions had been. The story of the Danish Jews is *sui generis*, and the behavior of the Danish people and their government was unique among all the countries in Europe—whether occupied, or a partner of the Axis, or neutral and truly independent. One is tempted to recommend the story as required reading in political science for all students who wish to learn something about the enormous power potential inherent in non-violent action and in resistance to an opponent possessing vastly superior means of violence. To be sure, a few other countries in Europe lacked proper "understanding of the Jewish question," and actually a majority of them were opposed to "radical" and "final" solutions. Like Denmark, Sweden, Italy, and Bulgaria proved to be nearly immune to anti-Semitism, but of the three that were in the German sphere of influence, only the Danes dared speak out on the subject to their German masters. Italy and Bulgaria sabotaged German orders and indulged in a complicated game of double-dealing and double-crossing, saving their Jews by a tour de force of sheer ingenuity, but they never contested the policy as such. That was totally different from what the Danes did. When the Germans approached them rather cautiously about introducing the yellow badge, they were simply told that the King would be the first to wear it, and the Danish government officials were careful to point out that anti-Jewish measures of any sort would cause their own immediate resignation. It was decisive in this whole matter that the Germans did not even succeed in introducing the vitally important distinction between native Danes of Jewish origin, of whom there were about sixty-four hundred, and the fourteen hundred German Jewish refugees who had found asylum in the country prior to the war and who now had been declared stateless by the German government. This refusal must have surprised the Germans no end, since it appeared so "illogical" for a government to protect people to whom it had categorically denied naturalization and even permission to work. (Legally, the prewar situation of refugees in Denmark was not unlike that in France, except that the general corruption in the Third Republic's civil services enabled a few of them to obtain naturalization papers, through bribes or "connections," and most refugees in France could work illegally, without a permit. But Denmark, like Switzerland, was no country *pour se débrouiller*[2].) The Danes, however, explained to the German officials that because the stateless refugees were no longer German citizens, the Nazis could not claim them without Danish assent. This was one of the few cases in which statelessness turned out to be an asset, although it was of course not statelessness per se that

---

2. For wangling—using bribery to circumvent bureaucratic regulations.

saved the Jews but, on the contrary, the fact that the Danish government had decided to protect them. Thus, none of the preparatory moves, so important for the bureaucracy of murder, could be carried out, and operations were postponed until the fall of 1943.

What happened then was truly amazing; compared with what took place in other European countries, everything went topsy-turvey. In August, 1943—after the German offensive in Russia had failed, the Afrika Korps had surrendered in Tunisia, and the Allies had invaded Italy—the Swedish government canceled its 1940 agreement with Germany which had permitted German troops the right to pass through the country. Thereupon, the Danish workers decided that they could help a bit in hurrying things up; riots broke out in Danish shipyards, where the dock workers refused to repair German ships and then went on strike. The German military commander proclaimed a state of emergency and imposed martial law, and Himmler thought this was the right moment to tackle the Jewish question, whose "solution" was long overdue. What he did not reckon with was that—quite apart from Danish resistance—the German officials who had been living in the country for years were no longer the same. Not only did General von Hannecken, the military commander, refuse to put troops at the disposal of the Reich plenipotentiary, Dr. Werner Best; the special S.S. units (Einsatz-kommandos) employed in Denmark very frequently objected to "the measures they were ordered to carry out by the central agencies"—according to Best's testimony at Nuremberg. And Best himself, an old Gestapo man and former legal adviser to Heydrich, author of a then famous book on the police, who had worked for the military government in Paris to the entire satisfaction of his superiors, could no longer be trusted, although it is doubtful that Berlin ever learned the extent of his unreliability. Still, it was clear from the beginning that things were not going well, and Eichmann's office sent one of its best men to Denmark—Rolf Günther, whom no one had ever accused of not possessing the required "ruthless toughness." Günther made no impression on his colleagues in Copenhagen, and now von Hannecken refused even to issue a decree requiring all Jews to report for work.

Best went to Berlin and obtained a promise that all Jews from Denmark would be sent to Theresienstadt[3] regardless of their category—a very important concession, from the Nazis' point of view. The night of October 1 was set for their seizure and immediate departure—ships were ready in the harbor—and since neither the Danes nor the Jews nor the German troops stationed in Denmark could be relied on to help, police units arrived from Germany for a

---

3. A camp for certain classes of prisoners who were to receive special treatment.

door-to-door search. At the last moment, Best told them that they were not permitted to break into apartments, because the Danish police might then interfere, and they were not supposed to fight it out with the Danes. Hence they could seize only those Jews who voluntarily opened their doors. They found exactly 477 people, out of a total of more then 7,800, at home and willing to let them in. A few days before the date of doom, a German shipping agent, Georg F. Duckwitz, having probably been tipped off by Best himself, had revealed the whole plan to Danish government officials, who, in turn, had hurriedly informed the heads of the Jewish community. They, in marked contrast to Jewish leaders in other countries, had then communicated the news openly in the synagogues on the occasion of the New Year services. The Jews had just time enough to leave their apartments and go into hiding, which was very easy in Denmark, because, in the words of the judgment, "all sections of the Danish people, from the King down to simple citizens," stood ready to receive them.

They might have remained in hiding until the end of the war if the Danes had not been blessed with Sweden as a neighbor. It seemed reasonable to ship the Jews to Sweden, and this was done with the help of the Danish fishing fleet. The cost of transportation for people without means—about a hundred dollars per person— was paid largely by wealthy Danish citizens, and that was perhaps the most astounding feat of all, since this was a time when Jews were paying for their own deportation, when the rich among them were paying fortunes for exit permits (in Holland, Slovakia, and, later, in Hungary) either by bribing the local authorities or by negotiating "legally" with the S.S., who accepted only hard currency and sold exit permits, in Holland, to the tune of five or ten thousand dollars per person. Even in places where Jews met with genuine sympathy and a sincere willingness to help, they had to pay for it, and the chances poor people had of escaping were nil.

It took the better part of October to ferry all the Jews across the five to fifteen miles of water that separates Denmark from Sweden. The Swedes received 5,919 refugees, of whom at least 1,000 were of German origin, 1,310 were half-Jews, and 686 were non-Jews married to Jews. (Almost half the Danish Jews seem to have remained in the country and survived the war in hiding.) The non-Danish Jews were better off than ever before, they all received permission to work. The few hundred Jews whom the German police had been able to arrest were shipped to Theresienstadt. They were old or poor people, who either had not received the news in time or had not been able to comprehend its meaning. In the ghetto, they enjoyed greater privileges than any other group because of the never-ending "fuss" made about them by Danish institutions and private persons. Forty-eight persons died, a figure that was not particularly high, in view of the average age of the group. When everything was over, it was the considered opinion of Eichmann that "for various reasons the action against the Jews in Denmark has been a failure," whereas the curious Dr. Best declared that "the objective of the operation was not to seize a great number of Jews but to clean Denmark of Jews, and this objective has now been achieved."

Politically and psychologically, the most interesting aspect of this incident is perhaps the role played by the German authorities in Denmark, their obvious sabotage of orders from Berlin. It is the only case we know of in which the Nazis met with *open* native resistance, and the result seems to have been that those exposed to it changed their minds. They themselves apparently no longer looked upon the extermination of a whole people as a matter of course. They had met resistance based on principle, and their "toughness" had melted like butter in the sun, they had even been able to show a few timid beginnings of genuine courage. That the ideal of "toughness," except, perhaps, for a few half-demented brutes, was nothing but a myth of self-deception, concealing a ruthless desire for conformity at any price, was clearly revealed at the Nuremberg Trials, where the defendants accused and betrayed each other and assured the world that they "had always been against it" or claimed, as Eichmann was to do, that their best qualities had been "abused" by their superiors. (In Jerusalem, he accused "those in power" of having abused his "obedience." "The subject of a good government is lucky, the subject of a bad government is unlucky. I had no luck.") The atmosphere had changed, and although most of them must have known that they were doomed, not a single one of them had the guts to defend the Nazi ideology. Werner Best claimed at Nuremberg that he had played a complicated double role and that it was thanks to him that the Danish officials had been warned of the impending catastrophe; documentary evidence showed, on the contrary, that he himself had proposed the Danish operation in Berlin, but he explained that this was all part of the game. He was extradited to Denmark and there condemned to death, but he appealed the sentence, with surprising results; because of "new evidence," his sentence was commuted to five years in prison, from which he was released soon afterward. He must have been able to prove to the satisfaction of the Danish court that he really had done his best.

1963

PIERRE BERTON

How Randolph Scott Saved the Northwest

"But," said Oliva Dionne, the father of the famous quintuplets
as he and his wife emerged, somewhat bewildered, from the New
York première of *The Country Doctor*, "it wasn't like that at all!
That's crazy!" Flashbulbs pop. Reporters scribble. The desk is going
to have fun with *that* quote: funny Papa Dionne with his quaint
accent and his store clothes.

It wasn't like that at all from Dionne's point of view; but the
world, including the press, had already bought the movie image of
the film father as a comic moron, a role in which John Qualen had
been typed for years. Qualen had only to look at the camera to get
a laugh—the dumb, ineffectual father who doesn't seem to know
where babies come from. There are a lot of jokes like that in *The
Country Doctor* but Oliva Dionne did not find them funny.

It wasn't like that at all in any of the movies made about Canadian historical events, with the possible exception of a brief four-
picture cycle of one-reelers made before the First World War. * * *
We can't be sure about these one-reelers because they no longer
exist. All we have are the critical reviews and the producer's blurbs,
which can't be taken as gospel. Certainly nothing made since that
time has borne much relationship to Canadian history.

*   *   *

No one, of course, expects motion pictures to be historically
accurate. American studios have distorted and mythologized their
own history and that of other countries just as much as they have
twisted the Canadian past. Playwrights do it all the time; Shakespeare, of course, did it—although Shakespeare never went around
boasting that his version of history was absolutely authentic.

All the same, it's an unfortunate accident that just as Canada was
emerging from the colonial shadows the most powerful educational
medium of all was developed by a friendly but alien power. We
can't blame Hollywood for ignoring the Canadian character and
lifestyle. But there's little doubt that the bludgeoning effect of the
motion picture first distorted our image by making us appear as a
nation of primitives, and then blurred it by confusing it with the
American image. No foreign myth makers could be expected to
reveal to us our own distinctive identity; that must be the task of
our own mass media. Hollywood made it hard for us to recognize
the Canadian identity because its movies masked it so effectively.

*   *   *

The Hollywood attitude to accuracy, as Garth S. Jowett has
pointed out in the *Journal of Popular Culture*, has been to *material*

things—to sets, costumes, and props, rather than to interpretive matters. DeMille probably believed his own press releases when they lauded his passion for authenticity. His sets *were* authentic. The backlot replica of Fort Carlton in *North West Mounted Police* was faithful in every detail to the original. So were the mounted police uniforms, except for the hats. He went to considerable trouble to make Walter Hampden, the Broadway actor, actually look like Big Bear, even to the extent of fitting him with brown contact lenses. It didn't occur to him to have Hampdén act as Big Bear would have acted; in spite of a superficial resemblance, the noted thespian sounded just liker any other Hollywood Indian, grunting away in his deep, mellow voice and carefully trimming all the definite and indefinite articles from his sentences.

In movies about the Canadian frontier—and most of the movies have been about the Canadian frontier—everything is right and everything is wrong. The small-town sets are often works of art— the wood on the false fronts carefully seasoned, the paint peeling to give an impression of age and decay—but they are American sets. The costumes are beautiful and, in the big productions, lovingly made, but they are all wrong because they, too, are American—cowboy outfits in the Canadian north, for instance. The fights are carefully staged, especially the gun-fights. Attention is paid to making the weapons fit the exact historical period—DeMille sent all the way to England in the middle of a war to get 1885 Enfields—but they are American gun-fights; Canadians didn't go around with six-shooters on their hips. The saloons, with their familiar bat-wing doors, their gilded mirrors, their oil paintings, and their long polished bars, are exquisite replicas of American saloons. The saloon is not really part of the Canadian style. For most of its frontier history, Canada has been dry: when the railway was being built, navvies furtively gulped bad whisky in log hovels hidden from the mounted police. That genuinely Canadian institution, the beer parlor of the twenties, thirties, and forties, has never been shown.

What Hollywood did for over half a century was to superimpose its vision of the old west, itself a mythological anachronism, onto the Canadian northwest. Hard-riding posses, men in cowboy outfits, necktie parties, covered wagons, painted Injuns, boot hills, vigilantes, and even tin stars were moved across the border with scarcely a change in the plot except for the presence of the movie Mounties who, all too often, acted like American town marshals.

It didn't occur to Hollywood and it didn't occur to Canadian audiences, either, that the Canadian concept of order imposed from above clashed with the American idea of rough frontier justice administered at grass-roots level by the people's choices. Nor did the moviemakers understand that in Canada the law arrived before the settlers did, in direct contrast to the American experience.

Although Hollywood exaggerated American frontier violence, the western society south of the border was demonstrably less stable than its Canadian counterpart. Shootings on the Canadian frontier were almost unknown. When a Texan on an Alberta ranch shot an adversary in the stomach in 1895, the *Fort McLeod Gazette* reported that it was only the second such killing since the paper was established in 1882. And, contrary to the impression given by the movies, the Canadian northwest was, to quote Jennings again, "one of the few examples in history of a frontier area settled with comparatively little racial friction."

These contrasts suggest that there *is* a difference between the American and the Canadian approach to frontier problems. Yet, as the *Daily Telegraph*'s critic remarked of *The Canadians*, "Saskatchewan might as well be in Texas, so traditional is the style." Almost two generations before, an American reviewer said much the same thing about a Hoot Gibson picture, *The Calgary Stampede*: "This is a typical Western with all the snap of the best examples of this class. . . . The action take[s] place on a ranch in Western Canada, which seems just like our own ranches. . . ." And why shouldn't it? The gun-play was there along with the ten-gallon hats.

It's a little ironic that the movies with the most Canadian-sounding titles are among the most American in style. * * * A good example is a picture called *'Neath Canadian Skies*, produced in 1948, which, if it wasn't for the movie Mounties, could just as easily have been called *'Neath Montana Skies*. Everything about it, including the mountains and the trees, is American: the hardrock mine in the wrong place, the villains with gunbelts who shoot strangers on sight, the townspeople all dressed like Mississippi gamblers and, of course, the inevitable saloon. Even the Mounties in this film act like an American posse, thundering along on their horses firing aimless volleys from their smoking pistols; and, when one of them goes undercover and disguises himself as a typical Canadian westerner, *he* wears a gunbelt too.

Three postwar movies, each dealing with a piece of frontier history in a different part of Canada, illustrate Hollywood's confusion about Canadian attitudes.

The Cariboo Trail is set in British Columbia in the early 1860s at the time of the gold rush.

Canadian Pacific is set in the Northwest during the building of the railway in 1883.

The Far Country is set in the Yukon Territory in the early days of the 1897–98 stampede.

The plots of these three films turn on the idea of strangers pouring into a lawless land and the tensions that such an influx can bring. The Good settlers—railwaymen, prospectors, and cowboys—

are faced with the Bad half-breeds, Indians, scalawags, and crooks who have taken the law into their own hands and who wish to frustrate the advance of civilization. All of these movies could easily have been set in the old west, given the Hollywood mythology. They could never have taken place north of the border because the conditions that existed in the American west simply weren't present anywhere in Canada.

In *The Cariboo Trail* Randolph Scott, in the role of Jim Redfern, a Montana cowboy, is taking cattle into the lawless Cariboo country. Scott literally shoots his way through British Columbia. At a toll bridge scoundrels attempt to charge Scott for passage; he drives on through, guns blazing. Shortly after that he and his partner meet a prospector named Grizzly, played by Gabby Hayes, the perennial comic of the Hopalong Cassidy westerns. "This is the Cariboo Trail, mister," Hayes warns them. "A broken heart for every rock, a dead man for every tree."

That night the scalawags from the toll bridge (those whom Scott hasn't shot full of holes) get their revenge by stampeding the cowboys' cattle. Scott springs into action once again, blasting into the night as men topple in agony from their horses. There is no coroner's inquest.

In the typical British Columbia town of Carson Creek, Scott learns that the entire Cariboo country is under the control of a rapscallion named Walsh, played with a sneer by Victor Jory. Walsh owns everything in town except the neighborhood saloon and gambling hall, identified as a Canadian institution by the presence of three large, if badly carved, totem poles. This environment is the scene of further gun-play: somebody tries to brain Scott with a sledgehammer but Scott, fast as always on the draw, kills him with a single shot.

There is no suggestion, of course, that the law in any form existed in the interior of British Columbia in the 1860s. Law enforcement is an individual matter. As Gabby Hayes tells Randolph Scott: "Up here in the gold country . . . a feller usually shoots first and buries his mistakes later." Life is cheap and nobody seems to be bothered by the corpses lying about in the underbrush, the streets, and the saloons. The Cariboo is the end of the earth: on the other side of the hills, in the mysterious Chilcotin, lies "Injun Country," totally unknown, full of war-whooping braves straight out of Peter Pan.

Hollywood's Cariboo is California in 1849. The real Cariboo was policed from the outset, not by the mounted police who had yet to be invented, but by order of the governor of the colony, James Douglas. This remarkable figure—he was, apparently, a mulatto with West Indian blood—acted decisively as soon as gold was discovered on the Fraser. He sent armed soldiers into the interior and backed them up with all the majesty of British justice, in the person of Judge Matthew Baillie Begbie. This Mephistophelian giant, tough but fair, was known as "the hanging judge of the Cariboo," although hanging was not his style. With this swift move Douglas saved British Columbia from the type of American mass invasion that had lost the empire its Oregon territory.

The last thing that Begbie would have stood for was a Cariboo gun-fight. Lawlessness was quickly stifled. Anybody who came up against the judge got summary treatment. Foreigners who didn't behave were hustled out of the country. The real history of the Cariboo is full of incredible stories and remarkable characters—a tapestry of folly, greed, avarice, eccentricity, profligacy, heroism, and romance. But Nat Holt's shoot-'em-up western might have been made in a foreign country, which of course it was, having been shot entirely in Colorado.

Holt was also the producer of *Canadian Pacific*. * * * Early press agentry suggested that Holt was going to do for Canada what DeMille had done for his own country with *Union Pacific*, a prospect designed to flatter both government and railway officials north of the border. Certainly the later picture derived from the earlier one but the technical production was far weaker, the acting more primitive, and the story much thinner. *Canadian Pacific*, too, was just another transplanted western.

The picture's antecedents were obvious. It was the stepson of *Union Pacific*, which was the stepson of John Ford's *The Iron Horse*. Both those movies had similar themes: attempts by renegades, profiteers, and Indians to prevent the transcontinental railway from being finished. "For three valiant years, Indians reddened the rails with the blood of the tracklayers," was the way a DeMille subtitle phrased it. The climax of both pictures was a bloody battle in which painted savages surrounded a work train and fought it out with the railwaymen.

Canadian Pacific borrowed shamelessly from both movies. DeMille's hero was a trouble-shooter played by Joel McCrea. ("You are the law and it's up to you to smash anything that delays us," General Dodge tells him.) Holt's hero was a trouble-shooter played by Randolph Scott. In John Ford's picture the villains try to kill the hero because he has discovered a pass through the mountains. In Holt's picture the villains try to kill the hero because he has discovered a pass through the mountains. In *Union Pacific* the trouble-shooter gets into a fight in a saloon and tears it down so the navvies can get back to work. In *Canadian Pacific* the trouble-shooter gets into a fight in a saloon and closes it up so the navvies can get back to work. In *The Iron Horse* the men rebel because the pay car fails to turn up. In *Canadian Pacific* the men rebel because the pay car fails to turn up. And the Canadian movie, like both of its predecessors, ends with a bloody battle between painted Indians and navvies holed up in a work train.

The violence in this film is remarkable even for a Hollywood western. Scott, in the role of Tom Andrews, surveyor and trouble-shooter (complete with Texas accent), has been given carte blanche by the Canadian Pacific Railway to do anything he wants with those two pearl-handled revolvers in his gunbelt, or with his fists. In an early scene he arrives at End of Track, spots a man he doesn't like, and walks over and punches him in the nose, knocking him to the ground. Then he kicks his prostrate victim and finally throws him out of camp. This action draws an admiring remark from a man identified as William Van Horne, who in real life was the vice-president of the railroad. "He's the best trouble boss in the country," says this Van Horne, overcome with delight at Scott's example of bossmanship. "He has to be quick with his fists." In *Canadian Pacific* Van Horne is a minor figure; it's Randolph Scott who runs things.

In another scene Scott comes across two men he suspects of steal-ing dynamite for their own nefarious purposes. Without a question or a challenge he pulls both guns from their holsters and opens fire, knocking both of them to the ground. His sidekick, played by J. Carroll Naish, accuses him of being a weakling for shooting them in the arms and not in the head.

There's a subplot in this picture involving a pretty nurse who thinks Scott is far *too* violent. She gets him to hang up his guns and promise her there'll be no more killing because bloodshed never solved anything. She loses out as the result of a gun-fight in a Holly-wood-style saloon (known as "the longest bar in the world") which has been set up beside the track. As in *Union Pacific* the railway's enemies have supplied free booze to the saloon to keep the navvies from working. When one of the patrons gets into an argument the bartender solves it by shooting him dead. This is the last straw for Andrews, who clearly believes that bloodshed solves *everything*. He eschews pacifism, retrieves his forsaken gunbelt, strides into the saloon, and in his role as surveyor/trouble-shooter/construction-boss/policeman arrests the guilty man behind the bar. When the bartender goes for his gun Scott plugs him and closes up the saloon as the picture moves on to its bloody climax.

Baker Street Irregulars[1] will recall the "singular incident of the dog in the night." "But," said Watson to the great detective, "the dog did nothing in the night." To which Holmes replied that *that* was the singular incident. In *Canadian Pacific* the singular incident was the fact that the mounted police did nothing in the movie.

---

1. Fans of the Sherlock Holmes stories of Sir Arthur Conan Doyle.

They weren't even shown. The Métis shot up the navvies; the Indians shot up the railway; Randolph Scott shot up everybody; but no movie Mountie appeared to make a report. Men rebelled and threatened violence; people were blasted to death by dynamite; corpses littered the track; but there wasn't a scarlet coat in evidence. This is remarkable when you consider that up to that point Hollywood had made at least two hundred movies about the mounted police.

Actually, the policing of the Canadian Pacific Railway during the construction period was one of the great triumphs of the NWMP. The divided and often opposing jurisdictions that plagued the American peace-keeping forces didn't exist in the Canadian northwest. From the Manitoba border to the Rockies the mounted police were in sole charge. Saloons were illegal; so was gambling; and *nobody* carried a gun. Because of this almost uncanny quiet the railroad was built across the prairies with a dispatch unique in the annals of North American track-laying.

The spectacle of an imported American surveyor in cowboy gear acting as a trouble-shooter for Van Horne, firing his six-guns at the nearest target, and killing men without a by-your-leave is so alien to the Canadian experience that it would be considered ludicrous were it not for the fact that it was believed. * * * The ultimate seal of approval was supplied by the *Motion Picture Herald,* which reported that "the program bears outward mark of the co-operation extended by the Dominion government and the Canadian Pacific Railway."[2]

The CPR company probably thought the film really *was* an accurate portrayal since it had demonstrated a remarkable lack of knowledge about its own history when *The Iron Horse* was released in 1925. According to the trade press CPR officials went to see that movie when it opened at the Lyric Theatre in New York and were so impressed that "they immediately began negotiations with the Fox Company to have the story and titles written to fit the building of the first Canadian transcontinental railroad. The conditions . . . were so similar . . . that with just a little changing, the picture could be made to fit the Canadian situation," it was pointed out.

The conditions were radically different, but nobody seemed to realize that. The necessary historical changes weren't made in *The Iron Horse,* but when the movie was released in Canada it was dedicated to the men who built the CPR. When it had its première in

2. Some of the non-trade reviews in the more sophisticated dailies were more realistic. Howard Barnes in the *New York Herald Tribune* tagged the movie as "merely a sprawling horse opera" and the *Christian Science Monitor* called it "a pseudo-documentary . . . whose resemblance to history is probably only coincidental" (MMA Photoplay clipping file) [Berton's note].

Montreal the *Gazette* reported that "except for the names applied to the historical participants in the film, it might serve with equal truth as a record of the construction against enormous odds of the Canadian Pacific."

The American idea of an untamed frontier, subdued by individual heroes armed with six-guns, was continued in *The Far Country*, another story about a cowboy from the American west—Wyoming this time—driving his herd of beef cattle into gold country. The picture is a nightmare of geographical impossibilities (a paddle-wheel riverboat leaving Skagway for Seattle, for instance), but the real incongruity is the major assumption on which the plot turns—that there was only one mounted policeman in all of the Canadian Yukon at the time of the gold rush and that he could not deal with the lawlessness. When James Stewart and Walter Brennan reach the Yukon border with their cattle (the geographic truth is that they would have had to drive the herd up the side of a mountain), the customs shack is empty.

"Where's the constable?" asks Brennan.

"Up on the Pelly River. Trouble with the Chilkats," someone replies, nicely garbling the geography but preserving the myth of the savage redskins. (The Chilkats in real life were making big money packing supplies over the passes.) "He's got a real tough job, that constable. He patrols some ten or twenty thousand square miles. Sometimes he don't get home for two or three months at a time."

The historical truth is that the Yukon Territory during the gold rush was the closest thing to a police state British North America has ever seen. The NWMP was stationed in the territory in considerable numbers long before the Klondike strike. They controlled every route into the Yukon and they brooked no nonsense. They collected customs duties, often over the wails of the new arrivals, made arbitrary laws on the spot about river navigation, and turned men back if they didn't have enough supplies, or if they simply *looked* bad. In true Canadian fashion, they laid down moral laws for the community. In Dawson the Lord's Day Act was strictly observed; it was a crime punishable by a fine to cut your own wood on Sunday; and plump young women were arrested for what the stern-faced police called "giving a risqué performance in a theater," generally nothing more than dancing suggestively on the stage in overly revealing tights.

In such a community, a gunbelt was unthinkable. One notorious bad man from Tombstone who tried to pack a weapon on his hip was personally disarmed by a young constable, who had just ejected him from a saloon for the heinous crime of talking too loudly. The bad man left like a lamb but protested when the policeman, upon discovering he was carrying a gun, told him to hand it over. "No man has yet taken a gun away from me," said the American. "Well, I'm taking it," the constable said mildly and did so, without further resistance. So many revolvers were confiscated in Dawson that they were auctioned off by the police for as little as a dollar and purchased as souvenirs to keep on the mantelpiece.

In 1898, the big year of the stampede, there wasn't a serious crime—let alone a murder—in Dawson. The contrast with Skagway on the American side, which *was* a lawless town run by Soapy Smith, the Denver confidence man, was remarkable. But in *The Far Country* Dawson is seen as a community without any law, which a Soapy Smith character from Skagway—he is called Gannon in the picture—can easily control. (In real life, one of Smith's men who tried to cross the border had all his equipment confiscated and was frogmarched[3] right back again by a mounted police sergeant.

When Stewart and Brennan hit town, men are being gunned down like rabbits. 'Where there's gold there's stealin' and where there's stealin' there's killin'," a bystander remarks. Stewart has hardly dipped his pan into the gravel of a creek before another killing takes place; it's explained that the corpse got into a little argument in a saloon.

Finally Stewart and his sidekick encounter the elusive lone Mountie who enters the Dawson Castle Saloon carrying another corpse over his shoulder. All the shooting and killing is too much for the redcoat. For years Hollywood pictures featured Mounties who cleaned up lawless towns single-handedly in the fact of fearful odds, but this one admits defeat in the following dialogue sequence:

"Yes, I'm the law. I represent the law in the Yukon Territory. About fifty thousand square miles of it."
"Then why aren't there more of you?"
"Because yesterday this was a wilderness. We didn't expect you to pour in by the thousands. Now that you're here, we'll protect you."
"When?"
"There'll be a post established here in Dawson early in May."
"What happens between now and May? You going to be here to keep order?"
"Part of the time."
"What about the rest of the time?"
"Pick yourselves a good man. Swear him in. Have him act as marshal. . . ."

The movie Mountie leaves and does not appear again in the picture. His astonishing suggestion—that an American town marshal, complete with tin star, be sworn in by a group of townspeople living

3. That is, he was carried face downward by four men, each holding a limb.

under British jurisprudence—is accepted. Naturally, they want to make Jimmy Stewart the marshal; he clearly fits the part. But Stewart is playing the role of the Loner who looks after Number One and so another man is elected to get shot. And he does. Others get shot. Even Walter Brennan gets shot. Stewart finally comes to the reluctant conclusion that he must end all the shooting with some shooting of his own. He pins on the tin star and he and the bully, Gannon, blast away at each other in the inevitable western climax.

To anybody with a passing knowledge of the Canadian north, this bald retelling of the story passes rational belief. Could such a motion picture really have been made? Did people actually believe it? Yes, they did. And reviewers on two continents, including Canada, saw nothing to complain about.

* * *

No one really expects foreign critics to have a first-hand knowledge of Canadian history. But I haven't been able to find a Canadian critic who set the record straight, either, even in Vancouver, with its strong Yukon connections. Les Wedman, praising the star's performance in the picture in the *Vancouver Province*, wrote with approval of how "in a blazing duel . . . Stewart brings law and order to Dawson."

Nothing has changed. Seeing *The Far Country* again on television took me back to a day in 1960 when a Hollywood movie company decided to make a series about the Klondike, based on my own history of the stampede. I met the executive producer of the series and the following dialogue took place:

ME: Uh. I guess you're going to have some kind of central character to kind of tie the story together, eh?

HIM: Oh, yes; we've figured that out.

ME: I thought maybe a dog driver . . .

HIM: No; we've got it worked out. He's going to be a U.S. marshal.

ME: A U.S. marshal?

HIM: Yes. He brings the law to Dawson City.

ME: But Dawson City is in Canada.

HIM: Is it? Really?

ME: Really.

HIM: Well, then, a U.S. marshal-type. He's elected by the miners, see, and –

ME: But they didn't *need* a marshal in Dawson. There wasn't any crime.

HIM: No crime? In Dawson City?

ME: You see they had these mounted police. You know – Mounties –

HIM: Oh yeah. The Mounties.

ME: And two hundred soldiers, all armed. They called that the Yukon Field Force.

HIM: Must have been a few murders, though.

ME: None.

HIM: Hold-ups? A few hold-ups?

ME: No holdups.

HIM: No murders? No hold-ups? No crime?

ME: Well, a guy got fined for going down to the Yukon River and chopping a hole in the ice and taking some water back to his cabin. You see it was Sunday, and in Canada we –

HIM: Yeah, yeah. I'm thinking. . . . (he thinks) I'm thinking maybe we ought to change the locale. . . .

ME: Well, if you want murders and holdups –

HIM: Maybe move it over to the American side. . . .

ME: To Skagway?

HIM: Yeah? Move the whole thing to Skagway! Then it would work!

ME: Yes. It would work all right in Skagway.

HIM: Then that's what we'll do.

And that, so help me, is exactly what they did.

1975

QUESTIONS

1. What is Berton's thesis? What is the function of the contrast he presents between Canada's actual history and the version found in Hollywood movies?

2. On p. 555 Berton makes the plausible assertion that only Canadian mass media can reveal the Canadian identity. In other selections, Kildare Dobbs describes the regions of Canada (pp. 372–376), and Fredelle Bruser Maynard describes the official, didactic effort in the Canadian Readers to guide Canadian children, to shape a Canadian identity (pp. 136–143). How would these authors respond to Berton's assertion? How would they respond to the movies he describes? In his final paragraph, Dobbs speaks of a Canadian self-image; what is the bearing of these remarks on Berton's essay?

3. On pp. 559–561 Berton establishes that the movie Canadian Pacific follows other railroad westerns more closely than Canadian history, and on p. 565 he shows a producer changing the fictional setting of a filmed television series from Canada to Alaska to avoid disturbing his conception of the potential story material. What is Berton's attitude toward such moviemaking? Does this attitude suggest a difference between the Canadian and the American, or rather between the historian and the moviemaker, or both?

4. Berton proves that the movies under discussion do not represent Canadian history or the Canadian identity. What do they accomplish? Using X. J. Kennedy's "Who Killed King Kong?" (pp. 261–264) as a model, suggest an interpretation of these movies, based on Berton's account of them, that might explain their success.

JOHN HOUSEMAN

The War of the Worlds

The War of the Worlds formed part of our general plan of contrasting shows.[1] No one, as I recall, was particularly enthusiastic about it. But it seemed good programming—following *Julius Caesar* (with the original Mercury cast and commentary by Kaltenborn out of Plutarch[2]), *Oliver Twist* (in which Orson played both the boy Oliver and the villainous Fagin), *Eighty Days Around the World*, *The Heart of Darkness*, *Jane Eyre* and before *Life with Father*, which was to be our next show—to throw in something of a scientific nature. We thought of Shiel's *Purple Cloud*, Conan Doyle's *Lost World* and several other well-known works of science fiction before settling on H. G. Wells's twenty-year-old novel, which neither Orson nor I remembered at all clearly. It is just possible that neither of us had ever read it.

Actually it was a narrow squeak. The men from Mars barely escaped being stillborn. Late Tuesday night—thirty-six hours before the first rehearsal—Howard Koch called me at the theater. He was in deep distress. After three days of slaving on H. G. Wells's scientific fantasy he was ready to give up. Under no circumstances, he declared, could it be made interesting or in any way credible to modern American ears. Koch was not given to habitual alarmism. To confirm his fears, Annie[3] came to the phone. "You can't do it, Houseman!" she whined. "Those old Martians are just a lot of nonsense! It's all too silly! We're going to make fools of ourselves! Absolute idiots!"

We were not averse to changing a show at the last moment. But the only other script available was an extremely dreary version of

1. In the series *Mercury Theatre of the Air*, named for the stage company of which Houseman and Orson Welles were cofounders and presiding geniuses; the series offered weekly broadcasts of adaptations of famous plays and fictional works.

2. H. V. Kaltenborn was a leading news commentator of the day, distinguished for his clipped, pedantic speech [Houseman's note]. Plutarch (46–120) was a biographer of famous Greeks and Romans, among the latter the dictator Julius Caesar.

3. Ann Froelich, who worked with Howard Koch, the show's regular scripwriter; Paul Stewart, mentioned later, was associate producer of the show.

Lorna Doone[4] which I had started during the summer and abandoned. I reasoned with Koch. I was severe. I taxed him and Annie
with defeatism. I gave them false comfort, I promised to come up
and help. When I finally got there—around two in the morning—
things were better. They were beginning to have fun laying waste
the State of New Jersey. Annie had stopped grinding her teeth. I
worked with them for the rest of the night and they went on
through the next day. Wednesday at sunset the script was finished.

Thursday, as usual, Paul Stewart rehearsed the show, then made
a record. We listened to it rather gloomily, between *Danton*
rehearsals, in Orson's room at the St. Regis, sitting on the floor
because all the chairs were still covered with coils of unrolled and
unedited film.[5] He was dead tired and thought it was a dull show.
We all agreed that its only chance of coming off lay in emphasizing
its newscast style—its simultaneous, eyewitness quality.

All night we sat up—Howard, Paul, Annie and I—spicing the
script with circumstantial allusions and authentic detail. Friday
afternoon it was sent over to CBS to be passed by the network
censor. Certain name alterations were requested. Under protest and
with a deep sense of grievance we changed the Hotel Biltmore to a
nonexistent Park Plaza, Trans-America to Inter-Continent, the Columbia Broadcasting Building to Broadcasting Building. Then the
script went over to mimeograph and I went back to the theater. We
had done our best and, after all, it was just another radio show.

Saturday, Paul Stewart rehearsed with sound effects and without
Welles. He worked for a long time on the crowd scenes, the roar of
cannon echoing in the Watchung Hills[6] and the sound of New
York Harbor as the ships with the last remaining survivors put out
to sea.

Around six we left the studio. Orson, phoning from the theater a
few minutes later to find out how things were going, was told by
one of the CBS sound men, who had stayed behind to pack up his
equipment, that it was not one of our better shows. Confidentially,
the man opined, it just didn't come off. Twenty-seven hours later,
quite a few of his employers would have found themselves a good
deal happier if he had turned out to be right.

On Sunday, October 30, at 8:00 P.M., E.S.T., in a studio littered
with coffee cartons and sandwich paper, Orson swallowed a second
container of pineapple juice, put on his earphones, raised his long
white fingers and threw the cue for the Mercury theme—the Tchai-
kovsky Piano Concerto No. 1 in B Flat Minor. After the music
dipped, there were routine introductions—then the announcement

---

4. Well-known romantic novel (1869)
by R. D. Blackmore.
5. A future Mercury Theatre stage
production was to have two filmed chase
scenes, which for several weeks Welles
had been trying to edit. Currently in
rehearsal was Georg Büchner's *Danton's
Death* (1835).
6. In northern New Jersey.

that a dramatization of H. G. Wells's famous novel, *The War of the Worlds*, was about to be performed. Around 8:01 Orson began to speak, as follows:

WELLES

We know now that in the early years of the twentieth century this world was being watched closely by intelligences greater than man's and yet as mortal as his own. We know now that as human beings busied themselves about their various concerns they were scrutinized and studied, perhaps almost as narrowly as a man with a microscope might scrutinize the transient creatures that swarm and multiply in a drop of water. With infinite complacence people went to and fro over the earth about their little affairs, serene in the assurance of their dominion over this small spinning fragment of solar driftwood which by chance or design man has inherited out of the dark mystery of Time and Space. Yet across an immense ethereal gulf minds that are to our minds as ours are to the beasts in the jungle, intellects vast, cool, and unsympathetic regarded this earth with envious eyes and slowly and surely drew their plans against us. In the thirty-ninth year of the twentieth century came the great disillusionment.

It was near the end of October. Business was better. The war scare was over. More men were back at work. Sales were picking up. On this particular evening, October 30th, the Crossley service estimated that thirty-two million people were listening in on their radios. . . .

Neatly, without perceptible transition, he was followed on the air by an anonymous announcer caught in a routine bulletin:

ANNOUNCER

. . . for the next twenty-four hours not much change in temperature. A slight atmospheric disturbance of undetermined origin is reported over Nova Scotia, causing a low pressure area to move down rather rapidly over the northeastern states, bringing a forecast of rain, accompanied by winds of light gale force. Maximum temperature 66; minimum 48. This weather report comes to you from the Government Weather Bureau. . . . We now take you to the Meridian Room in the Hotel Park Plaza in downtown New York, where you will be entertained by the music of Ramon Raquello and his orchestra.

At which cue, Bernard Herrmann led the massed men of the CBS house orchestra in a thunderous symphonic rendition of "La Cumparsita." The entire hoax might have been exposed there and then—but for the fact that hardly anyone was listening. They were being entertained by Charlie McCarthy.

The Crossley census, taken about a week before the broadcast, had given us 3.6 percent of the listening audience to Edgar Bergen's 34.7 percent. What the Crossley Institute (that hireling of the advertising agencies) deliberately ignored, was the healthy American habit of dial twisting. On that particular evening Edgar Bergen, in the person of Charlie McCarthy, temporarily left the air about 8:12 P.M. E.S.T., yielding place to a new and not very popular singer. At that point, and during the following minutes, a large number of listeners started twisting their dials in search of other entertainment. Many of them turned to us—and when they did, they stayed put! For by this time the mysterious meteorite had fallen at Grovers Mill in New Jersey, the Martians had begun to show their foul leathery heads above the ground, and the New Jersey State Police were racing to the spot. Within a few minutes people all over the United States were praying, crying, fleeing frantically to escape death from the Martians. Some remembered to rescue loved ones, others telephoned farewells or warnings, hurried to inform neighbors, sought information from newspapers or radio stations, summoned ambulances and police cars.

The reaction was strongest at points nearest the tragedy—in Newark, New Jersey, in a single block, more than twenty families rushed out of their houses with wet handkerchiefs and towels over their faces. Some began moving household furniture. Police switchboards were flooded with calls inquiring, "Shall I close my windows?"; "Have the police any extra gas masks?" Police found one family waiting in the yard with wet cloths on faces contorted with hysteria. As one woman reported later:

> I was terribly frightened. I wanted to pack and take my child in my arms, gather up my friends and get in the car and just go north as far as we could. But what I did was just sit by one window, praying, listening, and scared stiff, and my husband by the other sniffing, and looking out to see if people were running. . . .

In New York hundreds of people on Riverside Drive left their homes ready for flight. Bus terminals were crowded. A woman calling up the Dixie Bus Terminal for information said impatiently, "Hurry please, the world is coming to an end and I have a lot to do."

In the parlor churches of Harlem, evening service became "end of the world" prayer meetings. Many turned to God in that moment:

> I held a crucifix in my hand and prayed while looking out of my open window for falling meteors. . . . When the monsters were wading across the Hudson River and coming into New York, I wanted to run up on my roof to see what they looked like, but I couldn't leave my radio while it was telling me of their whereabouts.

> Aunt Grace began to pray with Uncle Henry. Lily got sick to her stomach. I don't know what I did exactly but I know I prayed harder and more earnestly than ever before. Just as soon as we were convinced that this thing was real, how petty all things on this earth seemed; how soon we put our trust in God!

The panic moved upstate. One man called up the Mt. Vernon Police Headquarters to find out "where the forty policemen were killed." Another took time out to philosophize:

> I thought the whole human race was going to be wiped out—that seemed
> more important than the fact that we were going to die. It seemed awful
> that everything that had been worked on for years was going to be lost
> forever.

In Rhode Island weeping and hysterical women swamped the
switchboard of the Providence *Journal* for details of the massacre,
and officials of the electric light company received a score of calls
urging them to turn off all lights so that the city would be safe from
the enemy. The Boston *Globe* received a call from one woman who
"could see the fire." A man in Pittsburgh hurried home in the
midst of the broadcast and found his wife in the bathroom, a bottle
of poison in her hand, screaming, "I'd rather die this way than
that." In Minneapolis a woman ran into church screaming, "New
York destroyed, this is the end of the world. You might as well go
home to die. I just heard it on the radio."

The Kansas City bureau of the AP received inquiries about the
"meteors" from Los Angeles; Salt Lake City; Beaumont, Texas; and
St. Joseph, Missouri. In San Francisco the general impression of listeners seemed to be that an overwhelming force had invaded the
United States from the air—was in process of destroying New York
and threatening to move westward. "My God," roared an inquirer
into a telephone, "where can I volunteer my services, we've got to
stop this awful thing!"

As far south as Birmingham, Alabama, people gathered in
churches and prayed. On the campus of a Southeastern college—

> The girls in the sorority houses and dormitories huddled around their
> radios trembling and weeping in each other's arms. They separated them-
> selves from their friends only to take their turn at the telephones to
> make long-distance calls to their parents, saying goodbye for what they
> thought might be the last time. . . .

There are hundreds of such items, gathered from coast to coast. At
least one book and quite a pile of sociological literature have
appeared on the subject of "the invasion from Mars." Many theories have been put forward to explain the "tidal wave" of panic that
swept the nation. Two factors, in my opinion, contributed to the
broadcast's extraordinarily violent effect. First, its historical timing.
It came within thirty-five days of the Munich crisis.[7] For weeks, the
American people had been hanging on their radios, getting most of
their news over the air. A new technique of "on-the-spot" reporting

---

7. The broadcast was on October 30,
1938. In September the prime ministers
of Great Britain and France had met in
Munich with Hitler and Mussolini and
ceded western Czechoslovakia to Germany in an effort to appease Hitler's
expansionism and prevent war.

had been developed and eagerly accepted by an anxious and news-hungry world. The Mercury Theatre of the Air, by faithfully copying every detail of the new technique, including its imperfections, found an already enervated audience ready to accept its wildest fantasies. The second factor was the show's sheer technical brilliance. To this day it is impossible to sit in a room and hear the scratched, worn, off-the-air recording of the broadcast without feeling in the back of your neck some slight draft left over from the great wind of terror that swept the nation. Even with the element of credibility totally removed it remains a surprisingly effective broadcast.

Beginning some time around two when the show started to take shape under Orson's hands, a strange fever seemed to invade the studio—part childish mischief, part professional zeal. First to feel it were the actors. I remember Frank Readick (who played the part of Carl Phillips, the network's special reporter) going down to the record library and digging up the recording of the explosion of the *Hindenburg* at Lakehurst. This is a classic reportage—one of those wonderful, unpredictable accidents of eyewitness description. The broadcaster is casually describing the routine landing of the giant dirigible. Suddenly he sees something. A flash of flame! An instant later the whole thing explodes. It takes him time—a full second—to react at all. Then seconds more of sputtering ejaculations before he can make the adjustment between brain and tongue. He starts to describe the terrible things he sees—the writhing human figures twisting and squirming as they fall from the white burning wreckage. He stops, fumbles, vomits, then quickly continues. Readick played the record to himself, over and over. Then, recreating the emotion in his own terms, he described the Martian meteorite as he saw it lying inert and harmless in a field at Grovers Mill, lit up by the headlights of a hundred cars, the coppery cylinder suddenly opening, revealing the leather tentacles and the terrible pale-eyed faces of the Martians within. As they began to emerge he froze, unable to translate his vision into words; he fumbled, retched, and then after a second continued.

A few moments later Carl Phillips lay dead, tumbling over the microphone in his fall—one of the first victims of the Martian ray. There followed a moment of absolute silence—an eternity of waiting. Then without warning, the network's emergency fill-in was heard—somewhere in a quiet studio, a piano, close on mike, playing "Claire de Lune," soft and sweet as honey, for many seconds, while the fate of the universe hung in the balance. Finally it was interrupted by the manly reassuring voice of Brigadier General Montgomery Smith, Commander of the New Jersey State Militia, speaking from Trenton and placing "the counties of Mercer and Middlesex as far west as Princeton and east to Jamesburg" under martial law! Tension—release—then renewed tension. Soon after that came an eyewitness account of the fatal battle of the Watchung Hills; then, once again, that lone piano was heard—now a symbol of terror, shattering the dead air with its ominous tinkle. As it played on and on, its effect became increasingly sinister—a thin band of suspense stretched almost beyond endurance.

That piano was the neatest trick of the show—a fine specimen of the theatrical "retard," boldly conceived and exploited to the full. It was one of the many devices with which Welles succeeded in compelling not merely the attention, but also the belief of his invisible audience. *The War of the Worlds* was a magic act, one of the world's greatest, and Orson was the man to bring it off.

For Welles, as I have said, was, first and foremost, a magician whose particular talent lay in his ability to stretch the familiar elements of theatrical effect far beyond their normal point of tension. For this reason (as we were discovering to our sorrow on Forty-first Street) his productions required more careful preparation and more perfect execution than most; like all complicated magic tricks, they remained, till the last moment, in a state of precarious balance. When they came off they gave, by virtue of their unusually high intensity, an impression of the greatest brilliance and power; when they failed—when something in their balance went wrong or the original structure proved to have been unsound—they provoked a particularly violent reaction of unease and revulsion. Welles's flops were louder then other men's. The Mars broadcast was one of his unqualified successes.

Among the columnists and public figures who discussed the affair during the next few days (some praising us for the public service we had rendered, some condemning us as sinister scoundrels), the most general reaction was one of amazement at the "incredible stupidity" and "gullibility" of the American public, who had accepted as real, in this single broadcast, incidents which in actual fact would have taken days or even weeks to occur. One explanation of our success lay in the fact that the first few minutes of our broadcast were strictly realistic in time and perfectly credible, though somewhat boring, in content. Herein lay the great tensile strength of the show; it was the structural device that made the whole illusion possible. And it could have been carried off in no other medium than radio.

Our actual broadcasting time, from the first mention of the meteorites to the fall of New York City, was less than forty minutes. During that time men traveled long distances, large bodies of troops were mobilized, cabinet meetings were held, savage battles fought on land and in the air. And millions of people accepted it—emotionally if not logically.

There is nothing so very strange about that. Most of us do the same thing, to some degree, most days of our lives—every time we look at a movie or a television show. Not even the realistic theater observes the literal unities; films, TV and, particularly, in its day, radio (where neither place nor time existed save in the imagination of the listener) have no difficulty in getting their audiences to accept the telescoped reality of dramatic time. Our special hazard lay in the fact that we purported to be not a play, but reality. In order to take advantage of the accepted convention, we had to slide swiftly and imperceptibly out of the "real" time of a news report into the "dramatic" time of a fictional broadcast. Once that was achieved—without losing the audience's attention or arousing their skepticism—once they were sufficiently absorbed and bewitched not to notice the transitions any more, there was no extreme of fantasy through which they would not follow us. If, that night, the American public proved "gullible," it was because enormous pains and a great deal of thought had been spent to make it so.

In the script, *The War of the Worlds* started extremely slowly— dull meteorological and astronomical bulletins alternating with musical interludes. These were followed by a colorless scientific interview and still another stretch of dance music. These first few minutes of routine broadcasting "within the existing standards of judgment of the listener" were intended to lull (or maybe bore) the audience into a false security and to furnish a solid base of realistic time from which to accelerate later. Orson, in directing the show, extended these slow movements far beyond our original conception. The interview in the Princeton Observatory—the clockwork ticking monontonously overhead, the woolly-minded professor mumbling vague replies to the reporters' uninformed questions—this, too, was dragged out to the point of tedium. Over my protests, lines were restored that had been cut at earlier rehearsals. I cried there would not be a listener left. Welles stretched them out even longer.

He was right. His sense of tempo, that night, was infallible. When the flashed news of the cylinder's landing finally came—almost fifteen minutes after the beginning of a fairly dull show—he was able suddenly to spiral his action to a speed as wild and reckless as its base was solid. The appearance of the Martians; their first treacherous act; the death of Carl Phillips; the arrival of the militia; the battle of the Watchung Hills; the destruction of New Jersey— all these were telescoped into a space of twelve minutes without overstretching the listeners' emotional credulity. The broadcast, by then, had its own reality, the reality of emotionally felt time and space.

At the height of the crisis, around 8:31, the Secretary of the Interior came on the air with an exhortation to the American people. It was admirably spoken—in a voice just faintly reminiscent of Franklin Delano Roosevelt's—by a young man named Kenneth Delmar, who later grew rich and famous as Senator Claghorn.[8]

THE SECRETARY

Citizens of the nation: I shall not try to conceal the gravity of the situation that confronts the country, nor the concern of your Government in protecting the lives and property of its people. However, I wish to impress upon you—private citizens and public officials, all of you—the urgent need of calm and resourceful action. Fortunately, this formidable enemy is still confined to a comparatively small area, and we may place our faith in the military forces to keep them there. In the meantime placing our trust in God, we must continue the performance of our duties, each and every one of us, so that we may confront this destructive adversary with a nation united, courageous, and consecrated to the preservation of human supremacy on this earth. I thank you.

Toward the end of this speech (circa 8:32 E.S.T.), Davidson Taylor, supervisor of the broadcast for the Columbia Broadcasting System, received a phone call in the control room, creased his lips, and hurriedly left the studio. By the time he returned, a few minutes later, pale as death, clouds of heavy smoke were rising from Newark, New Jersey, and the Martians, tall as skyscrapers, were astride the Pulaski Highway preparatory to wading the Hudson River. To us in the studio the show seemed to be progressing splendidly—how splendidly Davidson Taylor had just learned outside. For several minutes now, a kind of madness had been sweeping the continent: it was somehow connected with our show. The CBS switchboards had been swamped into uselessness, but from outside sources vague rumors were coming in of deaths and suicides and panic injuries by the thousands.

Taylor had orders to interrupt the show immediately with an explanatory station announcement. By now the Martians were across the Hudson and gas was blanketing the city. The end was near. We were less than a minute from the station break. Ray Collins, superb as the "last announcer," was choking heroically to death on the roof of Broadcasting Building. The boats were all whistling for a while as the last of the refugees perished in New York Harbor. Finally, as they died away, an amateur short-wave operator was heard, from heaven knows where, weakly reaching out for human companionship across the empty world:

2X2L Calling CQ
2X2L Calling CQ
2X2L Calling CQ
Isn't there anyone on the air?
Isn't there anyone?

---

8. A comic character in Fred Allen's popular radio show.

Five seconds of absolute silence. Then, shattering the reality of world's end—the announcer's voice was heard, suave and bright:

ANNOUNCER

You are listening to the CBS presentation of Orson Welles and the Mercury Theatre of the Air in an original dramatization of *The War of the Worlds*, by H. G. Wells. The performance will continue after a brief intermission.

The second part of the show was well written and sensitively played —but nobody heard it. It recounted the adventures of a lone survivor, with interesting observations on the nature of human society; it described the eventual death of the Martian invaders, slain—"after all man's defenses had failed by the humblest thing that God in his wisdom had put upon this earth"—by bacteriological action; it told of the rebuilding of a brave new world. After a stirring musical finale, Welles, in his own person, delivered a charmingly apologetic little speech about Halloween and goblins.

I remember, during the playing of the final theme, the phone starting to ring in the control room and a shrill voice through the receiver announcing itself as belonging to the mayor of some Midwestern city, one of the big ones. He was screaming for Welles. Choking with fury, he reported mobs in the streets of his city, women and children huddled in the churches, violence and looting. If, as he now learned, the whole thing was nothing but a crummy joke—then he, personally, was on his way to New York to punch the author of it on the nose! I hung up quickly. For we were off the air now and the studio door had burst open.

The following hours were a nightmare. The building was suddenly full of people and dark-blue uniforms. Hustled out of the studio, we were locked into a small back office on another floor. Here we sat incommunicado while network employees were busily collecting, destroying, or locking up all scripts and records of the broadcast. Finally the Press was let loose upon us, ravening for horror. How many deaths had *we* heard of? (Implying they knew of thousands.) What did *we* know of the fatal stampede in a Jersey hall? (Implying it was one of many.) What traffic deaths? (The ditches must be choked with corpses.) The suicides? (Haven't you heard about the one on Riverside Drive?) It is all quite vague in my memory and quite terrible.

Hours later, instead of arresting us, they let us out a back way and we scurried down to the theater like hunted animals to their hole. It was surprising to see life going on as usual in the midnight streets, cars stopping for traffic, people walking. At the Mercury the company was still rehearsing *Danton's Death*—falling up and down stairs and singing the "Carmagnole."[9] Welles went up on stage,

9. A song of the French Revolution of 1789, the setting for *Danton's Death*.

where photographers, lying in wait, caught him with his eyes raised to heaven, his arms outstretched in an attitude of crucifixion. Thus he appeared in a tabloid the next morning over the caption, "I Didn't Know What I Was Doing!" *The New York Times* quoted him as saying, "I don't think we will choose anything like this again."

We were on the front page for two days. Having had to bow to radio as a news source during the Munich crisis, the press was now only too eager to expose the perilous irresponsibilities of the new medium. Orson was their whipping boy. They quizzed and badgered him. Condemnatory editorials were delivered by our press-clipping bureau in bushel baskets. There was talk, for a while, of criminal action.

Then gradually, after about two weeks, the excitement subsided. By then it had been discovered that the casualties were not as numerous or as serious as had at first been supposed. One young woman had fallen and broken her arm running downstairs. Later the Federal Communications Commission held some hearings and passed some regulations. The Columbia Broadcasting System made a public apology. With that the official aspects of the incident were closed.

Of the suits that were brought against the network—amounting to over three-quarters of a million dollars for damages, injuries, miscarriages and distresses of various kinds—not one was substantiated. We did settle one claim, however. It was the particularly affecting case of a man in Massachusetts, who wrote:

> I thought the best thing to do was to go away. So I took three dollars twenty-five cents out of my savings and bought a ticket. After I had gone sixty miles I knew it was a play. Now I don't have money left for the shoes I was saving up for. Will you please have someone send me a pair of black shoes size 9B!

We did. And all the lawyers were very angry with us.

FRANCES FITZGERALD

Rewriting American History

Those of us who grew up in the fifties believed in the permanence of our American-history textbooks. To us as children, those texts were the truth of things: they were American history. It was not just that we read them before we understood that not everything that is printed is the truth, or the whole truth. It was that they, much more than other books, had the demeanor and trappings of authority. They were weighty volumes. They spoke in measured cadences: imperturbable, humorless, and as distant as Chinese emperors. Our teachers treated them with respect, and we paid them abject homage by memorizing a chapter a week. But now the textbook histories have changed, some of them to such an extent that an adult would find them unrecognizable.

One current junior-high-school American history begins with a story about a Negro cowboy called George McJunkin. It appears that when McJunkin was riding down a lonely trail in New Mexico one cold spring morning in 1925 he discovered a mound containing bones and stone implements, which scientists later proved belonged to an Indian civilization ten thousand years old. The book goes on to say that scientists now believe there were people in the Americas at least twenty thousand years ago. It discusses the Aztec, Mayan, and Incan civilizations and the meaning of the world "culture" before introducing the European explorers.

Another history text—this one for the fifth grade—begins with the story of how Henry B. Gonzalez, who is a member of Congress from Texas, learned about his own nationality. When he was ten years old, his teacher told him he was an American because he was born in the United States. His grandmother, however, said, "The cat was born in the oven. Does that make him bread?" After reporting that Mr. Gonzalez eventually went to college and law school, the book explains that "the melting pot idea hasn't worked out as some thought it would," and that now "some people say that the people of the United States are more like a salad bowl than a melting pot."

Poor Columbus! He is a minor character now, a walk-on in the middle of American history. Even those books that have not replaced his picture with a Mayan temple or an Iroquois mask do not credit him with discovering America—even for the Europeans. The Vikings, they say, preceded him to the New World, and after that the Europeans, having lost or forgotten their maps, simply neglected to cross the ocean again for five hundred years. Columbus is far from being the only personage to have suffered from time and revision. Captain John Smith, Daniel Boone, and Wild Bill Hickok —the great self-promoters of American history—have all but disappeared, taking with them a good deal of the romance of the American frontier. General Custer has given way to Chief Crazy Horse; General Eisenhower no longer liberates Europe single-handed; and, indeed, most generals, even to Washington and Lee, have faded away, as old soldiers do, giving place to social reformers such as William Lloyd Garrison and Jacob Riis. A number of black Americans have risen to prominence: not only George Washington Carver but Frederick Douglass and Martin Luther King, Jr. W. E.

B. Du Bois now invariably accompanies Booker T. Washington. In addition, there is a mystery man called Crispus Attucks, a fugitive slave about whom nothing seems to be known for certain except that he was a victim of the Boston Massacre and thus became one of the first casualties of the American Revolution. Thaddeus Stevens has been reconstructed—his character changed, as it were, from black to white, from cruel and vindictive to persistent and sincere. As for Teddy Roosevelt, he now champions the issue of conservation instead of charging up San Juan Hill. No single President really stands out as a hero, but all Presidents—except certain unmentionables in the second half of the nineteenth century—seem to have done as well as could be expected, given difficult circumstances.

Of course, when one thinks about it, it is hardly surprising that modern scholarship and modern perspectives have found their way into children's books. Yet the changes remain shocking. Those who in the sixties complained of the bland optimism, the chauvinism, and the materialism of their old civics text did so in the belief that, for all their protests, the texts would never change. The thought must have had something reassuring about it, for that generation never noticed when its complaints began to take effect and the songs about radioactive rainfall and houses made of ticky-tacky began to appear in the textbooks. But this is what happened.

The history texts now hint at a certain level of unpleasantness in American history. Several books, for instance, tell the story of Ishi, the last "wild" Indian in the continental United States, who, captured in 1911 after the massacre of his tribe, spent the final four and a half years of his life in the University of California's museum of anthropology, in San Francisco. At least three books show the same stunning picture of the breaker boys, the child coal miners of Pennsylvania—ancient children with deformed bodies and blackened faces who stare stupidly out from the entrance to a mine. One book quotes a soldier on the use of torture in the American campaign to pacify the Philippines at the beginning of the century. A number of books say that during the American Revolution the patriots tarred and feathered those who did not support them, and drove many of the loyalists from the country. Almost all the present-day history books note that the United States interned Japanese-Americans in detention camps during the Second World War.

Ideologically speaking, the histories of the fifties were implacable, seamless. Inside their covers, America was perfect: the greatest nation in the world, and the embodiment of democracy, freedom, and technological progress. For them, the country never changed in any important way: its values and its political institutions remained constant from the time of the American Revolution. To my generation—the children of the fifties—these texts appeared permanent just because they were so self-contained. Their orthodoxy, it seemed, left no handholds for attack, no lodging for decay. Who, after all, would dispute the wonders of technology or the superiority of the English colonists over the Spanish? Who would find fault with the pastorale of the West or the Old South? Who would question the anti-Communist crusade? There was, it seemed, no point in comparing these visions with reality, since they were the public truth and were thus quite irrelevant to what existed and to what anyone privately believed. They were—or so it seemed—the permanent expression of mass culture in America.

But now the texts have changed, and with them the country that American children are growing up into. The society that was once uniform is now a patchwork of rich and poor, old and young, men and women, blacks, whites, Hispanics, and Indians. The system that ran so smoothly by means of the Constitution under the guidance of benevolent conductor Presidents is now a rattletrap affair. The past is no highway to the present; it is a collection of issues and events that do not fit together and that lead in no single direction. The word "progress" has been replaced by the word "change": children, the modern texts insist, should learn history so that they can adapt to the rapid changes taking place around them. History is proceeding in spite of us. The present, which was once portrayed in the concluding chapters as a peaceful haven of scientific advances and Presidential inaugurations, is now a tangle of problems: race problems, urban problems, foreign-policy problems, problems of pollution, poverty, energy depletion, youthful rebellion, assassination, and drugs. Some books illustrate these problems dramatically. One, for instance, contains a picture of a doll half buried in a mass of untreated sewage; the caption reads, "Are we in danger of being overwhelmed by the products of our society and wastage created by their production? Would you agree with this photographer's interpretation?" Two books show the same picture of an old black woman sitting in a straight chair in a dingy room, her hands folded in graceful resignation; the surrounding text discusses the problems faced by the urban poor and by the aged who depend on Social Security. Other books present current problems less starkly. One of the texts concludes sagely:

Problems are part of life. Nations face them, just as people face them, and try to solve them. And today's Americans have one great advantage over past generations. Never before have Americans been so well equipped to solve their problems. They have today the means to conquer poverty, disease, and ignorance. The technetronic age has put that power into their hands.

Such passages have a familiar ring. Amid all the problems, the deus ex machina[1] of science still dodders around in the gloaming of pious hope.

Even more surprising than the emergence of problems is the discovery that the great unity of the texts has broken. Whereas in the fifties all texts represented the same political view, current texts follow no pattern of orthodoxy. Some books, for instance, portray civil-rights legislation as a series of actions taken by a wise, paternal government; others convey some suggestion of the social upheaval involved and make mention of such people as Stokely Carmichael and Malcolm X.[2] In some books, the Cold War has ended; in others, it continues, with Communism threatening the free nations of the earth.

The political diversity in the books is matched by a diversity of pedagogical approach. In addition to the traditional narrative histories, with their endless streams of facts, there are so-called "discovery," or "inquiry," texts, which deal with a limited number of specific issues in American history. These texts do not pretend to cover the past; they focus on particular topics, such as "stratification in Colonial society" or "slavery and the American Revolution," and illustrate them with documents from primary and secondary sources. The chapters in these books amount to something like case studies, in that they include testimony from people with different perspectives or conflicting views on a single subject. In addition, the chapters provide background information, explanatory notes, and a series of questions for the student. The questions are the heart of the matter, for when they are carefully selected they force students to think much as historians think: to define the point of view of the speaker, analyze the ideas presented, question the relationship between events, and so on. One text, for example, quotes Washington, Jefferson, and John Adams on the question of foreign alliances and then asks, "What did John Adams assume that the international situation would be after the American Revolution? What did Washington's attitude toward the French alliance seem to be? How do you account for his attitude?" Finally, it asks, "Should a nation adopt a policy toward alliances and cling to it consistently, or should it vary its policies toward other countries as circumstances change?" In these books, history is clearly not a list of agreed-upon facts or a sermon on politics but a babble of voices and a welter of events which must be ordered by the historian.

In matters of pedagogy, as in matters of politics, there are not two sharply differentiated categories of books; rather, there is a spec-

---

1. God from a machine. A reference to early plays in which a god, lowered to the stage by mechanical means, solved the drama's problems; thus, an artificial solution to a difficulty.

2. Radical black leaders of the 1960s.

trum. Politically, the books run from moderate left to moderate right; pedagogically, they run from the traditional history sermons, through a middle ground of narrative texts with inquiry-style questions and of inquiry texts with long stretches of narrative, to the most rigorous of case-study books. What is common to the current texts—and makes all of them different from those of the fifties—is their engagement with the social sciences. In eighth-grade histories, the "concepts" of social science make fleeting appearances. But these "concepts" are the very foundation stones of various elementary-school social-studies series. The 1970 Harcourt Brace Jovanovich[3] series, for example, boasts in its preface of "a horizontal base or ordering of conceptual schemes" to match its "vertical arm of behavioral themes." What this means is not entirely clear, but the books do proceed from easy questions to hard ones, such as —in the sixth-grade book—"How was interaction between merchants and citizens different in the Athenian and Spartan social systems?" Virtually all the American-history texts for older children include discussions of "role," "status," and "culture." Some of them stage debates between eminent social scientists in roped-off sections of the text; some include essays on economics or sociology; some contain pictures and short biographies of social scientists of both sexes and of diverse races. Many books seem to accord social scientists a higher status than American Presidents.

Quite as striking as these political and pedagogical alterations is the change in the physical appearance of the texts. The schoolbooks of the fifties showed some effort in the matter of design: they had maps, charts, cartoons, photographs, and an occasional four-color picture to break up the columns of print. But beside the current texts they look as naïve as Soviet fashion magazines. The print in the fifties books is heavy and far too black, the colors muddy. The photographs are conventional news shots—portraits of Presidents in three-quarters profile, posed "action" shots of soldiers. The other illustrations tend to be Socialist-realist-style[4] drawings (there are a lot of hefty farmers with hoes in the Colonial-period chapters) or incredibly vulgar made-for-children paintings of patriotic events. One painting shows Columbus standing in full court dress on a beach in the New World from a perspective that could have belonged only to the Arawaks.[5] By contrast, the current texts are paragons of sophisticated modern design. They look not like *People* or *Family Circle* but, rather, like *Architectural Digest* or *Vogue*. * * * The amount of space given to illustrations is far greater than

3. Major textbook publisher.
4. Socialist realism, which originated in the Soviet Union, is a style of art in which the communal labor of farmers and industrial workers is glorified in works of poster-like crudity.
5. American Indians, then inhabiting the Caribbean area.

it was in the fifties; in fact, in certain "slow-learner" books the pictures far outweigh the text in importance. However, the illustrations have a much greater historical value. Instead of made-up paintings or anachronistic sketches, there are cartoons, photographs, and paintings drawn from the periods being treated. The chapters on the Colonial period will show, for instance, a ship's carved prow, a Revere bowl, a Copley[6] painting—a whole gallery of Early Americana. The nineteenth century is illustrated with nineteenth-century cartoons and photographs—and the photographs are all of high artistic quality. As for the twentieth-century chapters, they are adorned with the contents of a modern-art museum.

The use of all this art and high-quality design contains some irony. The nineteenth-century photographs of child laborers or urban slum apartments are so beautiful that they transcend their subjects. To look at them, or at the Victor Gatto painting of the Triangle shirtwaist-factory fire, is to see not misery or ugliness but an art object. In the modern chapters, the contrast between style and content is just as great: the color photographs of junk yards or polluted rivers look as enticing as *Gourmet*'s photographs of food. The book that is perhaps the most stark in its description of modern problems illustrates the horrors of nuclear testing with a pretty Ben Shahn picture of the Bikini explosion,[7] and the potential for global ecological disaster with a color photograph of the planet swirling its mantle of white clouds. Whereas in the nineteen-fifties the texts were childish in the sense that they were naïve and clumsy, they are now childish in the sense that they are polymorphous-perverse. American history is not dull any longer; it is a sensuous experience.

The surprise that adults feel in seeing the changes in history texts must come from the lingering hope that there is, somewhere out there, an objective truth. The hope is, of course, foolish. All of us children of the twentieth century know, or should know, that there are no absolutes in human affairs, and thus there can be no such thing as perfect objectivity. We know that each historian in some degree creates the world anew and that all history is in some degree contemporary history. But beyond this knowledge there is still a hope for some reliable authority, for some fixed stars in the universe. We may know that journalists cannot be wholly unbiased and that "balance" is an imaginary point between two extremes, and yet

6. The reference is to John Singleton Copley (1738–1815), greatest of the American old masters; he specialized in portraits and historical paintings.
7. The Bikini atoll, part of the Marshall Islands in the Pacific, was the site of American nuclear-bomb testing from 1946 to 1958. Ben Shahn (1898–1969) was an American painter and graphic artist with strong social and political concerns.

we hope that Walter Cronkite will tell us the truth of things. In the same way, we hope that our history will not change—that we learned the truth of things as children. The texts, with their impersonal voices, encourage this hope, and therefore it is particularly disturbing to see how they change, and how fast.

Slippery history! Not every generation but every few years the content of American-history books for children changes appreciably. Schoolbooks are not, like trade books,[8] written and left to their fate. To stay in step with the cycles of "adoption"[9] in school districts across the country, the publishers revise most of their old texts or substitute new ones every three or four years. In the process of revision, they not only bring history up to date but make changes —often substantial changes—in the body of the work. History books for children are thus more contemporary than any other form of history. How should it be otherwise? Should students read histories written ten, fifteen, thirty years ago? In theory, the system is reasonable—except that each generation of children reads only one generation of schoolbooks. The transient history is those children's history forever—their particular version of America.

1979

---

8. Books written for a general audience, as opposed to textbooks.

9. Choice of required textbooks.

QUESTIONS

1. What sorts of difference does FitzGerald find between the history textbooks of the fifties and those of today? In what ways— according to what she states or implies—have they been improved? Does she see any changes for the worse?

2. By "rewriting" does FitzGerald mean changing the facts of history? What is the relationship between the facts of history and history textbooks? Does Thomas S. Kuhn's "The Route to Normal Science" (pp. 605–613) throw any light on this question?

3. Why does FitzGerald give the story about George McJunkin (p. 577)? Was his discovery important?

4. On p. 579 FitzGerald says that in the new texts "the word 'progress' has been replaced by the word 'change.'" What is the difference between these two words? What does the replacement imply?

5. Is FitzGerald showing that the newer textbooks give a truer account of American history?

Science

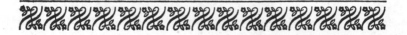

STEPHEN JAY GOULD

Of Bamboos, Cicadas, and the Economy of Adam Smith[1]

Nature usually manages to outdo even the most fanciful of human legends. Sleeping Beauty waited a hundred years for her prince. Bettelheim argues that her pricked finger represents the first bleeding of menstruation, her long sleep the lethargy of adolescence awaiting the onset of full maturity. Since the original Sleeping Beauty was inseminated by a king, rather than merely kissed by a prince, we may interpret her awakening as the beginning of sexual fulfillment (see B. Bettelheim, *The Uses of Enchantment*, A. Knopf, 1976, pp. 225–36).

A bamboo bearing the formidable name *Phyllostachys bambusoides* flowered in China during the year 999. Since then, with unerring regularity, it has continued to flower and set seed roughly every 120 years. *P. bambusoides* follows this cycle wherever it lives. In the late 1960s, Japanese stocks (themselves transplanted from China centuries before) set seed simultaneously in Japan, England, Alabama, and Russia. The analogy to Sleeping Beauty is not far-fetched, for sexual reproduction follows more than a century of celibacy in these bamboos. But *P. bambusoides* departs from the Brothers Grimm in two important ways. The plants are not inactive during their 120 year vigil—for they are grasses, and they propagate asexually by producing new shoots from underground rhizomes. Also, they do not live happily ever after, for they die after setting seed—a long wait for a short end.

Ecologist Daniel H. Janzen of the University of Pennsylvania recounts the curious tale of *Phyllostachys* in a recent article, "Why

1. Eighteenth-century Scottish economist, proponent of the doctrine of laissez faire, which held that government should not intervene in matters of commerce.

bamboos wait so long to flower" (*Annual Review of Ecology and Systematics*, 1976). Most species of bamboo have shorter periods of vegetative growth between flowerings, but synchroneity of seeding is the rule, and very few species wait fewer than 15 years before flowering (some may wait for more than 150 years, but historical records are too sparse to permit firm conclusions).

The flowering of any species must be set by an internal, genetic clock, not imposed from without by some environmental clue. The unerring regularity of repetition supplies our best evidence for this assertion, for we do not know any environmental factor that cycles so predictably to yield the variety of clocks followed by more than a hundred species. Secondly, as mentioned above, plants of the same species flower simultaneously, even when transplanted half a world away from their native habitat. Finally, plants of the same species flower together, even if they have grown in very different environments. Janzen recounts the tale of a Burmese bamboo only half a foot high that had been burned down repeatedly by jungle fires, but flowered at the same time as its unhurt companions standing 40 feet tall.

How can a bamboo count the passing years? Janzen argues that it cannot be measuring stored food reserves because starved dwarfs flower at the same time as healthy giants. He speculates that the calendar "must be the annual or daily accumulation or degradation of a temperature-insensitive photosensitive chemical." He finds no basis for guessing whether the cycles of light are diurnal (day-night) or yearly (seasonal). As circumstantial evidence for implicating light as a clock, Janzen points out that no accurately cycling bamboo grows within 5 degrees of latitude from the equator—for variations in both days and seasons are minimized within this zone.

The flowering of bamboo recalls a tale of striking periodicity better known to most of us—the periodical cicada, or 17-year "locust." (Cicadas are not locusts at all, but large-bodied members of the order Homoptera, a group of predominantly small insects including aphids and their relatives: locusts, along with crickets and grasshoppers, form the order Orthoptera.) The story of periodical cicadas is even more amazing than most people realize: for 17 years, the nymphs of periodical cicadas live underground, sucking juices from the roots of forest trees all over the eastern half of the United States (except for our southern states, where a very similar or identical group of species emerges every 13 years). Then, within just a few weeks, millions of mature nymphs emerge from the ground, become adults, mate, lay their eggs, and die. (The best accounts, from an evolutionary standpoint, will be found in a series of articles by M. Lloyd and H. S. Dybas, published in the journals *Evolution* in 1966 and *Ecological Monographs* in 1974). Most remarkable is the fact that not one, but three separate species of periodical cicadas follow precisely the same schedule, emerging together in strict synchrony. Different areas may be out of phase—populations around Chicago do not emerge in the same year as forms from New England. But the 17-year cycle (13 years in the south) is invariant for each "brood"—the three species always emerge together in the same place. Janzen recognizes that cicadas and bamboo, despite their biological and geographic distance, represent the same evolutionary problem. Recent studies, he writes, "reveal no conspicuous qualitative difference between these insects and bamboo except perhaps in the way they count years."

As evolutionists, we seek answers to the question "why." Why, in particular, should such striking synchroneity evolve, and why should the period between episodes of sexual reproduction be so long? As I have argued elsewhere, the theory of natural selection receives its strongest support when we devise satisfactory explanations for phenomena that strike us intuitively as bizarre or senseless.

In this case, we are confronted with a problem beyond the apparent peculiarity of such wastefulness (for very few seeds can sprout upon such saturated ground). The synchroneity of flowering or emergence seems to reflect an ordering and harmony operating upon the species as a whole, not upon its individual members. Yet Darwinian theory advocates no higher principle beyond individuals pursuing their own self-interest—i.e. the representation of their own genes in future generations. We must ask what advantage the synchroneity of sex provides for an individual cicada or bamboo plant.

The problem is similar to that faced by Adam Smith when he advocated an unbridled policy of laissez faire as the surest path to a harmonious economy. The ideal economy, Smith argued, might appear orderly and well balanced, but it would emerge "naturally" from the interplay of individuals who follow no path beyond the pursuit of their own best interests. The apparent direction toward a higher harmony, Smith argues in his famous metaphor, only reflects the operation of an "invisible hand."

As every individual . . . by directing (his) industry in such a manner as its produce may be of greatest value, intends only his own gain, he is in this as in many other cases led by an invisible hand to promote an end which was no part of his intention. . . . By pursuing his own interest he frequently promotes that of society more effectively than when he really intends to promote it.

Since Darwin grafted Adam Smith upon nature to establish his theory of natural selection, we must seek an explanation for apparent harmony in the advantage that it confers upon individuals. What, then, does an individual cicada or bamboo gain by indulging in sex so rarely and at the same time as all its compatriots?

In order to appreciate the most likely explanation, we must recognize that human biology often provides a poor model for the struggles of other organisms. Humans are slowly growing animals. We invest a great deal of energy in raising very few, late maturing offspring. Our populations are not controlled by the wholesale death of nearly all juvenile members. Yet many organisms follow a different strategy in the "struggle for existence": they produce vast numbers of seeds or eggs, hoping (so to speak) that a few will survive the rigors of early life. These organisms are often controlled by their predators, and their evolutionary defense must be a strategy that minimizes the chance of being eaten. Cicadas and bamboo seeds seem to be particularly tasty to a wide variety of organisms.

Natural history, to a large extent, is a tale of different adaptations to avoid predation. Some individuals hide, others taste bad, others grow spines or thick shells, still others evolve to look conspicuously like a noxious relative; the list is nearly endless, a stunning tribute to nature's variety. Bamboo seeds and cicadas follow an uncommon strategy: they are eminently and conspicuously available, but so rarely and in such great numbers that predators cannot possibly consume the entire bounty. Among evolutionary biologists, this defense goes by the name of "predator satiation."

An effective strategy of predator satiation involves two adaptations. First, the synchrony of emergence or reproduction must be very precise, thus assuring that the market is truly flooded, and only for a short time. Secondly, this flooding cannot occur very often, lest predators simply adjust their own life cycle to predictable times of superfluity. If bamboos flowered every year, seed eaters would track the cycle and present their own abundant young with the annual bounty. But if the period between episodes of flowering far exceeds the life-span of any predator, then the cycle cannot be tracked (except by one peculiar primate that records its own history). The advantage of synchroneity to individual bamboos and cicadas is clear enough: anyone out of step is quickly gobbled up (cicada "stragglers" do occasionally emerge in off years, but they never gain a foothold).

The hypothesis of predator satiation, though unproven, meets the primary criterion of a successful explanation: it coordinates a suite of observations that would otherwise remain unconnected and, in this case, downright peculiar. We know, for example, that bamboo seeds are relished by a wide variety of animals, including many vertebrates with long life spans; the rarity of flowering cycles shorter than 15 or 20 years makes sense in this context. We also know that the synchronous setting of seed can inundate an affected area. Janzen records a mat of seeds 6 inches deep below the parental plant in one case. Two species of Malagasy bamboos produced 50 kilograms of seed per hectare over a large area of 100,000 hectares during a mass flowering.

The synchrony of three species among cicadas is particularly impressive—especially since years of emergence vary from place to place, while all three species invariably emerge together in any one area. But I am most impressed by the timing of the cycles themselves. Why do we have 13 and 17 year cicadas, but no cycles of 12, 14, 15, 16, or 18? Thirteen and 17 share a common property. They are large enough to exceed the life cycle of any predator, but they are also prime numbers (divisible by no integer smaller than themselves). Many potential predators have 2–5-year life cycles. Such cycles are not set by the availability of periodical cicadas (for they peak too often in years of nonemergence), but cicadas might be eagerly harvested when the cycles coincide. Consider a predator with a cycle of five years: if cicadas emerged every 15 years, each bloom would be hit by the predator. By cycling at a large prime number, cicadas minimize the number of coincidences (every 5 × 17, or 85 years, in this case). Thirteen- and 17-year cycles cannot be tracked by any smaller number.

Existence is, as Darwin stated, a struggle for most creatures. The weapons of survival need not be claws and teeth; patterns of reproduction may serve as well. Occasional superfluity is one pathway to success. It is sometimes advantageous to put all your eggs in one basket—but be sure to make enough of them, and don't do it too often.

1977

STEPHEN JAY GOULD

Our Allotted Lifetimes

Meeting with Henry Ford in E. L. Doctorow's *Ragtime*, J. P. Morgan praises the assembly line as a faithful translation of nature's wisdom:

> Has it occurred to you that your assembly line is not merely a stroke of industrial genius but a projection of organic truth? After all, the interchangeability of parts is a rule of nature. . . . All mammals reproduce in the same way and share the same designs of self-nourishment, with digestive and circulatory systems that are recognizably the same, and they enjoy the same senses. . . . Shared design is what allows taxonomists to classify mammals as mammals.

An imperious tycoon should not be met with equivocation; nonetheless, I can only reply "yes, and no" to Morgan's pronouncement.

Morgan was wrong if he thought that large mammals are geometric replicas of small ones. Elephants have relatively smaller brains and thicker legs than mice, and these differences record a general rule of mammalian design, not the idiosyncracies of particular animals.

Morgan was right in arguing that large animals are essentially similar to small members of their group. The similarity, however, does not lie in a constant shape. The basic laws of geometry dictate that animals must change their shape in order to perform the same function at different sizes. I remind readers of the classical example, first discussed by Galileo in 1638: the strength of an animal's leg is a function of its cross-sectional area (length × length); the weight that the leg must support varies as the animal's volume (length × length × length). If a mammal did not alter the relative thickness of its legs as it got larger, it would soon collapse since body weight would increase much faster than the supporting strength of limbs. Instead, large mammals have relatively thicker leg bones than small mammals. To remain the same in function, animals must change their form.

The study of these changes in form is called "scaling theory." Scaling theory has uncovered a remarkable regularity of changing shape over the 25-millionfold range of mammalian weight from shrew to blue whale. If we plot brain weight versus body weight for all mammals on the so-called mouse-to-elephant (or shrew-to-whale) curve, very few species deviate far from a single line expressing the general rule: brain weight increases only two-thirds as fast as body weight as we move from small to large mammals. (We share with bottle-nosed dolphins the honor of greatest deviance from the curve.)

We can often predict these regularities from the physical behavior of objects. The heart, for example, is a pump. Since all mammalian hearts are similar in function, small hearts will pump considerably faster than large ones (imagine how much faster you could work a finger-sized toy bellows than the giant model that fuels a blacksmith's large forge). On the mouse-to-elephant curve for mammals, the length of a heartbeat increases between one-fourth and one-third as fast as body weight as we move from small to large mammals. The generality of this conclusion has just been affirmed in an interesting study by J. E. Carrel and R. D. Heathcote on the scaling of heart rate in spiders. They used a cool laser beam to illuminate the hearts of resting spiders and drew a crab spider-to-tarantula curve for eighteen species spanning nearly a thousandfold range of body weight. Again, scaling is very regular with heart rate increasing four-tenths as fast as body weight (or .409 times as fast, to be exact).

We may extend this conclusion for hearts to a very general statement about the pace of life in small versus large animals. Small animals tick through life far more rapidly than large ones—their hearts work more quickly, they breathe more frequently, their pulse beats much faster. Most importantly, metabolic rate, the so-called fire of life, scales only three-fourths as fast as body weight in mammals. Large mammals generate much less heat per unit of body weight to keep themselves going. Tiny shrews move frenetically, eating nearly all their waking lives to keep their metabolic fire burning at its maximal rate among mammals; blue whales glide majestically, their hearts beating the slowest rhythm among active, warmblooded creatures.

If we consider the scaling of lifetime among mammals, an intriguing synthesis of these disparate data seems to suggest itself. We have all had enough experience with mammalian pets of various sizes to understand that small mammals tend to live for a shorter time than large ones. In fact, the scaling of mammalian lifetime follows a regular curve at about the same rate as heartbeat and breath time—between one-fourth and one-third as fast as body weight as we move from small to large animals. (Again, *Homo sapiens* emerges as a very peculiar animal. We live far longer than a mammal of our body size should. I have argued elsewhere that humans evolved by a process called "neoteny"—the retention of shapes and growth rates that characterize juvenile stages of our primate ancestors. I also believe that neoteny is responsible for our elevated longevity. Compared with other mammals, all stages of human life—from juvenile features to adulthood—arise "too late." We are born as helpless embryos after a long gestation; we mature late after an extended childhood; we die, if fortune be kind, at ages otherwise reached only by the very largest warmblooded creatures.)

Usually, we pity the pet mouse or gerbil that lived its full span of a year or two at most. How brief its life, while we endure for the better part of a century. As the main theme of this column, I want to argue that such pity is misplaced (our personal grief, of course, is quite another matter; with this, science does not deal). J. P. Morgan of *Ragtime* was right—small and large mammals are essentially similar. Their lifetimes are scaled to their life's pace, and all endure for approximately the same amount of biological time. Small mammals tick fast, burn rapidly, and live for a short time; large ones live long at a stately pace. Measured by their own internal clocks, mammals of different sizes tend to live for the same amount of time.

Yet we are prevented from grasping this important and comforting concept by a deeply ingrained habit of Western thought. We are trained from earliest memory to regard absolute Newtonian time as the single valid measuring stick in a rational and objective world. We impose our kitchen clock, ticking equably, upon all things. We marvel at the quickness of a mouse, express boredom at the torpor of a hippopotamus. Yet each is living at the appropriate pace of its own biological clock.

I do not wish to deny the importance of absolute, astronomical time to organisms. Animals must measure it to lead successful lives. Deer must know when to regrow their antlers, birds when to migrate. Animals track the day–night cycle with their circadian rhythms; jet lag is the price we pay for moving much faster than nature intended. Bamboos can somehow count 120 years before flowering again.

But absolute time is not the appropriate measuring stick for all biological phenomena. Consider the song of the humpback whale. These magnificent animals sing with such volume that their sounds travel through water for thousands of miles, perhaps even around the world, as their leading student Roger S. Payne has suggested. E. O. Wilson has described the awesome effect of these vocalizations: "The notes are eerie yet beautiful to the human ear. Deep basso groans and almost inaudibly high soprano squeaks alternate with repetitive squeals that suddenly rise or fall in pitch." We do not know the function of these songs. Perhaps they enable whales to find each other and to stay together during their annual trans-oceanic migrations.

Each whale has its own characteristic song; the highly complex patterns are repeated over and over again with great faithfulness. No scientific fact that I have learned in the last decade struck me with more force than Payne's report that the length of some songs may extend for more than half an hour. I have never been able to memorize the five-minute first Kyrie of the B-minor Mass[1] (and not for want of trying); how could a whale sing for thirty minutes and then repeat itself accurately? Of what possible use is a thirty-minute repeat cycle—far too long for a human to recognize: we would never grasp it as a single song (without Payne's recording machinery and much study after the fact). But then I remembered the whale's metabolic rate, the enormously slow pace of its life compared with ours. What do we know about a whale's perception of thirty minutes? A humpback may scale the world to its own metabolic rate: its half-hour song may be our minute waltz.[2] From any point of view, the song is spectacular; it is the most elaborate single display so far discovered in any animal. I merely urge the whale's point of view as an appropriate perspective.

We can provide some numerical precision to support the claim that all mammals, on average, live for the same amount of biologi-

---

1. By Johann Sebastian Bach; the movement is woven together from many independent musical lines.

2. The reference is to the "Minute Waltz," by Frédéric Chopin, which is not only brief but fast-moving.

cal time. In a method developed by W. R. Stahl, B. Gunther, and E. Guerra in the late 1950s and early 1960s, we search the mouse-to-elephant equations for biological properties that scale at the same rate against body weight. For example, Gunther and Guerra give the following equations for mammalian breath time and heartbeat time versus body weight.

$$\text{breath time} = .0000470 \text{ body}^{0.28}$$
$$\text{heartbeat time} = .0000119 \text{ body}^{0.28}$$

(Nonmathematical readers need not be overwhelmed by the formalism. The equations simply mean that both breath time and heartbeat time increase about .28 times as fast as body weight as we move from small to large mammals.) If we divide the two equations, body weight cancels out because it is raised to the same power.

$$\frac{\text{breath time}}{\text{heartbeat time}} = \frac{.0000470 \ \text{body}^{0.28}}{.0000119 \ \text{body}^{0.28}} = 4.0$$

This says that the ratio of breath time to heartbeat time is 4.0 in mammals of any body size. In other words, all mammals, whatever their size, breathe once for each four heartbeats. Small animals breathe and beat their hearts faster than large animals, but both breath and heart slow up at the same relative rate as mammals get larger.

Lifetime also scales at the same rate to body weight (.28 times as fast as we move from small to large mammals). This means that the ratio of both breath time and heartbeat time to lifetime is also constant over the whole range of mammalian size. When we perform an exercise similar to that above, we find that all mammals, regardless of their size, tend to breathe about 200 million times during their lives (their hearts, therefore, beat about 800 million times). Small mammals breathe fast, but live for a short time. Measured by the sensible internal clocks of their own hearts or the rhythm of their own breathing, all mammals live about the same time. (Astute readers, having counted their breaths, may have calculated that they should have died long ago. But *Homo sapiens* is a markedly deviant mammal in more ways than braininess alone. We live about three times as long as mammals of our body size "should," but we breathe at the "right" rate and thus live to breathe about three times as much as an average mammal of our body size.)

The mayfly lives but a day as an adult. It may, for all I know, experience that day as we live a lifetime. Yet all is not relative in our world, and such a short glimpse of it must invite distortion in interpreting events ticking on longer scales. In a brilliant metaphor, the pre-Darwinian evolutionist Robert Chambers spoke of a mayfly watching the metamorphosis of a tadpole into a frog (from *Vestiges of the Natural History of Creation*, 1844):

Suppose that an ephemeron [a mayfly], hovering over a pool for its one April day of life, were capable of observing the fry of the frog in the waters below. In its aged afternoon, having seen no change upon them for such a long time, it would be little qualified to conceive that the external branchiae [gills] of these creatures were to decay, and be replaced by internal lungs, that feet were to be developed, the tail erased, and the animal then to become a denizen of the land.

Human consciousness arose but a minute before midnight on the geologic clock. Yet we mayflies, ignorant perhaps of the messages buried in earth's long history, try to bend an ancient world to our purposes. Let us hope that we are still in the morning of our April day.

1977

ARTHUR KOESTLER

Gravity and the Holy Ghost

"If I have been able to see farther than others," said Newton, "it was because I stood on the shoulders of giants." One of the giants was Johannes Kepler (1571–1630) whose three laws of planetary motion provided the foundation on which the Newtonian universe was built. They were the first "natural laws" in the modern sense: precise, verifiable statements expressed in mathematical terms; at the same time, they represent the first attempt at a synthesis of astronomy and physics which, during the preceding two thousand years, had developed on separate lines.

Astronomy before Kepler had been a purely descriptive geometry of the skies. The motion of stars and planets had been represented by the device of epicycles and eccentrics—an imaginary clockwork of circles turning on circles turning on circles. Copernicus, for instance, had used forty-eight wheels to represent the motion of the five known planets around the sun. These wheels were purely fictitious, and meant as such—they enabled astronomers to make more or less precise predictions, but, above all, they satisfied the dogma that all heavenly motion must be uniform and in perfect circles. Though the planets moved neither uniformly nor in perfect circles, the imaginary cogwheels did, and thereby "saved the appearances."

Kepler's discoveries put an end to this state of affairs. He reconciled astronomy with physics, and substituted for the fictitious clockwork a universe of material bodies not unlike the earth, freely floating and turning in space, moved by forces acting on them. His most important book bears the provocative title: *A New Astronomy Based on Causation, or Physics of the Sky* (1609). It contains the first and second of Kepler's three laws. The first says that the planets move around the sun not in circles but in elliptic orbits; the second says that a planet moves in its orbit not at uniform speed but at a speed that varies according to its position, and is defined by a simple and beautiful law: the line connecting planet and sun sweeps over equal areas in equal times. The third law establishes an equally elegant mathematical correlation between the length of a planet's year and its mean distance from the sun.

Kepler did not start his career as an astronomer, but as a student of theology (at the Lutheran University of Thuebingen); yet already as a student he was attracted by the Copernican idea of a sun-centered universe. Now Canon Copernicus's book, *On the Revolutions of the Heavenly Spheres,* had been published in the year of his death, 1543; that is, fifty years before Kepler first heard of him; and during that half century it had attracted very little attention. One of the reasons was its supreme unreadability, which made it into an all-time worst-seller: its first edition of a thousand copies was never sold out. Kepler was the first Continental astronomer to embrace the Copernican theory. His *Mysterium Cosmographicum,* published in 1597 (fifty-four years after Copernicus's death) started the great controversy—Galileo entered the scene fifteen years later.

The reason why the idea of a sun-centered universe appealed to Kepler was repeatedly stated by himself: "I often defended the opinions of Copernicus in the disputations of the candidates and I composed a careful disputation on the first motion which consists in the rotation of the earth; then I was adding to this the motion of the earth around the sun *for physical or, if you prefer, metaphysical reasons.*" I have emphasized the last words because they contain the leitmotif of Kepler's quest, and because he used the same expression in various passages in his works. Now what were those "physical or, if you prefer, metaphysical reasons" which made Kepler prefer to put the sun into the center of the universe instead of the earth?

My ceaseless search concerned primarily three problems, namely, the number, size, and motion of the planets—why they are just as they are and not otherwise arranged. I was encouraged in my daring inquiry by that beautiful analogy between the stationary objects, namely, the sun, the fixed stars, and the space between them, with God the Father, the Son, and the Holy Ghost. I shall pursue this analogy in my future cosmographical work.

Twenty-five years later, when he was over fifty, Kepler repeated his credo: "It is by no means permissible to treat this analogy as an empty comparison; it must be considered by its Platonic form and archetypal quality as one of the primary causes."

He believed in this to the end of his life. Yet gradually the analogy underwent a significant change:

The sun in the middle of the *moving* stars, himself at rest and yet the source of motion, carries the image of God the Father and Creator. He distributes his motive force through a medium which contains the moving bodies, even as the Father creates through the Holy Ghost.

Thus the "moving bodies"—that is, the planets—are now brought into the analogy. The Holy Ghost no longer merely fills the space between the motionless sun and the motionless fixed stars. It has become an active force, a *vis motrix*, which *drives* the planets. Nobody before Kepler had postulated, or even suspected, the existence of a physical force acting between the sun and the planets. Astronomy was not concerned with physical forces, nor with the causes of the heavenly motions, merely with their description. The passages which I have just quoted are the first intimation of the forthcoming marriage between physics and astronomy—the act of betrothal, as it were. By looking at the sky, not through the eyes of the geometrician only, but of the physicist concerned with natural causes, he hit upon a question which nobody had asked before. The question was: "Why do the planets closer to the sun move faster than those which are far away? What is the mathematical relation between a planet's distance from the sun and the length of its year?"

These questions could only occur to one who had conceived the revolutionary hypothesis that the motion of the planet—and therefore its velocity and the duration of its year—was governed by a physical force emanating from the sun. Every astronomer knew, of course, that the greater their distance from the sun the slower the planets moved. But this phenomenon was taken for granted, just as it was taken for granted that boys will be boys and girls will be girls, as an irreducible fact of creation. Nobody asked the cause of it because physical causes were not assumed to enter into the motion of heavenly bodies. The greatness of the philosophers of the scientific revolution consisted not so much in finding the right answers but in asking the right questions; in seeing a problem where nobody saw one before; in substituting a "why" for a "how."

Kepler's answer to the question why the outer planets move slower than the inner ones, and how the speed of their motion is related to their distance from the sun, was as follows:

There exists only one moving soul in the center of all the orbits; that is the sun which drives the planets the more vigorously the closer the planet is, but whose force is quasi-exhausted when acting on the outer planets because of the long distance and the weakening of the force which it entails.

Later on he commented: "If we substitute for the word 'soul' the word 'force,' then we get just the principle which underlies my 'Physics of the Skies.' As I reflected that this cause of motion *diminishes in proportion to distance* just as the light of the sun diminishes in proportion to distance from the sun, I came to the conclusion that this force must be substantial—'substantial' not in the literal sense but . . . in the same manner as we say that light is something substantial, meaning by this an unsubstantial entity emanating from a substantial body."

We notice that Kepler's answer came *before* the question—that it was the answer that begot the question. The answer, the starting point, was the analogy between God the Father and the sun—the former acting through the Holy Ghost, the latter through a physical force. The planets must obey the law of the sun—the law of God —the mathematical law of nature; and the Holy Ghost's action through empty space diminishes, as the light emanating from the sun does, with distance. The degenerate, purely descriptive astronomy which originated in the period of the Greek decline, and continued through the Dark and Middle Ages until Kepler, did not ask for meaning and causes. But Kepler was convinced that physical causes operate between heavenly, just as between earthly, bodies, and more specifically that the sun exerts a physical force on the planets. It was this conviction which enabled him to formulate his laws. Physics became the auxiliary matrix which secured his escape from the blocked situation into which astronomy had maneuvered itself.

The blockage—to cut a very long story short—was due to the fact that Tycho de Brahe[1] had improved the instruments and methods of star-gazing, and produced observational data of a hitherto unequaled abundance and precision; and the new data did not fit into the traditional schemes. Kepler, who served his apprenticeship under Tycho, was given the task of working out the orbit of Mars. He spent six years on the task and covered nine thousand folio-sheets with calculations in his small handwriting without getting anywhere. When at last he believed he had succeeded he found to his dismay that certain observed positions of Mars differed from those which his theory demanded by magnitudes up to eight minutes arc. Eight minutes arc is approximately one-quarter of the apparent diameter of the moon.

This was a catastrophe. Ptolemy, and even Copernicus, could

1. Danish astronomer (1546–1601).

afford to neglect a difference of eight minutes, because their observations were accurate only within a margin of ten minutes, anyway.
"But," Kepler wrote in the *New Astronomy*, "but for us, who by
divine kindness were given an accurate observer such as Tycho
Brahe, for us it is fitting that we should acknowledge this divine gift
and put it to use. . . . Henceforth I shall lead the way toward that
goal according to my ideas. For if I had believed that we could
ignore these eight minutes, I would have patched up my hypothesis
accordingly. But since it was not permissible to ignore them, those
eight minutes point the road to a complete reformation of astronomy. . . ."

Thus a theory, built on years of labor and torment, was instantly
thrown away because of a discord of eight miserable minutes arc.
Instead of cursing those eight minutes as a stumbling block, he
transformed them into the cornerstone of a new science. For those
eight minutes arc had at last made him realize that the field of
astronomy in its traditional framework was well and truly blocked.

One of the recurrent frustrations and tragedies in the history of
thought is caused by the uncertainty whether it is possible to solve a
given problem by traditional methods previously applied to problems which seem to be of the same nature. Who can say how many
lives were wasted and good minds destroyed in futile attempts to
square the circle, or to construct a *perpetuum mobile*?[2] The proof
that these problems are *insoluble* was in each case an original discovery in itself (such as Maxwell's second law of thermodynamics);[3]
and such proofs could only be found by looking at the problem from
a point of view outside its traditional matrix. On the other hand,
the mere knowledge that a problem is soluble means that half the
game is already won.

The episode of the eight minutes arc had convinced Kepler that
his problem—the orbit of Mars—was insoluble so long as he felt
bound by the traditional rules of sky-geometry. Implied in those
rules was the dogma of "uniform motion in perfect circles." *Uniform* motion he had already discarded before the crisis; now he felt
that the even more sacred one of *circular* motion must also go. The
impossibility of constructing a circular orbit which would satisfy all
existing observations suggested to him that the circle must be
replaced by some other curve.

The conclusion is quite simply that the planet's path is not a circle—it

2. A hypothetical machine which, once
set in motion, would continue in motion
forever unless stopped by some external
force or by its own the wearing out.
3. The second law of thermodynamics,
put forward not by James Clerk Maxwell,
but by Rudolf Julius Emmanuel Clausius
(1822–1888), provides an explanation of
why a perpetual-motion machine cannot
exist.

curves inward on both sides and outward again at opposite ends. Such a curve is called an oval. The orbit is not a circle but an oval figure.

This oval orbit was a wild, frightening new departure for him. To be fed up with cycles and epicycles, to mock the slavish imitators of Aristotle was one thing; to assign an entirely new, lopsided, implausible path for the heavenly bodies was quite another. Why indeed an oval? There is something in the perfect symmetry of spheres and circles which has a deep, reassuring appeal to the unconscious mind —otherwise it could not have survived two millennia. The oval lacks that archetypal appeal. It has an arbitrary, distorted form. It destroyed the dream of the "harmony of the spheres," which lay at the origin of the whole quest. At times he felt like a criminal, or worse: a fool. All he had to say in his own defense was: "I have cleared the Augean stables of astronomy of cycles and spirals, and left behind me only a single cartful of dung."

That cartful of dung—nonuniform motion in noncircular orbits —could only be justified and explained by arguments derived not from geometry, but from physics. A phrase kept humming in his ear like a catchy tune, and crops up in his writings over and again: there is a force in the sun which moves the planets, there is a force in the sun. . . . And since there is a force in the sun, there must exist some simple relationship between the planet's distance from the sun, and its speed. A light shines the brighter the nearer one is to its source, and the same must apply to the force of the sun: the closer the planet to it, the quicker it will move. This had been his instinctive conviction; but now he thought that he had found the proof of it. "Ye physicists, prick your ears, for now we are going to invade your territory." The next six chapters in the *Astronomia Nova* are a report on that invasion into celestial physics, which had been out of bounds for astronomy since Plato. He had found the second matrix which would unblock his problem.

That excursion was something of a comedy of errors—which nevertheless ended with finding the truth. Since he had no notion of the principle of inertia, which makes a planet persist in its tangential motion under its own momentum, and had only a vague intuition of gravity, he had to invent a force which, emanating from the sun, sweeps the planet round its path like a broom. In the second place, to account for the eccentricity of the orbits he had to postulate that the planets were "huge round magnets" whose poles pointed always in the same direction so that they would alternately be drawn closer to and be repelled by the sun. But although today the whole thing seems cockeyed, his intuition that there are *two antagonistic forces* acting on the planets, guided him in the right direction. A single force, as previously assumed—the divine Prime Mover and its allied hierarchy of angels—would never produce elliptic orbits and periodic changes of speed. These could only be the result of some dynamic tug of war going on in the sky—as indeed there is. The concept of two antagonistic forces provided rules for a new game in which elliptic orbits and velocities depending on solar distance has their legitimate place.

He made many mistakes during that wild flight of thought; but "as if by miracle"—as he himself remarked—the mistakes canceled out. It looks as if at times his conscious critical faculties had been anesthetized by the creative impulse, by the impatience to get to grips with the physical forces in the solar system. The problem of the planetary orbits had been hopelessly bogged down in its purely geometrical frame of reference, and when he realized that he could not get it unstuck he tore it out of that frame and removed it into the field of physics. That there were inconsistencies and impurities in his method did not matter to him in the heat of the moment, hoping that somehow they would right themselves later on—as they did. This inspired cheating—or, rather, borrowing on credit—is a characteristic and recurrent feature in the history of science. The latest example is subatomic physics, which may be said to live on credit—in the pious hope that one day its inner contradictions and paradoxes will somehow resolve themselves.

Kepler's determination of the orbit of Mars became the unifying link between the two formerly separate realms of physics and astronomy. His was the first serious attempt at explaining the mechanism of the solar system in terms of physical forces; and once the example was set, physics and cosmology could never again be divorced.

1964

QUESTIONS

1. What effect is produced by the essay's title, "Gravity and the Holy Ghost"? What relationship between the two terms in the title does the essay explore? Which of the two terms is more familiar to you; which do you think you know more about? Write an account of your understanding of them.
2. Why, according to Koestler, was it so difficult for Kepler to discard the notion of circular movement for the heavenly bodies, and why was it difficult to conceive of physical forces acting between the heavenly bodies? Are there any ideas in your own way of thinking that might be similarly difficult to discard or to accept? Perhaps Jacob Bronowski's essays "The Reach of Imagination" (pp. 99–106) and "The Nature of Scientific Reasoning" (pp. 600–604) may help you in thinking or writing about these questions.
3. What was the role of Tycho Brahe's observations, fact finding, data gathering, in the formulation of Kepler's thought? Did the

facts speak for themselves and make a true conception of the solar system evident at once? Explain the reasons for your answer.

4. On p. 597, Koestler says of Kepler, "Instead of cursing those eight minutes as a stumbling block, he transformed them into the cornerstone of a new science." What does this statement mean? Is a difference of such small scale between theory and observation necessarily significant in itself? If so, of what? Do you know of similar differences between expectation and actual behavior in your personal relationships? How have you handled such discrepancies?

JACOB BRONOWSKI

The Nature of Scientific Reasoning

What is the insight in which the scientist tries to see into nature? Can it indeed be called either imaginative or creative? To the literary man the question may seem merely silly. He has been taught that science is a large collection of facts; and if this is true, then the only seeing which scientists need to do is, he supposes, seeing the facts. He pictures them, the colorless professionals of science, going off to work in the morning into the universe in a neutral, unexposed state. They then expose themselves like a photographic plate. And then in the darkroom or laboratory they develop the image, so that suddenly and startlingly it appears, printed in capital letters, as a new formula for atomic energy.

Men who have read Balzac and Zola[1] are not deceived by the claims of these writers that they do no more than record the facts. The readers of Christopher Isherwood[2] do not take him literally when he writes "I am a camera." Yet the same readers solemnly carry with them from their schooldays this foolish picture of the scientist fixing by some mechanical process the facts of nature. I have had of all people a historian tell me that science is a collection of facts, and his voice had not even the ironic rasp of one filing cabinet reproving another.

It seems impossible that this historian had ever studied the beginnings of a scientific discovery. The Scientific Revolution can be held to begin in the year 1543 when there was brought to Copernicus, perhaps on his deathbed, the first printed copy of the book he had finished about a dozen years earlier. The thesis of this book is that

---

1. Honoré de Balzac and Émile Zola, nineteenth-century French novelists.
2. Modern English novelist and playwright.

the earth moves around the sun. When did Copernicus go out and record this fact with his camera? What appearance in nature prompted his outrageous guess? And in what odd sense is this guess to be called a neutral record of fact?

Less than a hundred years after Copernicus, Kepler published (between 1609 and 1619) the three laws which describe the paths of the planets. The work of Newton and with it most of our mechanics spring from these laws. They have a solid, matter-of-fact sound. For example, Kepler says that if one squares the year of a planet, one gets a number which is proportional to the cube of its average distance from the sun. Does anyone think that such a law is found by taking enough readings and then squaring and cubing everything in sight? If he does, then, as a scientist, he is doomed to a wasted life; he has as little prospect of making a scientific discovery as an electronic brain has.

It was not this way that Copernicus and Kepler thought, or that scientists think today. Copernicus found that the orbits of the planets would look simpler if they were looked at from the sun and not from the earth. But he did not in the first place find this by routine calculation. His first step was a leap of imagination—to lift himself from the earth, and put himself wildly, speculatively into the sun. "The earth conceives from the sun," he wrote; and "the sun rules the family of stars." We catch in his mind an image, the gesture of the virile man standing in the sun, with arms outstretched, overlooking the planets. Perhaps Copernicus took the picture from the drawings of the youth with outstretched arms which the Renaissance teachers put into their books on the proportions of the body. Perhaps he had seen Leonardo's drawings of his loved pupil Salai. I do not know. To me, the gesture of Copernicus, the shining youth looking outward from the sun, is still vivid in a drawing which William Blake in 1780 based on all these: the drawing which is usually called *Glad Day*.

Kepler's mind, we know, was filled with just such fanciful analogies; and we know what they were. Kepler wanted to relate the speeds of the planets to the musical intervals. He tried to fit the five regular solids into their orbits. None of these likenesses worked, and they have been forgotten; yet they have been and they remain the stepping stones of every creative mind. Kepler felt for his laws by way of metaphors, he searched mystically for likenesses with what he knew in every strange corner of nature. And when among these guesses he hit upon his laws, he did not think of their numbers as the balancing of a cosmic bank account, but as a revelation of the unity in all nature. To us, the analogies by which Kepler listened for the movement of the planets in the music of the spheres are far-fetched. Yet are they more so than the wild leap by which Rutherford and Bohr in our own century found a model for the atom in, of all places, the planetary system?

No scientific theory is a collection of facts. It will not even do to call a theory true or false in the simple sense in which every fact is either so or not so. The Epicureans held that matter is made of atoms two thousand years ago and we are now tempted to say that their theory was true. But if we do so we confuse their notion of matter with our own. John Dalton in 1808 first saw the structure of matter as we do today, and what he took from the ancients was not their theory but something richer, their image: the atom. Much of what was in Dalton's mind was as vague as the Greek notion, and quite as mistaken. But he suddenly gave life to the new facts of chemistry and the ancient theory together, by fusing them to give what neither had: a coherent picture of how matter is linked and built up from different kinds of atoms. The act of fusion is the creative act.

All science is the search for unity in hidden likenesses. The search may be on a grand scale, as in the modern theories which try to link the fields of gravitation and electromagnetism. But we do not need to be browbeaten by the scale of science. There are discoveries to be made by snatching a small likeness from the air too, if it is bold enough. In 1935 the Japanese physicist Hideki Yukawa wrote a paper which can still give heart to a young scientist. He took as his starting point the known fact that waves of light can sometimes behave as if they were separate pellets. From this he reasoned that the forces which hold the nucleus of an atom together might sometimes also be observed as if they were solid pellets. A schoolboy can see how thin Yukawa's analogy is, and his teacher would be severe with it. Yet Yukawa without a blush calculated the mass of the pellet he expected to see, and waited. He was right; his meson was found, and a range of other mesons, neither the existence nor the nature of which had been suspected before. The likeness had borne fruit.

The scientist looks for order in the appearances of nature by exploring such likenesses. For order does not display itself of itself; if it can be said to be there at all, it is not there for the mere looking. There is no way of pointing a finger or camera at it; order must be discovered and, in a deep sense, it must be created. What we see, as we see it, is mere disorder.

This point has been put trenchantly in a fable by Karl Popper. Suppose that someone wished to give his whole life to science. Suppose that he therefore sat down, pencil in hand, and for the next twenty, thirty, forty years recorded in notebook after notebook everything that he could observe. He may be supposed to leave out nothing: today's humidity, the racing results, the level of cosmic radiation and the stockmarket prices and the look of Mars, all would be there. He would have compiled the most careful record of nature that has ever been made; and, dying in the calm certainty of a life well spent, he would of course leave his notebooks to the Royal Society. Would the Royal Society thank him for the treasure of a lifetime of observation? It would not. The Royal Society would treat his notebooks exactly as the English bishops have treated Joanna Southcott's box.[3] It would refuse to open them at all, because it would know without looking that the notebooks contain only a jumble of disorderly and meaningless items.

Science finds order and meaning in our experience, and sets about this in quite a different way. It sets about it as Newton did in the story which he himself told in his old age, and of which the schoolbooks give only a caricature. In the year 1665, when Newton was twenty-two, the plague broke out in southern England, and the University of Cambridge was closed. Newton therefore spent the next eighteen months at home, removed from traditional learning, at a time when he was impatient for knowledge and, in his own phrase, "I was in the prime of my age for invention." In this eager, boyish mood, sitting one day in the garden of his widowed mother, he saw an apple fall. So far the books have the story right; we think we even know the kind of apple; tradition has it that it was a Flower of Kent. But now they miss the crux of the story. For what struck the young Newton at the sight was not the thought that the apple must be drawn to the earth by gravity; that conception was older than Newton. What struck him was the conjecture that the same force of gravity, which reaches to the top of the tree, might go on reaching out beyond the earth and its air, endlessly into space. Gravity might reach the moon: this was Newton's new thought; and it might be gravity which holds the moon in her orbit. There and then he calculated what force from the earth (falling off as the square of the distance) would hold the moon, and compared it with the known force of gravity at tree height. The forces agreed; Newton says laconically, "I found them answer pretty nearly." Yet they agreed only nearly: the likeness and the approximation go together, for no likeness is exact. In Newton's science modern sciences is full grown.

It grows from a comparison. It has seized a likeness between two

---

3. Joanna Southcott was a nineteenth-century English farm servant who claimed to be a prophetess. She left behind a box which was to be opened in a time of national emergency in the presence of all the English bishops. In 1927, a bishop agreed to officiate; when the box was opened, it was found to contain only some odds and ends.

unlike appearances; for the apple in the summer garden and the grave moon overhead are surely as unlike in their movements as two things can be. Newton traced in them two expressions of a single concept, gravitation: and the concept (and the unity) are in that sense his free creation. The progress of science is the discovery at each step of a new order which gives unity to what had long seemed unlike.

* * *

1953, 1965

QUESTIONS

1. In his opening paragraph Bronowski pictures what the "literary man," or perhaps the ordinary non-scientist, thinks of as the nature of science. Is this a fair representation of the layman's view? What features of science or of the presentation of science might contribute to the development of that view?
2. In his fourth paragraph Bronowski indicates that an electronic brain has little or no chance of making a scientific discovery. Do you agree? Why, or not?
3. Bronowski recounts the famous story of Newton and the apple. What general principle about science is he exemplifying in this story?
4. On p. 600 Bronowski describes a voice as having "not even the ironic rasp of one filing cabinet reproving another." Is that image more appropriate to the situation? Can you find other such uses of language in the selection?
5. Write an essay comparing Bronowski's description of the process of science with that given by Thomas S. Kuhn in "The Route to Normal Science" (pp. 605–613). In what respects are the views of these authors similar? Do they differ in any important ways? What sorts of language does each of them use to convey his thoughts? How would you account for differences in tone and usage?
6. In "The Reach of Imagination" (pp. 99–106) Bronowski shows the work of imagination in Newton's thinking of the moon as a huge ball, thrown hard, and in Galileo's imaginary experiment with unequal weights. In what particular ways do these examples relate to and supplement Bronowski's remarks on science in "The Nature of Scientific Reasoning"?

THOMAS S. KUHN
The Route to Normal Science

In this essay, 'normal science' means research firmly based upon one or more past scientific achievements, achievements that some particular scientific community acknowledges for a time as supplying the foundation for its further practice. Today such achievements are recounted, though seldom in their original form, by science textbooks, elementary and advanced. These textbooks expound the body of accepted theory, illustrate many or all of its successful applications, and compare these applications with exemplary observations and experiments. Before such books became popular early in the nineteenth century (and until even more recently in the newly matured sciences), many of the famous classics of science fulfilled a similar function. Aristotle's *Physica*, Ptolemy's *Almagest*, Newton's *Principia* and *Opticks*, Franklin's *Electricity*, Lavoisier's *Chemistry*, and Lyell's *Geology*—these and many other works served for a time implicitly to define the legitimate problems and methods of a research field for succeeding generations of practitioners. They were able to do so because they shared two essential characteristics. Their achievement was sufficiently unprecedented to attract an enduring group of adherents away from competing modes of scientific activity. Simultaneously, it was sufficiently open-ended to leave all sorts of problems for the redefined group of practitioners to resolve.

Achievements that share these two characteristics I shall henceforth refer to as 'paradigms,' a term that relates closely to 'normal science.' By choosing it, I mean to suggest that some accepted examples of actual scientific practice—examples which include law, theory, application, and instrumentation together—provide models from which spring particular coherent traditions of scientific research. These are the traditions which the historian describes under such rubrics as 'Ptolemaic astronomy' (or 'Copernican'), 'Aristotelian dynamics' (or 'Newtonian'), 'corpuscular optics' (or 'wave optics'), and so on. The study of paradigms, including many that are far more specialized than those named illustratively above, is what mainly prepares the student for membership in the particular scientific community with which he will later practice. Because he there joins men who learned the bases of their field from the same concrete models, his subsequent practice will seldom evoke overt disagreement over fundamentals. Men whose research is based on shared paradigms are committed to the same rules and standards for

605

scientific practice. That commitment and the apparent consensus it produces are prerequisites for normal science, i.e., for the genesis and continuation of a particular research tradition.

Because in this essay the concept of a paradigm will often substitute for a variety of familiar notions, more will need to be said about the reasons for its introduction. Why is the concrete scientific achievement, as a locus of professional commitment, prior to the various concepts, laws, theories, and points of view that may be abstracted from it? In what sense is the shared paradigm a fundamental unit for the student of scientific development, a unit that cannot be fully reduced to logically atomic components which might function in its stead? There can be a sort of scientific research without paradigms, or at least without any so unequivocal and so binding as the ones named above. Acquisition of a paradigm and of the more esoteric type of research it permits is a sign of maturity in the development of any given scientific field.

If the historian traces the scientific knowledge of any selected group of related phenomena backward in time, he is likely to encounter some minor variant of a pattern here illustrated from the history of physical optics. Today's physics textbooks tell the student that light is photons, i.e., quantum-mechanical entities that exhibit some characteristics of waves and some of particles. Research proceeds accordingly, or rather according to the more elaborate and mathematical characterization from which this usual verbalization is derived. That characterization of light is, however, scarcely half a century old. Before it was developed by Planck, Einstein, and others early in this century, physics texts taught that light was transverse wave motion, a conception rooted in a paradigm that derived ultimately from the optical writings of Young and Fresnel in the early nineteenth century. Nor was the wave theory the first to be embraced by almost all practitioners of optical science. During the eighteenth century the paradigm for this field was provided by Newton's *Opticks*, which taught that light was material corpuscles. At that time physicists sought evidence, as the early wave theorists had not, of the pressure exerted by light particles impinging on solid bodies.

These transformations of the paradigms of physical optics are scientific revolutions, and the successive transition from one paradigm to another via revolution is the usual developmental pattern of mature science. It is not, however, the pattern characteristic of the period before Newton's work, and that is the contrast that concerns us here. No period between remote antiquity and the end of the seventeenth century exhibited a single generally accepted veiw about the nature of light. Instead there were a number of competing schools and sub-schools, most of them espousing one variant or another of Epicurean, Aristotelian, or Platonic theory.[1] One group took light to be particles emanating from material bodies; for another it was a modification of the medium that intervened between the body and the eye; still another explained light in terms of an interaction of the medium with an emanation from the eye; and there were other combinations and modifications besides. Each of the corresponding schools derive strength from its relation to some particular metaphysic, and each emphasized, as paradigmatic observations, the particular cluster of optical phenomena that its own theory could do most to explain. Other observations were dealt with by *ad hoc* elaborations, or they remained as outstanding problems for further research.

At various times all these schools made significant contributions to the body of concepts, phenomena, and techniques from which Newton drew the first nearly uniformly accepted paradigm for physical optics. Any definition of the scientist that excludes at least the more creative members of these various schools will exclude their modern successors as well. Those men were scientists. Yet anyone examining a survey of physical optics before Newton may well conclude that, though the field's practitioners were scientists, the net result of their activity was something less than science. Being able to take no common body of belief for granted, each writer on physical optics felt forced to build his field anew from its foundations. In doing so, his choice of supporting observation and experiment was relatively free, for there was no standard set of methods or of phenomena that every optical writer felt forced to employ and explain. Under these circumstances, the dialogue of the resulting books was often directed as much to the members of other schools as it was to nature. That pattern is not unfamiliar in a number of creative fields today, nor is it incompatible with significant discovery and invention. It is not, however, the pattern of development that physical optics acquired after Newton and that other natural sciences make familiar today.

The history of electrical research in the first half of the eighteenth century provides a more concrete and better known example of the way a science develops before it acquires its first universally received paradigm. During that period there were almost as many views about the nature of electricity as there were important electrican experimenters, men like Haukshee, Gray, Desaguliers, Du Fay, Nollett, Watson, Franklin, and others. All their numerous concepts of electricity had something in common—they were partially derived from one or another version of the mechanico-corpuscular

1. The reference is to the three principal world views of ancient Greek philosophy.

philosophy that guided all scientific research of the day. In addition, all were components of real scientific theories, of theories that had been drawn in part from experiment and observation and that partially determined the choice and interpretation of additional problems undertaken in research. Yet though all the experiments were electrical and though most of the experimenters read each other's works, their theories had no more than a family resemblance.

One early group of theories, following seventeenth-century practice, regarded attraction and frictional generation as the fundamental electrical phenomena. This group tended to treat repulsion as a secondary effect due to some sort of mechanical rebounding and also to postpone for as long as possible both discussion and systematic research on Gray's newly discovered effect, electrical conduction. Other "electricians" (the term is their own) took attraction and repulsion to be equally elementary manifestations of electricity and modified their theories and research accordingly. (Actually, this group is remarkably small—even Franklin's theory never quite accounted for the mutual repulsion of two negatively charged bodies.) But they had as much difficulty as the first group in accounting simultaneously for any but the simplest conduction effects. Those effects, however, provided the starting point for still a third group, one which tended to speak of electricity as a "fluid" that could run through conductors rather than as an "effluvium" that emanated from non-conductors. This group, in its turn, had difficulty reconciling its theory with a number of attractive and repulsive effects. Only through the work of Franklin and his immediate successors did a theory arise that could account with something like equal facility for very nearly all these effects and that therefore could and did provide a subsequent generation of "electricians" with a common paradigm for its research.

Excluding those fields, like mathematics and astronomy, in which the first firm paradigms date from prehistory and also those, like biochemistry, that arose by division and recombination of specialties already matured, the situations outlined above are historically typical. Though it involves my continuing to employ the unfortunate simplification that tags an extended historical episode with a single and somewhat arbitrarily chosen name (e.g., Newton or Franklin), I suggest that similar fundamental disagreements characterized, for example, the study of motion before Aristotle and of statics before Archimedes, the study of heat before Black, of chemistry before Boyle and Boerhaave, and of historical geology before Hutton. In parts of biology—the study of heredity, for example—the first universally received paradigms are still more recent; and it remains an open question what parts of social science have yet acquired such paradigms at all. History suggests that the road to a firm research consensus is extraordinarily arduous.

History also suggests, however, some reasons for the difficulties encountered on the road. In the absence of a paradigm or some candidate for paradigm, all of the facts that could possibly pertain to the development of a given science are likely to seem equally relevant. As a result, early fact-gathering is a far more nearly random activity than the one that subsequent scientific development makes familiar. Futhermore, in the absence of a reason for seeking some particular form of more recondite information, early fact-gathering is usually restricted to the wealth of data that lie ready to hand. The resulting pool of facts contains those accessible to casual observation and experiment together with some of the more esoteric data retrievable from established crafts medicine, calendar making, and metallurgy. Because the crafts are one readily accessible source of facts that could not have been casually discovered, technology has often played a vital role in the emergence of new sciences.

But though this sort of fact-collecting has been essential to the origin of many significant sciences, anyone who examines, for example, Pliny's encyclopedic writings or the Baconian natural histories of the seventeenth century will discover that it produces a morass. One somehow hesitates to call the literature that results scientific. The Baconian "histories" of heat, color, wind, mining, and so on, are filled with information, some of it recondite. But they juxtapose facts that will later prove revealing (e.g., heating by mixture) with others (e.g., the warmth of dung heaps) that will for some time remain too complex to be integrated with theory at all. In addition, since any description must be partial, the typical natural history often omits from its immensely circumstantial accounts just those details that later scientists will find sources of important illumination. Almost none of the early "histories" of electricity, for example, mention that chaff, attracted to a rubbed glass rod, bounces off again. That effect seemed mechanical, not electrical. Moreover, since the casual fact-gatherer seldom possesses the time or the tools to be critical, the natural histories often juxtapose descriptions like the above with others, say, heating by antiperistasis (or by cooling), that we are now quite unable to confirm.[2] Only very occasionally, as in the cases of ancient statics, dynamics, and geometrical optics, do facts collected with so little guidance from pre-established theory speak with sufficient clarity to permit the emergence of a first paradigm.

2. Bacon [in the *Novum Organum*] says, "Water slightly warm is more easily frozen than quite cold" [Kuhn's note]; *antiperistasis*: an old word meaning a reaction caused by the action of an opposite quality or principle—here, heating through cooling.

This is the situation that creates the schools characteristic of the early stages of a science's development. No natural history can be interpreted in the absence of at least some implicit body of inter-twined theoretical and methodological belief that permits selection, evaluation, and criticism. If that body of belief is not already implicit in the collection of facts—in which case more than "mere facts" are at hand—it must be externally supplied, perhaps by a current metaphysic, by another science, or by personal and historical accident. No wonder, then, that in the early stages of the development of any science different men confronting the same range of phenomena, but not usually all the same particular phenomena, describe and interpret them in different ways. What is surprising, and perhaps also unique in its degree to the fields we call science, is that such initial divergences should ever largely disappear.

For they do disappear to a very considerable extent and then apparently once and for all. Furthermore, their disappearance is usually caused by the triumph of one of the pre-paradigm schools, which, because of its own characteristic beliefs and pre-conceptions, emphasized only some special part of the too sizable and inchoate pool of information. Those electricians who thought electricity a fluid and therefore gave particular emphasis to conduction provide an excellent case in point. Led by this belief, which could scarcely cope with the known multiplicity of attractive and repulsive effects, several of them conceived the idea of bottling the electrical fluid. The immediate fruit of their efforts was the Leyden jar, a device which might never have been discovered by a man exploring nature casu-ally or at random, but which was in fact independently devel-oped by at least two investigators in the early 1740's. Almost from the start of his electrical researches, Franklin was particularly con-cerned to explain that strange and, in the event, particularly reveal-ing piece of special apparatus. His success in doing so provided the most effective of the arguments that made his theory a paradigm, though one that was still unable to account for quite all the known cases of electrical repulsion.[3] To be accepted as a paradigm, a theory must seem better than its competitors, but it need not, and in fact never does, explain all the facts with which it can be con-fronted.

What the fluid theory of electricity did for the subgroup that held it, the Franklinian paradigm later did for the entire group of electricians. It suggested which experiments would be worth per-forming and which, because directed to secondary or to overly com-plex manifestations of electricity, would not. Only the paradigm did

3. The troublesome case was the mu-tual repulsion of negatively charged bodies [Kuhn's note].

the job far more effectively, partly because the end of interschool debate ended the constant reiteration of fundamentals and partly because the confidence that they were on the right track encouraged scientists to undertake more precise, esoteric, and consuming sorts of work.[4] Freed from the concern with any and all electrical phenomena, the united group of electricians could pursue selected phenomena in far more detail, designing much special equipment for the task and employing it more stubbornly and systematically than electricians had ever done before. Both fact collection and theory articulation became highly directed activities. The effectiveness and efficiency of electrical research increased accordingly, providing evidence for a societal version of Francis Bacon's acute methodological dictum: "Truth emerges more readily from error than from confusion."

We shall be examining the nature of this highly directed or paradigm-based research in the next section, but must first note briefly how the emergence of a paradigm affects the structure of the group that practices the field. When, in the development of a natural science, an individual or group first produces a synthesis able to attract most of the next generation's practitioners, the older schools gradually disappear. In part their disappearance is caused by their members' conversion to the new paradigm. But there are always some men who cling to one or another of the older views, and they are simply read out of the profession, which thereafter ignores their work. The new paradigm implies a new and more rigid definition of the field. Those unwilling or unable to accommodate their work to it must proceed in isolation or attach themselves to some other group.[5] Historically, they have often simply stayed in the departments of philosophy from which so many of the special sciences have been spawned. As these indications hint, it is sometimes just its reception of a paradigm that transforms a group previously inter-

4. It should be noted that the acceptance of Franklin's theory did not end quite all debate. In 1759 Robert Symmer proposed a two-fluid version of that theory, and for many years thereafter electricians were divided about whether electricity was a single fluid or two. But the debates on this subject only confirm what has been said above about the manner in which a universally recognized achievement unites the profession. Electricians, though they continued divided on this point, rapidly concluded that no experimental tests could distinguish the two versions of the theory and that they were therefore equivalent. After that, both schools could and did exploit all the benefits that the Franklinian theory provided [Kuhn's note].

5. The history of electricity provides an excellent example which could be duplicated from the careers of Priestley, Kelvin, and others. Franklin reports that Nollet, who at mid-century was the most influential of the Continental electricians, "lived to see himself the last of his Sect, except Mr. B.—— his *Eleve* [pupil] and immediate Disciple." More interesting, however, is the endurance of whole schools in increasing isolation from professional science. Consider, for example, the case of astrology, which was once an integral part of astronomy. Or consider the continuation in the late eighteenth and early nineteenth centuries of a previously respected tradition of "romantic" chemistry [Kuhn's note].

ested merely in the study of nature into a profession or, at least, a discipline. In the sciences (though not in fields like medicine, technology, and law, of which the principal *raison d'être* is an external social need), the formation of specialized journals, the foundation of specialists' societies, and the claim for a special place in the curriculum have usually been associated with a group's first reception of a single paradigm. At least this was the case between the time, a century and a half ago, when the institutional pattern of scientific specialization first developed and the very recent time when the paraphernalia of specialization acquired a prestige of their own.

The more rigid definition of the scientific group has other consequences. When the individual scientist can take a paradigm for granted, he need no longer, in his major works, attempt to build his field anew, starting from first principles and justifying the use of each concept introduced. That can be left to the writer of textbooks. Given a textbook, however, the creative scientist can begin his research where it leaves off and thus concentrate exclusively upon the subtlest and most esoteric aspects of the natural phenomena that concern his group. And as he does this, his research communiqués will begin to change in ways whose evolution has been too little studied but whose modern end products are obvious to all and oppressive to many. No longer will his researches usually be embodied in books addressed, like Franklin's *Experiments . . . on Electricity* or Darwin's *Origin of Species*, to anyone who might be interested in the subject matter of the field. Instead they will usually appear as brief articles addressed only to professional colleagues, the men whose knowledge of a shared paradigm can be assumed and who prove to be the only ones able to read the papers addressed to them.

Today in the sciences, books are usually either texts or retrospective reflections upon one aspect or another of the scientific life. The scientist who writes one is more likely to find his professional reputation impaired than enhanced. Only in the earlier, pre-paradigm, stages of the development of the various sciences did the book ordinarily possess the same relation to professional achievement that it still retains in other creative fields. And only in those fields that still retain the book, with or without the article, as a vehicle for research communication are the lines of professionalization still so loosely drawn that the layman may hope to follow progress by reading the practitioners' original reports. Both in mathematics and astronomy, research reports had ceased already in antiquity to be intelligible to a generally educated audience. In dynamics, research became similarly esoteric in the latter Middle Ages, and it recaptured general intelligibility only briefly during the early seventeenth century when a new paradigm replaced the one that had guided medieval research. Electrical research began to require translation for the layman before the end of the eighteenth century, and most other fields of physical science ceased to be generally accessible in the nineteenth. During the same two centuries similar transitions can be isolated in the various parts of the biological sciences. In parts of the social sciences they may well be occurring today. Although it has become customary, and is surely proper, to deplore the widening gulf that separates the professional scientist from his colleagues in other fields, too little attention is paid to the essential relationship between that gulf and the mechanisms intrinsic to scientific advance. .

Ever since prehistoric antiquity one field of study after another has crossed the divide between what the historian might call its prehistory as a science and its history proper. These transitions to maturity have seldom been so sudden or so unequivocal as my necessarily schematic discussion may have implied. But neither have they been historically gradual, coextensive, that is to say, with the entire development of the fields within which they occurred. Writers on electricity during the first four decades of the eighteenth century possessed far more information about electrical phenomena than had their sixteenth-century predecessors. During the half-century after 1740, few new sorts of electrical phenomena were added to their lists. Nevertheless, in important respects, the electrical writings of Cavendish, Coulomb, and Volta in the last third of the eighteenth century seem further removed from those of Gray, Du Fay, and even Franklin than are the writings of these early eighteenth-century electrical discoverers from those of the sixteenth century.[6] Sometime between 1740 and 1780, electricians were for the first time enabled to take the foundations of their field for granted. From that point they pushed on to more concrete and recondite problems, and increasingly they then reported their results in articles addressed to other electricians rather than in books addressed to the learned world at large. As a group they achieved what had been gained by astronomers in antiquity and by students of motion in the Middle Ages, of physical optics in the late seventeenth century, and of historical geology in the early nineteenth. They had, that is, achieved a paradigm that proved able to guide the whole group's research. Except with the advantage of hindsight, it is hard to find another criterion that so clearly proclaims a field a science.

1962

6. The post-Franklinian developments include an immense increase in the sensitivity of charge detectors, the first reliable and generally diffused techniques for measuring charge, the evolution of the concept of capacity and its relation to a newly refined notion of electric tension, and the quantification of electrostatic force [Kuhn's note].

QUESTIONS

1. What is Kuhn's thesis? How is the essay organized to develop that thesis?
2. What is the relationship, by Kuhn's account, of the science textbook to the nature and practice of science? Examine a textbook in your course in one of the natural or social sciences. Does it have the character Kuhn ascribes to textbooks? Does regarding the textbook in this light help you in your study of the subject?
3. What does Kuhn mean by a "paradigm" in science, and what advantages for science does he ascribe to it? Can you state the prevailing paradigm in sciences other than those he uses for illustration (for example, chemistry, biology, psychology)? Does the search for or finding of the paradigms help you to understand what these sciences are about?
4. What does Kuhn's essay suggest about the nature of a scientific fact, or the place of fact in science? By and large, does this conclusion accord, or disagree, with Jacob Bronowski's statement of the matter, in "The Reach of Imagination" (pp. 99–106)? Is it not the business of a science to observe and record the facts? What more should science do?

Prose Forms: Parables

When we read a short story or a novel, we are less interested in the working out of ideas than in the working out of characters and their destinies. In Dickens' Great Expectations, for example, Pip, the hero, undergoes many triumphs and defeats in his pursuit of success, only to learn finally that he has expected the wrong things, or the right things for the wrong reasons; that the great values in life are not always to be found in what the world calls success. In realizing this meaning we entertain, with Dickens, certain concepts or ideas that organize and evaluate the life in the novel, and that ultimately we apply to life generally. Ideas are there not to be exploited discursively, but to be understood as the perspective which shapes the direction of the novel and our view of its relation to life.

When ideas in their own reality are no longer the primary interest in writing, we have obviously moved from expository to other forms of prose. The shift need not be abrupt and complete, however; there is an area where the discursive interest in ideas and the narrative interest in characters and events blend. In allegory, for example, abstract ideas are personified. "Good Will" or "Peace" may be shown as a young woman, strong, confident, and benevolent in her bearing but vulnerable, through her sweet reasonableness, to the single-minded, fierce woman who is "Dissension." Our immediate interest is in their behavior as characters, but our ultimate interest is in the working out, through them, of the ideas they represent. We do not ask that the characters and events be entirely plausible in relation to actual life, as we do for the novel; we are satisfied if they are consistent with the nature of the ideas that define their vitality.

Ideas themselves have vitality, a mobile and dynamic life with a behavior of its own. The title of the familiar Negro spiritual "Sometimes I Feel Like a Motherless Child," to choose a random instance, has several kinds of "motion" as an idea. The qualitative identity of an adult's feelings and those of a child; the whole burgeoning possibility of all that the phrase "motherless child" can mean; the subtle differences in meaning—the power of context—that occur when it is a black who feels this and when it is a white; the speculative possibilities of the title as social commentary or psychological analysis —these suggest something of the "life" going on in and around the idea. Definition, analogy, assumption, implication, context, illustra-

615

tion are some of the familiar terms we use to describe this kind of life.

There is, of course, another and more obvious kind of vitality which an idea has: its applicability to the affairs of people in everyday life. Both the kind and extent of an idea's relevance are measures of this vitality. When an essayist wishes to exploit both the life in an idea and the life it comprehends, he or she often turns to narration, because there one sees the advantage of lifelike characters and events, and of showing through them the liveliness of ideas in both the senses we have noted. Ideas about life can be illustrated in life. And, besides, people like stories. The writer's care must be to keep the reader's interest focused on the ideas, rather than on the life itself; otherwise, he or she has ceased being essentially the essayist and has become the short-story writer or novelist.

The parable and the moral fable are ideal forms for this purpose. In both, the idea is the heart of the composition; in both the ideas usually assume the form of a lesson about life, some moral truth of general consequence; and in both there are characters and actions. Jesus often depended on parables in his teaching. Simple, economical, pointed, the parables developed a "story," but more importantly, applied a moral truth to experience. Peter asked Jesus how often he must forgive the brother who sins against him, and Jesus answered with the parable of the king and his servants, one of whom asked and got forgiveness of the king for his debts but who would not in turn forgive a fellow servant his debt. The king, on hearing of this harshness, retracted his own benevolence and punished the unfeeling servant. Jesus concluded to Peter, "So likewise shall my heavenly Father do also unto you, if ye from your hearts forgive not every one his brother their trespasses." But before this direct drawing of the parallel, the lesson was clear in the outline of the narrative.

Parables usually have human characters; fables often achieve a special liveliness with animals or insects. Swift, in "The Spider and the Bee," narrates the confrontation of a comically humanized spider and bee who debate the merits of their natures and their usefulness in the world of experience. The exchange between the two creatures is brilliantly and characteristically set out, but by its end, the reader realizes that extraordinary implications about the nature of art, of education, of human psychological and intellectual potential have been the governing idea all along.

The writer will be verging continually on strict prose narrative in writing the parable or fable, but through skill and tact he or she can preserve the essayist's essential commitment to the definition and development of ideas in relation to experience.

PLATO: The Allegory of the Cave

And now, I said, let me show in a figure how far our nature is enlightened or unenlightened: Behold! human beings living in an underground den, which has a mouth open towards the light and reaching all along the den; here they have been from their childhood, and have their legs and necks chained so that they cannot move, and can only see before them, being prevented by the chains from turning round their heads. Above and behind them a fire is blazing at a distance, and between the fire and the prisoners there is a raised way; and you will see, if you look, a low wall built along the way, like the screen which marionette players have in front of them, over which they show the puppets.

I see.

And do you see, I said, men passing along the wall carrying all sorts of vessels, and statues and figures of animals made of wood and stone and various materials, which appear over the wall? Some of them are talking, others silent.

You have shown me a strange image, and they are strange prisoners.

Like ourselves, I replied; and they see only their own shadows, or the shadows of one another, which the fire throws on the opposite wall of the cave?

True, he said; how could they see anything but the shadows if they were never allowed to move their heads?

And of the objects which are being carried in like manner they would only see the shadows?

Yes, he said.

And if they were able to converse with one another, would they not suppose that they were naming what was actually before them?

Very true.

And suppose further that the prison had an echo which came from the other side, would they not be sure to fancy when one of the passers-by spoke that the voice which they heard came from the passing shadow?

No question, he replied.

To them, I said, the truth would be literally nothing but· the shadows of the images.

That is certain.

And now look again, and see what will naturally follow if the prisoners are released and disabused of their error. At first, when any of them is liberated and compelled suddenly to stand up and turn his neck round and walk and look towards the light, he will suffer sharp pains; the glare will distress him and he will be unable to see the realities of which in his former state he had seen the shadows; and then conceive some one saying to him, that what he saw before was an illusion, but that now, when he is approaching nearer to being and his eye is turned towards more real existence, he has a clearer vision—what will be his reply? And you may further imagine that his instructor is pointing to the objects as they pass and requiring him to name them—will he not be perplexed? Will he not fancy that the shadows which he formerly saw are truer than the objects which are now shown to him?

Far truer.

And if he is compelled to look straight at the light, will he not have a pain in his eyes which will make him turn away to take refuge in the objects of vision which he can see, and which he will conceive to be in reality clearer than the things which are now being shown to him?

True, he said.

And suppose once more, that he is reluctantly dragged up a steep and rugged ascent, and held fast until he is forced into the presence of the sun himself, is he not likely to be pained and irritated? When he approaches the light his eyes will be dazzled and he will not be able to see anything at all of what are now called realities.

Not all in a moment, he said.

He will require to grow accustomed to the sight of the upper world. And first he will see the shadows best, next the reflections of men and other objects in the water, and then the objects themselves; then he will gaze upon the light of the moon and the stars and the spangled heaven; and he will see the sky and the stars by night better than the sun or the light of the sun by day?

Certainly.

Last of all he will be able to see the sun, and not mere reflections of him in the water, but he will see him in his own proper place, and not in another; and he will contemplate him as he is.

Certainly.

He will then proceed to argue that this is he who gives the season and the years, and is the guardian of all that is in the visible world, and in a certain way the cause of all things which he and his fellows have been accustomed to behold?

Clearly, he said, he would first see the sun and then reason about him.

And when he remembered his old habitation, and the wisdom of the den and his fellow-prisoners, do you not suppose that he would felicitate himself on the change, and pity them?

Certainly, he would.

And if they were in the habit of conferring honors among themselves on those who were quickest to observe the passing shadows and to remark which of them went before, and which followed after, and which were together; and who were therefore best able to draw conclusions as to the future, do you think that he would care for such honors and glories, or envy the possessors of them? Would he not say with Homer,

> Better to be the poor servant of a poor master,

and to endure anything, rather than think as they do and live after their manner?

Yes, he said, I think that he would rather suffer anything than entertain these false notions and live in this miserable manner.

Imagine once more, I said, such an one coming suddenly out of the sun to be replaced in his old situation; would he not be certain to have his eyes full of darkness?

To be sure, he said.

And if there were a contest, and he had to compete in measuring the shadows with the prisoners who had never moved out of the den, while his sight was still weak, and before his eyes had become steady (and the time which would be needed to acquire this new habit of sight might be very considerable) would he not be ridiculous? Men would say of him that up he went and down he came without his eyes; and that it was better not even to think of ascending; and if any one tried to loose another and lead him up to the light, let them only catch the offender, and they would put him to death.

No question, he said.

This entire allegory, I said, you may now append, dear Glaucon, to the previous argument; the prison-house is the world of sight, the light of the fire is the sun, and you will not misapprehend me if you interpret the journey upwards to be the ascent of the soul into the intellectual world according to my poor belief, which, at your desire, I have expressed—whether rightly or wrongly God knows. But, whether true or false, my opinion is that in the world of knowledge the idea of good appears last of all, and is seen only with an effort; and, when seen, is also inferred to be the universal author of all things beautiful and right, parent of light and of the lord of light in this visible world, and the immediate source of reason and truth in the intellectual; and that this is the power upon which he who would act rationally either in public or private life must have his eye fixed.

I agree, he said, as far as I am able to understand you.

Moreover, I said, you must not wonder that those who attain to this beatific vision are unwilling to descend to human affairs; for their souls are ever hastening into the upper world where they desire to dwell; which desire of theirs is very natural, if our allegory may be trusted.

Yes, very natural.

And is there anything surprising in one who passes from divine contemplations to the evil state of man, misbehaving himself in a ridiculous manner; if, while his eyes are blinking and before he has become accustomed to the surrounding darkness, he is compelled to fight in courts of law, or in other places, about the images or the shadows of images of justice, and is endeavouring to meet the conceptions of those who have never yet seen absolute justice?

Anything but surprising, he replied.

Any one who has common sense will remember that the bewilderments of the eyes are of two kinds, and arise from two causes, either from coming out of the light or from going into the light, which is true of the mind's eye, quite as much as of the bodily eye; and he who remembers this when he sees any one whose vision is perplexed and weak, will not be too ready to laugh; he will first ask whether that soul of man has come out of the brighter life, and is unable to see because unaccustomed to the dark, or having turned from darkness to the day is dazzled by excess of light. And he will count the one happy in his condition and state of being, and he will pity the other; or, if he have a mind to laugh at the soul which comes from below into the light, there will be more reason in this than in the laugh which greets him who returns from above out of the light into the den.

That, he said, is a very just distinction.

4th century B.C.

JONATHAN SWIFT: The Spider and the Bee

Things were at this crisis, when a material accident fell out. For, upon the highest corner of a large window, there dwelt a certain spider, swollen up to the first magnitude by the destruction of infinite numbers of flies, whose spoils lay scattered before the gates of his palace, like human bones before the cave of some giant. The avenues of his castle were guarded with turnpikes and palisadoes, all after the modern way of fortification. After you had passed several courts, you came to the center, wherein you might behold the constable himself in his own lodgings, which had windows fronting to each avenue, and ports to sally out upon all occasions of prey or defense. In this mansion he had for some time dwelt in peace and plenty, without danger to his person by swallows from above, or to his palace by brooms from below, when it was the pleasure of fortune to conduct thither a wandering bee, to whose curiosity a broken pane in the glass had discovered itself, and in he went; where expatiating a while, he at last happened to alight upon one of the outward walls of the spider's citadel; which, yielding to the unequal weight, sunk down to the very foundation. Thrice he endeavored to force his passage, and thrice the center shook. The spider within, feeling the terrible convulsion, supposed at first that nature was approaching to her final dissolution; or else that Beelzebub,[1] with all his legions, was come to revenge the death of many thousands of his subjects, whom his enemy had slain and devoured. However, he at length valiantly resolved to issue forth, and meet his fate. Meanwhile the bee had acquitted himself of his toils, and posted securely at some distance, was employed in cleansing his wings, and disengaging them from the ragged remnants of the cobweb. By this time the spider was adventured out, when beholding the chasms, and ruins, and dilapidations of his fortress, he was very near at his wit's end; he stormed and swore like a madman, and swelled till he was ready to burst. At length, casting his eye upon the bee, and wisely gathering causes from events (for they knew each other by sight), "A plague split you," said he, "for a giddy son of a whore. Is it you, with a vengeance, that have made this litter here? Could you not look before you, and be d——nd? Do you think I have nothing else to do (in the devil's name) but to mend and repair after your arse?" "Good words, friend," said the bee (having now pruned himself, and being disposed to droll) "I'll give you my hand and word to come near your kennel no more; I was never in such a confounded pickle since I was born." "Sirrah," replied the spider, "if it were not for breaking an old custom in our family, never to stir abroad against an enemy, I should come and teach you better manners." "I pray have patience," said the bee, "or you will spend your substance, and for aught I see, you may stand in need of it all, towards the repair of your house." "Rogue, rogue," replied the spider, "yet methinks you should have more respect to a person, whom all the world allows to be so much your betters." "By my troth," said the bee, "the comparison will amount to a very good jest, and you will do me a favor to let me know the reasons that all the world is pleased to use in so hopeful a dispute." At this the spider, having swelled himself into the size and posture of a disputant, began his argument in the true spirit of controversy, with a resolution to be heartily scurrilous and angry, to urge on his own reasons, without the least regard to the answers or objections of his opposite, and fully predetermined in his mind against all conviction.

"Not to disparage myself," said he, "by the comparison with such a rascal, what art thou but a vagabond without house or home, without stock or inheritance, born to no possession of your own, but a pair of wings and a drone-pipe? Your livelihood is an universal plunder upon nature; a freebooter over fields and gardens;

1. The Hebrew god of flies.

and for the sake of stealing will rob a nettle as easily as a violet. Whereas I am a domestic animal, furnished with a native stock within myself. This large castle (to show my improvements in the mathematics) is all built with my own hands, and the materials extracted altogether out of my own person."

"I am glad," answered the bee, "to hear you grant at least that I am come honestly by my wings and my voice; for then, it seems, I am obliged to Heaven alone for my flights and my music; and Providence would never have bestowed on me two such gifts, without designing them for the noblest ends. I visit indeed all the flowers and blossoms of the field and the garden; but whatever I collect from thence enriches myself, without the least injury to their beauty, their smell, or their taste. Now, for you and your skill in architecture and other mathematics, I have little to say: in that building of yours there might, for aught I know, have been labor and method enough, but by woful experience for us both, 'tis too plain, the materials are naught, and I hope you will henceforth take warning, and consider duration and matter as well as method and art. You boast, indeed, of being obliged to no other creature, but of drawing and spinning out all from yourself; that is to say, if we may judge of the liquor in the vessel by what issues out, you possess a good plentiful store of dirt and poison in your breast; and, tho' I would by no means lessen or disparage your genuine stock of either, yet I doubt you are somewhat obliged for an increase of both, to a little foreign assistance. Your inherent portion of dirt does not fail of acquisitions, by sweepings exhaled from below; and one insect furnishes you with a share of poison to destroy another. So that in short, the question comes all to this—which is the nobler being of the two, that which by a lazy contemplation of four inches round, by an overweening pride, feeding and engendering on itself, turns all into excrement and venom, produces nothing at last, but flybane and a cobweb; or that which, by an universal range, with long search, much study, true judgment, and distinction of things, brings home honey and wax."

1697   1704

JAMES THURBER: The Glass in the Field

A short time ago some builders, working on a studio in Connecticut, left a huge square of plate glass standing upright in a field one day. A goldfinch flying swiftly across the field struck the glass and was knocked cold. When he came to he hastened to his club, where an attendant bandaged his head and gave him a stiff drink. "What the hell happened?" asked a sea gull. "I was flying across a meadow when all of a sudden the air crystallized on me," said the goldfinch. The sea gull and a hawk and an eagle all laughed heartily. A swallow listened gravely. "For fifteen years, fledgling and bird, I've flown this country," said the eagle, "and I assure you there is no such thing as air crystallizing. Water, yes; air, no." "You were probably struck by a hailstone," the hawk told the goldfinch. "Or he may have had a stroke," said the sea gull. "What do you think, swallow?" "Why, I—I think maybe the air crystallized on him," said the swallow. The large birds laughed so loudly that the goldfinch became annoyed and bet them each a dozen worms that they couldn't follow the course he had flown across the field without encountering the hardened atmosphere. They all took his bet; the swallow went along to watch. The sea gull, the eagle, and the hawk decided to fly together over the route the goldfinch indicated. "You come, too," they said to the swallow. "I—I—well, no," said the swallow. "I don't think I will." So the three large birds took off together and they hit the glass together and they were all knocked cold.

Moral: He who hesitates is sometimes saved.

1955

FRANZ KAFKA: Parable of the Law

"Before the Law stands a doorkeeper. To this doorkeeper there comes a man from the country who begs for admittance to the Law. But the doorkeeper says that he cannot admit the man at the moment. The man, on reflection, asks if he will be allowed, then, to enter later. 'It is possible,' answers the doorkeeper, 'but not at this moment.' Since the door leading into the Law stands open as usual and the doorkeeper steps to one side, the man bends down to peer through the entrance. When the doorkeeper sees that, he laughs and says: 'If you are so strongly tempted, try to get in without my permission. But note that I am powerful. And I am only the lowest doorkeeper. From hall to hall, keepers stand at every door, one more powerful than the other. And the sight of the third man is already more than even I can stand.' These are difficulties which the man from the country has not expected to meet, the Law, he thinks, should be accessible to every man and at all times, but when he looks more closely at the doorkeeper in his furred robe, with his huge pointed nose and long thin Tartar beard, he decides that he had better wait until he gets permission to enter. The doorkeeper gives him a stool and lets him sit down at the side of the door. There he sits waiting for days and years. He makes many attempts to be allowed in and wearies the doorkeeper with his importunity. The doorkeeper often engages him in brief conversation, asking him about his home and about other matters, but the questions are put quite impersonally, as great men put questions, and always conclude with the statement that the man cannot be allowed to enter yet. The man, who has equipped himself with many things for his journey, parts with all he has, however valuable, in the hope of bribing the doorkeeper. The doorkeeper accepts it all, saying, however, as he takes each gift: 'I take this only to keep you from feeling that you have left something undone.' During all these long years the man watches the doorkeeper almost incessantly. He forgets about the other doorkeepers, and this one seems to him the only barrier between himself and the Law. In the first years he curses his evil fate aloud; later, as he grows old, he only mutters to himself. He grows childish, and since in his prolonged study of the doorkeeper he has learned to know even the fleas in his fur collar, he begs the very fleas to help him and to persuade the doorkeeper to change his mind. Finally his eyes grow dim and he does not know whether the world is really darkening around him or whether his eyes are only deceiving him. But in the darkness he can now perceive a radiance that streams inextinguishably from the door of the Law. Now his life is drawing to a close. Before he dies, all that he has experienced during the whole time of his sojourn condenses in his mind into one question, which he has never yet put to the doorkeeper. He beckons the doorkeeper, since he can no longer raise his stiffening body. The doorkeeper has to bend far down to hear him, for the difference in size between them has increased very much to the man's disadvantage. 'What do you want to know now?' asks the doorkeeper, 'you are insatiable.' 'Everyone strives to attain the Law,' answers the man, 'how does it come about, then, that in all these years no one has come seeking admittance but me?' The doorkeeper perceives that the man is nearing his end and his hearing is failing, so he bellows in his ear: 'No one but you could gain admittance through this door, since this door was intended for you. I am now going to shut it.' "

"So the doorkeeper deceived the man," said K. immediately, strongly attracted by the story. "Don't be too hasty," said the priest, "don't take over someone else's opinion without testing it. I have told you the story in the very words of the scriptures. There's no mention of deception in it." "But it's clear enough," said K., "and your first interpretation of it was quite right. The doorkeeper gave the message of salvation to the man only when it could no longer help him." "He was not asked the question any earlier," said the priest, "and you must consider, too, that he was only a doorkeeper, and as such fulfilled his duty." "What makes you think he fulfilled his duty?" asked K. "He didn't fulfill it. His duty might have been to keep all strangers away, but this man, for whom the door was intended, should have been let in." "You have not enough respect for the written word and you are altering the story," said the priest. "The story contains two important statements made by the doorkeeper about admission to the Law, one at the beginning, the other at the end. The first statement is: that he cannot admit the man at the moment, and the other is: that this door was intended only for the man. If there were a contradiction between the two, you would be right and the doorkeeper would have deceived the man. But there is no contradiction. The first statement, on the contrary, even implies the second. One could almost say that in suggesting to the man the possibility of future admittance the doorkeeper is exceeding his duty. At that time his apparent duty is only to refuse admittance and indeed many commentators are surprised that the suggestion should be made at all, since the doorkeeper appears to be a precisian with a stern regard for duty. He does not once leave his post during these many years, and he does not shut the door until the very last minute; he is conscious of the importance of his office, for he says: 'I am powerful'; he is respectful to his superiors, for he says: 'I am only the lowest doorkeeper'; he is not garrulous, for during all these years he puts only what are called 'impersonal questions'; he is not to be bribed, for he says in accepting a gift: 'I take this only to keep you from feeling that you have left something undone'; where his duty is concerned he is to be moved neither by pity nor rage, for we are told that the man 'wearied the doorkeeper with his importunity'; and finally even his external appearance hints at a pedantic character, the large, pointed nose and the long, thin, black, Tartar beard. Could one imagine a more faithful doorkeeper? Yet the doorkeeper has other elements in his character which are likely to advantage anyone seeking admittance and which make it comprehensible enough that he should somewhat exceed his duty in suggesting the possibility of future admittance. For it cannot be denied that he is a little simple-minded and consequently a little conceited. Take the statements he makes about his power and the power of the other doorkeepers and their dreadful aspect which even he cannot bear to see—I hold that these statements may be true enough, but that the way in which he brings them out shows that his perceptions are confused by simpleness of mind and conceit. The commentators note in this connection: 'The right perception of any matter and a misunderstanding of the same matter do not wholly exclude each other.' One must at any rate assume that such simpleness and conceit, however sparingly manifest, are likely to weaken his defense of the door; they are breaches in the character of the doorkeeper.

To this must be added the fact that the doorkeeper seems to be a friendly creature by nature, he is by no means always on his official dignity. In the very first moments he allows himself the jest of inviting the man to enter in spite of the strictly maintained veto against entry; then he does not, for instance, send the man away, but gives him, as we are told, a stool and lets him sit down beside the door. The patience with which he endures the man's appeals during so many years, the brief conversations, the acceptance of the gifts, the politeness with which he allows the man to curse loudly in his presence the fate for which he himself is responsible—all this lets us deduce certain feelings of pity. Not every doorkeeper would have acted thus. And finally, in answer to a gesture of the man's he bends down to give him the chance of putting a last question. Nothing but mild impatience—the doorkeeper knows that this is the end of it all—is discernible in the words: 'You are insatiable.' Some push this mode of interpretation even further and hold that these words express a kind of friendly admiration, though not without a hint of condescension. At any rate the figure of the doorkeeper can be said to come out very differently from what you fancied." "You have studied the story more exactly and for a longer time than I have," said K. They were both silent for a little while. Then. K. said: "So you think the man was not deceived?" "Don't misunderstand me," said the priest, "I am only showing you the various opinions concerning that point. You must not pay too much attention to them. The scriptures are unalterable and the comments often enough merely express the commentators' despair. In this case there even exists an interpretation which claims that the deluded person is really the doorkeeper." "That's a farfetched interpretation," said K. "On what is it based?" "It is based," answered the priest, "on the simple-mindedness of the doorkeeper. The argument is that he does not know the Law from inside, he knows only the way that leads to it, where he patrols up and down. His ideas of the interior are assumed to be childish, and it is supposed that he himself is afraid of the other guardians whom he holds up as bogies before the man. Indeed, he fears them more than the man does, since the man is determined to enter after hearing about the dreadful guardians of the interior, while the door-keeper has no desire to enter, at least not so far as we are told. Others again say that he must have been in the interior already, since he is after all engaged in the service of the Law and can only have been appointed from inside. This is countered by arguing that he may have been appointed by a voice calling from the interior, and that anyhow he cannot have been far inside, since the aspect of the third doorkeeper is more than he can endure. Moreover, no indication is given that during all these years he ever made any remarks showing a knowledge of the interior, except for the one remark about the doorkeepers. He may have been forbidden to do so, but there is no mention of that either. On these grounds the conclusion is reached that he knows nothing about the aspect and significance of the interior, so that he is in a state of delusion. But he is deceived also about his relation to the man from the country, for he is inferior to the man and does not know it. He treats the man instead as his own subordinate, as can be recognized from many details that must be still fresh in your mind. But, according to this view of the story, it is just as clearly indicated that he is really subordinated to the man. In the first place, a bondman is always subject to a free man. Now the man from the country is really free, he can go where he likes, it is only the Law that is closed to him, and access to the Law is forbidden him only by one individual, the doorkeeper. When he sits down on the stool by the side of the door and stays there for the rest of his life, he does it of his own free will; in the story there is no mention of any compulsion. But the doorkeeper is bound to his post by his very office, he does not dare go out into the country, nor apparently may he go into the interior of the Law, even should he wish to. Besides, although he is in the service of the Law, his service is confined to this one entrance; that is to say, he serves only this man for whom alone the entrance is intended. On that ground too he is inferior to the man. One must assume that for many years, for as long as it takes a man to grow up to the prime of life, his service was in a sense an empty formality, since he had to wait for a man to come, that is to say someone in the prime of life, and so he had to wait a long time before the purpose of his service could be fulfilled, and, moreover, had to wait on the man's pleasure, for the man came of his own free will. But the termination of his service also depends on the man's term of life, so that to the very end he is subject to the man. And it is emphasized throughout that the doorkeeper apparently realizes nothing of all this. That is not in itself remarkable, since according to this interpretation the doorkeeper is deceived in a much more important issue, affecting his very office. At the end, for example, he says regarding the entrance to the Law: 'I am now going to shut it,' but at the beginning of the story we are told that the door leading into the Law always stands open, and if it always stands open, that is to say at all times, without reference to life or death of the man, then the doorkeeper cannot close it. There is some difference of opinion about the motive behind the doorkeeper's statement, whether he said he was going to close the door merely for the sake of giving an answer, or to emphasize his devotion to duty, or to bring the man into a state of grief and regret in his last moments. But there is no lack of agreement that the doorkeeper will not be able to shut the door. Many indeed profess to find that he is subordinate to the man even in knowledge, toward the end, at least, for the man sees the radiance that issues from the door of the Law while the doorkeeper in his official position must stand with his back to the door, nor does he say anything to show that he has perceived the change." "That is well argued," said K., after repeating to himself in a low voice several passages from the priest's exposition. "It is well argued, and I am inclined to agree that the doorkeeper is deceived. But that has not made me abandon my former opinion, since both conclusions are to some extent compatible. Whether the doorkeeper is clear-sighted or deceived does not dispose of the matter. I said the man is deceived. If the doorkeeper is clear-sighted, one might have doubts about that, but if the doorkeeper himself is deceived, then his deception must of necessity be communicated to the man. That makes the doorkeeper not, indeed, a deceiver, but a creature so simple-minded that he ought to be dismissed at once from his office. You mustn't forget that the doorkeeper's deceptions do himself no harm but do infinite harm to the man." "There are objections to that," said the priest. "Many aver that the story confers no right on anyone to pass judgment on the doorkeeper. Whatever he may seem to us, he is yet a servant of the Law; that is, he belongs to the Law and as such is beyond human judgment. In that case one must not believe that the doorkeeper is subordinate to the man. Bound as he is by his service, even only at the door of the Law, he is incomparably greater than anyone at large in the world. The man is only seeking the Law, the doorkeeper is already attached to it. It is the Law that has placed him at his post; to doubt his dignity is to doubt the Law itself." "I don't agree with that point of view," said K., shaking his head, "for if one accepts it, one must accept as true everything the doorkeeper says. But you yourself have sufficiently proved how impossible it is to do that." "No," said the priest, "it is not necessary to accept everything as true, one must only accept it as necessary." "A melancholy conclusion," said K. "It turns lying into a universal principle."

1925

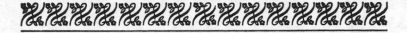

Philosophy and Religion

JAMES THURBER
The Owl Who Was God

Once upon a starless midnight there was an owl who sat on the branch of an oak tree. Two ground moles tried to slip quietly by, unnoticed. "You!" said the owl. "Who?" they quavered, in fear and astonishment, for they could not believe it was possible for anyone to see them in that thick darkness. "You two!" said the owl. The moles hurried away and told the other creatures of the field and forest that the owl was the greatest and wisest of all animals because he could see in the dark and because he could answer any question. "I'll see about that," said a secretary bird, and he called on the owl one night when it was again very dark. "How many claws am I holding up?" said the secretary bird, "Two," said the owl, and that was right. "Can you give me another expression for 'that is to say' or 'namely'?" asked the secretary bird. "To wit," said the owl. "Why does a lover call on his love?" asked the secretary bird. "To woo," said the owl.

The secretary bird hastened back to the other creatures and reported that the owl was indeed the greatest and wisest animal in the world because he could see in the dark and because he could answer any question. "Can he see in the daytime, too?" asked a red fox. "Yes," echoed a dormouse and a French poodle. "Can he see in the daytime, too?" All the other creatures laughed loudly at this silly question, and they set upon the red fox and his friends and drove them out of the region. Then they sent a messenger to the owl and asked him to be their leader.

When the owl appeared among the animals it was high noon and the sun was shining brightly. He walked very slowly, which gave him an appearance of great dignity, and he peered about him with large, staring eyes, which gave him an air of tremendous importance. "He's God!" screamed a Plymouth Rock hen. And the others took up the cry "He's God!" So they followed him wherever he went and when he began to bump into things they began to bump into things, too. Finally he came to a concrete highway and he started up the middle of it and all the other creatures followed him. Presently a hawk, who was acting as outrider, observed a truck coming toward them at fifty miles an hour, and he reported to the secretary bird and the secretary bird reported to the owl. "There's danger ahead," said the secretary bird. "To wit?" said the owl. The secretary bird told him. "Aren't you afraid?" He asked. "Who?" said the owl calmly, for he could not see the truck. "He's God!" cried all the creatures again, and they were still crying "He's God!" when the truck hit them and ran them down. Some of the animals were merely injured, but most of them, including the owl, were killed.

Moral: You can fool too many of the people too much of the time.

1955

JONATHAN EDWARDS
Sinners in the Hands of an Angry God[1]

Their foot shall slide in due time.
—DEUT. xxxii. 35[2]

In this verse is threatened the vengeance of God on the wicked unbelieving Israelites, who were God's visible people, and who lived under the means of grace; but who, notwithstanding all God's wonderful works towards them, remained (as ver. 28.)[3] void of counsel, having no understanding in them. Under all the cultivations of heaven, they brought forth bitter and poisonous fruit; as in the two verses next preceding the text. The expression I have chosen for my text, *Their foot shall slide in due time*, seems to imply the following things, relating to the punishment and destruction to which these wicked Israelites were exposed.

1. Only the first part of the sermon is printed here; the "application" is omitted.

2. The text appears in this context: "[32] For their vine is of the vine of Sodom, and of the fields of Gomorrah: their grapes are grapes of gall, their clusters are bitter: [33] Their wine is the poison of dragons, and the cruel venom of asps. [34] Is not this laid up in store with me, and sealed up among my treasures? [35] To me belongeth vengeance, and recompence; their foot shall slide in due time: for the day of their calamity is at hand, and the things that shall come upon them make haste." It occurs in the middle of a long denunciatory "song" addressed by Moses to the Israelites.

3. Verse 28: "For they are a nation void of counsel, neither is there any understanding in them."

1. That they were always exposed to *destruction;* as one that stands or walks in slippery places is always exposed to fall. This is implied in the manner of their destruction coming upon them, being represented by their foot sliding. The same is expressed, Psalm lxxiii. 18. "Surely thou didst set them in slippery places; thou castedst them down into destruction."

2. It implies that they were always exposed to sudden unexpected destruction. As he that walks in slippery places is every moment liable to fall, he cannot foresee one moment whether he shall stand or fall the next; and when he does fall, he falls at once without warning: Which is also expressed in Psalm lxxiii. 18, 19. "Surely thou didst set them in slippery places; thou castedst them down into destruction. How are they brought into desolation as in a moment!"

3. Another thing implied is, that they are liable to fall of *themselves,* without being thrown down by the hand of another; as he that stands or walks on slippery ground needs nothing but his own weight to throw him down.

4. That the reason why they are not fallen already, and do not fall now, is only that God's appointed time is not come. For it is said, that when that due time, or appointed time comes, *their foot shall slide.* Then they shall be left to fall, as they are inclined by their own weight. God will not hold them up in these slippery places any longer, but will let them go; and then, at that very instant, they shall fall into destruction; as he that stands on such slippery declining ground, on the edge of a pit, he cannot stand alone, when he is let go he immediately falls and is lost.

The observation from the words that I would now insist upon is this—"There is nothing that keeps wicked men at any one moment out of hell, but the mere pleasure of God"—By the *mere* pleasure of God, I mean his *sovereign* pleasure, his arbitrary will, restrained by no obligation, hindered by no manner of difficulty, any more than if nothing else but God's mere will had in the least degree, or in any respect whatsoever, any hand in the preservation of wicked men one moment. The truth of this observation may appear by the following considerations.

1. There is no want of *power* in God to cast wicked men into hell at any moment. Men's hands cannot be strong when God rises up. The strongest have no power to resist him, nor can any deliver out of his hands. He is not only able to cast wicked men into hell, but he can most easily do it. Sometimes an earthly prince meets with a great deal of difficulty to subdue a rebel, who has found means to fortify himself, and has made himself strong by the numbers of his followers. But it is not so with God. There is no fortress that is any defense from the power of God. Though hand join in hand, and vast multitudes of God's enemies combine and associate

themselves, they are easily broken in pieces. They are as great heaps of light chaff before the whirlwind; or large quantities of dry stubble before devouring flames. We find it easy to tread on and crush a worm that we see crawling on the earth; so it is easy for us to cut or singe a slender thread that any thing hangs by: thus easy is it for God, when he pleases, to cast his enemies down to hell. What are we, that we should think to stand before him, at whose rebuke the earth trembles, and before whom the rocks are thrown down?

2. They *deserve* to be cast into hell; so that divine justice never stands in the way, it makes no objection against God's using his power at any moment to destroy them. Yea, on the contrary, justice calls aloud for an infinite punishment of their sins. Divine justice says of the tree that brings forth such grapes of Sodom, "Cut it down, why cumbereth it the ground?" Luke xiii. 7. The sword of divine justice is every moment brandished over their heads, and it is nothing but the hand of arbitrary mercy, and God's mere will, that holds it back.

3. They are already under a sentence of *condemnation* to hell. They do not only justly deserve to be cast down thither, but the sentence of the law of God, that eternal and immutable rule of righteousness that God has fixed between him and mankind, is gone out against them, and stands against them; so that they are bound over already to hell. John iii. 18. "He that believeth not is condemned already." So that every unconverted man properly belongs to hell; that is his place; from thence he is, John viii. 23. "Ye are from beneath:" And thither he is bound; it is the place that justice, and God's word, and the sentence of his unchangeable law assign to him.

4. They are now the objects of that very same *anger* and wrath of God, that is expressed in the torments of hell. And the reason why they do not go down to hell at each moment, is not because God, in whose power they are, is not then very angry with them; as he is with many miserable creatures now tormented in hell, who there feel and bear the fierceness of his wrath. Yea, God is a great deal more angry with great numbers that are now on earth; yea, doubtless, with many that are now in this congregation, who it may be are at ease, than he is with many of those who are now in the flames of hell.

So that it is not because God is unmindful of their wickedness, and does not resent it, that he does not let loose his hand and cut them off. God is not altogether such an one as themselves, though they may imagine him to be so. The wrath of God burns against them, their damnation does not slumber; the pit is prepared, the fire is made ready, the furnace is now hot, ready to receive them; the flames do now rage and glow. The glittering sword is whet, and held over them, and the pit hath opened its mouth under them.

5. The *devil* stands ready to fall upon them, and seize them as his own, at what moment God shall permit him. They belong to him; he has their souls in his possession, and under his dominion. The scripture represents them as his goods, Luke xi. 12. The devils watch them; they are ever by them at their right hand; they stand waiting for them, like greedy hungry lions that see their prey, and expect to have it, but are for the present kept back. If God should withdraw his hand, by which they are restrained, they would in one moment fly upon their poor souls. The old serpent[4] is gaping for them; hell opens its mouth wide to receive them; and if God should permit it, they would be hastily swallowed up and lost.

6. There are in the souls of wicked men those hellish *principles* reigning, that would presently kindle and flame out into hell fire, if it were not for God's restraints. There is laid in the very nature of carnal men, a foundation for the torments of hell. There are those corrupt principles, in reigning power in them, and in full possession of them, that are seeds of hell fire. These principles are active and powerful, exceeding violent in their nature, and if it were not for the restraining hand of God upon them, they would soon break out, they would flame out after the same manner as the same corruptions, the same enmity does in the hearts of damned souls, and would beget the same torments as they do in them. The souls of the wicked are in scripture compared to the troubled sea, Isa. lvii. 20. For the present, God restrains their wickedness by his mighty power, as he does the raging waves of the troubled sea, saying, "Hitherto shalt thou come, but no further;" but if God should withdraw that restraining power, it would soon carry all before it. Sin is the ruin and misery of the soul; it is destructive in its nature; and if God should leave it without restraint, there would need nothing else to make the soul perfectly miserable. The corruption of the heart of man is immoderate and boundless in its fury; and while wicked men live here, it is like fire pent up by God's restraints, whereas if it were let loose, it would set on fire the course of nature; and as the heart is now a sink of sin, so if sin was not restrained, it would immediately turn the soul into a fiery oven, or a furnace of fire and brimstone.

7. It is no security to wicked men for one moment, that there are no visible means of death at hand. It is no security to a natural man, that he is now in health, and that he does not see which way he should now immediately go out of the world by any accident, and that there is no visible danger in any respect in his circumstances. The manifold and continual experience of the world in all ages, shows this is no evidence, that a man is not on the very brink of eternity, and that the next step will not be into another world. The

---

4. Satan, who appeared to Adam and Eve in the form of a serpent.

unseen, unthought-of ways and means of persons going suddenly out of the world are innumerable and inconceivable. Unconverted men walk over the pit of hell on a rotten covering, and there are innumerable places in this covering so weak that they will not bear their weight, and these places are not seen. The arrows of death fly unseen at noon-day; the sharpest sight cannot discern them. God has so many different unsearchable ways of taking wicked men out of the world and sending them to hell, that there is nothing to make it appear, that God had need to be at the expense of a miracle, or go out of the ordinary course of his providence, to destroy any wicked man, at any moment. All the means that there are of sinners going out of the world, are so in God's hands, and so universally and absolutely subject to his power and determination, that it does not depend at all the less on the mere will of God, whether sinners shall at any moment go to hell, than if means were never made use of, or at all concerned in the case.

8. Natural men's prudence and care to preserve their own lives, or the care of others to preserve them, do not secure them a moment. To this, divine providence and universal experience do also bear testimony. There is this clear evidence that men's own wisdom is no security to them from death; that if it were otherwise we should see some difference between the wise and politic men of the world, and others, with regard to their liableness to early and unexpected death: but how is it in fact? Eccles. ii. 16. "How dieth the wise man? even as the fool."

9. All wicked men's pains and *contrivance* which they use to escape hell, while they continue to reject Christ, and so remain wicked men, do not secure them from hell one moment. Almost every natural man that hears of hell, flatters himself that he shall escape it; he depends upon himself for his own security; he flatters himself in what he has done, in what he is now doing, or what he intends to do. Every one lays out matters in his own mind how he shall avoid damnation, and flatters himself that he contrives well for himself, and that his schemes will not fail. They hear indeed that there are but few saved, and that the greater part of men that have died heretofore are gone to hell; but each one imagines that he lays out matters better for his own escape than others have done. He does not intend to come to that place of torment; he says within himself, that he intends to take effectual care, and to order matters so for himself as not to fail.

But the foolish children of men miserably delude themselves in their own schemes, and in confidence in their own strength and wisdom; they trust to nothing but a shadow. The greater part of those who heretofore have lived under the same means of grace, and are now dead, are undoubtedly gone to hell; and it was not because they were not as wise as those who are now alive: it was not because they did not lay out matters as well for themselves to secure their own escape. If we could speak with them, and inquire of them, one by one, whether they expected, when alive, and when they used to hear about hell, ever to be the subjects of that misery: we doubtless, should hear one and another reply, "No, I never intended to come here: I had laid out matters otherwise in my mind; I thought I should contrive well for myself: I thought my scheme good. I intended to take effectual care; but it came upon me unexpected; I did not look for it at that time, and in that manner; it came as a thief: Death outwitted me: God's wrath was too quick for me. Oh, my cursed foolishness! I was flattering myself, and pleasing myself with vain dreams of what I would do hereafter; and when I was saying, Peace and safety, then suddenly destruction came upon me."

10. God has laid himself under *no* obligation, by any promise to keep any natural man out of hell one moment. God certainly has made no promises either of eternal life, or of any deliverance or preservation from eternal death, but what are contained in the covenant of grace, the promises that are given in Christ, in whom all the promises are yea and amen. But surely they have no interest in the promises of the covenant of grace who are not the children of the covenant, who do not believe in any of the promises, and have no interest in the Mediator of the covenant.

So that, whatever some have imagined and pretended about promises made to natural men's earnest seeking and knocking, it is plain and manifest, that whatever pains a natural man takes in religion, whatever prayers he makes, till he believes in Christ, God is under no manner of obligation to keep him a moment from eternal destruction.

So that, thus it is that natural men are held in the hand of God, over the pit of hell; they have deserved the fiery pit, and are already sentenced to it; and God is dreadfully provoked, his anger is as great towards them as to those that are actually suffering the executions of the fierceness of his wrath in hell, and they have done nothing in the least to appease or abate that anger, neither is God in the least bound by any promise to hold them up one moment; the devil is waiting for them, hell is gaping for them, the flames gather and flash about them, and would fain lay hold on them, and swallow them up; the fire pent up in their own hearts is struggling to break out: and they have no interest in any Mediator, there are no means within reach that can be any security to them. In short, they have no refuge, nothing to take hold of; all that preserves them every moment is in the mere arbitrary will, and uncovenanted, unobliged forbearance of an incensed God.

1741

QUESTIONS

1. Trace the steps by which Edwards gets from his text to his various conclusions about man's state. Are they all logical? What assumptions does he add to those implied by the text in developing his argument? (Before answering these questions you will probably want to check the entire context of the text in Deuteronomy xxxii.)

2. What kinds of evidence does Edwards use in supporting his argument? Are they equally valid?

3. How do the concrete details, the imagery, and the metaphors that Edwards uses contribute to the effectiveness of his argument?

4. One might make the assumption that a society's conception of hell reflects, at least indirectly, some of that society's positive values. What positive values are reflected in Edwards' picture of hell?

5. One of his pupils described Edwards' delivery: "His appearance in the desk was with a good grace, and his delivery easy, natural and very solemn. He had not a strong, loud voice, but appeared with such gravity and solemnity, and spake with such distinctness and precision, his words were so full of ideas, set in such a plain and striking light, that few speakers have been so able to demand the attention of an audience as he. His words often discovered a great degree of inward fervor, without much noise or external emotion, and fell with great weight on the minds of his hearers. He made but little motion of his head or hands in the desk, but spake as to discover the motion of his own heart, which tended in the most natural and effectual manner to move and affect others." Would this manner of delivery be effective for the sermon printed here? Explain.

C. S. LEWIS
Three Screwtape Letters

I

MY DEAR WORMWOOD,[1]

I note what you say about guiding your patient's reading and taking care that he sees a good deal of his materialist friend. But are you not being a trifle *naïf*? It sounds as if you supposed that *argument* was the way to keep him out of the Enemy's clutches. That might have been so if he had lived a few centuries earlier. At that time the humans still knew pretty well when a thing was proved and when it was not; and if it was proved they really believed it.

---

1. In these letters from Hell, Screwtape, an experienced devil, is counseling his nephew Wormwood, a neophyte tempter, who has ascended to Earth to begin his work.

They still connected thinking with doing and were prepared to alter their way of life as the result of a chain of reasoning. But what with the weekly press and other such weapons we have largely altered that. Your man has been accustomed, ever since he was a boy, to have a dozen incompatible philosophies dancing about together inside his head. He doesn't think of doctrines as primarily "true" or "false", but as "academic" or "practical", "outworn" or "contemporary", "conventional" or "ruthless". Jargon, not argument, is your best ally in keeping him from the Church. Don't waste time trying to make him think that materialism is *true*! Make him think it is strong, or stark, or courageous—that it is the philosophy of the future. That's the sort of thing he cares about.

The trouble about argument is that it moves the whole struggle onto the Enemy's own ground. He can argue too; whereas in really practical propaganda of the kind I am suggesting He has been shown for centuries to be greatly the inferior of Our Father Below. By the very act of arguing, you awake the patient's reason; and once it is awake, who can foresee the result? Even if a particular train of thought can be twisted so as to end in our favour, you will find that you have been strengthening in your patient the fatal habit of attending to universal issues and withdrawing his attention from the stream of immediate sense experiences. Your business is to fix his attention on the stream. Teach him to call it "real life" and don't let him ask what he means by "real".

Remember, he is not, like you, a pure spirit. Never having been a human (Oh that abominable advantage of the Enemy's!) you don't realise how enslaved they are to the pressure of the ordinary. I once had a patient, a sound atheist, who used to read in the British Museum. One day, as he sat reading, I saw a train of thought in his mind beginning to go the wrong way. The Enemy, of course, was at his elbow in a moment. Before I knew where I was I saw my twenty years' work beginning to totter. If I had lost my head and begun to attempt a defence by argument I should have been undone. But I was not such a fool. I struck instantly at the part of the man which I had best under my control and suggested that it was just about time he had some lunch. The Enemy presumably made the counter-suggestion (you know how one can never *quite* overhear what He says to them?) that this was more important than lunch. At least I think that must have been His line for when I said "Quite. In fact much *too* important to tackle at the end of a morning", the patient brightened up considerably; and by the time I had added "Much better come back after lunch and go into it with a fresh mind", he was already half way to the door. Once he was in the street the battle was won. I showed him a newsboy shouting the midday paper, and a No. 73 bus going past, and before he reached the bottom of the steps I had got into him an unalterable conviction that, whatever odd ideas might come into a man's head when he was shut up alone with his books, a healthy dose of "real life" (by which he meant the bus and the newsboy) was enough to show him that all "that sort of thing" just couldn't be true. He knew he'd had a narrow escape and in later years was fond of talking about "that inarticulate sense for actuality which is our ultimate safeguard against the aberrations of mere logic". He is now safe in Our Father's house.

You begin to see the point? Thanks to processes which we set at work in them centuries ago, they find it all but impossible to believe in the unfamiliar while the familiar is before their eyes. Keep pressing home on him the *ordinariness* of things. Above all, do not attempt to use science (I mean, the real sciences) as a defence against Christianity. They will positively encourage him to think about realities he can't touch and see. There have been sad cases among the modern physicists. If he must dabble in science, keep him on economics and sociology; don't let him get away from that invaluable "real life". But the best of all is to let him read no science but to give him a grand general idea that he knows it all and that everything he happens to have picked up in casual talk and reading is "the results of modern investigation". Do remember you are there to fuddle him. From the way some of you young fiends talk, anyone would suppose it was our job to *teach*!

Your affectionate uncle
SCREWTAPE

II

MY DEAR WORMWOOD,

I note with grave displeasure that your patient has become a Christian. Do not indulge the hope that you will escape the usual penalties: indeed, in your better moments, I trust you would hardly even wish to do so. In the meantime we must make the best of the situation. There is no need to despair; hundreds of these adult converts have been reclaimed after a brief sojourn in the Enemy's camp and are now with us. All the *habits* of the patient, both mental and bodily, are still in our favour.

One of our great allies at present is the Church itself. Do not misunderstand me. I do not mean the Church as we see her spread out through all time and space and rooted in eternity, terrible as an army with banners. That, I confess, is a spectacle which makes our boldest tempters uneasy. But fortunately it is quite invisible to these humans. All your patient sees is the half-finished, sham Gothic erection on the new building estate. When he goes inside, he sees the local grocer with rather an oily expression on his face bustling up to offer him one shiny little book containing a liturgy which neither of them understands, and one shabby little book containing corrupt texts of a number of religious lyrics, mostly bad, and in very small print. When he gets to his pew and looks round him he sees just that selection of his neighbours whom he has hitherto avoided. You want to lean pretty heavily on those neighbours. Make his mind flit to and fro between an expression like "the body of Christ" and the actual faces in the next pew. It matters very little of course, what kind of people that next pew really contains. You may know one of them to be a great warrior on the Enemy's side. No matter. Your patient, thanks to Our Father Below, is a fool. Provided that any of those neighbours sing out of tune, or have boots that squeak, or double chins, or odd clothes, the patient will quite easily believe that their religion must therefore be somehow ridiculous. At his present stage, you see, he has an idea of "Christians" in his mind which he supposes to be spiritual but which, in fact, is largely pictorial. His mind is full of togas and sandals and armour and bare legs and the mere fact that the other people in church wear modern clothes is a real—though of course an unconscious—difficulty to him. Never let it come to the surface; never let him ask what he expected them to look like. Keep everything hazy in his mind now, and you will have all eternity wherein to amuse yourself by producing in him the peculiar kind of clarity which Hell affords.

Work hard, then, on the disappointment or anticlimax which is certainly coming to the patient during his first few weeks as a churchman. The Enemy allows this disappointment to occur on the threshold of every human endeavour. It occurs when the boy who has been enchanted in the nursery by *Stories from the Odyssey* buckles down to really learning Greek. It occurs when lovers have got married and begin the real task of learning to live together. In every department of life it marks the transition from dreaming aspiration to laborious doing. The Enemy takes this risk because He has a curious fantasy of making all these disgusting little human vermin into what He calls His "free" lovers and servants—"sons" is the word He uses, with His inveterate love of degrading the whole spiritual world by unnatural liaisons with the two-legged animals. Desiring their freedom, He therefore refuses to carry them, by their mere affections and habits, to any of the goals which He sets before them: He leaves them to "do it on their own". And there lies our opportunity. But also, remember, there lies our danger. If once they get through this initial dryness successfully, they become much less dependent on emotion and therefore much harder to tempt.

I have been writing hitherto on the assumption that the people in the next pew afford no *rational* ground for disappointment. Of course if they do—if the patient knows that the woman with the absurd hat is a fanatical bridge-player or the man with squeaky boots a miser and an extortioner—then your task is so much the easier. All you then have to do is to keep out of his mind the question "If I, being what I am, can consider that I am in some sense a Christian, why should the different vices of those people in the next pew prove that their religion is mere hypocrisy and convention?" You may ask whether it is possible to keep such an obvious thought from occurring even to a human mind. It is, Wormwood, it is! Handle him properly and it simply won't come into his head. He has not been anything like long enough with the Enemy to have any real humility yet. What he says, even on his knees, about his own sinfulness is all parrot talk. At bottom, he still believes he has run up a very favourable credit-balance in the Enemy's ledger by allowing himself to be converted, and thinks that he is showing great humility and condescension in going to church with those "smug", commonplace neighbours at all. Keep him in that state of mind as long as you can.

> Your affectionate uncle
> SCREWTAPE

III

MY DEAR WORMWOOD,

I am very pleased by what you tell me about this man's relations with his mother. But you must press your advantage. The Enemy will be working from the centre outwards, gradually bringing more and more of the patient's conduct under the new standard, and may reach his behaviour to the old lady at any moment. You want to get in first. Keep in close touch with our colleague Glubose who is in charge of the mother, and build up between you in that house a good settled habit of mutual annoyance; daily pinpricks. The following methods are useful.

1. Keep his mind on the inner life. He thinks his conversion is something *inside* him and his attention is therefore chiefly turned at present to the states of his own mind—or rather to that very expurgated version of them which is all you should allow him to see. Encourage this. Keep his mind off the most elementary duties by directing it to the most advanced and spiritual ones. Aggravate that most useful human characteristic, the horror and neglect of the obvious. You must bring him to a condition in which he can practise self-examination for an hour without discovering any of those facts about himself which are perfectly clear to anyone who has ever lived in the same house with him or worked in the same office.

2. It is, no doubt, impossible to prevent his praying for his mother, but we have means of rendering the prayers innocuous.

Make sure that they are always very "spiritual", that he is always concerned with the state of her soul and never with her rheumatism. Two advantages will follow. In the first place, his attention will be kept on what he regards as her sins, by which, with a little guidance from you, he can be induced to mean any of her actions which are inconvenient or irritating to himself. Thus you can keep rubbing the wounds of the day a little sorer even while he is on his knees; the operation is not at all difficult and you will find it very entertaining. In the second place, since his ideas about her soul will be very crude and often erroneous, he will, in some degree, be praying for an imaginary person, and it will be your task to make that imaginary person daily less and less like the real mother—the sharp-tongued old lady at the breakfast table. In time, you may get the cleavage so wide that no thought or feeling from his prayers for the imagined mother will ever flow over into his treatment of the real one. I have had patients of my own so well in hand that they could be turned at a moment's notice from impassioned prayer for a wife's or son's "soul" to beating or insulting the real wife or son without a qualm.

3. When two humans have lived together for many years it usually happens that each has tones of voice and expressions of face which are almost unendurably irritating to the other. Work on that. Bring fully into the consciousness of your patient that particular lift of his mother's eyebrows which he learned to dislike in the nursery, and let him think how much he dislikes it. Let him assume that she knows how annoying it is and does it to annoy—if you know your job he will not notice the immense improbability of the assumption. And, of course, never let him suspect that he has tones and looks which similarly annoy her. As he cannot see or hear himself, this is easily managed.

4. In civilised life domestic hatred usually expresses itself by saying things which would appear quite harmless on paper (the *words* are not offensive) but in such a voice, or at such a moment, that they are not far short of a blow in the face. To keep this game up you and Glubose must see to it that each of these two fools has a sort of double standard. Your patient must demand that all his own utterances are to be taken at their face value and judged simply on the actual words, while at the same time judging all his mother's utterances with the fullest and most over-sensitive interpretation of the tone and the context and the suspected intention. She must be encouraged to do the same to him. Hence from every quarrel they can both go away convinced, or very nearly convinced, that they are quite innocent. You know the kind of thing: "I simply ask her what time dinner will be and she flies into a temper." Once this habit is well established you have the delightful situation of a human saying

things with the express purpose of offending and yet having a grievance when offence is taken.

Finally, tell me something about the old lady's religious position.
Is she at all jealous of the new factor in her son's life?—at all
piqued that he should have learned from others, and so late, what
she considers she gave him such good opportunity of learning in
childhood? Does she feel he is making a great deal of "fuss" about
it—or that he's getting in on very easy terms? Remember the elder
brother in the Enemy's story,[2]

Your affectionate uncle
SCREWTAPE

1942

2. The reference is to Jesus' parable
of the prodigal son. The younger brother, having gone out into the world and
spent his inheritance, was welcomed
back by the father with feasting and
celebration; this made the older brother,
who had stayed at home and labored
diligently for the father, angry and envious.

QUESTIONS

1. How would you state the serious underlying purpose of the
   Screwtape letters? Does Lewis derive advantages for that purpose
   by adopting a humorous manner? Can you show any instances in
   which that manner places familiar material in a new light?
2. What sort of characteristics does Lewis attribute to his devil
   Screwtape? Are they strange and unfamiliar, or are they human
   and familiar? What point does Lewis make by portraying his
   devil as he does?
3. Following Lewis, write another letter from Screwtape to Wormwood upon learning that Wormwood's subject has just been reading Jonathan Edwards' "Sinners in the Hands of an Angry God"
   (pp. 630–635) or Paul Tillich's "The Riddle of Inequality" (pp.
   643–649).
4. Try applying Lewis' method of irony to some other topic; write a
   letter or series of letters from an older student to a freshman on
   the subject of teachers, for example, or from one parent to
   another about their college-age children, or from an experienced
   government official to a newly elected one.

PAUL TILLICH

The Riddle of Inequality

> For to him who has will more be given; and from him
> who has not, even what he has will be taken away.
> —MARK iv. 25

One day a learned colleague called me up and said to me with
angry excitement: "There is a saying in the New Testament which
I consider to be one of the most immoral and unjust statements
ever made!" And then he started quoting our text: "To him who
has will more be given," and his anger increased when he continued:
"and from him who has not, even what he has will be taken away."
We all, I think, feel offended with him. And we cannot easily
ignore the offense by suggesting what *he* suggested—that the
words may be due to a misunderstanding of the disciples. It appears
at least four times in the gospels with great emphasis. And even
more, we can clearly see that the writers of the gospels felt exactly
as we do. For them it was a stumbling block, which they tried to
interpret in different ways. Probably none of these explanations satisfied them fully, for with this saying of Jesus, we are confronted
immediately with the greatest and perhaps most painful riddle of
life, that of the inequality of all beings. We certainly cannot hope to
solve it when neither the Bible nor any other of the great religions
and philosophies was able to do so. But we can do two things: We
can show the breadth and the depth of the riddle of inequality and
we can try to find a way to live with it, even if it is unsolved.

I

If we hear the words, "to him who has will more be given," we
ask ourselves: What *do* we have? And then we may find that much is
given to us in terms of external goods, of friends, of intellectual
gifts and even of a comparatively high moral level of action. So we
can expect that more will be given to us, while we must expect
that those who are lacking in all that will lose the little they already
have. Even further, according to Jesus' parable, the one talent[1] they
have will be given to us who have five or ten talents. We shall be
richer because they will be poorer. We may cry out against such
an injustice. But we cannot deny that life confirms it abundantly.
We cannot deny it, but we can ask the question, do we *really*
have what we believe we have so that it cannot be taken from
us? It is a question full of anxiety, confirmed by a version of our
text rendered by Luke. "From him who has not, even what he

---

1. A Middle Eastern coin at the time of Christ.

thinks that he has will be taken away." Perhaps our having of those many things is not the kind of having which is increased. Perhaps the having of few things by the poor ones is the kind of having which makes them grow. In the parable of the talents, Jesus confirms this. Those talents which are used, even with a risk of losing them, are those which we really have; those which we try to preserve without using them for growth are those which we do not really have and which are being taken away from us. They slowly disappear, and suddenly we feel that we have, lost these talents, perhaps forever.

Let us apply this to our own life, whether it is long or short. In the memory of all of us many things appear which we had without having them and which were taken away from us. Some of them became lost because of the tragic limitations of life; we had to sacrifice them in order to make other things grow. We all were given childish innocence; but innocence cannot be used and increased. The growth of our lives is possible only because we have sacrificed the original gift of innocence. Nevertheless, sometimes there arises in us a melancholy longing for a purity which has been taken from us. We all were given youthful enthusiasm for many things and aims. But this also cannot be used and increased. Most of the objects of our early enthusiasm must be sacrificed for a few, and the few must be approached with soberness. No maturity is possible without this sacrifice. Yet often a melancholy longing for the lost possibilities and enthusiasm takes hold of us. Innocence and youthful enthusiasm: we had them and had them not. Life itself demanded that they were taken from us.

But there are other things which we had and which were taken from us, because we let them go through our own guilt. Some of us had a deep sensitivity for the wonder of life as it is revealed in nature. Slowly under the pressure of work and social life and the lure of cheap pleasures, we lose the wonder of our earlier years when we felt intense joy and the presence of the mystery of life through the freshness of the young day or the glory of the dying day, the majesty of the mountains or the infinity of the sea, a flower breaking through the soil or a young animal in the perfection of its movements. Perhaps we try to produce such feelings again, but we are empty and do not succeed. We had it and had it not, and it has been taken from us.

Others had the same experience with music, poetry, the great novels and plays. One wanted to devour all of them, one lived in them and created for oneself a life above the daily life. We *had* all this and did not have it; we did not let it grow; our love towards it was not strong enough and so it was taken from us.

Many, especially in this group, remember a time in which the desire to learn to solve the riddles of the universe, to find truth has been the driving force in their lives. They came to college and university, not in order to buy their entrance ticket into the upper middle classes or in order to provide for the preconditions of social and economic success, but they came, driven by the desire for knowledge. They had something and more could have been given to them. But in reality they did not have it. They did not make it grow and so it was taken from them and they finished their academic work in terms of expendiency and indifference towards truth. Their love for truth has left them and in some moments they are sick in their hearts because they realize that what they have lost they may never get back.

We all know that any deeper relation to a human being needs watchfulness and growth, otherwise it is taken away from us. And we cannot get it back. This is a form of having and not having which is the root of innumerable human tragedies. We all know about them. And there is another, the most fundamental kind of having and not having—our having and losing God. Perhaps we were rich towards God in our childhood and beyond it. We may remember the moments in which we felt his ultimate presence. We may remember prayers with an overflowing heart, the encounter with the holy in word and music and holy places. We had communication with God; but it was taken from us because we had it and had it not. We did not let it grow, and so it slowly disappeared leaving an empty space. We became unconcerned, cynical, indifferent, not because we doubted about our religious traditions—such doubt belongs to being rich towards God—but because we turned away from that which once concerned us infinitely.

Such thoughts are a first step in approaching the riddle of inequality. Those who have, receive more if they really have it, if they use it and make it grow. And those who have not, lose what they have because they never had it really.

II

But the question of inequality is not yet answered. For one now asks: Why do some receive more than others in the very beginning, before there is even the possibility of using or wasting our talents? Why does the one servant receive five talents and the other two and the third one? Why is the one born in the slums and the other in a well-to-do suburban family? It does not help to answer that of those to whom much is given much is demanded and little of those to whom little is given. For it is just this inequality of original gifts, internal and external, which arouses our question. Why is it given to one human being to gain so much more out of his being human than to another one? Why is so much given to the one that much *can* be asked of him, while to the other one little is given and little *can* be asked? If this question is asked, not only about individual men but also about classes, races and nations, the everlasting question of political inequality arises, and with it the many ways appear in which men have tried to abolish inequality. In every revolution and in every war, the will to solve the riddle of inequality is a driving force. But neither war nor revolution can remove it. Even if we imagine that in an indefinite future most social inequalities are conquered, three things remain: the inequality of talents in body and mind, the inequality created by freedom and destiny, and the fact that all generations before the time of such equality would be excluded from its blessings. This would be the greatest possible inequality! No! In face of one of the deepest and most torturing problems of life, it is unpermittably shallow and foolish to escape into a social dreamland. We have to live now; we have to live this our life, and we must face today the riddle of inequality.

Let us not confuse the riddle of inequality with the fact that each of us is a unique incomparable self. Certainly our being individuals belongs to our dignity as men. It is given to us and must be used and intensified and not drowned in the gray waters of conformity which threaten us today. One should defend every individuality and the uniqueness of every human self. But one should not believe that this is a way of solving the riddle of inequality. Unfortunately, there are social and political reactionaries who use this confusion in order to justify social injustice. They are at least as foolish as the dreamers of a future removal of inequality. Whoever has seen hospitals, prisons, sweatshops, battlefields, houses for the insane, starvation, family tragedies, moral aberrations should be cured from any confusion of the gift of individuality with the riddle of inequality. He should be cured from any feelings of easy consolation.

III

And now we must make the third step in our attempt to penetrate the riddle of inequality and ask: Why do some use and increase what was given to them, while others do not, so that it is taken from them? Why does God say to the prophet in our Old Testament lesson that the ears and eyes of a nation are made insensible for the divine message?

Is it enough to answer: Because some use their freedom responsibly and do what they ought to do while others fail through their own guilt? Is this answer, which seems so obvious, sufficient? Now let me first say that it *is* sufficient if we apply it to ourselves. Each of us must consider the increase or the loss of what is given to him as a matter of his own responsibility. Our conscience tells us that we cannot put the blame for our losses on anybody or anything else than ourselves.

But if we look at others, this answer is not sufficient. On the contrary: If we applied the judgment which we *must* apply to anyone else we would be like the Pharisee in Jesus' parable.[2] You cannot tell somebody who comes to you in distress about himself: Use what has been given to you; for he may come to you just because he is unable to do so! And you cannot tell those who are in despair about what they are: Be something else; for this is just what despair means—the inability of getting rid of oneself. You cannot tell those who did not conquer the destructive influences of their surroundings and were driven into crime and misery that they should have been stronger; for it was just of this strength they had been deprived by heritage or environment. Certainly they all are men, and to all of them freedom is given; but they all are also subject to destiny. It is not up to us to condemn them because they were free, as it is not up to us to excuse them because they were under their destiny. We cannot judge them. And when we judge ourselves, we must be conscious that even this is not the last word, but that we like them are under an ultimate judgment. In it the riddle of inequality is eternally answered. But this answer is not ours. It is our predicament that we must ask. And we ask with an uneasy conscience. Why are they in misery, why not we? Thinking of some who are near to us, we can ask: Are we partly responsible? But even if we are, it does not solve the riddle of inequality. The uneasy conscience asks about the farthest as well as about the nearest: Why they, why not we?

Why has my child, or any of millions and millions of children, died before even having a chance to grow out of infancy? Why is my child, or any child, born feeble-minded or crippled? Why has my friend or relative, or anybody's friend or relative, disintegrated in his mind and lost both his freedom and his destiny? Why has my son or daughter, gifted as I believe with many talents, wasted them and been deprived of them? And why does this happen to any parent at all? Why have this boy's or this girl's creative powers been broken by a tyrannical father or by a possessive mother?

In all these questions it is not the question of our own misery which we ask. It is not the question: Why has this happened to *me*?

It is not the question of Job which God answers by humiliating him and then by elevating him into communion with him.[3] It is not the old and urgent question: Where is the divine justice, where is the divine love towards me? But it is almost the opposite question: Why has this *not* happened to me, why has it happened to the other

2. Praying in the temple, the Pharisee said, "God, I thank thee, that I am not as other men are, extortioners, unjust, adulterers . . . " (Luke xviii.11).

3. Job, one of God's favored servants, was stricken with afflictions. His ques-

tion, very briefly, was "Why?" God's answer was to remind Job of how powerless man was in comparison with God, and to refuse to explain His actions. After accepting this pronouncement, Job was elevated again into God's favor.

one, to the innumerable other ones to whom not even the power of Job is given to accept the divine answer? Why—and Jesus has asked the same question—are many called and few elected?

He does not answer; he only states that this is the human predicament. Shall we therefore cease to ask and humbly accept the fact of a divine judgment which condemns most human beings away from the community with him into despair and self-destruction? Can we accept the eternal victory of judgment over love? We cannot; and nobody ever could, even if he preached and threatened in these terms. As long as he could not see himself with complete certainty as eternally rejected, his preaching and threatening would be self-deceiving. And who could see himself eternally rejected?

But if this is not the solution of the riddle of inequality at its deepest level, can we trespass the boundaries of the Christian tradition and listen to those who tell us that this life does not decide about our eternal destiny? There will be occasions in other lives, as our present life is determined by previous ones and what we have achieved or wasted in them. It is a serious doctrine and not completely strange to Christianity. But if we don't know and never will know what each of us has been in the previous or future lives, then it is not really *our* destiny which develops from life to life, but in each life it is the destiny of someone else. This answer also does not solve the riddle of inequality.

There is no answer at all if we ask about the temporal and eternal destiny of the single being separated from the destiny of the whole. Only in the unity of all beings in time and eternity can a humanly possible answer to the riddle of inequality be found. *Humanly* possible does not mean an answer which removes the riddle of inequality, but an answer with which we can live.

There is an ultimate unity of all beings, rooted in the divine life from which they come and to which they go. All beings, non-human as well as human, participate in it. And therefore they all participate in each other. We participate in each other's having and we participate in each other's not-having. If we become aware of this unity of all beings, something happens. The fact that others have-not changes in every moment the character of my having: It undercuts its security, it drives me beyond myself, to understand, to give, to share, to help. The fact that others fall into sin, crime and misery changes the character of the grace which is given to me: It makes me realize my own hidden guilt, it shows to me that those who suffer for their sin and crime, suffer also for me; for I am guilty of their guilt—at least in the desire of my heart—and ought to suffer as they do. The awareness that others who *could* have become fully developed human beings and never *have*, changes my state of full humanity. Their early death, their early or late disintegration, makes my life and my health a continuous risk, a dying which is not yet death, a disintegration which is not yet destruction. In every death which we encounter, something of us dies; in every disease which we encounter, something of us tends to disintegrate.

Can we live with this answer? We can to the degree in which we are liberated from the seclusion within ourselves. But nobody can be liberated from himself unless he is grasped by the power of that which is present in everyone and everything—the eternal from which we come and to which we go, which gives us to ourselves and which liberates us *from* ourselves. It is the greatness and the heart of the Christian message that God—as manifest in the Cross of the Christ—participates totally in the dying child, in the condemned criminal, in the disintegrating mind, in the starving one and in him who rejects him. There is no extreme human condition into which the divine presence would not reach. This is what the Cross, the most extreme of all human conditions, tells us. The riddle of inequality cannot be solved on the level of our separation from each other. It is eternally solved in the divine participation in all of us and every being. The certainty of the divine participation gives us the courage to stand the riddle of inequality, though finite minds cannot solve it. Amen.

1963

GILBERT HIGHET

The Mystery of Zen

The mind need never stop growing. Indeed, one of the few experiences which never pall is the experience of watching one's own mind, and observing how it produces new interests, responds to new stimuli, and develops new thoughts, apparently without effort and almost independently of one's own conscious control. I have seen this happen to myself a hundred times; and every time it happens again, I am equally fascinated and astonished.

Some years ago a publisher sent me a little book for review. I read it, and decided it was too remote from my main interests and too highly specialized. It was a brief account of how a young German philosopher living in Japan had learned how to shoot with a bow and arrow, and how this training had made it possible for him to understand the esoteric doctrines of the Zen sect of Buddhism. Really, what could be more alien to my own life, and to that of everyone I knew, than Zen Buddhism and Japanese archery? So I thought, and put the book away.

Yet I did not forget it. It was well written, and translated into good English. It was delightfully short, and implied much more than it said. Although its theme was extremely odd, it was at least highly individual; I had never read anything like it before or since. It remained in my mind. Its name was *Zen in the Art of Archery*, its author Eugen Herrigel, its publisher Pantheon of New York. One day I took it off the shelf and read it again; this time it seemed even stranger than before and even more unforgettable. Now it began to cohere with other interests of mine. Something I had read of the Japanese art of flower arrangement seemed to connect with it; and then, when I wrote an essay on the peculiar Japanese poems called *haiku*, other links began to grow. Finally I had to read the book once more with care, and to go through some other works which illuminated the same subject. I am still grappling with the theme; I have not got anywhere near understanding it fully; but I have learned a good deal, and I am grateful to the little book which refused to be forgotten.

The author, a German philosopher, got a job teaching philosophy at the University of Tokyo (apparently between the wars), and he did what Germans in foreign countries do not usually do: he determined to adapt himself and to learn from his hosts. In particular, he had always been interested in mysticism—which, for every earnest philosopher, poses a problem that is all the more inescapable because it is virtually insoluble. Zen Buddhism is not the only mystical doctrine to be found in the East, but it is one of the most highly developed and certainly one of the most difficult to approach. Herrigel knew that there were scarcely any books which did more than skirt the edge of the subject, and that the best of all books on Zen (those by the philosopher D. T. Suzuki) constantly emphasize that Zen can never be learned from books, can never be studied as we can study other disciplines such as logic or mathematics. Therefore he began to look for a Japanese thinker who could teach him directly.

At once he met with embarrassed refusals. His Japanese friends explained that he would gain nothing from trying to discuss Zen as a philosopher, that its theories could not be spread out for analysis by a detached mind, and in fact that the normal relationship of teacher and pupil simply did not exist within the sect, because the Zen masters felt it useless to explain things stage by stage and to argue about the various possible interpretations of their doctrine. Herrigel had read enough to be prepared for this. He replied that he did not want to dissect the teachings of the school, because he knew that would be useless. He wanted to become a Zen mystic himself. (This was highly intelligent of him. No one could really penetrate into Christian mysticism without being a devout Christian; no one could appreciate Hindu mystical doctrine without accepting the Hindu view of the universe.) At this,

Herrigel's Japanese friends were more forthcoming. They told him that the best way, indeed the only way, for a European to approach Zen mysticism was to learn one of the arts which exemplified it. He was a fairly good rifle shot, so he determined to learn archery, and his wife co-operated with him by taking lessons in painting and flower arrangement. How any philosopher could investigate a mystical doctrine by learning to shoot with a bow and arrow and watching his wife arrange flowers, Herrigel did not ask. He had good sense.

A Zen master who was a teacher of archery agreed to take him as a pupil. The lessons lasted six years, during which he practiced every single day. There are many difficult courses of instruction in the world: the Jesuits, violin virtuosi, Talmudic scholars, all have long and hard training, which in one sense never comes to an end; but Herrigel's training in archery equaled them all in intensity. If I were trying to learn archery, I should expect to begin by looking at a target and shooting arrows at it. He was not even allowed to aim at a target for the first four years. He had to begin by learning how to hold the bow and arrow, and then how to release the arrow; this took ages. The Japanese bow is not like our sporting bow, and the stance of the archer in Japan is different from ours. We hold the bow at shoulder level, stretch our left arm out ahead, pull the string and the nocked arrow to a point either below the chin or sometimes past the right ear, and then shoot. The Japanese hold the bow above the head, and then pull the hands apart to left and right until the left hand comes down to eye level and the right hand comes to rest above the right shoulder; then there is a pause, during which the bow is held at full stretch, with the tip of the three-foot arrow projecting only a few inches beyond the bow; after that, the arrow is loosed. When Herrigel tried this, even without aiming, he found it was almost impossible. His hands trembled. His legs stiffened and grew cramped. His breathing became labored. And of course he could not possibly aim. Week after week he practiced this, with the Master watching him carefully and correcting his strained attitude; week after week he made no progress whatever. Finally he gave up and told his teacher that he could not learn: it was absolutely impossible for him to draw the bow and loose the arrow.

To his astonishment, the Master agreed. He said, "Certainly you cannot. It is because you are not breathing correctly. You must learn to breathe in a steady rhythm, keeping your lungs full most of the time, and drawing in one rapid inspiration with each stage of the process, as you grasp the bow, fit the arrow, raise the bow, draw, pause, and loose the shot. If you do, you will both grow stronger and be able to relax." To prove this, he himself drew his massive bow and told his pupil to feel the muscles of his arms: they were perfectly relaxed, as though he were doing no work whatever.

Herrigel now started breathing exercises; after some time he combined the new rhythm of breathing with the actions of drawing and shooting; and, much to his astonishment, he found that the whole thing, after this complicated process, had become much easier. Or rather, not easier, but different. At times it became quite unconscious. He says himself that he felt he was not breathing, but being breathed; and in time he felt that the occasional shot was not being dispatched by him, but shooting itself. The bow and arrow were in charge; he had become merely a part of them.

All this time, of course, Herrigel did not even attempt to discuss Zen doctrine with his Master. No doubt he knew that he was approaching it, but he concentrated solely on learning how to shoot. Every stage which he surmounted appeared to lead to another stage even more difficult. It took him months to learn how to loosen the bowstring. The problem was this. If he gripped the string and arrowhead tightly, either he froze, so that his hands were slowly pulled together and the shot was wasted, or else he jerked, so that the arrow flew up into the air or down into the ground; and if he was relaxed, then the bowstring and arrow simply *leaked* out of his grasp before he could reach full stretch, and the arrow went nowhere. He explained this problem to the Master. The Master understood perfectly well. He replied, "You must hold the drawn bowstring like a child holding a grownup's finger. You know how firmly a child grips; and yet when it lets go, there is not the slightest jerk—because the child does not think of itself, it is not self-conscious, it does not say, 'I will now let go and do something else,' it merely acts instinctively. That is what you must learn to do. Practice, practice, and practice, and then the string will loose itself at the right moment. The shot will come as effortlessly as snow slipping from a leaf." Day after day, week after week, month after month, Herrigel practiced this; and then, after one shot, the Master suddenly bowed and broke off the lesson. He said "Just then it shot. Not you, but *it*." And gradually thereafter more and more right shots achieved themselves; the young philosopher forgot himself, forgot that he was learning archery for some other purpose, forgot even that he was practicing archery, and became part of that unconsciously active complex, the bow, the string, the arrow, and the man.

Next came the target. After four years, Herrigel was allowed to shoot at the target. But he was strictly forbidden to aim at it. The Master explained that even he himself did not aim; and indeed, when he shot, he was so absorbed in the act, so selfless and unanxious, that his eyes were almost closed. It was difficult, almost impossible, for Herrigel to believe that such shooting could ever be effective; and he risked insulting the Master by suggesting that he ought to be able to hit the target blindfolded. But the Master accepted the challenge. That night, after a cup of tea and long meditation, he went into the archery hall, put on the lights at one end and left the target perfectly dark, with only a thin taper burning in front of it. Then, with habitual grace and precision, and with that strange, almost sleepwalking, selfless confidence that is the heart of Zen, he shot two arrows into the darkness. Herrigel went out to collect them. He found that the first had gone to the heart of the bull's eye, and that the second had actually hit the first arrow and splintered it. The Master showed no pride. He said, "Perhaps, with unconscious memory of the position of the target, *I* shot the first arrow; but the second arrow? *It* shot the second arrow, and *it* brought it to the center of the target."

At last Herrigel began to understand. His progress became faster and faster; easier, too. Perfect shots (perfect because perfectly unconscious) occurred at almost every lesson; and finally, after six years of incessant training, in a public display he was awarded the diploma. He needed no further instruction: he had himself become a Master. His wife meanwhile had become expert both in painting and in the arrangement of flowers—two of the finest of Japanese arts. (I wish she could be persuaded to write a companion volume, called *Zen in the Art of Flower Arrangement*; it would have a wider general appeal than her husband's work.) I gather also from a hint or two in his book that she had taken part in the archery lessons. During one of the most difficult periods in Herrigel's training, when his Master had practically refused to continue teaching him—because Herrigel had tried to cheat by *consciously* opening his hand at the moment of loosing the arrow—his wife had advised him against that solution, and sympathized with him when it was rejected. She in her own way had learned more quickly than he, and reached the final point together with him. All their effort had not been in vain: Herrigel and his wife had really acquired a new and valuable kind of wisdom. Only at this point, when he was about to abandon his lessons forever, did his Master treat him almost as an equal and hint at the innermost doctrines of Zen Buddhism. Only hints he gave; and yet, for the young philosopher who had now become a mystic, they were enough. Herrigel understood the doctrine, not with his logical mind, but with his entire being. He at any rate had solved the mystery of Zen.

Without going through a course of training as absorbing and as complete as Herrigel's, we can probably never penetrate the mystery. The doctrine of Zen cannot be analyzed from without: it must be lived.

But although it cannot be analyzed, it can be hinted at. All the hints that the adherents of this creed give us are interesting. Many are fantastic; some are practically incomprehensible, and yet unforgettable. Put together, they take us toward a way of life which is utterly impossible for westerners living in a western world, and nevertheless has a deep fascination and contains some values which we must respect.

The word Zen means "meditation." (It is the Japanese word, corresponding to the Chinese Ch'an and the Hindu Dhyana.) It is the central idea of a special sect of Buddhism which flourished in China during the Sung period (between A.D. 1000 and 1300) and entered Japan in the twelfth century. Without knowing much about it, we might be certain that the Zen sect was a worthy and noble one, because it produced a quantity of highly distinguished art, specifically painting. And if we knew anything about Buddhism itself, we might say that Zen goes closer than other sects to the heart of Buddha's teaching: because Buddha was trying to found, not a religion with temples and rituals, but a way of life based on meditation. However, there is something eccentric about the Zen life which is hard to trace in Buddha's teaching; there is an active energy which he did not admire, there is a rough grasp on reality which he himself eschewed, there is something like a sense of humor, which he rarely displayed. The gravity and serenity of the Indian preacher are transformed, in Zen, to the earthy live- liness of Chinese and Japanese sages. The lotus brooding calmly on the water has turned into a knotted tree covered with spring blossoms.

In this sense, "meditation" does not mean what we usually think of when we say a philosopher meditates: analysis of reality, a long- sustained effort to solve problems of religion and ethics, the logical dissection of the universe. It means something not divisive, but whole; not schematic, but organic; not long-drawn-out, but imme- diate. It means something more like our words "intuition" and "realization." It means a way of life in which there is no division between thought and action; none of the painful gulf, so well known to all of us, between the unconscious and the conscious mind; and no absolute distinction between the self and the external world, even between the various parts of the external world and the whole.

When the German philosopher took six years of lessons in archery in order to approach the mystical significance of Zen, he was not given direct philosophical instruction. He was merely shown how to breathe, how to hold and loose the bowstring, and finally how to shoot in such a way that the bow and arrow used him as an instrument. There are many such stories about Zen teachers. The strangest I know is one about a fencing master who undertook to train a young man in the art of the sword. The relationship of teacher and pupil is very important, almost sacred, in the Far East; and the pupil hardly ever thinks of leaving a master or objecting to his methods, however extraordinary they may seem. Therefore this young fellow did not at first object when he was made to act as a servant, drawing water, sweeping floors, gathering wood for the fire, and cooking. But after some time he asked for more direct instruction. The master agreed to give it, but produced no swords. The routine went on just as before, except that every now and then the master would strike the young man with a stick. No matter what he was doing, sweeping the floor or weeding in the garden, a blow would descend on him apparently out of nowhere; he had always to be on the alert, and yet he was constantly receiving unexpected cracks on the head or shoulders. After some months of this, he saw his master stooping over a boiling pot full of vegetables; and he thought he would have his revenge. Silently he lifted a stick and brought it down; but without any effort, without even a glance in his direction, his master parried the blow with the lid of the cooking pot. At last, the pupil began to understand the instinctive alertness, the effortless perception and avoidance of danger, in which his master had been training him. As soon as he had achieved it, it was child's play for him to learn the management of the sword: he could parry every cut and turn every slash without anxiety, until his opponent, exhausted, left an opening for his counterattack. (The same principle was used by the elderly samurai for selecting his comrades in the Japanese motion picture *The Magnificent Seven*.)

These stories show that Zen meditation does not mean sitting and thinking. On the contrary, it means acting with as little thought as possible. The fencing master trained his pupil to guard against every attack with the same immediate, instinctive rapidity with which our eyelid closes over our eye when something threatens it. His work was aimed at breaking down the wall between thought and act, at completely fusing body and senses and mind so that they might all work together rapidly and effortlessly. When a Zen artist draws a picture, he does it in a rhythm almost the exact reverse of that which is followed by a Western artist. We begin by blocking out the design and then filling in the details, usually working more and more slowly as we approach the completion of the picture. The Zen artist sits down very calmly; examines his brush carefully; prepares his own ink; smooths out the paper on which he will work; falls into a profound silent ecstasy of contemplation—during which he does not think anxiously of various details, composition, brushwork, shades of tone, but rather attempts to become the vehicle through which the subject can express itself in painting; and then, very quickly and almost unconsciously, with sure effortless strokes, draws a picture containing the fewest and most effective lines. Most of the paper is left blank;

only the essential is depicted, and that not completely. One long curving line will be enough to show a mountainside; seven streaks will become a group of bamboos bending in the wind; and yet, though technically incomplete, such pictures are unforgettably clear. They show the heart of reality.

All this we can sympathize with, because we can see the results. The young swordsman learns how to fence. The intuitional painter produces a fine picture. But the hardest thing for us to appreciate is that the Zen masters refuse to teach philosophy or religion directly, and deny logic. In fact, they despise logic as an artificial distortion of reality. Many philosophical teachers are difficult to understand because they analyze profound problems with subtle intricacy: such is Aristotle in his *Metaphysics*. Many mystical writers are difficult to understand because, as they themselves admit, they are attempting to use words to describe experiences which are too abstruse for words, so that they have to fall back on imagery and analogy, which they themselves recognize to be poor media, far coarser than the realities with which they have been in contact. But the Zen teachers seem to deny the power of language and thought altogether. For example, if you ask a Zen master what is the ultimate reality, he will answer, without the slightest hesitation, "The bamboo grove at the foot of the hill" or "A branch of plum blossom." Apparently he means that these things, which we can see instantly without effort, or imagine in the flash of a second, are real with the ultimate reality; that nothing is more real than these; and that we ought to grasp ultimates as we grasp simple immediates. A Chinese master was once asked the central question, "What is the Buddha?" He said nothing whatever, but held out his index finger. What did he mean? It is hard to explain; but apparently he meant "Here. Now. Look and realize with the effortlessness of seeing. Do not try to use words. Do not think. Make no efforts toward withdrawal from the world. Expect no sublime ecstasies. Live. All *that* is the ultimate reality, and it can be understood from the motion of a finger as well as from the execution of any complex ritual, from any subtle argument, or from the circling of the starry universe."

In making that gesture, the master was copying the Buddha himself, who once delivered a sermon which is famous, but was hardly understood by his pupils at the time. Without saying a word, he held up a flower and showed it to the gathering. One man, one alone, knew what he meant. The gesture became renowned as the Flower Sermon.

In the annals of Zen there are many cryptic answers to the final question, "What is the Buddha?"—which in our terms means "What is the meaning of life? What is truly real?" For example, one master, when asked "What is the Buddha?" replied, "Your name is Yecho." Another said, "Even the finest artist cannot paint him." Another said, "No nonsense here." And another answered, "The mouth is the gate of woe." My favorite story is about the monk who said to a Master, "Has a dog Buddha-nature too?" The Master replied, "Wu"—which is what the dog himself would have said.

Now, some critics might attack Zen by saying that this is the creed of a savage or an animal. The adherents of Zen would deny that—or more probably they would ignore the criticism, or make some cryptic remark which meant that it was pointless. Their position—if they could ever be persuaded to put it into words—would be this. An animal is instinctively in touch with reality, and so far is living rightly, but it has never had a mind and so cannot perceive the Whole, only that part with which it is in touch. The philosopher sees both the Whole and the parts, and enjoys them all. As for the savage, he exists only through the group; he feels himself as part of a war party or a ceremonial dance team or a ploughing-and-sowing group or the Snake clan; he is not truly an individual at all, and therefore is less than fully human. Zen has at its heart an inner solitude; its aim is to teach us to live, as in the last resort we do all have to live, alone.

A more dangerous criticism of Zen would be that it is nihilism, that its purpose is to abolish thought altogether. (This criticism is handled, but not fully met, by the great Zen authority Suzuki in his *Introduction to Zen Buddhism*.) It can hardly be completely confuted, for after all the central doctrine of Buddhism is—Nothingness. And many of the sayings of Zen masters are truly nihilistic. The first patriarch of the sect in China was asked by the emperor what was the ultimate and holiest principle of Buddhism. He replied, "Vast emptiness, and nothing holy in it." Another who was asked the searching question "Where is the abiding-place for the mind?" answered, "Not in this dualism of good and evil, being and non-being, thought and matter." In fact, thought is an activity which divides. It analyzes, it makes distinctions, it criticizes, it judges, it breaks reality into groups and classes and individuals. The aim of Zen is to abolish that kind of thinking, and to substitute—not unconsciousness, which would be death, but a consciousness that does not analyze but experiences life directly. Although it has no prescribed prayers, no sacred scriptures, no ceremonial rites, no personal god, and no interest in the soul's future destination, Zen is a religion rather than a philosophy. Jung points out that its aim is to produce a religious conversion, a "transformation": and he adds, "The transformation process is incommensurable with intellect." Thought is always interesting, but often painful; Zen is calm and painless. Thought is incomplete; Zen enlightenment brings a sense of completeness. Thought is a process; Zen illumination is a state. But it is a state which cannot be defined. In the Buddhist scriptures there is a dialogue between a master and a pupil in which the pupil tries to discover the exact meaning of such a state. The master says to him, 'If a fire were blazing in front of you, would you know that it was blazing?'

"Yes, master."

"And would you know the reason for its blazing?"

"Yes, because it had a supply of grass and sticks."

"And would you know if it were to go out?"

"Yes, master."

"And on its going out, would you know where the fire had gone? To the east, to the west, to the north, or to the south?"

"The question does not apply, master. For the fire blazed because it had a supply of grass and sticks. When it had consumed this and had no other fuel, then it went out."

"In the same way," replies the master, "no question will apply to the meaning of Nirvana, and no statement will explain it."

Such, then, neither happy nor unhappy but beyond all divisive description, is the condition which students of Zen strive to attain. Small wonder that they can scarcely explain it to us, the unilluminated.

1957

QUESTIONS

1. What difficulties does Highet face in discussing Zen? How does he manage to give a definition in spite of his statement that Zen "cannot be analyzed"?
2. Why does Highet describe the training in archery in such detail?
3. On page 657 Highet says that "Zen is a religion rather than a philosophy." How has he led up to this conclusion? What definitions of "religion" and "philosophy" does he imply?
4. By what means does Highet define "meditation"? Would other means have worked as well? Explain.
5. To what extent is Zen "the creed of a savage or an animal"? How does Highet go about refuting this charge?

JEAN-PAUL SARTRE
Existentialism

Man is nothing else but what he makes of himself. Such is the first principle of existentialism. It is also what is called subjectivity, the name we are labeled with when charges are brought against us. But what do we mean by this, if not that man has a greater dignity than a stone or table? For we mean that man first exists, that is, that man first of all is the being who hurls himself toward a future and who is conscious of imagining himself as being in the future. Man is at the start a plan which is aware of itself, rather than a patch of moss, a piece of garbage, or a cauliflower; nothing exists prior to this plan; there is nothing in heaven; man will be what he will have planned to be. Not what he will want to be. Because by the word "will" we generally mean a conscious decision, which is subsequent to what we have already made of ourselves. I may want to belong to a political party, write a book, get married; but all that is only a manifestation of an earlier, more spontaneous choice that is called "will." But if existence really does precede essence, man is responsible for what he is. Thus, existentialism's first move is to make every man aware of what he is and to make the full responsibility of his existence rest on him. And when we say that a man is responsible for himself, we do not only mean that he is responsible for his own individuality, but that he is responsible for all men.

The word "subjectivism" has two meanings, and our opponents play on the two. Subjectivism means, on the one hand, that an individual chooses and makes himself; and, on the other, that it is impossible for man to transcend human subjectivity. The second of these is the essential meaning of existentialism. When we say that man chooses his own self, we mean that every one of us does likewise; but we also mean by that that in making this choice he also chooses all men. In fact, in creating the man that we want to be, there is not a single one of our acts which does not at the same time create an image of man as we think he ought to be. To choose to be this or that is to affirm at the same time the value of what we choose, because we can never choose evil. We always choose the good, and nothing can be good for us without being good for all.

If, on the other hand, existence precedes essence, and if we grant that we exist and fashion our image at one and the same time, the image is valid for everybody and for our whole age. Thus, our responsibility is much greater than we might have supposed, because it involves all mankind. If I am a workingman and choose to join a Christian trade union rather than be a Communist, and if by being a member I want to show that the best thing for man is resignation, that the kingdom of man is not of this world, I am not only involving my own case—I want to be resigned for everyone. As a result, my action has involved all humanity. To take a more individual matter, if I want to marry, to have children, even if this marriage depends solely on my own circumstances or passion or wish, I am involving all humanity in monogamy and not merely myself. Therefore, I am responsible for myself and for everyone else. I am creating a certain image of man of my own choosing. In choosing myself, I choose man.

This helps us understand what the actual content is of such

rather grandiloquent words as anguish, forlornness, despair. As you will see, it's all quite simple.

First, what is meant by anguish? The existentialists say at once that man is anguish. What that means is this: the man who involves himself and who realizes that he is not only the person he chooses to be, but also a lawmaker who is, at the same time, choosing all mankind as well as himself, cannot help escape the feeling of his total and deep responsibility. Of course, there are many people who are not anxious; but we claim that they are hiding their anxiety, that they are fleeing from it. Certainly, many people believe that when they do something, they themselves are the only ones involved, and when someone says to them, "What if everyone acted that way?" they shrug their shoulders and answer, "Everyone doesn't act that way." But really, one should always ask himself, "What would happen if everybody looked at things that way?" There is no escaping this disturbing thought except by a kind of double-dealing. A man who lies and makes excuses for himself by saying "not everybody does that," is someone with an uneasy conscience, because the act of lying implies that a universal value is conferred upon the lie.

Anguish is evident even when it conceals itself. This is the anguish that Kierkegaard called the anguish of Abraham. You know the story: an angel has ordered Abraham to sacrifice his son; if it really were an angel who has come and said, "You are Abraham, you shall sacrifice your son," everything would be all right. But everyone might first wonder, "Is it really an angel, and am I really Abraham? What proof do I have?"

There was a madwoman who had hallucinations; someone used to speak to her on the telephone and give her orders. Her doctor asked her, "Who is it who talks to you?" She answered, "He says it's God." What proof did she really have that it was God? If an angel comes to me, what proof is there that it's an angel? And if I hear voices, what proof is there that they come from heaven and not from hell, or from the subconscious, or a pathological condition? What proves that they are addressed to me? What proof is there that I have been appointed to impose my choice and my conception of man on humanity? I'll never find any proof or sign to convince me of that. If a voice addresses me, it is always for me to decide that this is the angel's voice; if I consider that such an act is a good one, it is I who will choose to say that it is good rather than bad.

Now, I'm not being singled out as an Abraham, and yet at every moment I'm obliged to perform exemplary acts. For every man, everything happens as if all mankind had its eyes fixed on him and were guiding itself by what he does. And every man ought to say to himself, "Am I really the kind of man who has the right to act in such a way that humanity might guide itself by my actions?" And if he does not say that to himself, he is masking his anguish.

There is no question here of the kind of anguish which would lead to quietism, to inaction. It is a matter of a simple sort of anguish that anybody who has had responsibilities is familiar with. For example, when a military officer takes the responsibility for an attack and sends a certain number of men to death, he chooses to do so, and in the main he alone makes the choice. Doubtless, orders come from above, but they are too broad; he interprets them, and on this interpretation depend the lives of ten or fourteen or twenty men. In making a decision he cannot help having a certain anguish. All leaders know this anguish. That doesn't keep them from acting; on the contrary, it is the very condition of their action. For it implies that they envisage a number of possibilities, and when they choose one, they realize that it has value only because it is chosen. We shall see that this kind of anguish, which is the kind that existentialism describes, is explained, in addition, by a direct responsibility to the other men whom it involves. It is not a curtain separating us from action, but is part of action itself.

When we speak of forlornness, a term Heidegger was fond of, we mean only that God does not exist and that we have to face all the consequences of this. This existentialist is strongly opposed to a certain kind of secular ethics which would like to abolish God with the least possible expense. About 1880, some French teachers tried to set up a secular ethics which went something like this: God is a useless and costly hypothesis; we are discarding it; but, meanwhile, in order for there to be an ethics, a society, a civilization, it is essential that certain values be taken seriously and that they be considered as having an *a priori* existence. It must be obligatory, a *priori*, to be honest, not to lie, not to beat your wife, to have children, etc., etc. So we're going to try a little device which will make it possible to show that values exist all the same, inscribed in a heaven of ideas, though otherwise God does not exist. In other words—and this, I believe, is the tendency of everything called reformism in France— nothing will be changed if God does not exist. We shall find ourselves with the same norms of honesty, progress, and humanism, and we shall have made of God an outdated hypothesis which will peacefully die off by itself.

The existentialist, on the contrary, thinks it very distressing that God does not exist, because all possibility of finding values in a heaven of ideas disappears along with Him; there can no longer be an *a priori* Good, since there is no infinite and perfect consciousness to think it. Nowhere is it written that the Good exists, that we must be honest, that we must not lie; because the fact is we are on a plane where there are only men. Dostoievsky said, "If God didn't exist, everything would be possible." That is the very starting point of existentialism. Indeed, everything is permissible if God does not exist, and as a result man is forlorn, because neither within him nor without does he find anything to cling to. He can't start making excuses for himself.

If existence really does precede essence, there is no explaining things away by reference to a fixed and given human nature. In other words, there is no determinism, man is free, man is freedom. On the other hand, if God does not exist, we find no values or commands to turn to which legitimize our conduct. So, in the bright realm of values, we·have no excuse behind us, nor justification before us. We are alone, with no excuses.

That is the idea I shall try to convey when I say that man is condemned to be free. Condemned, because he did not create himself, yet, in other respects is free; because, once thrown into the world, he is responsible for everything he does. The existentialist does not believe in the power of passion. He will never agree that a sweeping passion is a ravaging torrent which fatally leads a man to certain acts and is therefore an excuse. He thinks that man is responsible for his passion.

The existentialist does not think that man is going to help himself by finding in the world some omen by which to orient himself. Because he thinks that man will interpret the omen to suit himself. Therefore, he thinks that man, with no support and no aid, is condemned every moment to invent man. Ponge, in a very fine article, has said, "Man is the future of man." That's exactly it. But if it is taken to mean that this future is recorded in heaven, that God sees it, then it is false, because it would really no longer be a future. If it is taken to mean that, whatever a man may be, there is a future to be forged, a virgin future before him, then this remark is sound. But then we are forlorn.

To give you an example which will enable you to understand forlornness better, I shall cite the case of one of my students who came to see me under the following circumstances: his father was on bad terms with his mother, and, moreover, was inclined to be a collaborationist;[1] his older brother had been killed in the German offensive of 1940, and the young man, with somewhat immature but generous feelings, wanted to avenge him. His mother lived alone with him, very much upset by the half-treason of her husband and the death of her older son; the boy was her only consolation.

The boy was faced with the choice of leaving for England and joining the Free French forces—that is, leaving his mother behind —or remaining with his mother and helping her to carry on. He was fully aware that the woman lived only for him and that his going

---

1. With the occupying German army, or its puppet government in Vichy.

off—and perhaps his death—would plunge her into despair. He was also aware that every act that he did for his mother's sake was a sure thing, in the sense that it was helping her to carry on, where-as every effort he made toward going off and fighting was an uncertain move which might run aground and prove completely useless; for example, on his way to England he might, while passing through Spain, be detained indefinitely in a Spanish camp; he might reach England or Algiers and be stuck in an office at a desk job. As a result, he was faced with two very different kinds of action: one, concrete, immediate, but concerning only one individual; the other concerned an incomparably vaster group, a national collectivity, but for that very reason was dubious, and might be interrupted en route. And, at the same time, he was wavering between two kinds of ethics. On the one hand, an ethics of sympathy, of personal devotion; on the other, a broader ethics, but one whose efficacy was more dubious. He had to choose between the two.

Who could help him choose? Christian doctrine? No. Christian doctrine says, "Be charitable, love your neighbor, take the more rugged path, etc., etc." But which is the more rugged path? Whom should he love as a brother? The fighting man or his mother? Which does the greater good, the vague act of fighting in a group, or the concrete one of helping a particular human being to go on living? Who can decide *a priori?* Nobody. No book of ethics can tell him. The Kantian ethics says, "Never treat any person as a means, but as an end." Very well, if I stay with my mother, I'll treat her as an end and not as a means; but by virtue of this very fact, I'm running the risk of treating the people around me who are fighting, as means; and, conversely, if I go to join those who are fighting, I'll be treating them as an end, and, by doing that, I run the risk of treating my mother as a means.

If values are vague, and if they are always too broad for the concrete and specific case that we are considering, the only thing left for us is to trust our instincts. That's what this young man tried to do; and when I saw him, he said, "In the end, feeling is what counts. I ought to choose whichever pushes me in one direction. If I feel that I love my mother enough to sacrifice everything else for her—my desire for vengeance, for action, for adventure—then I'll stay with her. If, on the contrary, I feel that my love for my mother isn't enough, I'll leave."

But how is the value of a feeling determined? What gives his feeling for his mother value? Precisely the fact that he remained with her. I may say that I like so-and-so well enough to sacrifice a certain amount of money for him, but I may say so only if I've done it. I may say "I love my mother well enough to remain with her" if I have remained with her. The only way to determine the value of this affection is, precisely, to perform an act which confirms and defines it. But, since I require this affection to justify my act, I find myself caught in a vicious circle.

On the other hand, Gide has well said that a mock feeling and a true feeling are almost indistinguishable; to decide that I love my mother and will remain with her, or to remain with her by putting on an act, amount somewhat to the same thing. In other words, the feeling is formed by the acts one performs; so, I cannot refer to it in order to act upon it. Which means that I can neither seek within myself the true condition which will impel me to act, nor apply to a system of ethics for concepts which will permit me to act. You will say, "At least, he did go to a teacher for advice." But if you seek advice from a priest, for example, you have chosen this priest; you already knew, more or less, just about what advice he was going to give you. In other words, choosing your adviser is involving yourself. The proof of this is that if you are a Christian, you will say, "Consult a priest." But some priests are collaborating, some are just marking time, some are resisting. Which to choose? If the young man chooses a priest who is resisting or collaborating, he has already decided on the kind of advice he's going to get. Therefore, in coming to see me he knew the answer I was going to give him, and I had only one answer to give: "You're free, choose, that is, invent." No general ethics can show you what is to be done; there are no omens in the world. The Catholics will reply, "But there are." Granted —but, in any case, I myself choose the meaning they have.

When I was a prisoner, I knew a rather remarkable young man who was a Jesuit. He had entered the Jesuit order in the following way: he had had a number of very bad breaks; in childhood, his father died, leaving him in poverty, and he was a scholarship student at a religious institution where he was constantly made to feel that he was being kept out of charity; then, he failed to get any of the honors and distinctions that children like; later on, at about eighteen, he bungled a love affair; finally, at twenty-two, he failed in military training, a childish enough matter, but it was the last straw.

This young fellow might well have felt that he had botched everything. It was a sign of something, but of what? He might have taken refuge in bitterness or despair. But he very wisely looked upon all this as a sign that he was not made for secular triumphs, and that only the triumphs of religion, holiness, and faith were open to him. He saw the hand of God in all this, and so he entered the order. Who can help seeing that he alone decided what the sign meant?

Some other interpretation might have been drawn from this series of setbacks; for example, that he might have done better to turn carpenter or revolutionist. Therefore, he is fully responsible for the interpretation. Forlornness implies that we ourselves choose our being. Forlornness and anguish go together.

As for despair, the term has a very simple meaning. It means that we shall confine ourselves to reckoning only with what depends upon our will, or on the ensemble of probabilities which make our action possible. When we want something, we always have to reckon with probabilities. I may be counting on the arrival of a friend. The friend is coming by rail or streetcar; this supposes that the train will arrive on schedule, or that the streetcar will not jump the track. I am left in the realm of possibility; but possibilities are to be reckoned with only to the point where my action comports with the ensemble of these possibilities, and no further. The moment the possibilities I am considering are not rigorously involved by my action, I ought to disengage myself from them, because no God, no scheme, can adapt the world and its possibilities to my will. When Descartes said, "Conquer yourself rather than the world," he meant essentially the same thing.

The Marxists to whom I have spoken reply, "You can rely on the support of others in your action, which obviously has certain limits because you're not going to live forever. That means: rely on both what others are doing elsewhere to help you, in China, in Russia, and what they will do later on, after your death, to carry on the action and lead it to its fulfillment, which will be the revolution. You even *have* to rely upon that, otherwise you're immoral." I reply at once that I will always rely on fellow-fighters insofar as these comrades are involved with me in a common struggle, in the unity of a party or a group in which I can more or less make my weight felt; that is, one whose ranks I am in as a fighter and whose movements I am aware of at every moment. In such a situation, relying on the unity and will of the party is exactly like counting on the fact that the train will arrive on time or that the car won't jump the track. But, given that man is free and that there is no human nature for me to depend on, I cannot count on men whom I do not know by relying on human goodness or man's concern for the good of society. I don't know what will become of the Russian revolution; I may make an example of it to the extent that at the present time it is apparent that the proletariat plays a part in Russia that it plays in no other nation. But I can't swear that this will inevitably lead to a triumph of the proletariat. I've got to limit myself to what I see.

Given that men are free and that tomorrow they will freely decide what man will be, I cannot be sure that, after my death, fellow-fighters will carry on my work to bring it to its maximum perfection. Tomorrow, after my death, some men may decide to set up Fascism, and the others may be cowardly and muddled enough to let them do it. Fascism will then be the human reality, so much the worse for us.

Actually, things will be as man will have decided they are to be. Does that mean that I should abandon myself to quietism? No. First, I should involve myself; then, act on the old saw, "Nothing ventured, nothing gained." Nor does it mean that I shouldn't belong to a party, but rather that I shall have no illusions and shall do what I can. For example, suppose I ask myself, "Will socialization, as such, ever come about?" I know nothing about it. All I know is that I'm going to do everything in my power to bring it about. Beyond that, I can't count on anything. Quietism is the attitude of people who say, "Let others do what I can't do." The doctrine I am presenting is the very opposite of quietism, since it declares, "There is no reality except in action." Moreover, it goes further, since it adds, "Man is nothing else than his plan; he exists only to the extent that he fulfills himself; he is therefore nothing else than the ensemble of his acts, nothing else than his life."

According to this, we can understand why our doctrine horrifies certain people. Because often the only way they can bear their wretchedness is to think, "Circumstances have been against me. What I've been and done doesn't show my true worth. To be sure, I've had no great love, no great friendship, but that's because I haven't met a man or woman who was worthy. The books I've written haven't been very good because I haven't had the proper leisure. I haven't had children to devote myself to because I didn't find a man with whom I could have spent my life. So there remains within me, unused and quite viable, a host of propensities, inclinations, possibilities, that one wouldn't guess from the mere series of things I've done."

Now, for the existentialist there is really no love other than one which manifests itself in a person's being in love. There is no genius other than one which is expressed in works of art; the genius of Proust is the sum of Proust's works; the genius of Racine is his series of tragedies. Outside of that, there is nothing. Why say that Racine could have written another tragedy, when he didn't write it? A man is involved in life, leaves his impress on it, and outside of that there is nothing. To be sure, this may seem a harsh thought to someone whose life hasn't been a success. But, on the other hand, it prompts people to understand that reality alone is what counts, that dreams, expectations, and hopes warrant no more than to define a man as a disappointed dream, as miscarried hopes, as vain expectations. In other words, to define him negatively and not positively. However, when we say, "You are nothing else than your life," that does not imply that the artist will be judged solely on the basis of his works of art; a thousand other things will contribute toward summing him up. What we mean is that a man is nothing else than a series of undertakings, that he is the sum, the organization, the ensemble of the relationships which make up these undertakings.

When all is said and done, what we are accused of, at bottom, is not our pessimism, but an optimistic toughness. If people throw up to us our works of fiction in which we write about people who are soft, weak, cowardly, and sometimes even downright bad, it's not because these prople are soft, weak, cowardly, or bad; because if we were to say, as Zola did, that they are that way because of heredity, the workings of environment, society, because of biological or psychological determinism, people would be reassured. They would say, "Well, that's what we're like, no one can do anything about it." But when the existentialist writes about a coward, he says that this coward is responsible for his cowardice. He's not like that because he has a cowardly heart or lung or brain; he's not like that on account of his physiological make-up; but he's like that because he has made himself a coward by his acts. There's no such thing as a cowardly constitution; there are nervous constitutions; there is poor blood, as the common people say, or strong constitutions. But the man whose blood is poor is not a coward on that account, for what makes cowardice is the act of renouncing or yielding. A constitution is·not an act; the coward is defined on the basis of the acts he performs. People feel, in a vague sort of way, that this coward we're talking about is guilty of being a coward, and the thought frightens them. What people would like is that a coward or a hero be born that way. . . .

From these few reflections it is evident that nothing is more unjust than the objections that have been raised against us. Existentialism is nothing else than an attempt to draw all the consequences of a coherent atheistic position. It isn't trying to plunge man into despair at all. But if one calls every attitude of unbelief despair, like the Christians, then the word is not being used in its original sense. Existentialism isn't so atheistic that it wears itself out showing that God doesn't exist. Rather, it declares that even if God did exist, that would change nothing. There you've got our point of view. Not that we believe that God exists, but we think that the problem of His existence is not the issue. In this sense existentialism is optimistic, a doctrine of action, and it is plain dishonesty for Christians to make no distinction between their own despair and ours and then to call us despairing.

QUESTIONS

1. What are some of the methods or devices Sartre uses to define existentialism? Why does he use more than one method or device? Compare the techniques that Sartre uses with those Highet uses in defining Zen (pp. 649–658).

2. What is the significance of the words "if existence really does precede essence"? What does this mean? What is the force of "if"? Why does Sartre repeat the words later in the essay?
3. Why does Sartre use three separate terms—anguish, forlornness, despair? What, if any, are the differences among them?
4. Sartre makes a distinction between treating "any person as a means . . . [and] as an end" (p. 663). What are the implications of this distinction?

Notes on Composition

SAYING SOMETHING THAT MATTERS
Thesis • Assumptions • Fact and Opinion •
Understanding and Emotions

THE MEANS OF SAYING IT
DEFINING: *Example • Negation • Comparison and Contrast • Analysis*
Cause or Effect • End or Means
MARSHALING EVIDENCE: *Facts • Authority • "Common Consent"*
DRAWING CONCLUSIONS: *Deduction • Induction • Analogy*

AND THE STYLE
Diction • Metaphor • Repetition and Variation • Tone
Point of View • Persona • Irony • Audience

Saying Something That Matters

There is no point in the hard labor of writing unless you expect to *do* something to your readers—perhaps add to their store of information, perhaps get them to change their minds on some issue that you care about. Determining just what that something is, is half the battle; hence the importance of knowing your main point, your central purpose in writing, your **thesis**. It may seem that this step—perhaps in the form of a "thesis sentence" or exact statement of the main point—is inevitably prior to everything else, but in actual practice the case is more complicated. Few good writers attain a final grasp of their thesis until they have tried setting down their first halting ideas at some length; to put it another way, you discover more precisely what it is you have to say in the act of trying to say it. Formulating and refining upon a thesis sentence as you work your way through a piece of writing helps you see what needs to be done at each stage; the finished piece, though, instead of announcing its thesis in any one sentence, may simply imply it by the fact of its unity, the determinate way the parts hang together. There is probably no single sentence in E. B. White's "Once More to the Lake" (p. 56) that will serve satisfactorily to represent the entire essay in miniature, yet clearly such a sentence could be formulated: The pleasure of recapturing the past is heavily qualified by an adult awareness of the inevitability of change. But whether you state the

669

main point or leave it to be inferred, you need to decide what your piece is about, what you want to say about it, why, and to whom.

Sometimes a thesis will rest on **assumptions**, related ideas that the writer doesn't mention directly but depends upon the reader to understand and agree to, or—if the real purpose is deception—to overlook and hence fail to reject. Machiavelli (p. 503) appears to assume that it is more important for a prince to stay in power than to be a "good" man. You may feel the question is highly ambiguous, or you may disagree sharply. But even if you decide, finally, that you can live with Machiavelli's assumption, you will have acquired a fuller understanding of what he is saying, and of your own relationship to it, for having scrutinized what is being taken for granted. The habit of scrutiny guards you against the careless or cunning writer whose unstated assumptions may be highly questionable. The same habit, turned on your own mind when you become the writer, can save you from the unthinking use of assumptions that you would be hard pressed to defend.

Some theses lend themselves to verification by laboratory methods or the like; they deal with **questions of fact**. The exact order of composition of Shakespeare's plays could conceivably be settled finally if new evidence turned up. Whether or not the plays are great literature, on the other hand, is a **question of opinion**; agreement (though not hard to reach in this instance) depends on the weighing of arguments rather than on tests or measurements. Not that all theses can be neatly classified as assertions either of fact or of opinion (consider 'Shakespeare's influence has been greater than Newton's"); still, the attempt to classify your own effort can help you understand what you really want to do.

Sometimes writers address themselves specifically to their readers' **understanding**, sometimes chiefly to their **emotions**. Although the processes of thinking and feeling are almost always mixed, still it is obvious that a description of a chemical process and a description of a candidate you hope to see elected to office will differ considerably in tone and emphasis. Accordingly you need to give some thought to the kind of result you hope to produce: perhaps simply an addition of information, perhaps a change of attitude, perhaps a commitment of the will to action.

The Means of Saying It

No worthwhile thesis comes without work, and the work of arriving at a thesis is much like the work of writing itself—developing, elaborating, refining upon an idea that is perhaps at first hazy. For convenience the process may be divided into setting bounds, or defining; marshaling evidence; and drawing conclusions.

DEFINING in a broad sense may be thought of as what you do to answer the question "What do you mean?" It sets bounds by doing two things to an idea: grouping it with others like it and showing how it differs from those others. "An island is a tract of land" (like a lot or prairie or peninsula) "completely surrounded by water and too small to be called a continent" (and therefore different from a lot, etc.). This process of classifying and distinguishing may take many forms, depending on the kind of thing you are dealing with and your reason for doing so. (Artifacts, for example, can hardly be defined without reference to purpose; a lock is a device *for securing* a door; a theodolite is an instrument used *to measure* horizontal or vertical angles). Some of the standard methods are these: by giving **examples**, pointing to an instance as a short way of indicating class and individual characteristics ("*That* is a firebreak"; "A liberal is a man like Jefferson"); by **negating**, explaining what your subject is *not*—i.e., using the process of elimination ("Love vaunteth not itself, is not puffed up"); by **comparing and contrasting**, noting the resemblances and differences between your subject and something else ("A magazine is sometimes as big as a book but differs in binding and layout"); by **analyzing**, breaking down a whole into its constituent parts ("A play may be seen as exposition, rising action, and denouement"); by seeking a **cause** of the thing in question or an **effect** that it has produced ("Scurvy is the result of a dietary deficiency and often leads to anemia"); or by attributing to a thing an **end** or **means**, seeing it as a way of fulfilling purpose or as the fulfillment of a purpose ("Representation is the end of the electoral system and the means to good government").

When we turn to specimens of writing, we see immediately that the various methods of defining may serve not only for one-sentence "dictionary" definitions but also as methods of organizing paragraphs or even whole essays, where unfolding the subject is in a sense "defining" it, showing where its boundaries lie. Kildare Dobbs (p. 372) explains the diversity of Canada by comparing its regions with one another and with their southern neighbor, the United States. William Golding (p. 83) analyzes thought in general into three distinct "grades" as he recounts his own intellectual development as a schoolboy. The choice of method in the above examples, it will be noted, is not random; each author selects according to his purpose in writing, and what suits one purpose exactly might be exactly wrong for another.

MARSHALING EVIDENCE. Once you have said what you mean, the next question is likely to be "How do you know?" Marshaling evidence may be thought of as what you do to answer that question. Where the matter at hand involves questions of fact, **factual evidence** will be most directly appropriate. (A diary, a letter—perhaps a cryptogram hidden in the text —might prove even to die-hard Baconians that Shakespeare himself did in fact write the plays which have been credited to him). Writers on scientific subjects inevitably draw chiefly on facts, often intricately arrayed, to support their conclusions. But it should not be assumed that factual evidence turns up mainly in scientific writing. Dorothy Gies McGuigan's account (p. 539) of what it took for a woman to achieve a doctoral degree in the seventeenth century is obviously based on facts in the form of historical documents. Anthony Burgess (p. 320), adopting a less direct strategy, adduces many familiar facts that seem to point to the imminent breakdown of American society, but then, through a combination of factual and other kinds of evidence, tries to show that such signs are misleading.

Factual evidence is generally thought to carry more weight than any other kind, though the force of a fact is greatly diminished if it is not easily verifiable or attested to by reliable witnesses. Where factual evidence is hard to come by (consider the problems of proving that Bacon did not write Shakespeare's plays), the opinion of **authorities** is often invoked, on the assumption that the people most knowledgeable in a field are most likely to judge truly in a particular case. The testimony of authorities is relevant, of course, not only in questions of fact but also in questions of opinion. Francis Bacon (p. 219), for example, invokes Solomon and Job to support his ideas about revenge. In general, however, the appeal to authority in matters of opinion has lost the rhetorical effectiveness it once had, perhaps because there is less agreement as to who the reliable authorities are.

As changes in the nature of the question draw in a larger and larger number of "authorities," evidence from authority shades into what might be called "the **common consent** of mankind," those generalizations about human experience that large numbers of readers can be counted upon to accept and that often find expression in proverbs or apothegms: "Risk no more than you can afford to lose" and "The first step toward Hell is half-way there." Such generalizations, whether proverbial or not, are a common ground on which writer and reader meet in agreement. Your task as writer is to find and present the ones applicable to your particular thesis and then demonstrate that applicability.

DRAWING CONCLUSIONS. One of the ways of determining the consequences of thought—that is, drawing conclusions—is the process of applying generalizations (**deduction**): "If we should risk no more than we can afford to lose, then we had better not jeopardize the independence of our universities by seeking federal aid." Another way of arriving at conclusions is the process of **induction**, which consists in forming generalizations from a sufficient number of observed instances: "Since universities A, B, and C have been accepting federal aid through research grants for years without loss of independence, it is probably safe for any university to do so." Typically deduction and induction work reciprocally, each helping to supply for the other the materials upon which inference operates. We induce from experience that green apples are sour; we deduce from this generalization that a particular green apple is sour. A third kind of inference, sometimes regarded as only a special kind of deduction or induction, is **analogy**, the process of concluding that two things which resemble each other in one way will resemble each other in another way also: "Federal aid has benefited mental hospitals enormously, and will probably benefit universities just as much." An analogy proves nothing, although it may help the reader see the reasonableness of an idea and is often extremely valuable for purposes of illustration, since it makes an unknown clearer by relating it to a known.

Turning to our essays, we can see something of the variety of ways in which these three kinds of inference manifest themselves: Samuel Johnson (p. 220) deducing from men's customary unwillingness to pay more than a thing is worth the conclusion that the pyramids are a monument to human vanity; Wallace Stegner arguing from a series of particular instances to the general conclusion that a community may be judged by what it throws away (p. 6); Stephen Jay Gould turning to the legend of Sleeping Beauty for an analogy to the propagation of bamboos (p. 584).

Such a list of examples suggests that in good writing the conclusions we draw, the consequences of thought, are "consequential" in more than one sense: not only do they follow logically from the evidence considered, they are also *significant*; they relate directly or indirectly to aspects of our lives that we care about. To the questions suggested earlier as demands for definition and evidence, then, we must add a third. "What do you mean?" calls for precision yet admits answers vast in scope. "How do you know?" trims the vastness down to what can be substantiated, but may settle for triviality as the price of certainty. The appropriate question to raise finally, then, is simply "So what?" and the conclusions we as writers draw need to be significant enough to yield answers to that question. We have come full circle back to the idea of saying something that matters.

And the Style

One theory of style in writing sees form and content as distinct: style is the way a thing is said, the thing itself an unchanging substance that can be decked out in various ways. Mr. Smith not only *died*, he *ceased to be*, he *passed away*, he *croaked*, he *was promoted to glory*—all mean "the same thing." According to a second theory, however, they are ways of saying different things: variations in **diction** imply variations in reference. To say that Smith *ceased to be* records a private and secular event; to say that he *was promoted to glory* (a Salvation Army expression) rejoices in an event of a different order altogether. Content and form in this view are inseparable; a change in one is a change in the other.

In **metaphor** we can see that the two theories, instead of contradicting each other, are more like the two sides of a coin; when one idea is expressed in terms of another, it is the same and yet not the same. To view the passage from life to death as if it were a promotion from one military rank to a higher one is to see a common center of reference and widening circles of association at the same time. This seeing *as if* opens up a whole range of expression, since many meanings reside in the relationship between the two parts of a comparison rather than in either part by itself. Charles Lamb (p. 222), ironically extolling borrowers over lenders, exclaims "What a careless, even deportment hath your borrower!" and then adds "what rosy gills!" His metaphor seems to suggest, approximately, that the borrower's healthy contentment depends on a certain fishlike obliviousness, yet no paraphrase captures the humorous aptness of the metaphor itself.

But style is by no means dependent on diction and metaphor alone. Grammatical relationships yield a host of stylistic devices, most of which can be described in terms of **repetition and variation**. Repetition may exist at every level; as commonly understood, its chief application is to the word (including the pronoun as a word-substitute), but the same principle governs the use of parallelism (repetition of a grammatical structure) within and between sentences, even between paragraphs. Failure to observe that principle—that similarity in idea calls for similarity in form—can be detected wherever a change in form implies that a distinction is being made when actually none is relevant to the context: "Their conversation was interrupted by dinner, but they resumed their discussion afterwards"; "She rolled out the dough, placed it over the pie, and pricked holes in it. She also trimmed off the edge." The corollary of the principle of appropriate repetition is the principle of appropriate variation—that difference in idea calls for difference in form. For every failure to repeat when repetition is called for there is a corresponding failure to vary when variation is called for: "Their discussion was interrupted when class discussion of the day's assignment began"; "It had been raining for many days near the river. It had been rising steadily toward the top of the levee." Failures of this sort, which suggest a similarity in idea or parallelism in thought where none exists, often strike the ear as a lack of euphony or appropriate rhythm: "A boxer must learn to react absolutely instantly"; "The slingshot was made of strips of inner tubes of tires of cars." The principle of appropriate variation applies, too, to sentences as wholes: if a separate sentence is used for each detail, or if every sentence includes many details, the reader may be given a false impression of parallelism or equality of emphasis. Here again variation may be a way to avoid misleading grammatical indications of meaning. In a writer like Samuel Johnson (p. 220), who works deliberately for a high degree of parallelism, correspondence between repetition and sameness of meaning, or variation and difference of meaning, is perhaps most conveniently illustrated.

All stylistic techniques come together to supply an answer to the question "Who is behind these words?" Words are spoken in a particular tone of voice, but **tone** is not limited to speech; written words convey a tone, too, a tone inferred by the reader from the way something is said and the context in which it occurs. Related to tone is **point of view**, the position from which you approach and deal with your subject: as an insider or an outsider, critic or apologist, and so on.

Tone and point of view contribute, along with other stylistic considerations, to the total impression the reader forms of you as a person. The quality of that impression—your **persona** (which may or may not resemble your actual personality)—obviously has much to do with the reader's willingness to be convinced. Honesty and straightforwardness come first—though the honesty of an ignoramus and the straightforwardness of a fool are unlikely to win assent. Some more sophisticated approaches to the adoption of a persona employ **irony**: you assume a character that the reader can see is at odds with your real intention. Whether direct or ironic, the chosen role must be suited to your **audience**; clearly your sense of who your readers are has a bearing on the kind of role you adopt. And your role must also be suited to your subject and to your own talents; it must be one you can play effectively. You may want to try out several to see what each implies: are you an expert or a humble seeker after truth? a wry humorist or a gadfly deliberately exacerbating hidden guilt? Even writers working in the same general territory—S. J. Perelman (p. 311) and Herb Goldberg (p. 292), for example, both deal with supposed aspects of the American character—may present sharply different personalities to their readers in their characteristic handling of both thought and expression. A self will be revealed in every phrase you set down—even in details of spelling, grammar, and punctuation, which, if ineptly handled, may suggest to your readers a carelessness that destroys their confidence.

Authors

Woody Allen (1935–)
Pseudonym of Heywood Allen Konigsberg; American comedian, writer, actor, film director; author of *Getting Even*, **Without Feathers*.

Maya Angelou (1924)
American actress, journalist, television-script writer, civil-rights worker; author of **I Know Why the Caged Bird Sings, Just Give Me a Cool Drink of Water 'fore I Die*.

Hannah Arendt (1906–1975)
German-American political analyst (New School for Social Research); author of *The Origins of Totalitarianism, The Human Condition, *Eichmann in Jerusalem, On Revolution, On Violence, Men in Dark Times, Crises of the Republic*.

Matthew Arnold (1822–1888)
English man of letters, poet, literary critic; author of *Poems, Essays in Criticism, *Culture and Anarchy, Literature and Dogma*.

Roger Ascham (1515–1568)
English scholar, tutor of Queen Elizabeth I; author of **Toxophilus, The Scholemaster*.

Isaac Asimov (1920–)
American author, professor of biochemistry (Boston University School of Medicine); author of 200 books, including *The Stars, Like the Dust, Of Time and Space and Other Things, An Easy Introduction to the Slide Rule, *The Left Hand of the Electron, Nightfall and Other Stories, ABC's of the Earth*.

Sir Francis Bacon (1561–1626)
English politician, statesman, philosopher; author of **Essays, Advancement of Learning, *New Organon, New Atlantis*.

Russell Baker (1925–)
American journalist, essayist (*The New York Times*); author of *All Things Considered, An American in Washington, Our Next President*.

Kayla F. Bernheim (1946–)
American psychologist, clinical director of Threshold (an adolescent treatment center in Rochester, N.Y.); coauthor of **Schizophrenia*.

Pierre [Francis de Marigny] Berton (1920–)
Canadian writer, broadcaster, former editor (*Maclean's Magazine*); author of *Klondike, Adventures of a Columnist, The Last Spike, The National Dream, Drifting Home, *Hollywood's Canada*.

Ambrose Bierce (1842–1914?)
American short-story writer, journalist; author of *Tales of Soldiers and Civilians, The Cynic's Word Book* (retitled **The Devil's Dictionary*).

William Blake (1757–1827)
English poet, artist, engraver; author of *Songs of Innocence, Songs of Experience, *The Marriage of Heaven and Hell, The Book of Thel*.

Wayne C. Booth (1921–)
American literary critic, dean (University of Chicago); author of *The Rhetoric of Fiction, The Rhetoric of Irony*.

Jacob Bronowski (1908–1974)
English critic, statesman, senior fellow and trustee of Salk Institute for Biological Studies; author of *The Poet's Defence, The Common Sense of Science, *Science and Human Values, The Identity of Man, Nature and Knowledge.*

Jerome S. Bruner (1915–   )
American psychologist (Harvard University); author of *The Process of Education, Toward a Theory of Instruction, Processes of Cognitive Growth, The Relevance of Education.*

Art Buchwald (1925–   )
American newspaper columnist, humorist; author of *Paris After Dark, Is It Safe to Drink the Water?, Getting High in Government Circles, *I Never Danced at the White House.*

Edward Bunker (1933–   )
American writer, former addict and inmate of San Quentin and Folsom state prisons; author of *Straight Time, No Beast So Fierce* (novels).

[John] Anthony Burgess [Wilson] (1917–   )
English novelist; author of *A Clockwork Orange, Re Joyce, The Novel Now, MF, Tremor of Intent, Enderby, Nothing Like the Sun, The Wanting Seed* (novels), *Urgent Copy* (essays).

[Arthur] Joyce [Lunel] Cary (1888–1957)
Anglo-Irish novelist, poet, political philosopher; author of *Aissa Saved, The Horse's Mouth, Mister Johnson, The Captive and the Free* (novels), *A Case for African Freedom, Power in Men, The Process of Real Freedom.*

Lord Chesterfield (1694–1773)
Philip Dormer Stanhope, fourth earl; English statesman, diplomat, well-known letter writer (*Letters to His Son*).

Samuel Langhorne Clemens (Mark Twain) (1835–1910)
American humorist, itinerant journalist, critic, novelist; author of *Roughing It, Tom Sawyer, Life on the Mississippi, Huckleberry Finn,* *A Connecticut Yankee in King Arthur's Court.*

Peter Cohen (1939–   )
Swiss businessman, graduate of the Harvard Business School (1970); author of *The Gospel According to the Harvard Business School.*

[William] Robertson Davies (1913–   )
Canadian novelist, playwright, critic, Master of Massey College (University of Toronto); author of the trilogy *Fifth Business, The Manticore, World of Wonders* (novels), more than a dozen plays, three books on the Stratford, Ontario, drama festival, and *One Half of Robertson Davies* (essays).

Thomas De Quincey (1785–1859)
English essayist, critic; author of *Confessions of an English Opium Eater, *Autobiographic Sketches.*

Joan Didion (1934–   )
American writer; author of *Run River, Play It As It Lays* (novels), *Slouching Towards Bethlehem.*

Kildare Dobbs (1923–   )
Canadian writer; author of *Running to Paradise, Reading the Time.*

Margaret Donaldson (1926–   )
Scottish psychologist (University of Edinburgh); author of *A Study of Children's Thinking, *Children's Minds.*

John Donne (1573–1631)
English poet, clergyman, Dean of St. Paul's Cathedral; author of *Songs and Sonnets, *Devotions upon Emergent Occasions.*

Jonathan Edwards (1703–1758)
American Puritan preacher and theologian in Massachusetts Bay Colony.

Loren Eiseley (1907–   )
American anthropologist, historian of science (University of Pennsylvania); author of *The Immense Journey, Darwin's Century, The Firmament of Time, The Mind as Nature, Francis Bacon and the Modern Dilemma, The Unexpected Universe, The Invisible Pyramid, *The Night Country, All the Strange Hours.*

Ralph Waldo Emerson (1803–1882)
American essayist, poet, expositor of the intellectual movement known as Transcendentalism; author of *Nature, Representative Men, English Traits, *Journal.*

Frances FitzGerald (1940–)
American journalist, writer (*The New Yorker, Atlantic*); author of *Fire in the Lake: The Vietnamese and Americans in Vietnam;* winner of Pulitzer Prize for her reporting of the Vietnam War.

Janet Flanner (Genêt) (1892–1978)
American writer, foreign correspondent (*The New Yorker*); author of *The Cubical City, American in Paris, Men and Monuments, Paris Journal.*

Linda Bird Francke
American journalist (*The New York Times*).

Benjamin Franklin (1706–1790)
American statesman, delegate to the Continental Congress and Constitutional Convention, ambassador to France during the American Revolution, inventor, newspaper publisher, practical philosopher; author of *Poor Richard's Almanack, *Autobiography.*

Erich Fromm (1900–1980)
German-American psychoanalyst; author of *Psychoanalysis and Religion, The Sane Society, Sigmund Freud's Mission, The Dogma of Christ and Other Essays on Religion, Psychology and Culture, The Heart of Man.*

Robert Frost (1874–1963)
American poet, lecturer, teacher.

Northrop Frye (1912–)
Canadian literary critic (University of Toronto); author of *Anatomy of Criticism, Design for Learning, *The Educated Imagination.*

John Kenneth Galbraith (1908–)
Canadian-American economist (Harvard University), broadcaster, writer; author of *The Affluent Society, The New Industrial State, Money, The Age of Uncertainty.*

Willard Gaylin (1925–)
President of the Institute of Society, Ethics, and the Life Sciences in Hastings, New York; author of *In the Service of Their Country: War Resisters in Prison.*

Erving Goffman (1922–)
American psychologist, essayist; author of *The Presentation of Self in Everyday Life, Asylums, Strategic Interaction.*

Herb Goldberg (1937–)
American psychotherapist (California State University, Los Angeles); author of *The Hazards of Being Male.*

William Golding (1911–)
English novelist, poet; author of *Lord of the Flies, Pincher Martin.*

Rose K[ohn] Goldsen (1918–)
American sociologist (Cornell University), broadcaster, writer (*Human Behavior*); author of *What College Students Think, *The Show and Tell Machine.*

Stephen Jay Gould (1941–)
American scientist (Harvard University), writer (*Natural History*); author of *Ever Since Darwin.*

Nathaniel Hawthorne (1804–1864)
American novelist, short-story writer, essayist; author of *Twice-told Tales, Mosses from an Old Manse, The Scarlet Letter, The House of the Seven Gables.*

Gilbert Highet (1906–)
Scottish-American classicist (Columbia University); author of *The Classical Tradition, The Art of Teaching, The Anatomy of Satire, *Talents and Geniuses.*

John [Caldwell] Holt (1923–)
American educator; author of *How Children Fail, How Children Learn, Underachieving School, What Do I Do Monday?*

John Houseman (1902–)
Theatrical and motion-picture producer, director, actor, educator (Juilliard School); author of *Run-Through.*

Thomas Jefferson (1743–1826)
Third president of the United States, first secretary of state, founder of the University of Virginia,

drafter of the *Declaration of Independence and the statute of Virginia for religious freedom, founder of the Democratic party; also renowned for his talents as an architect and inventor.

Samuel Johnson (1709–1784)
English lexicographer, critic, moralist, journalist (*The Idler*, *The Rambler*); author of *A Dictionary of the English Language, Lives of the Poets;* subject of Boswell's *Life*.

Carl Gustav Jung (1875–1961)
Swiss psychiatrist, a founder of analytic psychology; author of *Analytical Psychology, The Undiscovered Self, Man and His Symbols, *Modern Man in Search of a Soul, Psychology and Religion, A Theory of Psychoanalysis*.

Franz Kafka (1883–1924)
Czech novelist and short-story writer; author of *The Trial, The Castle, Amerika*.

Horace M. Kallen (1882–1974)
American pragmatic philosopher (New School for Social Research), pupil of William James; author of *Art and Freedom, Cultural Pluralism and the American Idea, *Indecency and the Seven Arts, Culture and Democracy in the United States*.

X. J. Kennedy (1929–   )
Pseudonym of Joseph C. Kennedy; poet, critic, professor of English (Tufts University); author of *Nude Descending a Staircase, An Introduction to Poetry*.

Martin Luther King, Jr. (1929–1968)
American Negro clergyman, civil-rights leader, president of Southern Christian Leadership Conference; winner of Nobel Peace Prize; author of *Stride Toward Freedom, Why We Can't Wait*.

Arthur Koestler (1905–   )
Hungarian-English writer; author of *Darkness at Noon* (novel), *The Ghost in the Machine, The Case of the Midwife Toad*.

Joseph Wood Krutch (1893–1970)
American literary and social critic; author of *The Modern Temper, The Measure of Man, Human Nature and the Human Condition*.

Elisabeth Kübler-Ross
Psychologist; author of *On Death and Dying* (1969).

Thomas Kuhn (1922–   )
American historian of science (Princeton University); author of *The Copernican Revolution, Planetary Astronomy in the Development of Western Thought, *The Structure of Scientific Revolutions*.

Charles Lamb (1775–1834)
English essayist, critic; author of *Essays of Elia* and, with his sister Mary, *Tales from Shakespeare*.

Lewis H. Lapham (1935–   )
American writer, journalist, editor (*Harper's Magazine*).

Margaret Laurence (1926–   )
Canadian writer; author of *The Stone Angel, A Jest of God, A Bird in the House, The Diviners* (fiction), *Heart of a Stranger*.

Fran Lebowitz
American writer; author of *Metropolitan Life*.

Doris Lessing (1919–   )
British novelist; author of *Children of Violence, Briefing for a Descent into Hell, The Summer Before the Dark* (novels), *A Small Personal Voice*.

Richard R. J. Lewine (1947–   )
American psychologist (University of Massachusetts); coauthor of *Schizophrenia*.

C[live] S[taples] Lewis (1898–1963)
English novelist, essayist; author of *The Pilgrim's Regress, *The Screwtape Letters*.

John Livingston Lowes (1867–1945)
American literary critic, scholar

(Harvard University); author of *Geoffrey Chaucer, The Road to Xanadu.*

Niccolò Machiavelli (1469–1527)
Florentine statesman, political philosopher during the reign of the Medici; author of *The Art of War, History of Florence, Discourses on Livy, *The Prince.*

[John] Hugh MacLennan (1907–   )
Canadian novelist, essayist, professor (McGill University); author of *Barometer Rising, Two Solitudes, The Watch That Ends the Night* (novels), **The Other Side of Hugh MacLennan* (essays).

Fredelle Bruser Maynard (1922–   )
Canadian journalist, writer on child development; author of *Guiding Your Child to a More Creative Life, *Raisins and Almonds* (memoirs).

Joyce Maynard (1954–   )
Canadian-American writer (*The New York Times*); author of *Looking Back: A Chronicle of Growing Old in the Sixties.*

Dorothy Gies McGuigan (1914–   )
American historian (University of Michigan); author of *Metternich and the Duchess, The Habsburgs.*

N. Scott Momaday (1934–   )
American Indian writer, poet; author of *The Names, *The Way to Rainy Mountain* (nonfiction); *Angle of Geese and Other Poems, The Gourd Dancer* (poetry).

Desmond Morris (1928–   )
English zoologist, writer; author of *The Naked Ape, Intimate Behavior, The Human Zoo, The Biology of Art, *Manwatching.*

Toni Morrison (1931–   )
American writer; author of *The Bluest Eye.*

John Henry Newman (1801–1890)
English Catholic prelate, cardinal; author of *Tracts for the Times,* *The Idea of a University, Apologia pro Vita Sua.*

Peter C. Newman (1929–   )
Canadian journalist, editor (*Maclean's Magazine*); author of *Renegade in Power: The Diefenbaker Years, The Canadian Establishment, Bronfman Dynasty, *Home Country* (essays).

George Orwell (1903–1950)
Pseudonym of Eric Blair; English novelist, essayist, social commentator, satirist of totalitarianism; author of *Down and Out in Paris and London, Homage to Catalonia, Nineteen Eighty-Four, Animal Farm.*

Walter Pater (1839–1894)
English man of letters; author of *Studies in the History of the Renaissance, Marius the Epicurean, Appreciations.*

S[idney] J[oseph] Perelman (1904–1979)
American humorist, writer for motion pictures; author of *One Touch of Venus, *Vinegar Puss, Eastward Ha!*

Robert Pirsig (1928–   )
American writer, educator; author of *Zen and the Art of Motorcycle Maintenance.*

Plato (427?–347 B.C.)
Greek philosopher, pupil and friend of Socrates, teacher of Aristotle, founder of the Academy; author of *The Republic* and other dialogues.

Norman Podhoretz (1930–   )
American writer, former editor of *Commentary*; author of *Doings and Undoings, The Fifties and After in American Writing, Making It.*

Betty Rollin
American writer, actress; author of *I Thee Wed; First, You Cry.*

Carl Sagan (1934–   )
American space scientist (Cornell University), writer; author of *The Dragons of Eden, The Cosmic

Connection, Intelligent Life in the Universe (with I. S. Shklovsky), *Planetary Exploration.*

Jean-Paul Sartre (1905–1980)
French philosopher, playwright, novelist, story writer, social and literary critic, winner of Nobel Prize; author of *Existentialism, Existentialism and Humanism, No Exit, The Wall, Imagination, Of Human Freedom, The Problem of Method, The Words, The Transcendence of the Ego.*

Jonathan Schell (1943–)
Writer, (*The New Yorker*); author of *The Village of Ben Suk, The Military Half, *The Time of Illusion.*

Chief Seattle (1790?–)
American Indian, chief of the Duwampo tribe in Washington Territory.

Richard B. Sewall (1908–)
American scholar, biographer (Yale University); author of *The Vision of Tragedy, The Life of Emily Dickinson.*

Laurence Sheehan
American free-lance sportswriter, collaborator with Arthur Ashe and Stan Smith on books about tennis.

B[urrhus] F[rederic] Skinner (1904–)
American psychologist (Harvard University); author of *Science and Human Behavior, Walden Two, Beyond Freedom and Dignity.*

Wallace Stegner (1909–)
American essayist, novelist, professor (Stanford University); author of *Remembering Laughter, The Women on the Wall, Beyond the Hundredth Meridian, A Shocking Star, *Wolf Willow, All the Little Live Things, Gathering of Zion: The Story of the Mormon Trail.*

Benjamin Stein
American journalist, writer, editor (*Wall Street Journal*); author of *The View from Sunset Boulevard, Dreemz.*

John Steinbeck (1902–1969)
American novelist, columnist, winner of Nobel Prize; author of *In Dubious Battle, Of Mice and Men, The Grapes of Wrath, East of Eden, *Journal of a Novel: The East of Eden Letters.*

Laurence Sterne (1713–1768)
English cleric, novelist, humorist; author of *Tristram Shandy, A Sentimental Journey, Sermons.*

Jonathan Swift (1667–1745)
Irish satirist, poet, churchman; author of *Gulliver's Travels, A Tale of a Tub, *The Battle of the Books.*

Dylan Thomas (1914–1953)
Welsh poet, story writer, radio script writer, broadcaster; author of *Collected Poems (1934–1952), Under Milk Wood* (verse drama), *Adventures in the Skin Trade and Other Stories, Portrait of the Artist as a Young Dog.*

Lewis Thomas (1913–)
American physician, educator, medical administrator; author of *The Lives of a Cell, *The Medusa and the Snail.*

Henry David Thoreau (1817–1862)
American philosopher, essayist, naturalist, poet, disciple of Emerson; author of *Walden,* "Civil Disobedience," *Journals.*

James Thurber (1894–1961)
American humorist, cartoonist, social commentator (*The New Yorker*), playwright; author of *My Life and Hard Times; *Fables for Our Time; *Men, Women, and Dogs; The Beast in Me and Other Animals.*

Paul Tillich (1886–1965)
German-American theologian; author of *The Interpretation of History, The Shaking of the Foundations, Systematic Theology, The Dynamic of Faith, Christianity and the Encounter of the World Religions.*

John Updike (1932–)
American novelist, story writer, poet; author of *Rabbit, Run; The Centaur; Of the Farm; Couples; Bech; Rabbit Redux* (novels); *The Same Door; Pigeon Feathers; The Music School* (stories).

E. B. White (1899–   )
American essayist, poet, journalist *(The New Yorker);* author of *One Man's Meat,* **The Wild Flag,* **The Second Tree from the Corner.*

Edward O. Wilson (1929–   )
American biologist (Harvard University), Curator of Entomology at Museum of Comparative Zoology there; author of *The Insect Societies, Sociobiology,* **On Human Nature.*

Tom Wolfe (1931–   )
American essayist, story writer, social critic; author of **The Kandy-Kolored Tangerine-Flake Streamline Baby, The Pump House Gang, Radical Chic and Mau-Mauing the Flak Catchers.*

Virginia Woolf (1882–1941)
English novelist, essayist, critic; author of *Mrs. Dalloway, To the Lighthouse* (novels), *The Common Reader, Granite and Rainbow,* **The Second Common Reader* (essays).

William Zinsser (1922–   )
American journalist, writer, teacher (Yale University); author of *The City Dwellers, On Writing Well, Pop Goes America.*

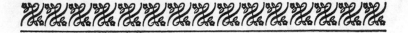

Index

ACKNOWLEDGMENTS

Allen: From *Without Feathers*, by Woody Allen. Copyright © 1972, 1973, 1974, 1975 by Woody Allen. Reprinted by permission of Random House, Inc.

Angelou: From *I Know Why the Caged Bird Sings*, by Maya Angelou. Copyright © 1969 by Maya Angelou. Reprinted by permission of Random House, Inc.

Arendt: From *Eichmann in Jerusalem* by Hannah Arendt. Copyright © 1963, 1964 by Hannah Arendt. Reprinted by permission of Viking Penguin Inc.

Asimov: "The Eureka Phenomenon," copyright © 1971 by Mercury Press, Inc., from *The Left Hand of the Electron*, by Isaac Asimov. Reprinted by permission of Doubleday & Company, Inc.

Baker: "Summer Beyond Wish," © 1977/78 by The New York Times Company. Reprinted by permission.

Bernheim & Lewine: Selection is reprinted from *Schizophrenia* by Kayla F. Bernheim & Richard R. J. Lewine, with the permission of W. W. Norton & Company, Inc. Copyright © 1979 by Kayla F. Bernheim and Richard R. J. Lewine.

Berton: "How Randolph Scott Saved the Northwest" from *Hollywood's Canada* by Pierre Berton. Reprinted by permission of McClelland & Stewart.

Booth: "Boring from Within: The Art of the Freshman Essay," from an address to the Illinois Council of College Teachers in 1963. Reprinted by permission of the author.

Bronowski: "The Nature of Scientific Reasoning" from *Science and Human Values* by J. Bronowski. Copyright © 1956, 1965 by J. Bronowski. Reprinted by permission of Julian Messner, a Simon & Schuster division of Gulf & Western Corporation. "The Reach of Imagination" from *American Scholar*, Spring 1967. Reprinted by permission of the American Academy and Institute of Arts and Letters.

Bruner: "Freud and the Image of Man," from *Partisan Review* XXIII, #3. Copyright 1956, by *Partisan Review*. Reprinted by permission of the publisher.

Buchwald: Reprinted by permission of G. P. Putnam's Sons from *I Never Danced at the White House* by Art Buchwald. Copyright © 1971, 1972, 1973 by Art Buchwald.

Bunker: "Let's End the Dope War: A Junkie's View of the Quagmire" by Edward Bunker, from *The Nation*, June 25, 1977. Copyright © 1977 The Nation Associates.

Burgess: "Is America Falling Apart?" © 1971 by The New York Times Company. Reprinted by permission.

Cary: From "On the Function of the Novelist," © 1949 by The New York Times Company. Reprinted by permission.

Cohen: Excerpted from "What Would You Do? The Case Method of Business Education," from *The Gospel According to the Harvard Business School*, by Peter Cohen. Copyright © 1973 by Peter Cohen. Reprinted by permission of Doubleday & Company, Inc.

Davies: "A Few Kind Words for Superstition," reprinted by permission of Newsweek.

Didion: "On Going Home" and "On Keeping a Notebook" from *Slouching Towards Bethlehem* by Joan Didion. Copyright © 1966, 1968 by Joan Didion. Reprinted with the permission of Farrar, Straus and Giroux, Inc.

Dobbs: Excerpt from *Canada*, by Peter Varley and Kildare Dobbs. Reprinted by permission of The Macmillan Company of Canada Limited and Thames and Hudson Ltd.

Donaldson: Selection is reprinted from *Children's Minds* by Margaret Donaldson, with the permission of W. W. Norton & Company, Inc., and Bolt & Watson Ltd. Copyright © 1978 by Margaret Donaldson. Originally published by Fontana Books.

Eiseley: "The Brown Wasps" is reprinted by permission of Charles Scribner's Sons from *The Night Country* by Loren Eiseley. Copyright © 1971 by Loren Eiseley.

FitzGerald: From *America Revised* by Frances FitzGerald. Originally published in *The New Yorker*. Reprinted by permission of Little, Brown and Co. in association with the Atlantic Monthly Press.

Flanner: From *Paris Was Yesterday* by Janet Flanner. Copyright 1940 by Janet Flanner, © renewed 1968 by Janet Flanner. Reprinted by permission of Viking Penguin Inc.

Francke: "The Body Count in the Battle of the Sexes" © 1977 by The New York Times Company. Reprinted by permission.

Fromm: From *The Forgotten Language* by Erich Fromm. Copyright 1951 by Erich Fromm. Reprinted by permission of Holt, Rinehart and Winston, Publishers.

Frost: From *Selected Prose of Robert Frost* edited by Hyde Cox and Edward Connery Lathem. Copyright 1939, 1954, © 1966, 1967 by Holt, Rinehart and Winston. Copyright 1946, © 1959 by Robert Frost. Copyright © 1956 by The Estate of Robert Frost. Reprinted by permission of Holt, Rinehart and Winston, Publishers.

Frye: From *The Educated Imagination* by Northrop Frye. Reprinted by permission of Indiana University Press and the author.

687

Galbraith: From *The Affluent Society*, 3rd edition revised by John Kenneth Galbraith. Copyright © 1958, 1969, 1976 by John Kenneth Galbraith. Reprinted by permission of Houghton Mifflin Company.

Gaylin: "What You See Is the Real You" © 1977 by The New York Times Company. Reprinted by permission.

Goffman: "Reality and Contrivance," from *The Presentation of Self in Everyday Life*, by Erving Goffman. Copyright © 1959 by Erving Goffman. Reprinted by permission of Doubleday & Company, Inc.

Goldberg: Reprinted by permission of Herb Goldberg from *The Hazards of Being Male* by Herb Goldberg. © 1976 Herb Goldberg.

Golding: From *Holiday Magazine*, August 1961. Copyright © 1961 by William Golding. Reprinted by permission of Curtis Brown, Ltd.

Goldsen: Adapted from *The Show and Tell Machine: How Television Works and Works You Over* by Rose K. Goldsen. Copyright © 1975, 1977 by Rose K. Goldsen. Reprinted by permission of The Dial Press. Selection from Sesame Street Theme reprinted by permission of Children's Television Workshop.

Gould: "Our Allotted Lifetimes" by Stephen Jay Gould, reprinted with permission from *Natural History Magazine* August/September 1977. Copyright © the American Museum of Natural History, 1977. "Of Bamboos, Cicadas, and the Economy of Adam Smith" is reprinted from *Ever Since Darwin* by Stephen Jay Gould, with the permission of W. W. Norton & Company, Inc. Copyright © 1977 by Stephen Jay Gould. Copyright © 1973, 1974, 1975, 1976, 1977 by the American Museum of Natural History.

Highet: From *Talents and Geniuses*, Copyright © 1957 by Gilbert Highet. Reprinted by permission of Curtis Brown, Ltd.

Holt: From *Redbook*, November 1967. Copyright © 1967 by McCall Corporation. Reprinted by permission of John Holt Associates.

Houseman: "The War of the Worlds" from *Run-Through*. Copyright © 1972 by John Houseman. Reprinted by permission of SIMON & SCHUSTER, A Gulf & Western Corporation.

Jung: From *Modern Man in Search of a Soul*. Reprinted by permission of Harcourt Brace Jovanovich, Inc.

Kafka: From *The Trial*, Definitive Edition, Revised, by Franz Kafka, translated by Willa and Edwin Muir. Copyright 1937, © 1956 and renewed 1965 by Alfred A. Knopf, Inc. Reprinted by permission of the publisher and Schocken Books Inc.

Kallen: Selection is reprinted from *Indecency and the Seven Arts* by Horace M. Kallen, with the permission of Liveright Publishing Corporation. Copyright 1930 by Horace Liveright, Inc. Copyright renewed © 1958 by Horace M. Kallen.

Kennedy: From *Dissent*, Spring 1960. Reprinted by permission of *Dissent*.

King: "Letter from Birmingham Jail"—April 16, 1963—from *Why We Can't Wait* by Martin Luther King, Jr. Copyright © 1963 by Martin Luther King, Jr.

Koestler: Reprinted with permission of Macmillan Publishing Co., Inc. and A. D. Peters & Co. Ltd. from *The Act of Creation* by Arthur Koestler. Copyright © Arthur Koestler 1964, 1969.

Krutch: "Picasso versus Picasso" (under title "Modern Painting") from *And Even If You Do: Essays on Man, Manners & Machines* by Joseph Wood Krutch. Copyright © 1967 by Joseph Wood Kruth. By permission of William Morrow & Company.

Kübler-Ross: Reprinted with permission of Macmillan Publishing Co., Inc. from *On Death and Dying* by Elisabeth Kübler-Ross. Copyright © 1969 by Elisabeth Kübler-Ross.

Kuhn: From *The Structure of Scientific Revolutions*, copyright © 1962 by the University of Chicago Press. Reprinted by permission of the publishers.

Lane: From *Up from Under*, copyright © 1971 by *Up From Under, A Magazine by, for, and about Women*, 339 Lafayette St., New York, NY 10012. Reprinted by permission of the publisher.

Lapham: From *Harper's Magazine*. Copyright © 1976 by Harper's Magazine. All rights reserved. Reprinted from the September 1976 issue by special permission.

Laurence: "Where the World Began" from *Heart of a Stranger* by Margaret Laurence. Reprinted by permission of McClelland & Stewart and JCA Literary Agency, Inc.

Lebowitz: From *Metropolitan Life* by Fran Lebowitz. Copyright © 1974, 1975, 1976, 1977, 1978 by Fran Lebowitz. Reprinted by permission of E. P. Dutton.

Lessing: From *A Small Personal Voice*. Copyright © 1956, 1957, 1959, 1963, 1966, 1968, 1971, 1972, 1974 by Doris Lessing. Reprinted by permission of the Author and her Agents, James Brown Associates, Inc.

Lewis: Reprinted with permission of Macmillan Publishing Co., Inc. from *The Screwtape Letters* by C. S. Lewis. © C. S. Lewis 1942.